The New Russia

The New Russia

A Handbook of Economic and Political Developments

Ian Jeffries

RoutledgeCurzon
Taylor & Francis Group

First Published in 2002
by RoutledgeCurzon
11 New Fetter Lane, London EC4P 4EE

Simultaneously published in the USA and Canada
by RoutledgeCurzon
29 West 35th Street, New York, NY 10001

RoutledgeCurzon is an imprint of the Taylor & Francis Group

Typeset in Janson by LaserScript Ltd, Mitcham, Surrey
Printed and bound in Great Britain by
Antony Rowe Ltd, Chippenham, Wiltshire

British Library Cataloguing in Publication Data
A catalogue record of this book is available from the British Library

Library of Congress Cataloguing in Publication Data
A catalogue record for this book has been requested

ISBN 0–7007–1621–1

CONTENTS

TABLES

ACKNOWLEDGEMENTS

The mammoth task of keeping up to date with rapidly changing economic and political events in Russia would not have been possible without the help of a magnificent library staff, certain other individuals and the portering/cleaning staff in general. Individuals deserving of particular mention are the following (in alphabetical order): Gwen Bailey (Library); Pam Beardsmore, Michele Davies (Library); Dianne Evans (Library); Ray Jones (Library); Nigel O'Leary (Economics); Lis Parcell (Library); Ann Preece (Library); Paul Reynolds (Library); Kathy Sivertsen (Library); Clive Towse (Library); Ray Watts (Library); Chris West (Library).

The earliest possible access to quality newspapers and magazines has, as always, been ensured by the excellent Kays Newsagency, owned and managed by Russell Davies.

Professor Michael Kaser and Professor Paul Hare have continually provided external support and encouragement.

This is not (and is not meant to be) original research but a broad-brush painting of the overall economic and political picture. I make use of a range of secondary sources in English. Apart from journals and books, the sources include the following:

1. Reports such as the European Bank for Reconstruction and Development's (EBRD's) *Transition Report*, the United Nations' *World Economic and Social Survey*, the United Nations Economic Commission for Europe's *Economic Survey of Europe*, the United Nations Economic and Social Commission for Asia and the Pacific's *Economic and Social Survey of Asia and the Pacific*, the World Bank's *Transition*, the IMF's *World Economic Survey* and the OECD's *Economic Outlook*.
2. Quality newspapers such as the *International Herald Tribune (IHT)*, *Financial Times (FT)*, *The Times*, *The Guardian*, *The Independent*, *The Telegraph* and *The Baltic Times*.
3. Weeklies such as *The Economist* and the *Far Eastern Economic Review (FEER)*.
4. Quarterlies/Monthlies/Fortnightlies such as *Russian Economic Trends*, *Business Central Europe*, *Eastern Europe* (*EEN*, formerly *Eastern Europe*

Newsletter), *The World Today*, *Asian Survey*, *Current Digest of the Post-Soviet Press* (*CDSP*, before 5 February 1992 known as *Current Digest of the Soviet Press*), *Transition* and *Finance and Development*.

A review in the *Times Higher Education Supplement* (29 October 1993) kindly referred to my 'meticulous referencing', even though detailed referencing has the potential to be tiresome to readers. But since this is not original research and I am deeply indebted to many sources, I feel it necessary to make every effort to acknowledge the material used. It is not always feasible to name the correspondents or contributors, but I try, as far as possible, to ensure that credit goes where it is due. Partly for this reason and partly for accuracy I make extensive use of quotations.

Ian Jeffries
Centre of Russian and East European Studies, University of Wales

INTRODUCTION AND OVERVIEW

INTRODUCTION

The Soviet Union was the world's largest country in terms of land area, occupying a sixth of the earth's land surface excluding Antarctica. Stalin and his successors succeeded in making the Soviet Union one of the world's two 'superpowers' in terms of conventional and nuclear military capacity. The USSR (Union of Soviet Socialist Republics) comprised fifteen republics (based on the most populous nationalities). In 1990 the population was 290.1 million, the third largest after China and India. Russia dwarfed the other Soviet republics, e.g. its population of 148.5 million in 1990 represented 51.2 per cent of the Soviet total. 'Russia may be still nearly twice the size of the United States, but it is a quarter smaller than the Soviet Union. Of its present territorial extent ... less than 10 per cent is arable ... The United States' population of 264 million people is nearly 80 per cent larger than the 148 million population of today's Russia ... In the Soviet Union only 55 per cent of the people were ethnic Russians. In today's Russia that figure is 81.5 per cent, with less than 20 per cent of the population belonging to fourteen acknowledged minority nationalities. It has not been so homogeneous since the eighteenth century' (William Pfaff, *IHT*, 22 April 1998, p. 9).

On the eve of the First World War Russia (an empire which, unlike the British Empire for example, was essentially in one piece) was still a relatively backward, agrarian country. But the economic potential in the shape of a rich and varied natural resource endowment was enormous, despite climatic, transport and soil difficulties. There was actually considerable industrial growth during thirty years prior to 1913, the level of output doubling during the 1890s for instance. In 1913 Russia accounted for only just over 4 per cent of world industrial output (compared with 10 per cent in 1941 and about 20 per cent in the mid-1980s). In 1917 Russia ranked as the fifth industrial power in the world and the fourth in Europe (Aganbegyan 1988b: 45–7). But *per capita* income in 1913 was less than 40 per cent of France's, about 33 per cent of Germany's, 20 per cent of Britain's and 10 per cent of the USA's (Gregory and Stuart 1990: 36). Agriculture employed 72 per cent of the workforce

(82 per cent of the population was rural) and contributed over 50 per cent of national product (Gregory and Stuart 1990: 39). Serfdom had been abolished only in 1861 and the attempted switch to capitalist agriculture after 1906 came too late. The commodity structure of foreign trade was typical of a poor country, with exports of primary commodities, especially grain, paying for imports of manufactures, especially capital goods. A high birth rate of around forty-four per thousand in 1913 was coupled with a relatively high death rate of around twenty-seven per thousand, the infant mortality rate being about 237 per thousand. Sixty per cent of the population over the age of ten was illiterate (Gregory and Stuart 1990: 39).

The Bolsheviks came to power in October/November 1917. They were led by Lenin, who died on 21 January 1924 after a series of strokes starting in the summer of 1922. Stalin ruthlessly outmanoeuvred his rivals for the leadership, having Trotsky assassinated in Mexico in 1940 for example. Stalin (who died in 1953) became one of history's greatest tyrants.

It was the so-called 'bourgeois revolution' of February/March 1917 that actually overthrew Tsar Nicholas II, although it was the Bolsheviks who murdered the Tsar and his family on 17 July 1918. The Kerensky regime was toppled in October/November 1917 and with it went the chance of a democratic future. The problem of specifying the months of the revolutions arise because the Julian calendar was used until February 1918. According to that calendar, the start of the Bolshevik Revolution was 25 October 1917. But thereafter, with the Gregorian calendar in use, the Revolution was celebrated on 7 November. In 1903 the Social Democratic Labour Party had split into a so-called 'majority' and 'minority' factions (from which the words 'Bolshevik' and 'Menshevik' derive). Lenin ensured an early exit from the First World War. The Treaty of Brest-Litovsk (with considerable loss of territory) was signed on 3 March 1918 with Germany, Austria-Hungary, Turkey and Bulgaria. (The treaty was annulled on 13 November 1918.)

There was no detailed economic blueprint from the works of Marx and Engels to guide the Bolsheviks in 1917. Marx saw society inevitably progressing through various stages of development, namely primitive society, slavery, feudalism, capitalism, socialism and communism. Marx essentially provided a critique of capitalism, but socialism was only vaguely defined. There was to be the 'conscious social regulation of production' (as opposed to the 'anarchy' of the market), the 'common' ownership of the means of production, and distribution according to work (as opposed to need under communism).

The early years after the revolution saw state takeovers (without compensation) in banking, foreign trade and key industries like iron and steel. All land was nationalized, and the national debt, equivalent to 120 per cent of national income in 1917, was repudiated. The period of 'War Communism' lasted from 1918 to 1921. The overriding aim was to win the civil war against the Whites, who were aided by capitalist intervention from the spring of 1918 to September 1919. Nationalization was taken to extremes, with enterprises employing only one person in some cases. The market was replaced by a form of moneyless administration, local authorities mainly, with the central state practising campaign methods. Labour was directed and increasingly paid in kind, while agricultural products were compulsorily requisitioned. Although allowing resources to be concentrated at the front, war communism was not sustainable as a peacetime mechanism, and gave way to the New Economic Policy (NEP; 1921–28), the study of which became topical in the Gorbachev era. Concessions were made to private enterprise, especially in retail trade, although the state still retained control of the 'commanding heights' like metallurgy, armaments, fuels, and banking. The market mechanism was restored to a large extent. There were even (not very successful) attempts to attract foreign capital and enterprise. One of the world's classic hyperinflations was checked by output increases, a decreasing reliance on the printing press to finance budget deficits and confidence inspired by a new currency. The pre-First World War output levels were broadly regained towards the end of the NEP period, planning institutions such as Gosplan were established, planning techniques were developed and the future was explored in a rigorous 'industrialization debate'.

The Soviet command economy was introduced after 1928. The details will be discussed in the individual chapters on the economy, but at this point it is necessary to explain the goals which Stalin set out to achieve. The Soviet Union being the only socialist country in what was perceived to be a hostile capitalist environment and thus in danger of an all-out invasion, the basic aim was to catch up with and surpass the leading capitalist countries, especially in terms of heavy industrial capacity and military power. This was encapsulated in a famous 1931 speech by Stalin: 'We are fifty or a hundred years behind the advanced countries. We must make good this distance in ten years. Either we do it, or we shall go under.' (For a fuller quotation see Ellman 1979: 13.)

During the 1930s the state used its allocative powers to devote the historically high figure of around a quarter of national output to investment (Bergson 1961: 237). Consumption was held down to a level judged adequate to maintain political stability and work incentives. Sectoral priority was awarded to industry, specifically about 40 per cent of total investment (Kaplan 1953: 52). Within industry priority was given to 'heavy' industry (some 84 per cent of industrial investment during the First Five Year Plan 1928–32 going to heavy industry). The share in total industrial production of producer goods rose from 39.5 per cent in 1928 to 61.2 per cent in 1940 (Ellman 1979: 139). (Industry was divided into category 'A', producer goods, and category 'B', consumer goods.) The 'leading links' were iron and steel, heavy engineering ('machine building'), mining, electric power generation, and armaments. In a quantitative sense, foreign trade did not play a large strategic role; exports reached their lowest share as a proportion of national income of only 0.5 per cent in 1937. Nevertheless, the Soviet Union was able to import vital capital goods embodying the latest technology.

Stalin maintained that it was possible to build 'socialism in one country' (socialism being the penultimate stage on the path to communism, where there is distribution according to need and no class conflict). Eastern European countries (excluding Yugoslavia and Albania) did not become satellites of the Soviet Union until after the defeat of Hitler's Germany in 1945. The USA became the Soviet Union's chief foe and rival 'superpower' in the Cold War era.

(The above issues are discussed in Chapter 1.)

A bewildering number of economic changes were introduced in the Soviet Union, especially after the mid-1960s. (See Chapter 1 and the introductions to Chapters 2 to 7.) But right to the end of the 1980s the economic system remained recognizably a command economy. The Gorbachev era (11 March 1985–25 December 1991) was remarkable, although mainly as regards domestic politics (democratization) and international politics (the end of the Cold War).

Gorbachev put political reform before economic reform. (See Chapter 10.) Democratization broke the monopoly of power held by the Communist Party of the Soviet Union (CPSU) and eventually included the formation of new parties. The first round of voting for the Congress of People's Deputies held in March 1989 was partially free (and the reserved seats were envisaged to go on the following occasion) and a surprising number of independent and radical deputies were elected. Gorbachev opened the possibility of the secession of republics from the Soviet Union (although the ultimate approval of the Russian Congress of People's Deputies was still needed).

Mikhail Gorbachev was a star internationally (he was awarded the Nobel Peace Prize on 15 October 1990) but he was subsequently reviled by many Russians for what they saw as his role in the economic and political disintegration of the Soviet Union. Gorbachev made a grave mistake in not putting himself forward for popular election as Soviet president and so did not gain the political legitimacy of his arch opponent Yeltsin. Gorbachev won a miserly 0.51 per cent of the vote in the first round of the Russian presidential election held on 16 June 1996 (although he was brave to stand at all).

Glasnost and *perestroika* became household terms during the Gorbachev era. Radical economic reform was not implemented, although concessions to the private sector and direct foreign investment, for example, were important for their time. Gorbachev blew hot and cold as regards radical economic reform, hopping between the political poles in order to preserve the integrity of the country. He finally plumped for the market, but by then it was too late; radical economic reform never left the paper and the country disintegrated. Russia under the humane Gorbachev (unlike China under Deng Xiaoping) put political reform ahead of economic reform. This weakened central political control to such as degree that the old economy started to fall apart in the absence of a new one. Output growth was negative in 1990 and 1991. The Soviet Union did not collapse because of its economic weaknesses, however.

The economic system could have trundled on despite falling further and further behind in relative terms. It was the collapse of the political system that was the key. Command economies can survive only if commands are generally obeyed. Gorbachev was not a tyrant who was willing to use the security forces to enforce compliance at home or in Eastern Europe. The Soviet political system was, ironically, also undermined by the very success of foreign policy. The end of the Cold War deprived the Communist Party of an important source of legitimacy. (The issues in this paragraph are discussed in Chapters 1 and 10.)

Late 1989 saw the momentous and unexpected collapse of communism in Eastern Europe. Soon afterwards (late 1991) the Soviet Union disintegrated. (See Chapter 10.) It was truly ironic that the abortive August 1991 coup in the Soviet Union (against Gorbachev), designed to preserve the country, put the final nail in its coffin. 'Communism' (more formally 'socialism') had thus lost the Cold War battle against 'capitalism', although Boris Yeltsin more accurately described it as a victory for both sides: 'The winners in this war were all those who opposed totalitarianism and defended democracy – in West and East' (speech in London given on 10 November 1992).

The fact that the Soviet Union disintegrated in a relatively peaceful manner is truly remarkable. (See Chapter 10.) This is not to underestimate the bitter conflicts, for example, in Tajikistan, in Georgia (over Abkhazia, for instance) and between Azerbaijan and Armenia (over Nargorno-Karabakh). The potential for strife in a Soviet Union armed to the teeth with nuclear weapons was frightening – some 65 million of the former Soviet citizens lived outside their ethnic republics; 25 million of these were Russians stranded in the 'near abroad' (the Russian term for the other former Soviet republics). Russia itself, of course, has not been free of strife. Yeltsin dissolved parliament on 21 September 1993 and blasted the White House into submission on 4 October (Chapter 12), while the first invasion of Chechenia (Chapter 11), colossally destructive in human and material terms, began on 11 December 1994 and did not effectively end until August 1996.

The origins of the second Chechen war (see Chapter 11) have usually been traced to the invasion of the neighbouring province of Dagestan by large numbers of Islamic extremists (mostly Chechens but also foreigners) on 7 August 1999, especially when an independent Islamic state was proclaimed three days later (without the support of many of the local Dagestanies, who were, in fact, overwhelmingly against the extremists). (Vladimir Putin became acting prime minister on 9 August.) But periodic clashes between Russian forces and Chechen rebels had occurred well before August 1999. In January 2000 former prime minister Sergei Stepashin said that a plan had been discussed in March 1999 to invade Chechenia, with the aim of establishing a buffer zone along the Terek river north of Grozny. The second war is also generally seen as an act of revenge by Russian generals humiliated by the first one.

Many civilians lost their lives in bomb attacks in Russia proper (on 2, 4, 9, 13 and 16 September 1999). The authorities blamed (without ever providing convincing evidence) Chechen extremists. (There was another bomb explosion in Moscow on 8 August 2000, but this time Putin warned against jumping to conclusions regarding Chechens.) On 30 September 1999 large numbers of Russian troops invaded Chechenia. Most remaining rebels fled Grozny (with heavy loss of life) on 1 February 2000. Lessons had been learned not only from the first Chechen war but also from the 1999 Nato attack on Serbia. Massive bombing preceded the movement of Russian ground forces. Russian used the media in a propaganda war, with independent journalists and international organizations kept at arms length. The Russian journalist Andrei Babitsky, a critic of the war, became internationally known as a result of his poor treatment at the hands of the Russian authorities. International condemnation of Russia centred on the disproportionate and indiscriminate use of force, which led to the deaths of many civilians and to colossal destruction within Chechenia. There were many complaints about the behaviour of marauding Russian troops, allegedly including executions, rape and looting. Criticism was also aimed at so-called 'filtration' camps (detention centres or internment camps meant to filter rebels from civilians), where allegations included torture, rape and killings. But the seriousness of the concern was not matched by commensurate action by the international community, no doubt owing to factors such as general acceptance of Russian sovereignty over Chechenia and of the importance of nuclear-armed Russia in wider terms. This is not to underestimate the importance of the actions taken by the Council of Europe on 6 April 2000 (even though Russia's response was sufficient to avoid suspension) and by the United Nations Human Rights Commission on 25 April 2000.

There was significant public disapproval of the government during the first Chechen war. Public opinion (and the Russian Orthodox Church) has remained supportive during the second, although continuing losses among Russian troops in the predictable guerrilla war that followed early Russian successes have eroded popular support somewhat. Indeed, the second Chechen war is arguably the most important single factor explaining the meteoritic rise of Vladimir Putin from relative obscurity to president. Russians overwhelmingly accept the official explanation that Chechen rebels were responsible for the September 1999 bombings on Russian soil which led to the loss of many civilian lives. Chechen 'independence' proved to be an anarchic affair, with the lawless province associated with banditry and kidnapping. Hostage-taking became a high earner of hard currency and international aid organizations were increasingly forced to give Chechenia a wide berth. 'Chechen bands have taken about 1,300 hostages since 1996 and about 700 have been released' (*The Times*, 27 November 1999, p. 16). Hostages have also been murdered. All these events reinforced the prejudice against ethnic Chechens in the minds of many ethnic Russians.

President Aslan Maskhadov of Chechenia (democratically elected in a generally free and fair election on 27 January 1997) was unable to control extremists (whether criminal, Islamic or both). Russia did next to nothing for Chechenia after the 31 August 1996 Khasavyurt agreement signed by Alexander Lebed and Aslan Maskhadov. (The agreement effectively made Chechenia independent, although a referendum was to establish its final status in a referendum to have been held in December 2001. Putin has repudiated the agreement.) 'The tragedy of the Russians' ham-fisted brutality is that they might have attracted the support of most Chechens had they tried to work peacefully with Mr Maskhadov to expel the extremist groups' (Anatol Lieven, *IHT*, 1 December 1999, p. 8). Yeltsin refused Maskhadov's offers to negotiate after the second war started, while Putin has laid down conditions for direct personal talks with Maskhadov (such as handing over the Islamic extremists or at least joining with Russian forces to capture them) that the Chechen president cannot possibly fulfil. On 8 June 2000 Putin imposed direct presidential rule over Chechenia.

The need to ensure the lumbering and failing giant's successful transition to democracy and the market is of paramount importance. The question about how to handle the transition in Russia has thus not surprisingly led to immense controversy and problems. It is little wonder that Russia can produce such contrasting views. (See Chapter 1.) (For example, the decision to release most prices in 'big bang' fashion in January 1992 was immensely controversial, critics arguing that savings were decimated in real terms, that the monopolistic structure of the economy was inappropriate and that an inflationary spiral could develop. See Chapter 2.)

It is remarkable how Russia has arisen relatively peacefully from the ashes of the Soviet Union and how its people taken readily to relatively free parliamentary and presidential elections after a history of oppression and servitude. The Soviet (and Tsarist) legacy was a weakly developed civil society. But progress on this front has been disappointing and Russia is a country riddled with crime and corruption. (See Chapter 1.) (Organized crime has reached beyond Russia's frontiers, even to Western countries.) A 'financial oligarchy' quickly became unimaginably wealthy in ways which largely did not involve creating wealth. The small number of 'financial oligarchs' quickly accumulated both immense economic wealth (through such mechanisms as export licences, tariff concessions and corrupt privatization schemes) and considerable political power (enhanced by media ownership). (In Chapter 12 the entry for 30 October 1996 provides details about the seven top businessmen. See also entries for the summer of 2000.) The financial crisis after August 1998 took its toll, but some fared better than others. Boris Berezovsky's fall from his position of influence within presidential circles was spectacular. Equally spectacular was his comeback! As regards the Putin era, Berezovsky was instrumental in helping set up a new, pro-Putin party (Unity), which did so well in the December 1999 general election. But Berezovsky fell from grace during the summer 2000 offensive against some of the oligarchs. Throughout he has remained immensely wealthy and outspoken. (See below.)

Many ill-gotten gains have found their way abroad, a large part of 'capital flight' being illegal. (See Chapter 3.) Money laundering via Western banks situated abroad certainly involves Russian mafia money. But these banks are also useful tax avoidance mechanisms.

Among the causes of crime and corruption (the abuse of public office for personal gain) are the weakness of central government in certain respects (such as ensuring the rule of law) coupled with often copious regulations in other respects (such as licences). Other causes include a poorly developed civil society. Putin has vowed to institute a 'dictatorship of the law'.

Anders Åslund provides some startling statistics. 'A small group of businessmen enriched themselves and then corrupted many of Russia's politicians and officials. They have conspired to stymie economic reforms, which would stimulate growth and help the overall population, because reform threatens their domination. Russian suffers not from too free a market but from corruption thriving on their excessive regulations erected by a large and pervasive state' (Åslund 1999b: 64). 'Russia's elite started making their fortunes in the Soviet Union's last years, mostly from three sources: commodity exports, subsidized credits and food imports. The best way of making a killing between the late 1980s and 1993 was to buy commodities such as metals or oil at low, state-controlled prices in Russia and then sell them abroad at world prices ... Gorbachev's partial liberalization let thousands of enterprises pursue foreign trade. In 1988 state enterprise managers were allowed to set up private co-operatives for arbitrage with "their" government-owned businesses. Managers of state companies bought oil from their enterprises privately, extracted export licences and quotas from corrupt officials, and sold the oil abroad at the market price ... In 1992 the Russian price of oil was still 1 per cent of the world market price. A few state enterprise managers, government officials, politicians and commodity traders amassed no less than $24 billion, or 30 per cent of Russia's GDP, in this peak year of gains from commodity trading. These profits gradually dwindled. Eventually the reformers succeeded in deregulating commodity prices, but only after managers had extracted billions of dollars from their state enterprises. Business elites had an alternative way of making money in the early 1990s: cheap credits from the Russian central bank ... In 1992, while inflation was 2,500 per cent, the bank issued credits at 10 or 25 per cent a year ... Many Russian bankers became rich ... Only in late 1993 did the reformers manage to end this pilfering. A third way of making big money in the transition period was through food-import subsidies ... A food importer paid only 1 per cent of the going exchange rate when purchasing essential foods from abroad, but could easily resell them relatively freely on the domestic market and pocket the subsidy. These imports were paid for with Western "humanitarian" export credits that were added to Russia's state debt. Total import subsidies were 17.5 per cent of Russia's GDP in 1992. These profits were highly concentrated, benefiting a limited number of traders in Moscow who operated through the old state agricultural monopolies ... Altogether, the gains from these three parasitic business activities amounted to no less than 79 per cent of GDP in 1992 ... The rise of the oligarchs was the result of slow and partial reforms. If commodity prices, exports and imports had been allowed to prevail, these fortunes would never have been made. Russian enterprises would have been forced to restructure to survive ... The managers of companies ... in total obtained at most 4 per cent of GDP from privatization, a trifle compared with the profits made through regulated exports, subsidized credits and import subsidies' (pp. 65–8). 'Today the Russian bureaucracy, government, parliament and regional governments are deeply corrupt' (p. 70).

Grotesque inequalities in income and wealth have arisen. While the financial oligarchs have become obscenely rich and powerful in the ways described, vast numbers of Russian citizens (especially many older people) have become pauperized and demoralized. Factors such as the stoicism of a long-suffering people and the weakness of civil society (including trade unions) help explain the lack of a violent reaction. (See Chapter 9.)

There is increasing recognition among analysts of transitional economies in general that the institutional basis of a market economy takes a long time to put in place. (See Chapter 1.) Just think how long it has taken the Western countries to develop appropriate political, legal and economic institutions and attitudes (including informal codes of behaviour such as 'gentlemen's agreements'). And yet even today massive financial scandals, for example, arise periodically. In transitional economies there is a vital need for an efficient and honest legal system to enforce contracts and property rights. The vacuum that exists when the state is too weak to fulfil these vital functions is quickly filled by organized crime. What is particularly disturbing about countries like Russia is the common occurrence of links between the mafia and corrupt officials.

'It is widely believed that a liberal economy is inconsistent with a strong government. But in fact a liberal economic systems *needs* a strong government. It needs one because a liberal economy presumes laws and rules that are the same for everyone, and the only way to ensure such uniformity is through a strong government. One that tolerates no exceptions. One that cannot be bought. One that is capable of meeting out punishment' (Pyotr Aven, the president of Alphabank and former minister of foreign economic relations in Russia, *CDSP*, 1999, vol. 51, no. 7, p. 5). 'Key institutional foundations ... [include] an effective judicial and law enforcement system, the creation of a healthy commercial banking system, and a coherent policy for changing the structure of incentives so as to encourage entrepreneurship and fixed investment rather than rent-seeking and asset stripping' (United Nations Economic Commission for Europe, *Economic Survey of Europe 1998*, New York: United Nations, 1998, p. 10). 'Among the most damaging of the mistaken conclusions that were drawn early on in the transition process, both by Western advisers and by policy makers in Moscow, was that the Russian state remained too strong. The need to scale back inefficient spending, and to create room for private inefficient spending is a necessary task for which a strong public administration is required; but this is a quite different task from *restructuring* the state so that it is strong enough and capable to perform the functions required to support a market economy' (p. 9). 'Russian public administration is infamous for its lack of transparency and corruption' (p. 34).

The European Bank for Reconstruction and Development stresses the importance of institutional change in the next phase of transition in general. 'Some aspects of a market economy can and have been created quickly in transition economies, in particular through market liberalization and privatization. However, developing the institutions and business practices required for a well-functioning market economy takes much longer' (EBRD 1998b: iv). 'The imbalance has continued to widen between the earlier successes of privatization and liberalization and the more difficult structural and institutional challenges of the next phase of transition. These challenges include corporate governance and enterprise restructuring, financial sector reforms, infrastructure reform, and fiscal and social reforms … The challenges of the next phase … require a substantial and constructive role of the state at a time when its capacity is still underdeveloped and subject to capture by powerful economic interests' (pp. vi–vii).

Privatization of the non-agricultural sectors of the economy has been very rapid. (See Chapter 5.) But the gigantic task has been undertaken in ways which have been controversial and at times downright scandalous:

1. Even the first stage of privatization (1 October 1992–1 July 1994) has been severely criticised, e.g. the favouring of 'insiders' (existing workers and managers), leading to problems such as a lack of enterprise restructuring and of corporate control, and asset-stripping by owner-managers. The main argument put forward in support of 'insider' privatization was that speedy privatization was necessary to make the reform process irreversible and thus a weak central state (in a society not generally enamored with privatization) had to 'bribe' the 'insiders' in general and the powerful managerial lobby in particular. Critics felt that a rapid and more equitable first stage of privatization could have been achieved by means of a more conventional and thus more extensive voucher (mass) privatization programme in order to gain public support. (In such a programme all eligible citizens are allotted vouchers, for free or at nominal cost, which can be used to buy the bulk of shares in the enterprises on offer.) Well-regulated investment funds could help overcome the problems of corporate governance, while a small percentage of shares distributed for free or on favourable terms to 'insiders' would have been adequate as an incentive to efficiency.

Gaddy and Ickes (1998a) comment generally on marketization and industrial privatization in the context of what they call a 'virtual economy'. 'Most of the

Russian economy has not been making progress toward the market or even marking time. It is actively moving in the other direction. Over the past six years Russian companies, especially in the manufacturing sector, have indeed changed the way they operate, but to protect themselves against the market rather than join it. What has emerged is a new kind of economic system with its own rules and its own criteria for success and failure. The new system can be called Russia's virtual economy because it is based on an illusion about almost every important parameter: prices, sales, wages, taxes and budgets … It is the real cause of the web of wage, supply and tax arrears from which Russia cannot seem to extricate itself' (pp. 53–4). 'Although Russia formally has privatized most of its industrial sector, the pace of economic restructuring is still grossly inadequate to ensure stable economic growth … Enterprises continue to trade with one another without the use of money – either by not paying each other at all or by using non-monetary means, such as barter or promissory notes, called vecksels … What explains the failure of Russian enterprises to restructure? … The environment induces them [managers] to postpone or avoid restructuring … Formal activities of enterprises … are reflected in official statistics and result in the cash payment of taxes. But below the surface Russian enterprises engage in informal activities, as a means of survival and as a response to the structure of taxation and the weak system of corporate governance. Informal activities involve non-monetary transactions: the "soft" goods are sold against promissory notes such as vecksels or exchanged for other goods and services (barter). These transactions – including taxes paid in kind – occur outside the formal monetary system and consequently are much less observable, contrary to "hard goods" that are produced and sold through monetary transactions (for cash) in the formal economy … Initially, barter was seen as a natural response by some enterprises to the high inflation that prevailed in Russia after prices were liberalized. But the use of barter has increased despite financial liberalization. This could be explained by the shortage of liquidity, as high interest rates made it hard for enterprises to borrow. The impetus to barter, however, often comes from the seller. This suggests other motivations for the widespread use of barter, including its usefulness in beating Russia's onerous tax system' (pp. 2–3). 'Tax offsets fundamentally change the set of choices available to Russian enterprise directors. By allowing enterprises to pay taxes in "soft goods" (that is, output for which there is no effective demand), tax offsets provide an incentive to avoid restructuring' (p. 3). 'Hard goods sold for cash yield monetary tax liabilities as well as income that must be paid to shareholders and other stakeholders … On the plus side, high-effort goods are easier to translate into cash, which may be needed to procure important inputs … Russia appears to be generating a dual economy. Alongside a modernizing private sector [there exists] a paternalistic, unrestructured industrial sector' (p. 5).

'The central problem of the Russian economy is simple. The country has a large number of enterprises that are continuing to operate even though they are producing obsolete products of little value ... A complex web of barter transactions and subsidies keeps inefficient companies alive. Under current law many resource-producing companies are forced to continue supplying inputs to technically bankrupt enterprises ... Instead of payments the resource supplying companies are given a credit against their tax liability' (James Gwartney, *FT*, 9 May 2000, p. 27).

Thus privatization has not eliminated 'soft budget constraints'. 'In an attempt to understand why economic reform has failed in Russia we looked at the performance of ten representative sectors ... In Russia the more productive companies are often the least profitable. Thus, more productive companies are not gaining market share and not pushing less productive firms out. In nine out of the ten sectors the direct cause of low economic performance is market distortions that prevent equal competition. The distortions come from attempts to address social concerns, corrupt practices and lack of information. In the manufacturing sectors regional governments channel implicit federal subsidies to unproductive companies. Such subsidies take the form of lower tax and energy payments, and are allegedly intended to prevent companies from shutting down and laying off workers [distortions can also take forms such as different import tariffs and differential access to government-controlled export infrastructure: p. 19]. This puts potentially productive companies at a cost disadvantage, blocking investments and growth on their part ... We found the other often mentioned reasons for Russia's economic problems to play a much smaller role (e.g. poor corporate governance and lack of a transport infrastructure)' (McKinsey Global Institute 1999: 8–9).

2. It is difficult not to agree with Jeffrey Sachs's view of privatization in sectors such as oil and gas: 'When the economic reforms got underway in 1992 Russia's vast natural resources provided unparalleled opportunities for theft by officials. Oil, gas, diamond and metal ore deposits were nominally owned by the state and thus by nobody. They were ripe for stealing – or for "spontaneous privatization" as Russians cynically call it ... When natural resource enterprises were privatized the system was often skirted or compromised by ad hoc decrees and hidden arrangements ... It is hard to know who owns Gazprom, the partly privatized natural gas giant, whose first chairman was Viktor Chernomyrdin, the prime minister' (*IHT*, 6 December 1995, p. 10).

The 1995 'shares-for-loans' scheme was simply a scandal. Valuable assets were in effect transferred cheaply into the hands of the financial oligarchs, encouraged by factors such as collusion among the permitted potential bidders (foreigners being typically excluded from bidding). The most blatant cases were the ones where the eventual purchaser was the (legally permitted) organizer of the auction! A political quid pro quo has been detected in the shape of the massive, self-interested help (financial and via their extensive media) given by the oligarchs in the successful campaign to reelect President Yeltsin in 1996 (after being very low in the polls earlier on).

Dmitri Vasiliev, who resigned on 15 October 1999 as head of the federal securities commission, stated: 'Not much was done to ensure the protection of investors … It is absolutely clear that we have not received the full support of other state bodies concerning investor problems.' The difficulties of protecting property rights and enforcing contracts can affect even big international players, as, for example, BP Amoco found in late 1999.

More recent sales of state assets have been more above board. (See Chapter 5.)

Putin does not intend any major overturning of previous privatizations. (See below and Chapter 12.)

The privatization picture in agriculture contrasts starkly with that in industry. (See Chapter 6.) Although the private plot has rapidly grown in importance, progress with private (peasant) farms has been very slow. Hindering factors included the conservatism of the countryside, the uncertainty of life in the new market economy and resistance from many Soviet-era managers. But regional variations are apparent, with areas such as Nizhny Novgorod more go-ahead as regards agricultural reform. President Yeltsin and the State Duma could not agree on a new land code, the main sticking point being the question of land sales. In the absence of a federal code a number of provinces (such as Saratov and Samara) have passed their own laws on land sales. The more cordial relations between the new State Duma (elected in December 1999) and President Vladimir Putin (elected in March 2000) should ensure more rapid progress on issues such as the land code.

Direct foreign investment in Russia is tiny compared with that in China. (See Chapter 4.) There was a significant increase in 1996, but the financial crisis soon knocked the recovery on the head. The value of direct foreign investment can be illustrated in the case of banking. The drawbacks of shielding generally weak, poorly regulated and even corrupt domestic banks from the competition provided by foreign banks were clearly illustrated when the financial crisis hit Russia in August 1998. Depositers need to have confidence in banks and loans have to be allocated with profitability rather than cronyism in mind. Factors deterring direct foreign investment in general include heavy, arbitrary and erratic taxes, the weakness of property rights and contract enforcement, the slowness in approving production sharing agreements in the oil sector, and the extraordinary degree of crime and corruption. (Oil and natural gas have always been among the strongest magnets for direct foreign investment. The rapid recovery of the economy from the financial crisis of August 1998 was greatly helped by the high world price of oil. In turn this considerably enhanced the attractiveness of the energy sector. Other sectors have also benefited.)

There was hyperinflation in 1992. It took three attempts to bring inflation under control. (See Chapter 7.) Yeltsin admitted on 16 February 1995 that 'Two serious attempts were made to curb inflation in the years of reform … The third attempt must be a success.' The two earlier attempts led to tortuous negotiations with the IMF and a huge decline in the nominal exchange rate of the rouble against the US dollar. Inflation had fallen to relatively low levels by 1997, despite the fact that inter-enterprise arrears weakened monetary policy. The currency reform of 1 January 1998 was a success, lessons having been learned from the mistakes of earlier reforms such as that in July 1993. But the financial crisis of August 1998 exposed Russia's fundamental weaknesses. The Russian government defaulted on domestic debt and was forced to allow the rouble to float. 'The Russian government was forced to devalue the rouble on 17 August 1998; it also announced a unilateral rescheduling of most of its short-term debt into long-term securities and the imposition of a ninety-day moratorium on payments by Russian banks and enterprises on much of their foreign debt' (United Nations, *World Economic and Social Survey 1999*, p. 57).

An aspect of globalization was the financial turmoil which affected many emerging market economies (a term which include the transitional economies) and which became known as the Asian financial crisis. (See Chapter 7.) Mexico was hit in 1994, but attention was centred on events after July 1997 when the currency of Thailand came under speculative attack. The panic spread to other Asian countries (such as Indonesia). As regards the transitional countries, it is interesting to ask why Russia was devastated by the Asian financial crisis while China and former communist countries such as Hungary and Poland escaped relatively unscathed.

On 17 August 1998 Russia itself actually became the cause of further financial turmoil. (See Chapter 7.) This happened despite the fact that Russia is now considered to be a minnow in world economic terms. 'Russia's economy... is about the size of Switzerland's' (*The Economist*, 31 October 1998, p. 108). ('Russia's economy [is] smaller than that of the Netherlands': *The Economist*, 18 December 1999, p. 13.) 'It is easy to forget that Russia is a small economy, whose trade links with the West are tiny. Western Europe's exports to Russia, for example, account for well under 0.5 per cent of GDP. However, it is already clear that the impact of this crisis will be greatly disproportionate to Russia's size' (*FT*, 29 August 1998, p. 10). 'The country now accounts for less than 1 per cent of global GDP; its entire federal budget is dwarfed by the size of US military spending' (*FT*, 23 December 1998, p. 2). 'According to the IMF, Russia's GDP in 1999 was just 2 per cent of that of the USA' (*FT*, 3 June 2000, p. 14).

The main point to make is that the countries most adversely affected suffer from *fundamental weaknesses*, weaknesses cruelly exposed by the Asian financial turmoil. In Asia, for example, there is the phenomenon of 'crony capitalism' (such as incestuous links between government and companies and between banks and 'their' companies in the allocation of capital funds). Let us analyse what has happened to Russia.

Ironically, Russia seemed to be turning the corner in 1997, e.g. the economy grew (although only barely) for the first time since 1989, inflation was modest (after hyperinflation in 1992), direct foreign investment was markedly higher than in 1996 and the balance of payments on current account was still in surplus. Thus it should not be forgotten that events outside Russia (including falling world market prices for oil and gas, which are vitally important exports) played a part in its recent demise. The chilling effects of the Asian financial crisis were kept at bay in the autumn of 1997 and the spring of 1998, albeit at the expense of dramatic rises in interest rates. So what went wrong on 17 August 1998 when the Russian government defaulted on its domestic debt and was forced to allow the rouble to float? What are the fundamental weaknesses of the Russia economy which have dramatically distanced it even further from the economies of, say, Hungary and Poland?

Russia's inability to raise sufficient tax revenue to finance the *central* (federal) government's essential activities is crucial to gaining an understanding of the crisis. On 23 June 1998 Sergei Kiriyenko (prime minister 23 March–23 August 1998) stated: 'If the state does not learn to collect taxes it will cease to exist.' Anatoli Chubais had earlier (17 April 1997) thought likewise: 'Russia is experiencing a monstrous state budget crisis, whose parameters, if truth be told, call into question the ability of the state to perform its functions' (*FT*, 18 April 1997, p. 2). 'The government is basically bankrupt. New York City collects more in municipal taxes than Russia collects federal taxes' (Boris Fyodorov, a former finance minister, *FT*, 18 February 1999, p. 14). 'Deputy finance minister Mikhail Kasyanov said Wednesday [10 February 1999] that the IMF wanted Russia to double its tax collection ... "The IMF considers that the revenues of the federal budget should be 17 per cent to 18 per cent of GDP", said Mr Kasyanov' (*IHT*, 11 February 1999, p. 13). 'Russia's inability to collect taxes is rapidly becoming the greatest threat to its economic and political stability. The current government cannot raise the revenues needed to run a modern state. Since economic reforms began in 1992 federal tax revenues have fallen from about 18 per cent of Russia's GDP to less than 10 per cent in 1997 – compared with about 31 per cent in Austria, 27 per cent in Germany and 18 per cent in the USA' (Treisman 1998: 55). 'A different model is now gaining currency among political and economic analysts, who say that Russia is in imminent danger of becoming a "failed state", not breaking into pieces as the Soviet Union did in December 1991, but simply ceasing to function as a cohesive federal government' (David Hoffman, *IHT*, 27 February 1999, p. 1).

It is important to note the stress on the federal level. 'The concern is not that the government does not collect enough taxes. In fact, it collected 32 per cent of Russia's GDP last year [1997], the same proportion that the United States does. The problem is rather that Russia has no actual tax system. In practice, taxation is a free negotiation between the ubiquitous tax inspectors and taxpayers, meaning that the strong win and small entrepreneurs are chased out of business' (Anders Åslund, *IHT*, 29 April 1998, p. 10). 'The problem is an arbitrary tax system, with excessively high rates and ruthless government officials ... The present system is so arbitrary that you are more likely to be forced to pay a penalty if you pay your taxes than if you ignore them altogether. Moreover, excessive rates make it impossible to collect taxes. Until recently penalties have been extraordinarily high and big enterprises presume they can be negotiated away ... Apparently many big companies enjoy immunity ... One serious problem is that taxes tend to stop at the regional level, where budgets are extremely wasteful' (Anders Åslund, *The World Today*, July 1998, pp. 185–6). 'The tax system must be simplified and tax rates reduced. The current system stifles growth, penalizes honesty and encourages evasion' (James Gwartney, *FT*, 9 May 2000, p. 27). (Other important factors hindering tax collection is the weakness of the tax ethic – the 'social contract' being eroded because of the central government's poor record in providing social services in return for taxes – and the widespread use of barter.)

Features of the Putin tax reforms, introduced in 2000, included the following: the overall tax burden was reduced; the share of the tax burden borne by businesses was lowered at the expense of the consumer; the tax system was simplified in order to increase transparency, equality of treatment and willingness to pay (e.g. a flat rate personal income tax and a unified employers' social security tax). (See Chapter 7.)

A budget deficit occurs when a government spends more than it raises in tax revenue. The size of the budget and the way it is financed have a crucial bearing on the control of inflation. The budget deficit can be financed by (1) increasing the money supply, (2) borrowing from the private sector of the economy and/or from foreigners, or (3) some combination of (1) and (2). ('When government spending exceeds tax revenues the difference is financed by selling government bonds. If these are sold to the public then the net effect on the money supply is zero. But if they are purchased by the central bank the money supply rise that accompanies the deficit is not offset: this is known as "printing money" or "monetizing the deficit"': *The Economist*, 20 November 1999, p. 142.) (It is now the federal budget, rather than the consolidated state budget, which includes the regions, which is now the central focus of debate: *RET*, 1994, vol. 3, no. 2, p. 9. Unlike local budgets the federal budget can be financed by money creation: *RET*, 1994, vol. 3, no. 3, p. 10. Note also the increasing stress on the 'primary' federal budget deficit or surplus, i.e. excluding the snowballing state debt servicing.)

Russia conquered the hyperinflation which occurred in 1992 when a massive budget deficit was financed entirely by printing money. By 1997 inflation was at a relatively modest level. This was achieved by gradually reducing reliance on the printing press to finance persistently high (though generally declining) budget deficits. The federal budget deficit in 1995 was financed almost entirely by bond sales and external credits (*RET*, 1995, vol. 4, no. 4, p. 5). The federal budget deficit has remained stubbornly high, though, with problems on both the tax and spending sides (despite, as regards the latter, delays in the payment of state wages and pensions, a policy which is non-sustainable in the long run). The federal budget deficit (according to the

IMF definition) was 7.9 per cent of GDP in 1996, 7 per cent in 1997 and 5 per cent in 1998 (*RET*, Monthly Update, 20 January 1999, p. 24, and 10 February 1999, p. 10). (The federal budget deficit was 5.8 per cent in 1993, 9.8 per cent in 1994 and 5.2 per cent in 1995: *RET*, 2000, vol. 9, no. 1, p. 118.) (IMF definition: 'Privatization receipts and net sales of state gold reserves are counted as deficit financing': *RET*, Monthly Update, 10 February 1999, p. 24. The EU's Maastricht criterion as regards the budget deficit is a maximum of 3 per cent of GDP.)

But heavy dependence on *short-term borrowing* ultimately proved to be unsustainable. Servicing the national debt took up an increasing proportion of government expenditure and investors became increasingly unwilling to roll over their loans. The crunch finally came. 'The Russian authorities have been forced to attract increasing amounts of foreign funds to finance the deficit: by selling Treasury bills to foreigners and by borrowing from the international financial markets. This has resulted in an increase in the exposure of Russia to volatile short-term foreign capital' (United Nations Economic Commission for Europe 1998b: 24–5). 'Russia's most immediate problem is that it has too large a short-term government debt in comparison with international reserves' (Anders Åslund, *Transition*, 1998, vol. 9, no. 3, pp. 10–11). 'The current crisis in Russia arose largely from a failure of the state – its inability to collect taxes, to enforce laws, to manage its employees and to pay them' (EBRD 1998b: iv). 'At the root of Russia's macroeconomic problems have been persistently high federal budget deficits' (p. 14). The fundamental causes of the budget deficit were political: an inability to rein in government spending, weak tax discipline among politically influential firms and an excessive devolution of revenue to regional governments ... Politicians have been unwilling to draw sharp distinctions between public and private property or to impose hard budget constraints on large enterprises, both out of fear of the unemployment implications and to preserve rent-seeking opportunities for powerful vested interests' (pp. 14–15). 'From 1995 the federal government financed much of its deficit by issuing short-term (less than one year) rouble-denominated Treasury bills (GKOs) and longer-dated coupon-bearing bonds (OFZs). Foreigners rushed into the high-yielding Russian debt market and, by the end of 1997, held an estimated 33 per cent of the total stock of GKOs and OFZs (p. 13). Foreign investors in the GKO market were at first obliged, and many later chose, to hedge themselves against the risk of devaluation by buying dollar forward contracts with Russian banks. The hedge contracts increased the exposure of the Russian banking system to declines in the rouble (p. 14).

A word or two may be in order about the controversies surrounding exchange rate regimes and controls on capital flows. After mid-August 1998 the nominal rate of exchange of the rouble against the US dollar quickly plunged from over six to over twenty. There was a vociferous debate prior to 17 August 1998 about the policy of defending the rouble on the foreign exchange market.

'A devaluation in Russia would be catastrophic ... The greatest achievement of the reformers has been to bring low inflation and financial stability. If they cannot even do that they will lose all credibility ... A devaluation would lead to an immediate increase in inflation and, even worse, to bank failures. And bank failures would lead to bankruptcies of enterprise. Unemployment would rise on a massive scale ... Without the Asian debâcle, there would be no crisis now in Russia. The G7 nations need to put together a stabilization fund of at least $10 billion which would be available for the Russian government' (Richard Layard, *The Independent*, 29 May 1998, p. 23). 'Devaluation is not necessary because the rouble is not overvalued. Last year Russia had a huge trade surplus of $20 billion and it has had similar trade surpluses for years ... Devaluation would undermine what little remaining confidence there was in the rouble and the exchange rate would drop by 80 to 90 per cent' (Anders Åslund, *Transition*, 1998, vol. 9, no. 3, pp. 10–11). (Åslund was an early adviser to the Russian government.)

Jeffrey Sachs, who was an economic adviser to the Russian government from December 1991 to January 1994, thinks the opposite. He believes that exchange rates should generally float. 'It is neither worthwhile nor feasible to twist monetary policy to soothe panicky investors, especially at the cost of internal depression. The only real exception to floating rates comes at the start of stabilization from extreme inflations, when exchange rate targeting is more efficient than monetary targeting' (*The Economist*, 12 September 1998, p. 24). 'Emerging market currencies should be allowed to float, since countries with pegged currencies too often run out of foreign reserves' (Jeffrey Sachs, *The Independent*, 1 February 1999, p. 11).

My own view is that is makes no sense to use vital foreign exchange reserves to try to defend the exchange rate of a currency under attack in a deregulated world of massive and highly mobile private capital flows. There is an inherent weakness with adjustable peg exchange rate regimes, since private speculators are on an essentially 'one-way bet'. All that is at risk is relatively modest transactions costs since a currency under heavy attack is not going to strengthen. (Britain found this out to its cost when it was forced to leave the exchange rate mechanism of the European Monetary Mechanism in September 1992 and George Soros, for example, made a fortune.) Thus much IMF aid to Russia was wasted in a futile defence of the currency. It would be far better, for example, to use what should be generous Western aid to strengthen the legal and regulatory system and to encourage the development of civil society (the self-organization of individuals in society).

Proponents of 'big bang'/'shock therapy' have always recommended rapid current account convertibility of currencies in transitional economies. But the Asian financial crisis has reinforced the view that capital account liberalization ought to be a much slower and selective process. 'Premature liberalization of capital markets ... was one cause of the current crisis ... Developing countries should impose their own supervisory controls on short-term international borrowing by domestic financial institutions' (Jeffrey Sachs, *The Economist*, 12 September 1998, p. 24). Naturally, there is considerable debate about the merits of imposing controls on short-term capital flows. Critics argue, for example, that such controls are not very effective and that it would be better to concentrate on basic problems such as regulation.

The effects of the financial crisis on Russia were profoundly adverse at first in terms of output, but the rebound was surprisingly rapid:

After GDP grew (by 0.8 per cent) in 1997, the economy returned to negative growth the following year (GDP falling by 4.6 per cent). The financial crisis led to sharp declines in real incomes and savings, a rise in the proportion of the population in poverty, increasingly shortages and difficulties in gaining access to bank deposits. (Social unrest, however, continued to be very limited.)

The IMF predicted that GDP in Russia would fall by 7 per cent in 1999 before stabilizing in 2000. The IMF report said: 'In the absence of coherent stabilization and reform policies, however, there would remain a risk of high inflation and continued economic contraction; access to international financial markets would be unlikely to resume; and much of the progress tentatively achieved in some areas during 1991–98 would be lost' (*FT*, 21 April 1999, p. 6). 'For 1999 the usually judicious IMF had forecast that Russian GDP would slump by 9 per cent' (Anders Åslund, *IHT*, 19 January 2000, p. 8).

There were fears that hyperinflation would return as a result of a massive increase in the money supply. This did not happen, but the monthly inflation rate rose noticeably at first. In July 1998 prices grew only 0.2 per cent month-on-month. The monthly inflation rate was 15.3 per cent in August (year-on-year), 38.4 per cent in September, 4.5 per cent in October and 5.7 per cent in November 1998 (*RET*, Monthly Update, 4 September 1998, p. 1).

There was a sharp fall in imports immediately following the mid-August 1998 crisis. In September 1998 imports fell by 65 per cent compared with the previous month (*RET*, Monthly Update, 4 September 1998, p. 1). On 6 October 1998 prime minister Yevgeni Primakov said: 'The rouble's collapse has resulted in a sharp decline in food imports, which in recent years have accounted for half our food supplies' (*CDSP*, 19998, vol. 50, no. 40, p. 5). Food imports fell by 60 per cent in September 1998 (*CDSP*, 1998, vol. 50, no. 46, p. 7). (The share of imported goods in retail sales peaked at 53 per cent in 1995: *RET*, Monthly Update, 30 January 1998, p. 4.)

'Gloomy forecasts predicting hyperinflation and a deep recession have not yet been realized. In spite of the collapse of Russia's banking system and the breakdown of its financial markets, the country appears to have started on the path of real growth by taking advantage of the rouble devaluation that has made Russian goods more competitive' (*RET*, Monthly Update, 14 May 1999, p. 1). 'At that time [August 1998] forecasts were made predicting hyperinflation and a rapid reduction in production ... This gloomy scenario [however] did not materialize. Instead the economy has been on a path of recovery with impressive growth rates in industrial production. Inflation has come down ... [Central bank chairman] Gerashchenko's actions have been very different from that of 1992–4 ... Emissions have been kept at a reasonable level ... Two events in particular have provided the foundation for the industrial recovery and healthy export environment. These are the devaluation of the rouble in August 1998 and the agreement made by OPEC in March 1999 to limit world oil supply, bringing surging world market oil prices ... The real exchange rate has depreciated 43 per cent since July 1998 ... A devaluation of this magnitude ... gives domestic producers and exporters a competitive edge. For Russia this has materialized in the form of strong growth in industrial production, driven mainly by import substitution and an improved situation for exporters, many of which have their costs in roubles and revenues in dollars ... The devaluation has had a positive impact on Russia's current account and trade account, mainly due to the effect on imports' (*RET*, Monthly Update, 10 September 1999, pp. 3–6). 'In the first nine months of the year [1999] the federal government exceeded its tax collection target by 27 per cent, while the expenditure target was more or less kept' (*RET*, 1999, vol. 8, no. 4, p. 4).

'GDP rose 3.2 per cent [in 1999] ... thanks largely to a surge in industrial output [which rose by 8.1 per cent]. While a boost in world oil prices contributed usefully, the main gains came from import substitution prompted by the 80 per cent decline in the rouble's international value. Exports stayed roughly constant, but imports dropped by more than a third' (*FT*, Survey, 10 May 2000, p. ii).

'The 1998 financial crash seems to have been a catalyst for more profound change. By imposing tough budget constraints the crash convinced many Russian businessmen that they could no longer live off the state but had to make real money in the market. Meanwhile the much-publicized barter economy is dwindling' (Anders Åslund, *IHT*, 19 January 2000, p. 8).

'By destroying the government debt market and devaluing the rouble the crash has forced companies to look for investment opportunities' (*Business Central Europe*, May 2000, pp. 35–6).

There are many concerns about Russia's long-term prospects since many fundamental weaknesses remain.

'The rouble is rising against the dollar. Coupled with [rising] inflation this erodes the competitiveness that Russian has enjoyed since devaluation. So the economy remains acutely vulnerable. Its fragility is a result of the lack of structural reform since the financial crisis ... Investment, though up a bit on the pitiful levels of last year [1999], is still paltry when set against Russia's modernization needs' (*The Economist*, 8 July 2000, p. 125). (In 1999 investment in fixed assets rose by 1 per cent: *CDSP*, 2000, vol. 52, no. 11, p. 17.)

Stanley Fischer, acting managing director of the IMF (6 April 2000): 'The good macroeconomic performance since early 1999 cannot be sustained without a broad-based acceleration of structural reforms ... The sustained growth that is needed will require an acceleration in economic reforms to spur investment and strengthen exports as well as comprehensive tax and expenditure reforms' (*FT*, 7 April 2000, p. 10; *IHT*, 7 April 2000, p. 15).

'The positive effects of the past year were almost guaranteed by the devaluation. They have also been substantially helped by the oil price rise. But there is no persuasive evidence that the devaluation has led to, or even been used for, reforming the Russian economy and improving its prospects in the longer term' (Clifford Gaddy, *Post-Soviet Affairs*, 2000, vol. 16, no. 1, p. 17). 'What real 1999 increment in production, in monetization and in fiscal balance has occurred is the result of massive devaluation coupled with a very fortuitous rise in energy and resource prices, and is unsustainable without massive investment and structural change' (Richard Ericson, p. 18).

President Vladimir Putin (8 July 2000): 'Russia's economic weaknesses continues to be another serious problem. The widening gap between the advanced countries and Russia is pushing us into the ranks of third-world countries. The figures showing current economic growth should not put our minds at ease ... The current growth has very little to do with the revamping of the economic mechanism. It is largely the result of favourable foreign economic conditions' (*CDSP*, 2000, vol. 52, no. 28, p. 5).

Prime minister Mikhail Kasyanov: 'While Russia's economic performance has improved significantly since the financial crisis of August 1998 much of the improvement is the result of one-off events. The challenge for Russia today is to implement extensive structural reforms that will ensure long-term economic growth and macroeconomic stability' (*FT*, 20 July 2000, p. 23).

'There is a strong consensus that in order to attain sustainable economic growth further progress must be made in the area of structural reforms' (*RET*, 2000, vol. 9, no. 1, p. 4).

'For sustainable growth to be achieved, Russia will have to make significant progress in improving the investment climate, in enterprise restructuring and in eliminating barter, non-payments and arrears' (EBRD 2000a: 3).

'The new-found profitability of a number of industrial firms may be related not only to the weaker rouble and strong export prices, but also to severely repressed domestic prices for energy and transportation. This latter factor continues to raise questions about the quality and sustainability of current industrial growth' (OECD, *Economic Outlook*, June 2000, p. 146).

Other effects of the financial crisis were as follows:

1. The Asian financial crisis had a devastating effect on stock markets. 'Between March and August [1998] the Moscow stock exchange, which was the world's best-performing market in 1997, lost more than 80 per cent of its value' (*Transition*, 1998, vol. 9, no. 4, p. 7). The Russian Trading System (RTS) index reached a 1997 peak of 571.6 on 6 October (*IHT*, 3 June 1998, p. 1). On 17 September 1998 the RTS index was only 51.7. 'The RTS stock index ... slid 85 per cent last year [1998], when it was the world's worst' (*IHT*, 23 February 1999, p. 13).

A rally soon followed, however. 'If Russia's stock market was labelled the worst performing stock market of 1998, the first three months of 1999 told a different story. The Moscow Times dollar index, which fell 87 per cent during the course of 1998, rose 58.9 per cent in the first three months of 1999, making Russia one of the world's best performing markets so far this year. A recent boost was given by expectations of part of the defaulted GKOs being swapped for equity (under the restructuring deal foreign holders of GKO Treasury bills will receive 10 per cent in cash which can then be invested in certain shares, decided by the ministry of finance, on the stock market) and by progress in the government's negotiations with the IMF. Equally the recent increase in the world market price of oil has aroused interest in the shares of oil companies' (*RET*, Monthly Update, 13 April 1999, pp. 15–16). 'The equity market, which slumped by more than 90 per cent last year [1998], is up 145 per cent in 1999, making it the best performing stock market in the world' (*FT*, 9 July 1999, p. 15). The stock market has gyrated since then. *The Economist* publishes the value of the Russian stock markets in dollar terms: on 3 March 1999 the figure was 73.3; on 29 March 2000 it was 232.4; on 28 June 2000 it was 170.2; on 30 August 2000 it was 240.0; on 18 October 2000 it was 184.0; on 1 November 2000 it was 194.1; on 22 November 2000 it was 166.2.

2. Russia's gold and foreign exchange reserves, already low, continued to fall. On 7 August 1998 they stood at $17 billion (*IHT*, 22 August 1998, p. 4), while on 26 March 1999 the figure was $10.9 billion (*IHT*, 2 April 1999, p. 13). There were increased restrictions on hard currency trading. (The reserves were later boosted by factors such as rapidly rising world oil prices. 'Russian gross gold and currency reserves have begun to increase, moving from roughly $11 billion in the first three quarters of 1999 to over $16 billion by April 2000': OECD, *Economic Outlook*, June 2000, p. 146. 'International reserves rose sharply from $12.5 billion at the end of 1999 to $23 billion by August 2000': EBRD 2000b: 202.)

3. The regions of Russia began to adopt policies (in some cases unconstitutional) which weakened federal control. These policies (in many cases temporary) included refusal to send funds to the central government, price controls and restrictions on the transport of food to other regions of Russia.

4. Antiseminism stirred up by individuals like Albert Makashov (a communist member of parliament) seeking scapegoats for the increasing misery. The crisis gave further ammunition to previous attacks on the Jewish financial oligarchs. 'Six of the seven oligarchs are Jewish' (David Hoffman, *IHT*, 9 April 1999, p. 5).

5. Deep-seated commercial banking problems were severely exacerbated by the events of mid-August 1998.

'Facing substantial margin calls and refusal of creditors to roll over their liabilities, Russian banks bought foreign exchange to repay debts, in the process drying up their liquidity and creating interbank loan defaults' (Desai 2000: 51).

Government attempts to free up the jammed payments system have included several attempts to offset debts and liabilities with the aid of central bank loans. Some bank deposits have been transferred to the reliable state savings bank, Sberbank (which holds around 80 per cent of retail deposits: *RET*, Monthly Update, 11 November 1998, p. 2). Bank mergers have been encouraged. But there has been no fundamental restructuring of the commercial banking system.

6. Russia's credibility in international financial circles was severely dented. Funding by the IMF became even more necessary for any significant funding from other international sources. Direct foreign investment fell sharply.

Detailed negotiations with banks about rescheduling domestic debt have not helped, since the terms of the final deal have been essentially forced upon creditors. (See Chapter 7.) Various estimates have been made, implying more or less confiscatory terms. 'The whole package is worth about 4 cents on the dollar' (*FT*, 18 December 1998, p. 4). 'The ministry's current derisory, restructuring offer would leave debt-holders with about 5 cents in the dollar' (*The Economist*, 20 March 1999, p. 109). 'Bondholders are now contemplating a restructuring deal worth – at best – one solitary cent in the dollar' (*The Economist*, 24 April 1999, p. 99).

'Russia made a return to the domestic debt market in February [2000] as the government issued a modest 2.5 billion roubles in new short-term GKOs. This is the first issue since the August 1998 crisis' (*RET*, Monthly Update, 10 March 2000, p. 16).

Russia has also at times effectively (though not formally) defaulted on its sovereign debt, disguised by payment delays and formal reschedulings. Defaults (in effect) have not only applied to Soviet-era debt. Rolled over IMF loans have on occasion avoided formal defaults (which the IMF is not permitted to condone) on loans the institution has made since 1992. (See Chapters 7 and 8.)

Russia's record of fulfilling IMF conditions has been poor and there is a debate about whether some funds have been used corruptly. (See Chapters 7 and 8.) Another criticism often heard is that some Western countries (especially the USA) twist the IMF's arms behind the scenes to continue funding for broader political reasons. Russia's prowess as a military (especially nuclear) power in the world far outstrips its economic importance and funding has in fact continued after various delays and adjustments. The IMF itself was sympathetic to reformist prime minister Sergei Kiriyenko. On 13 July 1998 there was an agreement in principle to provide a $22.6 billion loan package of new ($17.1 billion) and old ($5.5 billion) loans (of which the IMF was to provide $15.1 billion, the World Bank $6 billion and Japan $1.5 billion). But, as before, Russia failed to meet many of the conditions laid down. The State Duma, for example, failed to pass critical aspects of government fiscal policy. On 20 July 1998 the IMF board released the first tranche, but reduced the amount from $5.6 billion to $4.8 billion. Some of the IMF loan

($3.8 billion, according to the government) was used in a vain attempt to defend the value of the rouble against the dollar. On 11 September 1998 Viktor Gerashchenko became chairman of the central bank for the second time. But there has been no massive increase in the money supply and thus no return to hyperinflation.

On 5 February 1999 the State Duma approved the 1999 budget at its fourth and final reading by 308 votes to fifty-eight. The 1999 budget envisaged revenues of 473.8 billion roubles, expenditures of 575.1 billion roubles, and thus a deficit (after interest payments) of 101.3 billion roubles (2.53 per cent of GDP). Part of the deficit was to be financed by central bank credits (32.7 billion roubles) (*RET*, Monthly Update, 10 February 1999, p. 11). As regards external debt obligations, $9.5 billion was budgeted compared with $17.5 billion actually due (p. 12). Total federal revenues were to amount to 11.84 per cent of GDP (almost 10 per cent arising from taxes) and federal expenditures to 14.38 per cent of GDP. The planned federal budget deficit of 2.54 per cent of GDP arose despite a primary budget surplus of 1.64 per cent of GDP (*RET*, Monthly Update, 13 April 1999, p. 1). But assumptions underlying the draft budget (such as those relating to inflation, the exchange value of the rouble and foreign funding) were generally considered to be unrealistic.

On 29 March 1999 Michel Camdessus (managing director of the IMF), on a visit to Moscow, said that a framework agreement had been reached on an IMF loan. An IMF mission was to visit Moscow to work out the details of the programme, which would then be submitted for approval to the board. The size of the loan was not revealed. A joint statement said: 'The parties have agreed on a primary budget surplus of 2 per cent of GDP to be realized in 1999 and most of the measures needed to achieve it.' Earlier the IMF had demanded a surplus of 3.5 per cent.

'Stanley Fischer ... [first deputy managing director of the IMF] added that the IMF had relaxed its negotiating stance on a Russian primary surplus of 3.5 per cent because it would have resulted in "unrealistically large cuts in pensions" and civil service salaries' (*FT*, 1 April 1999, p. 4). Russia is facing more than $6 billion in foreign debt repayments through July and a total of $17.5 billion in 1999 as a whole, including $4.5 billion owed to the IMF (*IHT*, 30 March 1999, pp. 1, 4). 'Russia owes the IMF $19 billion, making it one of the lender's largest debtors' (*IHT*, 8 April 1999, p. 13).

On 28 April 1999 it was announced that the IMF had reached a preliminary agreement to lend Russia $4.5 billion over the following eighteen months. But the cheque never left Washington, being merely transferred from one accounts to the other to avoid formal default by Russia and to ensure that the aid is used for the purposes specified. The Fund insisted on things like strengthened bankruptcy laws, improved tax collection, a restructured banking system and a rise in the value-added tax from 15 per cent to 20 per cent. Michel Camdessus said Russia had agreed to provide the IMF with an explanation of how earlier loans had been used. Funds from the World Bank and Japan (a package totalling $7.8 billion including the IMF loan) were conditional on a definite IMF agreement.

On 29 July 1999 the IMF executive board approved a loan of $4.5 billion. 'The money will be used for refinancing the country's debt to the Fund' (*RET*, Monthly Update, 10 August 1999, p. 13). The IMF planned to extend $4.5 billion during the course of 1999 and 2000. The first tranche of $640 million was to be disbursed on 1 August 1999 (*RET*, 1999, vol. 8, no. 3, p. 84).

'The Russian central bank lied to the IMF in 1996 about the level of its foreign exchange reserves ... an auditor's report has concluded ... The report from PricewaterhouseCoopers concluded that the central bank channelled assets through Fimaco, based in the Channel Island tax haven of Jersey ... Central bank reserves had been overstated by $1.2 billion in the middle of 1996. But Stanley Fischer, deputy managing director of the IMF, said there was no evidence of "large-scale misappropriation of money" through Fimaco. He also said the auditors found no evidence of wrongdoing in the handling of $4.8 billion lent to Russia in July 1998 ... Apart from $1 billion that went, as agreed, to the budget, the rest went in foreign exchange intervention ... It [the central bank] would in future exclude any deposits from reserves' (*FT*, 29 July 1999, p. 2). 'In 1996 the central bank left the IMF with the impression that $1.2 billion remained in its currency reserves when it fact the money had been rerouted elsewhere' (*IHT*, 6 August 1999, p. 13). 'Most attention has been focussed on Fimaco's 1996 operations, when the central bank used it as a backdoor conduit to invest in Russia's short-term Treasury bills, known as GKOs, which were then just becoming available to foreigners ... The central bank shifted money through Fimaco, a subsidiary of Eurobank, a French bank in which the Russian central bank owns 78 per cent ... In Russia the central bank, together with its affiliate Sberbank, were known to dominate 50 per cent of the GKO market' (*IHT*, 31 July 1999, p. ii).

On 25 August 1999 the government submitted a draft of the 2000 budget to the State Duma. Assumptions included an inflation rate in the range 18 to 22 per cent, an exchange rate of thirty-two roubles to the US dollar and a GDP growth rate of 1.5 per cent. The budget deficit was projected at 1.1 per cent of GDP, with a primary surplus of 3.1 per cent of GDP (*RET*, Monthly Update, 10 September 1999, p. 14).

'A decision [was made] this week by the IMF to further postpone delivery of a long-awaited $640 million credit ... Originally due to be delivered in September ... the loan was postponed after the fund, at the urging of leading industrial countries, pressed for new conditions, aimed largely at structural economic reforms, in part as a result of the Russian financial scandals. Failure to meet those conditions, which include measures setting higher standards of accountability and openness for Russian financial institutions, have been cited by IMF spokesmen as the reasons for the latest delay' (*IHT*, Wednesday 8 December 1999, p. 6). 'The IMF's decision to delay the next disbursement of a $640 million tranche [was] ostensibly for technical financial reasons' (*FT*,

9 December 1999, p. 8). 'The IMF said it would delay disbursement of further credits to Russia because Moscow had not implemented agreed structural reforms, including more effective bankruptcy legislation and improved banking regulations' (*FT*, 13 December 1999, p. 10). (The tranche was delayed in the midst of Western criticism of the way Russia was conducting the war in Chechenia.) 'Russia completed its loan repayments for 1999 to the IMF' (*IHT*, 29 December 1999, p. 13).

'The federal budget deficit, calculated on a cash basis, comprised 1.7 per cent of GDP in 1999 ... A very small part of the federal deficit was financed by foreign borrowing ... The bulk of the deficit was financed with credits from the central bank' (*RET*, 2000, vol. 9, no. 1, p. 66). The finance ministry says the primary budget surplus in 1999 was 2.2 per cent of GDP (p. 95). The federal budget deficit, according to the IMF definition, was 1.7 per cent in 1999 (*RET*, Monthly Update, 11 August 2000, p. 25). (IMF definition: 'Privatization receipts and net sales of state gold reserves are counted as deficit financing': *RET*, 10 February 1999, p. 24.)

'On 26 August [2000] the draft budget was submitted to the Duma ... For the first time a balanced budget is being proposed ... Interest payments (which exactly equal the primary surplus since the deficit is zero) are envisaged at ... 3.1 per cent of GDP. The first reading of the draft in the Duma is scheduled for 22 September' (*RET*, Monthly Update, 15 September 2000, p. 12).

'This is the first balanced budget in all the years of reform. Not counting debt service, revenues will exceed expenditures by 3.1 per cent of GDP. The extra revenue will go towards paying off our foreign debt, [finance minister] Kudrin said. Russia is supposed to pay back $14.5 billion next year [2001], but that is if the Paris Club does not agree to restructure Soviet debts. Right now the government is optimistic, so the budget reflects about $6 billion in debt service and $4.5 billion in payments on the principal. In other words, the government is planning to pay only about $10.5 billion altogether' (*Kommersant*, 10 August 2000, p. 2: *CDSP*, 2000, vol. 52, no. 32, p. 10).

'[On 6 October 2000] the lower house of parliament approved the country's first ever balanced budget ... The Duma approved the budget in the first reading' (*FT*, 7 October 2000, p. 8).

The extent to which the West should provide aid in general, and on what terms, is a subject of considerable debate. (See Chapter 8.) Critics express concern, for example, that aid can actually hinder the implementation of vital economic reforms. Personally, I have always been at one with Sachs in his view that the West is very shortsighted when it comes to providing aid. The West lost a golden opportunity in the very early stages of the transition, for example, to help the reformist government set up the institutions necessary for successful market-orientated reforms. Jeffrey Sachs's controversial attacks on the IMF make entertaining reading. Russia's foreign debt, however, is relatively small given the size and endowment of its economy. Russia is actually a net international creditor, being owed more than it owes. But the problem is that most of the debt owed to Russia by poor and current/former communist countries will never be repaid. On 17 September 1997 Russia became a member of the Paris Club of creditor nations.

Chapter 9 deals with economic performance, health and the environment. GDP growth rates were negative from 1990 to 1996. There were a number of false dawns and the return to positive growth in 1997 was followed by a return to negative growth in 1998 as a result of the financial crisis. Note that the official figures for output tend to overstate the contraction to some degree owing to factors such as the generally improving quality of products, greater reliability of statistics, and the inadequate account taken of the contribution of the expanding private sector (much of it in the black economy). Some argue that electricity consumption is a better guide to real overall economic performance. Living standards need also to take account of the black economy, the end of endemic shortages and the rise in the quality of goods. Inequality in the distribution of income and wealth has reached obscene proportions.

There have been profound structural changes in the Russian economy, such as the growing importance of services at the expense of manufacturing industry. But the overall investment record has been abysmal, greatly hindering restructuring. (See Table 9.1.)

The hyperinflation of 1992 was conquered and by 1997 the inflation rate was not much into double figures. The 1998 inflation rate was not too bad since increases in the money supply were held in reasonable check.

The relatively low rate of unemployment, even using standard international definitions, are arousing considerable interest. One factor, it is argued, is the flexibility of the market, which allows real wages to fall.

The typical surplus on the balance of payments on current account has been a bright spot in a generally bleak overall economic performance.

In 1999, in contrast to early forecasts, GDP growth turned decidedly positive owing to such factors as the large depreciation of the rouble and rapidly rising world oil prices. Inflation did not take off. (In 1999 GDP was an estimated 57 per cent of the 1989 level: EBRD 2000b: 65.)

The demographic picture in modern Russia is depressing. Between the end of 1992 and the end of 1999 the population of Russia had fallen from 148.6 million to 145.5 million. Male life expectancy fell from a peak of 65 years in 1987 to a low of 57.6 years in 1994. In 1998 the figure was 61.8 years, only to fall once again to 59.8 years the following year.

The reformers did badly in the general election of 12 December 1993 and ensured that friction between the weak parliament and the powerful president continued. (See Chapter 12.) But the fact that there was a good turnout for a reasonably fair election in which generally embryonic parties participated was a remarkable achievement in itself. In the December 1995 election for the State Duma the big winner (as expected) was the Communist Party of the Russian Federation, profiting from the pain of transition experienced by large sections of the population. (See Chapter 12.) Zhirinovsky's Liberal Democratic Party did much better than expected but worse than in the 1993 election. Grigori Yavlinsky's party (Yabloko) did worse than expected. Prime minister Chernomyrdin's new party (Our Home is Russia) performed disappointingly but still ended up as the second largest party in parliament. Alexander Lebed's Congress of Russian deputies did much worse than expected. Friction between parliament and president continued. But both the general election of 1995 and the presidential election of 1996 seemed to show that there was no going back for the Russian people. What the majority seemed to want was a fairer, more protected, more gradual, more orderly and less corrupt transition to a new system.

The draft of the new constitution was published on 9 November 1993, providing for a strong presidency and a weak parliament. (See Chapter 12.) This followed the violent dénouement of President Boris Yeltsin's quarrel with parliament in the shape of the blasting of the 'White House' into submission on 4 October 1993. But Yeltsin continued to be generally at odds with parliament. Given the power of the presidency, Yeltsin's recurrent illnesses and erratic (at times even bizarre) behaviour caused considerable concern both at home and abroad. Even a successful quintuple heart-bypass operation on 5 November 1996 did not end Yeltsin's health problems and frequent absences and his unpredictability. Out of the blue, for example, he dismissed the long-time prime minister Viktor Chernomyrdin and the entire cabinet on 23 March 1998. Yeltsin had great difficulty in getting the State Duma to accept as his candidate for prime minister the young, little known and reformist Sergei Kiriyenko (made acting prime minister on 23 March 1998 but not approved until 24 April 1998). He, in turn, was dismissed on 23 August 1998 but Yeltsin failed altogether in his attempt to persuade the State Duma to reinstate Viktor Chernomyrdin to his old position. It took a long time before it became clear that Yeltsin would not run for a third term as president. Before his health took a decisive turn downwards he chopped and change his statements, one minute saying he would run again for a 'third' term as president and the next minute saying he would not. (Only two terms are allowed, but there was the constitutional problem of whether Yeltsin was eligible to run again, since he was elected for the 'first' time when Russia was still part of the Soviet Union. On 5 November 1998 the constitutional court ruled that Yeltsin could not seek a third term as president, but the court did not actually examine the issue of whether he had a legal right to run for election again.) The State Duma considered five impeachment charges against Yeltsin, namely illegally conspiring to to destroy the Soviet Union in 1991, overthrowing the constitutional order and violently dispersing the elected parliament in 1993, illegally unleashing the (first) war in Chechenia, undermining national defence by ruining Russia's armed forces, and committing 'genocide' against the Russian people by pushing market reforms that led to falling birth rates, shortened life expectancy and widespread poverty. But the State Duma failed (on 15 May 1999) to get the required minimum number of votes (300) for any charge, including what was generally considered to be the most likely to succeed (the one referring to Chechenia) which received 283 votes. Yeltsin did not succeed in getting the Council of the Federation to accept the dismissal of the chief prosecutor, Yuri Skuratov. (President-elect Vladimir Putin did succeed and quickly, on 19 April 2000.) The assassination of the reformist politician Galina Staravoitova in St Petersburg on 20 November 1998 shocked even the more cynical interpreters of the Russian scene.

But Yeltsin was generally seen as reliable and predictable in certain regards:

1. There was a 'honeymoon' period with the West despite Russia's humiliation at the precipitous decline in her international status. Friction over issues such as Nato expansion brought this period to an end and there was international concern over Yeltsin's two-fold use of force in Chechenia (as has already been discussed). But Yeltsin was still viewed in the West as someone who was broadly a 'friend' and as someone who could be relied to keep Russia broadly on track as regards political democracy and economic reform. (Jack Matlock, a former US ambassador to the Soviet Union: 'In a meeting in Moscow last December [1999] Mr Yeltsin's spokesman told me that his boss was determined to go down in history as the person who made the restoration of communism impossible': *IHT*, 29 March 2000, p. 8.) At home he comfortably won the 1996 presidential (albeit with the media/economic help of the financial oligarchs and with the help of extravagant gestures/promises) on a platform of looking forward not backwards and was seen as the only alternative to a president of the extreme left or right. (See Chapter 12.) Despite harsh criticism of Nato's decision to start bombing Yugoslavia on 24 March 1999, Yeltsin promised that Russia would not intervene or even provide arms to Slobodan Milosevic. In fact he appointed Viktor Chernomyrdin as his special envoy on the crisis and Russia played an important mediating role.

The crisis over Kosovo was in fact brought to an end with the aid of Russian diplomacy. (See Chapter 13.) When Nato started bombing the Federal Republic of Yugoslavia on 24 March 1999 relations between Russia and Nato sunk to their lowest level since the disintegration of the Soviet Union. Russia suspended co-operation with Nato and participation in the Partnership for Peace programme and did not accept the invitation to attend the fiftieth anniversary of Nato (on 23 April 1999). But Yeltsin, despite harsh words, ensured that the arms embargo (imposed by the UN Security Council on 31 March 1998) was not broken and the peace plan drawn up by Russian special envoy Viktor Chernomyrdin and Finnish president Martti Ahtisaari was accepted by the Federal Republic of Yugoslavia on 3 June and by the UN Security Council on 10 June 1999. The role of and command structure relating to Russian troops in the international peacekeeping force in Kosovo was resolved (so it seemed) after considerable discussion and extra tension brought about by Russia's success in getting some of its troops into Kosovo ahead of Nato forces, taking control of Pristina airport on 12 June. Relations between Russia and Nato then improved rapidly and Yeltsin himself attended the final day of the G8 meeting on 18–20 June 1999. But soon afterwards further prickly discussions took place. It was not until 5 July 1999 that an announcement was made, although not all details were revealed. At any rate Russian troops began to be deployed in Kosovo, welcomed by ethnic Serbs there but given a generally hostile reception by ethnic Albanians, who see Russia as an ally of Serbia.

2. Yeltsin was generally seen as obsessed with holding on to power. (See Chapter 12.) (He also liked to take credit when things went right and blamed members of the government when things went wrong.) Until Vladimir Putin (seen as strong enough to ensure Yeltsin's post-retirement immunity from corruption charges) Yeltsin dismissed anyone perceived of as a real rival and played off one individual or group against another so that he could act as ultimate arbiter. Yeltsin personally went into steep decline during the financial crisis (although he bounced back after Nato began to bomb Yugoslavia on 24 March 1999). In such a powerful presidential system this was potentially extremely destabilizing, but the practical running of the country was left largely in the pragmatic hands of Yevgeni Primakov. He became acting prime minister on 10 Setember 1998 and gained State Duma approval (on the first vote) the following day. Primakov gained broad approval across the political spectrum and provided essential political stability. Even so Yeltsin on occasion hinted that even Primakov was not indispensable and actually dismissed the prime minister on 12 May 1999, allegedly on the grounds slowness as regards economic reform. Factors explaining the slowness of a comprehensive economic package included a broad cabinet containing members with significantly different views. The government was faced with the problem of reconciling priorities such as payment of wage and pension arrears with avoiding hyperinflation through an over-reliance on printing money to finance the budget deficit (and so regain access to international aid and finance).

Next in the merry-go-round of prime ministers was Sergei Stepashin, who was made acting prime minister on 12 May 1999 and approved by the State Duma on 19 May on the first vote. But Yeltsin clearly did not see him as likely to win the next presidential election or strong enough to protect Yeltsin and members of his family from any corruption charges. The failure to prevent the Fatherland-All Russia bloc turning into an opposition centre of power was also a commonly listed reason for Stepashin's dismissal.

Yeltsin dismissed Sergei Stepashin on 9 August 1999 and nominated the almost unknown Vladimir Putin as prime minister (the post being approved by the State Duma on 16 August in the first round of voting).

Vladimir Putin's meteoric rise from relative obscurity to president (on 26 March 2000) is truly remarkable. (See Chapter 12.) A new party (Unity), based almost entirely on support for Putin, came second only to the Communist Party in the party list seats in the 19 December 1999 election for the State Duma. Yeltsin saw him as his successor and a man strong enough to protect the Yeltsin family after the presidential election. This manufactured succession succeeded despite Yeltsin's rapidly declining popularity. ('In the wake of the August [1998] financial crisis Mr Yeltsin's approval rating fell to just 2 per cent': *FT*, Survey, 10 May 2000, p. i.) It succeeded in large part because of the popularly-supported Chechen war. It is not possible to totally discredit the idea that the bombings in Russian cities, officially attributed to Chechen terrorists, were actually the result of a Kremlin conspiracy.

Putin was born on 7 October 1952 and became a middle-ranking KGB agent in the Soviet era. He worked in the GDR and learned to speak German. In the new Russia he became first deputy mayor of St Petersburg under Anatoli Sobchak, a leading reformer whose reputation was later sullied by corruption allegations. Among Putin's important duties was the attraction of foreign investment. On 25 July 1998 Putin was appointed head of the Federal Security Service and on 29 March 1999 he also became secretary of the 'security council'. (Details of Putin's career can be found in the entry for 9 August 1999.)

Boris Yeltsin unexpectedly announced his resignation as president at around mid-day on 31 December 1999. Prime minister Vladimir Putin became acting president (as of midday) until the holding of a presidential election. Putin immediately signed a decree entitled 'On guarantees to the President of the Russian Federation after he leaves office and to the members of his family': 'After leaving office the President of the Russian Federation enjoys immunity. After leaving office the President of the Russian Federation may not be prosecuted on criminal charges, subjected to administrative penalties, detained, arrested or subjected to search, interrogation or personal inspection. The immunity enjoyed by the President of the Russian Federation after he leaves office extends to his places of residence and of work, the vehicles and means of communications he uses, all documents and baggage belonging to him and his correspondence.'

The presidential election was held on 26 March 2000. (See Chapter 12.) There were eleven candidates, but the only thing in doubt was whether prime minister and acting president Vladimir Putin would win in the first round. In fact, he did, with 52.64 per cent of the vote. Gennadi Zyuganov (leader of the Russian Federation Communist Party) came second with 29.34 per cent. Grigori Yavlinsky (leader of Yabloko) came a distant third, with 5.84 per cent. Vladimir Zhirinovsky (leader of the Liberal democratic Party of Russia) was fifth, with 2.72 per cent of the vote. (Zhirinovsky ran in the general election as leader of Zhirinovsky's Bloc because of trouble registering with the electoral commission. 'Vladimir Zhirinovsky ... has supported the Kremlin on crucial votes': *IHT*, 21 December 1999, p. 6. 'Mr Zhirinovsky ... has proved to be Mr Yeltsin's unfailing parliamentary ally': *FT*, 21 December 1999, p. 6.)

Vladimir Putin was sworn in as president on 7 May 2000. Putin: 'For the first time in all of Russian history supreme power is being handed over in the most democratic and simplest possible way – through the will of the people, legitimately and peacefully ... The peaceful transfer of power is a crucial element of the political stability that you and I have dreamed of, that we have striven for and tried to achieve.' Putin nominated Mikhail Kasyanov as prime minister.

('The leaders of Mr Primakov's All-Russia movement, including the presidents of Tatarstan [Mintimir Shaimiyev], Bashkortostan [Murtaza Rakhimov] and Ingushetia [Ruslan Aushev], and the governor of St Petersburg [Vladimir Yakovlev], said they had unanimously decided to support Mr Putin': *FT*, 6 January 2000, p. 1. On 4 February 2000 Yevgeni Primakov announced that he would not run in the presidential election. On the opening day of the new parliament last month [January] a pro-Putin party known as Unity allied itself with the opposition Communists and took control of the parliament's top leadership positions. One goal of the manoeuvre, analysts say, was to block Mr Primakov from being elected speaker': *IHT*, 5 February 2000, p. 5. Unity's parliamentary start was not smooth. Members of various other parties were so upset by an agreement between Unity and the Communist Party over the election of a speaker and control over most committees that they started a boycott of the State Duma. The boycott lasted from the opening session on 18 January 2000 to 9 February 2000.)

Although Putin did not formally campaign, he received a great deal of publicity in the media. 'In preliminary findings released yesterday [27 March] an observation team from OSCE concluded that it had seen no evidence of significant fraud that would have affected the outcome. In a more critical report the European Institute of the Media attacked the disproportionately large and favourable coverage given to Mr Putin on television and in newspapers' (*FT*, 28 March 2000, p. 10). Apart from the general popularity of the second Chechen war, Putin was commonly seen as the strong leader needed to combat the high degree of corruption and crime in Russia and to strengthen Russia's international status. Other factors working in his favour were an improving economic situation and a generally pro-reform stance.

Putin's attitude towards the 'oligarchs' has aroused considerable interest. (See chapter 12.) In June, July and August 2000 there were moves (some later reversed) against a number of the oligarchs and/or the companies that they represent. The reaction was mixed one, however. Although the moves were generally popular in Russia because of the typically poor reputation of the 'oligarchs', concerns were expressed about threats to media freedom because of the control over important sections of the media exercised by 'oligarchs' critical of Putin (such as Vladimir Gusinsky and Boris Berezovsky). (There are more general concerns about Putin's attitude towards the media, e.g. his signing, on 12 September 2000, of a new information security doctrine, which critics consider to be a possible threat to media freedom.) The major events were as follows:

1. On 13 June 2000 Vladimir Gusinsky (president of Media-Most) was arrested for alleged fraud. The formal charge was 'large-scale embezzlement' of state funds. The loss to the state was said to amount to about $10 million and was related to the privatization at a low price of a St Petersburg television company (Channel 11). The following day seventeen leading businessmen signed an open letter condemning the arrest. The seventeen included Vladimir Potanin (Interros), Anatoli Chubais (UES), Mikhail Friedman (Alfa Group), Pyotr Aven (Alfa Bank), Mikhail Khodorkovsky (Yukos), Rem Vyakhirev (Gazprom)and Valdimir Yevtushenkov (Systema). Among those who did not sign were Boris Berezovsky, Roman Abramovich and Vagit Alekperov. Gusinsky was released from prison on 16 June and then went to Spain. In late July 2000 it was announced that the case against Vladimir Gusinsky was to be dropped, owing, prosecutors say, to 'lack of the fact of a crime'.

'The Russian prosecutors office said Tuesday [19 September] it had begun investigating a claim that the country's biggest independent media group was trying to back out of a takeover agreement with the Gazprom natural gas monopoly. The investigation ... comes at Gazprom's request ... Gazprom is demanding that ... Vladimir Gusinsky ... honour a July agreement to yield control of his company [Media-Most] to settle debts to Gazprom. Mr Gusinsky says the agreement was forced on him at "gunpoint, so to say" and under pressure from the Kremlin. He has vowed not to sell out ... One of the provisions of the 20 July agreement, disclosed for the first time in documents made public Monday [18 September], suggest that the Kremlin was prepared to make a deal with Mr Gusinsky under which he would not be subject to prosecution as long as he remained silent and did not criticise the government ... In late July charges were dropped and Mr Gusinsky was permitted to leave the country. He has not returned to Russia [from Spain] ... Gazprom, which is 38 per cent owned by the state ... has made a $211 million loan secured by 20 per cent of Media-Most shares, and another loan, for $262 million, due next summer, is backed by another 20 per cent of the company ... Media-Most ... includes radio, print and a pay television system, as well as NTV. Mr Gusinsky's news magazine, Itogi, is a partner of Newsweek ... On 20 July Mr Gusinsky signed a deal to settle all debts with Gazprom for $773 million, which comprised forgiveness of the outstanding $473 million in loans, plus an additional $300 in cash from Gazprom. But just two days earlier Mr Gusinsky made a sworn statement saying that he was being forced to make a deal by the press minister, Mikhail Lesin, a point man for the Kremlin' (*IHT*, 20 September 2000, p. 13).

'The president, like prime minister Kasyanov, considers Mr Lesin's actions "unacceptable"' (*CDSP*, 2000, vol. 52, no. 39, p. 5).

'Russian prosecutors began a criminal embezzlement investigation Thursday [28 September] against the heads of companies belonging to Media-Most ...

The prosecutors were acting on accusations that Media-Most had hidden assets abroad to avoid having them seized by Gazprom' (*IHT*, 29 September 2000, p. 4). 'The deputy prosecutor said yesterday [28 September] that the fraud charges were made because Media-Most shares used as security for the [Gazprom] loan had been moved to offshore funds … Mikhail Kasyanov, the prime minister, said yesterday that Mr Lesin [the press minister] has "acted improperly in signing a document on relations between the two for-profit companies"' (*The Independent*, 29 September 2000, p. 14). 'The prosecutor general's office has instituted criminal proceedings in response to an appeal by Gazprom-Media. The company complained that this April nearly all of Media-Most's assets were transferred out of the holding company, leaving it no longer in possession of controlling stakes in its constituent companies. Meanwhile, Gazprom still holds 40 per cent of media-Most as collateral for two loans to the company, one of $211 million, the other of $275 million. Gazprom executives contend that the withdrawal of assets has devalued its collateral and damaged its interests' (*CDSP*, 2000, vol. 52, no. 39, p. 5).

'Media-Most … yesterday [18 October] said it had reached an outline agreement with Gazprom … in a deal that would preserve its independence from the state. The vaguely worded statement … also hinted that the heavily indebted Media-Most was in talks with a significant international investor' (*FT*, 19 October 2000, p. 11). 'Vladimir Gusinsky … and Gazprom have agreed that Mr Gusinsky can pay off his debt to the monopoly in a way that will allow his media group to remain independent, according to officials on both sides. The deal means that Mr Gusinsky will be allowed to use company stock to settle his $211.6 million debt, plus interest of $36.9 million, as the two parties had originally envisioned' (*IHT*, 20 October 2000, p. 8).

'Russia's general prosecutor yesterday [1 November] … summoned … Vladimir Gusinsky and Boris Berezovsky … who are currently outside Russia … to appear in Moscow on 13 November, with the threat of prison and international arrest warrants if they failed to show up … for questioning about alleged criminal business dealings … The general prosecutor's office said it now had sufficient proof [in the case of Boris Berezovsky] to bring charges of large-scale theft … in relation to alleged embezzlement from the state airline Aeroflot … Separately it accused Mr Gusinsky of "deceit and abuse of trust" and embezzlement in securing more than $300 million in loans from Gazprom' (*FT*, 2 November 2000, p. 12).

'Russian prosecutors yesterday [13 November] issued an arrest warrant for Vladimir Gusinsky … as news emerged of a debt agreement which would see Mr Gusinsky lose control of key parts of his empire. Under a deal signed on Saturday [11 November] Gazprom … will emerge as the largest single shareholder in NTV, Russia's leading private channel, with 46 per cent of the company's shares. An additional 19 per cent in NTV will be sold to outside investors' (*FT*, 14 November 2000, p. 9). '[Gazprom] on Tuesday [14 November] suddenly backed out of ... [the] agreement' (*IHT*, 15 November 2000, p. 15).

'Boris Berezovsky yesterday [15 November] refused to attend a Moscow court to face charges of embezzlement' (*The Times*, 16 November 2000, p. 19). (Berezovsky, like Gusinsky, was still out of the country.)

'Media-Most ... yesterday [17 November] said it had signed an agreement to swap its debt for equity with Gazprom. The deal ... would give him [Gusinsky], Gazprom and an outside investor yet to be found blocking stakes ... A Media-Most executive said the deal ... paved the way for a restructuring of the group's debts while preserving its independence from the dominance of any of the shareholders' (*FT*, 18 November 2000, p. 10).

2. On 21 June 2000 a lawsuit was launched against Norilsk Nickel.

'Masked and armed police yesterday [28 June] raided a Siberian company controlled by two of Russia's influential business oligarchs ... TNK, an oil subsidiary of the Alfa group owned by Pyotr Aven and Mikhail Friedman ... The action was related to an investigation concerning the sale in 1997 to a subsidiary of Alfa of shares in TNK previously owned by the state ... Legal action was launched in Moscow last week against the Russian commodities group Norilsk Nickel ... A Moscow court [decided] to question the legality of the ... privatization of Norilsk Nickel, controlled by Vladimir Potanin' (*FT*, Thursday 29 June 2000, p. 10). 'The conduct of my company Interros is now being questioned by the Moscow prosecutor' (Vladimir Potanin, *FT*, 29 June 2000, p. 27).

3. 'Yesterday [11 July] Russian authorities ... accused the chairman of Lukoil, the country's largest oil company, of tax evasion ... Prosecutors yesterday also targeted Vladimir Potanin, chairman of Interros, the financial holding company that controls ... Norilsk Metal. They said Mr Potanin must pay $140 million to make up the amount they said he underpaid for a 38 per cent stake in the enterprise ... The case against Media-Most involves charges ranging from invasion of privacy by security guards to financial skullduggery. Authorities are especially interested in the links between the television company and Gazprom' (*FT*, 12 July 2000, p. 10).

4. 'Russian authorities yesterday [12 July] launched their third big criminal tax investigation in a month, fresh evidence that President Vladimir Putin is mounting a serious attack against the country's most powerful businessmen, or oligarchs. The probe into an alleged $600 million tax fraud at Avtovaz, Russia's largest car maker, follows investigations into the tax affairs of Media-Most and of Vagit Alekperov, chairman of Lukoil, the country's biggest oil company ... The probe at Avtovaz is significant because the company has in the past been linked with Boris Berezovsky ... Yesterday Mr Berezovsky said he had ended his links with Avtovaz and denied claims by industry analysts that he retained control' (*FT*, 13 July 2000, p. 10).

'The prosecutor general of Russia on Thursday [3 August] unexpectedly halted a criminal investigation into illegal business practices by senior executives at Russia's largest automaker, Avtovaz ... Avtovaz ... is run by a former first deputy prime minister, Vladimir Kadannikov, while its cars are distributed through the Logovaz network set up by Boris Berezovsky ... Tax officials on 7 July began an investigation ... Tax officials alleged that Avtovaz had hidden the sales of about 200,000 cars by assigning them all the same identification number. But the prosecutor's office told Interfax that an inquiry had shown that the tax police did not have sufficient evidence to begin a criminal inquiry' (*IHT*, 4 August 2000, p. 5).

5. The Audit Chamber, a parliamentary watchdog, announced on 14 July 2000 that it was to investigate whether UES (Unified Energy System), the electricity monopoly headed by Anatoli Chubais, had illegally sold more than 15 per cent of its shares to foreigners 1992. The Audit Chamber is headed by Sergei Stepashin (*The Times*, 15 July 2000, p. 16; *The Guardian*, 15 July 2000, p. 16; *FT*, 15 July 2000, p. 12; *IHT*, 17 July 2000, p. 4).

6. On 28 July 2000 Putin met twenty-one leading businessmen. Boris Nemtsov conceived the idea. Among those not invited to attend were Boris Berezovsky, Roman Abramovich and Vladimir Gusinsky. Anatoli Chubais was in Finland on business. Putin said: 'I only want to draw your attention straight away to the fact that you have yourselves formed this very state through the political or quasi-political structures under your control. So perhaps what one should do least of all is blame the mirror ... We have to discuss what is to be done so that relations [between business and government] can be democratic, absolutely civilized and transparent.'

'*Kommersant* was told by a participant in the meeting that the president said everything they had expected him to. That it is necessary to strengthen the right of private ownership. That law enforcement agencies do not and will not have orders to harass businessmen, and that they are supposed to fight crime, not business. And, finally, that there has not been, nor will be, any revision of the outcomes of privatization ... [Putin] "Are you prepared, right now, to renounce the idea of installing your own people in government agencies?" ... Virtually the only guest he criticized personally was Sibneft president Yevgeni Shvidler. "Why is Sibneft paying so little in taxes?"' (*Kommersant*, 29 July 2000, p. 1; *CDSP*, 2000, vol. 52, no. 31, p. 8).

7. On 10 August 2000 tax police raided the headquarters of the oil company Sibneft and took away some documents. 'The action seemed to be a direct blow against Roman Abramovich, who has a controlling interest in Sibneft and has been named frequently by the Russian press as both a close confidant of the family circle of former president Boris Yeltsin and of those around Mr Putin' (*FT*, 11 August 2000, p. 6).

8. Boris Berezovsky (in an open letter to President Putin on 4 September 2000): 'Last week a high-ranking official on your staff issued me an ultimatum: to place under state management the block of shares in ORT [Russian Public Television] that I control, or to follow in the footsteps of Gusinsky – to all appearances Butyrka prison was meant ... If I accept the ultimatum Russia

will cease to have television news and in its place will have television propaganda controlled by your advisers … Building on the idea of creating a civil society I have decided to place the block of ORT shares that I control under the management of journalists and other members of the creative intelligentsia. I feel certain that a similar step by the state, an initiative that you could take, would enable our country's number one television channel to completely respond to its name – "Russian Public Television"' (*CDSP*, 2000, p. 52, no. 36, pp. 1–3). (On 7 September Berezovsky revealed that the official was the president's chief of staff, Alexander Voloshin: p. 5.)

'Mr Berezovsky … controls 49 per cent of the network … ORT is the most watched television channel … The state owns 51 per cent of it' (*IHT*, 5 September 2000, p. 4).

'Boris Berezovsky named "creative intellectuals" Thursday [7 September] to whom he would give control over his … 49 per cent share in ORT … He proposed turning them over in trust for four years to a committee of what he called creative intellectuals. Most of those on Mr Berezovsky's list worked at ORT or at newspapers he controls, although the list also included an employee of the US-funded Radio Liberty and a novelist' (*IHT*, 8 September 2000, p. 8). (Details are to be found in *CDSP*, 2000, vol. 52, no. 36, p. 4.)

At first attention was focussed on Putin's statements to discover the drift of the new president's general way of thinking. But more concrete policies began to emerge (see Chapter 12):

1. Putin released a policy statement on 28 December 1999: 'Russia will not soon become, if it will ever become, a second edition, say, of the USA or England, where liberal values have deep historical traditions. A strong state is not an anomaly for Russians, and not something that must be fought against, but on the contrary the source and guarantee of order, the initiator and main engine of any change … [Russia] wants a restoration of a guiding and regulatory role of the state … Our state and its institutions have always played an exceptionally important role in the life of the country and its people … [There is need for] a comprehensive system of state regulation of the economy … [Russians] are not ready to abandon traditional dependence on the state and become self-reliant individuals … Russia has reached its limit of political and socio-economic upheaval, cataclysms and radical reforms … [There will be no resort to] experiments … radicalism … revolutionary extremism … [There is need for a long-term strategy of] market and democratic reforms implemented only by evolutionary, gradual and prudent methods … Everything depends on us, and us alone, on our ability to see the size of the threat, to pool forces and set our minds to hard and lengthy work … [Russia's decline has been caused by] our mistakes and miscalculations.'

2. Putin published an open letter on 25 February 2000: 'The stronger the state, the freer the individual … [What is needed is] dictatorship of the law … It [the state] must set equal rules and comply with them … The essence of [economic] regulation is not to stifle the market and extend bureaucratic

control into new branches – but quite the contrary ... Our priority is to protect the market against illegal intervention, both bureaucratic and criminal' (*FT*, 26 February 2000, p. 5, and 28 February 2000, p. 22; *IHT*, 3 March 2000, p. 5; *Business Central Europe*, April 2000, p. 44).

3. A statement was released by Putin on 31 March 2000: 'The West misunderstands our thesis about a strong Russian state. It interprets it as an increase in the use of force, the law enforcement agencies and the security services. We have something completely different in mind, an effective state. It is a state which does not just stick to the rules of the game but is able to guarantee the same rule for everyone ... What we are talking about is a strong state where rules are secured by laws and their observation is guaranteed ... Strengthening the state and continuing market reforms are the principles on which the work of the government will be based ... Pro-market professionals [will be brought into government].'

4. Putin (his first state of the nation speech given on 8 July 2000): 'Only a strong ... an effective and democratic state can protect civil, political and economic freedoms ... The key role the government should play in the economy is, without a doubt, the protection of economic freedom. Our strategic policy is as follows: less administrative bureaucracy and more entrepreneurial freedom – freedom to produce, trade and invest ... The government's task is to co-ordinate the operations of state institutions that ensure the functioning of the market. We won't achieve stable development without genuinely independent courts and an effective system of law-enforcement agencies ... It won't be possible in the immediate future for the state to cease its involvement in the development of some sectors of our economy ... such as the defence-industry complex. The state will continue to keep strategically important branches of the economy under its constant attention ... Protection of ownership rights must be ensured ... A second area is ensuring equal conditions for competition ... A third area is freeing entrepreneurs from administrative oppression ... A fourth area is reducing the tax burden ... The customs system must be radically simplified and the duties on goods must be made uniform ... The fifth area is the development of the financial infrastructure ... The sixth area is a realistic social-welfare policy ... We are insisting on one kind of dictatorship – dictatorship of the law' (*CDSP*, 2000, vol. 52, no. 28, p. 6).

5. In June 2000 the government adopted a decidedly market-orientated economic reform programme. Comprising both short-term and long-term elements, the programme was drawn up by the Centre for Strategic Studies under its head (and subsequently minister of economic development and trade) German Gref. (See Chapter 12.)

6. Putin has stressed the need to preserve the cohesion of the federation and to revise past generous treaties with members. For example, on 22 March 2000 he said: 'Experience has shown that at the time that treaty [with Tatarstan] was the right solution, and maybe even the only viable one ... [But] the

constitution stipulates that all Federation members are equal ... [and] Tatarstan ... understands that ... [We have to] bring everything in conformity with the constitution' (*CDSP*, 2000, vol. 52, no. 12, p. 3). '"Russia was founded as a super-centralized state from the very start. This is inherent in its genetic code, traditions and people's mentality", Mr Putin said before the presidential elections' (*FT*, Survey, 10 May 2000, p. v).

On 13 May 2000 President Putin issued a decree organizing Russia into seven administrative districts, each to be overseen by a presidential representative. (See Chapter 11.) '[The decree says that its aims are] to facilitate the Russian Federation president's exercise of his constitutional powers, increase the effectiveness of federal bodies of state power and improve the system for monitoring compliance with their decisions' (*CDSP*, 2000, vol. 52, no. 20, p. 1). '[Existing] envoys rely on local leaders for housing, favours and even jobs for family members' (Michael Wines, *IHT*, 15 May 2000, p. 7). 'Under Mr Yeltsin both the envoys and many federal agencies became willing captives of the governors, who supplied the favours the Kremlin could or would not provide' (Michael Wines, *IHT*, 22 May 2000, p. 7). ('Five of the seven "super governors" are military, police or security service officers ... Sergei Kiriyenko ... [is the president's representative] in the Volga region ... That left Leonid Drachevsky as the only civilian besides Mr Kiriyenko': *The Independent*, 20 May 2000, p. 16. 'Mr Putin has tapped the the military and security services for five of the seven super-administrators': *IHT*, 20 May 2000, p. 1.)

'It was clear that the decree was intended to create the basis for a much broader recentralization of power. A few days later Putin addressed the nation on the subject and the Kremlin submitted four bills to the State Duma ... The authority leakage of the 1990s was largely a consequence of the Kremlin's weakness – of Boris Yeltsin's unpopularity and his need for regional support in battles with parliament. The situation is now reversed ... His successor is now acting with the Duma to bring the regions to heel' (Tompson 2000a: 14–16).

On 17 May 2000 President Vladimir Putin proposed to revise the composition of the Council of the Federation.

Putin (in a television address): 'The bills being submitted to the Duma continue the line that was begun by my 13 May decree establishing federal districts. This line is aimed at strengthening the unity of the state ... First is a proposal to change the principles for forming the Federation Council ... [which] is made up of representatives of the executive and legislative branches of government. But the constitution does not say that these representatives necessarily have to be the top officials of a region – the governors, republic presidents and heads of regional governments. Yet that is precisely how things are today. I believe that regional leaders should focus their energy on the specific problems of their own regions ... And they should have representatives who engage in lawmaking, but on a regular and professional basis, not once a month, the way things are now ... The second significant proposal involves introducing procedures for removing regional leaders from office and dissolving legislative assemblies that adopt acts that conflict with federal laws ... The third proposal ... [is that] if, under certain conditions, the head of a region can be removed by the country's president, then the regional leader should have a similar right with respect to lower-ranking authorities' (*CDSP*, 2000, vol. 52, no. 20, p. 5).

'The Kremlin submitted four bills to the State Duma. The first would change the mechanism for forming the Federation Council. The constitution says only that each member of the federation has two representatives, one each from its executive and legislative branches. An ordinary federal law has made the chamber an assembly of governors and speakers of regional legislatures ... The law before the Duma would require the regions to appoint individuals to represent the executive and legislature in the council. This would reduce the governors' power and status – and deprive them of parliamentary immunity ... The second bill would empower the president to ask the supreme court to remove a governor guilty of two or more violations of federal law or the constitution. He would be able to ask the State Duma to dissolve the legislature of a federation member on the same grounds ... The bill would allow him to suspend those under investigation for legal violations even without the supreme court's approval. Governors suspended by the president or removed by the court would be replaced by "temporary" presidential appointees ... A third bill would extend similar powers to the governors over the municipal and other lower-level authorities ... The president would be given analogous powers over sub-regional governments ... The new federal districts, not coincidentally, correspond with the country's major military districts' (Tompson 2000a: 14–15).

'Mr Putin unexpectedly went on nationwide television Wednesday evening [17 May] to announce that and other initiatives he said were aimed at "strengthening and cementing Russian statehood"' (*IHT*, 18 May 2000, p. 5). 'On Wednesday he proposed to evict all eighty-nine governors and the leaders of their legislators from their guaranteed seats in the Federation Council' (*IHT*, 22 May 2000, p. 7). 'Mr Putin's plan would remove the governors and other regional leaders from the Federation Council and replace them with regional representatives of lesser prestige and power. Half would be chosen by the regional parliaments and half would be chosen by the governor or regional executive. The governors would lose their immunity from prosecution as well as their parliamentary seats' (*IHT*, 24 June 2000, p. 2).

'Right now governors and chairman of province legislative assemblies automatically become deputies to the upper house of parliament. The president has proposed that instead the governors and province deputies choose the senators ... The governors would lose their deputy's immunity' (*CDSP*, 2000, vol. 52, no. 20, p. 6).

'[On 23 June 2000] the State Duma passed the bill on new procedures for forming the Federation Council on second and third (final) readings. The governors suffered defeat in almost all key areas; the deputies rejected the majority of their amendments … Regional leaders will have to clear their protégés [i.e. their nominees for executive branch representative in the Federation Council] with their regional legislatures (a procedure similar to the State Duma's confirmation of the prime minister). The second senator from a region will be elected by the local legislators on the basis of a nomination by the chairman of the house. In addition, an alternative senate candidate may be nominated by one-third of the deputies to a legislative assembly or province Duma … Under the law the election of all members of the Federation Council must be completed by 1 February 2001' (*CDSP*, 2000, vol. 52, no. 6, p. 1).

Even the Council of the Federation eventually passed the bills. The vote on 26 July 2000 was 119 votes to eighteen.

'President Vladimir Putin said Thursday [31 August 2000] that he would include regional officials in a new council [the "state council"] as consolation for losing their seats in the Federation Council … but stressed that it would only be an advisory body … saying: "Today these powers can only be consultative. What will happen in the future we will think over and decide with regional leaders"' (*IHT*, 1 September 2000, p. 7). 'President Vladimir Putin inaugurated Russia's new "state council" on Wednesday [22 November] and warned the long-powerful regional bosses who sit on the advisory body not to challenge the authority of his government … Mr Putin created the council on 1 September … The council has eighty-nine members plus the president … [Putin]: "The state council can set the direction of the country, but it must not replace parliament or the government … The most important part of our joint work is reinforcing the chain of command. That means control from the federal centre and effective feedback" … Political analysts say the new "state council" is a toothless body whose main role is to reconcile regional chiefs to their loss of influence by giving the appearance of having the president's ear four times a year' (*IHT*, 23 November 2000, p. 2).

President Putin has a far smoother relationship with the State Duma as a result of the general election of 19 December 1999 than Yeltsin ever did. (Chapter 12.) Half of the 450 seats in the State Duma were allotted on the basis of party lists. The other members were directly elected from 225 constituencies (although there was no constituency election in Chechenia because of the war there). Six (out of twenty-six) parties won enough seats in the party list section to enter the State Duma. The percentage of the vote and the number of seats won (225 in total) were as follows:

1. Russian Federation Communist Party (led by Gennadi Zyuganov), 24.29 per cent and sixty-seven.
2. Unity, 23.32 per cent and sixty-four.
3. Fatherland-All Russia, 13.33 per cent and thirty-seven.
4. Union of Rightist Forces, 8.52 per cent and twenty-four.

5. Zhirinovsky's Bloc, 5.98 per cent and seventeen.
6. Yabloko, 5.93 per cent and sixteen.

A total of 441 deputies were elected to the Duma, 225 from federal party lists and 216 in single-seat districts (*CDSP*, 1999, vol. 51, no. 52, pp. 5–6: results as of 29 December 1999).

The distribution of the 216 deputies in single-member districts was as follows: Russian Federation Communist Party, forty-seven; Unity, nine; Fatherland-All Russia, twenty-nine; Union of Rightist Forces, five; Zhirinovsky's Bloc, zero; Yabloko, four; other parties, seventeen; independents, 105. A second round of voting was scheduled for the eight single-member district seats where the majority of the electorate voted against all the candidates on the ballot paper. Elections were not held in Chechenia, the ninth vacant seat (Sakwa 2000: 101).

Although the Communist Party remained the largest single party in the State Duma, there was a dramatic, 'last-minute' increase in support for Unity and the Union of Rightist Forces:

1. The Unity governors' bloc, headed by emergency situations minister Sergei Shoigu, was formed on 24 September 1999.

'The new association is clearly the Kremlin's final attempt to get a "party of power" of its own into the running' (*CDSP*, 1999, vol. 51, no. 39, p. 13). 'It was created only three months ago and has not even published a party programme' (*FT*, 17 December 1999, p. 20). 'Unity is three months old and has no political programme or regional infrastructure' (*The Guardian*, 18 December 1999, p. 15). Prime minister Putin endorsed Unity in late November 1999 (*IHT*, 22 December 1999, p. 6). Boris Berezovsky, who was instrumental in helping to set up Unity, won a seat in Karachayevo-Cherkessia in the north Caucasus (thus gaining immunity from prosecution).

'The surprise winners of the election were two parties [Unity and the Union of Rightist Forces] ... that emerged out of the political wilderness in the last few months, boosted by their backing of a popular war in Chechenia and supported by a ferocious propaganda campaign waged by the Kremlin and its allies' (Celestine Bohlen, *IHT*, 21 December 1999, p. 1). 'The big victor from the poll was undoubtedly Vladimir Putin, the prime minister, whose ruthless prosecution of the war in Chechenia has won him a dramatic rise in popularity. The bloc he invented, known as Unity, has emerged with almost as many votes as the Communist Party, despite having no policy platform, and no regional organization. It is simply the Kremlin's party' (*FT*, editorial, 21 December 1999, p. 18).

2. The Union of Rightist Forces was formed on 24 August 1999. It is led by Sergei Kiyiyenko (New Force), Boris Nemtsov (Young Russia) and Irina Khakmada (Common Cause). (Voice of Russia, headed by Samara province governor Konstantin Titov, agreed to form a bloc with it.) Other important figures include Yegor Gaidar and Anatoli Chubais. ('Mr Putin ... said last

week that he could agree with parts of the economic platform of the rightist party. Leaders of the Right Forces, who publicly have supported the prime minister's tough conduct of the Chechenia war despite the misgivings of some of their backers, have returned the compliment by endorsing Mr Putin for president': *IHT*, Tuesday 21 December 1999, p. 1.)

Both Unity and the Union of Rightist Forces were overtly supported by prime minister Vladimir Putin, himself experiencing a rapid rise from obscurity to widespread popularity as a result of what was generally perceived to be a justified and successful prosecution of the war in Chechenia. He was widely perceived to be exercising strong leadership and restoring national pride.

The prospering of Unity and the Union of Rightist Forces mirrored the decline in the fortunes of Fatherland-All Russia. 'Mr Putin and his Kremlin allies showed great skill in destroying political opponents ... [Fatherland-All Russia] was widely expected just four months ago to lead at the polls. Under withering attack it won only third place ... The Kremlin used its control of the two leading television stations to smear Mr Luzhkov and his allies relentlessly with charges of corruption and murder, based on half-truths and outright fabrications. The government's tax authorities harassed media outlets which refused to hew the line. To be sure, Mr Luzhkov responded in kind, but it was an unfair battle. His media and financial resources pale compared with the Kremlin's' (Thomas Graham, *IHT*, 22 December 1999, p. 6). 'In the campaign both Mr Luzhkov and Mr Primakov were pummelled by a steady stream of negative, sometimes vicious, broadcasts on national television channels controlled by the Kremlin and its allies' (*IHT*, 21 December 1999, p. 1). 'The media was strongly opposed to the Fatherland-All Russia alliance' (*FT*, 21 December 1999, p. 18). 'The first and second television channels unashamedly favoured the Kremlin' (*The Independent*, 21 December 1999, p. 10). (The Fatherland-All Russia bloc is led by Yevgeni Primakov and Yuri Luzhkov. 'A left-of-centre party is now coalescing around the Our Fatherland is All Russia bloc founded by Yuri Luzhkov, Moscow's mayor, and several regional governors': *FT*, 13 August 1999, p. 2. 'Mintimir Shaimiyev [president of Tatarstan] leads the regional governors allied to Mr Luzhkov': *The Economist*, 14 August 1999, p. 14.)

Ironically, the war in Chechenia hardly registered as a debating point during the election, although Yabloko suffered from Grigori Yavlinsky's call on 9 November 1999 for peace talks and a halt to the massive offensive, albeit subject to strict conditions. (Sergei Stepashin joined forces with Yabloko on 24 August 1999.) Economic issues were also sidelined by war in Chechenia. 'The great issues facing Russia – in particular how to extricate the country from its prolonged socio-economic depression – were not even debated' (Thomas Graham, *IHT*, 22 December 1999, p. 6). But the war was not the only factor accounting for the muting of economic issues. The economy had returned to positive growth much more quickly than generally predicted after the crisis of

August 1998, helped by the huge depreciation of the rouble (which improved the competitiveness of Russian products) and the marked increase in world oil prices. In addition, there had been a narrowing of views on economic policy. 'A study of the economic programmes of the main parties, conducted by the Carnegie Moscow Centre, found that there had been a notable convergence of thinking about the main economic challenges facing Russia and how to address them' (*FT*, 17 December 1999, p. 20).

'International observers assessed the electoral campaign positively, while noting that state-run television had proved "very biased" … Their biggest criticism was reserved for the Russian media' (*FT*, 21 December 1999, pp. 1, 6).

The Russian armed forces are in generally pretty poor shape and painful decisions have to be taken about their size and configuration. The loss of the nuclear-powered submarine *Kursk* and its entire crew of 118 on 12 August 2000 and the bungled domestic rescue attempt seemed to epitomize the state of the armed forces. The loss did not do Putin's reputation for decisiveness any good either (a tarnishing that was enhanced by Putin's belated recognition of Vojislav Kostunica's win over Slobodan Milosevic in the first round of the 24 September 2000 presidential election in Yugoslavia). (See Chapters 12 and 13.) Performance in the first Chechen war was disastrous. A much improved performance in the second one is still turning out to be costly in lives lost as the promised early end to the conflict proved to be predictably false, Chechen fighters adopting guerrilla tactics. (See Chapter 11.) Coupled with the rush to expand Nato eastwards, the decline of conventional military capacity has driven Russia into increasing dependence on nuclear weapons. (See Chapter 13.) A new national security doctrine was decreed on 10 January 2000 by acting president Vladimir Putin. In December 1997 Yeltsin's strategy declared that nuclear weapons would only be used 'in the case of a threat to the very existence of the Russian Federation as a sovereign state'. The new doctrine states: 'The Russian Federation considers it possible to use military force to guarantee its national security according to the following principles: the use of all forces and equipment at its disposal, including nuclear weapons, in case of the need to repel armed aggression if all other means of resolving the crisis have been exhausted or proved ineffective'. The general election of December 1999 and the presidential election of March 2000 proved to be a catalyst in security matters.

The State Duma ratified the Start 2 treaty on 14 April 2000. (See Chapter 13.) The ratification was conditional, e.g. on the USA not withdrawing from or violating the 26 May 1972 Anti-Ballistic Missile Treaty. In this regard, Russia has rejected the US proposal to set up a national missile defence (NMD) system, a missile shield to defend the whole of US territory against a small number of strategic (intercontinental) nuclear missiles from what are now called 'states of concern' (formerly 'rogue states') such as North Korea, Iran and Iraq. Russia has suggested collaboration with Europe and the USA to jointly develop a programme using theatre anti-missile systems allowed under the 1972 ABM treaty to shoot down missiles just after launching (in the so-called 'boost phase'). The USA says that this system would be too slow in setting up and would involve US anti-missile systems outside US territory. President Clinton left the question about deployment of the NMD to his successor.

The State Duma ratified the Comprehensive Test Ban Treaty on 21 April 2000. Also on 21 April 2000 the 'security council' approved a new security doctrine.

At first the Commonwealth of Independent States (CIS) seemed to be merely a way of allowing a 'peaceful divorce'. (See Chapter 10.) After 1993 Russia's military and economic dominance (especially its supplies of energy and raw materials) gave it a temporary boost. Political and economic desperation drove the more reluctant countries to become members and only the Baltic States of Estonia, Latvia and Lithuania refused to join. Each of the twelve CIS countries now has its own currency. Belarus favours economic and political union with Russia, while at the other extreme Azerbaijan and Georgia are among the least keen on the CIS. Overall the CIS is a failing organization. 'The CIS has failed to integrate the Soviet successor states in any meaningful sense. Although on paper it has been a forum for several ambitious projects of co-operation, in reality the CIS has been gradually emptied of responsibility and has been witness to a diminishing base of collaborative activities' (Sakwa and Webber 1999: 379). 'Whereas in 1991 trade between the current members of the CIS constituted 21 per cent of their combined GDP, today this has fallen to around 6 per cent' (p. 407). 'The CIS provides a forum for diplomacy, informal discussions and the voicing of grievances ... Yet it is clear that the achievements of the CIS are few in number' (p. 408). 'The presidents of Russia, Belarus, Kazahstan, Kyrgyzstan and Tajikistan – the countries of the customs union – have held a meeting in Minsk. An attempt was made at the meeting to accelerate the establishment of a free trade zone, which is being held back by the Russian position ... Russia is the only one that has not ratified the free trade treaty. This is because if the treaty takes effect the Russian Treasury will lose millions in revenue from transporting energy resources abroad' (*Kommersant*, 24 May 2000, p. 11; *CDSP*, 2000, vol. 52, no. 21, p. 21). 'We are becoming economic strangers to one another. The customs union has been in an embryonic state for more than four years now, its five members [Russia, Belarus, Kazakhstan, Kyrgyzstan and Tajikistan] in no hurry to fully co-ordinate their trade legislation. Furthermore, all of these countries are trying to gain admission to the WTO, and Kyrgyzstan has already joined it. Yet the WTO has completely different rules. Restoring all production relations within the framwork of the Soviet division of labour is not realistic. And the hard currency the post-Soviet republics need so desperately cannot be earned by trading with one another – everyone in the CIS is poor' (Semyon Novoprudsky, *Izvestia*, 17 June 2000, p. 1; *CDSP*, 2000, vol. 52, no. 25, p. 16). 'The new Russian government will not have a ministry for CIS affairs, which has been abolished by presidential decree. The ministry's functions will be transferred to the foreign ministry and the ministry of economics ... This is the second time the commonwealth ministry has been abolished. The first time was in April 1998 ... Six months later, however, the commonwealth ministry was reestablished ... True, economic ties with the CIS countries were none the better for it ... Overall management will be the [Russian] security council's job. Putin's new plan accords priority to bilateral ties, with all integration efforts to be based on security' (*Kommersant*, 25 May 2000, p. 11; *CDSP*, 2000, vol. 52, no. 21, p. 22).

In the West economics has grown worryingly apart from other academic disciplines and become increasingly specialized and abstract. It is imperative to be aware of historical, political and social factors when analyzing economic developments in Russia. Early concern was expressed at the role of those who were essentially theoreticians in actual government. For example, the eminent and long-time radical economist Nikolai Shmelev commented as follows on the relatively young group of economists led by Yegor Gaidar formulating policy in Russia: 'These new smart guys are judging their policy mostly from economic textbooks rather than real life ... They are much more brutal than we are. This is a highly painful surgical operation without any anesthesia' (*IHT*, 5 February 1992, p. 9).

I think it essential to analyze both economic and political events. For example, the privatization programmes chosen by Russia have been profoundly affected by political factors such as the weakness of the central government, the power of the managerial lobby, corruption and Boris Yeltsin's reelection prospects in the mid-1990s. The Asian financial crisis cruelly exposed Russia's fundamental political and economic weaknesses.

OVERVIEW OF THE BOOK

I hope that this volume will provide an overview of the main ideas involved in and the events occurring during the transition to democracy and the market in Russia. But I feel it is only right to reveal my limitations as an academic in trying to attempt such a broad overview of economic and political events:

1. I am not a political scientist. Thus I present the main political events in a largely chronological order in the hope my conscientious, day-by-day updating will in some degree compensate. I present a 'quarry' rather than an in-depth analysis of Russian politics.

2. I am not an econometrician and thus cannot analyze economic data in any sort of sophisticated manner. Indeed, I am mostly interested in how the economic and political system has actually changed. But I think the reader should be aware of the broad economic magnitudes and these I present in tables that are meant to be as simple as possible. There are often many differing estimates and not infrequently the same source changes the figures from one issue to the next! Rather than drawing up immensely complicated

tables showing a multitude of estimates, I have tried to look for the most representative figures. These usually speak for themselves and thus I avoid tediously stating the obvious.

3. I am not an economic theorist, but I hope that the logical arrangements of chapters on actual economic events (i.e. covering the measures outlined in the 'big bang'/'shock therapy' package) may enlighten readers to some degree. My primary task is to inform and hopefully provide some insights into complex issues. I thus minimize my personal views and allow the reader to make up his or her own mind.

Part One deals with the economy. With advice from leading Western economists such as Jeffrey Sachs and Anders Åslund, Russia initially chose to follow a course of 'big bang'/'shock therapy'. This involved a programme of rapid and comprehensive market transformation and of macroeconomic stabilization. The three 'izms' of 'big bang'/'shock therapy' are liberalization, privatization and stabilization. The liberalization chapters (1 to 4 respectively) cover the transition from command planning to the market, prices, foreign trade and foreign investment. Also dealt with in Chapter 1 are the raging controversies over the general transitional path adopted by Russia after 1992, the concept of the 'virtual economy' and the reasons for and extent of crime and corruption. Privatization in the non-agricultural sectors is the realm of Chapter 5 and privatization in agriculture is that of Chapter 6. Chapter 7 is devoted to macroeconomic stabilization and discusses how the hyperinflation of 1992 was caused and how it was conquered; the Russian financial crisis of August 1998 is dealt with at length here. Jeffrey Sachs (a former adviser to the Russian government) recommends a 'social safety net' (especially an unemployment compensation scheme; dealt with in Chapter 9, which covers economic performance) and sees the need for a generous international aid (and trade) policy (foreign aid and debt being dealt with in Chapter 8). Most chapters begin with an overview of the relevant aspect of the Soviet economy.

Part Two concerns mainly political developments. Chapter 10 covers the following: the dissolution of the Soviet Union (the events prior to the 19–21 August 1991 abortive coup, the coup itself, the Union Treaty, the role of Boris Yeltsin and the Russian republic, the control of the economy in the immediate aftermath of the coup attempt, and the Economic Community); the Commonwealth of Independent States (CIS); economic relations between Russia and the other countries of the former Soviet Union (the payments mechanism, subsidies, the rouble zone, demographic aspects of the CIS and later developments in the CIS). Chapter 11 deals with the federal state and the two Chechen wars. The federal state section covers political features, demographic features and the economics of the federal state (devolution and differentiation, transfers, economic associations, bilateral agreements between the centre and individual members of the federation, local politics, including the 1996–97 elections, and the Putin reforms). The extensive section on the two Chechen wars includes the background, the toll, public opinion, international opinion and a chronology of developments. Chapter 12 presents a chronology of political developments in the period 1992–2000, including the following: the dissolution of parliament on 21 September 1993 and the attack on the 'White House' on 4 October 1993; the search for a new constitution; the general election of 12 December 1993; the general election of 17 December 1995; the reelection of Yeltsin as president on 3 July 1996; the merry-go-round of prime ministers; the general election of 19 December 1999; the resignation of Yeltsin on 31 December 1999 and the meteoric rise of Vladimir Putin from relative obscurity to president (elected on 26 March 2000); the Putin reforms. Chapter 13 covers military affairs, disarmament agreements, the Partnership for Peace and Nato expansion: the armed forces (their size and and proposals for reduction, the problems and future of conscription, the poor state of the armed forces, and the threat of the theft of nuclear and other material); defence doctrine; international treaties and agreements; and the Kosovo crisis.

PART ONE

ECONOMIC DEVELOPMENTS

THE TRANSITION TO THE MARKET: INTRODUCTION

The question about how to handle the transition from plan to market (from 'communism' to 'capitalism') in Russia has led to immense controversy and problems. There are two broad approaches in theory, 'gradualism' and 'big bang'/'shock therapy'. While China chose the former course, Russia chose the fast track approach to changing its economic system (although it took three attempts to bring inflation under control and the implementation of reforms was often slow). First, a word about terms (all of which are to be found in the glossary). 'Big bang'/'shock therapy' is a programme of rapid and comprehensive market transformation, comprising a package of interdependent measures. The terms 'big bang' and 'shock therapy' are often used interchangeably, while the term 'shock therapy' is more often than not used in a broad sense to cover both (i) severe austerity measures and (ii) a rapid and comprehensive change in the economic system. But at times the term has been used in a narrower sense, referring only to (i). This point is dealt with in the chapter on macroeconomic stabilization. Leading exponents of 'big bang'/'shock therapy', such as Sachs, Åslund and Balcerowicz, advocate the following measures:

1. *Liberalization.* This includes the end of central planning and the freeing of prices in the context of a liberal international trade regime. Rapid current account convertibility of the currency is recommended. Chapter 1 deals with the transition from command planning to the market, Chapter 2 deals with prices, Chapter 3 with foreign trade and Chapter 4 with foreign investment.

2. *Privatization.* The rapid expansion of the private sector through deregulation (i.e. freedom of entry into sectors of the economy by new enterprises) and the privatization of state enterprises is recommended. It is recognized that large privatization will take longer than small privatization. In the meantime the remaining state enterprises will need to be disciplined by measures such as demonopolization, exposure to domestic and foreign competition, and the ending of 'soft budget constraints'. Chapter 5 deals with non-agricultural privatization and Chapter 6 with agricultural privatization.

3. *Stabilization.* Macroeconomic stabilization is needed in order to bring inflation under control. Chapter 7 is devoted to this topic.

Proponents such as Jeffrey Sachs also recommend a 'social safety net' (especially an unemployment compensation scheme; dealt with in Chapter 9) and see the need for a generous international aid (and trade) policy (foreign aid and debt being dealt with in Chapter 8).

CHAPTER ONE

THE TRANSITION FROM COMMAND PLANNING TO THE MARKET

COMMAND PLANNING IN THE SOVIET ERA

Before embarking on an analysis of command planning, it is important to understand the pivotal role played by the Communist Party of the Soviet Union (CPSU). The CPSU dominated economic, political and social life in this one-party state, e.g. it formulated and implemented economic policies.

Command planning was introduced in the Soviet Union after 1928. The basic allocative decisions about what to produce and in what quantities were taken by the state (used as an instrument by the CPSU), although in reality the whole economic hierarchy had to be involved in decision-making. The enterprise manager, for example, had some decision-making autonomy with regard to input substitution and production choice within the aggregate plan target.

The State Planning Commission (Gosplan) was at the apex of the planning pyramid, branch ministries (called 'commissariats' before 1946) were at the intermediate level and enterprises (production units) were at its base. Between 1957 and 1965 the basic intermediate link was the 'regional economic council'. This was not a decentralization of decision-making. Most branch ministries were dismantled for largely political reasons, many of Khrushchev's opponents being found in them. But there were also economic problems such as 'empire building', caused by strong pressures for ministries to be self-sufficient in input supply. Bureaucracy and unnecessary crosshauls were also causes of concern. But regional self-sufficiency proved to be an even greater problem and unnecessary crosshauls were not eliminated with regional economic councils. Thus branch ministries regained their predominance.

The State Planning Commission received instructions about basic economic magnitudes from the party, especially the Politburo, relating to growth rates of national income and of its sub-categories of consumption, investment and defence, and to vitally important goods. These instructions were relayed via the state apparatus, especially the Council of Ministers, and Gosplan combined these with the data/requests/proposals flowing upwards from the hierarchy to draw up plans of varying duration by means of 'material balances' (the aim being roughly to equate the major sources of supply and demand for particular commodities). The annual, quarterly and monthly plans were operational; medium (five-year) plans and perspective plans of at least fifteen years' duration were much more highly aggregated and were operational only in relation to the investment plan. Many projects were spread over a number of years and thus longer-term plans were needed for guidance. In later reforms annual plans were meant to be drawn up within the context of the allegedly more important five-year plan, but in reality changing targets and economic conditions ensured that the annual plan remained the operational one.

It is vital to stress the distortion of information flowing up the hierarchy. For example, in trying to achieve as low an output plan as possible enterprises have an incentive to understate capacity (see below). A reliable source of information, however, is what enterprises have already achieved. This accounts for the persistence of the so-called 'ratchet effect' despite its severe problems (see below), planners essentially setting output targets on the basis of what had been produced in the last plan period plus a bit more.

The Soviet economy suffered endemic supply problems, the reasons including the following:

1. Balances were heavily aggregated, the number of balances being far fewer than the number of 'commodities'. Even by 1981 the annual plan involved Gosplan drawing up material balances for only 2,044 products (though crucially important ones), Gossnab (the State Committee for Material and Technical Supply) 7,500, and ministries 25,000 (Schroeder 1982: 75). By way of contrast, Nikolai Shmelev (*Novy Mir*, 1987, no. 6, p. 136) put the number of items in industrial production alone at around 24 million.

2. The 'iterative' problem. If, for example, the output of a particular good were increased, in the early years of planning usually only the first-order iteration (repetition) was carried out (i.e. estimates made of the effects on direct inputs). Further iterations (effects on the inputs needed to produce the increased inputs and so on) were ignored. For this reason excess demand was tackled as much as possible by, for example, reducing both the use of inputs per unit of output ('tightening of norms') and the consumption element of final demand (i.e. using the consumer sector as a buffer), as opposed to changing supply (i.e. increasing output).

Although stockpiles of goods could arise on occasion (see below), one of the basic features of the Soviet Union was widespread shortages, i.e. it was a 'shortage' economy. This will be pursued later, but some of the ill effects of shortages need stressing at this stage:

1. The opportunity cost of queues to consumers and the rest of society in terms of foregone work and leisure was enormous.

2. The 'soft budget constraint' (see below) shielded enterprises from bankruptcy and thus encouraged inefficiency. In turn, workers were generally

guaranteed a job for life. This tended to have a deleterious effect on incentives, which were further undermined by the fact that widespread shortages ensured that money income was not an automatic command over real goods and services.

3. There was a loss of the benefits of specialization as enterprises and ministries attempted to produce as many inputs as they could themselves because of the unreliability of the materials allocation system.

Material balancing was never supplanted by other techniques as the core of command planning and was improved over time (e.g. by a greater number of iterations). For instance, the first input-output table to be drawn up was for the year 1959. But input-output played only a peripheral role in planning, e.g. variant analysis and in the final stages of planning for checking consistency, consistency in the sense that supply equals demand. Linear programming (despite some practical use, for example, at level of the enterprise) also played only a marginal role in reality (Jeffries 1993: 110–12).

The allocation of most non-labour inputs was handled by the 'materials allocation' system – the administrative distribution of raw materials, intermediate goods and capital goods. The supplying and using enterprises were matched centrally and the all-important document was the *naryad* (allocation certificate), which specified the quantity of the product and the supplying organization.

Command planning was well-named in the sense that the production unit (the enterprise) eventually received plan targets in the shape of a technical-industrial-financial plan (*tekhpromfinplan*). But since it was impossible for central planners to produce detailed, concrete plans in the abstract, the economic hierarchy had to be involved, with the emphasis in the traditional system on vertical as opposed to horizontal (i.e. enterprise to enterprise) linkage. More specifically tentative, crudely balanced output targets ('control figures') were passed down the planning pyramid to be increasingly disaggregated (made more detailed) by ministries and enterprises. Suggestions/requests (the *zayavka* being an input indent, for example) were made at each echelon and passed back up the hierarchy. While the centre's major allocative decisions were preserved, this process of haggling and bargaining could be influential, as in suggested input substitution to meet a given output target. Annual plans were often late and were frequently changed; failure to fulfil by one enterprise had repercussions on others. (It is worth noting at this point the importance of informal linkages that oiled the wheels of the economic mechanism in reality. Examples include, as is to be seen below, shady deals and downright illegal relationships between enterprises.)

It is important to note that two areas of the economy were left, in more normal times, largely to the market mechanism, namely the distribution of consumer goods and the allocation of manpower. These were interrelated in both a micro- and a macro-economic sense. Wages and salaries paid out in the production sector constituted the main means of payment for the consumer goods and services made available in the plan (which, in turn, provided the main incentive to work), while avoidance of inflation meant matching the cash (rouble notes and coins) injected into the economy with the aggregate supply of consumer goods and services at established prices.

As regards the *distribution of consumer goods* there was essentially consumer choice (as opposed to sovereignty) in the command economy. This meant that consumers could choose among the consumer goods and services made available in the plan, rather than being able to determine the allocation of resources, as in a competitive market economy. As discussed in the section on pricing, queues were an endemic feature of the Soviet economy. Among the cause of queues were prices for consumer goods and services being typically below market-clearing levels and the restricted number of poorly organized distribution outlets. Queues imposed considerable economic and social costs on the Soviet consumer. Plokker (1990: 404) quoted a 1988 Soviet source, which estimated that the average family may have spent one month per year standing in queues. Shleifer and Vishny cited another Soviet estimate that 30 million man-years were spent in queues annually, some 25 per cent of the waking time of every adult (1991: 347). But it is worth noting that the opportunity cost of time spent queuing was lower for groups such as pensioners and the Soviet élite had the best of both worlds – assured access to scarce goods and services (e.g. via special shops and hospitals) at low or even zero prices! The poor quality, non-availability and erratic supply of many consumer goods and services, coupled with the frequency of queues and rationing, provided a breeding ground for activities of varying degrees of legality. Black markets were rife.

As regards the *allocation of manpower*, the fulfilment of plan output targets obviously required the necessary labour and non-labour inputs. But there were contrasting ways of obtaining them. While the latter were essentially administratively allocated by means of the materials allocation system, the former mainly involved the use of the market mechanism, with administrative methods and moral suasion also employed. The internal passport system, introduced in 1932, helped to control the geographical movement of people.

The command planning solution of labour direction, although used during the Second World War, was ruled out in more normal circumstances because of adverse effects on incentives (the War Communism period of 1918–21 being informative in this respect). Market forces were heeded when the planners determined basic wage differentials, while the state controlled the education system, including the number of places available for particular courses of study. The industrial worker's pay crudely consisted of two parts: (1) a state-guaranteed basic wage, which varied according to industrial branch, skill and region; and (2) the residual. This residual was affected by bonuses, related to such factors as plan fulfilment and the nature of the job (dangerous working conditions, for example). This formal system enabled the state to encourage labour to move to desired industries and regions and to adopt the desired skills. In addition, there was *de facto* room to manoeuvre for the enterprise manager, even within the constraints of an enforced wage fund, by manipulating norms and skill designations, for example. In the early period piece rates, as opposed to time rates, were dominant.

The non-market elements in manpower allocation varied enormously over time. Forced labour camps were busy as a result of the collectivization of agriculture and Stalin's purges. Although used for activities such as mining in inhospitable places, the camps served a mainly political function. (The declassification of NKVD files on the labour camp system for 1934–60 have resolved some of the long-standing disputes among Western historians. Estimates of the labour camp population at the end of the 1930s varied between 2 million and 9 million or more. It is now known that 3.3 million people were confined in prisons, camps, colonies and labour settlements. The number peaked in 1953 at 5.5 million and fell to 1 million in 1959: *The Economist*, 2 March 1996, p. 99. The NKVD or People's Commissariat for Internal Affairs controlled the security apparatus and was the predecessor of the KGB.) High labour turnover during the 1930s, seen as a threat to plan fulfilment, was combated by means such as the 'work book'. This was introduced in 1938 and held by the enterprise manager; without it a worker could not, in principle, find another job. Increasingly harsh legislation eventually made even absenteeism and lateness criminal offences. Graduates of universities and technical schools were assigned to a place of work for two or three years. Moral suasion exercised by the party could be seen in operation, for example, when students and workers helped out at harvest time.

Trade unions were an arm of the state in the traditional model. They were organized along industrial lines with the result that worker and manager belonged to the same union. There was no collective bargaining between trade unions and management about basic wage and salary differentials, although the former exercised some marginal consultative roles. Strikes were considered to be counter-revolutionary and in any case unnecessary, although they were not actually outlawed in the constitution. This reduced the role of trade unions to the transmission of party policies, ensuring favourable conditions for plan fulfilment, protecting workers' interests (legal requirements as to health and safety, for example) and administering the social security system relating to sickness, work injury and pensions. (On 9 October 1989 the Supreme Soviet passed a law relating to labour disputes. Strikes were permitted as long as they met a number of conditions. They could not be politically inspired. They could not take place in key sectors such as transport, communications, fuel, energy and defence. Strikes also had to be approved by a majority vote of the relevant work force and a conciliation process had to be attempted. Illegal strikes were still held, however, such as those by coal miners.)

Unemployment was officially declared to be eliminated by the end of 1930 (*CDSP*, 1988, vol. XL, no. 4, p. 4); work was regarded not only as a right but as a legal obligation. (Article 60 of the 1977 constitution stated that: 'The refusal of socially useful work is incompatible with the principles of socialist society.') The Gorbachev era was far more frank about unemployment and the need for unemployment pay. At the end of 1990 the unemployment rate was in the range of 3 to 6 per cent (Oxenstierna 1992: 59). Adirim (1989: 460) proffered an overall figure of 6.2 per cent, including 'open' unemployment (people without a job), 'concealed' unemployment (people with a job providing insufficient work and earnings) and 'indirect' unemployment (people with a job, but with pay so inadequate that they are forced to search for additional work). It was recognized that the unemployment rate was especially high in republics such as Azerbaijan and Uzbekistan (Nikolai Shmelev, *Novy Mir*, 1987, no. 6, p. 148; *CDSP*, 1989, vol. XLI, no. 44, p. 6). The first case of unemployment pay involved those losing their jobs as a result of ministerial reorganization in 1985, being eligible for full pay for three months without affecting pension and other social security rights; normally pension rights were adversely affected if unemployment lasted more than a month. In 1966 central authorization was given to the fifteen republics of the Soviet Union to set up State Committees of Labour Utilization.

At the bottom of the planning pyramid was the *state industrial enterprise*. The typical industrial enterprise was a state-owned plant, operating on the principle of one-man responsibility and control (*edinonachalie*) by a director appointed by the state (more strictly by the communist party). (The *nomenklatura* system – list of key posts – was one in which the party made all important appointments.) Lower levels of management included the deputy director and chief engineer, complemented by the party cell and the trade union branch. The basic function of the industrial enterprise was to fulfil its 'technical, industrial and financial plan' (*tekhpromfinplan*), which appeared at the end of a haggling and bargaining process. The operational plans (annual, quarterly and monthly) were expressed in terms of plan targets ('success indicators'), varying over time in terms of number and priority as particular problems arose. There was no 'all-round' indicator such as profit in a market economy. Instead, production decisions were broken down into individual targets. Output targets, however, were typically paramount. (Enterprises producing goods for export or using imported commodities were shielded from the world market by the state monopoly of foreign trade and payments. This separation of Soviet and foreign industrial firms greatly aggravated the problems already experienced with product quality since the disciplining force of world competition was absent. This is discussed in greater detail in the section on foreign trade.)

The industrial enterprise was a financially separate and accountable unit operating on a *khozraschyot* (economic accounting) basis, for the purpose of efficiently implementing the plan. Prices were fixed by the state and the enterprise account had to be kept in the local branch of the State Bank (Gosbank). The purpose of the latter was to help ensure plan compliance, the idea being that only payments in conformity with the plan should be permitted. Budgetary grants covered fixed capital needs and Gosbank had a monopoly over the granting of short-term credit, available at a nominal rate of interest which was fixed to cover only administrative costs. Management motivation involved negative consequences for non-fulfilment of the plan, such as loss of bonuses, expulsion from the party and its associated privileges, and possible imprisonment or even capital punishment for 'economic sabotage' during the darkest periods. Positive incentives were associated with fulfilment and overfulfilment. Bonus, socio-cultural and investment funds were linked to success indicators, especially output.

Although the traditional system played a crucial role in carrying out Stalin's goals, micro-economic problems of a severe kind arose:

1. There was a neglect of user need. Output had only to be produced and not sold in the traditional Soviet economic system, while emphasis on one indicator led to neglect of others. The result was that quantity was stressed at the expense of quality. For example, physical indicators such as weight, number, or length resulted in too large, small or narrow objects respectively being produced, relative to user need. This neglect of the qualitative aspects of production was especially acute in low-priority sectors involved in heterogeneous output, such as textiles, and helps explain the seemingly paradoxical phenomenon of stockpiles of unsaleable products in a situation of general consumer goods scarcity. The problem persisted. In the mid-1980s it was estimated that only between 7.0 and 18 per cent of Soviet manufacturing output met world standards (Shmelev, *Novy Mir*, 1987, no. 6, p. 148).

2. There was a tendency to understate productive capacity. The director had an incentive to provide such false information in the hope of achieving a 'slack' plan, one that called for less than feasible output, since no bonuses were paid for anything less than 100 per cent fulfilment. ('Taut' planning prevailed in general, with pressure to maximize output from given resources.) Although extra bonuses were available for overfulfilment, the director was careful not to overfulfil by too much, since that would endanger fulfilment of subsequent plans. The 'ratchet effect' (known in Eastern Europe as the 'base-year approach') meant that a particular period's achievement was the starting point for next period's plan: 'planning from the achieved level', as it was also called (Birman 1978). The ratchet effect was a persistent problem because of its simplicity of use by data-deficient planners; in a world of distorted information planners could rely on what had already been produced in the previous period and they simply added a bit more.

3. There was a tendency to over-indent for non-labour inputs and to hoard these as well as labour. Manpower was hoarded to meet unforeseen needs or the frequent changes in plans and to compensate for the erratic supply of inputs (catching up on production when they did arrive). These non-labour inputs too were hoarded, owing, for example, to the horrendous supply problems associated with the materials allocation system and to the fact that

capital was a factor free to the enterprise. This led to such phenomena as *tolkachi* (expediters, unofficial supply agents, who bartered with each other, among other things) and a powerful inducement to self-sufficiency in the supply of inputs; parts of Soviet industry were notoriously non-specialized.

4. There was the problem of 'storming' (*shturmovshchina*). This was the mad rush to fulfil plans at the end of the planning period (such as the month), explained by such factors as the bonus system, delays in receiving inputs from other enterprises and the unwillingness of enterprises to show early eagerness in an environment where plans typically arrived late and were frequently changed (Bleaney 1988: 63).

5. There was an anti-innovation bias at the micro level. Innovation is the application of new ideas about products and techniques to the production process. New priority large-scale technologies, in armaments for example, were readily dealt with by command economies. (Although technology generally lagged behind the West, the Soviet Union was much more successful in areas such as armaments and space vehicles.) But vital, spontaneous, micro-level innovation was hindered by the traditional Soviet economic system: there was no competitive pressure to stay in business as in market economies; the incentive system meant jeopardizing short-term plan fulfilment and the prospect of 'ratchet effects'; state-determined prices might have meant adverse effects on value indicators; there were the aforementioned problems of input supply; R&D, which traditionally took place in specialized organizations within ministries, was separated from production (Berliner 1976); there was frequent shifting around of managers to prevent 'familiness' (friendliness developing between the various individuals within an enterprise; coalitions could thwart the enterprises' superiors).

One of the fundamental problems of the Soviet economy was the existence of the 'soft budget constraint', to use Kornai's famous term (Kornai 1992b: 7). Any losses made by state enterprises were automatically made good by the state; thus enterprises were not allowed to go bankrupt and workers were shielded from unemployment. This automatic bailout was a recipe for disaster in terms of efficiency. 'No state-run enterprises could ever go bankrupt. The result of that situation was the bankruptcy of the whole [Soviet] system' (Alexander Yakovlev, *Moscow News*, 19–26 January 1992, p. 11).

There were other problems affecting the Soviet economy which furthered the cause of economic reform. One of these was the so-called 'scattering' (excessive spread) of investment resources (*raspilenie sredstv*), construction projects whose completion times were excessive relative both to plan norm and to those taken in Western countries. Responsible factors included the greater ease involved in obtaining resources to complete projects as opposed to starting them, the absence of a capital charge before the mid-1960s, the tendency of output-orientated indicators to reward starting more than finishing, and the absence of the threat of bankruptcy in the event of investment failure. As the Soviet economy developed it became more complex

Table 1.1 The Soviet Union: average annual rates of growth of NMP, GNP and GDP (%)

Measure	*1928–37*	*1951–55*	*1956–60*	*1961–65*	*1966–70*	*1971–75*	*1976–80*	*1981–85*	*1986*	*1987*	*1988*	*1989*	*1990*	*1991*
NMP[1]	16.3	11.0	9.2	8.5	7.1	5.1	3.9	3.2	4.1	2.3	4.4	3.0	−4.0	−15.0
Bergson (GNP)	5.0–5.5	–	–	–	–	–	–	–	–	–	–	–	–	–
Joint economic Committee of the US Congress (GNP)	–	5.5	–	5.1	5.2	3.8	2.7	2.4	3.9	0.5	1.5	–	–	–
CIA (GNP)	–	–	–	–	5.1	3.0	2.3	1.9	3.8	1.3	1.5	1.4	–	–
UNECE (GDP)	–	–	–	–	–	–	–	–	–	2.9	5.5	3.0	−2.3	−17.0
IMF (GDP)	–	–	–	–	–	–	–	–	–	–	–	–	−0.4	−9.0

1. Net Material Product differs from the United Nations 'system of national accounts', mainly because of the exclusion of so-called non-productive services, such as defence, general administration, education, finance and credit, and transport and communications serving households.

Source: Jeffries (1993: 40); Schroeder (1986: 20); Ofer (1987: 1778); D. Dyker, The Soviet Economy, London: Crosby Lockwood, 1976, p. 18; Z. Fallenbuchl in *Canadian Slavonic Papers*, vol. XXX, no. 3, 1988, p. 306; *CDSP*, vol. XLII, no. 9, 1990, p. 17; vol. XLIV, no. 1, 1992, p. 5; Hanson P. (1990a: 110); *Economic Affairs*, vol. 10, no. 6, p. 8; United Economic Commission for Europe (1992: 1, 105); IMF, *World Economic Outlook* (April 1992).

to plan. Soviet growth was of an 'extensive' type (largely due to increases in inputs, rather than to greater efficiency in the use of inputs). (Only one-third of growth was accounted for by the rise in efficiency, compared with around two-thirds in Western countries: Gregory and Stuart 1990: 488.) The drying up of the traditional sources of inputs (such as the influx of manpower from the countryside, increases in participation rates – especially among women – and increases in the proportion of national income devoted to investment) put massive pressure on the Soviet Union to adopt a more 'intensive' pattern of growth. Environmental problems became severe (owing to factors such as the stress on output growth at all cost, the arms race, the self-interest of various groups in the economy, secrecy and the lack of any effective opposition groups).

Official Soviet figures for the rate of growth of Net Material product (NMP) show a long-term downward trend. Western estimates for Gross National Product (GNP) and Gross Domestic product (GDP) are lower and also show a downward trend (see Table 1.1). Gorbachev called the Brezhnev era a 'period of stagnation'. In 1990–91 the Soviet economy experienced negative growth as the old system disintegrated before a new one could be introduced. Towards the end of 1991 the Soviet Union itself ceased to exist as a political entity.

Economic reform in the Soviet era

Gorbachev put political reform (democratization) ahead of economic reform. The Soviet system was still recognizably a command economy even by the late 1980s, but the changes undertaken are not to be underestimated (especially those introduced by Gorbachev, 1985–1991). The aim was to *improve* the Soviet economic system (as opposed to replacing it). Stalin died in 1953 and this paved the way for reform. At the Twentieth Congress of the CPSU in 1956 Nikita Khrushchev (who lost power in 1964) denounced the 'cult of personality'. This eased the restrictions on debate. The 1960s was a decade of reform experiments followed by gradual and more general application (although some of the reforms were later retracted). The general aspects of industrial reforms up to the Gorbachev era were as follows:

1. A decentralization of decision-making to enterprises over details and greater 'indirect steering' of the economy via 'economic levers' such as taxes, credit policy and prices. The 'success indicator' system was amended, e.g. a reduction in the number (although increased on occasion as particular problems arose) and a change in emphasis to cope with particular problems (such as profit, sales and labour productivity). This found reflection in changes in the bonus system for incentive purposes.

2. The following is a summary of specific problems and the reforms meant to overcome them:

i. 'Ratchet effect': e.g. increased emphasis on Five Year Plans.
ii. Labour hoarding: Shchekino Chemical Combine (wage savings boosting the income of remaining workers and managers).
iii. 'Counter-plans' (slack plan problem): higher bonuses for originally higher plan targets.
iv. 'Net output': to overcome excessive use of inputs.
v. Worker brigades: increased incentives (payment by results) and self-discipline (basic output targets and inputs given). (Brigades represented one of the more successful reforms.)
vi. A move to long-term credits instead of capital grants for more efficient use of capital. (Investment decision-making was improved by the use of the Coefficient of Relative Effectiveness or CRE, a sort of interest rate: Jeffries 1993: 112–13.)

On balance these brought about some improvements. But the basic problems remained unsolved, enabling Gertrude Schroeder to talk famously about a 'treadmill of reform' (Schroeder 1982).

3. Larger enterprises (mainly horizontally integrated). The aims included a streamlining and improving of central planning (fewer units to control) and an encouragement of technological progress by integrating R&D and production. In 1973 the 'production association' became the main production unit.

Mikhail Gorbachev became General Secretary of the Communist Party of the Soviet Union (CPSU) on 11 March 1985. Gorbachev did not *intend* to destroy the Soviet Union. He wanted to end the Cold War and, as far as domestic matters were concerned, he desired a more humane society and a more efficient economic system. At first Gorbachev talked about 'democratization' (e.g. greater involvement of people in society and at work), but he later allowed independent parties to emerge. A number of terms became famous. *Perestroika* meant 'restructuring' (all-round economic and social reform). *Glasnost* ('openness') meant the need to admit problems before they could be tackled. Political reforms preceded economic reform (the opposite sequence to that chosen by China). The problem was that a 'command' economy relies on commands being obeyed most of the time. Thus the economic system started to disintegrate. Gorbachev admitted that 'The old system fell apart even before the new system began to work'. Life was complicated by the 'war of laws' with Yeltsin's Russian republic (i.e. when the latter's laws and decrees conflicted with federal ones). Gorbachev zigzagged between political poles to try to achieve his aim (arguably necessary to take the CPSU along with him). Gorbachev did not commit himself whole-heartedly to a switch to a market system until it was too late to save the country from disintegrating. He resigned as president (the first Soviet leader to do so, although he was never elected by popular vote) of the Soviet Union 25 December 1991. On 16 June 1996 he received a derisory 0.51 per cent of the popular vote in the Russian presidential election.

In the Gorbachev era industrial reform preceded agricultural reform (the opposite to that chosen by China). The general aspects of industrial reform were as follows:

1. A decentralization of decision-making, to enterprises (especially those producing consumer goods) and to the regions. Gosplan was to focus on 'strategic' matters and there was to be a greater emphasis on indirect steering.
2. A stronger link between performance and reward.
3. An increased stress on the quality of goods.
4. A greater stress on 'intensive' growth in general by encouraging technological progress. (The Soviet Union continually fell behind in areas outside armaments and space technology.)
5. An increase in the size of production units.

The 1987 Law on the State Enterprise (Association) seemed a significant development at first. 'Self-management' implied a greater involvement of the work force in plan determination. 'Full economic accounting' and 'self-financing' implied no automatic subsidies, i.e. imposition of a hard budget restraint. This was something envisaged but not actually attained. There was to be greater leeway in wage determination. There were experiments in elected management but these were later terminated. 'State orders' were intended to be based on voluntary contracts and to leave spare capacity to adapt to market demand. But in reality 'state orders' were little different from plan orders (commands). Wholesale trade was supposed to become the norm. But it did not happen to any great extent because the abolition of the material allocations would have meant the end of central planning.

In the late Gorbachev era a number of programmes were presented as ways towards a market-based economy with a much larger private sector. In October 1990 the Supreme Soviet approved the 'Basic Directions for the Stabilization of the Economy and the Changeover to the Market'. But none of the programmes were implemented because the Soviet Union disintegrated (Jeffries 1993: 70–4).

Gorbachev became preoccupied with preserving the Soviet Union as a country and economic reform was put on the back burner. He saw the need for greater central control as a prerequisite to a shift to the market. (The weakness of the central government and widespread corruption/criminality provided Gorbachev with ammunition to attack Yeltsin, his old enemy.) As we have already seen, Gorbachev unsuccessfully sought for political and economic agreement among the Soviet republics to preserve the Soviet Union, albeit as a voluntary union.

FROM PLAN TO MARKET

Progress towards a market mechanism in Russia after 1992 proved to be rapid in many respects. Former advisers to the Russian government, such as Jeffrey

Sachs (from the USA) and Anders Åslund (from Sweden) at first saw a great deal to be encouraged by. 'Much progress has been made in the area of privatization ... Great advances have been made in dismantling price controls and abolishing the planning system' (Sachs, *The Independent*, 11 October 1993, p. 18). 'The Russia emerging today is very different from what pessimists have prophesied ... Most of the Russian economy ... has been privatized in just two years. Russia has already become a market economy, but one in the midst of long-overdue and massive restructuring. In short, Russia has undergone fundamental changes and appears to be on the right track' (Åslund 1994b: 58). 'More daunting is the task of building a system of law,' but 'the situation ... is far from hopeless' (p. 59). 'Russia already has a functioning market economy characterized by real economic interests that defend themselves' (Åslund, *IHT*, 25 April 1995, p. 8). (Sachs and Åslund, of course, were always aware of the problems and their criticisms grew over time, as will be seen. 'The core problem is that Russia has had far-too-slow reforms and has allowed a small group of big businessmen to become too rich ... The very rich in Russia made their fortunes on rent-seeking from 1991 to 1993. The two most important sources of revenues were export rents and subsidized credits ... Thanks to low state controlled prices for commodities, people with connections could ... get permission to sell them at world market prices ... [while] subsidized credits were issued on a discretionary basis to certain companies in 1992 ... With their riches these businessmen have bought into Russian politics in order to attain a degree of state intervention that is to their liking. If commodity prices and export prices had been deregulated earlier, interest rates been brought up to a market level earlier and the exchange rate been unified earlier, most of the initial rents could have been avoided': Åslund 1999a: 84–5. 'Many argue that Russia has fared badly because its "shock therapy" reforms were too fast and radical. But all measures show that Russia's economy is not very liberalized, and the financial collapse [of August 1998] made it obvious that Russia's problems were actually caused by reforms that were too slow and partial. A small group of businessmen enriched themselves and then corrupted many of Russia's politicians and officials. They have conspired to stymie economic reforms, which would stimulate growth and help the overall population, because reform threatens their domination. Russia suffers not from too free a market but from corruption thriving on their excessive regulations erected by a large and pervasive state': Åslund 1999b: 64.)

'After Russia's 1995 programme with the IMF brought inflation under control and the budget under control, the country embarked on a new programme with the IMF, with the goal of completing macroeconomic stabilization and moving ahead rapidly on structural reform. This did not happen because of Russia, not the West: the framework of assistance was in place, but the Russian government failed to deliver for complex reasons, one of them the health of President Boris Yeltsin. The 1996–8 programme was an on-and-off affair, with the IMF repeatedly delaying payments while policies got back on track … What went wrong with Russia? The basic problem was not the omission from the programme of some critical element, such as tax or legal reform. Rather, the problems arose from the Byzantine interaction of business and political interests in Russia, where the process of reform was often defeated by those seeking control over natural resources and the nascent market economy… On the speed of reform there were two elements of shock therapy in Russia – price liberalization in 1992 and privatization in 1992–5. On both the decision to move fast was made by the Russian government. In a different political environment more gradual privatization, after the creation of legal and institutional frameworks for a market economy, could have made more sense. But that was not the view of the Russian policymakers. In other respects reform has been too slow, not too fast. If Russia had implemented the 1996 reforms its economy would now be stronger, incomes would be higher and it would have avoided the 1998 collapse. Capital flight estimated at $10 billion to $20 billion a year, would be much smaller' (Stanley Fischer, first deputy managing director of the IMF, *FT*, 27 September 1999, p. 26). 'Joseph Stiglitz [chief economist of the World Bank] restated his disapproval of Russia's privatization programme, saying the system encourages "asset stripping" that has seen "billions and billions of dollars taken out of the country" … Mr Stiglitz said that privatization had gone ahead without a sufficient legal framework. As a result, he said, "rather than providing incentives for wealth creation, there have been incentives for asset stripping". "Providing free capital mobility has been an open invitation for people to take out billions, in fact billions and billions, of dollars out of the country", he said … Mr Stiglitz said the West assumed that a rules-based legal and financial infrastructure would emerge "spontaneously … [But] privatization by itself has not been a guarantee for success" … Rather than becoming wealthier, he said, Russia has become poorer' (*IHT*, 27 January 2000, pp. 1, 17).

Progress towards the market has been traced by others. 'Commercial relations between enterprises, based on freely agreed contracts, have supplanted administrative allocation in most parts of the economy. The market economy is rapidly taking over' (*RET*, 1993, vol. 2, no. 1, p. 5). 'The results of the widespread deregulation of 1992 continued to be felt. Queues virtually disappeared, and increasingly goods became allocated by market mechanisms rather than bureaucratic methods. There remains, however, a good deal of managed trade between enterprises' (*RET*, 1993, vol. 2, no. 4, p. 5). 'Russia has made great economic progress in 1995 … financial markets have developed … there are clear signs of economic restructuring at the enterprise level (*RET*, 1995, vol. 4, no. 4, p. 3). 'Contrary to the popular view, Russia is emerging as a success story of capitalism and market forces … a consistent picture of a vibrant and growing economy – an economy increasingly trusted by the international financial markets and US companies … Russia is successfully converting to a market economy' (Shama 1996: 111–13).

But even President Boris Yeltsin has sounded an early note of caution: 'Several important elements of market relations have appeared recently: economic freedom, the right of ownership and functioning markets for goods and services. But it is too early to say that the Russian economy is living according to the laws of the market. What we have now is a combination of new but still weak market mechanisms and old command levers. The administrative-distributive system has not vanished without trace; it has assumed new forms' (part of Boris Yeltsin's speech to a joint session of parliament delivered on 24 February 1994: *CDSP*, 1994, vol. XLVI, no. 8, p. 7). (On 30 March 1999 Yeltsin delivered his annual state of the nation speech: 'We are bogged down halfway between a planned, command economy and a workable market one. We have created a freakish model, a hybrid of the two systems': *CDSP*, 1999, vol. 51, no. 13, p. 14; *IHT*, 31 March 1999, p. 6.)

But much more trenchant criticism of the way Russia's transition has been handled is not hard to find:

1. Russia's black humour has been brought to bear. 'Russia, which managed to discredit the idea of socialism, is going to do the same with capitalism' (a Russian joke, quoted by Shlapentokh 1993: 19). 'Under the leadership of Lenin, Brezhnev, Gorbachev and others we were brought to the edge of a great abyss. But under the leadership of Boris Yeltsin we have taken a great step forward' (a popular joke circulating in 1993).

'There is the almost unimaginable economic and political disaster in Russia. As others have said, it took the Russian experience of capitalism to make Soviet communism look good' (John Kenneth Galbraith, *IHT*, 13 October 1998, p. 6).

'Everything Marx told us about communism was false. But it turns out that everything he told us about capitalism was true' (quoted by Freeland 2000: 14).

2. John Gray (*The Guardian*, 11 March 1994, p. 22) is very critical of the advice given by former advisers such as Sachs and Åslund: 'In Russia ... market institutions exist outside any framework of law or civil society, in a kind of anarcho-capitalism of nomenklaturist privatization and of competing mafias. To suppose that such wild or anarchic capitalism will converge on any Western model, in a process of slow evolution, is a dangerous delusion. It is far more likely to issue in precipitate economic collapse ... or in an authoritarian political backlash, as has already occurred in Russia ... The truth is that we cannot know what mix of economic policies and institutions will be best for the Russian peoples. Their problems will be solved, in so far as they are soluble, by skilful improvisation, encompassing the development of policies offering a safety net for those dislocated by unemployment, not by the importation of bankrupt Western models.'

3. 'Russia's transition to the market, largely on the advice of Western governments, has been handled so abruptly and hastily that it has given capitalism an almost irretrievably bad name, at least among a majority of the

current generations of Russians' (Jonathan Steele, *The Guardian*, 19 May 1994, p. 26).

4. 'The major mistake of reformers is that they followed the habitual revolutionary road – "to destroy the foundations and then ..." But even a fool can see that what is required in this case is an evolutionary approach, a smooth and slow transition. The old economic mechanism has to be preserved, but reanimated from below' (Alexander Solzhenitsyn, *Moscow News*, 29 July–4 August 1994, p. 13). 'The destructive course of events in the last decade has come about because the government, while ineptly imitating foreign models, has completely disregarded the country's creativity and particular character as well as Russia's centuries-old spiritual and social traditions' (Alexander Sozhenitsyn, *IHT*, 7 January 1997, p. 8).

5. 'The bonds holding the state, political system and society together have slackened – the result of trying to carry out simultaneous political and economic revolutions in a society unready for them. Economic reform has been too ambitious and doctrinaire. This has caused the old state-run system to be replaced not by a true market economy, but by an unstable semi-market system, preyed on by a growing army of *mafiosi* and bribe-taking officials' (Peter Reddaway, *IHT*, 14 January 1995, p. 6).

6. Jerry Hough (*IHT*, 13 January 1996, p. 6) offers the following critique: 'The economists dominating Western policy have not intended to weaken Russia, but they have to recognize that their advice has not worked. The West has been pushing reforms based on pure ideology in almost total disregard of local conditions ... Capitalism is very diverse. Saudi Arabia has nationalized its oil industry; the Pacific Rim countries have had high tariffs and a strong industrial policy; America has artificial farm price supports; Europe is moving towards a common currency. To say that Russian adoption of such policies is an abandonment of "reform" and a reimposition of empire is ideological nonsense. The West has been following a harsh policy not unlike what the world imposed on Germany from 1919 to 1933. It is time to change the policy.'

7. 'Much of the advice was ruinously bad, misunderstanding the change possible in a society ignorant of market-place functions and lacking the legal, institutional and social basis for capitalism – singularly the naive and ideological version of cutthroat capitalism preached on the editorial page of *The Wall Street Journal* and by the followers of Ronald Reagan and Margaret Thatcher. These treated Russia as the site for experiments unacceptable to the public in their own countries' (William Pfaff, *IHT*, 26 November 1996, p. 8). 'Some economists in the West still talk about Russia's new "businessmen" as the equivalent of nineteenth-century American "robber barons". But [they] ... created the American steel industry ... established the American oil industry ... built and consolidated great railroads. They enriched themselves while doing so, and ruined others, but left their fortunes to philanthropy. What has Boris Berezovsky built for Russia? What have these "businessmen" done for

Russia, other than appropriate its wealth?' (William Pfaff, *IHT*, 3 September 1998, p. 8).

8. 'We have learned from what happened in the Soviet Union that the successor to communism might not be democracy but "kleptocracy", where an economic elite rips off all the state assets. One reason that happened in Russia was that there was no rule-of-law foundation in place when the USSR collapsed' (Thomas Friedman, *IHT*, 11 March 1997, p. 8).

9. 'While Russia has its economic success stories, many aspects of the economy suggest that it is moving toward a corporatist market in which corruption is rampant. The most important of these trends is the rise of the Russian oligarchs, who have created a form of robber-baron capitalism. Far from creating an open market, Russia has consolidated a semi-criminal oligarchy that was already largely in place under the old Soviet system ... These nomenklatura capitalists' ... market of insider deals and political connections stands in the way of an open economy that would benefit all Russian citizens ... Those who believe that the capitalism of the robber barons will eventually give way to a market economy that benefits all in society, as occurred in the United States at the turn of the century, are mistaken. America had an established middle class with a work ethic and a government that remained largely free of robber-baron infiltration. The American tycoons were still investing in their own country. Russia's robber barons are stifling their homeland's economic growth by stealing from Russia and investing abroad. In the late 1990s Russia has no emerging middle class and the oligarchy, which is deeply involved in the government, can alter policy for its private benefit' (Yavlinsky 1998: 69–70).

10. 'Russia's underlying problem is an unprecedented, all-encompassing economic catastrophe – a peacetime economy that has been in a process of relentless destruction for nearly seven years ... So great is Russia's economic and social catastrophe that we must now speak of another unprecendented development: the demodernization of a twentieth-century country. When the infrastructures of production, technology, science, transportation, heating and sewage disposal disintegrate; when tens of millions of people do not receive earned salaries, some 75 per cent of society lives below or barely above the subsistence level, and at least 15 million people are actually starving; when male life expectancy has plunged to fifty-seven years, malnutrition has become the norm among schoolchildren, once eradicated diseases are again becoming epidemic, and basic welfare provisions are disappearing; when even highly educated professionals must grow their own food in order to survive, and well over half the nation's economic transactions are barter – all this, and more, is indisputable evidence of a tragic transition to a premodern era ... Russian economists and politicians across the spectrum are now desperately trying to formulate alternative economic policies that might save their nation – ones more akin to Franklin Roosevelt's New Deal than to the neo-liberal monetarist orthodoxies of the US State and Treasury departments, the IMF,

the World Bank and legions of Western advisers, which have done so much to abet Russia's calamity' (Stephen Cohen, *IHT*, 21 August 1998, p. 8).

11. 'Most of the Russian economy has not been making progress toward the market or even marking time. It is actively moving in the other direction. Over the past six years Russian companies, especially in the manufacturing sector, have indeed changed the way they operate, but to protect themselves against the market rather than join it. What has emerged is a new kind of economic system with its own rules and its own criteria for success and failure. The new system can be called Russia's virtual economy because it is based on an illusion about almost every important parameter: prices, sales, wages, taxes and budgets. At its heart is the pretence that the economy is much larger than it really is. This pretence allows for a larger government and larger expenditures than Russia can afford. It is the real cause of the web of wage, supply and tax arrears from which Russia cannot seem to extricate itself. The virtual economy is robust, deep-rooted and broadly popular' (Gaddy and Ickes 1998b: 53–4). 'The share of barter payments among all industrial enterprises in Russia has now reached more than 50 per cent' (p. 56). 'At its [the virtual economy's] heart are many enterprises that produce goods but take away rather than add value. This sector has survived six years of market reform. The reasons are complex, but the most important is that enterprises can now operate in Russia without paying their bills. This is possible because value is redistributed to them from other sectors of the economy. One way this is done is through tax arrears, which are a form of continued budget subsidies. More important, however, is direct redistribution from the value-producing sectors of the economy, primarily the natural resources sector' (pp. 56–7). 'The virtual economy masks the non-viability of the value-subtracting manufacturer ... The virtual economy has arisen for two fundamental reasons: most of the Russian economy, especially its manufacturing sector, takes away value, and most of its participants in the economy pretend that it does not. Barter, tax arrears and other non-monetary methods of payment turn out to be the main mechanism used to sustain the pretence. The pretence is what causes all the non-payment difficulties. There is less value produced than there are claims on it ... At the same time the system dictates a certain minimum requirement for cash, called the cash constraint. Most enterprises must sell their products for cash in order to pay wages. This explains the ironic feature of the virtual economy that while it is itself a non-market system, it depends upon the market. It is only the market that allows some of the economy's products to be realised for the cash needed to payworkers ... Some of the products can be sold inside Russia. But the main source of cash is outside, on the world market' (pp. 59–60). 'Russia's GDP may be even smaller than the official figures suggest, even after taking into account the underreporting of the hidden economy' (p. 62). 'The virtual economy ... could not have developed to the extent it has, and arguably might not have become as corrupt and inefficient as it has, unless over $70 billion had been infused from the outside since 1992' (p. 65).

'The unprecedented reliance on non-monetary exchange (NME) among industrial enterprises is one of the most remarkable features of Russia's post-Soviet economic transformation' (Tompson 1999: 256). 'Enterprises have tended to avoid the rouble in transactions not because it is too weak and inflation-prone but because it is too valuable – too valuable, at any rate, to be employed at prevailing nominal prices' (p. 261). 'Industry's "virtual" prices are too high. Too high, that is, to pay in money: rather than lowering prices, Russian industrial enterprises avoid paying one another in roubles. The result is the emergence of the "virtual economy" ... in which official [virtual: p. 257] prices do not reflect the actual values at which transactions take place' (p. 262). 'Firms engage in NME in order to discount nominal prices which remain well above market-clearing levels. The mechanisms which prevent a convergence between formal and actual transaction values include asset valuation rules, depreciation schedules, tax regulations and an inadequate bankruptcy mechanism' (p. 256). 'In the absence of recourse to bankruptcy, barter has become the only way for many enterprises to recover debts ... The seller may be in a position where cutting off deliveries to bad debtors is effectively impossible, as has tended to be the case with the gas, electricity and rail monopolies in recent years' (p. 271). 'The virtual economy ... is primarily an industrial phenomenon' (p. 262). 'The virtual economy is in essence a non-transparent system of subsidies which, by grossly distorting prices and concealing the true relative costs of various activities, has helped many enterprises that would otherwise have failed to maintain the appearance that they are both larger and more profitable that they are' (p. 273). 'Non-monetary settlements basically involve the settling of transactions at effective prices that are below the recorded prices: because agents are often unable, for various reasons, to lower their nominal prices, de facto discounts are extended by accepting payment in forms other than money. Every Russian manager knows that a rouble in "live money" (cash or bank money) is worth more than a rouble in any other form (barter, offsets or bills of exchange' (Tompson 2000b: 617).

'The central problem of the Russian economy is simple. The country has a large number of enterprises that are continuing to operate even though they are producing obsolete products of little value ... A complex web of barter transactions and subsidies keeps inefficient companies alive. Under current law many resource-producing companies are forced to continue supplying inputs to technically bankrupt enterprises ... Instead of payments the resource supplying companies are given a credit against their tax liability' (James Gwartney, *FT*, 9 May 2000, p. 27).

('By 1994–6, in lieu of barter, many suppliers (creditors) began to demand that buyers (debtors) sign an invoice indicating the delivery of a good or service, its value, and the date payment would be expected; this creates a paper debt instrument in the form of trade or commercial credit, Dubbed *vekselia* from the German *wechsel*, or bill of exchange, these paper debt instruments had the advantage they could be endorsed by the seller and passed on in trade. In this way *velselia* served as a privately-issued means of payment': Shirley Gedeon, Review, *Comparative Economic Studies*, 2000, vol. XLII, no. 2, p. 114.)

('There are many explanations for the "barter" phenomenon ... Accounting practices, including an extraordinarily inept tax provision, refusing to recognize that goods might be sold at a loss, helped to conceal price cutting by using a different and discounted "currency". In this they were aided and abetted by both local and central government. No one trusted the banks, who ... took weeks to transfer funds, in a depreciating currency, and, given the tax-free returns available on GKOs, the banks had no incentive to lend to industry. The tax authorities had the right to collect money from companies' bank accounts, which discouraged companies from paying their sales proceeds into them. The credit crunch created arrears on business payments (including tax payments) and these were systematized as barter transactions and veksels. Government exacerbated this by, in effect, using the system to provide soft credit to industry': John Chown, *Times Literary Supplement*, 28 January 2000, p. 5. 'Value-added tax ... is based on anticipated enterprise activity; it comes directly and automatically out of the enterprise bank account as soon as the account contains anything. Thus all monetary revenues are automatically confiscated until the full VAT is paid. This provides a tremendous incentive to expand barter relations and non-cash arrangements, accepting payment and profits only in the form of storable materials': Ericson 1998: 4.)

(According to Goskomstat, about 70 per cent of industrial shipments are exchanged through barter. Another survey of medium-sized manufacturing enterprises gives a figure of 40 per cent, compared with only 6 per cent in 1992: *RET*, Monthly Update, 17 March 1997, p. vi. By June 1998 overdue payables on company balance sheets totalled 1,126 billion roubles or over 40 per cent of GDP and barter accounted for 50 per cent of industrial sales: EBRD 1998b: 16. Non-monetary forms of payments accounted for about 60 per cent or more of the average industrial firm's sales: p. 186.)

12. 'In order to identify the most important causes of low economic performance in Russia, we studied in detail ten representative economic sectors. Specifically, we examine why Russian companies are not restructuring and expanding faster, and why foreign companies are not investing more in Russia' (McKinsey Global Institute 1999: 1). The ten sectors together account for over 15 per cent of total employment (p. 11). 'In an attempt to understand why economic reform has failed in Russia we looked at the performance of ten representative sectors – software, steel, general merchandise and food retailing, hotels, oil, housing construction, cement, confectionary and dairy – and related their performance to that of the overall Russian economy. We also gauged the productivity of those industries against best practices around the world ... Overall labour productivity is indeed very low. Our ten industries averaged only 19 per cent of US productivity levels, with software leading the

group at 38 per cent and cement only 7 per cent. Soviet legacy assets – which were operated at roughly 30 per cent of the US labour productivity in 1992 – have had their labour productivity halved. This precipitous drop results from the fact the industries have not adjusted their labour force despite sharp drops in demand from Russian consumers who now have access to products from around the world. Roughly 25 per cent of Russian industrial capacity is currently in sub-scale or obsolete assets, which are still operating and fully staffed, but should be shut down. Assets since 1992 are surprisingly unproductive [new assets – put in place since 1992 – achieve only 30 per cent of the US productivity level: p. 13]. Almost no new capacity is being added in the oil and consumer goods industries, the sectors of the economy with the greatest potential for fast performance improvement. New assets are either well below efficient scale – as in housing construction and software, or under capitalized – as in open-air markets. Despite high competition intensity, the competition is unequal and it causes low productivity. Price decontrol and privatization did successfully stimulate competition. Paradoxically, however, in Russia the more productive companies are often the least profitable. Thus, more productive companies are not gaining market share and not pushing less productive firms out. In nine out of the ten sectors the direct cause of low economic performance is market distortions that prevent equal competition. The distortions come from attempts to address social concerns, corrupt practices and lack of information. In the manufacturing sectors regional governments channel implicit federal subsidies to unproductive companies. Such subsidies take the form of lower tax and energy payments, and are allegedly intended to prevent companies from shutting down and laying off workers [distortions can also take forms such as different import tariffs and differential access to government-controlled export infrastructure: p. 19]. This puts potentially productive companies at a cost disadvantage, blocking investments and growth on their part. In the service sectors, where employment should grow, investments by efficient companies are discouraged by the presence of well connected unproductive incumbents who benefit from favourable regulations, weak law enforcement and privileged access to land or government procurements' (pp. 8–9). 'Inequalities tending to favour low productivity incumbents … are often put in place to achieve social objectives, namely protecting existing jobs, but in many cases the suspicion is that they also serve the personal financial interests of government officials in collusion with businessmen' (p. 17). 'Furthermore, these sector level market distortions are key contibutors to macroeconomic instability, because they reduce government revenues and increase its expenditures. Macroeconomic instability itself is another important deterrent to investments. We found the other often mentioned reasons for Russia's economic problems to play a much smaller role (e.g. poor corporate governance and lack of a transport infrastructure)' (pp. 8–9). 'Obsolete … steel and cement plants are avoiding shutdowns by paying for only a fraction of their energy bills … Regional governments channel implicit federal energy subsidies to these companies by letting arrears to federal suppliers (Gazprom and UES) accumulate at the local gas and electricity distribution companies. These energy distribution companies are often under effective control of the regional governments … Financially sound companies end up paying taxes and energy bills "for themselves and the other guy"' (p. 19). 'In food retail … modern high productivity formats are still almost entirely absent from Russia with less than 1 per cent market share, against already 18 per cent in Poland (growing fast)' (p. 15). 'Because the products of Russian packaged software companies are systematically pirated they lack the resources to invest in the development of innovative products … The other sub-sector in the software industry, project services, proves by reaching 72 per cent of the US productivity level that, with equal conditions, of competition, a whole economic sector can reach high productivity. There are no market distortions in this sector for two reasons: first, it is completely new, with no incumbents to be protected, and, second, its customized nature makes it immune to piracy' (p. 23). 'Our sector studies show that almost three-quarters of the old assets are still economically viable and could achieve up to 65 per cent of US productivity with limited upgrade investments combined with modern forms of organization' (p. 15).

13. Mikhail Gorbachev: 'I hope that the bitter experience of recent years has taught all of us not to expect miracles. By now we have seen that overnight revolutions and shocks make good headlines; so do flashy ideas from whiz kids with little or no experience outside the ivory tower. But we neeed long-term, persistent work to build a civil society and a healthy economy that serves the people' (*IHT*, 7 January 2000, p. 8).

14. 'Yeltsin's great accomplishment, and Putin's most precious inheritance, is the destruction of the Soviet Union and of the communist regime that controlled it … But Yeltsin's great failure, and Putin's most poisonous inheritance, was his inability to build healthy new institutions to take the place of the Soviet ones he razed … The single most important cause of Yeltsin's failures was where he began – ruling a country devastated by seventy years of communism and centuries of authoritarianism before that. Russian history's most crippling legacy was the lack of civil society. Even under tsarism Russian civil institutions had been notoriously underdeveloped. Under the Bolsheviks they were systematically destroyed: political parties were banned, the press was severely censored, religion was suppressed and trade unions became arms of the Communist Party. In this atomised community social interaction was governed by a perversion of the golden rule: inform on your neighbour as he is certain to inform on you … [Another] problem was Russia's collapsing state … Russian will only free itself of the oligarchs once it has built a vocal and energetic civil society and an effective yet democratically elected state. Yeltsin has shown that you cannot build capitalist democracy from the top down' (Freeland 2000: 14).

Crime and corruption

Among the causes of crime and corruption (the abuse of public office for personal gain) are the weakness of central government in certain respects (such as ensuring the rule of law) coupled with often copious regulations in other respects (such as licences). Other causes include a poorly developed civil society.

President Vladimir Putin (8 July 2000): 'In our country ... we have too much government intervention in spheres where there should not be any and a lack of intervention in areas where they are needed. Today there is too much government involvement in property ownership, entrepreneurship and, to some extent, consumption. On the other hand, the government remains passive when it comes to the creation of a single economic space in the country, the mandatory enforcement of laws, and protection of property rights' (*CDSP*, 2000, vol. 52, no. 28, p. 6).

'The reformers ... have been unable to abolish highly corrupted and inefficient controls on international and internal trade ... these controls, such as export licences, are not only economically unjustified, but are also the seedbed of Russia's extraordinary corruption' (Jeffrey Sachs, *The Independent*, 11 October 1993, p. 18).

'Many argue that Russia has fared badly because its "shock therapy" reforms were too fast and radical. But all measures show that Russia's economy is not very liberalized, and the financial collapse [of August 1998] made it obvious that Russia's problems were actually caused by reforms that were too slow and partial. A small group of businessmen enriched themselves and then corrupted many of Russia's politicians and officials. They have conspired to stymie economic reforms, which would stimulate growth and help the overall population, because reform threatens their domination. Russian suffers not from too free a market but from corruption thriving on their excessive regulations erected by a large and pervasive state' (Åslund 1999b: 64). 'Russia's elite started making their fortunes in the Soviet Union's last years, mostly from three sources: commodity exports, subsidized credits and food imports. The best way of making a killing between the late 1980s and 1993 was to buy commodities such as metals or oil at low, state-controlled prices in Russia and then sell them abroad at world prices ... Gorbachev's partial liberalization let thousands of enterprises pursue foreign trade. In 1988 state enterprise managers were allowed to set up private co-operatives for arbitrage with "their" government-owned businesses. Managers of state companies bought oil from their enterprises privately, extracted export licences and quotas from corrupt officials, and sold the oil abroad at the market price ... In 1992 the Russian price of oil was still 1 per cent of the world market price. A few state enterprise managers, government officials, politicians and commodity traders amassed no less than $24 billion, or 30 per cent of Russia's GDP, in this peak year of gains from commodity trading.

These profits gradually dwindled. Eventually the reformers succeeded in deregulating commodity prices, but only after managers had extracted billions of dollars from their state enterprises. Business elites had an alternative way of making money in the early 1990s: cheap credits from the Russian central bank ... In 1992, while inflation was 2,500 per cent, the bank issued credits at 10 or 25 per cent a year ... Many Russian bankers became rich ... Only in late 1993 did the reformers manage to end this pilfering. A third way of making big money in the transition period was through food-import subsidies ... A food importer paid only 1 per cent of the going exchange rate when purchasing essential foods from abroad, but could easily resell them relatively freely on the domestic market and pocket the subsidy. These imports were paid for with Western "humanitarian" export credits that were added to Russia's state debt. Total import subsidies were 17.5 per cent of Russia's GDP in 1992. These profits were highly concentrated, benefiting a limited number of traders in Moscow who operated through the old state agricultural monopolies ... Altogether, the gains from these three parasitic business activities amounted to no less than 79 per cent of GDP in 1992 ... The rise of the oligarchs was the result of slow and partial reforms. If commodity prices, exports and imports had been allowed to prevail, these fortunes would never have been made. Russian enterprises would have been forced to restructure to survive ... The managers of companies ... in total obtained at most 4 per cent of GDP from privatization, a trifle compared with the profits made through regulated exports, subsidized credits and import subsidies' (pp. 65–8). 'Clearly privatization has not caused Russia's economic problems ... The problem is that businesses are formally private but that state officials' extensive and arbitrary interventions limit property rights ... Russia's greatest problem is that a few operators have made fortunes on inconsistent government regulations and subsidies. True, widespread corruption in the late 1980s sealed the fate of the communist dictatorship and facilitated its peaceful end, as many members of the elite became more concerned with creating their own wealth than with promoting socialism. But the Soviet directors made so much money that they soon bought the state. Today the Russian bureaucracy, government, parliament and regional governments are deeply corrupt ... The first crop of corrupt big businessman has lost most of its money' (pp. 69–70). 'The financial crash [of August 1998] brought huge losses to almost all big Russian businessman' (p. 73). (Note that some financial oligarchs fared better than others, e.g. Boris Berezovsky retained his wealth and temporarily regained his political influence.) ('The crisis tore through the ranks of the oligarchs, the heads of the big business groups. Groups with skilful managers and/or access to export earnings survived but those with big exposures to banking and other loss-making activities are struggling': *FT*, Survey, 10 May 2000, p. ii.)

On 10 November 1996 thirteen people attending a memorial service in a Moscow cemetary were killed in a bomb explosion thought to be related to gang warfare and a greater number were injured. The criminal interest was connected with the tax concessions formerly granted to various organizations, in this case an Afghan War veterans association. On 17 November 1996 a block of flats in Dagestan, mainly occupied by military border troops and their families, was destroyed by a bomb explosion. The mafia were suspected because of their involvement in smuggling.

The extent of organized crime can be indicated by the following:

1. The Analytical Centre for Social and Economic Policy (a presidential think-tank) estimates that 70 to 80 per cent of all private firms (local and foreign) and virtually all cafes, restaurants and retail shops pay 10 to 20 per cent of their earnings to mafia groups (*Business Central Europe*, July–August 1994, p. 27)

2. The Ministry of Internal Affairs estimates that more than 3,000 criminal groups, using threats and blackmail, have established control over 40,000 businesses, including more than 400 banks, nearly 50 stock exchanges and almost 1,500 enterprises in the government sector of the economy (*Transition*, November–December 1995, vol. 6, nos 11–12, p. 7).

3. The Russian mafia is not a single organization but a collection of perhaps 3,000 to 4,000 groups employing more than 25,000 people. Several hundred of these groups now span the countries of the former Soviet Union and Central and Eastern Europe and sometimes reach the West (World Bank 1996: 97).

4. 'The Russian mafia now controls more than 40 per cent of the total economy' (Louise Shelley, *Transition*, February 1997, vol. 8, no. 1, p. 7).

5. 'The director of the FBI told the US Congress this week that "highly sophisticated" Russian mafia groups were establishing bases in Europe and the USA and posed a threat to the authority of the Kremlin itself. His warnings followed a report from a Washington think-tank which described Russia as "an emergent criminal-syndicalist state" and estimated that two-thirds of the economy was already under the sway of racketeers' (Chrystia Freeland, *FT*, 4 October 1997, p. 2).

6. In late 1998 the Russian prosecutor general said that organized crime controlled nearly 50 per cent of the economy. 'Prosecutors estimate 50 per cent of all commercial banks and 40 per cent of state-owned companies are criminally controlled, thus affecting between 40 per cent and 50 per cent of Russia's GDP. Russia's natural gas, oil and coal sectors have been particularly hard hit by organized crime units' (*Transition*, December 1998, vol. 9, no. 6, p. 27).

7. 'Although all figures in this area are inherently unreliable, the Russian interior ministry has estimated that organized crime controls 40 per cent of the economy; other estimates are even higher. Half of Russia's banks are thought to be controlled by crime syndicates' (*The Economist*, 28 August 1999, pp. 17–18).

8. 'Over 200 large Russian organized crime groups are operating out of fifty-eight countries around the world, according to new estimates reported by a US-based think-tank. Russia's August 1998 financial crisis reduced criminals'

opportunities to make money domestically and accelerated their expansion abroad, into North America, Israel, Brazil, Columbia, Austria, Turkey, Hungary, Poland and Sri Lanka, the global organized crime project of the Centre for Strategic and International Studies said, citing figures compiled by the FBI. Russian groups are forging links with transnational criminal organizations, including US syndicates, the Cali drug cartels and the Sicilian mafia, warned the project' (*FT*, 5 July 2000, p. 8).

There is general concern about crime and corruption, even though the picture is not entirely negative. 'Some [criminal groups] fill market gaps created by inadequate government institutions, providing security services for new private businesses or helping to enforce contracts (for example by collecting debts for banks, a significant number of which maintain close links with organized crime). But the value of these services is dwarfed by the sums these powerful criminal groups extort from private businesses' (World Bank 1996: 97). Even former advisers are dismayed by the degree of corruption: 'It will be no surprise if the Russian government is handed a stinging defeat in the parliamentary elections [of 17 December 1995] ... The people are burdened by an unending economic and social crisis. They resent the staggering government corruption that has compromised economic reform and led to several years of inflation and privations. Russia has always lacked a political tradition, even the rhetoric, of civic-mindedness. Few politicians even profess a standard of public service or public morality. Although virtually all post-communist states have experienced corruption scandals (largely because civil society is weak and still unorganized), Russia's corruption is singularly deep. One reason is that the Communist Party Central Committee, the breeding ground of much of today's leadership, was profoundly corrupt ... In the Soviet Union's waning years senior apparatchiks converted political power into financial stakes in the emerging market economy' (Jeffrey Sachs, *IHT*, 6 December 1995, p. 10). 'The post-Soviet state is so corrupt that the only way back to economic growth seems to be by restricting and minimizing it' (Anders Åslund, *IHT*, 19 March 1997, p. 8).

Despite general concern, a more pessimistic and a more optimistic view of Russia's long-term prospects as regards crime and corruption can be distinguished. On the more pessimistic wing of the debate are the following:

1. Stephen Handelman (1994) describes a deeply disturbing degree of criminality. 'Organized crime is the most explosive force to emerge from the wreckage of Soviet communism. The so-called Russian mafiya has undermined reform, spawned extraordinary levels of violence in major cities, and helped fuel a growing ultra-nationalist backlash ... Russia's crime syndicate constitutes a serious threat to post-Soviet democracy ... The "mafiya", Russian-style, is a hydra-headed phenomenon that feeds on the emerging market economy' (p. 83). Between 3,000 and 4,000 gangs operate in Russia. Although total gang membership is estimated at less than 100,000, 'the hazy boundary between criminal and legal business activity has allowed mafiya

groups to penetrate most areas of the Russian economy, giving them disproportionate influence' (p. 83). According to the Russian Ministry of Internal Affairs (MVD), organized crime controlled as much as 40 per cent of the turnover in goods and services by 1993. No criminal enterprise of this complexity could have succeeded without the support and encouragement of officials at every level. According to government investigators, more than half the criminal gangs in 1992 had ties with government. A number of cartels are fronts for the former Soviet elites, the '*nomenklatura* capitalists' (p. 84). The mixture of unbridled capitalism, organized crime and official chicanery has produced a crisis of government (p. 88). 'Russia's policy-makers committed a fundamental mistake: they tried to develop a free market before constructing a civil society in which such a market could safely operate' (p. 89). 'The danger is especially apparent outside the urban centres of Moscow and St Petersburg, where local crime lords and their government allies have filled the vacuum created by the departure of communist authority' (p. 90).

2. Thomas Friedman (*IHT,* 4 May 1995, p. 8) considers that: 'It is not the street crime that threatens Russia. It is the official corruption, the cheating of the state and businesses by their own employees and the Mafia, which, if unchecked, is going to undermine Russian reform from within. It is already eroding the credibility of the government and courts, diverting resources, lowering tax revenues and driving away investors … rampant corruption could leave all those left out of the game looking for a man-on-horseback, maybe a fascist, to crack down.'

3. 'Probably the most damaging aspect of Russian organized crime activity is its contribution to large-scale capital flight … A specialist on capital flight reported at a recent Ministry of Interior conference in Moscow that $150 billion had been exported from Russia since 1991. This figure may be high but conservative estimates are still more than $50 billion. A minimum of 40 per cent of the estimated $2 billion in monthly capital flight is attributable to organized crime groups … Russian organized crime secured a massive transfer of state property because the privatization occurred rapidly, on a huge scale, without legal safeguards, and without transparency … The Russian mafia now controls more than 40 per cent of the total economy. In some sectors, such as consumer markets, real estate and banking, their role is even greater … Organized crime groups are dominating both legitimate and illegitimate economic sectors simultaneously. The new owners, often uninterested in making their enterprises function, drain the resources and transfer the proceeds abroad, exacerbating the problems of both capital flight and nonpayment of wages' (Louise Shelley, *Transition*, February 1997, vol. 8, no. 1. p. 7).

4. A survey of top executives and directors of US, British, German and Scandinavian companies revealed that Russia is considered to be the most corrupt country, followed by Nigeria (*IHT,* 4 November 1997, p. 14).

5. In 1997 a group called Transparency International ranked corruption in fifty-two countries as judged by global executives and country specialists.

Russia ranked fourth (*IHT*, 10 September 1998, p. 8). In 1998 the survey by Transparency International placed Russia twelfth out of eighty-five in terms of corrupt countries to do business (*IHT*, 24 September 1999, p. 23). Of the ninety-nine countries ranked in 1999 Cameroon was the most corrupt at number ninety-nine. Russia was ranked at eighty-two. Denmark, at number one, was the least corrupt (*Transition*, 1999, vol. 10, no. 5, pp. 1–3). In 2000 Russia again came in at number eighty-two (*Business Central Europe*, October 2000, p. 63).

On the more optimistic side of the debate are the following:

1. A common argument is that today's criminals will eventually turn into advocates of law and order in order to protect their gains from future criminals.

2. 'The stage is now set for a long and intense struggle between law and crime, but there is little reason to believe that society will lose' (Åslund 1994b: 69). 'After an astounding 50 per cent surge in the number of registered crimes from 1990 to 1992, the rate levelled off in 1993 and dropped by 6 per cent in 1994' (Åslund, *IHT*, 25 April 1995, p. 8).

3. 'It [organized crime] is the only counterweight to the greater number of firms backed by corrupt officials which now engage in ruthless monopolistic practices ... Only the local criminal mafia may be able to resist the ex-Party mafia, if the two are not one and the same' (Edward Luttwak, *The Guardian*, 31 July 1995, p. 11).

4. 'The absence of effective and legitimate public institutions to enforce contracts and compel enterprises to meet their economic obligations, stimulates the appearance of agencies for private protection ... Of course, "protection" can become prohibitively costly as it blends into extortion ... The mafia, its coercive means notwithstanding, provides a service without which many economic transactions might not take place' (Burawoy 1996: 1111).

A chronology of further developments

17 November 1998. A statement is issued by two colonels, two majors and a senior lieutenant of the Federal Security Bureau (successor to the KGB), claiming that senior officials (although not its director, Vladimir Putin) were using the organization to carry out assassinations, seize hostages and extort money from businesses: 'Officials have begun using the FSB not for its constitutional goals of protecting the state but to settle accounts with undesirable persons, to carry out private political and criminal orders for a fee, and sometimes simply as an instrument to earn money ... Our aim is to draw public attention to the deviations in the work of the Federal Security Bureau that are exceedingly dangerous for society and which have become features of its activities. We do not want the shadow of the criminal actions of a number of officials to be cast on the service and its honest officials ... The order [given in December 1997] to assassinate ... Boris Berezovsky, unfortunately, is not an exceptional event in the present life of the FSB.' Lt-Col Alexander Litvinenko claims that an officer accused him of 'preventing patriots from the motherland from killing a Jew who robbed half his country'. It was alleged that the agency's problems began under the former director, Nikolai Kovalev (*The Independent*, 18 November 1998, p. 13; *The Telegraph*, 18 November 1998, p. 16).

Yeltsin has ordered an enquiry into charges that members of the FSB (which is responsible for investigating organized crime, terrorism and foreign intelligence operations) plotted to kill Boris Berezovsky. Litvinenko and the other agents alleged that the agency was infested by a 'criminal group' that had been using it 'for their own private political purposes, including settling accounts with unwanted people'. The agents stressed that the plots had unravelled before Vladimir Putin took command in August 1998. But Putin said that he had written evidence that that some of the complaining agents were themselves rogues who had pushed illegal crime-fighting methods. He claimed that some of them had been personal bodyguards for Berezovsky before working for the FSB. Putin ridiculed the allegations (Michael Wines, *IHT*, 23 November 1998, p. 8).

2 February 1999. Yuri Skuratov resigns as chief prosecutor, 'for reasons of health'.

3 February 1999. 'Russia's acting chief prosecutor yesterday [3 February] criticised the country's courts for being too lenient, and said an explosion in corruption among officials ranked among the world's worst in that respect. "Corruption among Russian bureaucrats has reached unprecedented levels", said Yuri Chaika. Only Venezuela, Nigeria, Pakistan and Cameroon do worse than us" ... On Tuesday [2 February] a high-profile raid by the general presecutor's office ... took place at Sibneft, an oil group linked to the "oligarch" Boris Berezovsky' (*FT*, 4 February 1999, p. 2).

'Russia's chief prosecutor suddenly resigns, officially for health reasons ... In private conversations Kremlin aides acknowledged that there was more to Mr Skuratov's abrupt exit than a bad heart, the ailment with which he was admitted Monday [1 February] to the Kremlin hospital. They said Mr Yeltsin's displeasure had been a long time building, first over Mr Skuratov's failure to bring to the most publicized Russian crimes to trial and, more recently, over his failure to move against outspoken neo-fascist and antisemitic politicians ... The prosecutor's foot-dragging in bringing a case against Albert Makashov – a communist member of parliament who in October called for Jews to be driven out of Russia – was linked to the resurgence last weekend of a small splinter neo-fascist group in Moscow ... The interior ministry announced Wednesday [3 February] that it had arrested a former justice minister, Valentin Kovalyov, on charges of embezzlement ... The police confirmed Wednesday night that they had found evidence of illegal wiretapping during a citywide raid of offices and apartments linked to Boris Berezovsky ... now the most public target of what seems to be prime minister

Yevgeni Primakov's opening shot in a crackdown on economic crime and corruption. Mr Primakov sent out a warning last week when he said that an amnesty of 94,000 prisoners would free cells needed to house an incoming wave of corrupt officials and businessmen … Armed Russian federation agents … swooped this week through the offices of Sibneft, a Berezovsky-controlled oil company, and Atoll, a Berezovsky-controlled security company. Atoll has been accused of serving as Mr Berezovsky's private intelligence agency, secretly spying on top Russian officials and even members of President Boris Yeltsin's family. The raids [are] seen as the final blows to Mr Berezovsky's dwindling prestige and influence' (Celestine Bohlen, *IHT*, 5 February 1999, p. 5).

4 February 1999. 'Masked, camouflaged special troops raided an office affiliated with Aeroflot, the national airline in which Mr Berezovsky has had major interests. The raids Thursday [4 February] marked the second time this week that investigators stormed into a business linked to Mr Berezovsky. On Tuesday [2 February] they seized documents and videotapes from Sibneft, a leading oil company that also has ties to Mr Berezovsky. They said they found evidence there that he ran an intelligence operation to tap the phones of Mr Yeltsin's family' (*IHT*, 6 February 1999, p. 11).

4 March 1999. Yeltsin asks the other members of the CIS to agree to dismiss Boris Berezovsky as executive chairman of the CIS 'for exceeding his powers and failing to carry out orders'.

17 March 1999. The Council of the Federation refuses to accept the resignation of Yuri Skuratov.

Yuri Skuratov (in his speech to the Council of the Federation): 'I could sense almost physically that, for some people, the activity of law-enforcement agencies had become like a thorn in their side, that we had touched on a sore spot, so to speak. Especially when we started looking into instances in which enterprises had been privatized or converted into joint stock companies illegally, or into unlawful activity in the banking system, and into management of the economy and abuses by very high-ranking officials. I am very sorry to say that certain forces have skilfully managed to wedge themselves between the president and the prosecutor general … First of all the influential people who made their mark in dubious operations in the market for GKOs [short-term government binds] … A big contribution to the process of getting me out of office was made by the oligarchs … The cases they are most interested in are the ones involving the Aeroflot airline company, the AvtoVAZ [Volga Automotive Plant] joint stock company, the Atoll private security company and others' (*CDSP*, 1999, vol. 51, no. 11, p. 1).

'In his speech to the Federation Council Mr Skuratov had earlier denied that he was ill and said he would continue in his work if he was backed by parliament. He explained his resignation had been prompted by "certain forces" who had driven a wedge between him and the president. Mr Skuratov said his investigations had uncovered dubious practices in the government debt market ... Mr Skuratov implied that Boris Berezovsky ... had been one of those behind a campaign to discredit him ... Last month [February] he [Skuratov] disclosed that the central bank had channelled billions of dollars of its hard currency reserves through an obscure, Jersey-based fund management group called Fimaco' (*FT*, 18 March 1999, p. 3).

18 March 1999. 'After meeting Thursday [18 March] with both Mr Skuratov and prime minister Yevgeni Primakov, Mr Yeltsin directed the Russian security council to form a commission to investigate Mr Skuratov's alleged "misdeeds, which bring disgrace to the honour of a prosecutor, and his violations of the prosecutor's oath"' (*IHT*, 19 March 1999, p. 1).

23 March 1999. Prosecutor-general Yuri Skuratov sends a team into the Kremlin to seize documents as part of a corruption probe. The documents seized concern the Kremlin's dealings with a Swiss construction firm, which renovated large parts of the Kremlin and other government buildings. There have been rumours of bribery in relation to the award of contracts (*The Guardian*, 24 March 1999, p. 17; *The Independent*, 24 March 1999, p. 13).

'Russia's chief prosecutor's office has confirmed that it is investigating corruption inside the Kremlin itself, aiming at members of President Yeltsin's inner circle. Acting on orders from Yuri Skuratov ... investigator's have seized documents from the offices of the presidential administration's powerful property-management office, headed by Pavel Borodin ... Until now Russia's periodic anti-corruption campaigns have steered clear of the Kremlin ... Mr Borodin's property-management office is a vast empire of office buildings, apartment blocks, clinics, country houses and vacation spas used by government employees. The investigation of the office followed a raid on 22 January by Swiss investigators of Mabetex, a construction company ... that does extensive business throughout the former Soviet Union ... Accusations that have surfaced during Mr Skuratov's investigation suggest that Mabetex paid Kremlin officials to secure the lucrative contracts' (Celestine Bohlen, *IHT*, 25 March 1999, p. 7).

2 April 1999. Yeltsin suspends Yuri Skuratov from his position as chief prosecutor. The decision led to a debate about the legality of the move.

'Under the 1993 constitution the prosecutor is appointed and relieved from his post by the Federation Council on the nomination of the president. However, a separate law says that if the prosecutor is under investigation he can be suspended, which is the action that Mr Yeltsin took Friday [2 April]. The investigation of Mr Skuratov centres on who paid for the prostitutes [shown on a videotape with Skuratov], according to the news agency Interfax, which ... said a businessman paid for the prostitutes in exchange for Mr Skuratov's promise to delay three criminal cases against the businessman' (*IHT*, 3 April 1999, p. 2).

Yeltsin unilaterally dismisses Boris Berezovsky as executive secretary of the CIS. A plane carrying him from Paris was refused permission to enter Russian airspace and landed instead in Ukraine. At the CIS conference Yeltsin succeeded in winning confirmation of Yuri Yarov as the new executive secretary. Yarov became Yeltsin's first deputy chief of staff in the summer of 1996 but was dismissed in December 1998 (*CDSP*, 1999, vol. 51, no. 14, pp. 19–20).

6 April 1999. 'Russia's chief prosecutor issued an arrest warrant Tuesday [6 April] for Boris Berezovsky ... Officials in the prosecutor's office said Mr Berezovsky [who is in France] ... had been charged with money laundering and "illegal entrepreneurship" as part of a scheme that diverted Aeroflot's foreign currency proceeds to a Geneva-based company that they were said to control ... While Mr Yeltsin recently ordered Mr Skuratov removed from his post a second time, corruption inquiries under Mr Skuratov's deputy seem to have continued apace' (*IHT*, 7 April 1999, p. 5).

'Mr Berezovsky ... lost his immunity from prosecution last week [2 April] when he was fired as secretary of the CIS and stripped of his diplomatic immunity. But Mr Berezovsky claimed he had been prevented from defending himself at a meeting of CIS leaders in Moscow when his aircraft was denied access to Russian airspace' (*FT*, 7 April 1999, p. 3).

'Russia's prosecutor general Yuri Skuratov issued arrest warrants for ... Boris Berezovsky, head of the conglomerate Logova, and Alexander Smolensky, head of the defunct bank SBS-Agro ... Both [were] charged with embezzlement' (*Business Central Europe*, May 1999, p. 12).

The charges against Alexander Smolensky include money laundering (*RET*, 1999, vol. 8, no. 2, p. 95).

9 April 1999. 'Interior minister Sergei Stepashin said Friday [9 April] that he would not arrest Boris Berezovsky even though there is a warrant out for the billionaire businessman ... "Berezovsky will arrive in Russia, present his explanations and this, I hope, will be the end of the incident", Mr Stepashin said' (*IHT*, 10 April 1999, p. 2).

14 April 1999. The warrant for Berezovsky's arrest is withdrawn. (The arrest warrant for Alexander Smolensky was withdrawn on 20 April.)

18 April 1999. Berezovsky returns to Russia. (He went into hospital the following day.)

21 April 1999. For the second time the Council of the Federation votes (by seventy-nine to sixty-one) not to accept the resignation of Yuri Skuratov.

26 April 1999. Boris Berezovzky is formally charged with money-laundering and barred from leaving Moscow while prosecutors investigate his case. He is accused of expatriating hard currency profits from the state airline Aeroflot to a shell company in Switzerland he had set up. It is alleged that he ran the state airline for several years by naming his cronies to the board of directors (*IHT*, 27 April 1999, p. 5). Berezovsky is charged with illegal business activities, money laundering and continuing business activities when he held a state post (*FT*, 27 April 1999, p. 3).

18 August 1999. 'Billions of dollars have been channelled through the Bank of New York in the last year in what is believed to be a major money-laundering operation by Russian organized crime, US law enforcement officials say ... Investigators say that as much as $10 billion may have flowed through the bank ... since early last year [1998] ... On Wednesday [18 August] the Bank of New York said it had suspended two employees [one was dismissed on 27 August] ... "The bank of New York has been co-operating with the office of the United States Attorney for the Southern District of New York in a confidential investigation of the use of bank facilities to transfer funds from Russia to other countries", the bank said in a statement' (*IHT,* 20 August 1999, p. 3). '[US] federal investigators believe that the amount of money moved through the Bank of New York – at least $4.2 billion and possibly as much as $10 billion – was so large that Russian organized crime figures linked to the investigation could be directly responsible for only a small part of it ... Investigators say Semion Mogilevich [a reputed head of Russian organized crime] used a company called Benex to launder funds through the Bank of New York ... Investigators say it is very likely that the bulk of the money that flowed through the bank is tied to corporate embezzlement and political graft in Russia. And Russia's securities markets, marred by rampant insider trading, have long been considered easy for public officials to manipulate ... A powerful Russian industrialist whose empire is under investigation in the money laundering inquiry at the Bank of New York has alleged that a large part of the billions of dollars moved through the bank was controlled by Russian officials protecting their fortunes by shipping their money abroad before Russian markets collapsed last year [1998] ... Mikhail Khodorkovsky [chairman of the oil company Yukos; he was chairman of the now-insolvent Menatep bank, which did business with the Bank of New York] said ... that many Russian officials began selling government securities in 1998 because they had inside knowledge about government deliberations in the months leading to a decision to permit the devaluation of the rouble' (*IHT,* 30 August 1999, p. 6).

'The investigation now under way in the United States will, it is hoped, determine where the money that went through the Bank of New York came from. Our theory is that Russia's ill-fated Treasury bills – the GKOs – will account for much of it' (Boris Nemtsov and Ian Bremmer, *IHT,* 4 September 1999, p. 8).

'The scandal has confirmed Russia's status as the world's leading kleptocracy. The story broke on 19 August, when the Bank of New York ... admitted co-operating with an investigation into alleged money-laundering of as much as $10 billion ... Crime is not at the margin of [Russian] society: it is at its very centre. Although all figures in this area are inherently unreliable, the Russian interior ministry has estimated that organized crime controls 40 per cent of the economy; other estimates are even higher. Half of Russia's banks are thought to be controlled by crime syndicates' (*The Economist,* 28 August 1999, pp. 17–18).

26 August 1999. 'A tide of Russian financial scandals yesterday [26 August] reached the walls of the Kremlin, putting under pressure the daughters of

Boris Yeltsin and the president himself. Allegations that credit card slips signed by Mr Yeltsin and his daughters [Tatiana Dyachenko and Yelena Okulova] had been found in a [January 1999] raid on the Lugano offices of Mabetex, a Swiss company contracted to renovate the Kremlin, prompted the Yeltsin administration to issue a carefully worded denial of wrongdoing ... The implication that the Yeltsin family was using Mabetex as its personal bank on shopping sprees could be an acute embarrassment in the lead-up to the presidential elections next June [2000] ... The Mabetex controversy has arisen again in the wake of revelations by the New York Times that British and US authorities are investigating the source of $10 billion channelled through Russian accounts at the Bank of New York in 1998 and 1999. The investigation into alleged money-laundering operations appears to be widening its scope. US and UK law enforcement officials believe it has brought to the surface a much wider pattern of illicit money transfers involving some Western banks, offshore centres, Russian organized crime and people close to the Yeltsin government' (*FT*, 27 August 1999, p. 16). In January 1999 the Russian prosecutor-general's office revealed that it had been co-operating with the Swiss authorities to investigate the activities of the Lugano-based Mabetex company. It is alleged that Mabetex paid bribes to Kremlin officials to win lucrative renovation contracts. Soon after airing the allegations, Yuri Skuratov, the prosecutor-general, was sacked by Yeltsin (*FT*, 1 September 1999, p. 2).

30 August 1999. 'A Russian investigator has said in a television interview that published accounts of bribes paid to Kremlin officials by a Swiss construction company were "98 per cent true" and could be backed up by evidence in his files. The investigator, Georgi Chuglazov, a deputy in the office of the prosecutor-general, made the comments Monday night [30 August] after he was barred at the last minute from joining a delegation from the office that was to leave Tuesday [31 August] for Switzerland. Mr Chuglazov confirmed that he had been removed Friday [27 August] as head of the investigation into Mabetex ... Last week the Italian newspaper Corriere della Sera reported detailed charges against the inner circle of Mr Yeltsin and his family. The newspaper ... said that $1 million channelled by Mabetex through accounts used by Pavel Borodin, head of the property management office of the Kremlin, had been labelled "pocket money" for members of Mr Yeltsin's family during an official trip to Hungary several years ago. The paper also reported that Mr Yeltsin's family had been given access to credit cards that were paid by the president of Mabetex' (*IHT*, 1 September 1999, p. 5).

3 September 1999. 'Prosecutors in Switzerland who are investigating suspected money laundering by officials at high levels of the Russian government have ordered Swiss banks to provide information about ... [twenty-four] Russians who might have accounts in Switzerland and have frozen [since July] at least fifty-nine bank accounts ... The Russians under investigation include Pavel Borodin, the powerful head of the Russian president's property management team, as well as his wife, daughter and son-in-law, and Oleg Soskovets, a former deputy prime minister heavily involved in the military industry and in weapons exports. The Swiss investigation was opened in response to requests made last spring by the chief prosecutor in Moscow, Yuri Skuratov, who was subsequently fired by President Boris Yeltsin but technically remains in office because parliament rejected his dismissal. The investigation has continued under Mr Skuratov's deputies (*IHT*, 6 September 1999, p. 9).

'In an article published Saturday [4 September] an Italian newspaper [Corriere della Sera] reported that Pavel Borodin, head of the Kremlin's property management office since 1993, was one of the three signatories on a Swiss bank account opened by Mabetex in March 1995. The newspaper also said that Russian investigators believe that two other bank accounts, opened in the names of two of Mr Borodin's deputies code-named "Cinderella" and "Tsarina", were put at the disposal of the two Yeltsin daughters ... The report in Corriere della Sera ... largely corroborated a report in July in Vestiya, a Russian investigative newspaper, that Mr Borodin was one of three names listed on at account at Gotthard Bank ... The other signatories were Mr Borodin's daughter ... and ... the president of Mabetex' (*IHT*, 7 September 1999, p. 10).

Samuel Berger (President Clinton's national security adviser): 'In early 1997 Vice-President Al Gore pressed prime minister Viktor Chernomyrdin to back money-laundering and anti-crime bills, which the Duma and Federation Council subsequently approved. We feel that President Yeltsin should not have vetoed the money-laundering law' (*IHT*, 7 September 1999, p. 10).

'A Swiss investigation has uncovered evidence that a Swiss construction company that received major Kremlin contracts paid tens of thousands of dollars of bills charged to credit cards in the names of President Boris Yeltsin and his two daughters, law enforcement officials say. The company, Mabetex, also provided $1 million that was transferred several years ago to a Hungarian bank account intended for Mr Yeltsin's benefit, the officials say ... In all, Mabetex poured $10 million to $15 million into the bank or credit card accounts for numerous Russian officials, say officials close to the investigation ... Yuri Skuratov, then Russia's chief prosecutor, asked for ... [Swiss] help in November [1998]. Swiss investigators found that Mabetex had opened bank accounts for Pavel Borodin ... The company also set up accounts and credit cards for numerous other Russian officials, mostly in Mr Borodin's department, or their relatives, the sources said' (*IHT*, 9 September 1999, pp. 1, 12). 'A Swiss investigation has uncovered evidence that ... [the president of Mabetex] paid roughly $10 million in bribes to high-ranking officials in Moscow, law enforcement sources have said ... The Swiss general prosecutor ... confirmed the Kremlin's statement that neither Mr Yeltsin nor his daughters have Swiss bank accounts in their names' (*IHT*, 15 September 1999, p. 5).

'Pavel Borodin is head of the directorate of presidential affairs … [which] publishes no accounts … [It is] unaccountable … [It] inherited the assets of the Communist Party, the former Soviet government and parliament and of most other well-endowed Soviet-era institutions (such as the health ministry that ran holiday homes for the elite), which between them owned most of the desirable property in Russia. The DPA, says Mr Borodin, now owns property in seventy-eight countries … Its turnover, of $2.5 billion last year [1998], comes from 200 separate businesses, including hotels, airlines, five car fleets and Russia's elite official hospital, which also takes private patients. Its core competence is construction … The number of employees has risen tenfold in six years, to 100,000 (*The Economist*, 18 September 1999, p. 111).

12 September 1999. 'Swiss bank accounts linked to Boris Berezovsky have been frozen, a top prosecutor [in Moscow] said Sunday [12 September]. Russian media have linked him to an investigation into whether money belonging to the state-controlled airline Aeroflot was misappropriated through two Swiss companies' (*IHT*, 13 September 199, p. 1).

15 September 1999. Yuris Skuratov: 'An analysis of the central bank's use of the account where the IMF stabilization loan was deposited showed that $4.4 billion was sold from that account between 23 July and 17 August 1998. Of that money $3.9 billion was sold directly to Russian and foreign banks, bypassing the trading session at the Moscow Interbank Currency Exchange [MICEX]. Only $471 million went to support the rouble exchange rate on MICEX. Another $100 million went for intervention on other [currency] exchanges.'

'Mr Skuratov claimed that almost $4 billion of an IMF bailout was sold by the Russian central bank to Russian insider banks … Bypassing the main exchange forum in Moscow the dollars were sold to eighteen Russian banks using their accounts at the Bank of New York, he said … The insider banks used the $3.9 billion to convert their rouble-denominated short-term Treasury bills or GKOs into dollars' (*The Independent*, 16 September 1999, p. 17).

'Mr Skuratov … named two of the banks as Oneximbank and SBS-Agro' (*The Times*, 16 September 1999, p. 20).

21 September 1999. Swiss banks have frozen $16.8 million worth of Russian accounts suspected of being linked to a money-laundering case involving the Bank of New York (*IHT*, 22 September 1999, p. 23).

23 September 1999. Michel Camdessus (managing director of the IMF): 'Russia, for us, is a programme that has worked … [Russia's economy, in relation to expectations, is] overperforming … Nothing has been found [to justify allegations of misuse of IMF funds]' (*IHT*, 24 September 1999, p. 13).

'No evidence has so far been presented that the current money laundering scandal involves the diversion of IMF loans' (Stanley Fischer, first deputy managing director of the IMF, *FT*, 27 September 1999, p. 26).

'Almost no responsible officials in the USA and Russia governments, nor those in international lending organizations, will admit publicly that their funds or foreign aid have been misused ... According to the audit committee of the Russian Duma, the $600 million [World Bank] loan provided in 1996 for the coal mines seems to have disappeared with little evident restructuring ... IMF officials have not addressed the claim that senior [Russian] central bank officials took [IMF] funds and invested them in high-yielding government securities back in Russia and kept the proceeds for their personal use. The central bank also has a long history of taking dollars borrowed from the IMF. Instead of selling them all at auction to prop up the rouble, as it is supposed to do, it sets aside a substantial portion at a lower rate for a few selected banks owned by a few favoured oligarchs. Moreover, these transfers have a habit of taking place immediately before a sharp devaluation of the rouble. Many of those dollars then quickly find their way back to the West' (Marshall Goldman, *IHT*, 15 October 1999, p. 10).

13 October 1999. The Council of the Federation (for the third time) refuses to endorse the dismissal of Yuri Skuratov. This time the vote was ninety-eight to fifty-two.

5 November 1999. 'The Russian prosecutor's office unexpectedly terminated a high-profile corruption investigation on Friday [5 November], saying that charges would not be filed against magnate Boris Berezovsky in a case involving charges of diversion of cash from the national airline, Aeroflot, into a pair of Swiss companies. The prosecutor, Nikolai Volkov, said he had signed an order on Thursday [4 November] terminating the criminal enquiry. He told the Interfax news agency that Mr Berezovsky remained a "witness" and that two fomer Aeroflot executives were still under investigation. It was not clear why the case was abruptly closed down, but Mr Volkov said the evidence collected so far did not support preliminary charges brought in April ... Mr Volkov suggested that the enquiry might continue by saying that the investigation had stopped "for this period of time" ... Court papers made public in Lausanne on 16 October alleged that Mr Berezovsky and two executives of Aeroflot hid some $600 million in hard currency in Switzerland. The figure was given to Swiss authorities by Russian investigators who asked for help. The Russian investigators said, according to the court papers, that Mr Berezovsky and the other two ... took $400 million in Aeroflot profits and $200 million in air traffic fees and hid the money in two Swiss companies ... The two companies were raided by Swiss authorities in July and their bank accounts frozen' (*IHT*, 6 November 1999, p. 4).

27 January 2000. 'Swiss prosecutors issued [several days ago] an arrest warrant for Pavel Borodin, the Kremlin's former estates manager, on charges of money laundering' (*The Times*, 28 January 2000, p. 18).

'It emerged yesterday [27 January] that a Swiss magistrate has issued an international arrest warrant for a top state official on suspicion of money laundering ... against Pavel Borodin, the former head of presidential affairs at the Kremlin under Boris Yeltsin and currently the state secretary responsible for the Russia-Belarus union. The warrant comes after investigations carried out over the last year into the alleged payment of bribes to top Russian officials by the Swiss-based construction company Mabetex in exchange for government contracts ... Mr Putin ... appointed Mr Borodin to his current position ... [but] he himself worked as Mr Borodin's deputy when he came to Moscow in the mid-1990s before being made head of the FSB, the KGB's successor body, and then prime minister last August [1999]' (*FT*, 28 January 2000, p. 9). (Borodin was appointed manager of the Kremlin's property department in 1993: *FT*, 29 January 2000, p. 8. On 10 January 2000 Vladimir Putin demoted Pavel Borodin from head of the Kremlin's management office to state secretary of the Russia-Belarus union.)

31 January 2000. 'A new criminal case of abuse of office has been opened up against Yuri Skuratov' (*The Independent*, 1 February 2000, p. 17).

16 February 2000. 'A former employee of the Bank of New York and her husband have admitted laundering at least $7 billion through the bank, much of it for Russian nationals hoping to evade customs duties and local taxes. In a New York federal court, Lucy Edwards and Peter Berlin also pleaded guilty to a range of other offences. They included setting up a branch of a foreign bank without regulatory permission, operating an illegal wire transfer business, fraudulently obtaining visas, bribing a bank official, accepting illicit payments and laundering them offshore ... Until now the couple had been charged only with the relatively minor offence of operating an illegal money transfer business. The Russian-born couple surrendered to the FBI as part of a deal with prosecutors on Tuesday [15 February], after flying from London' (*FT*, 17 February 2000, p. 14).

'A former Bank of New York executive [Lucy Edwards] and her husband [Peter Berlin] pleaded guilty Wednesday [16 February] to money-laundering charges, admitting they accepted $1.8 million to arrange an elaborate scheme purportedly linked to the Russian mob ... The couple admitted allowing Russian bankers to set up unlicensed banking operations ... so the Russian could launder large amounts of money and evade taxes in Russia and the United States. The pleas were the first major admissions in the international scam involving as much as $10 billion. Ms Edwards told the court she was approached by Russian bankers in late 1995 and they then agreed that her husband would open an account at the Bank of New York to obtain software that would enable them to bank illegally. In exchange Ms Edwards and her husband were paid a percentage of the money transferred through accounts' (*IHT*, 17 February 2000, p. 5). 'A former Bank of New York executive and her husband [admitted] that they helped move billions of dollars out of Russia in a vast, secret scheme to avoid paying taxes and customs duties there. For four years, working at the behest of figures who controlled two Moscow banks, Lucy Edwards and Peter Berlin set up front companies and eased the way for more than 160,000 electronic transactions worth more than $7 billion from banks in Russia [Depozitarno-Kliringovy Bank and Commercial Bank Flamingo] to the Bank of New York and the rest of the world ... The

Russian bankers eventually paid them a total of $1.8 million, which was deposited in offshore accounts to hide it from the [US] Internal Revenue Service ... Ms Edwards ... [said] the Russians acknowledged [in August 1999] that they were trying to avoid paying steep Russian taxes and customs duties' (*IHT*, 18 February 2000, p. 7).

'After about two years of investigating the movement of billions of dollars through the Bank of New York, [US] federal law enforcement officials now say much of the money involved tax evasion by Russian businesses, and that the investigators are prepared to help Moscow if Russia wishes to pursue the cases on its own' (*IHT*, 16 September 2000, p. 1).

19 April 2000. The Council of the Federation votes 133 to ten in favour of President-elect Vladimir Putin's recommendation to dismiss Yuri Skuratov as chief prosecutor. 'In January [2000] Mr Skuratov accused Mr Putin of shielding corrupt aides who had served under Mr Yeltsin' (*IHT*, 20 April 2000, p. 5).

10 July 2000. Oleg Belonenko, the chief executive of the huge Uralmash company (which makes heavy industrial machinery in Yekaterinburg) is shot dead.

CHAPTER TWO

PRICES

PRICES IN THE SOVIET ERA

In the traditional system industrial producer prices were formally fixed by the state on the basis of planned branch average cost of production and a small profit mark-up on costs. The aim was to ensure overall branch profitability while providing an incentive to lower costs. Costs included labour, raw materials, intermediate inputs, interest on short-term credits, and depreciation (though not allowing for technical obsolescence), but excluded a capital charge and a rental charge reflecting favourable location or plant modernity. Prices were not efficiency prices, but they were not, of course, meant to play an important allocative role (factor substitution being one area where they were active.) Instead, in line with the essential passivity of money, they served as a means of control and evaluation (*khozraschyot* and value indicators, for example). Prices were fixed for long periods of time, partly for administrative reasons and partly the better to assess enterprise performance over time. Domestic prices were separated from world prices by the state foreign trade monopoly.

For consumer goods the difference between the wholesale price (based on average cost), including the mark-up of the wholesale organization where appropriate, and the retail price, less the retail mark-up, was the 'turnover tax'. Since the general rule in the case of goods such as consumer durables was to try to set the retail price at market clearing levels, the turnover tax was generally price-determined (i.e. a residual). The tax was price determining only when it was in effect an excise tax of a given amount. Retail prices (unlike wholesale prices) reflected demand to varying extents. But market-clearing prices were typically not achieved, either because demand was wrongly estimated in the first place or because demand may have changed over time (prices often being set for extended periods of time). If the price was too low (as was typically the case), then excess demand resulted and other forms of market clearing, such as queues, had to be employed. If the price was set too high, then excess supply caused stockpiles of commodities. (The poor quality of many Soviet consumer goods may be seen in this context as demand being less than that estimated by planners.)

It is important to note that the state deliberately underpriced some consumer goods and services and these were either formally rationed or distributed through queues, literally or in the form of long waiting lists. Foodstuffs (such as bread, dairy products and meat in the postwar period), transport fares and housing rents were typically heavily subsidized and remained constant for decades for political and income distribution reasons. (In 1987 Gorbachev remarked that bread was so cheap that children used loaves as footballs. Farmers illegally fed bread instead of fodder to livestock because the former was cheaper than the latter.) In 1985 rents for state housing, fixed in 1928, took up only 3 per cent of an average family budget (Trehub 1987: 29). Queues were usually allowed to form for foodstuffs in state retail outlets and there were periods when rationing was general (such as in the first half of the 1930s). There was, of course, a substantial black market for many consumer goods and services, where prices reflected supply and demand.

Price reform in the Soviet era

Historically the infrequent wholesale price changes that actually occurred usually involved increases in order to reflect rising costs and to reduce subsidies, the aim being to allow most enterprises to operate profitably. Prices, however, were generally fixed on a cost-plus basis, although the profit mark-up was later on capital and was high enough to allow for the payment of a capital charge. This was introduced in 1965 and normally at 6 per cent of the undepreciated value of an enterprise's fixed and working capital. The charge was not formally counted as a cost, but was reflected in price indirectly through the higher mark-up. The second half of the 1960s also saw the introduction of rental charges. These were paid by those industrial enterprises particularly favourably situated and/or endowed with modern machinery.

Deviations from standard practice included a move towards marginal cost pricing in extractive industries (oil, natural gas and iron ore). In 1967, for example, oil prices were based on the costs of average-sized enterprises working under worse-than-average conditions, with the more favourably situated fields making rental payments to the state. There were also moves towards world price levels for oil and gas. Earlier, in 1964, 'analogue' pricing had been introduced for new and improved products. This involved pricing in relation to improvements, in the form of higher quality, lower costs and so on, compared with the most analogous product. A lower limit (roughly the old cost-plus basis) and an upper limit (based on the improvements in use value) were fixed, with prices set nearer the upper limit the greater the shortage of the products, thus taking some account of demand. There also developed a system of producer price surcharges for above-standard quality and price reductions for below-standard goods. A three-tier system of prices was introduced in the Gorbachev era: fixed (e.g. for energy and basic consumer goods), range, and free (for luxury goods). A presidential decree of 4 October 1990 allowed enterprises to negotiate wholesale prices (albeit with state-determined maximum levels of profitability, with all excess profits going to federal and republican budgets in equal amounts), with exceptions such as oil, gas, electricity, rail charges, military products and farm supplies. But radical price reform was never implemented in the Soviet era.

PRICE LIBERALIZATION IN RUSSIA

In theory transitional economies are faced with the choice of releasing prices from state control at once (in 'big bang' fashion) or of allowing the market to determine gradually more and more prices over time. In reality, of course, not all prices are released at once even in the case of a 'big bang' strategy, with energy prices and housing rents being typical exceptions. On 2 January 1992 Russia broadly took the former course of action and began the transition to a market economy in earnest by liberalizing many prices.

The reasons for 'big bang' price liberalization

Yegor Gaidar was the main architect of Russia's economic reform programme. He was appointed deputy prime minister and minister of economics and finance in the Russian federation on 7 November 1991. On 21 February 1992 he lost the economics portfolio. But having been made joint first deputy prime minister, he retained control of overall economic strategy even when he lost the finance ministry on 2 April 1992. On 15 June 1992 Gaidar was made acting prime minister. But on 9 December 1992 the Congress of People's Deputies rejected Gaidar as prime minister. On 14 December Yeltsin presented a list of five candidates for prime minister, including Gaidar. But Gaidar came a poor third with only 400 votes. The winner, Viktor Chernomyrdin, came first with 621 votes. Chernomyrdin was endorsed as prime minister and he remained in the post until 23 March 1998.

The specific reasons why most prices were liberalized in early 1992 were revealed in articles written by Yegor Gaidar in 1992 (*FT*, 22 January 1992, p. 15, and 4 March 1992, p. 17):

1. To reduce queues and to restore confidence in the rouble (much of the trade between enterprises having become barter). (In a general sense queues and forced substitution of goods are eliminated when price controls are ended. The benefits of the elimination of queues include more leisure time and greater incentives to work since money income can command control over goods and services. There is the argument that the welfare costs of monopoly are less than those of queues. Controls over prices and the consequent shortages encourages corruption and 'rent-seeking', i.e. the seeking of favours such as subsidies from the government.)

2. Once expected, price rises must take place right away because otherwise supplies would be withheld from the market in anticipation of future rises, while consumers would try to speed up purchases. The rapid liberalization of prices would increase supplies in the market as both dishoarding and increased production ensued. Prices would then start to fall.

3. To reduce the 'monetary overhang'. Repressed inflationary pressures are eased as the 'monetary overhang' (forced savings) is eroded. The release of most price controls leads to an immediate increase in open inflation. (In January 1992 the monthly inflation rate was 245.3 per cent.) Tight fiscal and monetary policies would be needed to ensure that inflation would be gradually brought under control.

4. Gaidar argues that it was not possible to privatize or even introduce anti-monopoly policy before price liberalization. (Note that a liberalization of foreign trade provides competition in the shape of imports.)

There are arguments in favour of 'big bang' price liberalization not specifically mentioned by Gaidar: (1) the need to make use of a political 'honeymoon' period to make painful economic decisions; (2) market-determined prices lead to a more efficient allocation of resources; (3) with price controls it is difficult to determine the reasons why some enterprises perform poorly and this encourages 'rent-seeking'.

The critics of rapid price liberalization put forward the following arguments:

1. Factors such as the decimation of the real value of savings could lead to social unrest. The danger is enhanced when increases in money wages and pensions are not kept in line with price rises. (Widespread social unrest did not occur. Reasons include the patience of the long-suffering Russian people and the impediments to the development of civil society during the Tsarist and Soviet periods.)

2. The Soviet legacy was a structure of industry dominated by large state-owned enterprises. Releasing most prices in these circumstances would not bring forth the desired increase in output, while monopoly profits on a large scale would be made. Thus prices are best released gradually, in line with privatization (defined broadly to include the creation of new firms) and the creation of more competitive conditions through demonopolization and the regulation of remaining monopolies. (As discussed below, monopoly was one of the reasons why some price controls were maintained.) Grigori Yavlinsky was one of the strongest defenders of this line of reasoning and he also feared that hyperinflation would follow in the absence of demonopolization and privatization. He also stressed the need for real economic co-operation and co-ordination among the former Soviet republics (*CDSP*, 1992, vol. XLIV, no. 5, p. 3).

Note that there are a dissenting voices on the question of monopoly. 'One of the greatest myths is that Soviet production was enormously monopolized. The truth is the opposite. In the USSR, there were surprisingly many producers of various goods and the big enterprises were not dominant and not even particularly big by any international comparison. The problem was instead the regulation of the market that created trade monopolies ... since the Russian belief was that the economy was dominated by gigantic producer monopolies, the anti-monopoly policy was characterized by price regulation, which further entrenched the trade monopolies. In reality, however, more liberalization and stabilization were needed, so that enterprises could compete and would feel forced to compete, as otherwise they would run out of money' (Åslund 1996: 8). Boone and Fedorov (Fyodorov) (1997: 173) cite the findings of Brown, Ickes and Ryterman (1994) that Russian industry is no more monopolized than that in the West. They found that only forty-three out of 21,391 civilian manufacturing enterprises constituted monopolies at the national level, and enterprises with 35 per cent of market share accounted for only 4 per cent of all employment.

3. There is also the general point that tight fiscal and monetary policy is needed to prevent hyperinflation from occurring. (Hyperinflation did occur in 1992.) McKinnon (1994) believes that 'it was a major mistake for the Russian Federation, in January 1992, to suddenly decontrol virtually all prices within the state sector and to stop trying to enforce normal patterns of delivery within that sector' (p. 459). 'The big bang argument for total price decontrol is flawed if the important actors bidding for scarce resources have soft budget constraints ... until budget constraints are hardened, uncontrolled bidding by state enterprises will cause the producer price level to increase indefinitely' (p. 462).

4. The liberalization of most prices should have been synchronized with the start of large-scale Western aid.

5. China's generally successful policy of gradual economic reform after 1978 showed that gradual price liberalization is feasible. (The counter-argument is that China's circumstances were different from those of Russia and hence the Chinese model is not relevant.)

The course of price liberalization

Approximately 90 per cent of consumer goods and 80 per cent of producer goods were freed from direct administrative regulation (*CDSP*, 1992, vol. XLVI, no. 9, p. 1). In early 1992 about 80 per cent of wholesale prices and 90 per cent of retail prices were freed of administrative controls (EBRD 1995a: 55). Prices were liberalized for most goods on 2 January 1992. Most federal controls were lifted, except on utilities, transport, telecommunications, energy and certain foods (*RET*, 1993, vol. 2, no. 1, pp. 7, 23; no. 4, p. 28). (As regards wages and salaries the aim was that these should not be raised commensurately in most cases. Deputy prime minister Alexander Shokin remarked that 'One of the fundamental principles of the concept of social protection during the changeover to a market is that increases in income should not lag behind increases in prices by more than 30 per cent': *CDSP*, 1992, vol. XLIV, no. 14, p. 30.)

Housing rents were frozen pending privatization. In some cases even those prices that remained controlled were raised substantially, e.g. basic consumer goods such as bread and milk. (Yegor Gaidar stated that basic consumer goods were raised by 300 per cent on average: *FT*, 22 January 1992, p. 15.) Even so-called 'contract' prices were subject to guidelines, such as a maximum 25 per cent trade mark-up on the producer's price for state trade enterprises not converted to 'commercial operations' (*CDSP*, 1992, vol. XLIV, no. 9, p. 3). On 16 January 1992 Yeltsin set a 50 per cent maximum producer's margin.

On 7 March 1992 all federal controls on consumer goods (and federal subsidies) were abolished. Local authorities retained the right to impose maximum prices on consumer goods, but subsidies had to be met from local budgets. Local authorities increasingly reduced their own control. Local authorities directly control municipal transport prices and public housing rents. Indirect price controls through profitability limits also affect for many industries, e.g. the 600 enterprises officially designated as monopolies face a profitability limit of 25 per cent (*RET*, 1992, vol. 1, no. 2, p. 16; 1993, vol. 2, no. 1, pp. 7, 23; 1993, vol. 2, no. 4, p. 28).

The majority of goods and services are now sold at free-market prices. Since the beginning of 1994 there have been no price controls on goods and services officially designated as monopolies (other than those considered natural monopolies, e.g. gas and some transport and communications). Previously monopoly prices were controlled either by setting an upper limit, a maximum coefficient of price increase or a marginal profitability level (although there was frequently evasion of these controls) (*RET*, 1994, vol. 3, no. 1). The prices of products and services of natural monopolies continue to be regulated at the federal and local levels (e.g. electricity and heating supply, railway tariffs, basic communication services, housing and communal services). Since the beginning of 1994 other monopolies have not been subject to price regulation, but the authorities interfere if monopoly power is abused. At the regional and local levels there is price regulation of basic foods, some non-food goods and some services (e.g. direct price-fixing and limits on trade mark-ups and profitability). But there were fewer of these by mid-1994 (*RET*, 1994, vol. 3, no. 2). Monopoly prices in 1996 were not to be increased by more than industrial prices (*RET*, 1995, vol. 4, no. 3, p. 38). A decree regulating the pricing policy of natural monopolies was issued on 17 July 1996: (1) the government was to continue with the policy of permitting electricity tariffs to grow by no more than 80 per cent of the industrial price index; (2) price increases for crude oil transportation, railway freight transportation and gas supply for industrial purposes would be limited to 100 per cent of the industrial price index over the next six months; (3) communication services during the second half of 1996 would have their prices capped for each quarter at 100 per cent of the industrial price index rise of the previous quarter (*RET,* Monthly Update, 26 August 1996, p. 4). A 7 February 1997 decree tied increases in electricity rates, rail transport costs and oil transport fees to the rate of wholesale price inflation in industry (*RET,* 1997, no. 1, p. 162).

The prices of commodities such as oil and gas have gradually been raised to world levels. (Note that export quotas and inadequate pipeline capacity increased domestic supply and thus helped keep prices below world market levels.) Some estimates of this progress are as follows:

1. In the summer of 1992 the price of a tonne of oil was about 2,000 roubles or 10 to 20 per cent of the world price (Lipton and Sachs 1992: 231).

2. In early 1993 the price of natural gas was only 5 to 10 per cent of the world price and in the case of oil around one-quarter in February 1993 (IMF, *World Economic Outlook*, May 1993, p. 61).

3. Layard (*Economics of Transition*, 1993, vol. 1, no. 3, p. 359) claims that in June 1993 the domestic price of oil was only 13 per cent of the world price and the price of natural gas was only 4 per cent of the West European price.

4. Average commodity prices on the commodity exchanges are gradually approaching world price levels. By the start of 1994 domestic prices merged with world prices for petrol, but the crude oil price is still 50 per cent of the world price (*RET,* 1994, vol. 3, no. 1). In September 1994 the price of crude oil was about 30 per cent of the world level, the price of petroleum being higher because of a higher share of taxes (*RET,* 1994, vol. 3, no. 3, p. 46). In December 1993 the domestic price of crude oil was 58 per cent of the world price, but by December 1994 it was only 25 per cent (*RET,* 1995, vol. 3, no. 4, p. 44). *RET* now takes user prices reported by Goskomstat rather than prices listed on the Russian commodity exchanges (*RET,* 1995, vol. 4, no. 1, pp. 44–5). Domestic crude oil prices reached the world price level during the fourth quarter of 1995 after adjusting for export taxes and transport costs (*RET,* 1995 vol. 4, no. 4, pp. 44–5). In December 1995 crude oil prices rose to nearly 55 per cent of the world level from about 45 per cent in June. By September 1995 prices of petrol and diesel fuel reached world prices regardless of the measure used. Only heating oil is still below the world price (p. 46).

5. Domestic oil prices have been liberalized. In August 1996 crude oil prices stood at about 65 per cent of the world price levels, while prices for oil products are above their international levels (EBRD 1996b: 170).

(See Russian financial crisis for more recent developments in pricing.)

CHAPTER THREE

FOREIGN TRADE

THE SOVIET ERA

In 1937 Soviet exports reached an all-time low of 0.5 per cent of national product, although this was due to a combination of deliberate isolation ('socialism in one country'), Western embargoes and deteriorating commodity terms of trade (i.e. the prices of primary products falling relative to imported manufactures). In 1913 the figure had been 10.4 per cent and in 1929 3.1 per cent (Gregory and Stuart 1990: 325). The Soviet Union's share of world trade turnover in 1990 was only about 4.5 per cent (compared with the USA, 16.3 per cent; West Germany, 12 per cent; and Japan, 9.5 per cent) (*RET*, 1993, vol. 2, no. 4, p. 85).

In the traditional Soviet economic system the state had a monopoly of foreign trade and payments, the purpose being to help carry out party policy and shield the domestic from the international economy. The institutional hierarchy ran from the State Planning Commission to the Ministry of Foreign Trade and on to the foreign trade corporations, which normally specialized in a particular product or group of products and which operated on a *khozraschyot* basis. The industrial enterprise was assigned to a foreign trade corporation. The industrial enterprise that produced the good designated in its *tekhpromfinplan* as an export did not receive the world price but the domestic wholesale price, with appropriate adjustments in case of factors such as quality differences. The ultimate user of an import was charged the price of its nearest domestic substitute.

With direct control exercised over exports and imports, tariffs lost their conventional significance as protectors of home industry and sources of budgetary revenue. Two-tariff schedules were used, however, as bargaining levers with the West in the quest for 'most favoured nation' treatment (the lowest tariff applying to all).

In the traditional Soviet economic system the rouble was an inconvertible currency. It was not freely convertible into gold or other currencies and was not, therefore, subject to supply and demand forces in world foreign exchange markets. There was a multiple exchange rate system (the term 'coefficients' was often used), with various rates for different products or groups of products. The separation of domestic and world prices resulting from the state monopoly of foreign exchange ensured that exchange rates were arbitrarily determined (with the exception of the tourist rate of exchange), with a tendency towards overvaluation. (Comecon – the Council of Mutual Economic Assistance – was founded in January 1949 and held its last meeting on 28 June 1991. Within this communist trading bloc there was also the phenomenon of 'goods inconvertibility'. If, for example, the Soviet Union had a trade surplus with another communist country, this could not be automatically converted into a claim on particular goods. The claim could only be met by negotiations with the latter country, which would then have to make provision in its central plan. See Jeffries 1993: Chapter 2 for an analysis of Comecon.)

In the traditional Soviet system exports were viewed as a means of paying for the import of goods either totally unavailable or in short supply at home, goods deemed essential to fulfil national plans; exports were not seen, for example, as a means of achieving full employment. Inefficient domestic prices and arbitrarily determined exchange rates precluded a meaningful calculation of the gains from trade. The commodity structure of trade was determined by political factors (sales of armaments, for example), domestic resource endowment (the Soviet Union was the world's largest producer of oil) and the relative inefficiency of the economic system (reflected, for example, in difficulties selling manufactured goods in Western markets).

The separation of Soviet and foreign firms, except for perhaps contact over minor details such as precise delivery times, severely aggravated the problem of quality in production and marketing. Industrial enterprises produced according to plan and were unaffected by either competition in or, in any automatic sense, the movement of prices on the world market.

The erosion of the state monopoly of foreign trade began in the late Soviet era. On 1 January 1987 twenty ministries and departments (e.g. chemicals) and seventy-six major individual enterprises (e.g in automobile production and heavy engineering) were granted the right to engage in foreign trade on their own behalf and to retain a portion of export earnings for their own use. The experiment was later extended. As of 1 April 1989 any state or co-operative whose output was competitive on the foreign market was allowed to trade independently (Jeffries 1993: 57–8).

The rouble was made somewhat less inconvertible. In November 1989 the first hard currency auction took place. This meant that there was an official (i.e. not black) market determined rate. (The multiple exchange rate system was made less complex.) Although the auctions covered only a small part of hard currency exchange, it was an important inducement for direct foreign investment, i.e. profits earned from sales within the Soviet Union could be repatriated. Previously hard currency earned from exports had been required (Jeffries 1993: 58–9).

FOREIGN TRADE IN RUSSIA BETWEEN JANUARY 1992 AND THE FINANCIAL CRISIS OF AUGUST 1998

Foreign trade has been liberalized and the rouble made more convertible. Russia's trade has become far more orientated towards the advanced Western countries.

The liberalization of foreign trade

Foreign trade has been liberalized, although on occasion there have been reversals. It is worth stressing here that quantitative restrictions on trade (such as import and export quotas) are a major source of corruption. Export quotas, for example, may be deemed necessary when domestic prices are legally restricted below world market levels. But selling at higher world market prices gives rise to large profits and thus the administrators who deal with licences become targets for bribes.

Important stages in the deregulation of foreign trade are as follows:

1 January 1992. A presidential decree came into force which drastically limited the requirements on licensing and mandatory registration of participants in foreign trade transactions, extending the right to conduct foreign trade operations to all domestic enterprises (*RET*, 1997, no. 3, p. 133).

1 July 1992. In order to maintain budget revenues, the export tax on raw materials was doubled to an average of 40 per cent. Previously exporters of raw materials paid export taxes at an average rate of 20 per cent and had to surrender 40 per cent of their foreign exchange earnings at approximately half the market rate. The surrender represented an additional 20 per cent tax, so that the effective tax rate remained unchanged. As regards imports there were no tariffs until the government introduced a 5 per cent tariff on 1 July 1992. (Medicine and food were zero rated and luxury goods such as cars were rated at 10 per cent.) The tariff was increased to an average rate of 15 per cent on 1 September 1992 (*RET*, 1992, vol. 1, no. 2, p. 31). Up to 1 July 1992 exporters had to sell 10 per cent of their hard currency earnings to the central bank at the market exchange rate. As of 1 July 1992 this was increased to 20 per cent and at the same time exporters became obliged to sell 30 per cent of their earnings to commercial banks (*RET*, 1993, vol. 2, no. 4, pp. 41–2). Thus all exporters were subject to mandatory sales of half their foreign exchange earnings at the newly unified ('market') rate, 30 per cent to the central bank and 20 per cent to commercial banks to be sold on the domestic hard currency market. Importers were free to buy dollars on the production of a certificate of import. Private citizens were free to buy dollars for any purpose but they were not allowed to take more than $500 outside the country except to pay for authorized travel. Foreigners still had limited rights to take out dollars (though they could repatriate profits) and enterprises could only buy dollars for purposes of import. The exchange rate was not actually fully unified on

1 July 1992 since organizations buying centralized imports continued to receive their foreign exchange at a price below the market rate (*RET*, 1992, vol. 1, no. 2, p. 33). (For later developments, see the exchange rate below.)

In the second half of 1992 onwards trade liberalization was partially reversed. Export licensing was reintroduced and quantitative restrictions were imposed on more than 70 per cent of exports. In 1992–93 trade liberalization mainly concerned imports (*RET*, 1997, no. 3, pp. 133–4). The key feature of trade in 1992 was the existence of export quotas for raw materials. These were allocated by administrative methods. The raw material quotas were regularly violated. (Illegal exports of raw materials may have amounted to more than $5 billion.) For this reason, in early 1993 a programme of centralized exports for raw materials was introduced: Russian producers sold goods to the government at rouble prices and the government then sold the goods on the world market at a mark-up averaging 30 per cent of the rouble purchasing price. The coverage of both VAT and excise taxes was expanded to include imports as of February 1993. The 20 per cent VAT was applied to all imported goods except some types of food, medicine, clothing and furniture. The government subsidized imports of critical materials like grain and medicines (*RET*, 1993, vol. 2, no. 4, pp. 41–2).

11 June 1993. Russia formally applied to join Gatt.

1 July 1993. The rules governing the mandatory sale of 50 per cent of hard currency earnings were changed. Henceforth all 50 per cent had to be sold on currency exchanges rather than 20 per cent (the remaining 30 per cent having previously been bought by the central bank) (*CDSP*, 1993, vol. XLV, no. 26, p. 25).

1 November 1993. The number of commodities subject to export taxes was reduced from fifty-three to twenty-nine and the average level of export tax was reduced. All import subsidies were to be abolished at the beginning of 1994 (*RET*, 1993, vol. 2, no. 4, pp. 54–6). On 10 November 1993 duties were raised on a range of imported goods, chiefly alcohol, tobacco and cars (p. 101).

A 1 November 1993 resolution cut export tariffs by half on average. Import subsidies were to be halted, with the exception of centralized purchases of medicines. There was to be a sharp reduction in the list of products subject to licensing and quotas. Import tariffs were to be set at 5 per cent to 15 per cent (*CDSP*, 1993, vol. XLV, no. 44, pp. 21–2).

23 May 1994. A presidential decree stated that quotas and licences were to be scrapped as of 1 July 1994, including oil and gas but excluding certain materials subject to international agreements (such as uranium, aluminium and diamonds). All tax concessions for exporters (mainly for energy supplies) were also to be removed. Import tariffs were to be raised, including, for the first time, tariffs on food.

1 July 1994. Two new decrees appeared. The first one prolonged, until the end of 1994, the existing procedure for exporting oil and petroleum products on the basis of previously distributed quotas. All tax exemptions for exporters of oil for state needs were to be retained and only specifically authorized organizations had the right to export oil. The second decree, issued by the government, was concerned mainly with those highly exportable 'strategic commodities' (such as natural gas, electricity and timber) which ceased to be regulated by export quotas. These were to become subject to a special registration procedures. The decree also retained export quotas for a number of specific commodities agreed with the EU (e.g. aluminium and textile articles). The existing special export regime for goods like weapons and nuclear materials was left untouched (*RET*, 1994, vol. 3, no. 2, pp. 7, 65–6).

December 1994. It was proposed that, as of 1 January 1995, oil export quotas were to be scrapped and domestic producers obliged to supply up to 65 per cent of output to the domestic market. Exports would continue to be regulated by tariffs and other methods, while the system of fourteen approved 'special exporters' would be maintained.

31 December 1994. Chernomyrdin signed a resolution (which needed to be approved) lifting the export quotas but ruling out domestic quotas. The fourteen approved 'special exporters' would remain, as would export taxes. The existing pipeline capacity was to be allocated by a government committee, largely on the basis of each oil producer's total output (*RET*, Monthly Update, 17 January 1995, p. 3).

In 1994 and 1995 the export regime was increasingly liberalized. The 1995 law banned all quantitative restrictions except for cases in which national security and domestic market exigencies dictate otherwise. Quantitative restrictions on imports could be introduced under certain circumstances. The government has eliminated the category of special exporters as well as privileges to various economic entities and regions (*RET*, 1997, no. 3, pp. 133–4).

6 March 1995. Yeltsin signed two more decrees (effective 25 May 1995). These revoked special trading privileges, e.g. exemptions from import duties (*FT*, 7 March 1995, p. 1).

Yeltsin signed two decrees on 6 March 1995 liberalizing foreign trade:

1. Abolition of the special dispensations granted for export and import operations granted certain groups (e.g. athletes and disabled people), enterprises (e.g. Gazprom) and regions.

2. 'Restricting exports of goods and services by establishing mandatory amounts of deliveries to the domestic market is not permitted' (exceptions to this rule include defence). The system of special exporters was abolished (*CDSP*, 1995, vol. XLVII, no. 10, p. 5).

25 March 1995. The system of special exporters was abolished and quotas for domestic supplies were banned except in special circumstances (*RET*, Monthly Update, 21 March 1995, p. 2). Quantitative restrictions on exports and imports can be introduced by the government only if they are necessary for the implementation of international agreements. Exports cannot be limited by insisting upon a compulsory level of supply for the domestic market (*RET*, 1995, vol. 4, no. 1, p. 76). Any oil producing company can now gain access to the pipelines; capacity is initially allocated in proportion to output, but can then be traded (p. 4).

1 October 1995. All exemptions on import duties were officially revoked. They had been set to expire on 1 July 1995 but survived because all the exempted organizations were reported to have received individual documents allowing them to defer payment of duties for several years (*FT*, 2 October 1995, p. 3).

December 1995. Export taxes were to be eliminated as of 1 January 1996, except for oil and gas for which taxes were to be halved (*RET*, Monthly Update, 15 December 1995, p. 7).

1 April 1996. Export taxes on oil were halved and abolished for all other products, including natural gas.

1 July 1996. Export taxes on oil were eliminated.

By the fourth quarter of 1996 the maximum import tariff had been reduced to 30 per cent (except for alcohol) (EBRD 1997a: 32).

The exchange rate

5 May 1992. A single (unified) exchange rate for the rouble was to be established on 1 July 1992 and the rouble was then to float for a month in order to find a defendable level of perhaps eighty to the US dollar. The rouble was to become internally convertible as regards current account transactions on 1 August 1992 at a rate fixed against the US dollar, with the rouble allowed to move 7.5 per cent either side of par. A stabilization fund provided by the West would be available to defend the rouble if necessary (*FT*, Survey, 13 May 1992, p. iv).

1 July 1992. The unified rate for the rouble was actually set at 125.26 to the US dollar. This was based on the average market rate over the previous month and compared with a market rate of 144 on that particular day on the Moscow Interbank Currency exchange. But the rate quickly became that established on the exchange at its twice-weekly auctions. The rouble soon plummeted against the US dollar in nominal terms, as can seen in Table 3.1. (Table 3.1 shows the nominal value of the rouble on the Moscow Interbank Currency Exchange. An appreciation of the rouble in real terms against the US dollar means that rouble depreciation in nominal terms has been slower than the differential between the Russian and US inflation rates.)

The exchange rate was unified in mid-1992 and the rouble was allowed to float. The rouble is convertible for most current account purposes, including profit repatriation for foreign investors. There are restrictions on the capital account (EBRD 1994: 35, 111).

December 1994. The central bank ordered the exchange to impose a maximum daily fluctuation of 10 per cent in the rouble exchange rate with effect from 1 January 1995.

Table 3.1 Russia: the nominal value of the rouble on the Moscow Interbank Currency Exchange (no. of roubles to $1)

1992		1993		1994		1995		1996		1997		1998[2]	
Date	*Roubles*	*Date*	*Roubles*	*Date*	*Roubles*	*Date*	*Roubles*	*Date*	*Roubles*	*Date*	*Roubles*	*Date*	*Roubles*
14 January	180	14 January	442	14 January	1,356	13 January	3,776	9 January	4,668	9 January	5,595		
18 February	170	18 February	559	18 February	1,567	18 January	3,883						
17 March	161	18 March	667	18 March	1,722	25 January	3,988						
14 April	155	15 April	779	15 April	1,793	26 January	4,004						
14 May	128	18 May	934	18 May	1,880	16 February	4,293	26 February	4,793	18 February	5,659		
16 June	119	16 June	1,104	16 June	1,959	15 March	4,744						
16 July	136	16 July	1,020	15 July	2,024	11 April	4,991						
18 August	163	18 August	985	18 August	2,141	12 April	5,008						
15 September	204	15 September	1,010	15 September	2,301	29 April	5,130					27 May	6.18
15 October	338	15 October	1,116	10 October	3,081	2 June	4,943						
17 November	448	17 November	1,201	11 October[1]	3,926	8 June	4,911						
17 December	416	17 December	1,247	12 October	3,736	9 June	4,943						
				13 October	2,994	20 June	4,546						
				14 October	2,988	27 June	4,516	28 June	5,105	30 June	5,766	29 June	6.22
				17 October	2,996	7 July	4,581			31 July	5,809	21 July	6.26
				17 November	3,157	11 July	4,550					13 August[3]	6.36
				29 November	3,232	24 August	4,428						
				9 December	3,261	7 September	4,479						
				12 December	3,323	15 September	4,465						
				14 December	3,368	16 October	4,506	18 October	5,434				
				15 December	3,383	8 November	4,523						
				16 December	3,395	16 November	5,534			4 December	5,945		
				29 December	3,550	31 December	5,570			10 December	5,924		

1. 'Black Tuesday.'
2. The currency reform of 1 January 1998 knocked three zeros off the denomination rouble, e.g. 1,000 old roubles equals 1 new rouble.
3. 'Black Thursday.'

5 July 1995. It is announced that for the period 6 July–1 October 1995 the central bank will keep the exchange rate within a band of 4,300–4,900 roubles to the US dollar (*IHT*, 6 July 1995, p. 13). On 24 August 1995 the duration of the band was extended to the end of 1995 (*The Economist*, 2 September 1995, p. 103). (On 24 August a banking crisis began, with banks ceasing to lend to each other. In order to ease the liquidity crisis the central bank stepped in with short-term loans to a number of large banks and with purchases of government bonds.)

30 November 1995. It was announced that between 1 January 1996 and 30 June 1996 a band of 4,550–5,150 roubles to the US dollar would apply. 'A gradual managed devaluation of the rouble ... is the declared policy of the government and the Central Bank of Russia' (United Nations, *World Economic and Social Survey*, 1996, p. 62). In 1995 the rouble appreciated 72 per cent against the US dollar in real terms (p. 29).

16 May 1996. A new exchange rate regime was announced. The 'crawling corridor', to be implemented as of 1 July 1996, would start at the 5,000–5,600 roubles to the US dollar range and be adjusted on a daily basis until the range 5,500–6,100 rouble to the US dollar range was reached by the end of 1996. The rouble would be allowed to fall by about 1.5 per cent a month.

1 June 1996. The rouble was made convertible on current account in line with the Article 8 of the IMF. (Tight restrictions would remain on the capital account.) This would mean the end of regulations requiring exporters to surrender part of their exchange earnings (*FT*, 17 May 1996, p. 2; *IHT*, 17 May 1996, p. 16).

26 November 1996. It was announced that the 'crawling corridor' would start in 1997 at 5,500–6,100 roubles to the US dollar and end the year at 5,750–6,350 roubles to the US dollar.

'To stabilize exchange rate expectations the central bank introduced an exchange rate band in July 1995. The band's shape was changed one year later to allow for a gradual depreciation of the rouble. The rate of exchange rate depreciation slowed steadily, from 23.5 per cent in 1995, to 16.5 per cent in 1996 and to only 6.7 per cent in 1997' (Balino 1998: 39).

1 January 1998. Three zeros were knocked off the denomination of the rouble on 1 January 1998. From the beginning 1998 until the end of 2000 the rouble was to have a 'central' exchange rate of 6.2 new roubles to the US dollar, inside a corridor with rates 15 per cent either side of the central rate (i.e. the band would be 5.25 to 7.15 new roubles to the US dollar). It was also an aim to achieve an average exchange rate of 6.1 new roubles in 1998 and in the following two years if conditions allowed. 'The announcement [on 10 November 1997] was made earlier than expected in order to help reduce the pressure the rouble had come under from world financial turbulence' (*RET*, Monthly Update, 24 November 1997, p. 4). (The world financial turbulence started in July 1997 in Thailand: p. iv.) The real exchange rate to the US dollar remained roughly constant throughout 1996 and 1997 (*RET*, 1998, no. 1, p. 38).

'The monetary authorities continue to target the exchange rate in order to achieve financial stabilization' (*RET*, 1997, no. 1, p. 51). 'Over the course of the year [1996] there was on average an appreciation of the real rate, compared to the whole of 1995' (p. 53).

'Between 1992 and 1996 the RUR [rouble] appreciated massively versus the dollar in real terms ... in 1995 and 1996, respectively, [by] 38 per cent and 26 per cent ... Although an exchange rate anchor remains a paramount goal of the CBR, developments in 1997 suggest that the central bank would like to maintain a stable exchange rate to ensure competitiveness. As such, we expect the nominal exchange rate to devalue in line with the anticipated rate of inflation in 1998 (8–9 per cent)' (Deutsche Bank Research, *Russia*, 12 March 1998, pp. 6–7).

On 31 March 1998 the governor of the central bank said that the rouble had to be devalued in line with inflation in order to help exporters to compete globally (*FT*, 1 April 1998, p. 2).

(For later developments, see the Asian financial crisis.)

The volume and geographical distribution of foreign trade

In 1992 the volume of foreign trade fell by 23 per cent (*CDSP*, 1993, vol. XLV, no. 6, p. 10). In 1992 exports fell by 25 per cent and imports fell by 21 per cent (*Moscow News*, 18 February 1993, p. 4).

The Gatt's annual world trade report noted that in 1991 the former Soviet Union had been among the world's top twenty traders, but that its successor is now not even among the top twenty-five (*IHT*, 29 March 1993, p. 7).

In 1995 domestic production of consumer goods fell to 48 per cent of its 1991 level and was still shrinking at the start of 1996. The market share of imports has soared from an average of 12 per cent in 1991 to 56 per cent in 1995, by official reckonings. When smuggled goods and 'personal imports' are added the true proportion of foreign consumer goods is probably higher still (*The Economist*, 13 April 1996, pp. 71–2).

Trade with the former Comecon countries fell by more than 56 per cent in 1992. Trade with other socialist countries also fell sharply, but that with industrial economies was similar to 1991 (*RET*, 1993, vol. 2, no. 4, pp. 41–2). In 1993 the EU took about 50 per cent of Russian exports, minerals accounting for 44 per cent and wood products 14 per cent. The value of these exports was $17.4 billion, while EU exports to Russia came to $13.5 billion. One-third of EU exports were electrical machines and parts, while processed foodstuffs made up 16 per cent (*FT*, 25 June 1994, p. 2). Nearly two-thirds of exports now go to the West and two-thirds of imports come from the West (*RET*, 1994, vol. 3, no. 2, p. 7). In 1994 some 70 per cent of exports went to industrialized countries, particularly the EU (*Transition*, January–February 1995, p. 20). In a February 1995 speech Yeltsin stated that the CIS countries accounted for only 20 per cent of foreign trade, compared with 56 per cent in 1991 (*CDSP*, 1995, vol. XLVII, no. 8, p. 13).

'The EU accounts for almost 40 per cent of all Russian external trade' (*FT*, 26 May 2000, p. 21).

'At the end of this month [October] President Vladimir Putin will travel to Paris to sign a series of energy contracts with EU leaders ... With North Sea oil diminishing Europe will soon be importing as much as 85 per cent of its energy supplies. Currently Russia provides only about 20 per cent of Europe's natural gas needs and 16 per cent of its oil supplies, and EU officials say they hope the energy pact will soon lead to a doubling of imports from Russia ... Russia also plans to increase its electricity exports to the West' (*IHT*, 21 October 2000, pp. 1, 21).

'The EU and Russia yesterday [30 October] took the first steps towards long-term co-operation in the energy sector ... [at the] sixth EU-Russia summit ... But yesterday's talks on energy underlined the still cautious nature of relations between Russia and the EU. The two sides agreed to institute an "energy dialogue" as a first stage towards defining the details of a partnership between them. Whereas a month ago there was talk in Brussels of the EU doubling its annual purchases of gas from Russian in return for large-scale investment, yesterday's meeting resulted in no targets or figures. Instead, a high level working group ... will study all options for boosting EU imports of gas, oil and electricity from Russia in the period to 2020' (*FT*, 31 October 2000, p. 10).

'Last month ... Gazprom reached a deal with four West European energy firms to boost its supplies to the West dramatically. It is setting up a consortium with Germany's Ruhrgas and Wintershall, Gaz de France and Italy's Snam, which will invest $2 billion in a new pipeline. The aim is to increase Russia's gas supplies to Western Europe by 50 per cent. The deal came only a few days after Russia's President Vladimir Putin met with Romano Prodi, head of the European Commission, to discuss a long-term plan to double Russia's gas supplies to Western Europe ... The new pipeline will head through Belarus, Poland and Slovakia, but it misses Ukraine' (*Business Central Europe*, November 2000, p. 16).

Russia and the EU

5 April 1993. EU foreign ministers agreed to widen the terms of the European Commission's mandate for negotiating a partnership agreement with Russia to include the attainment of a free-trade agreement 'when economic and political circumstances in Russia are suitable'. But eventual membership of the EU was not an issue.

24 June 1994. Russia and the EU signed a partnership and co-operation agreement, which involved a strengthening of political and economic ties. Russia was recognized as an economy in transition rather than a state trading country. The main specific economic elements were as follows:

1. A relaxation of trade restrictions. Tariffs would be gradually lowered, with the possibility of a free-trade agreement after 1998 if Russia made

sufficient progress along the path of a market economy. In the meantime EU quotas on imports from Russia would be removed (with the exception of certain textile and steel products; agricultural products were unaffected by the agreement), while Russia could introduce limited import restrictions in sectors facing severe job losses or market shares. Safeguard clauses could be activated by either side to counter sudden surges of imports proved to be substantially harmful to domestic producers (e.g. uranium from Russia).

2. Measures to improve the business environment in Russia for foreign investors, e.g. removing obstacles to the free flow of capital and profit repatriation. (Once established in Russia, EU companies could not be subjected to restrictive legislation for three years following the passage of any new law: *FT*, 25 June 1994, p. 2.)

3. The 1993 presidential decree restricting the activities of foreign banks in Russia would be scrapped by 1996. The five banks which had already been given licences prior to the decree would be immediately freed of the restrictions. (See foreign investment below for details.)

17 July 1995. The EU and Russia signed a trade agreement (delayed by the EU as a protest against the handling of the Chechen crisis).

27 April 1998. The EU agrees to remove Russia from a list of 'non-market' economies. The decision revises the EU's criteria for judging 'dumping'. The EU will now use Russia's own price information rather than prices from Western producers to determine (on a case-by-case basis) whether Russia is selling goods below cost. Russia is not designated as a market economy, but the new policy will enable the EU to take account of cases where market conditions exist. EU anti-dumping actions affect 1.1 per cent of Russian trade and only fourteen out of 146 existing EU anti-dumping duties target Russia. EU exports to Russia in 1997 amounted to Ecu 18.7 billion ($20.61 billion). Russia's exports to the EU were worth Ecu 21.5 billion (*IHT*, 28 April 1998, p. 13).

Capital flight

'There are many reasons why some Russians have chosen either to take their savings abroad or to hold them domestically in dollars. The collapse in the value of the rouble in the early 1990s and the accompanying annihilation of savings in banks have made people justifiably wary of the rouble as a store of value. Second, capital flight has been driven by the desire to avoid Russian taxes. Third, poor definition and protection of property rights during privatization has led managers and entrepreneurs to launder their gains abroad' (*RET*, Monthly Update, 3 April 1998, p. 7). 'Capital flight has been a sign of Russia's failure to establish a functioning market environment. Macroeconomic instability and institutional deficiencies, such as the lack of confidence in the domestic banking system and disincentives to reinvest company profits, have encouraged companies and individuals to move their money offshore.

Efforts to combat the problem by introducing capital restrictions have had limited success' (*RET,* Monthly Update, 11 February 2000, p. 3). 'The real solution to the problem of capital flight is to improve the investment climate by continued reforms, especially institutional reforms that would protect any investor, foreign as well as domestic; tax reform to ensure transparency and equal treatment; and the introduction of international systems of accounting to create a better framework for capital investments. In addition, a main priority should be to speed up bank restructuring and to increasingly allow foreign banks into the retail market, creating a competitive pressure on Russian banks … As long as companies and individuals do not have trust in the domestic banking system, and there is a lack of other investment opportunities, it must be considered rational behaviour to either keep one's money outside the banking system or to move it abroad' (p. 9).

Estimates vary considerably, not least because it is difficult to define let alone measure:

1. Capital flight rose from a cumulative total of $10.6 billion in 1991 to $43.1 billion in 1994. The legally held portion rose from $7.6 billion to $24.9 billion; this consists of enterprises' hard currency deposits in Russian banks plus cash dollars, held mostly by individuals, including those operating in the grey economy. The illegal portion increased from $3 billion to $18.2 billion; this consists of assets mainly held abroad, as cash, securities or real property. In 1994 most of the increase was in interest earned and there was little new export of illegal capital (*RET,* Monthly Update, 14 April 1995, p. 4). Capital flight was running at roughly $10 billion a year in 1992, 1993 and 1994. But it stopped in 1995 as normal financial conditions developed, with positive real interest rates on rouble assets (*RET,* Monthly Update, 22 April 1996, p. 5). 'A recent encouraging sign is that flight capital appears to have begun to return in the form of loans to the banking and corporate sectors' (*RET,* Monthly Update, 3 April 1998, p. 7).

'A large share of the money moved abroad has left Russia via the trade account by use of false contracts, over-reporting imports and under-reporting exports. Several attempts have been made to quantify the amount of money that has left the country illegally or semi-legally … Estimated capital flight between 1993 and 1998 was $68.3 billion according to [*RET*'s] estimate 1 and $77.6 billion for estimate 2' (*RET,* Monthly Update, 11 February 2000, p. 3). The figure for estimate 2 reached a peak of nearly $20 billion in 1997 (with estimate 1 reaching a peak in 1996). In 1999 the estimated figure for estimate 2 is about $14 billion (p. 4). 'On top of capital flight an estimated $30 billion to $40 billion is held in "mattresses" inside Russia' (p. 9).

2. According to the World Bank's definition, capital flight includes not only illegal capital exports but also currency substitution in the domestic economy. Capital flight amounted to $8.2 billion in 1992, $10.6 billion in 1993 and $7.4 billion in 1994 (DIW, *Economic Bulletin,* 1996, vol. 33, no. 2, p. 13). 'The capital balance also reflects some problems … "other assets" and "errors and

omissions" show a considerable amount of non-patriated foreign trade revenues or capital flight, which official estimates put at roughly $20 billion, a substantial increase compared to the previous year' (Deutsche Morgan Grenfell, *Focus: Eastern Europe*, 3 March 1997, p. 41).

3. Åslund is quoted as saying that 'To judge from conversations with well informed businessmen and government officials, 10 to 20 per cent of the oil and at least one-third of the metals exported from Russia in 1992 were smuggled out of the country. Naturally the revenues from these sales stayed in bank accounts abroad (*FT*, 1 June 1993, p. 38). In 1994 capital flight fell to $5 billion (Anders Åslund, *IHT*, 25 April 1995, p. 8).

4. 'Probably the most damaging aspect of Russian organized crime activity is its contribution to large-scale capital flight ... A specialist on capital flight reported at a recent ministry of interior conference in Moscow that $150 billion had been exported from Russia since 1991. This figure may be high but conservative estimates are still more than $50 billion. A minimum of 40 per cent of the estimated $2 billion in monthly capital flight is attributable to organized crime groups' (Louise Shelley, *Transition*, February 1997, vol. 8, no. 1. p. 7).

5. On 15 October 1993 a scheme to tackle the problem of illegal capital flight was announced. The banks would be involved in monitoring foreign exchange earnings, as of January 1994 in the case of the exporters of strategic commodities (such as oil and precious metals) and March 1994 for the others.

6. 'Before the elections there was a huge amount of capital flight. Now people are bringing so much money back in that the central bank has to buy dollars to keep the rouble from rising too much' (Yegor Gaidar, *IHT*, 5 August 1996, p. 6).

7. Capital flight amounted to $60 billion in the period 1996 to 1998 (*FT*, 31 December 1998, p. 19). Official figures for capital flight show a fall from $25 billion in 1998 to $15 billion in 1999 (*FT*, 5 February 2000, p. 6).

8. The Russian finance ministry estimates that capital flight was about $25 billion in 1999 (*IHT*, 14 February 2000, p. 19).

9. 'An estimated $50 billion or more dollar bills currently [lie] under Russian mattresses' (Reginald Dale, *IHT*, 11 April 2000, p. 11).

CHAPTER FOUR

DIRECT FOREIGN INVESTMENT

THE SOVIET ERA

Lenin tried to attract foreign capital and enterprise during the New Economic Policy of 1921–28. But he was not very successful. 'At the end of the NEP there were only fifty-nine foreign concessions, accounting for less than 1 per cent of the output of state industry' (Gregory and Stuart 1986: 63). Stalin forbad such concessions and it was not until 1 January 1987, under Gorbachev, that direct foreign investment was next allowed. Even then only a few selected sectors were granted access and foreign ownership of joint ventures was limited to a maximum of 49 per cent. More sectors became eligible and on 26 October 1990 wholly foreign-owned firms were permitted (Jeffries 1993: 59–60).

RUSSIA SINCE 1992

Peitsch draws attention to the distinction between direct foreign investment and foreign portfolio investment. 'An investment is considered to constitute direct foreign investment when a lasting relationship is established between a legal person or entity resident in one country (the foreign investor) and an entity resident in another country (the foreign investment enterprise) in which the foreign investor obtains a controlling interest. This type of investment can be contrasted with (foreign) portfolio investment, in which the investor is not interested in exerting significant influence over management decisions' (Barbara Peitsch, *The OECD Observer*, April–May 1995, no. 193, p. 32).

What is striking about Russia is that the volume of direct foreign investment (DFI) is relatively small for such a huge country, even taking account of the noticeable increase since 1996. The most obvious comparison is with China. Actual (utilized) DFI in China was $33.8 billion in 1994 and $38 billion in 1995 (second in the world behind the USA's $60 billion out of a world total of $315 billion). In 1996 DFI was $42 billion and the cumulative total at the end of that year was $177.2 billion. In 1997 the figure was $45 billion. (*FT*, 6 February 1996, p. 5; 9 January 1997, p. 3; 27 May 1997, p. 10;

21 October 1997, p. 18; 16 February 1998, p. 2; *The Economist*, 26 August 1995, p. 60.) (See Table 9.1 for EBRD figures for net foreign direct investment.)

'In 1996 Russia received only slightly more than Hungary, a country with the population less than a tenth of the size of Russia's. In 1995 Hungary received twice as much FDI as Russia' (*RET*, Monthly Update, April 1998, p. 5).

Various estimates for Russia are as follows:

1. By the end of 1993 direct foreign investment totalled around $2 billion (in 1992 $290 million flowed in and in 1993 $400 million) (Deutsche Bank, *Focus: Eastern Europe*, 1994, no. 107, pp. 1–6).

2. At the end of 1993 total foreign investment amounted to $2.7 billion, an increase of $1.4 billion for the year (*Transition*, 1994, vol. 5, no. 6, p. 19).

3. Foreign direct investment amounted to $2 billion in the period 1990–93: $100 million in 1991, $800 million in 1992 and $1.1 billion in 1993 (EBRD 1994: 123).

4. At an international conference held in Moscow on 27 June 1994 it was revealed that the cumulative total of foreign investment was $2.7 billion (*IHT*, 28 June 1994, p. 2).

5. Net direct foreign investment was -$400 million in 1990, -$100 million in 1991, -$112 million in 1992, $682 million in 1993, $256 million in 1994 and $920 million in 1995 (United Nations Economic Commission for Europe 1996: 149). According to the United Nations Economic Commission for Europe, the stock of foreign direct investment was valued at just over $3 billion at the end of 1994 and $3.3 billion at the end of June 1995. About 60 per cent was in mining and manufacturing, notably in energy and engineering (Frances Williams, *FT*, 18 January 1996, p. 5).

6. Goskomstat estimates that foreign direct investment in 1995 came to $2.8 billion. Of this $1.9 billion was direct foreign investment and the remainder mostly in the form of private credits (*RET*, Monthly Update, 13 June 1996, p. 7). Foreign direct investment was $2.5 billion in 1996 and $2.8 billion in the first half of 1997 (*RET*, 1997, no. 4, p. 4).

7. By 1 November 1995 foreign investment amounted to over $6 billion (*Transition*, 1996, vol. 7, no. 1, p. 17).

8. Cumulative direct foreign investment in the period 1992–95 amounted to a mere $4 billion, much of it by food and drink manufacturers with international brands and ready-made markets (*The Economist*, 13 April 1996, p. 72).

9. Direct foreign investment was $6.2 billion in 1997 (*RET*, 1998, no. 2, p. 24). The Asian financial crisis brought this rapidly improving situation to an end.

10. In 1998, according to the UN, direct foreign investment in Russia was $2.2 billion or only $15 *per capita*. In the Czech Republic the figure was $243 per head. In Poland, which attracted $5.1 billion in 1998, the figure per head was $132 (*FT*, 19 January 2000, p. 21). 'According to official figures, direct foreign investment across the country was just $4.2 billion in 1999, up from $3.3 billion in 1998 and down from a peak of $5.3 billion in 1997' (*FT*, 4 April 2000, p. 23).

11. Direct investment in 1998 was $3.361 billion and in 1999 it was $4.26 billion (*CDSP*, 2000, vol. 52, no. 11, p. 17).

In 1998 world direct foreign investment amounted to $430 billion (*RET*, Monthly Update, 11 March 1999, p. 1). Between 1993 and 1998 Russia attracted $9.2 billion. Close to 50 per cent of direct foreign investment came from the USA (mainly in the oil and mineral sectors), followed by Germany and other EU countries (increasingly focused on the consumer goods sectors). In 1995 food processing was the largest recipient (mainly to supply the domestic market), followed by the fuel and oil sector (p. 5).

The significance of DFI can be judged in other ways:

1. In 1992 joint ventures accounted for 11 per cent of total exports (*Moscow News*, 29 October 1993, p. 7). In 1994 enterprises with foreign investment were responsible for 17 per cent of exports (Barbara Peitsch, *The OECD Observer*, April–May 1995, no. 193, p. 32).

2. Enterprises with foreign capital accounted for only 1 per cent of the 'total production of goods and services' (*CDSP*, 1993, vol. XLV, no. 40, p. 33).

3. 'Foreign investment enterprises' accounted for 0.5 per cent of total employment and more than 2 per cent of total output (Frances Williams, *FT*, 18 January 1996, p. 5).

4. In 1997 foreign companies and joint ventures accounted for 3 per cent of GDP and 9 per cent of exports (*FT*, Survey, 15 April 1998, p. ix).

5. A Moscow bank reckons that about $4.3 billion of foreign investment in Russia has gone to Moscow, some two-thirds of the total (*The Economist*, 6 September 1997, p. 38). 'It is interesting to look at where most of the cash [direct foreign investment] has been going. The Moscow region is the easy answer. The capital has attracted almost half of Russia's $10.3 billion foreign investment to date. But some intrepid foreigners have ventured further, mainly to the second city of St Petersburg or the oil-rich Krasnoyarsk. The far east of the country has also attracted investment, to exploit its proximity to Asia. Russia's heavy industrial interior, meanwhile, remains largely untouched' (*Business Central Europe*, February 1999, p. 60).

(Note that on 21 November 1996 Russia raised $1 billion on the international bond market. This was the first international issue since Tsarist times.)

Changes have been made to the regulations governing direct foreign investment:

1. Direct foreign investment in some sectors (such as banking, insurance and heavy industry when damage to the environment could result) requires authorization. The defence sector is closed to foreign investment, as is gambling (Barbara Peitsch, *The OECD Observer*, April–May 1995, no. 193, pp. 32–4).

2. The laws on joint ventures have been repeatedly changed over the past year and foreigners have lost any shred of preferential treatment (*The Economist*, 27 February 1993, p. 100).

3. A presidential decree of 23 May 1994 awarded a three-year profit tax holiday for joint ventures registered after 1 January 1994 with at least 30 per cent foreign ownership and worth at least $10 million, provided that they are not liquidated within six years. In the fourth year enterprises would pay a quarter of the usual tax rate and half in the fifth year (*CDSP*, 1994, vol. XLVI, no. 21, p. 9).

4. There have been changes in the regulations governing banks. Crédit Lyonnais Russie (St Petersburg) was the first to obtain a licence in December 1991. New regulations were published on 15 April 1993. Foreign banks could open only one branch office besides their head office, while the total capital of all foreign banks operating in Russia could not exceed 12 per cent of the aggregate capital of the Russian commercial banks in 1993 (the annual limit would vary). Parliament was due to consider finalizing a bill excluding, until January 1996, banks with more than 50 per cent foreign participation from dealing with Russian customers, including joint ventures, i.e. confining them to transactions with foreign nationals and non-resident legal entities. But parliament was dissolved by Yeltsin on 21 September 1993. The ban finally came into force on 19 November 1993, although those banks already dealing with residents as of 15 November were allowed to continue. Of the twelve foreign banks that had by then received licences, only two (Crédit Lyonnais Russie and BNP-Dresdner) already had resident clients (*Moscow News*, 19–25 August 1994, p. 10). Finance Minister Fyodorov justified the move in terms of protecting Russian banks from losing their best clients and staff during the transitional stage. A presidential decree of 10 June 1994 lifted the restrictions on banks from those countries with which Russia had signed investment protection agreements. The partnership and co-operation agreement with the EU of 24 June 1994 immediately lifted the restrictions on the five EU banks which had already been given licences prior to the November 1993 decree, namely Crédit Lyonnais Russie and Société Générale of France, Ing and ABN-Amro of the Netherlands, and Dresdner of Germany. The restrictions would be scrapped for other banks by 1996.

The drawbacks of shielding generally weak, poorly regulated and even corrupt domestic banks from the competition provided by foreign banks were clearly illustrated when the financial crisis hit Russia in August 1998. Depositers need to have confidence in banks and loans have to be allocated with profitability rather than cronyism in mind.

'Viktor Gerashchenko announces [27 April 1999] that the share of foreign capital in the Russian banking system may be increased from the current 12 per cent to 25 per cent' (*RET*, 1999, vol. 8, no. 2, p. 96).

5. A Russian law on 'production sharing' became operational in January 1996. The law concerns the exploitation of natural resources, including oil and minerals. Under production sharing an investor enters into a contract with the state, which grants it exploitation rights for a particular geographical area together with an exemption from all present and future taxes other than those

expressly defined in the agreement. In return the state receives an agreed percentage of the production after the investor has recouped his investment costs (EBRD 1996a: 10). Production-sharing agreements are recognized in international law (*RET*, Monthly Update, 11 March 1999, p. 6). The contentious new law on 'production-sharing agreements' was signed by Yeltsin at the end of December 1995. It sets a framework for contracts between the state and private domestic and foreign investors in oil and other mineral resources, fixing the general principles under which private investors have to cede a proportion of output to the government in the form of taxes and royalties. 'The resulting text is vague and rambling and satisfies nobody ... foreign oil companies ... fear that the provisions for rewriting agreements in the wake of "changed circumstances" will enable the Russian government to claw back profits from investors who do better than expected ... [and foreign oil companies] ... also dislike the law's insistence on specific, separate parliamentary approval of "strategic" agreements, and also of any agreements that the government wants to reach without going through an open tender or an auction.' Other worries include a restriction on any investor's freedom to transfer or mortgage property rights, the law saying that this will require the state's consent. Provisions relating to the settlement of disputes fail to guarantee an investor's right to international arbitration (merely making this one possible option) and Russia is not obliged to waive its sovereign immunity in any dispute. Some of these shortcomings may be remedied by writing clauses into individual agreements (*The Economist*, 20 January 1996, p. 80). 'The Duma has been dragging its heels on production-sharing legislation for three years. It has approved a mere seven agreements out of a list of 230, and has yet to amend a dozen other laws that conflict with the principle of production-sharing' (*The Economist*, 15 November 1997, p. 96). The production sharing law requires parliament's approval to exploit certain areas, including the continental shelf. Russia has the right to cancel deals if world oil markets move sharply and western companies' ability to sue in international courts is limited. The law is unclear on some tax issues (*FT*, 29 March 1996, p. 7). On 9 December 1998 the State Duma passed amendments to oil production-sharing legislation that removed the main obstacles confronting foreign investors. The new law opens up 30 per cent of Russia's hydrocarbon resources for production-sharing agreements. Under the old law only 10 per cent of Russia's strategic minerals were eligible. 'Production-sharing agreements will now prevail over both existing and future Russian legislation. Until now foreign companies have been worried that new laws could undermine any deals they might make' (*FT*, 10 December 1998, p. 3).

The trend towards more favourable regulations has helped increase volume of DFI. But significant obstacles remain. Burton and Juzaitis, for example, point to a number of these. There are heavy VAT and profit taxes imposed on direct investments by foreigners. Alternative forms of investment have arisen in response, such as placing money in special tax-free investment funds or making capital contributions to existing Russian companies. The newness of the relevant investment laws, the unknown status of numerous proposed laws and the volatile political situation are hindrances (Rodney Burton and Diane Juzaitis, *IHT*, 25 March 1995, p. 21).

Investment is so risky in Russia that investors require an extremely high expected return. A survey was carried out in February 1995 of twenty Western investment banks, brokerages and accounting firms, along with several major companies engaged in direct foreign investment. The disincentives, in order of ranking, were as follows:

1. Legal disincentives were the most serious (average rank 1.7), especially fears about shareholder rights, weak contract enforcement and securities regulation.

2. Economic disincentives (2.9), especially high inflation, the incoherence of the tax system and exchange rate fluctuations.

3. Political disincentives (3.0), especially scepticism about commitment to reform, fears about renationalization and doubts about parliamentary elections.

4. Financial disincentives (3.7), especially lack of information about potential business partners, repatriation of profits and lack of a credit rating in Russia.

5. General disincentives (4.1), especially the worldwide retreat from emerging markets, fear of crime/the mafia and discrimination against foreigners.

6. Logistic disincentives (5.6), especially the communications infrastructure, the transport infrastructure and technological constraints (*RET*, Monthly Update, 21 March 1995, pp. 3–4).

'Russia, which has prevented foreigners from participating in many privatization auctions, banned them from owning land, and limited their role in the banking sector, has been receiving a correspondingly small amount of FDI. In 1996 Russia received only slightly more than Hungary, a country with a population less than a tenth the size of Russia's. In 1995 Hungary received twice as much FDI as Russia ... However, FDI into Russia has been growing' (*RET*, Monthly Update, 3 April 1998, p. 5).

The main problems stated by foreign investors and importers are as follows:

1. A high tax burden and unfair taxation combined with a complicated tax system.

'One investor revealed that the tax burden for investors could be as high as 55 per cent to 66 per cent, but the actual tax burden depends very much on one's connections. A well-connected business can significantly reduce its tax bill. This ad hoc system creates uncertainty and risk, thus discouraging much needed investments.'

2. A lack of international accounting standards. ('Russian accounting make it very difficult for foreign companies to evaluate the financial situation of potential acquisitions or partners': p. 6.)

3. An unclear and over-bureaucratic system of standards, licensing and certification.

4. Crime and corruption.

5. Unsatisfactory protection of property rights.

6. Problems with customs and checkpoints.

7. The devaluation of August 1998 hurt investors relying on imports (*RET*, Monthly Update, 11 March 1999, p. 7).

'Russia has lost out because of the inability or unwillingness of its government to tackle a huge number of fiscal, legal and cultural obstacles that frighten away investors of all kinds. Taxation is so complicated and changeable that it verges on the arbitrary, the more so when administered by a bureaucracy within which corruption is endemic. Exchange controls and customs regulations operate similarly. Anything connected with property is fraught with uncertainties over title and contract. Civil law is full of loopholes' (*The Economist*, 13 April 1996, p. 72).

'By the summer of 1995 no more than $1–2 billion of the $50–70 billion which the [oil] industry needs to arrest its decline, and which foreign oil companies were reportedly ready to invest in Russia, had actually been committed. Oil output from joint ventures in 1995 accounted for less than 6 per cent of the Russian total ... I examine those factors – inadequate legal guarantees, high taxes and export regulation – which have deterred foreign oil companies from making greater investments in Russia' (Watson 1996: 429).

'The annual flow of foreign direct investment into Russia was only an average of $20 *per capita* between 1994 and 1999, substantially less than the annual $220 received by Hungary or the $134 received by the Czech Republic ... With the help of the European Business Club in Moscow we surveyed [in the spring of 2000] almost fifty European enterprises that conduct business in Russia ... Our survey shows that ... the most pressing problem foreign direct investors in Russia face is connected neither with criminality, nor corruption, but simply an inadequate and ever changing tax law. Next in line come problems with property and creditor rights, customs, the risk of political change, macroeconomic instability, a weak banking sector, the Russian accounting system, and only then corruption. The risk of expropriation, harassment from federal and local government, and payment arrears from clients are considered to be of medium-level importance. Finally, problems with the Russian work force or management, Russian suppliers, crime, racket and barter are seen as being of moderate significance ... Even though improvements in a wide range of areas will be required before Russian can create a good investment climate, foreign direct investment ... appears to be a much more attractive prospect than the general view in the Western press would suggest. Still there should be swift progress on at least the most pressing issues. Improving the tax law seems an absolute priority. As indicated by the low significance of tax incentives for investment and location decisions, foreign companies are not asking for temporary better treatment or tax rates far below international standards; however, they are looking for a reasonable, transparent and predictable tax system. A strengthening of the banking system is also very important for increasing the attractiveness of foreign direct investment … Finally, improving customs authorities – still too often perceived as arbitrary and corrupt – is one of the more urgent tasks' (*RET*, Monthly Update, 14 June 2000, pp. 3–11).

CHAPTER FIVE

THE PRIVATE NON-AGRICULTURAL SECTOR

THE PRIVATE NON-AGRICULTURAL SECTOR IN THE SOVIET ERA

In the traditional Soviet economic system the legal private industrial sector was negligible. Private enterprise was severely limited as regards area and employment. Handicrafts, agriculture and certain consumer services were acceptable, but selling goods made by other people was not allowed. The employment of another person outside the immediate family in the production of goods for sale was illegal. Direct taxes were heavier than normal.

In the Gorbachev era non-state activity was significantly expanded. In and after 1987 there were major concessions to private activity. In 1990 the hiring of labour outside the immediate family was allowed and private retail trade legalized. Independent and voluntary co-operatives were also permitted (although many co-operatives were formed by existing enterprises hiving off activities to escape planning controls). 'Destatization' is a wider concept than privatization (although that was the final stage). In the early stages of 'destatization' there was to be the formation of joint stock companies with all shares owned by the state (but independent of ministries). Also included were worker-ownership and leasing. 'Destatization' featured in various programmes to shift to the market in the late Gorbachev period.

PRIVATIZATION IN THE NON-AGRICULTURAL SECTORS OF THE RUSSIAN ECONOMY SINCE 1992

Since in the Soviet period the industrial sector was almost entirely state-owned, privatization has been a gigantic undertaking. As in other transitional economies, a distinction is made between 'small' and 'large' privatization (the latter category including both medium-sized and large enterprises). Specifically, a 'small' enterprise in Russia is one with less than 200 employees and which had assets of less than 1 million roubles as of 1 January 1992. A 'medium-sized' enterprise employs between 200 and 1,000 people and had assets worth between 1 million and 50 million roubles as of 1 January 1992.

The respective figures for a 'large' enterprise are over 1,000 employees and over 50 million roubles of assets. The speed of Russian privatization has been extremely rapid and the methods employed in large privatization have been highly controversial.

Before embarking on the process of privatization it is worth mentioning the problem of the social welfare services offered by Soviet-era enterprises and their subsequent divestiture. 'Prior to 1991 ... enterprises owned housing, kindergartens, sports centres, hospitals and polyclinics and, especially in the mono-cities, operated public transport. Following privatization the heavy costs of supporting these social services has encouraged many enterprises to divest these assets; indeed, divestiture has normally been an explicit condition of privatization' (Healey *et al.* 1999: 263). 'Prior to 1991 the enterprise housing stock amounted to 65 per cent of the municipal stock of Russia, with one in five citizens living in housing owned by his or her enterprise. In addition, at least one million people (mainly young workers) lived in dormitories owned by enterprises ... Enterprises' healthcare ... services were available to an estimated 20 to 33 per cent of Russian citizens' (p. 267). 'Between 1993 and 1997 the divestiture of social assets was very rapid. During this period approximately 80 per cent of housing, 76 per cent of kindergartens, 75 per cent of children's recreation camps, 82 per cent of polyclinics and hospitals, and 84 per cent of culture and sports facilities were moved wholesale into municipal ownership, together with approximately 70 per cent of sanatoriums and 60 per cent of preventoriums ... The share of social assets retained by enterprises varies considerably from one region to another ... Most of the divestitures took place in the period 1993–95 ... By 1995 many of the commercially viable enterprises had been privatized and had disposed of their social assets, leaving a rump of enterprises that either could not or would not restructure ... "Dilapidated housing" and other excessively depreciated assets, cannot, at least in principle, be transferred to the municipalities. They must first be partially or completely restored or demolished and rebuilt. For obvious reasons many privatized enterprises lack the financial resources to undertake such wholesale renovation ... "Discarded" social assets are, as a rule, given top priority and taken over by municipalities ... They have a statutory responsibility for the social sphere of the city or town, with the residents of "abandoned" houses typically turning for help not to enterprises but to their local administrations' (pp. 270–2). 'The municipalities have generally been unwilling or unable to properly finance and manage the social assets divested by privatized enterprises over the period 1993–7, with the result that social services have deteriorated or collapsed altogether ... The competitiveness of those enterprises still operating social services is being damaged by the resultant drain on productive resources ... A vicious circle is underway whereby allowing social assets to remain in the ownership of enterprises erodes the tax base and reduces the federal, regional and local revenues available for social policy reform' (p. 279).

The first stage of privatization, 1 October 1992–1 July 1994

The first stage of privatization is often referred to as the 'voucher' ('mass') stage of privatization. But it is better described as the stage of 'insider' privatization, the term 'insider' referring to existing workers and managers. The return (restitution) of property to former owners or their heirs was ruled out (owing to factors such as its probable general unpopularity and the relatively long period that had elapsed since property was expropriated).

The privatization programme was passed by parliament on 11 June 1992 and President Yeltsin outlined the voucher scheme on 19 August of that year. All citizens (including children born before 1 September 1992) would be eligible and vouchers could be used (i) to buy shares in privatized enterprises or private investment funds or (ii) sold (even to foreigners).

Citizens were to be able to obtain their vouchers between 1 October and 31 December 1992 (many authorities later extending the period by one month), vouchers being exchangeable for shares during 1993. (By the end of January 1993 96 per cent of the population had received their vouchers. The vouchers would be redeemed by the central government and cash raised would go to regional and local governments.) For a small registration fee of 25 roubles vouchers worth 10,000 roubles (corresponding to the historical book value) could be obtained. Although in nominal terms the vouchers were worth only around two months' average salary (earned in mid-1992), they would be used 'to acquire property at the old prices on the last balance-sheet appraisals of enterprises' (*CDSP*, 1992, vol. XLIV, no. 34, p. 7).

Sales of regional property are carried out locally. The process of privatization has taken on a decidedly regional character, with reformist Nizhny Novgorod, for example, attracting considerable attention. The mayor of Moscow, Yuri Luzhkov, was powerful enough to reject the government's voucher privatization programme and enriched the capital with sales and leasing.

Small privatization

Small enterprises (many in domestic trade) are typically the property of municipal governments, with privatization largely decentralized. Small enterprises are sold either through unconditional auctions or tender offers (in which the purchaser accepts some stipulations regarding such things as employment). Preference is given to workers by granting a 30 per cent discount on the auction price to successful bids from workers' collectives. The collectives are also allowed to spread 75 per cent of their payments over three years at zero interest. It is, therefore, not surprising that at the end of 1992 worker collectives owned 60 per cent of the shares in privatized small-scale enterprises, other firms owned 27 per cent and individuals owned 13 per cent. (See *RET*, 1993, vol. 2, no. 1, pp. 5, 8, 50–2, for the details of both small-scale and large-scale privatization.) 'Small' privatization is naturally easier than 'large' privatization and the process has been very rapid. By the end of March 1994 more than 70 cent of all small-scale retail, catering and personal service enterprises were under private ownership (*RET*, Monthly Update, 30 April 1994, p. 14). More than 75 per cent of small-scale activity was in private ownership by mid-1994 (*RET*, 1994, vol. 3, no. 2, p. 82). At the end of June 1994 the market share of private enterprises was 75 per cent in retail trade, 66 per cent in catering and 77 per cent in personal services (*RET*, 1994, vol. 3, no. 3, p. 96).

Large privatization

The first stage of large privatization process involved employees deciding upon one of the three options. If the enterprise collective was unable to agree on any option, Option 1 was selected by default. (Privatization was banned in areas such as mineral and water resources, military property, the central bank, and radio and television centres. Permission for privatization was required in, for example, weapons, machinery for the nuclear power industry, the fuel and energy complex, commercial banking, news agencies, enterprises in any sector that occupied dominant positions in the federal or local markets, enterprises with more than 10,000 employees, enterprises in rail, air and water transport, and the production of alcoholic drinks: *CDSP*, 1992, vol. XLIV, no. 26, pp. 33–4.) The three options were as follows:

1. In Option 1 workers were given 25 per cent of (non-voting) shares, with the option of buying 10 per cent of (voting) shares at a 30 per cent discount on 1991 book value. A three-year installment plan was available and vouchers could be used. Managers had the option of buying 5 per cent of the voting shares at 1991 book value.

2. In Option 2, subject to a two-thirds majority vote, workers and managers could buy 51 per cent of the voting shares at a discount and with deferred payments. Employees had the right to buy up to 51 per cent of their enterprise's capital at 1.7 times 1991 book value. Up to 50 per cent of the value of the stock could be paid for with vouchers. Shares not given or sold to employees were to be sold at auction to the general public. Thirty-five per cent of shares were to be sold in exchange for vouchers. The remainder were to be sold for cash. Workers and managers were free to use their vouchers and cash to buy these shares too.

3. In Option 3 a group of employees (not necessarily the entire work collective) could agree to reorganize an enterprise. The agreement had to be approved by at least two-thirds of the work collective and had to be in effect for one year. The group was obliged to reorganize the enterprise within one year, investing the employees' personal money in an amount at least 200 times the minimum wage for each member of the group. If the terms of the agreement were met, the group members would receive the right to acquire

20 per cent of the ordinary shares at face value. In addition, all enterprise employees, including members of the group, could acquire an additional 20 per cent of the shares on the same terms as Option 2.

Option 2 proved to be by far the most popular of the three. By July 1994 more than 70 per cent of all enterprises had been privatized under Option 2. Another 21 per cent of enterprises chose Option 1 (*RET*, 1994, vol. 3, no. 2, pp. 79–80). By the end of June 1994 workers and managers at 73 per cent of all privatized large enterprises had selected Option 2 whereas only 25 per cent had chosen Option 1 (McFaul 1996a: 293). Some 70 per cent of industrial enterprises have been privatized. Two-thirds of shares ended up in the hands of employees of those enterprises (Åslund 1994b: 68). In over 65 per cent of the 18,000 privatized medium-sized and large enterprises management and employees have majority ownership, whereas non-state outsiders control only 20 per cent of these enterprises (EBRD 1997b: 195).

The speed of privatization has been very rapid (enterprises being considered privatized if they are over half privately owned). (See Table 5.1.) ('It is generally forgotten that nearly half of Russian industry is still really owned by the state': *Business Central Europe*, November 1999, p. 41.) The following estimates give some idea of the speed:

1. In January–October 1992 the private sector accounted for only 6.7 per cent of industrial output (United Nations Economic Commission for Europe 1993: 215). The number of medium-sized and large enterprises (out of roughly 14,500) privatized were as follows: December 1992, eighteen; January 1993, 105; February 1993, 201; March 1993, 378; April 1993, 558; mid-1993, more than 2,300; September 1993, about 4,500; October 1993, over 5,000. (Various issues of *RET*, *CDSP*, *The Economist*, *FT* and *IHT*.)

2. By 1 July 1994 some 14,000 medium-sized and large enterprises had been privatized. Two-thirds of the industrial labour force is now employed by privatized firms. More than 40 million Russians became shareholders in either privatized enterprises or investment funds (Maxim Boycko and Andrei Shleifer, *Transition*, 1994, vol. 5, no. 9, p. 8).

3. 'By now two-thirds of Russian industry, big and small, is in private hands' (Richard Layard, *FT*, 3 June 1994, p. 17). Around 86 per cent of Russia's industry is in mainly private hands (Richard Layard, *FT*, 14 March 1995, p. 20).

4. By 1 July 1994 more than 40 million Russians became share owners in enterprises or in investment funds. More than 75 per cent of the industrial labour force had moved into the private sector. The government has retained a controlling share in some 358 enterprises and a 'golden share' (with veto power over strategic enterprise decisions) in 211 enterprises (*RET*, 1994, vol. 3, no. 2, pp. 79–80). Thus over half of all workers in Russia now work in private enterprise (p. 8). By 1 July 1994 15,052 medium-sized and large industrial enterprises had been sold through voucher auctions (*RET*, 1994, vol. 3, no. 3, pp. 93–4). The workers accounted for 84 per cent of total industrial employment (p. 94; a figure of 81 per cent was later given: 1995, vol. 3, no. 4,

Table 5.1 Russia: privatization

Date		*Total no. of enterprises privatized*	*Percentage of industrial workers in private enterprises (workers in medium-sized and large industrial enterprises)*
1992	March	1,352	
	April	2,995	
	May	5,855	
	June	8,933	
	July	12,015	
	August	17,230	
	September	22,572	
	October	29,235	
	November	34,932	
	December	46,815	0.2
1993	January	54,243	1.1
	February	57,989	2.0
	March	59,495	4.6
	April	66,000	8.6
	May	68,000	11.3
	June	72,000	15.5
	July	78,000	19.1
	August	81,000	22.9
	September	82,000	26.8
	October	83,000	30.9
	November	86,000	35.1
	December	89,000	40.0
1994	January	91,000	43.1
	February	93,000	49.1
	March	95,000	54.0
	April	98,000	59.8
	May	99,000	65.0
	June	102,000	81.8

Source: Russian Economic Trends (various issues)

p. 94). By the end of 1995 the total number of privatized enterprises exceeded 122,000, 10,000 of which had been privatized in the course of the year (*RET*, 1995, vol. 4, no. 4, p. 98). By the end of September 1995 77.2 per cent of the total number of industrial enterprises were privatized, producing 88.3 per cent of industrial production and employing 79.4 per cent of industrial personnel (p. 99).

Various estimates have also been made of the importance of the private sector as a whole in the economy:

1. Around 75 per cent of economic activity is now generated in the private sector (Anatoli Chubais, quoted in *IHT*, 6 February 1996, p. 1).

2. Rough estimates in mid-year of the private sector as a percentage of GDP are provided by the EBRD: 1990, 5 per cent; 1991, 5 per cent; 1992, 25 per cent; 1993, 40 per cent; 1994, 50 per cent; 1995, 55 per cent; 1996, 60 per cent;

1997, 70 per cent; 1998, 70 per cent; 1999, 70 per cent; 2000, 70 per cent (EBRD 1999b: 24, 260, and 2000b: 14, 204).

Private enterprises that originated in the private sector (i.e. not as converted state enterprises) accounted for 25 per cent of GDP in 1994 and 38 per cent in 1996. Over the period the GDP share of state enterprises fell from 38 per cent to 23 per cent (United Nations, *World Economic and Social Survey*, 1997, p. 27).

The first stage of large privatization was mired in controversy. Among the common objections were the following:

1. Rapid and more equitable privatization could have been achieved by means of a more conventional and thus more extensive voucher (mass) privatization programme in order to gain public support. (In such a programme all eligible citizens are allocated vouchers, for free or at nominal cost, which can be used to buy the bulk of shares in the enterprises on offer.) (Alexander Solzhenitsyn concluded thus: 'The [privatization] campaign's first step was the government's issuing of vouchers to each citizen that supposedly represented his "share" of all the national wealth accumulated under the communists. In reality, the total value of all the vouchers represented only a small fraction of 1 per cent of that wealth': *IHT*, 7 January 1997, p. 8.)

2. There was often ignorance about the value of vouchers and shares among ordinary people. 'Valeri Bykov ... seized control of Kras [Krasnoyarsk aluminium smelter] ... the second largest in the world ... earning $1 billion a year ... "They were privatizing it", he says. "All the workers were given shares, but no one believed in them. You could buy them for almost nothing at the factory gates. My partner and I bought 20 per cent"' (Andrew Harding, *The Guardian*, 27 November 1999, p. 18). Pressure was also sometimes put on workers to sell against their will.

3. The preference given to existing workers and managers ('insiders') would hinder the necessary adaption of enterprises to harsher market conditions, especially when 'soft budget constraints' and payments arrears operate (and thus bankruptcy is not a serious threat). It was felt that investment would be neglected at the expense of wages. (See, for example, Sutela 1994: *The Economist*, 20 November 1993, p. 48, and 12 March 1994, p. 46; Brzezinski 1994; Boris Fyodorov, *IHT*, 17 October 1994, p. 2.)

While Boone and Fedorov (Fyodorov) see many positive features of the privatization process, they are not unaware of some problems. 'There are several incentives operating today that suggest insider owners may still wait before they restructure enterprises or divest assets. When there are outstanding shares held by the state, or by workers with weak control rights, it is only normal that a director would want to take actions to limit the market value of these shares so that management or friendly entities can buy up the remaining shares at low prices' (Boone and Fedorov 1997: 181).

'Financial discipline, would, it was anticipated, start to to force secondary trading in shares of insider-dominated companies and introduce outside ownership ... First [however], insiders – particularly the workers in the newly privatized firms – deeply feared outside ownership and a loss of control (and jobs). Second, because the financial and physical conditions of many firms were unattractive, not many outsiders were interested in acquiring their shares. Third, there was an acute lack of defined property rights, institutional underpinnings, and safeguards for transparent secondary trading; this further discouraged outside investors. Fourth, various Russian governments failed to put in place supporting policies and institutions – such as hard budget constraints, reasonable taxes and services, and mechanisms to permit and encourage new business entrants – that might have channelled enterprise activity to productive ends' (Nellis 1999: 17). 'Itzhak Goldberg argues for a particular form of reprivatization. He suggests that the principal obstacle to progressive restructuring in privatized firms in Russia and elsewhere is the excessive concentration of ownership in the hands of insiders, who lack the means and incentives to lead the firms forward. Goldberg accepts the futility of renationalization and argues instead for increasing the capital in privatized firms and then immediately diluting the stakes of insiders by selling the new shares to external investors' (p. 19).

Filatotchev *et al.* (1999a) surveyed more than 300 enterprises of different sizes in the period 1995–6. 'The major findings of the research are that managers are hostile towards outside ownership, and they effectively collude with other employees to preserve insider control. We also provide evidence that the gradual accumulation of shares by managers is not based on a profit motive alone, but is also driven by their efforts to preserve insider control' (p. 483). 'It has sometimes been argued that insider ownership in Russian firms will be a short-lived phenomenon, because the tradability of shares combined with insiders' desire for portfolio diversification will ensure a fairly rapid dilution of their equity stake. Our findings suggest that this is a simplistic view – insider control may exist for quite long periods of time. In Russia insider control is associated with particularly low levels of outside monitoring, because managers and employees effectively collude to keep outside influence low, and the legal rights of outside shareholders are proving difficult to enforce' (p. 500). 'Using data from a recent survey we show that insider control in firms privatized in 1992–4 through the voucher process ... is insecure and dependent on managers' support. For employees investment in insider control appears to have been motivated by employment income insurance rather than expected excess returns on the equity. Managers are predominantly the same individuals as before privatization and display considerable hostility to outside investors, probably because they fear dismissal should outsiders gain control' (Filatotchev *et al.* 1999b: 129). 'There is a striking degree of managerial sympathy with the concerns of employees, such as the preservation of employment, and considerable hostility to outside investors' (p. 146). 'Insider control is, however, likely to become steadily less important in the Russian economy through two mechanisms: many industrial firms will continue to lose labour and shrink relatively as the service sector grows, and in well-performing firms managers may feel after a certain time that they have signalled sufficient quality to risk giving outsiders control' (p. 147). 'Despite insider control firms are shedding labour quite rapidly through voluntary resignations (p. 129). 'Russian firms have shed labour in response to declining sales' (p. 146).

4. Existing managers would become increasingly powerful given the weakness of trade unions and the fear of unemployment among workers. (See, for example, McFaul 1996a.)

5. 'Most large enterprises are run by insiders who disregard the owners' rights' (Yavlinsky 1998: 78).

'Insiders typically focus on maintaining control over their firms than on restructuring. Maintenance of "pocket" share registrars (i.e. registrars controlled by the firm), manipulation of voting procedures and obstacles to board representation of outside shareholders have been widely used as defence mechanisms to preserve insider control' (EBRD 1997b: 195).

'A 25 per cent stake in a Russian company is widely regarded as the minimum requirement to wield any influence over the management' (*FT*, 27 June 2000, p. 23).

6. Corporate governance (control) would also be hindered by the newness and fewness of investment funds. Whereas Czech investment funds collected 70 per cent of privatization vouchers, Russian investment funds attracted only 6 per cent (*Business Central Europe*, May 1996, p. 48). Some investment funds (such as MMM in 1994) were essentially pyramid schemes (which rely on new subscriptions to pay off existing investors and are therefore inherently doomed to fail).

7. Gaddy and Ickes (1998a) comment on industrial privatization in general. 'Although Russia formally has privatized most of its industrial sector, the pace of economic restructuring is still grossly inadequate to ensure stable economic growth ... Enterprises continue to trade with one another without the use of money – either by not paying each other at all or by using non-monetary means, such as barter or promissory notes, called vecksels. (These are notes, issued by commercial banks, governments and enterprises, that serve as an alternative medium of exchange.) Estimates of the share of sales made in the form of barter or other non-monetary forms run as high as 70 per cent' (p. 1). 'What explains the failure of Russian enterprises to restructure? One popular argument is that Russian management is inadequate. We support an alternative explanation: managers are rational and the environment induces them to postpone or avoid restructuring ... Formal activities of enterprises ... are reflected in official statistics and result in the cash payment of taxes. But below the surface Russian enterprises engage in informal activities, as a means of survival and as a response to the structure of taxation and the weak system of corporate governance. Informal activities involve non-monetary transactions: the "soft" goods are sold against promissory notes such as vecksels or exchanged for other goods and services (barter). These

transactions – including taxes paid in kind – occur outside the formal monetary system and consequently are much less observable, contrary to "hard goods" that are produced and sold through monetary transactions (for cash) in the formal economy ... Initially, barter was seen as a natural response by some enterprises to the high inflation that prevailed in Russia after prices were liberalized. But the use of barter has increased despite financial liberalization. This could be explained by the shortage of liquidity, as high interest rates made it hard for enterprises to borrow. The impetus to barter, however, often comes from the seller. This suggests other motivations for the widespread use of barter, including its usefulness in beating Russia's onerous tax system' (pp. 2–3). 'Tax offsets fundamentally change the set of choices available to Russian enterprise directors. By allowing enterprises to pay taxes in "soft goods" (that is, output for which there is no effective demand), tax offsets provide an incentive to avoid restructuring' (p. 3). 'Hard goods sold for cash yield monetary tax liabilities as well as income that must be paid to shareholders and other stakeholders ... On the plus side, high-effort goods are easier to translate into cash, which may be needed to procure important inputs ... Russia appears to be generating a dual economy. Alongside a modernizing private sector, a paternalistic, unrestructured industrial sector continues to hang on, and even to regenerate' (p. 5). 'Russia's virtual economy is based on illusion, or pretence, about almost important parameter of the economy: prices, sales, wages, taxes and budgets. At its heart is the ultimate pretence that the Russian economy is larger than it really is ... Industry in the Soviet economy was subsidized by underpriced raw materials and insufficient charges for capital. The economy appeared to have a large manufacturing sector that produced value; in fact, manufacturing destroyed value, but this was masked by arbitrary pricing. The roots of the virtual economy lie in the maintenance of this pretence ... Russia's economy is probably even smaller than official figures suggest (not bigger, as many people say)' (p. 4). 'The share of barter payments among all industrial enterprises in Russia has now reached more than 50 per cent' (Gaddy and Ickes 1998b: 56). 'GDP may be even smaller than the official figures suggest, even after taking into account the underreporting of the hidden economy' (p. 62). (See the references to Gaddy and Ickes in Chapters 1 and 8. The virtual economy is discussed at length in Gaddy and Ickes 1998b.)

8. 'At the start of the transition industrial behemoths employed the large majority of the workforce. During the years of partial liberalization under Mikhail Gorbachev's policy of *perestroika*, managers took de facto control over most of these enterprises. In their search for rapid privatization reformers saw little alternative but to transfer the de facto control of managers into de jure ownership rights. Having developed very close relationships with government authorities at all levels under the Soviet period, these managers-turned-owners used their influence to protect their enterprises from potential outside owners, from competition by new market entrants and from restructuring

plans that would force substantial layoffs. To keep these enterprises alive in their enfeebled condition required a massive drain on public resources and a reliance on wasteful practices, such as barter, to conceal the real state of affairs. The Russian experience is the most powerful example of the damaging consequences of insider ownership, which are particularly severe when insiders have inherited or developed strong ties to government' (EBRD 1998b: 3–4). 'Around 60 per cent of Russia's medium-sized and large companies are majority owned by insiders. The dominance of managers also extends to many companies with substantial outside ownership. Minority shareholders have frequently been subjected to a range of abuses including restricted access to shareholder meetings, share dilutions and discriminatory transfer pricing and share swaps with holding companies, especially in the oil and gas sector' (pp. 186–7).

9. In the section entitled 'the impact of privatization on productivity performance', Brown and Earle conclude in their article that: 'On average privatized firms in Russia appear to perform somewhat better than do state firms, but the best performance appears in companies that have large, concentrated outside stakeholders.' They add that: 'In mid-1994 most Russian firms were left with continued domination by insiders and the state. Subsequent sales of blocks of shares have been quite slow, as have secondary sales of shares by workers' (Brown and Earle 1999: 30).

10. 'On the speed of reform there were two elements of shock therapy in Russia – price liberalization in 1992 and privatization in 1992–5. On both the decision to move fast was made by the Russian government. In a different political environment more gradual privatization, after the creation of legal and institutional frameworks for a market economy, could have made more sense. But that was not the view of the Russian policymakers. In other respects reform has been too slow, not too fast. If Russia had implemented the 1996 reforms its economy would now be stronger, incomes would be higher and it would have avoided the 1998 collapse. Capital flight estimated at $10 billion to $20 billion a year, would be much smaller' (Stanley Fischer, first deputy managing director of the IMF, *FT*, 27 September 1999, p. 26).

11. 'Joseph Stiglitz [chief economist of the World Bank] restated his disapproval of Russia's privatization programme, saying the system encourages "asset stripping" that has seen "billions and billions of dollars taken out of the country" ... Mr Stiglitz said that privatization had gone ahead without a sufficient legal framework. As a result, he said, "rather than providing incentives for wealth creation, there have been incentives for asset stripping". "Providing free capital mobility has been an open invitation for people to take out billions, in fact billions and billions, of dollars out of the country", he said ... Mr Stiglitz said the West assumed that a rules-based legal and financial infrastructure would emerge "spontaneously ... [But] privatization by itself has not been a guarantee for success" ... Rather than becoming wealthier, he said, Russia has become poorer' (*IHT*, 27 January 2000, pp. 1, 17).

12. 'While the original rationale for Russia's rapid privatization was to prevent asset stripping by managers in state-owned enterprises, owner-mangers have significantly degraded their firms' assets. Efforts made to limit this asset degradation have, in recent years, been successfully blocked by a coalition of enterprise insiders and regional governments, together with their allies in the Duma ... Owner-managers ... [have] insufficient incentives ... to restructure firms and maximize their value over the long run. First, owner-mangers perceive their titles to firms as uncertain, temporary and subject to expropriation ... Second, maximizing value is a reasonable objective only if that value can be realized through the sale of the ownership rights in enterprises. Given the illiquidity of Russia's relatively underdeveloped capital markets, both pubic and private, firms rarely change hands and managers therefore have little incentive to increase the firms' value. Third, because dividends are taxable and have to be shared with other stockholders, mainly employees, owners have been more inclined to withdraw cash from their enterprises by requesting reimbursement for fictitious expenses or engaging in other types of theft. Even in those enterprises where only a minority of shares are held by management, managers use a variety of techniques to ensure they have de facto control. They have often taken to (illegally) imposing bans on the selling of firms to outsiders, placing limits on share ownership, and using implicit threats against workers who violate these policies' (Desai and Goldberg 2000: 15).

Arguments in favour of the method of privatization adopted in stage one include the following:

1. Rapid privatization was essential to make the transition to a Western-type economy irreversible. The political situation, especially the weakness of the central government in a country not generally enamoured with privatization, meant that there was no option to in effect bribing 'insiders' (especially the powerful managerial lobby). (See, for example, Boycko *et al.* 1994.)

2. Once clear private property rights have been established (especially in conditions of tight monetary policy), market share dealing will empower 'outside' owners (including foreigners) to exercise corporate governance. There will be changes in management and a more efficient use of resources in general. (See, for example, Åslund 1994b; Joseph Blasi, *IHT*, 1 July 1994, p. 4, and *The Economist*, Survey, 12 July 1997, p. 12; Fan and Schaffer 1994; Maxim Boycko and Andrei Shleifer, *Transition*, 1994, vol. 5, no. 9, p. 8; Buck *et al.* 1994; EBRD 1994: 34, and 1996b: 170.)

'Although privatization has not been as successful as the reformers hoped, some positive changes have been implemented. Many Soviet-era managers have been replaced, which is often a precondition for restructuring ... A recent broad survey shows substantial market-directed restructuring, although this process has been much faster in countries with more radical reforms' (Åslund 1999b: 70). 'Barter is abating, from 54 per cent of industrial firms' sales in August 1998 to 46 per cent in January 1999' (p. 76).

3. Some see positive aspects in the increasing power of managers. 'Managers now own around a third of shares in the typical firm, which gives them a powerful incentive to maximise shareholder value, and restructuring is going ahead fast' (Richard Layard, *FT*, 14 March 1995, p. 20). 'When enterprises are controlled by their rank-and-file employees, they tend to be slow to restructure and likely to accumulate inter-enterprise and tax arrears; but when management has control, firms have been far more likely to reorient themselves towards success in the new market conditions' (*RET*, 1996, vol. 5, no. 2, p. 123). Krueger (1995) believes that the ability of Russian managers to adjust to new circumstances has generally been underestimated.

4. Corporate governance is being improved, e.g. through greater legal protection for the rights of 'outside' shareholders and through the activity of Financial–Industrial Groups (FIGs).

'Problems in the area of corporate governance, resulting from a combination of privatization to insiders and the lack of shareholders' rights, are often mentioned as key to Russia's underperformance. The existing governance environment gives the current managers more incentives to divert the company cash flow to their own trading firms, than to restructure or invest. Such cash diversions have been commonly mentioned in the steel, cement and oil sectors. However, in these industries battles for corporate control are now coming to an end in most of the viable assets, allowing management to focus on increasing long-term value of the company' (McKinsey Global Institute 1999: 27).

The registration of official FIGs began soon after the adoption of a presidential decree on FIGs in December 1993. By 1998 the official registry of FIGs listed seventy-five groups, including a total of 1,212 firms with 3,330,000 employees. A great number of informal FIGs have also emerged (*RET*, 1999, vol. 8, no. 3, p. 6).

'Corporate governance remains handicapped by the continued concentration of ownership in the hands of insiders (workers and management). However, commercial banks are an increasingly active influence. They have taken large equity stakes in many enterprises and are exercising external control, partly in the framework of Financial–Industrial Groups. Recent evidence suggests that real restructuring is coming mainly from this source ... In mid-1996 there were about thirty-five such officially registered FIGs ... While these groups may create useful synergies between banks and industry they may also cause remonopolization and reduced transparency within the economy' (EBRD 1996b: 170). While in the top 100 largest enterprises outsiders have an ownership stake well above the average, the wide dispersion of these shareholdings often ensures a controlling position for the management. 'Insiders typically focus on maintaining control over their firms than on restructuring. Maintenance of "pocket" share registrars (i.e. registrars controlled by the firm), manipulation of voting procedures and obstacles to board representation of outside shareholders have been widely used as defence mechanisms to preserve insider control. However, recent high-profile cases of enforcing improved corporate governance and respect of shareholder rights (Gazprom, Unified Energy System, Mosenergo and Novolipetsk) are encouraging signs ... Recent evidence suggests that roughly 25 per cent of the medium-sized and large companies are engaged in serious restructuring, many of them being members of Financial and Industrial Groups (FIGs). About half of the medium-sized and large companies have not as yet undertaken any meaningful restructuring' (EBRD 1997b: 195). In early 1997 there were over sixty officially registered FIGs, although many more were operating without official registration (p. 196).

But the impact of FIGs has not been seen entirely in a positive light. 'The seven major FIGs control over 40 per cent of the economy and 1997 has seen a clear tightening of this grip': Business Central Europe 1997: 32. On 20 February 1998 Boris Nemtsov declared that the failure to establish control over monopolies had already resulted in a 'dictatorship' of Financial–Industrial Groups. ('Unless we establish control over monopolies and rebuff the increasingly insolent industrial groups a gloomy end awaits us. We can expect economic collapse, as happened with the Asian Tigers': *IHT*, 21 February 1998, p. 9.)

FIGs (Financial–Industrial Groups) are officially defined as 'a group of enterprises, institutions, organizations, lending and financial institutions and investment institutions' (Johnson 1997: 334). Johnson breaks FIGs down into two major groups:

1. Industry-led FIGs tend to be based on old industrial ties or branch ministries, concentrated in depressed industrial sectors (especially defence) and located in the regions. Banks have joined these FIGs but they are usually weak local banks (often so-called 'pocket banks' directly controlled by the enterprises involved) or banks that have provided little actual support to other members of the group. 'Most industry-led FIGs have engaged in almost no active enterprise restructuring on their own' (p. 334). 'The member-enterprises have banded together at the behest of the state in hopes of finding a way out of their restructuring dilemmas without yielding control to outsiders' (p. 361).

2. Bank-led FIGs emerged as the largest banks began to acquire shares of privatized or privatizing enterprises, tending to focus on lucrative export or consumer industries and succeeding in gaining control over many leading enterprises (p. 334).

'We find that, whereas industry-led FIGs for the most part represent failed efforts by enterprise managers and conservative politicians to salvage uncompetitive industrial ventures without restructuring them, bank-led FIGs have acquired powerful and potentially pivotal positions in the Russian economy today. These bank-led FIGs have used various methods to advance their interests, including lobbying the government for privileges, colluding with each other, and beginning to take more active roles in restructuring

Russian enterprises. The bank-led FIGs reached a crucial decision point in 1997, a time when they were weighing to what extent they were willing and able to pursue the difficult task of enforcing effective corporate governance in Russia's struggling enterprises. Moreover, 1997 represented a crucial point in the development of Russia's financial sector, as the political and economic ascendance of the bank-led FIGs pushed Russia ever further along the path of developing a German-centred investment system, as opposed to a more open, capital-markets-centred, US-style investment system' (pp. 335–6).

'Banks garnered their unique position in the Russian economy in great part because of two early government decisions with unexpected consequences: the rapid liberalization of the Soviet financial system under Gorbachev in 1987–88, and Russia's attempts to implement shock therapy in 1992 ... The liberalization allowed thousands of undercapitalized banks to spring up with the direct participation of state, regional and party authorities. The failed attempt to implement shock therapy, then, had a twofold effect, allowing the best-connected and most-established bankers to make money in the highly inflationary, unstable environment while impoverishing in relative terms most other domestic economic actors. This left the leading bankers in a good position to expand their political influence. Since 1993 the political power of the bank-led FIGs, driven by their status as economic heavyweights, has come from three major sources: their acquisitions in the Russian media; their activity in campaign finance; and the revolving door between executive positions in the banks and government' (p. 348). Bank-led FIGs have manipulated the institution of 'authorized' banks. By 1996 the big banks held the accounts, for example, of the tax authorities, the customs authorities and the finance ministry (which also took out bank loans, guaranteed by government, to cover temporary budgetary shortfalls). Bank-led FIGs have acquired enterprises cheaply in the 'shares-for-loans' programme and have hampered the activities of foreign investors in Russian markets (p. 351).

(The government has decided to shift the government and customs accounts from 'authorized banks' to the central bank: *RET*, 1997, no. 3, p. 109. On 24 September 1997 Yeltsin said that in 1998 all federal government accounts would be transferred from commercial banks to the federal treasury: *RET*, 1997, no. 4, p. 105.)

('In a country where a bank transfer takes a week or so to go through, banks profit hugely from inflation': *The Economist*, 19 September 1998, p. 114.)

Privatization after 1 July 1994

After the first stage of privatization ended on 1 July 1994 attention switched to sales for cash. In 'strategic sectors', including energy, metals and armaments, the state would retain the right to hold a 51 per cent stake for a further three years (*RET*, 1994, vol. 3, no. 3, p. 93). Other key changes included:

1. The attraction of 'strategic private investors' for the sake of corporate governance. The scheme would allow investors to acquire 'substantial stakes' in enterprises (*RET*, 1994, vol. 3, no. 3, p. 93). The programme was designed to attract 'strategic investors' through direct sales of shares representing 20 per cent of state assets (*Transition*, 1994, vol. 5, no. 6, p. 19). An important aim was to try to sell large blocks of shares (more than 51 per cent of authorized capital) to 'major strategic investors' (*CDSP*, 1994, vol. XLVI, no. 15, p. 22).

2. Reduced privileges for 'insiders'. Workers would either be able to buy up to 20 per cent of the enterprise that employs them at a 30 per cent discount or 51 per cent at the market price. One of the options would allow the enterprise to give 25 per cent of the non-voting stock away and to sell a further 10 per cent of voting stocks to employees at a discount (*RET*, 1994, vol. 3, no. 3, p. 94).

3. The enterprise could retain 51 per cent of the revenue raised from its privatization and these funds were to be used for investment. The other 49 per cent would be split between the federal and local governments.

A presidential decree of 11 May 1995 established new rules for distributing the proceeds from sales of shares in federally-owned enterprises: 55 per cent of the funds was to go to the federal budget (up from 10 per cent), 10 per cent to republican budgets, 4 per cent to local budgets, and 14 per cent to the enterprise itself (down from 51 per cent) (*CDSP*, 1995, vol. XLVII, no. 19, p. 15; *RET*, 1995, vol. 4, no. 1, p. 95).

4. Regions would be given greater authority. For example, local authorities would have the right to set the price, above a government-established minimum threshold, at which shares in privatized enterprises could be sold to the public.

The second stage of privatization was slow in getting off the ground, in part owing to depressed share prices (*RET*, Monthly Update, 21 March 1995, p. 10).

Privatization of the oil and gas industries

Oil and gas are key sectors in the Russian economy. Russia is the third largest producer of oil in the world, behind Saudi Arabia and the USA (*IHT*, 6 July 1994, p. 6). Thus the way the energy sectors have been privatized have attracted particular attention.

Structure and privatization

The oil industry has been split up into a number of corporations, with the state holding company Rosneft acting as overseer. The state was initially concerned to have a controlling stake in each corporation for at least three years, while up to 15 per cent of shares could go to foreigners. According to Joskow *et al.* (1994: 365), there are a number of competing integrated oil production and refining enterprises, separated from pipeline transport and product distribution enterprises. Companies such as Lukoil have become well known in the West.

In contrast, the natural gas industry is still dominated by Gazprom (which was turned into a joint stock company). The company is huge, although estimates of its importance vary somewhat:

1. Gazprom controls 24 per cent of the world's known natural gas reserves, supplies nearly a fifth of total West European gas demand and is Russia's largest single source of hard currency (*FT*, 10 January 1995, p. 17, and 27 March 1995, p. 19). Gazprom, which benefits from special tax breaks not available to other enterprises, employs 360,000 people directly and supports 6 million. The company controls a fifth of the world's natural gas reserves, is the largest gas exporter to Europe and accounts for an estimated 8 per cent of GDP (*FT*, 1 April 1996, p. 21). Gazprom holds 25 per cent of the world's natural gas reserves (*FT*, 1 November 2000, p. 25).

2. Gazprom is the largest gas company in the world, accounting for 22 per cent of world production (*Business Central Europe*, March 1995, p. 41).

3. Gazprom supplies about 30 per cent of Western Europe's natural gas. Foreigners own less than 3 per cent of the company's stock (*IHT*, 2 July 1996, p. 13). Gazprom accounts for 22 per cent of world gas production, a third of global reserves and a fifth of Russia's export earnings (*IHT*, 5 July 1996, p. 8). Gazprom owns a third of the world's known gas reserves and supplies a quarter of Europe's gas (*IHT*, 17 February 2000, p. 9).

4. Gazprom supplies up to 40 per cent of the world demand for natural gas. Gazprom's 1995 gross income amounted to 8 per cent of GDP (*CDSP*, 1996, vol. XLVIII, no. 22, p. 18).

The ownership of Gazprom shares, especially by individuals, is not entirely clear:

1. 'It is hard to know who owns Gazprom, the partly privatized natural gas giant, whose first chairman was Viktor Chernomyrdin, the prime minister' (Jeffrey Sachs, *IHT*, 6 December 1995, p. 10).

2. 'In early 1993 … Gazprom gained the right to buy 10 per cent of its shares from the state, without any competition and often for token sums … Gazprom was directed to sell those shares on the securities market within a six-month period and to earmark the proceeds for the development of the major gas fields on the Yamal peninsula … However … the 10 per cent stake was never offered on the market. Instead, those shares were sold in December 1995 at nominal value to various subsidiaries and friendly companies: 4.3 per cent went to Gazprom's pension fund, almost 1 per cent went to Gazprombank, and a 4.7 per cent stake … was purchased by Stroitransgaz … a construction company created by Gazprom structures … Today that company is responsible for most of the construction work on the Yamal-Europe natural gas pipeline and at the Urengoi and Yamburg gas fields … However, the Gazprom-created company has gradually and imperceptibly slipped from under the natural monopoly's control, and today Gazprom owns just 0.03 per cent of the company's total stock. Meanwhile, a controlling interest is now held by a group of private investors … that has very close ties

to Gazprom ... [Stroitransgaz is] owned largely by relatives and associates of top Gazprom executives' (*Noviye Izvestia*, 2 September 1999, pp. 1–2: *IHT*, 1999, vol. 51, no. 36, p. 10).

3. In 1994 half Gazprom's shares were exchanged for vouchers in closed privatization auctions, going in large part to managers, employees and residents in gas-producing regions. Gazprom itself purchased an additional 10 per cent of shares at par value from the government, which owns the remaining 40 per cent. Shares cannot be registered in new owners' names without management approval. Gazprom's tax compliance is low and is allowed to retain billions in a tax-free 'stabilization fund' for investment (World Bank 1996: 119).

4. On 25 April 1994 28.7 per cent of Gazprom's shares were publicly auctioned for vouchers reserved for Russian citizens. Gazprom was to buy 10 per cent of its own shares (all or some of which could, later on, be sold to foreigners). The staff of Gazprom already owned 15 per cent of the shares (since February 1994), 5.2 per cent were to be reserved for inhabitants of the Yamal-Nenetsk autonomous region in the far north and the state would hold the remaining roughly 40 per cent for at least three years (*FT*, 23 February 1994, and 27 April 1994, p. 3). In 1994 34 per cent of its shares were sold for privatization vouchers in a closed auction held mainly in gas-producing regions. Employees hold an additional 15 per cent share, while the state retains a 40 per cent stake. Later in 1995 it was planned to sell to foreign investors 9 percentage points of the 10 per cent of the shares held by the company (*FT*, 10 January 1995, p. 17, and 27 March 1995, p. 19). The sale of 9 per cent of its shares to foreigners was postponed on 26 March 1995 (*FT*, 27 March 1995, p. 19). (Foreigners own less than 3 per cent of the company's stock: *IHT*, 2 July 1996, p. 13. On 15 May 1997 it was confirmed that foreign investors would be allowed to purchase no more than 9 per cent of Gazprom's shares: *RET*, 1997, no. 2, p. 120.)

5. The government owns 40.87 per cent of Gazprom. Foreign investors already hold a separate 9 per cent stake. Gazprom also has two strategic partners (Royal Dutch/Shell Group and Ente Nazionale Idrocarburi of Italy), which hold equity stakes (*IHT*, 12 June 1998, p. 19).

Although the state has a 40 per cent stake, only 5 per cent of shares were originally directly controlled by the state. The remaining 35 per cent of shares were left under the control of Gazprom's management (*IHT*, 16 April 1997, p. 15). On 13 May 1997 it was announced that a new ten-member board (headed by Boris Nemtsov, who was keen to lower gas prices) was to oversee Gazprom. The state would regain control of the whole 40 per cent stake. It was revealed that in 1993 certain members of Gazprom's management had been given future share options to buy the 35 per cent on highly favourable terms. This concession was withdrawn (*IHT*, 14 May 1997, pp. 1, 7). The salary of Gazprom's chairman would henceforth be a percentage of the dividend paid to the government. Other companies would have open access to Gazprom's pipelines (*FT*, 26 May 1997, p. 22, and 27 May 1997, p. 22).

On 28 May 1997 a presidential decree ended Gazprom's veto over the sale of shares on the internal, secondary market. This market is supposed to be closed to foreigners (who are thus supposed to be confined to foreign markets). 'Theoretically, the domestic market is closed to outside investors, but foreigners have bought shares through grey funds, vehicles set up by foreign fund managers to exploit legal loopholes. Buying shares on the local market has been attractive, as they are trading at about one-third the price of the stock offered to foreigners.' The 28 May decree sought to close the loopholes in the legislation by, for example, establishing a broad definition of foreign investors. The grey funds were allowed to keep current holdings but forbidden to buy additional shares (*FT*, 29 May 1997, p. 36).

Gazprom's debt to the government amounted to over 14.8 trillion (14,800 billion) roubles. Gazprom agreed (on 14 April 1997) to pay half its tax debt (about $1.2 billion) by 10 June 1997. A 28 April 1997 decree specified that the unified network would not be broken up, but Gazprom that would lose its monopoly of new gas deposits (which would instead be auctioned off). Gazprom would have to publish annual reports (*RET*, 1997, no. 2, p. 119). The chairman of Gazprom presented a restructuring plan involving the shedding of about 100,000 people from its payroll (pp. 120–1). On 14 April 1997 Gazprom announced that it would hive off some of its subsidiaries, releasing up to a quarter of its 375,000 workers (*Transition*, 1997, vol. 8, no. 3, p. 13). Gazprom claims that it is owed 70 trillion roubles by its customers (p. 15).

On 30 June 2000 Dmitri Medvedev, acting deputy head of the presidential administration and 'a key ally of President Vladimir Putin', became chairman of Gazprom, replacing former prime minister Viktor Chernomyrdin as head of the board. 'The government holds a 38 per cent stake in the company, which is the world's largest natural gas producer, with about a quarter of the world's reserves. It is also the largest and richest company in Russia, contributing a quarter of total federal tax revenues.' Minority shareholders managed to gain management representation for the first time on 30 June, electing two members to the eleven-member board. They were the deputy head of Germany's Ruhrgas AG (which owns 4 per cent of Gazprom) and former Russian finance minister Boris Fyodorov. Four members were nominated by the state, giving it five seats, while four members, including the chief executive, Rem Vyakhirev, who has been in the position for seven years. 'He has come under criticism for a lack of disclosure about the company's operations' (*IHT*, 1 July 2000, p. 11). 'Vladimir Putin … increased his control over Gazprom, the country's gas monopoly which holds a quarter of the world's reserves, by installing a close ally as the chairman of the board of directors. Dmitri Medvedev, thirty-four, a first deputy head of the Kremlin administration, was voted into the post at the company's annual general meeting … Gazprom's own executives, who held six of the eleven seats on the board, have not only lost an ally in Mr Chernomyrdin, a former chief executive … but also seen two of their own candidates ousted in favour of minority shareholder representatives ... Both Boris Fyodorov from the Russian fund UFG and ... the deputy head of Ruhrgas of Germany were elected to the board. Ruhrgas owns 3.5 per cent of Gazprom. Rem Vyakirev, Mr Chernomyrdin's protégé and Gazprom's chief executive, retained his position and his place on the board in spite of apparent antagonism towards Mr Putin. He stated earlier this week that he intended to remain until May next year [2001]. However, Gazprom's four executives on the new board are out-numbered by the five representatives of the Russian state – which holds a 38 per cent stake – including German Gref, the economics minister, who is another close ally of Mr Putin' (*FT*, Wednesday 1 July 2000, p. 8).

'Gazprom has been accused of transfer pricing much of its profits away to Itera, a little-known Florida registered company which the Russian press links to top Gazprom management. Itera denies that it is owned by Gazprom management and says it is the victim of a political vendetta' (*FT*, Survey on the World Economy, 22 September 2000, p. xvi). 'The directors of Gazprom ... yesterday [27 October 2000] banned their top managers from transferring assets or making any transactions involving its shares without the approval of the board' (*FT*, 28 October 2000, p. 10). 'Last week it emerged that relatives of its past and present management own large stakes in Stroitransgaz, a gas pipe construction company that not only receives large contracts from Gazprom, but has also acquired 4.8 per cent of the gas monopoly for $2.5 million. Brokers estimate that the minimum market price for those shares in 1995, the year of the transaction, would have been about $80 million ... Itera ... [was] set up eight years ago ... Today it is the second largest natural gas company in Russia ... "Itera is growing and Gazprom is shrinking", says Boris Fyoderov, a former finance minister under Mr Yeltsin who now represents minority shareholders on Gazprom's board ... The board plans to discuss Gazprom's relationship with Itera this month' (*FT*, Wednesday 1 November 2000, p. 25).

Critics of the way oil and gas have been privatized

Severe critics include even former advisers such as Sachs and Åslund:

1. Jeffrey Sachs (*IHT*, 6 December 1995, p. 10) draws a contrasting picture of privatization in various sectors. 'When the economic reforms got underway in 1992 Russia's vast natural resources provided unparalleled opportunities for theft by officials. Oil, gas, diamond and metal ore deposits were nominally owned by the state and thus by nobody. They were ripe for stealing – or for "spontaneous privatization" as Russians cynically call it. The main method of legal privatization, a combination of selling and giving shares to the people, was amazingly honest when it involved manufacturing enterprises, although some managers later abused it. But when natural resource enterprises were privatized the system was often skirted or compromised by ad hoc decrees and hidden arrangements. The biggest plums, the oil and gas enterprises, are worth tens of billions of dollars. The Soviet state earned vast sums on sales,

especially exports, but much of this income now flows to a few private pockets, creating shortfalls in the government's budget. Until recently government licences to export oil were given free to insiders, at a cost to the budget of billions of dollars a year.' In a later article Sachs wrote: 'In the past three years, under IMF auspices, Russia has been borrowing short-term funds from abroad to keep a corrupt and mismanaged government afloat. The Fund stood by as the government squandered tens of billions of dollars by transferring state-owned oil and gas companies to cronies at cut-rate prices' (*IHT*, 5 June 1998, p. 8).

2. Åslund (Business Central Europe 1995: 15) makes similar points. 'The oil and gas company executives were the prime advocates of low oil and gas prices. They bought oil at the domestic price on their own account and sold it abroad at the world market price ... The low domestic prices caused their companies losses, but that made shares in loss-making enterprises cheaper and the oil executives bought undervalued stock in the companies they managed for their illicit personal gains. This double fraud came to light in 1995 and it cannot survive for much longer.'

3. 'The [energy] industry's present managers are mostly the people who ran the energy industry when it was the property of the state. They were handed it virtually as a gift, in the guise of its privatization, and at a stroke were made rich and powerful. Their principal political ally is Mr Yeltsin's prime minister, Viktor Chernomyrdin' (William Pfaff, *IHT*, 13 June 1996, p. 8). '"Oligarchs" have profited from what were described as privatizations of Russian industry but were actually appropriations of Russia's state assets by people in power and their associates' (William Pfaff, *IHT*, 2 September 1999, p. 8).

Later developments in oil and gas privatization:

4 November 1997. A presidential decree lifts the 15 per cent limit (established in 1992) on foreign shareholding in Russian oil companies (*CDSP*, 1997, vol. XLIX, no. 45, p. 15).

17 November 1997. BP buys a 10 per cent stake in Sidanko (for $571 million). Oneximbank is the main shareholder in Sidanko, Russia's fourth largest oil company. Royal Dutch/Shell announces a strategic alliance with Gazprom, one aspect of which is a commitment by the former to invest $1 billion in a convertible bond to be issued in early 1998 (i.e. convertible into Gazprom shares in the future). Joint development projects are planned in both cases (*FT*, 18 November 1997, p. 1; *The Economist*, 24 January 1998, p. 76).

19 January 1998. Yukos (Russia's second largest oil producer) and Sibneft (fifth largest), announce plans to merge. The new company will be called Yuksi, 60 per cent held by Yukos. Eastern Oil was acquired by Yukos in December 1997 and East Siberian Oil and Gas was recently acquired by Sibneft, both at privatization sales. Yuksi will have about 22 per cent of Russia's crude oil production, will surpass Lukoil (20 per cent) as Russia's largest oil company and will be the world's third largest oil company in terms of production behind Royal Dutch/Shell and Exxon. Yuksi will be the world's largest oil company by proven reserves. The chief executive of Yuksi will be Mikhail Khodorkovsky (chairman of Yukos). Boris Berezovsky is thought to own about 90 per cent of Sibneft, but he denies this. (*IHT,* 20 January 1998, p. 11; *FT,* 20 January 1998, p. 26; *The Times*, 20 January 1998, p. 33; *The Independent*, 20 January 1998, p. 21; *The Telegraph*, 20 January 1998, p. 26; *The Economist*, 24 January 1998, pp. 5, 74, 76; *Business Central Europe*, February 1998, p. 27.) But merger talks were called off on 25 May 1998, reasons including recent sharp falls in world oil prices and financial uncertainty in Russia.

23 March 1998. The French oil company Elf Aquitaine pays $528 million for a 5 per cent stake in Yuksi (*IHT,* 24 March 1998, p. 13; *FT,* 24 March 1998, p. 25).

26 May 1998. There are no bids for a 75 per cent plus one share stake in Rosneft (the oil company), the starting price of which was set at $2.1 billion plus a $400 million tax arrears and investment obligation. Reasons included recent sharp falls in world oil prices and financial uncertainty in Russia. On 2 June the offer price was reduced to $1.6 billion plus a $62.5 million investment requirement. (*IHT,* 26 June 1998, p. 15, and 4 July 1998, p. 12; *FT,* 3 June 1998, p. 2, and 4 July 1998, p. 20.)

3 July 1998. Royal Dutch/Shell withdraws from the bid for Rosneft.

7 July 1998. BP withdraws from the bid for Rosneft.

10 July 1998. Owing to the absence of bidders, the Rosneft sale scheduled for 21 July is put off until 27 October 1998.

2 November 1998. Yeltsin signs a decree allowing the sale of up to 5 per cent of Gazprom. The 5 per cent stake may be sold in parts. The decree confirms a rise in the limit for foreign participation in Gazprom from 9 per cent to 14 per cent (*FT,* 3 November 1998, p. 3). The following day it was reported that Russia had put on sale 2.5 per cent of Gazprom at a starting price of $651 million. Payments would be in roubles at the market rate on the sale date (*IHT,* 5 November 1998, p. 17). The single-lot 2.5 per cent stake was to be sold before the end of 1998 (*FT,* 5 November 1998, p. 2).

19 December 1998. It is announced that Germany's Ruhrgas has bought a 2.5 per cent stake in Gazprom for $660 million, $9 million more than the $651 million the minimum asking price. The head of the federal property fund says that most of the proceeds will be be injected into the federal budget. Rurhgas has to retain the stake for at least five years (*FT,* 21 December 1998, p. 2; *IHT,* 21 December 1998, p. 15). The government now owns a 38.37 per cent stake in Gazprom (*FT,* 7 August 1999, p. 2).

26 August 1999. The government increases its representation on Gazprom's eleven-person board from four to five (*FT,* 27 August 1999, p. 3). The state, which owns 35 per cent of the stock, increases its representation on the board of directors to five. Rem Vyakhirev remains chairman (*CDSP,* 1999, vol. 51, no. 34, p. 17).

29 October 1999. 'An obscure Cyprus-based business on Friday [29 October] appeared to have won the bidding for a significant stake in Lukoil ... in a partial-privatization process that had been criticised by some observers as being geared towards a bid from the company's own executives. Reforma Investments bid just over $200 million for a 9 per cent stake in Lukoil ... Under the terms of the auction the privatization process required two competing bids and a minimum tender price of $200 million ... The sale required partial payment in cash, with the remaining half of the money coming in the form of investment commitments ... The sale, plus a further 1 per cent stake, will also reduce the Russian state's stake from 28 per cent to 18 per cent. A further 9 per cent of Lukoil is owned by Arco [Atlantic Richfield Company], 6 per cent by the staff pension fund, and the remainder by a range of individuals and funds' (*FT*, 1 November 1999, p. 29).

'In October the state property ministry sold a 9 per cent government equity stake in Lukoil ... The parties standing behind the offshore firm were not disclosed. Under the terms of the auction the winner has to invest $240 million in the company in the next six months' (*RET*, Monthly Update, 12 November 1999, p. 13). 'The buyer, a Cyprus-registered company, is thought to be owned by Lukoil itself' (*RET*, 1999, vol. 8, no. 4, p. 99).

23 November 1999. An agreement is signed in Moscow by the Blue Stream Pipeline Company, comprising Gazprom and ENI (Italy), on the design and construction of a gas pipeline to connect Russia with Turkey under the Black Sea (*RET*, 1999, vol. 8, no. 4, p. 100).

26 November 1999. 'BP Amoco yesterday [26 November] raised the prospect of cutting back its activities in Russia after what it claimed was the illegal forced sale of its principal oil investment in western Siberia to a local competitor. Chernogorneft, the main oil producing subsidiary of Sidanko, the Russian group in which BP Amoco has taken effective control, was sold out of bankruptcy to the Tyumen Oil Company (TNK) for $176 million ... BP Amoco purchased a 10 per cent stake in Sidanko in 1997, but both the Russian company and a number of its subsidiaries were pushed into bankruptcy in the wake of the financial crisis in August last year [1998] ... Sidanko, along with leading Western creditors including the EBRD and the US Ex-Im Bank, found themselves squeezed into a minority on the creditors' committee of Chernogorneft, over which TNK exercised increasing control in the past few months. A series of court appeals by the foreign creditors failed, and in spite of their claims that the rise in oil prices over the past few months meant Chenogorneft ought to have easily been able to pay off its debts, a court-appointed bankruptcy administrator pushed ahead with his plan to hold an auction' (*FT*, 27 November 1999, p. 15).

'Chernogorneft ... sits astride the northern part of the huge Samotlor oil field in western Siberia ... Tyumen Oil Company already controls the southern part of the field ... Sidanko said the bankruptcy process was flawed and the auction unnecessary ... The EBRD said Friday [26 November] that the sale was a "sham ... in violation of a legal injunction issued earlier in the week and was wholly contrary to the concepts of fairness and transparency".

Among those contesting the sale is BP Amoco ... and Renaissance Capital Group's Sputnik Fund, which includes investments of George Soros and the Harvard Endowment ... [Tyumen's] bid was a small fraction of the company's 125,000 barrels a day crude oil output, worth about $1.1 billion a year at current prices ... BP Amoco said it believed the tender was illegal and that Chernogorneft was a viable, profit-making company ... Mr [Vladimir] Potanin's holding company, Interros, which owns 40 per cent of Sidanko, also protested, saying the sale "was conducted in an atmosphere of unprecendented pressure on the court system"' (*IHT*, 27 November 1999, p. 11). 'Sputnik, BP Amoco and some other Chernogorneft creditors say that ... Tyumen Oil has used the bankruptcy process, reportedly through tampering with the courts, to strip away Sidanko's most valuable assets. It had been widely predicted that Tyumen oil would buy Chernogorneft in a court-supervised auction ... similar to the way the company acquired another Sidanko unit, Kondpetroleum, several weeks ago at a rock-bottom price. Critics of Tyumen Oil say the company has used the courts to appoint its own people as external managers of bankrupt Sidanko units to swing the auctions in their favour' (*IHT*, 25 November 1999, p. 17).

'The bankruptcy process itself is often used as another channel for asset-stripping, with the appointment of lenient administrators' (EBRD 1999b: 259).

On Tuesday 21 December 1999 the Clinton administration (on the grounds of national interest) blocked a $500 million loan guarantee for the Tyumen Oil Company from the US Export-Import Bank (*IHT*, 22 December 1999, p. 4). (The loan guarantee was unblocked on 3 April 2000: *FT*, 4 April 2000, p. 15.) 'BP Amoco appears poised to conclude an agreement ... Tyumen Oil would return Chernogorneft to Sidanko and in return receive a stake in Sidanko of 25 per cent of equity plus one share ... BP Amoco would keep the 10 per cent stake it bought in Sidano in 1997, but its voting rights would be the same as Tyumen Oil's. Such holdings are known as "blocking stakes", which would give both concerns seats on the Sidanko board and enough leverage to influence the company's activities' (*IHT*, 22 December 1999, p. 11). 'After shaking up Sidanko, which is bankrupt, BP Amoco could then increase its voting rights in Sidanko to 25 per cent plus one share from the present 20 per cent. However, its direct equity stake would remain at 10 per cent' (*FT*, 22 December 1999, p. 17). '[On 22 December] BP Amoco and OAO Tyumen Oil Company settled a dispute over control of a Siberian production unit, helping the Western giant salvage a $571 million investment in Russia. The accord returns the unit, which controls part of Russia's biggest oil field, to Tyumen Oil's rival OAO Sidenko, of which BP Amoco owns 10 per cent. Tyumen Oil's shareholders will get 25 per cent of Sidanko and work with BP Amoco to develop the field' (*IHT*, 23 December 1999, p. 11). 'Shareholders in the Russian oil group TNK scored a victory over the multinational BP Amoco by persuading it to co-operate in future operations within the country and to acquire over a quarter of the equity in Sidanko. In an agreement signed yesterday [22 December], TNK's principal shareholders – Alfa Group and Access/Renova – will receive 25 per cent plus one share in Sidanko, the Russian oil group in which BP Amoco holds a 10 per cent stake. In exchange TNK's shareholders will hand back debt-free Chernogorneft, Sidnako's principal oil producing subsidiary ... The deal has cost TNK about $200 million compared with $484 million paid by BP Amoco for a 10 per cent stake in Sidanko acquired in 1997, since when a sharp rise in world oil prices has helped increase the value of the investment ... The deal means that TNK's owners, including "oligarchs" Mikhail Friedman and Peter Aven, will be co-operating with another oligarch, Vladimir Potanin, whose Interros group has the largest shareholding in Sidanko' (*FT*, 23 December 1999, p. 25).

'Shareholders of OAO Sidanko ... have agreed to return $484 million in assets of its subsidiary OAO Chernogorneft to BP Amoco PLC' (*IHT*, 26 August 2000, p. 11).

The 'shares-for-loans' scheme

On 31 August 1995 a presidential decree described what was to prove a highly controversial 'shares-for-loans' scheme, allowing certain Russian banks to assume management control of state shares in selected enterprises for use as collateral in return for loans. The low level of privatization revenue raised by that time was a major consideration. (In 1995 the government raised only 6 trillion roubles from privatization, compared with the 9.3 trillion roubles expected: *The Economist*, 6 January 1996, p. 63.) Interest was to be paid and the loan was to be repaid within three years at the original value 'adjusted' for the intervening change in the rouble value of the Ecu. If the lender and the state property committee agreed, the former could at any time sell the shares and keep the 'adjusted' value of the loan plus 30 per cent of the excess of the sale price over that value. For each block of shares there would be a competition and the block would be awarded to the one offering the largest loan. For strategic decisions the voting rights of shares could be exercised only with the agreement of the state property committee (*RET*, Monthly Update, 19 September 1995, p. 11). On 2 November 1995 the president signed a decree deferring the earliest date when investors could be given permission to sell the acquired shares from 1 January 1996 to 1 September 1996 (*RET*, Monthly Update, 14 November 1995, p. 10). In certain cases foreign investors were not allowed to participate in the auction (announced on 17 October 1995) and the winner was required to invest in the enterprise and pay its tax arrears (*RET*, 1995, vo. 4, no. 3, p. 93).

The first round of mortgage auctions began on 17 November 1995. But the 'shares-for-loans' scheme was ended on 28 December 1995 owing to vociferous criticism:

1. 'The complications and lack of transparency engendered by this measure will probably decrease the value of the shares to be sold and reduce interest in the auctions. There are also concerns that the auctions will not be free and

competitive: banks which are charged with management of the auctions are also permitted to take part in the auction.' Despite the fact that large blocks of shares in some of the best known enterprises were on offer, there were few bidders [owing to collusion among the potential bidders: see below], leading to low bids. The 38 per cent stake in the largest nickel producer in the country, Norilsk Nikel, was won by Oneximbank (United Export-Import Bank), Russia's largest private commercial bank and the bank responsible for organizing the auction. One bidder who offered a much higher price was not allowed to take part in the auction, allegedly 'because the bank that guaranteed the bid had insufficient capitalization'. A 40.1 per cent stake in the oil company Surgut was sold to its pension fund. 'One concern is that the government will lose control over state shares which it continues to own under this scheme. While there are safeguards, and limits on the decision rights of winners ... there may still be problems in overseeing enterprises during this period' (*RET*, 1995, vol. 4, no. 3, pp. 93–4, 100–2). 'The most controversial feature of the auctions was that banks acting as depositors and organizers of the auctions were also allowed to participate in them. Out of the twelve auctions which actually took place (four were stopped because of lack of bids), six were won by the banks acting as depositors for companies affiliated with them. Another four of the companies were won by organizations linked to the companies themselves and only two companies ended up in the hands of outsiders. The distribution of the winning bids around the starting price shows the degree of competition on these auctions. The lack of transparent procedures, and restrictions on participation and competition, have led to widespread concerns over corruption ... The proceedings illustrate how the controversy over the shares-for-loans scheme also reflects a struggle by management to avoid outside control of their enterprise' (*RET*, 1995, vol. 4, no. 4, pp. 101–2). 'The banks were allowed to impose tender conditions [such as future investment] on the buyer of the stake that would be difficult for any unaffiliated company to fulfil' (*RET*, 1997, no. 1, p. 151). 'In each of the shares-for-loans sales the winner of the mortgage auction skewed the subsequent sale in its own favour by imposing conditions that would be extremely expensive for outside bidders to fulfil' (*RET*, 1997, no. 3, p. 103). (Since late 1996 in a few cases the state shares held as collateral under the shares-for-loans scheme have been auctioned off, typically to a connected party of the original loan: EBRD 1997a: 32.)

'Contrary to expectations, the government has so far decided not to pay back any of the loans, so it is almost certain that the banking groups will opt to buy up the shares themselves in order to consolidate their control over the enterprises ... It remains to be seen how the banks decide to treat their new acquisitions. There is some anecdotal evidence that some banks are making serious attempts to improve the management of the enterprises in their possession' (*RET*, 1996, vol. 5, no. 3, pp. 123–4). (The government did not repay loans by 1 September 1996: *Business Central Europe*, October 1996, p. 63.)

2. 'Russia's big financial-industrial groups limited competition among themselves, ensuring they all bought state assets at knock-down prices in the controversial "shares-for-loans" privatization schemes' (John Thornhill, *FT*, 8 April 1998, p. 30).

3. '[In] earlier auctions ... the tycoons collaborated to gain huge shares of industry for a fraction of their actual worth' (Yavlinsky 1998: 70).

4. 'In practice, there may be little competition, and lenders will probably have understandings with the management of the companies involved. The result may well be a series of *de facto* management buy-outs, mostly at below-market prices' (*The Economist*, 18 November 1995, p. 100). 'The scheme became bogged down in accusations that it [the government] was handing over Russia's best companies to a small group of insiders at a fraction of their market price' (Business Central Europe 1995: 34).

5. Russia's largest private bank, Oneximbank, was the initiator of the loans-for-shares scheme 'whose blatant favourism ignited a political scandal that inflamed the presidential campaign and cost Anatoli Chubais ... his job ... When the auctions began last fall it became all too obvious that a fix was in. Foreign investors were barred from bidding for the most desirable assets, and the same banks that were assigned by the government to organize the auctions ended up winning them, and usually at only a fraction over the minimum bid. Shares in some of Russia's largest oil conglomerates, including Lukoil and Yukos, were sold off for what Western analysts considered to be a fraction of their real value' (Alessandra Stanley, *IHT*, 29 January 1996, p. 11).

6. 'When the time came for the government to decide whether to repay the loans and thus reclaim their shares (in late 1996 or in 1997 depending on the shares in question), it declined to do so for financial reasons. The bank-led FIGs [financial-industrial groups] that had acquired the shares in trust were thus required by law to sell them via a tender to complete the privatization process. In all four instances the bank-led FIGs "sold" the shares back to themselves in auctions they also organized. Such sales represented a way of circumventing the government because, according to the terms of the original 1995 shares-for-loans deal, whenever the auction winners sold their shares the government was entitled to 70 per cent of the profits. These incestuous transactions released the bank-led FIGs from that obligation, leaving them free to sell these companies later and keep the profits for themselves. Conducting such closed auctions necessitated that no other group be willing or able to submit a competitive bid' (Johnson 1997: 355).

7. 'Afraid that it had no political allies, the desperate Yeltsin administration decided to create some. The Kremlin's vehicle was the shares-for-loans privatization scheme, which, over a few months in the autumn of 1995, transferred controlling stakes in some of Russia's most valuable companies to government insiders at a fraction of their potential worth. The programme provoked instant and outraged attacks at home and abroad. But it paid dividends at the ballot box on 3 July 1996, when Mr Yeltsin cruised to victory,

aided by the vigorous organizational and material support of the small group of bankers he had made into billionaires' (Chrystia Freeland, *FT*, Survey, 9 April 1997, p. i). 'Loans-for-shares strutted on to the political stage … at a cabinet meeting of the Russian government on 30 March 1995 … Thanks to the scheme he was about to pitch to the cabinet, within two years *Business Week* would estimate that his empire accounted for 10 per cent of Russia's GDP … [Vladimir] Potanin's proposal amounted to … a crude trade of property for political support which promised to keep the communists out of the Kremlin in exchange for wildly enriching Potanin and the business cartel he has assembled … By the end of the year [1995] the government had privatized the behemoths of the Russian economy, including the world's dominant producer of nickel and several reserve rich oil companies, selling them for a fraction of their potential market value … For Russia's market reformers it was a necessary pact, made morally permissible by their absolute faith in the curative powers of private property, however it may have been acquired. Shortly after the loans-for-shares deal, [Anatoli] Chubais explained … "They steal and steal and steal … They [the country's businessmen] are stealing absolutely everything and it is impossible to stop them. But let them steal and take their property. They will then become owners and decent administrators of this property" … In Vladimir Putin's Russia there is not very much left to steal' (Chrystia Freeland, *FT*, Weekend, 27 May 2000, p. ix). 'The scheme was so brazen and so byzantine that it was months, if not years, before the rest of the world woke up to it. At heart loans-for-shares was a crude trade of property for political support. In exchange for some of Russia's most valuable companies (including several oil firms and the world's largest nickel mine), a group of businessmen – the oligarchs – threw their political and financial muscle behind the Kremlin' (Freeland 2000: 14).

('It is highly unlikely that seven bankers control 50 per cent of the Russian economy, as the deputy secretary of the "security council" [Boris Berezovsky] recently boasted to a Western newspaper': *RET*, 1996, vol. 5, no. 3, p. 118.)

'The oligarchs extorted a heavy price for their support of Yeltsin. They received shares in the most valuable state-owned companies as security against loans they made to the state budget in an infamous "loans for shares" scheme. After Yeltsin won the election these companies were put up for auction and the oligarchs divided them up among themselves' (George Soros, *The New York Review of Books*, 2000, vol. XLVII, no. 6, p. 12).

8. Pyotr Aven, the president of Alphabank and former minister of foreign economic relations (*CDSP*, 1999, vol. 51, no. 7, p. 3): 'Based on Alphabank's experience participating (on the whole unsuccessfully) in such auctions, I can assert that in all the "major" deals the winner was known in advance, before the bidding. The whole thing really amounted to a select group of businessmen being "appointed" millionaires (or even billionaires), with the idea that they would become the main sources of support for the current regime.'

9. 'The "loans-for-shares" scheme, in which major Russian banks obtained shares in firms with strong potential as collateral for loans to the state – turned into a fraudulent shambles, which drew criticism from many, including supporters of the first, mass phase of Russian privatization' (Nellis 1999: 17).

10. 'The loans-for-shares deals at the end of 1995 were a scandal ... A few large banks were allowed to privatize some large enterprises in auctions they themselves controlled. In fact, only fifteen enterprises were involved and in some cases sold only a small share of their stocks. But a few huge cash cows did change hands, most notably three big oil companies: Yukos, Sibneft and Sidanko. No qualitative change accompanied these takeovers. The new majority owners did not behave like self-interested proprietors but just continued the management theft, primarily by selling the products below market prices to their own trading companies, letting the old companies deteriorate' (Åslund 1999b: 69–70).

11. In a reference to privatization as a whole in Russia, Martin Wolf cites the following estimate: 'One estimate is that in Russia assets worth between $50 billion and $60 billion were privatized for just $1.5 billion' (*FT*, 10 November 1999, p. ii).[1]

12. 'Sibneft [Russia's sixth largest oil company] is only about four year's old ... Like a number of leading oil companies, Sibneft sprang from a now-notorious programme called "loans for shares" in which the Kremlin handed out stakes in major industries – almost always to insider friends – as collateral for loans it never repaid. In Sibneft's case a company tied to Boris Berezovsky ... won the rights to 51 per cent of the stock in 1995. In return for a $100 million loan he got control of a company then valued at roughly $600 million, including Russia's best oil refinery and proven petroleum reserves larger than those of Texaco Inc' (Michael Wines, *IHT*, 29 December 1999, p. 13).

13. Vladimir Potanin bought Norilsk Nickel for $170 million in 1997. The company is now worth $1.5 billion (*The Times*, 22 June 2000, p. 16).

Vladimir Potanin (president of the holding company Interros): 'I am known as an oligarch ... [one of the ones who] were first called the "seven bankers" and later the oligarchs ... [Privatization] vouchers were either bought up by the financial institutions or ended up in the hands of the old nomenklatura, the so-called "red directors" who became the real owners of many factories. More often than not these red directors happened to be hopeless owners ... So in 1995 the state decided it had to sell property to effective owners. This was when the idea of "loans-for-shares" emerged. Although I do not deny that I was the author, I would like to point out that the concept was changed to a great extent as a result of political pressure on government from the red directors. The original scheme was simple: the government gained loans collateralized by shares of the companies for sale. The government was supposed to draw up an agreement that included a commission for sale within three years ... instead of selling a company for a low price the sale was postponed for three years, during which the company was prepared for flotation. The reward for this task was 30 per cent of the increase in price during that period. There was supposed to be tender, with the winner being the company willing to work for the least remuneration. Participation in the shares would not be limited ... In some case the scheme worked as it was originally planned. For example, 38 per cent of Norilisk Nickel was used as collateral for a $170 million loan in 1995. The shares were sold in 1997 at a far higher price, with $250 million going to the state budget, more than $300 million invested in the company and about $130 million used to pay off company debt. But that came later. During the initial loans-for-shares auctions the red directors and the old nomenklatura pressured the government, which was itself far from united. Red directors lobbied for the sale of non-controlling stakes, no access to foreign investors and other measures. The government gave in and changed the scheme. This was later criticised and rightly so' (*FT*, 29 June 2000, p. 27).

Vladimir Potanin's Interros company is the controlling shareholder in the Norilsk Nickel mining complex, the world's largest producer of palladium and nickel, 'accounting for 2 per cent of Russia's GDP' (*FT*, 1 July 2000, p. 8).

Crime, corruption and privatization

A number of analysts have made the link between crime, corruption and privatization:

1. 'Russia's new private sector is dominated by former but still intact Soviet monopolies seized by ex-communist officials who have become the core of a semi-criminalized business class' (Stephen Cohen, *IHT*, 13 December 1996, p. 8).

2. 'Who could have expected that the new, "democratic" authorities would themselves openly and impudently fire the starting gun for the unconstrained plundering of the national wealth for the benefit of certain individuals appointed by the authorities from the old nomenklatura and the "nouveaux riches" – through export licences and quotas, preferential customs treatment for imports and, finally, the divvying up of state property among [enterprise] directors in the course of "Chubais-style" privatization?' (Nikolai Shmelev, *CDSP*, 1997, vol. XLIX, no. 1, pp. 5–6).

3. 'In the guise of privatization, the population has been swindled of its national resources and industry by the people who are now manipulating its politics' (William Pfaff, *IHT*, 22 April 1998, p. 9).

4. 'Russian organized crime groups secured a massive transfer of state property because the privatization occurred rapidly, on a huge scale, without legal safeguards, and without transparency ... The Russian mafia now controls more than 40 per cent of the total economy. In some sectors, such as consumer markets, real estate and banking, their role is even greater ... Organized crime groups are dominating both legitimate and illegitimate economic sectors simultaneously. The new owners, often uninterested in making their enterprises function, drain the resources and transfer the proceeds abroad,

exacerbating the problems of both capital flight and nonpayment of wages' (Louise Shelley, *Transition*, February 1997, vol. 8, no. 1. p. 7).

Further developments in privatization

24 June 1997. A new law on privatization is passed by the State Duma. It was passed by the Council of the Federation in early July and signed by the president on 25 July 1997. Under the constitution laws passed by the State Duma override presidential decrees and government resolutions (*RET*, 1997, no. 3, p. 105). 'Previously, privatization had proceeded on the basis of presidential decrees and government resolutions. The new law endorses most existing methods of privatization, but bans shares-for-loans auctions and investment tenders. In addition, it makes it easier for the government to reclaim property in cases where privatization laws were violated or tender conditions not fulfilled' (p. 100). 'The new law does not mark a break with the current privatization policy: instead it collects and tightens regulations on existing auction procedures, with certain modifications; it clarifies the state's prerogatives in strategic enterprises in which it has retained a "golden share"; and lays down stringent penalties for buyers who fail to fulfil auction conditions' (p. 103). The details are as follows:

1. 'Investment tenders' are abolished owing to the difficulties of verification. ('Investment tenders' are those in which the government sets a price for the stake to be sold and then awards it to the bidder who pledged to invest the most in the enterprise.) The conditions that may be attached to 'commercial tenders with investment conditions' are clarified. (Here the government specifies a minimum level of investment and then awards the stake to the bidder offering the highest price.) A new possible form of tender is introduced, namely the 'commercial tender with social conditions', in which the winner may be required to maintain a certain level of employment, retrain workers, refrain from reducing worker benefits or changing the enterprise's area of operations, or to implement environmental clean-ups (p. 103).

2. Competitive tenders are to be held for the right to manage state shares in the run-up to privatization and then to organize the auction. The new law explicitly prohibits any side deals between the organizer of the auction and any one of the participants (p. 103). (Organizers of privatization tenders are no longer allowed to make bids: Deutsche Morgan Grenfell, *Focus: Eastern Europe*, 5 September 1997, p. 43.)

3. The new law clarifies the state's control rights in enterprises in which it has a 'golden share' or a minority ownership stake in the interests of national security, public health or the public interest (p. 104). ('Golden shares' give the state, for example, a seat on the enterprise's board of directors and the power to veto major changes.)

4. Tender winners are not allowed to take full possession of their shares until they have completed the required investment programme. If they

ultimately do not meet the conditions the state takes back the property . This applies retroactively. In cases where privatization rules are violated the state can apply to the courts to take back the property (p. 105).

5. The new law gives workers a veto over their enterprise's privatization plan, although after two such vetoes the government must choose a plan (p. 106).

6. The government will seek parliamentary approval for its annual privatization targets (p. 121).

7. The privatization of particularly large enterprises requires a presidential decree: Deutsche Morgan Grenfell (*Focus: Eastern Europe*, 5 September 1997, p. 43).

18 July 1997. The Alfa Group (one of the largest financial-industrial groups without an oil company) buys 40 per cent of the Tyumen Oil Company in a tender in which it pledges more than the minimum investment (*RET*, 1997, no. 3, p. 106).

25 July 1997. A consortium (Mustcom) comprising Oneximbank, Deutsche Morgan Grenfell, Morgan-Stanley and George Soros win the auction for a 25 per cent stake (plus one share) in Svyazinvest. This gives Mustcom a veto over any attempt to change the charter of Svyazinvest. Svyazinvest (established in 1995) is a telecommunications holding company, with controlling stakes of 51 per cent in eighty-five (out of eighty-seven) regional telecommunications companies. It also has a controlling stake in Rostelcom (the dominant long-distance and international provider of telephone services). (In 1997 the government added its 38 per cent stake in Rostelcom to the charter capital of Svyazinvest.) A further 24 per cent of Svyazinvest was to be sold to Russian investors in 1998, with the state retaining a 51 per cent stake. (*RET*, 1997, no. 3, pp. 106–7, 121; *FT*, 26 July 1997, p. 2; *IHT*, 26 July 1997, p. 11.) (Rostelcom controlled some 80 per cent of telephone lines, practically all long-distance domestic traffic and much of the international traffic. The state owned 51 per cent of shares and 22 per cent of shares were to be offered to the public on 14 March–12 April 1994: *FT*, 18 February 1994, p. 2.)

'That, its enemies argue, is the game [prisoners' dilemma] which Oneximbank played last year when it broke with a collusive agreement among Russia's business barons and bid high for the government's 25 per cent stake in Svyazinvest, the national telecommunications holding company. Before that bid, Russia's big financial-industrial groups limited competition among themselves, ensuring they all bought state assets at knock-down prices in the controversial "shares-for-loans" privatization schemes' (John Thornhill, *FT*, 8 April 1998, p. 30).

'This auction was to be the first where competitive bids were held for a privatizing company. Unlike earlier auctions, where the tycoons collaborated to gain huge shares of industry for a fraction of their actual worth, during the Svyazinvest auction the leaders of the rival industrial syndicates could not agree on who would get the company and were therefore forced to bid against each other. The "bankers' war" that ensued was fought not with bullets but through allegations of graft aired by their media outlets. As a result, some of these tycoons were removed from their government posts and corruption charges were levelled against Chubais and his privatization team' (Yavlinsky 1998: 70).

'The auction precipitated a knockdown, drag-out fight among the oligarchs, a falling out among thieves. Some of the oligarchs were eager to make the transition to legitimacy while others resisted it because they were incapable of working in a legitimate manner. The main opponent of the auction and its outcome was Boris Berezovsky. After his allies lost the auction he vowed to destroy Chubais ... Berezovsky revealed that Chubais had received $90,000 from a phony book contract, which was in fact the other oligarchs' payment for his service as Yeltsin's campaign manager ... [Berezovsky] genuinely believed that he and the oligarchs had bought the government by paying for Yeltsin's reelection [in 1996] and that the government had reneged on the bargain by allowing a genuine auction for Svyazinvest. He was determined to bring down Chubais for betraying him ... The $90,000 Chubais received in the form of a phony book contract caused his temporary downfall' (George Soros, *The New York Review of Books*, 2000, vol. XLVII, no. 6, p. 14).

5 August 1997. It is announced that the Svift group (affiliated to Oneximbank which has been managing the shares under the shares-for-loans scheme) has won the tender for 38 per cent of the shares in Norilsk Nikel. The conditions of the tender include investment, the paying off of debt to the pension fund and a sum to finance the enterprise's social assets transferred to the municipal government (*RET*, 1997, no. 3, p. 106).

'The auction was conducted by Oneximbank itself, because it had already gained provisional control of the group in the notorious "loans for shares" swap of 1995. Only one other bidder was allowed, and the price paid by Oneximbank was far below the shares' market value' (*FT*, editorial, 11 August 1997, p. 13). Oneximbank had held the Norilsk stake for the government in trust. Oneximbank officials were part of the auction's tender committee' (*IHT*, 16 August 1997, p. 11). 'The bank already controlled Norilsk and a sister firm was running the tender' (*Business Central Europe*, September 1997, p. 17). 'It was organized by a Oneximbank subsidiary and there were only two bidders.' Oneximbank's partners include George Soros ('whose Quantum fund put up much of the money'). Oneximbank 'is effectively the local frontman for a Western financial consortium, comprising not only Mr Soros but also a couple of investment banks like Deutsche Morgan Grenfell, a subsidiary of the powerful German Bank' (p. 31).

(See Vladimir Potanin, above.)

13 August 1997. Alfred Kokh resigns as privatization minister and is replaced by Maxim Boycko.

15 August 1997. Yeltsin: 'The whole furore over Svazinvest and Norilsk Nikel is linked with the perception that certain banks are apparently closer to the soul of Alfred Kokh than others. That should not be the case. Everything should be fair, open and legal.'

30 September 1997. A presidential decree transforms the state property committee into the state property ministry (*RET,* 1997, no. 4, p. 106).

15 October 1999. Dmitri Vasiliev, head of the federal securities commission, resigns.

Vasiliev: 'Only half the work was done on the market from the standpoint of investor protection, despite the fact that I have been working on this for five years. Yes, we have established a government agency whose objectives are to protect investors' rights. But at the same time I think that from the standpoint of civil society not much was done to ensure the protection of investors ... The commission is in a rather difficult position. It is absolutely clear that we have not received the full support of other state bodies concerning investor problems.'

'Earlier this year [1999] Mr Vasiliev clashed with Yukos ... over a series of planned share issues. Yukos's minority investors had protested that these share issues would massively dilute their ownership. Mr Vasiliev said he had received no response from the tax service or the interior ministry after he had passed on information to suggesting Yukos might have violated tax laws and court orders' (*FT,* 16 October 1999, p. 8).

'Mr Vasiliev had launched an investigation of Yukos ... which had diluted the stock held by minority shareholders and moved the shares to obscure offshore tax havens. Yukos is run by Mikhail Khodorkovsky ... Mr Vasiliev said he ran into a brick wall trying to investigate the share dilution. Both Russian government agencies and the offshore havens refused to co-operate, he said' (*IHT,* 16 October 1999, p. 9).

'Dmitri Vasiliev's ... departure coincided with a major setback for the Russian securities commission ... on a test case of minority shareholder rights. The commission had begun an investigation of Yukos [run by Mikhail Khodorkovsky] ... which diluted the stock held by minority shareholders in its oil-producing minorities. The goal appeared to be to wrest control of the subsidiaries from minority shareholders ... As Mr Vasiliev was resigning the securities commission voted to approve the share dilution of one of the three Yukos subsidiaries ... a victory for Mr Khodorkovsky' (*IHT,* 5 November 1999, pp. 13, 15).

'In another case a court this week ordered foreign investors to return to the state their share in the Lomonosov porcelain factory in St Petersburg. The decision, in effect a renationalization of the plant, was an "extremely dangerous precedent", Mr Vasiliev said ... This week ... workers at the plant [the Vyborg pulp and paper mill near the border with Finland] have for more than a year fought to keep out new owners who are foreign investors. On Thursday [14 October], after a court ruling upheld the rights of the new owners to take control, riot police stormed the factory, setting off a confrontation with the workers. The new owners were unable to take control of the factory, which is still being guarded by the workers, who say they fear layoffs' (*IHT*, 16 October 1999, p. 9). 'The Vyborg Pulp and Paper … is in receivership because of debts' (*IHT*, 5 November 1999, p. 13).

'Local Russian security men opened fire on workers occupying a paper and pulp factory, owned by a British-registered company, outside St Petersburg [in Vyborg] early yesterday [14 October], wounding two of them. The security unit known as Taifun [Typhoon], which is part of the justice ministry, was trying to enforce a court order returning the factory, taken over and run by workers since 1998, to private control … The company [Alchem], registered in Britain and Switzerland, is reported by local news agencies to be owned by Russian entrepreneurs … A state commission has now been set up to consider the future ownership of the plant. The workers challenge the legality of its original privatization and want the plant returned to state ownership. They claim the price was "ridiculous" and that actually only 12 per cent of it had been paid' (*The Independent*, 15 October 1999, p. 16).

'The workers claim that Alchem, which owns a majority stake in the the factory, intends to close the plant down and sell its equipment' (*The Times*, 15 October 1999, p. 19).

On 15 October 1999 it was announced that the authorities had given up trying to enforce the court ruling. The special police and marshals of the court had vacated the premises the day before (*CDSP*, 1999, vol. 51, no. 42, p. 9).

The details of the Lomonosov Porcelain Factory case are to be found in *CDSP* (1999, vol. 51, no. 41, p. 9). 'The St Petersburg court of arbitration has upheld the suit filed by the state property ministry and annulled the privatization of the Lomonosov factory, creating a very dangerous precedent. The problem is that the infractions committed in the course of privatizating the Lomonosov factory date back to 1993, and since then the factory's shares have changed hands many times. The current principal shareholders, the United States-Russia Investment Fund [capitalized by the American government] and Kohlberg Kravis Roberts and Company, had nothing to do with what happened six years ago. But they are the ones that are now being stripped of their shares in the factory. Considering the pace at which Russian privatization was carried out, it would be safe to say that a great many investors who have purchased Russian stocks could find themselves in a similar position … Yesterday [12 October] the federal securities commission chairman Dmitri Vasiliev himself filed a request for clarification with the state property ministry. Vasiliev is insisting that the ministry determine and publish as soon as possible a list of enterprises whose privatization involved violations of the law. Vasiliev's position is understandable. And yet the beginning of any effort to compile such a list would signify the onset of a large-scale revision of the results of privatization … The court showed no doubt whatsoever that the privatization of Lomonosov had been illegal. But the problem is that the state property ministry (back then when it was still the state property committee), which is still the plaintiff in the present case, had itself previously approved that same privatization – and then for five years had turned a blind eye to the infractions. They were detected only when a special state commission investigating the buy-up of the shares in Lomonosov by foreign investors accidentally came across them ... It remains to be seen what the foreign investors will get in place of their shares ... The ministry's position ... is based on the premise that there simply was not any privatization, but rather theft of state property ... On 28 January 1993 the enterprise operated under lease reregistered itself as the Lomonosov Porcelain Factory Closed-type Joint Stock Company and the shareholders counted the leased property as their investment in the company's authorized capital. That property still belonged to the state ... Shares were traded in subsequent transactions' (*Kommersant*, 13 October 1999, pp. 1, 4). 'In 1993 ... all the shares were distributed among the factory employees ... The shares in a closed-type joint stock company could be sold only to other shareholders ... Then in 1998 ... one shareholder [of this languishing enterprise] ... "gave away" one of his shares to ... a foreign investment firm ... And once he did the the recipient of that gift became a legal shareholder in Lomonosov. At that point the same [one shareholder] ... sold ... another 217 of his shares, which he could now legally do ... In August of that same year a brisk buy-up of shares held by the employee "owners" began. For their part, the employees, who had virtually ceased being paid, saw no other recourse ... By November foreign fims owned 64 per cent of Lomonosov. It was at this point that Lomonosov's workers ... started clamouring to every possible government authority: "We won't surrender the pride of Russia to the control of foreigners!"' (*Noviye Izvestia*, 13 October 1999, pp. 1, 4).

'Earlier this month [April 2000] the US-Russia Investment Fund won a court ruling that appeared to bring to an end challenges brought by former "red directors" and the federal state property ministry, questioning the legality of the controlling stake it acquired last year [1999] in Lomonosov, the historic St Petersburg porcelain factory' (*FT*, 4 April 2000, p. 23).

19 September 2000. It is announced that Tyumen Oil has won a government auction to buy an 85 per cent stake in a smaller oil producer, Onaco, for $1.1 billion. 'The deal represents the country's biggest asset sale since 1997' (*IHT*, 20 September 2000, p. 13).

'A state-owned company is sold to the highest bidder, with no visible foul play ... for $1.1 billion – more than double the starting price ... [But] foreigners were not allowed to bid, and some of the local contenders are linked by a murky web of connections' (*The Economist*, 23 September 2000, p. 112).

'Continued depressed asset prices and unclear policies resulted in modest and controversial privatization achievements over the past year. The few high-profile privatization deals, including the sale of minority government stakes in Lukoil and Tyumen Oil Company, were characterized by limited transparency and favours to insiders. The reform programme promises a new approach to privatization and foresees a reduction of the 27,000 state-owned companies to about 3,000 over the next few years ... Privatization of twenty major companies is currently earmarked for 2001, including large shareholding blocks in Slavnest and Rosneft and the sale of smaller stakes in Gazprom, Lukoil, Svyazinvest and Aeroflot ... Over the past year the level of payments arrears has substantially declined, while the share of barter transactions in industrial sales dropped from 46 per cent at the start of 1999 to 31 per cent by April 2000' (EBRD 2000b: 202–3).

NOTE

1 'Five years ago state properties worth at least $5 billion were given away for only $1 billion' (Andrei Illarionov, economic adviser to President Putin, *Kommersant*, 16 December 2000, p. 1: *CDSP*, 2000, vol. 52, no. 51, p. 7).

CHAPTER SIX

AGRICULTURE

THE SOVIET ERA

All land in the Soviet Union belonged to the state, although other bodies were allowed use of it. The main agricultural production unit in the early system was not the state farm (*sovkhoz*), but the collective farm (*kolkhoz*). Collectivization during the 1930s was forced, bloody and brutal. Only a nominally independent co-operative, the *kolkhoz* was subject to state plans and delivery quotas at state-determined prices which sometimes bordered on the confiscatory. In 1936 the compulsory procurement price for wheat, plus handling costs, was fifteen roubles a tonne; this wheat was sold to state milling enterprises at 107 roubles per tonne, the turnover tax thus amounting to ninety-two roubles (Nove 1961: 99). During the 1930s the compulsory procurement price for potatoes of 3.6 roubles a tonne contrasted with free market prices varying between thirty-seven and 200 roubles a tonne.

Peasant income for work on the collective farm was residual in nature, constituting that remaining from gross revenue after deduction of all other costs, including social security and equipment. The workday (*trudoden*) was not literally a calendar day, but each particular piece of work was valued at so many workdays. Its value was not known until the end of the year, the residual being divided by the total number of workdays earned. This uncertainty, the infrequency and low levels of remuneration (in kind as well as in money), the negligible impact of individual effort on total farm income, and the fact that the burden of a poor harvest was placed on the shoulders of the peasants (there was even a man-made famine in areas such as the Ukraine) had a disastrous effect on incentives. Peasants devoted so much time to their private plots that a minimum number of days of collective work had to be introduced. Although severely restricted in terms of size and livestock holdings, these plots were a vital source of peasant cash income and of supply of such products as fruit and vegetables, dairy products and meat, which were either consumed in the household or sold on the free market. Private plots contributed 25 per cent of total agricultural output even in the late Soviet period. 'We are dealing with a sector which ... still contributes over 25 per cent of total agricultural production and is still vitally important as a producer of potatoes, vegetables, eggs, fruit, meat and daily produce ... The little plots ... (most often 0.25 ha) receive a disproportionate amount of care and attention ... [this] helps explain the ... fact that 3 per cent of the sown area produces 25 per cent or more of the produce' (Nove 1977: 123).

There is still controversy about the role of agriculture as a source of forced savings, but collectivization provided food for the rapidly growing urban labour force, raw materials (like cotton) for industry and agricultural products for export (generally at relatively low cost to the state), and encouraged the movement of labour necessary for rapid industrialization. It was also hoped that collectivization would reap the benefits of industrial mechanization applied to large-scale farming units and secure party control in the countryside. Over time the average size of Soviet farm units increased. In 1937 the average collective farm comprised seventy-six households, but by the mid-1980s the number had increased to 484 (working 6,400 ha of agricultural land). Over the same period of time the state farm employed, on average, 285 and 529 workers respectively (working 16,200 ha latterly).

The cost of collectivization was great. In the short term there was a reduction in agricultural output of around a fifth during 1928–32 and massive slaughter of livestock by unwilling peasants. The long-run health of the sector also suffered, agriculture often being described as the Achilles heel of the economy. Apart from the income distribution system in collective farms (exacerbated by the large size of these multi-product farms, which made the link between effort and reward even more tenuous), the central planning of agriculture faced special problems. These problems included the following: (1) the variety of constantly changing local conditions and difficulties of supervision; (2) the vital importance of a *timely* supply of (typically scarce) inputs in a sector dominated by seasonal factors (e.g. spare parts for repair and maintenance); and (3) the fact that land and produce could be put to better use, as far as farmers were concerned. Other factors explaining the poor shape of Soviet agriculture were geographical features (deficiencies with regard to climate and soil), the poor rural infrastructure (e.g. roads) and the ageing rural opulation. The environmental legacy was quite horrendous, e.g. the effects of cotton production (via irrigation and fertilizers) on the poisoning and drastic shrinking of the Aral Sea.

In the postwar period there were a number of important developments:

1. Agriculture became heavily subsidized. But the heavy investment in agriculture was often wastefully used, e.g. the Virgin Lands campaign of the 1950s.

2. The state farm overtook the collective farm in importance (state farms being used in the Virgin Lands campaign). But the two farms more and more resembled one another, e.g. in 1964 collective farmers became entitled to state pensions, while in 1966 collective farmers were paid the same rate as state farm workers for work actually done.

3. There was a decentralization of decision-making to small, lower-level units (often family members in reality) called 'links', 'brigades' and the like. Broad output targets were set and basic inputs provided, but there were no work schedules and payment was by result.

4. Prices were increased for agricultural products.

5. Gorbachev stressed the leasing of land (and equipment) for up to 100 years if necessary. But did not approve of private land ownership. One aspect of the 'war of laws' was that Yeltsin introduced private ownership of land in 1990 in the Russian republic in direct contradiction to the Soviet constitution (see below).

6. Extra incentives included hard currency used by the state to buy agricultural products. In the Russian republic 'harvest '90 cheques', introduced in July 1990, supposedly guaranteed access to scarce consumer goods. There were experiments in shareholding in state and collective farms.

AGRICULTURE IN RUSSIA

In 1992 26 per cent of the population were rural and agriculture accounted for 20 per cent of employment in the period 1990–92 (industry 46 per cent and services 34 per cent) (*The Economist*, Survey, 8 April 1995, p. 4).

'In 1991 the government spent about 12 per cent of its budget on the agricultural sector; by 1998 that had dropped to 1 per cent' (*FT*, Survey, 10 May 2000, p. vi).

Laws and decrees relating to private land ownership

3 December 1990. The Russian Federation's Second Congress of the People's Deputies adopted legislation permitting private land ownership, although individuals were able to sell land only after ten years and even then only to the state. Private land ownership was codified in the Land Code of April 1991.

The 27 December 1990 Law on Peasant Farms allowed 'every able-bodied citizen' who possessed 'specialized agricultural knowledge or past specialized training' to organize a peasant farm. (Jeffries 1993: 69; Wegren 1994: 222, and 1997: 961.)

(Note that the legislation is an example of the so-called 'war of laws', since the Soviet constitution banned private land ownership.)

27 December 1991. Yeltsin's land decree specified that collective and state farms were to reorganize themselves and decide their future forms of organization by 1 March 1992. They were to re-register by 1 January 1993. (More than three-quarters of state and collective farms had actually been reregistered by the beginning of 1993: *CDSP*, 1993, vol. XLV, no. 5, p. 22.) Unprofitable farms were to be declared bankrupt by 1 February 1992 (to be taken over by profitable enterprises or, as a last resort, have their assets sold at auction). The options were as follows: to form a joint stock company (where farmers hold shares); to form an agricultural co-operative; to divide the farm into individual private farms; to remain as before as state or collective farms.

The chairman of any farm was obliged to allow individual farmers to withdraw with a share of the land and of property such as equipment. Land was to be divided up equally, but, in the case of property, factors such as past wages, age and qualifications were to be taken into account. If a member's request for a plot of land was not satisfied within a month of submission, the farm chairman could be fined three months' salary. Recipients of land shares were allowed to exchange their shares or to lease the rights to their shares. Farm members were permitted to sell their land plots 'to other citizens' if they retired from farming, inherited the plot, wanted to organize a farm elsewhere, or intended to invest the proceeds in rural processing, retailing, construction or other businesses.

The Russian Land Code of 1991 stated that any citizen at least eighteen years old who had experience in agriculture and the corresponding skills, or who had past specialized training, could receive land. (Jeffries 1993: 94; Wegren 1992b: 657–61, 1994: 222, and 1997: 961–2.)

March 1992. A presidential decree allowed the sale of the plots of privatized state and municipal enterprises (Wegren 1997: 962).

October 1992. A presidential decree allowed the sale, on an experimental basis, of private garden and housing plots in Ramenskii raion in Moscow oblast (Wegren 1997: 962).

December 1992. The Russian Supreme Soviet legalized the sale of land. But agricultural land could only be sold if used for subsidiary agriculture (private plots), dacha (building) plots, collective gardening or plots around individual housing. If land was used for these types of agricultural production then it could be sold without a moratorium. In other cases, if the land was used for purposes other than those stated above, had been received free, and was held in ownership, then the owner had to wait for ten years before the land could be sold. If the land plot in question had been purchased then a five-year wait was required. In both cases the price of land would be at negotiated market prices. However, market prices would only apply to the sale or purchase of land up to the size norms established by local soviets (councils). If the size of land plot exceeded established norms then the owner could retain the excess in lifetime use with the right of inheritance, or, if he wished to sell, he could do so through the local soviet at a 'negotiated price' determined by the local soviet. (Wegren 1997: 962; Siszov 1993: 500.)

27 October 1993. A presidential decree reinforced the legal status of land shares within an agricultural enterprise and reiterated the right to conduct land transactions. The right to buy land would be given to all existing members of collective and state farms, including pensioners and children. Members of state and collective farms would receive a certificate (voucher in effect) of land ownership entitling them to a share of the farm's land based on share sizes that had been previously established during farm organization.

(According to *The Economist*, the first certificate entitled each holder to a certain number of hectares, calculated by dividing the area of the farm by the number of claimants, while the second certificate entitled the holder to a share of farm assets such as buildings and machinery, the value of each individual certificate depending on how many years the holder has worked on the farm: *The Economist*, 18 June 1994, p. 55.) These certificates would be used in auctions to bid for farm land and property or could be sold to their fellow farmers (the first certificates being issued on 23 October 1993). But physical land plots continued to be held by the collective and were only distributed if a person decided to leave the parent farm. The decree annulled previous restrictions on land sales and allowed the owner to sell his land shares. The decree stated that: 'Citizens and juristic persons who own land have the right to sell, bequeath, give away, mortgage, lease or exchange land, or pass it wholly or in part as a contribution to the authorized capital of joint stock companies, associations and co-operatives, including those with foreign investments.' 'The owners of land have the right ... to sell shares in land to other members of the collective, as well as to other citizens and juristic persons, for the production of agricultural products. At the same time, members of the collective are to take preference over other purchasers in acquiring shares of land.'

Regions would decide the maximum amount of land an individual could own. The use of hired farm labour would not be allowed, i.e. owners must work the land themselves or form co-operatives. Potential owners would have to have an agricultural education and some farming experience. Local authorities would have the right to take back land left uncultivated or used 'irrationally'. (The decree was primarily aimed at agricultural land, but local authorities would be allowed to change the use to commercial.) The aim was to promote viable private farms. Foreigners would be allowed to rent land ('under certain conditions'), but not to buy land themselves (although joint ventures would be able to buy land). (Wegren 1997: 962–3, 966; Jeffries 1996: 220.)

The 27 October 1993 decree also said that 'as of [1 January] 1994, compulsory deliveries and other forms of forced taking of agricultural products for state resources are to be abolished'. Yeltsin signed a decree entitled 'liberalizing the grain market in Russia' on 27 December 1993 (*CDSP*, 1993, vol. XLV, no. 52, p. 24). Before this decree Wegren was able to report that 'Although in reality the state continues to require obligatory deliveries to it, state prices are much more influenced by market prices' (Wegren 1994: 217). 'Early in 1993 the government created a federal grain fund to which farms of all types were required to deliver grain. The Law on Grain, signed by Yeltsin in May 1993, states that the government will select, on a competitive basis, purchasers who will buy grain at negotiated, market prices ... In reality, state purchasers are simply the state grain elevators ... and there is no competitive selection process. Grain elevators are issued state credits to buy grain. The prices offered by these grain elevators are state-set firm prices ... The federal grain fund requires a farm to deliver about one-third of its grain to state elevators, while the local grain fund requires another 10–12 per cent ... in October 1993 obligatory deliveries were abolished, although food funds will remain during 1994' (p. 237). The central reforms in 1993 were the freeing of grain prices, the decision to procure grain, meat and milk at market prices, and the lifting of the time limit on the sale of land (*RET*, 1993, vol. 2, no. 4, p. 52).

7 March 1996. A presidential decree restated that a person had the right to bequeath, sell, give away, exchange, lease, transfer the rights of, or use his land shares without the consent of other shareholders. The owner of land shares was allowed to request conversion to a physical plot of land for the operation of a private farm. A land share owner could also sell or lease the physical plot of land to a private farmer, rural household or agricultural enterprise for agricultural use. As before, the share owner could invest his shares in a farm enterprise, or (if he decided to retain possession of his shares) to lease use rights to an agricultural producer. New stipulations allowed localities to increase the maximum size of a land plot for use as a private plot. The amount of land that could be leased was 'unlimited'. Municipalities were permitted to obtain land shares from individuals in order to redistribute to citizens or to sell to corporate enterprises engaged in agricultural production (Wegren 1997: 963).

The presidential decree of 7 March 1996 entitled any agricultural worker to claim his share of the farm's land and to sell, bequeath or mortgage it. The same applied to private plots and dachas. The aim was to introduce registration procedures by mid-1996. As regards urban land, enterprises would have the right not only to buy their land but also to sell it. Condominiums would be given their land and have the right to sell it (*RET*, Monthly Update, 21 March 1996, p. 3). According to the 7 March 1996 decree, land defined as agricultural could only be used for this purpose (*RET*, 1996, vol. 5, no. 1, p. 107). The decree made it easier for farmers to buy and sell their holdings and for the first time allowed the trading of privately owned 'household plots' (p. 129).

The decree, which parliamentarians challenged as unconstitutional, says that the owners of farm land (including those who hold it indirectly through shares in collective farms) can buy, sell or mortgage their land, provided it stays in agricultural use and in Russian hands. The decree also allows a free market in the smallholdings tended by some 40 million people, which have until now been passed on only through inheritance (*The Economist*, 16 March 1996, p. 104).

Yeltsin's March 1996 decree means that every peasant who rents a garden plot now owns it. The sale of land to foreigners and the sale of any urban land are prohibited (Michael Specter, *IHT*, 19 March 1996, p. 2).

Despite the fact that the right of private ownership of land was guaranteed by the Congress of People's Deputies in late 1990, in reality the exercise of this right ran up against serious legal and administrative restrictions. Since early 1991, as a result of reforms aimed at the transformation of former collective farms and state farms into joint stock companies and the legal registration of private land ownership, about 40 million people have acquired ownership of plots of land. Another 12 million residents of rural areas have become owners of shares in newly formed agro-industrial associations and joint stock companies. The most important restriction on the rights of owners of property shares (such as farm equipment, animals and buildings) and land shares in disposing of their property was that they wanted to withdraw and sell those shares, they had to obtain the consent of other former members of the collective farm. The new decree guarantees that the owners of shares of land in reorganized collective farms and state farms are free to exercise their rights (to bequeath the land, use it to engage in private farming, sell it, give it away or exchange it) without the consent of the other former members of the collective farm (*CDSP*, 1996, vol. XLVIII, no. 10, pp. 1–2). The only thing that cannot be done with a share is to use it for a purpose other than agriculture (p. 4). Of the 12 million, only 8 million have received certificates of ownership (p. 3). The executive branch must issue certificates to all 12 million members of collective farms, joint stock companies and limited liability partnerships by the end of 1996 (p. 5).

The new land code

A new land code has yet to be agreed, with the restrictions suggested by the State Duma resisted by Yeltsin. On 14 July 1995 the State Duma passed the first reading of the new land reform bill. Agricultural land would remain the property of the state or legal entities. Private individuals would be able only to lease it or have the right to use it for life. The sale of agricultural land would be prohibited (*RET*, 1995, vol. 4, no. 2, pp. 129–30). On 22 November 1995 the State Duma refused to support the Land Code on second reading. The text had undergone no conceptual changes in comparison with the version adopted on first reading on 14 July 1995. The Land Code, while recognizing in principle the existence of private land ownership along with state and municipal ownership, for all practical purposes reduces it solely to the right to own garden plots. The law allows only these parcels of land to be bought and sold without restriction, taking all other land out of real circulation. Parcels of land transferred to agricultural organizations that were created from former collective farms are the organizations' property, along with the land shares held by the organizations' members. Private farms are granted parcels of land for lifetime possession and the landholders may pass the land on to their heirs, but they do not have the right to sell or lease it. Sub-leasing of agricultural land is restricted to a five-year period and is possible only in cases specifically stipulated by law. The government spoke out categorically against adoption of the Land Code (*CDSP*, 1995, vol. XLVII, no. 47).

In November 1997 Saratov province adopted a law on land, which, for the first time anywhere in Russia, authorized the buying and selling of agricultural land. The province did this in the absence of a federal land code, which the province will adapt to when passed (*CDSP*, 1997, vol. XLIX, no. 47, p. 17).

On 26 November 1997 Yeltsin signed a presidential decree 'on the sale to citizens and juristic persons of parcels of land on which construction will be done in urban and rural communities or of leasing rights to that land'. This decree would remain in force until a land code was passed. The decree covered only land in cities and settlements, i.e. about 3 per cent of all land (*CDSP*, 1997, vol. XLIX, no. 47, pp. 13–14). 'The presidential decree has not brought about a revolution in the area of land legislation. After all, today more than fifty regions have normative acts regulating land relations, many of which, in one way or another, permit the buying and selling of land. For example, Saratov-model draft laws on the unrestricted sale of land have been prepared in the Jewish Autonomous Province, Tataria, Sverdlovsk Province and Samara. In the regions opponents of buying and selling land are in the minority' (p. 13). 'St Petersburg, Novgorod, Barnaul, Nizhny Novgorod, Tver and several other cities ... already have functioning markets in land intended for construction purposes ... In a number of cities local decisions have also granted this right to juristic persons, including foreign ones. For instance ... St Petersburg ... Novgorod' (p. 14). In the absence of a federal law members of the federation have the right to regulate land relations as an object of joint jurisdiction (*CDSP*, 1998, vol. XLIX, no. 52, p. 7). On 5 March 1998 the first land auction was held in Balakovo (Saratov province). Governor Dmitri Ayatskov began to implement the president's decree on the sale of plots of land for private construction, reaffirming his loyalty to the president's land policy. The auction was for twenty-four plots of land, including land earmarked for the construction of cafés, shops and private homes. A 20 ha plot of farmland was sold to a grain products joint stock company which intended to grow vegetables and grain. Eighteen of the twenty-four plots of city-owned land were sold. Proceeds went into the municipal treasury (*CDSP*, 1998, vol. 50, no. 10, p. 15). The Saratov administration does not allow the sale of land to foreigners, but foreign investors can lease land for fifty years (*FT*, Survey, 15 April 1998, p. viii).

On 26 December 1997 Yeltsin offered to compromise with the State Duma and a working party was set up. Yeltsin suggested a free market for land in urban areas and a more tightly controlled system for the private ownership of agricultural land. He proposed a ban on selling agricultural land to foreigners, a requirement that land may only be sold to people who prove their ability to cultivate it, and that land must be used for farming for up to fifteen years following a sale (*IHT*, 27 December 1997, p. 4).

On 26 December 1997 Yeltsin delivered an opening statement at the first roundtable meeting: 'In our country different regions have different types of land. I believe that our approach should be diversified too. Commercial transactions in urban industrial land must be introduced right away. This land makes up only 3 per cent of Russia's territory ... We should introduce transactions in farmland only under strict state oversight ... In general we know what this should entail: a complete ban on the sale of any tract of land involving a change in its designated use during the first few years after its acquisition, and restrictions on the categories of persons having the right to acquire land. If you want to operate a farm, show us your skills, your qualifications. A ban on the sale of land to foreigners. I could go on with this list' (*CDSP*, 1998, vol. XLIX, no. 52, p. 6).

The State Duma approved a new version of the Land Code on 23 April 1998. But the president's representative stated that all the president's proposals had been interpreted 'exactly contrary to their intent'; the new version ignored both the priority of federal over local laws and citizens' rights to private ownership of land (*CDSP*, 1998, vol. 50, no. 17, p. 18). The Council of the Federation approved the new version on 20 May 1998. The new version would legalize the 'right of ownership without the right to sell', or 'the right of permanent (indefinite) use or lease', which in effect would abrogate the right of inheritance. In addition, if a landowner changes his mind about being a farmer property would be returned to the state or municipal ownership, with no reimbursement except for money spent on improving property. The regions are not waiting for a federal law. Saratov Province and Tatarstan are not the only places where private ownership of land has been legalized. Either the buyout of farmland already being used by the purchaser or lifetime leasing (sometimes with the right of inheritance) has been authorized in almost fifty regions (*CDSP*, 1998, vol. 50, no. 20, p. 15).

On 26 June 1998 the Samara Province Duma adopted a law on land. On the question of buying and selling land the law settles in favour of active capitalist relations. It also gives citizens and juristic persons the right to acquire parcels of land as property, enjoy lifelong possession with the right of inheritance, lease land or use it on a permanent and indefinite basis. There is provision for the possibility of confiscating parcels of land from owners or tenants if the land is being used for purposes other than those intended or if significant environmental deterioration results from its use. A provision making it possible to sell land to foreign citizens was proposed by the Samara Province administration but did not make it into the final version approved by the Duma (*CDSP*, 1998, vol. 50, no. 26, p. 15). The first auctions are to take place in October 1998. In recent years Samara Province has totally abolished the government monopoly on land. More than 70 per cent of agricultural land and 11 per cent of the land in cities and towns has been turned into private property. The Samara law is based on Chapter 25 of the Russian Federation Civil Code, which states that Russian Federation citizens and juristic persons have the right to own parcels of land. It grants the right of hereditary ownership, permanent use (without a time limit) and leasing. No one may oblige citizens or juristic persons to purchase parcels of land and no one may be denied the purchase of land unless stipulated otherwise by federation legislation. The Samara law stipulates that foreign citizens, persons without citizenship and foreign juristic persons may only hold plots of land as established by federal and province legislation on leasing rights (*CDSP*, 1998, vol. 50, no. 29, p. 17).

The Moscow city government and Duma announced on 10 December 1998 that from January 1999 land in Moscow would be eligible for sale to private owners, but only for capital construction within the framework of specific projects of the Moscow authorities. 'Land laws exist in forty-eight regions of Russia and they are in the process of being adopted in two more (Kaliningrad and Rostov provinces). All these laws differ from one another. For example, in fourteen regions (including Dagestan, Kalmykia and the republic of Sakha) farmland may not be bought or sold. Regional laws also differ substantially in the restrictions they place on buying and selling parcels of land, especially agricultural land' (*CDSP*, 1999, vol. 50, no. 50, p. 17).

The Nizhny Novgorod experiment

The October 1993 presidential decree dealt with the distribution of certificates (vouchers) to farm members, entitling them to bid for land and property (see above). A pilot scheme involving six collective and state farms in the Nizhny Novgorod area was announced on 26 October 1993. Help was given by the International Finance Corporation. Encouragement was given to form co-operatives (in order to create viable units) and most in fact did this (John Lloyd, *FT*, 2 April 1994, p. 26). The resulting farms were large-group farms (Van Atta 1994: 185). The employees in all five farms decided to split the farms into smaller 'enterprise farms'. But none were divided into individual family farms (EBRD 1996b: 23).

On 10 March 1994 prime minister Chernomyrdin paid a visit and said that 'I am convinced this programme should become the national programme for all Russia. I have supported it and will support it'; he also said, however, that the scheme would be used 'as the basis' for the national programme. Agriculture minister Alexander Zaveryukha also expressed support.

As of early February 1995 seven agricultural enterprises in Nizhny Novgorod Province had gone through a reform process based on this model. Heavy pressure from the agrarian lobby had postponed the plan to make the programme a national one (*CDSP*, 1995, vol. XLVII, no. 7, p. 12).

But 'efforts to repeat it [the Nizhny Novgorod scheme] across the country have got nowhere' (*The Economist*, 11 March 1995, p. 36). 'Nizhny Novgorod is the only region in Russia to have tried systematically breaking up its collective farms – ninety of them so far' (*The Economist*, 25 March 1995, p. 52). In 1993–94 the members of five collective farms agreed to rearrange their assets into forty-two smaller farms run on commercial lines (*The Economist*, 16 March 1996, p. 104). By April 1996 103 collective farm auctions had been conducted in Nizhny Novgorod, yielding 372 private farms, 114 joint stock companies and fifty-nine mixed partnerships (*The Economist*, 29 June 1996, p. 99). (By mid-1995 sixty-eight farms enterprises had gone through the process. In the period 1993–94 there were created, out of five farms, twenty collective enterprises, seventeen family farms and six individual businesses: World Bank 1996: 59.)

'Although the scheme was repeated in other regions, it did not become regular practice. Because the mechanism is voluntary, it does not provide much incentive for managers who often prefer to keep the present structure unchanged' (*RET*, 1996, vol. 5, no. 1, p. 107).

The development of private farming

A clear distinction needs to be made between private plots (which accounted for about a quarter of agricultural output in the Soviet period) and newly formed private ('peasant') farms. There were two main ways for an individual to receive land free from the state in order to begin peasant farming operations: (1) from a Special Land Fund; initially this consisted of land that state or collective farms did not want, were not using, or which had been used unproductively in the recent past; only this sort of land was available under Gorbachev, but in early 1991 Yeltsin signed a decree that allowed up to 10 per cent of a farm's land to be withdrawn and placed in this fund; and (2) from a state or collective farm (Wegren 1994: 222). Private ('peasant') farms refer to farms which were created voluntarily by individuals who withdrew from state and collective farms or who obtained land from state land funds that were established at the local level. Collective or state farm members were able to obtain land directly from the parent farm free of charge during farm reorganization (1992–94), while urban dwellers who wished to undertake private farming received land from a land fund. Prior to December 1993 urbanites received land free, but after that date they had to purchase the land. Farm members wishing to withdraw from a parent farm continue to be able to obtain land free of charge, but once reorganization was completed this land was allotted from land funds, not from the farm itself (Wegren 1996: 114–15). Note that private farmers do not own all their land. Some 39 per cent of the land allotted to private farming had become the farmers' own property, 32 per cent was held in lifelong heritable possession and 29 per cent was leased (*CDSP*, 1993, vol. XLV, no. 5, p. 22).

Private ('peasant') farms have made slow progress, in contrast to rapid privatization in the non-agricultural sectors. This can be seen in Table 6.1 and in the figures provided by *RET*. The percentage contribution to gross agricultural output for 1990, 1991, 1992 and 1993 respectively by type of enterprise was as follows: agricultural enterprises (such as collective farms, state farms, joint stock companies, partnerships and co-operatives, which together had 90 per cent of cultivated land at the beginning of 1994), 76, 72,

Table 6.1 Russia: private farms

End of year	*No. of private farms*	*Average size (ha)*	*Agricultural land (%)*	*Agricultural output (%)*	*Average number employed*
1990	4,432	46.3			
1991	49,013	42.0	0.6		
1992	182,787	42.5	3.65	1.0	3
1993	270,000	43.0	5.0	2.0	
1994	279,200	43.0	4.8	1.7	
1996	280,000		5.2	1.9	
1997	274,000		5.7	2.2	
1999				2.1	

Sources: Russian Economic Trends (various issues), United Nations Economic Commission for Europe (1993: 206), Wegren (1992b: 646, 665; 1998: 83), Siszov (1993: 501), Shaw (1992: 554), Nikonov (1992: 1159–60), *CDSP* (various issues), Pallot (1993: 112); Amelina 1999: 20.

66 and 62; household plots (5 per cent of cultivated land), 24, 28, 33 and 36; new private farms (5 per cent of cultivated land), 0, 0, 1 and 2 (*RET*, 1994, vol. 3, no. 2, pp. 62–3). 'The number of private farmers has remained at roughly 280,000 for a long time now. The amount of land they are tilling is not increasing either. It is now 6 per cent of all farmland, although 49 per cent of the land used for agriculture has technically been divided up among shareholders' (*Izvestia*, 14 January 1998, p. 2; cited in *CDSP*, 1998, vol. 50, no. 2, p. 8).

'The number of individual farms ... decreased from a peak of 280,000 in 1996 to 274,000 at the end of 1997. Individual farms produce just 2 per cent of recorded agricultural output on 6 per cent of agricultural land. The remaining 48 per cent is produced on tiny private plots – averaging one-third of a hectare – by rural and urban workers for whom this is a part-time occupation or by pensioners for whom it supplements retirement benefits.' The shares, respectively, of agricultural production and agricultural land use accounted for by collective enterprises are as follows: 1991, 68.8 per cent and 91.2 per cent; 1994, 54.5 per cent and 82.8 per cent; 1997, 49.9 per cent and 80.4 per cent. The number of collective enterprises was 27,000 in 1997, roughly the same as in 1991 (Amelina 1999: 19).

Wegren (1992a: 120) argues that collective and state farmers have overwhelmingly preferred to devote their energies to their private plots rather than venture into outright private farming. 'Only 3 per cent of agricultural workers are private farmers, and their number is falling. Moreover, because farmland is deemed to have no value, banks will not treat it as collateral, so credit is almost unobtainable. The countryside is starved of investment ... Russians are likely to be dependent on their ... little family plots for some time to come. These plots are now thought to provide 50 per cent of the food produced in Russia ... illustrating the way that Russia really is a subsistence economy' (*The Economist*, Survey, 12 July 1997, p. 17).

'Yeltsin has been largely successful in creating a new set of rural institutions in the Russian countryside. But the underlying culture has changed very little ... a collectivist and egalitarian culture still exists in the countryside' (Wegren 1994: 216). 'One of the most striking features of land reform in Russia is the lack of spontaneous decollectivization by collective and state farm workers themselves ... by 1 July 1993 over 90 per cent of all state and collective farms had reorganized. Of those farms which had reorganized ... *collective* forms of organization retained much more popularity than expected ... the most popular forms of reorganization were: joint stock companies, which retain collective ownership; the retention of a farm's previous status, chosen by more than one-third of reorganized farms; and the creation of "comrade societies with limited responsibility", a form chosen by more than half of the farms undergoing reorganization ... of the farms that remained intact after reorganization ... an overwhelming 92 per cent chose a form of collective labour organization' (p. 219). 'Despite the increased ease of land acquisition, most economic regions in European Russia had not more than 10 per cent of cultivated land allocated to private farmers. Thus, even after five years of land reform the Russian agricultural sector was still dominated by large collective farms and their successors which controlled around 90 per cent of agricultural land, with private farmers possessing only about 5 to 6 per cent of all agricultural land. The remaining land was used for small individual farming such as private plots' (Wegren 1996: 120–1). 'In most cases the farm and farm property remained intact. Former state and collective farms remained intact by forming joint stock farms, limited partnerships, or retaining their previous status. For example, about 83 per cent of former state and collective farms either retained their previous status or reorganized as a joint stock farm. Most farmers transferred their land shares to the parent farm ... On 1 January 1995 former state and collective farms and their legal successors held about 87 per cent of agricultural land (not including land reserves and forest funds), although technically this land was now private, not state, property' (Wegren 1997: 970).

'The option preferred by the overwhelming majority of land share owners/ agricultural workers in Russia to date has been to lease their land back to the enterprise which issued it for a predetermined period (often five years) in return for an annual rental payment made by the enterprise in cash or kind. That is, the vast majority of rural workers have not opted to try private farming on their land shares either individually or in groups' (Kitching 1998: 18). But the importance of the private plot has increased (p. 20). 'There has been a tendency, certainly in the Western media and scholarly literature, to assume that over the majority of Russia, where more "radical" reforms of the Nizhny Novgorod type have not occurred, there must have been "stagnation" and the "mere continuation" of old Soviet collective and state farms in a slightly new juridical guise ... The result of the slump [in agricultural production] has been to turn the majority of these farms into more or less pure "subsistence" entities engaged in the self supply of food for their members and (as far as possible) of the inputs necessary for that food production – but withdrawing mainly or totally from market supply. At the same time, however, a small minority of these former state and collective farms (about 10–15 per cent of them in all four regions studied) have come to dominate marketed production of food and other agricultural crops .... The clue to the survival of this small minority of enterprises has been their success in a form of "crisis management", a success determined largely (in my view) by the contacts and abilities of their farm management' (pp. 19–20). The survey data show that a much higher proportion of private plot output is marketed on 'survivor' farms than 'collapsing' farms. 'On "collapsing" farms ... private plot production increases ... are almost entirely for subsistence use ... In effect ... such farms have become little more than "servicing agencies" and "input providers" to "subsistence" private plot production ... The 10–15 per cent of "survivor" farms in our four survey regions do not merely dominate the marketed production of collectively produced grain and feed crops ... their work forces now also dominate the marketed production of fruit, vegetable and livestock products coming from private plots in these regions' (pp. 21–2).

'The term "collective farm" may not disappear for at least another fifty years, although the term "state farm", closely related in meaning, has already practically gone out of use ... In the first years of reform ... it was illegal even to call oneself a collective farm. Farms came up with such curious names as Lenin Collective Farm Closed-Type Joint Stock Company or 22nd Party Congress Collective Farm Limited Liability Partnership. After a few years collective farms were once again allowed to call themselves collective farms ... There are actually a lot more collective farms than it appears. Only 13.6 per cent of the country's 27,300 agricultural enterprises are officially called collective farms ... almost 4,000 of them ... But, with very rare exceptions, all the rest of the open-type joint stock companies, limited liability partnerships, closed-type joint stock companies, agricultural co-operatives, associations and silent partnerships are actually collective farms. The collective farms are currently losing the economic race. Not to privately owned farms, though, but to private plots' (Yelena Yakovleva, *Izvestia*, 15 March 2000, p. 2: *CDSP*, 2000, vol. 52, no. 12, p. 16).

A number of factors have hindered the development of private farms:

1. The uncertainties of life in the new market economy.
2. Resistence from many of the Soviet-era managers.
3. Wegren (1996) argues that 'Private farmers have not been successful in defending their interests because they are politically weak, a fact that led them to seek out urban alliances whose interests differ from private farmers, and because of intrarural divisions that have weakened the efforts by agrarians to defend their interests' (p. 106) 'What has been crucial to the private farming movement is state financing and access to state-subsidized credits ... The rise

and fall of the private farm movement correlates with the financial support shown by the Russian government. The political weakness of rural liberals has meant that private farmers have not fared well in defending the issues that are most critical to the fate of private farming' (p. 122). (At the end of September 1993 state-subsidized credits to private farmers were ended: p. 111.) Factors hindering the development of private farming include the lack of an adequate rural infrastructure, problems of input supplies ('channels of trade for farm inputs has remained highly monopolized': p. 117), state payment arrears, underdeveloped market trade channels, and the quantity and quality of land allocated (pp. 116–20).

4. A lack of machinery suitable for small farms (as well as difficulties in obtaining other inputs) hinders the development of the 260,000 private farms (*The Economist*, 7 August 1993, p. 64).

5. In a survey 80 per cent of farmers named high prices for equipment and building materials as the chief hindrance to the development of their farms (*CDSP*, 1993, vol. XLV, no. 5, 23).

The army and farming

'The Russian army currently provides itself with nearly 30 per cent of the farm products it requires and the defence ministry has plans to raise that level to at least 50 per cent in the near future ... Immediately after the default [of August 1998] commercial suppliers refused to deliver produce to army units ... With its own state farms the military has firm supply contracts. Today there are eighty-four state farms that – without taking a single soldier or officer on their payrolls – have put themselves on a military footing ... Russia has about 30,000 agricultural enterprises [in total]. State farms have been amazingly persistent in begging the army to sign them up ... The terms on which a farm "joins the army" are as follows. First, it has to lose everything: its land, which only fairly recently was transferred to farm workers, its buildings and its equipment are all made over to the state for no monetary compensation. The only thing the peasants get in return is a reliable sales market ... [But] payments are constantly being delayed ... The defence ministry ... makes no investments in its state farms ... Occasionally a few of them will disagree with their fellow farmers' decision and will strike off on their own, but after a year or two they usually ask to be let back in. The free market usually proves the ruin of many an individual farmer' (*Moskovskiye Novosti*, December 21–7 1999, p. 14: *CDSP*, 1999, vol. 51, no. 52, p. 12).

CHAPTER SEVEN

MACROECONOMIC STABILIZATION

THE SOVIET FINANCIAL SYSTEM

Any economy that wishes to reap the benefits of extensive specialization and exchange needs money to function as a medium of exchange, unit of account, store of value and standard for deferred payments. The command economy used money, the experience of War Communism (1918–21) being influential here. But, given that resources were largely centrally allocated, it played an essentially passive role. This is best illustrated by repeating the point that an enterprise's non-labour inputs were distributed administratively; it was the *naryad* that was the vital piece of paper, money being automatically forthcoming. Price tags were attached to items of expenditure and revenue in order for it to be possible to draw up the account necessary for purposes of evaluation and control. (Note, however, that since market elements were important, differential wage rates actively influenced manpower allocation, and consumers often exercised choice over the goods and services made available in the plan.) Money was needed because it was impossible to plan physically the output of every single good and in order to monitor performance.

The concept of the total money supply in a command economy was not very meaningful because there were two payments circuits, 'household cash' and 'deposit transfer'. The latter circuit comprised the bookkeeping changes that covered practically all inter-enterprise transactions, while the former had implications for macro financial equilibrium. The state was concerned to keep a balance between the cash injected into the economy, largely via the paying out of wages and salaries, and the supply of consumer goods and services made available under the plan at established prices, in order to avoid inflationary pressures. This can be expressed with the aid of an equation: $PQ = Y + TP - S - T$, where P is the general retail price level (i.e. average retail price), Q is the quantity of consumer goods and services, Y is household income in the form of wages and salaries earned in the production of *all* goods and services, TP is transfer payments, such as pensions, paid out to households, S is household savings, and T is direct taxes levied on households.

In principle the Soviet Union was thus able to prevent open and repressed inflation. It is interesting and instructive, therefore, to examine why significant open inflation was a feature of the 1930s. While plans for the production of consumer goods were generally underfulfilled, there was a large leakage of cash into the system through the overdrawing of wage funds. This originated in (1) the high level of labour turnover, which itself was the result of a predominantly undisciplined labour force, recently arrived from the countryside, in search of higher earnings; and (2) the plight of enterprise directors desperate for labour to fulfil the all-important output targets. Managers indulged in all sorts of activities, such as artificial upgrading, to get round state-determined wage rates. The State Bank allowed wage fund transgressions for fear of jeopardizing output plans. (The leak associated with Y was later plugged by tighter regulations, which specified, for example, that overspending had to be made good within a matter of months.)

There were attempts to correct the financial imbalance by encouraging household savings (S), including what were in effect forced bond sales, but the massive increases in direct taxes that would have been needed were ruled out by the necessity to preserve work incentives. What was left was P. Retail prices were increased to move nearer to market clearing levels (thus causing turnover taxes, which were usually price-determined, to increase) and to soak up some of the excess purchasing power. (Note that in the 1930s the Soviet Union experienced full employment and open inflation while the reverse situation existed in the capitalist West.)

If retail prices are not raised sufficiently to achieve financial equilibrium, the result is 'repressed' inflation, which takes the form of queues, rationing and blocked purchasing power (i.e. forced savings or 'monetary overhang'). The extent to which repressed inflation existed in the Soviet Union in later decades, however, was a very controversial point. The sceptics pointed to the coexistence of stockpiles and queues, and considered rapidly rising savings accounts as normal consumer behaviour. By the late 1980s, however, the evidence was strongly in favour of repressed inflation. Nikolai Shmelev (*CDSP*, 1989, vol. XLI, no. 44, p. 6), for example, estimated 150 billion to 200 billion roubles of 'hot money' (sometimes called 'mobile' money) that people would have spent immediately if goods were available. The Soviet government's estimate of the monetary overhang at the end of 1989 was 165 billion roubles, while Marrese (1990: 57) put the figure at 233 billion roubles. Burgeoning budget deficits (120 billion roubles in 1989 or about 12 per cent of national income) were increasingly financed by printing money, while mounting difficulties were experienced on the production side.

'Monetary overhang' may be seen as an unplanned accumulation of cash and savings accounts because of the lack of desired goods and services. Work incentives are severely adversely affected by the uncertainty of being able to translate money income into command over real goods and services. Converting repressed into open inflation by allowing prices to rise brings its own political dangers, while removing a given overhang by one-off measures provides no long-term cure; the root causes of the problem must be tackled by such measures as reducing the budget deficit (or rather the part of the deficit financed by printing money).

Various proposals were put forward for removing the monetary overhang:

1. The most radical proposal was a comprehensive monetary reform involving the substitution of a new money. The problems here include panic buying if such a reform were even suspected and the fact that better-off citizens tend to hold much of their wealth in the form of real estate, valuables and hard currency. A partial monetary reform was implemented via the 22 January 1991 decree: 50 and 100 rouble notes were no longer legal tender (limits being placed on the amount that could be converted), allegedly aimed at 'speculation, corruption, smuggling, forgery, unearned income, and normalizing the monetary situation and the consumer market'; limits were also placed on the amount of savings that could be withdrawn monthly in the form of cash for the first half of 1991.

2. Partial measures to remove the overhang included such proposals as bond sales, the sale of housing and industrial assets, and the resale of more imports at high mark-up rates. One concrete measure, effective 1 January 1991 (though scrapped a year later), involved the imposition of a 5 per cent turnover tax on goods for production and technical purposes, consumer goods, jobs performed and paid services (the revenue being used for social and economic progress, to support the needy members of society and for stabilizing currency circulation), and the setting up of a stabilization fund (revenue raised from social security funds, depreciation funds, windfall profits resulting from excessive price rises, and the sale of shares) used to support enterprises adversely affected by circumstances beyond their control in the transition to the market, scientific research, the conversion of defence enterprises to civilian production and special republican subsidies. Indeed 1991 was the beginning of the end for the Soviet Union, financial chaos playing its part as output levels plummeted.

Real resource flows were determined in the plan, but were also reflected in the 'consolidated' budget at all levels of government. The major elements of expenditure were for the 'national economy', especially capital grants and subsidies, and for socio-cultural purposes, such as health and education. The budgetary category of defence significantly underestimated the real total, with elements such as weapons research tucked away under other headings. On the revenue side, the outstanding point to note was the overwhelming reliance on indirect rather than direct taxes. One important reason for this was to preserve the wage differentials needed for incentives in a market environment. The turnover tax was more important than profit payments in the early years. Since resource allocation was determined in the plan, the budget played a role in the quest for financial equilibrium.

Banking was a state monopoly in the traditional economic system. The State Bank (Gosbank) was a 'monobank', that is, there was not the separation between the central bank and private commercial banks to be found in the West. Gosbank fulfilled the following functions in that it: issued cash; had a monopoly of gold and foreign exchange reserves (a specialized Foreign Trade Bank dealing with international payments); acted as the fiscal agent of government, collecting budgetary revenue and disbursing current expenditures (a separate Construction Bank handling the doling out of investment grants); had a monopoly of short-term credits for working capital purposes in line with the state plan; monitored plan fulfilment by enterprises by means of the obligatory account. The Savings Bank serviced the needs of individuals. The overriding task then, reflecting the essentially passive role of money, was to aid plan fulfilment. Contrast this with the active exercise of monetary (and fiscal) policy in market economies.

MACROECONOMIC STABILIZATION BEFORE THE FINANCIAL CRISIS OF AUGUST 1998

Introduction

Western-type financial institutions have been developed, e.g. a conventional central bank, private banks, stock exchanges and a bond market. But the major concerns of this section are to analyze how hyperinflation was conquered, to discuss remaining problems as regards macroeconomic stabilization and to study the role of the IMF.

Hyperinflation (conventionally defined as an annual inflation rate of at least 1000 per cent) occurred in 1992. Macroeconomic stabilization here refers to an acceptable inflation rate, achieved especially by means of appropriately tight fiscal and monetary policy. Before explaining how hyperinflation was conquered, it may be helpful to say something about the meaning of the term 'shock therapy'. It was argued that before hyperinflation had been overcome Russia had not implemented 'shock therapy', e.g. Åslund and Layard (1993). Here it is important to bear in mind that a narrow definition was being used, namely macroeconomic stabilization measures (as opposed to a broad definition which includes rapid and comprehensive change in the economic system). 'The reformers have been completely stymied in macroeconomic stabilization' (Jeffrey Sachs, *The Independent*, 11 October 1993, p. 18).

In his state-of-the-nation speech on 16 February 1995 Yeltsin stated that: 'Two serious attempts were made to curb inflation in the years of reform … For various reasons the job was not implemented in full. The third attempt must be a success.' The early failure can be explained by a number of factors behind the increase in the money supply:

1. Powerful lobby groups were catered for.

The then finance minister Yegor Gaidar (*CDSP*, 1994, vol. XLVI, no. 6, p. 9) admits that although 'in those first months of 1992 a serious step was taken … within just a few months our policy began to spin its wheels. Under pressure from lobbying groups, particularly in the former Supreme Soviet, our firm line in budget and monetary policy was broken.'

Mikhail Berger of *Izvestiya* thinks that 'shock therapy' (in the narrow meaning of the term) in Russia lasted just sixteen days. It ended on 18 January 1992, when the decision to provide state subsidies to the coal mining industry was taken (*CDSP*, 1994, vol. XLVI, no. 3, p. 3).

The high growth of money in the third quarter of 1994 was due to a large credit injection at the end of the summer for agriculture, the northern regions and the defence industry (*RET*, Monthly Update, 17 November 1994, p. 7).

In late summer 1994 4,200 billion roubles' worth of soft credits went to defence and investments (*FT*, 12 October 1994, p. 25).

In early October 1994 the ministry of defence was awarded extensive credit to cover its energy debt (*IHT*, 11 October 1994, p. 11).

Sachs argued that 'the general cause of the rouble's downward trend is easy to pinpoint. After pursuing a tight monetary policy for half a year, the government and the central bank flooded the market with new credits in the last three months to cover the government's budget deficit and relieve favoured enterprises of bulging debts' (*IHT*, 17 October 1994, p. 8). 'Russian monetary policy has been in the hands of a few powerful people who understand little and care little about normal monetary policy and instead view central bank credits as a resource to be manipulated at will for short-run advantage' (p. 8).

2. There were early attempts (encouraged by the IMF) to preserve the rouble zone.

'In 1992–95 Russia suffered extreme rates of inflation of over 1,000 per cent in 1992 (annual average) and not falling below 100 per cent until 1996 … What were the reasons behind this development? Russia in 1991 inherited an economy characterized by a monetary overhang and repressed inflation, signified by a rapid increase in aggregate demand and shortages … The budget deficit reached … 19 per cent of GDP in 1991. The decision to liberalize 90 per cent of prices in January 1992 led to a price jump of 245 per cent and by the summer the monetary overhang had been eliminated. Efforts to tighten monetary policy in 1992–94 failed mainly due to attempts to preserve the rouble zone which after the break-up consisted of fifteen independent countries, each with their own central bank. And although the CBR [Central Bank of Russia], under the leadership of Viktor Gerashchenko, was the only one allowed to print roubles the central banks of other CIS countries (and initially also the Baltic States) could issue credits. This meant that monetary policy span out of control … More countries started to introduce their own currency or issue monetary surrogates. Furthermore, much of the credits issued by CIS central banks were used to finance imports of Russian commodities, mainly oil and gas, which meant that pressure was also put on the CBR and the Russian government by Russian exporters to continue looser monetary policy. As a result by mid-1992 the granting of concessional credits to agriculture and industry intensified. At the same time Russia was unable to increase tax revenues or reduce expenditures and as a result continued to run a large budget deficit. And without access to domestic capital markets and a lack of willingness by the West to lend money to Russia, the only source of finance was the printing presses. This policy resulted in a rapid growth of the money supply' (*RET*, Monthly Update, 8 December 1998, pp. 1–2). 'There are, however, other ways for the CBR to increase the money supply than simply printing new notes. Whenever the CBR grants direct credits to commercial banks this has an expansionary effect on the money supply. But this would also show up as an increase in base money [consisting of currency in circulation – designated as MO – and commercial bank reserves required to be held at the CBR: p. 11] ... Equally, the CBR can reduce the reserve-deposit ratio, enabling commercial banks to use additional funds for their own purposes' (p. 4).

'Poorly designed monetary arrangements following the collapse of the Soviet Union impeded an effective monetary policy. The Gosbank disappeared and monetary policy functions were vested in the central banks of the countries in the rouble area. Russia and the former republics (except the Baltics) agreed to maintain the rouble as their common currency. The central bank of Russia became the sole issuer of cash, but all the central banks could grant credit. Those credits increased rouble deposits with the central banks in the area, which could be used for both interregional and intraregional trade ... Because payments between rouble area countries were automatically settled, the central bank of Russia could not control them ... Several attempts to co-ordinate monetary policy among central banks in the rouble area failed. To deal with this problem the Russian central bank centralized all interstate transactions in Moscow and decided to settle them only to the extent that each other country in the rouble area had funds in its bilateral account with Russia. If a country had a deficit it had to negotiate a "technical credit" to cover it' (Balino 1998: 37). 'In July 1993 the problems of the rouble area led Russia to introduce the Russian rouble and demonetize the pre–1993 roubles. This marked the end of the rouble area and the beginning of Russia's full monetary independence ... The central bank of Russia made all its lending more expensive by making the interbank lending rate the basis for its lending. This encouraged banks to rely on the central bank only as a lender of last resort ... In early 1996 the central bank introduced two Lombard facilities (which provided short-term credit, collateralized with government securities, to banks): one in the form of an auction and the other in the form of a standing facility at a fixed (nonpenal) rate ... In 1996 ... the central bank allowed bank primary dealers to get uncollateralized overnight credit at a penal rate ... [Since] 1996 the central bank [has] ... monitored interbank market rates, and if they fall below the level it deems desirable, it offers overnight deposits to selected banks ... In late 1996 it started repurchase operations (using Treasury bills) ... In addition to developing market-based instruments the central bank continued to use changes in reserve requirements ... It extended them to foreign exchange deposits' (p. 38).

Currency reforms

The July 1993 currency reform may be seen as a bungled anti-inflationary move, which reduced confidence in the rouble. The gradual replacement of old notes had been decided upon before, but on Saturday 24 July 1993 the chairman of the Russian central bank, Viktor Gerashchenko, made a surprise and dramatic announcement about the currency. All rouble notes printed before 1993 (specifically 1961–92 notes) were to be invalid as of 12.01 a.m. on Monday 26 July. Russian citizens were to have until 7 August to change up to 35,000 old roubles; additional sums were to be placed in the state savings bank, where they would not be able to be withdrawn for six months and would earn interest at the 'established rate' (generally thought to be significantly below inflation).

The alleged reasons for the move were as follows: (1) to reduce inflation; (2) to counter illegal activities (only legally earned roubles would be exchangeable); (3) to make counterfeiting more difficult; (4) to force other republics still using the rouble to synchronize monetary and fiscal policy with Russia (the bank claimed that rouble notes from other republics were undermining Russia's monetary policy and that it would be ready to supply them with new roubles if they would synchronize their monetary and fiscal policies with Russia's: *CDSP*, 1993, vol. XLV, no. 30, p. 5), otherwise they would not be issued with 1993 rouble banknotes and would thus have to introduce their own currency (the finance ministry estimated that 20 per cent of all roubles were held outside Russia: *The Guardian*, 26 July 1993, p. 6). It has also been suggested that the recent strengthening of the rouble against the US dollar was also a factor in the sense that roubles accumulated through dollar sales made a tempting target (*Moscow News*, 30 July 1993, p. 2). (Note that 'citizens of other states who are temporarily in the Russian Federation' would only be able to exchange up to 15,000 roubles and even then only on 26 July. The rest would have to go into the state savings bank.)

Yeltsin did not cancel the ruling, but a decree issued on 26 July substantially diluted it. The maximum amount of old rouble notes Russian citizens could exchange was raised to 100,000 and the period of time was extended to 31 August. In addition there was to be no quantity limit on the exchange of 10,000 rouble notes dated 1992 and all pre–1993 notes of ten roubles or less could still be used up to the end of August. (The official aim of forcing individuals to place sums exceeding 100,000 old roubles in bank accounts earning interest at a rate well below inflation was to make entrepreneurs declare untaxed revenues: *FT*, 16 August 1993, p. 2.)

The currency ruling of the central bank was ill prepared, e.g. there was a wholly inadequate supply of new notes. There was much confusion, distress, panic buying of goods and panic selling of old notes. The prime minister had been involved in the decision and called a surprise cabinet meeting the day before the announcement (at which Chubais and Sergei Shakhrai had apparently spoken against the decision), but the finance ministry was not invited (Fyodorov was in the USA at the time and was not informed) and Yeltsin was on holiday (it is not clear whether he knew in advance of the announcement). This led to the allegation that the unpopular currency reform was a move inspired by parliament (parliament, to which the central bank is accountable, had gone into recess the day before the announcement) and the central bank in order to undermine Yeltsin. (Note that, shortly before, parliament had passed measures to counter various Yeltsin policies and the to-and-fro battle continued until the president dissolved parliament on 21 September 1993.)

Boris Fyodorov said that his ministry 'did not take part in the preparation of this decision and considers it to be economically and politically harmful'. He described it as 'useless and unjustified' and 'a deliberate political provocation aimed at causing dissatisfaction among the population with the president, his government and the course he is pursuing ... a direct deception of the people ... [and] ... a blow against economic reforms'. He called for the resignation of the chairman of the central bank, Viktor Gerashchenko. 'The action undertaken by the central bank of Russia to exchange old paper money is illegal from a juridical standpoint; it is senseless from an economic standpoint; from a political standpoint it is certainly harmful to Russia's interests, since it is a flagrant provocation aimed at undermining the people's confidence in the president, the government and the social and economic policy that is being pursued; and, finally, from a moral standpoint it insults and mocks the people of Russia' (Boris Fyodorov, *CDSP*, 1993, vol. XLV, no. 31, p. 5).

General criticisms of the central bank ruling by reformers and government advisers included the following: (1) old roubles would actually be encouraged to flood into Russia from the other republics to be exchanged on the black market, while old unexchanged rouble notes would flow from Russia into the other countries still using them; (2) it would undermine confidence in the rouble (just at the time, moreover, when the exchange rate against the US dollar was beginning to stabilize); (3) there was no consultation with other countries and international organizations; loss of confidence in Russia could lead to the loss of aid; (4) trade links between the republics of the former Soviet Union would be further impaired; (5) it was possibly a way to cover up corruption and mismanagement, while the real criminals would either hold their wealth in forms such as hard currency or find a way round the regulations. Åslund discerned criminal motives in the central bank's action. He argues that it was no coincidence that it was taken 'immediately after the central bank's audit by the firm Coopers & Lybrand, according to whose report the passing of questionable sums through the bank cannot be ruled out ... It seems to me that there is only one explanation ... The central bank sold money to other republics and the central bank's officers got something for it.'

A number of measures have been taken since the July 1993 currency reform. On 4 October 1993 the central bank announced that as of 1 January 1994 all transactions in foreign cash were to be banned and that all enterprises had to return foreign banknotes to banks by 31 December 1993. But Russian citizens and enterprises would still have the right to maintain foreign currency accounts. Transactions by hard currency credit and charge cards would still be permitted. Permission to trade in foreign cash was to cease on 1 November.

On 22 September 1997 the central bank announced that as of 1 November 1997 the use of hard currency credit cards was to be banned. But the order was not to affect duty-free shops or to prevent individuals from opening hard currency bank accounts. The central bank estimated that the volume of hard currency payments in shops had fallen from 60 per cent of total sales in 1995 to 18 per cent in the first half of 1997 (*IHT*, 23 September 1997, p. 16).

The successful currency reform of 1 January 1998 (announced on 4 August 1997) knocked three zeros off the denomination of rouble notes, e.g. a 1,000 rouble note became one new rouble note. The kopek was reintroduced, replacing the ten-rouble note. Old notes were to be used until the end of 1998, while they could be exchanged for new notes at banks until the end of 2002. (Since 1 January 1998 there has been a 2 per cent tax on money converted from dollars to roubles: *IHT*, 3 January 1998, p. 11.)

The rouble and the banking system

Despite legal moves to bolster the use of the rouble, Western currencies (particularly the US dollar) continued to play a very important role in the Russian economy even before the financial crisis of August 1998. That crisis seriously undermined the credibility of the rouble.

'Russia has a very low stock of bank savings in roubles. M2 (rouble bank deposits plus cash in circulation) is just 13.5 per cent of GDP, with rouble deposits just 9 per cent of GDP' (*RET*, Monthly Update, 7 May 1998, p. 1). The current low stock of rouble deposits is explained by the decimation by inflation of the real value of savings in 1992–3 and the slow growth of rouble deposits and rouble cash holdings. 'Household rouble deposits have grown slowly. While this may be partly explained by the relatively low savings rate of 10 per cent of gross income, the main reason is that most of these savings are held in cash dollars' (p. 2). 'Russia has been a capital exporter. And the willingness of both foreigners and Russians to hold roubles is still limited regardless of the Russian economy's relatively strong external position. The key point is that both households and enterprises hold much of their savings in foreign currency and most of this is outside the domestic banking system. The Russian economy is in effect still a two-currency economy. About half of annual household savings are in cash dollars. Many firms spirit capital away offshore. Many transactions, particularly those in the black economy are settled in dollars. Households use cash dollars for transactions that in other countries would be conducted through the banking system.' The common use of dollars is explained by factors such as historic high rates of inflation, expectations of exchange rate depreciation and poor government finances. 'However, the recent improvements in these macro indicators has not been accompanied by a significant increase in rouble deposits, pointing to the importance of other, structural reasons for the use of dollars. The two main reasons are tax avoidance (leading to transactions being settled outside the domestic banking system, be it abroad or domestically in cash) and inefficient and uncompetitive banks' (p. 3). 'To accelerate the structural transformation of the banking sector, it needs to be more competitive. The experience of other countries has shown that the best way to achieve this is to open the sector to foreign participation' (p. 7).

Enterprise arrears

Inter-enterprise debt is worth discussing at this point because monetary policy is weakened.

'The attempt to impose a tight credit policy in a financially underdeveloped economy is the fundamental cause of the explosion of inter-enterprise arrears' (Ickes and Ryterman 1993: 250). 'An outcome of the debt accumulation has been a breakdown in economic stabilization. And, more ominously, arrears have proven to be a safety valve that enables enterprises to postpone adjustment ... Arrears arise because enterprises find the adjustment to markets costly. When enterprises provide credit to trading partners of unknown viability, they discover that they can obscure their own viability. This loss of information undermines the commitment of government to policies such as bankruptcy and liquidation ... To prevent the creation of new arrears, their primary underlying cause – the absence of financial discipline due to the underdevelopment of the financial system – must be addressed' (pp. 232–4). 'Soon after the clearing process was completed estimates of the level of inter-enterprise arrears appeared which suggested that, by January 1993, the 5 trillion rouble level had been reached, approximately 20 per cent of GNP. This explosion in the level of inter-enterprise arrears clearly indicates that the combination of mutual clearing and pre-payment failed to stem the flow of new arrears. In particular, it failed because the Russian government and the central bank failed to signal their commitment to impose financial discipline on enterprises' (p. 240).

'Russia has witnessed relentless growth of payment arrears ever since it began transition to a market economy. Non-payments have been pervasive: from the state to its employees and providers of goods and services, from taxpayers to the state, and from firm to firm ... [There have been] recurrent suggestions that all arrears should be consolidated and all debts undone in one big settlement. Several tax amnesties carried out in October 1993, January 1996 and March 1997 were efforts in this direction ... [But] each amnesty was followed by another jump in tax arrears. It seems that non-compliant taxpayers interpreted each tax amnesty as a promise of further forgiveness and acted accordingly. In the same vein the government has also offered to settle its own debts against tax arrears by offering mutual offsets on several occasions since March 1994. In fact, non-monetary offsets were continuously on offer from March 1994 to February 1998 when they were stopped in response to IMF pressure. But the idea of offset schemes has been revived since the crisis of August 1998 under the new name of "targeted finance", which is an attempt to repay government debt for goods and services supplied in 1997 and 1998. Offsets have been particularly large at the end of each year. Periods of large offsets coincide with a reduced flow of federal tax arrears, but the effect is only temporary and tax arrears promptly build up again ... There have been a few highly publicized attempts at ... eliminating the flow of its own arrears ... such as the drive to pay off salary and pension arrears in full by the end of 1997. But such initiatives have meant pulling resources from other budget commitments so that, in the end, overall government arrears did not decline' (*RET*, 1999, vol. 8, no. 1, p. 25).

Inter-enterprise debt (arrears) grew from 48 billion roubles at the beginning of 1992 to over 3,000 billion (70 per cent of GDP) by mid-1992 (IMF, *World Economic Outlook*, May 1993, p. 61). Inter-enterprise debt was essentially eliminated during the payments crisis in summer 1992 by a massive credit injection, but by summer 1993 the debt had reportedly reached 60 per cent (in real terms) of the pre-crisis level (OECD, *Economic Outlook*, December 1993, p. 116).

By December 1994 inter-enterprise debt amounted to 196,000 billion roubles (*RET*, 1995, vol. 3, no. 4, p. 112).

Inter-enterprise debt is the largest category of total enterprise arrears, amounting to 63.8 per cent as of 1 June 1994. The second largest category is tax arrears, followed by bank loan arrears and then wage arrears (*Transition*, 1994, vol. 5, no. 9, p. 5).

Bribery of managers to deliver without payment is another reason for arrears (*The Guardian*, 29 May 1998, p. 14).

A number of measures have subsequently been taken to deal with the problem, including the following:

1. A decree of 20 October 1993 stated that all inter-enterprise debt had to be converted into three-month promissory notes. Non-payment of these bills on maturity would lead to automatic bankruptcy, although privatization could take place by swapping debt for equity. An insolvent enterprise could also be leased by an outside investor, who would be able to purchase (at a discount) 20–30 per cent of the shares of the enterprise if it was still operating after a year (*RET*, 1993, vol. 2, no. 4, p. 65). The promissory notes would enable creditors to sell debt to others, who could then try to recover the amount owing through the bankruptcy procedures.

2. A presidential decree of 20 December 1994, effective 1 January 1995, concerned non-payment. The bill for an item delivered under contract must

be paid within three months of receipt of the item. If the bill is not paid the money owed to the enterprise is written off as a loss; bankruptcy agencies acquire the right to recover the money as state revenue (*CDSP*, 1995, vol. XLVI, no. 51, p. 23).

Incomes policy

Another way of tackling inflation is by means of an incomes policy.

After January 1992 enterprises were free to set the wages of their employees. But 'excessive' wage increases were subject to punitive taxation (EBRD 1994: 35). An increase in the wage fund that exceeded the level of price increases by more than 70 per cent was subject to a fine (*RET*, 1994, Monthly Update, 30 June 1994, p. 3; *CDSP*, 1994, vol. XLVI, no. 21, pp. 9–10). But the tax on excessive wage increases, covering both state and non-state enterprises, was scrapped at the start of January 1996 (EBRD 1996b: 171; Deutsche Bank, *Focus: Eastern Europe*, 1996, no. 160, p. 4).

The conquering of hyperinflation: the budget deficit and its financing

A budget deficit occurs when a government spends more than it raises in tax revenue. The size of the budget and the way it is financed have a crucial bearing on the control of inflation. The budget deficit can be financed by (1) increasing the money supply, (2) borrowing from the private sector of the economy and/or from foreigners, or (3) some combination of (1) and (2). ('When government spending exceeds tax revenues the difference is financed by selling government bonds. If these are sold to the public then the net effect on the money supply is zero. But if they are purchased by the central bank the money supply rise that accompanies the deficit is not offset: this is known as "printing money" or "monetizing the deficit"': *The Economist*, 20 November 1999, p. 142.)

Basically what happened in Russia is that the budget deficit was reduced as a percentage of GDP and (1) was decreased while (2) was increased in importance. Inflation was consequently brought under control by 1997. 'The method of stabilization has been straightforward: the end of monetary financing of the budget deficit. This was accomplished … by issuing short-term Treasury bills (GKOs), longer-term Treasury bills (OFZs) and other notes, along with lending from the IMF' (Ickes *et al.* 1997: 110).

Hyperinflation in 1992 was caused by a massive budget deficit that was financed entirely by printing money. The money supply was swollen by a factor of 7.4 in 1992 and 4.8 in 1993 (Gaidar, *CDSP*, 1994, vol. XLVI, no. 6, p. 9). According to Andrei Illarionov, the money supply increased by 130 per cent in 1991, 640 per cent in 1992 and 380 per cent in 1993; Illarionov resigned as chief economic adviser to the prime minister on 8 February 1994 (*CDSP*, 1994, vol. XLVI, no. 6, p. 14). 'Central bank credit in the second half of 1992 increased dramatically, with devastating implications for the government's stabilization programme ... Between June and October central bank credit to commercial banks trebled ... These credits were than lent on to enterprises, often at interest rates that were highly subsidized' (Ickes and Ryterman 1993: 238–9).

By 1997 inflation was at a relatively modest level (an estimated 14.7 per cent). This was achieved by gradually reducing reliance on the printing press to finance persistently high (though generally declining) budget deficits. Tighter control was gradually attained over the money supply. A positive interest rate was achieved in November 1993 and after February 1994 Russia had 'a real interest rate of about 100 per cent a year – the highest rate in the world' (Åslund 1994b: 63). 'For the past year Russia has had some of the highest real interest rates in the world' (*The Economist*, 8 October 1994, p. 24). Both nominal and real interest rates went down as inflationary pressures abated. The nominal interest rate the central bank charged commercial banks for credit rose from 20 per cent on 1 January 1992 to 210 per cent on 15 October 1993. It then fell, reaching 21 per cent on 1 October 1997. Russia then had to react to the effects of the Asian financial crisis, which had begun in July 1997 in Thailand. The interest rate was increased to 28 per cent on 10 November 1997 and reached 42 per cent on 2 February 1998. The interest rate was then reduced to 39 per cent on 17 February 1998, to 36 per cent on 2 March 1998 and to 30 per cent on 16 March 1998. (Later developments will be discussed in the Asian/Russian financial crisis.)

The federal budget deficit has remained stubbornly high, however, with problems on both the tax and spending sides (despite, as regards the latter, delays in the payment of state wages and pensions, a policy which is non-sustainable in the long run: see below). The federal budget deficit (according to the IMF definition) was 7.9 per cent of GDP in 1996, 7.0 per cent in 1997 and 5 per cent in 1998 (*RET*, Monthly Update, 20 January 1999, p. 24, and 10 February 1999, p. 10). (The federal budget deficit was 5.8 per cent in 1993, 9.8 per cent in 1994 and 5.2 per cent in 1995: *RET*, 2000, vol. 9, no. 1, p. 118. The federal budget deficit, according to the IMF definition, was 5.4 per cent in 1995 and 1.7 per cent in 1999: *RET*, Monthly Update, 11 August 2000, p. 25.) (IMF definition: 'Privatization receipts and net sales of state gold reserves are counted as deficit financing': *RET*, 10 February 1999, p. 24. The EU's Maastricht criterion as regards the budget deficit is a maximum of 3 per cent of GDP.) The federal budget deficit in 1995 was financed almost entirely by bond sales and external credits (*RET*, 1995, vol. 4, no. 4, p. 5). But heavy dependence on *short-term borrowing* ultimately proved to be unsustainable, as will be seen in the section on the Asian/Russian financial crisis below.

It is important to stress that it is now the *federal* budget (rather than the consolidated state budget, which includes the regions) which is now the central focus of debate (*RET*, 1994, vol. 3, no. 2, p. 9). Unlike local budgets the federal budget can be financed by money creation (*RET*, 1994, vol. 3, no. 3, p. 10).

'The concern is not that the government does not collect enough taxes. In fact, it collected 32 per cent of Russia's GDP last year [1997], the same proportion that the United States does' (Anders Åslund, *IHT*, 29 April 1998, p. 10). The media reports Russian tax revenues at about 10 per cent of GDP. However, that is only federal tax revenues, which are less than one-third of the total. In 1997 revenues were no less than 32 per cent of GDP when the regional and local budgets, as well as extra-budgetary funds (notably the pension fund) are included. The Russian state collects as large a share of GDP as the American state does. 'One serious problem is that taxes tend to stop at the regional level, where budgets are extremely wasteful. About one-third of those expenditures are on subsidies to enterprises, which tend to converge on corruption. Another third is housing and communal support which is directed to the wealthiest, and barely one-third goes to socially desirable purposes. Cleaning up corruption at the regional level will be a complex task lasting years. In the short term the only plausible solution is to try to starve regional authorities of funds' (Anders Åslund, *The World Today*, July 1998, vol. 54, no. 7, pp. 185–6).

The budget deficit, its financing and the role of the IMF before the financial crisis of August 1998: a detailed chronology

The definition of the budget deficit varies between countries and can vary over time in the same country, as it has done in Russia. A distinction has been made, for example, between the budget deficit on a 'rouble cash flow basis' and that on an 'overall government deficit on an accrual basis'. The former excludes (1) extra-budgetary funds such as the Pension Fund, (2) off-budget interest rate subsidies and import subsidies and (3) unpaid obligations to the domestic economy and to foreign creditors (*RET*, 1993, vol. 2, no. 4, p. 10).

In 1992 the large budget deficit was financed entirely by increasing the money supply ('monetization' of the budget deficit). This caused hyperinflation. Conquering hyperinflation meant reducing the budget deficit as a proportion of GDP and reducing the proportion of the deficit financed by printing money. Russia began issuing domestic debt in the spring of 1993. GKOs are short-term (less than one year) Treasury bills, while OFZs are longer-dated federal bonds. Foreigners were banned from investing in GKOs until late 1996 (*IHT*, 9 March 1999, p. 8.)

Critics of IMF loans express concern that Russia has often failed to meet conditions laid down and yet aid has still been forthcoming. Russia has suffered only periodic delays in receiving aid. Those in favour of continued aid to Russia point, for example, to the wider political benefits of maintaining stability in Russia. (See Chapter 8.)

The consolidated budget deficit on a 'rouble cash flow basis' was 20 per cent in 1991 (*RET*, 1993, vol. 2, no. 3, pp. 6, 9). In 1992 the budget deficit on a 'rouble cash flow' basis was 4.7 per cent of GDP, but the 'overall government deficit on an accrual basis' was of the order of 20 per cent of GDP (*RET*, 1993, vol. 2, no. 4, p. 10).

An international aid package worth $24 billion was announced on 1 April 1992 to be financed by the G7 and other Western countries (in part via institutions like the IMF). (See Chapter 8 for details.) The aid package was conditional (including targets for reducing the budget deficit and inflation rates) and the main monitoring agency was to be the IMF. On 5 August 1992 the IMF agreed to release $1 billion in spite of considerable concern about Russia's progress in meeting its commitments.

A G7 meeting in Tokyo on 15–16 April 1993 agreed on a $43.4 billion aid package, which was larger than expected. There was more old than new, but the exact proportion was not clear. Included was a $3 billion 'systemic transformation facility' from the IMF. Not only was this new, but some of the conditions laid down were also new. The first instalment of $1.5 billion was to be disbursed simply when a commitment to economic change was made (the IMF actually approved the first tranche on 30 June 1993), although the second depended on the curbing of inflation and the budget deficit. The second tranche, due in September, was delayed because of the IMF's concern that its conditions were not being met (*IHT*, 21 September 1993, p. 13). It was not until 22 March 1994 that Michel Camdessus, the managing director of the IMF, agreed in principle to the second tranche; formal IMF approval had to wait until 20 April 1994. The agreed conditions included cutting planned expenditure programmes in the event of tax deficiencies and/or spending overruns and a target monthly inflation rate of 7 per cent by the end of 1994.

In the first quarter of 1994 credit from the central bank accounted for 82 per cent of the total budget shortfall (*RET*, 1994, vol. 3, no. 1, p. 12). In the first half of 1994 central bank financing amounted to 80 per cent of the federal budget shortfall. But in order to reduce this inflationary method of finance the government now also sells government bonds and gold certificates. Net borrowing through these operations yielded a sum equivalent to nearly 14 per cent of the federal budget deficit. The remaining 6 per cent was covered by the partial sale of the IMF loan received in April 1994 (*RET*, 1994, vol. 3, no. 2, p. 13). ('In 1994 72 per cent of the state budget deficit was covered by credits from the central bank, that is, by printing money that had nothing behind it': Anatoli Chubais, *CDSP*, 1995, vol. XLVII, no. 22, p. 7.)

It is now the federal budget, rather than the consolidated state budget (including the regions), which is now the central focus of debate. The federal budget has now been adjusted to include all interest rate subsidies, all foreign currency income and outlays and the formerly extra-budgetary production funds (the social funds, which are larger, remaining outside the budget) (*RET*, 1994, vol. 3, no. 2, p. 9). Unlike local budgets the federal budget can be financed by money creation. The federal budget deficit (on a cash flow basis) in 1993 was 10.4 per cent of GDP (*RET*, 1994, vol. 3, no. 3, p. 10).

The 1995 budget was outlined by prime minister Chernomyrdin on 27 October 1994 in a speech to the State Duma, which approved it on 23 December. The budget deficit was to be kept to 7.8 per cent of GDP and the monthly inflation rate was to be reduced to 1 per cent by the end of 1995. Just under half was to be financed by borrowing from abroad, especially from the IMF.

On 28 January 1995 the State Duma passed a law (which needed to be ratified by the Council of the Federation) banning the central bank from financing the budget by credits not approved in the budget (*RET,* Monthly Update, 21 February 1995, p. 2).

On 7 February 1995, after three weeks of negotiations, the IMF suspended negotiations about a $6.25 billion stand-by loan and a $6 billion stabilization fund. The IMF was concerned about unfavourable fiscal and monetary trends, exacerbated by the cost of the war in Chechenia. Negotiations were resumed on 23 February and the following day the State Duma passed the budget for 1995 on its third reading. The budget deficit was to be a satisfactory 7.8 per cent of GDP and the aim was to bring the monthly inflation rate down to under 2 per cent by the end of 1995. The State Duma failed to override Yeltsin's veto of the proposed massive increase in the minimum monthly wage from 20,500 roubles to 54,500 roubles.

Yeltsin issued three decrees on 1 March 1995. One aim was to exercise tighter control over fiscal policy. Only the president would henceforth be able to permit spending greater than or revenue less than that envisaged in the budget, while the tax and import duty exemptions enjoyed by certain companies and organizations engaged in foreign trade were cancelled.

On 10 March 1995 Michel Camdessus announced that he was recommending the IMF board to permit the stand-by loan, but that it should be paid out in monthly rather than quarterly tranches in order to ensure compliance with the terms. When the State Duma passed the budget on its fourth reading on 15 March 1995 (the Council of the Federation gave its approval on 22 March) it was announced that the budget deficit would be 5.6 per cent of GDP, owing to GDP being greater than first calculated. The deficit of 73.2 trillion roubles was to be financed by the issuing of domestic bonds (30.6 trillion roubles) and by foreign loans (42.6 trillion roubles), primarily from the IMF (*IHT,* 23 March 1995, p. 7). The IMF's decision to lend Russia $6.4 billion, announced on 10 March 1995, would help the government to finance two-fifths of the deficit (*The Economist*, Survey, 8 April 1995, p. 19).

The IMF approved a $6.8 billion stand-by loan on 11 April 1995.

The budget adopted for 1995 included no central bank credits (the 5,000 billion credits voted for the first quarter did not break the rule, since the government planned to repay them later in the year). But it was still possible for the central bank to buy a limited amount of Treasury bills on the secondary market, thereby expanding the money base. The deficit was to be financed by issues of Treasury bills and private saving certificates and by foreign borrowing (*RET*, Monthly Update, 21 February 1995, p. 2).

The projected budget deficit for 1995 was 5.5 per cent of GDP, compared with roughly 10 per cent in 1994 and 15 per cent in 1993 (after allowing for quasi-budgetary credits) (*RET*, Monthly Update, 14 April 1995, p. 2). The consolidated budget deficit in 1994 was 9.9 per cent of GDP. The federal deficit on a cash flow basis was 10.4 per cent of GDP (close to the 9.6 per cent planned), of which more than 70 per cent was financed with credits from the central bank (*RET*, 1995, vol. 3, no. 4, pp. 4, 9). Between January and October 1995 the federal budget deficit was kept down to 3.5 per cent of GDP. Some 60 per cent of the deficit was financed by increases in the holdings of government debt by the Russian public. The rest was financed by Treasury bills bought in the secondary market by the central bank and by the sale of Ministry of Finance dollars to the central bank (*RET*, Monthly Update, 15 December 1995, p. 6).

The federal budget deficit in 1995 was 2.9 per cent of GDP, the lowest since reforms began in 1992. The deficit was financed almost entirely via bond sales and external credits (*RET*, 1995, vol. 4, no. 4, p. 5). In 1994 about two-thirds of the deficit was financed through central bank credits to the government. In 1995 this pattern was reversed, with all of the deficit being financed through non-inflationary means. While most of the financing came from foreign credits, it was internal financing that really entered the spotlight. In 1995 the sales of securities accounted for 47.9 per cent of the deficit compared with 19.3 per cent in 1994 (pp. 11–12).

'The budget deficit is no longer financed by inflationary CBR [central bank] credits but largely by sales of debt to the private sector' (p. 3). Some two-thirds of the budget deficit in 1995 was financed by net receipts from the sale of Treasury bills (*RET*, 16 January 1996, p. 3). The budget deficit has been financed mainly by foreign and domestic borrowing, rather than money creation (p. 6). In 1995 the budget deficit was financed primarily by non-inflationary means and included sales of securities (48 per cent) and foreign credits (52 per cent) (*RET*, Monthly Update, 13 February 1996, p. 7).

The 1996 budget was approved by the State Duma on 6 December 1995, with the budget deficit targeted at 3.85 per cent of GDP and the average monthly inflation rate at 1.9 per cent. The vote 'paves the way for a relatively stable fiscal environment for the upcoming year. This is the first time in the history of independent Russia that the budget has been approved by the legislative branch before the beginning of the new fiscal year' (*RET*, Monthly Update, 15 December 1995, 6; 16 January 1996, pp. 3, 8).

The 1996 federal budget deficit (excluding interest payments on domestic government debt) was 3.3 per cent of GDP, below the 3.85 per cent target. But high yields on government securities pushed the more inclusive IMF definition deficit up to 7.7 per cent of GDP, which was above target. The consolidated general government deficit (which includes the deficits of the central and local authorities but excludes four extra-budgetary funds) was 4.2 per cent (compared with 3.4 per cent in 1995). In 1996 the government continued the policy adopted in 1995 of relying on non-inflationary financing of the budget deficit. Thus central bank credits did not account for any share of the deficit financing (compared with over 50 per cent in 1994) (*RET*, 1997, no. 1, pp. 5, 8, 18). In 1996 the federal budget deficit (including interest payments on short-term debt and excluding privatization revenues) was 7.7 per cent of GDP (*RET*, Monthly Update, 23 September 1997, p. vi).

On 22 February 1996 Michel Camdessus announced that he was recommending that the IMF board permit (which it did on 26 March) a $10.2 billion stand-by loan over three years (with $4.1 billion allotted for 1996). Once again the loan would be paid out in monthly tranches in order to ensure compliance with the terms, which included the following: maximum target budget deficits as a proportion of GDP of 4 per cent in 1996, 3 per cent in 1997 and 2 per cent in 1998; a monthly inflation rate of 1 per cent by the end of 1996; the elimination of tariffs on oil and gas exports (a 1 April 1996 deadline for the abolition of export tariffs on natural gas and for a 50 per cent reduction in oil tariffs; oil export tariffs have to be phased out altogether by 1 July 1996).

But on 22 July 1996 the IMF announced that it was to delay the July tranche of $330 million largely because of unsatisfactory tax revenue. Then on 21 August 1996 the IMF announced that it had decided to release the July tranche of $330 million. On 24 October 1996 the IMF delayed payment of the October tranche of $336 million again largely because of dissatisfaction with the amount of tax revenue raised. The government admitted that during the first nine months of 1996 budget revenue reached only 71 per cent of that predicted for the period and tax revenue 64.6 per cent of that predicted (*IHT*, 26 October 1996, p. 15). 'Improved revenue performance' led the IMF to release the October tranche on 13 December 1996.

The draft budget for 1997 submitted to the Duma called for a federal deficit of 3.3 per cent of GDP. This excluded interest payments on GKO debt. Once these interest payments and local and extra-budgetary deficits are included, the general government deficit would possibly be as much as 7 to 8 per cent of GDP. It should be possible to finance this deficit in a non-inflationary way through new bond issues and foreign loans (*RET*, Monthly Update, 13 September 1996, p. 6). The draft federal budget for 1997 foresees a deficit of 3.3 per cent of GDP. But in addition to this interest payments on GKOs amount to something like 2 per cent of GDP at least and local budgets and extra-budgetary funds are likely to be in deficit. Thus the general government budget may be as high as 7 to 8 per cent of GDP (*RET*, Monthly Update, 22 October 1996, pp. 5–6).

The federal budget deficit for 1997 (counting privatization receipts and net sales of state gold reserves as government revenues) was 6.1 per cent of GDP, with a 'primary deficit' (deficit minus interest payments) of 1.7 per cent of

GDP (*RET*, Monthly Update, 3 March 1998, pp. 1–2). (The general government budget deficit, including deficits run by regional and local governments, was over 6.5 per cent of GDP: p. 1.) The federal budget deficit for 1997 according to the IMF definition came to 6.8 per cent of GDP (p. 9). In 1997 the federal budget deficit was 6.8 per cent of GDP, compared with 7.7 per cent in 1996. The enlarged budget deficit (including the deficits of regional and local governments and the surpluses run by off-budget funds) was likely to remain below 8 per cent of GDP (*RET*, 1998, no. 1, p. 73).

On 3 September 1997 the IMF approved a $700 million tranche of its three-year $10 billion loan (*RET*, 1997, no. 4, p. 104). On 31 October 1997 the IMF delayed issuing a $700 million tranche of the three-year $10 billion loan until at least early 1998 because of unsatisfactory tax collection (p. 107).

The draft budget for 1998 before the State Duma sets the deficit at 4.5 per cent of GDP and predicts debt service expenditures of 4.4 per cent of GDP (the same as in 1997), leaving a 'primary deficit' of 0.1 per cent of GDP (*RET*, Monthly Update, 3 March 1998, pp. 1–2). The State Duma did not pass the (amended) 1998 budget (on its fourth and final reading) until 4 March 1998. The vote was 252 to 129. There was to be a federal deficit of 5 per cent of GDP and a primary deficit of 0.6 per cent of GDP. The Duma approved a clause that allowed the government to implement proportional spending cuts across all items if revenue was lower than planned (*RET*, 1998, no. 1, p. 74). The budget law allowed the government to make proportional spending cuts (i.e. to 'sequester') without submitting a revised budget to the Duma (p. 80).

The Duma agreed that the government could cut spending by 5 per cent without its approval, or 10 per cent with its approval, if revenue collection falls short (*Business Central Europe*, April 1998, p. 17).

On 19 February 1998 IMF managing director Michel Camdessus, on a visit to Russia, announced that Russia and the IMF had agreed to extend the $10 billion three-year loan programme for another year (the original one having been planned to end in early 1999). Additional funding (not specified) would be available. The date of release of the next $700 million tranche was not specified either. The credits available under the newly agreed 1998 IMF programme would begin flowing only after a regular quarterly review (*IHT*, 20 February 1998, p. 15; *FT*, 20 February 1998, p. 2).

On 29 May 1998 the IMF recommended that $670 million be released by the end of June 1998.

Problems of expenditure control and of raising tax revenue

Even before the financial crisis of August 1998 dramatically exposed the dangers of relying too heavily on short-term borrowing, questions were raised as to the sustainability of macroeconomic stabilization through such means of expenditure control as delays in paying state wages and pensions.

Problems of expenditure control

The ability to control government expenditures by delaying payment of wages in the state sector and (to a lesser extent) of pensions can be explained by a number of factors. 'The lesson of the past few years has been that in post-communist Russia, workers have almost no political muscle … Discredited by years of co-operation with the communists and further enfeebled by the country's bleak economic conditions, even trade unions are barely able to organize protest … At first hesitantly, and now with increasing boldness, the government has learned that it can pursue the toughest financial stabilization programmes with little fear of a political backlash … The impotence of Russian workers, whose wage arrears are again mounting, is the biggest reason why the Kremlin has managed to defend its hard won financial stabilization, especially in the wake of the financial turmoil caused by the Asian crisis. In the long run, however, the lack of political institutions through which everyone, even the dispossessed, can express their grievances, may prove to be one of the greatest flaws in the emerging new Russia … [if] charismatic nationalist and populist politicians … devise a way of tapping the anger of the unpaid workers, Russia's post-communist establishment could be overturned' (Chrystia Freeland, *FT,* 1 April 1998, p. 2).

In February 1995 Yeltsin complained that the work of the government commission on the non-payment problem had been unsatisfactory (*CDSP,* 1995, vol. XLVII, no. 7, p. 4).

'The budget deficit targets have been achieved through the government failing to pay all its obligations – even including wages, where the wages arrears of central and local governments are now 20 per cent of all wage arrears. This situation needs to be reformed, through expenditure commitments based on realizable forecasts of tax revenue' (*RET,* Monthly Update, 16 December 1996, p. vii). In the first three-quarters of 1996 realized budget expenditure was only 75 per cent of budget levels (p. 110). Some arrears have been paid off periodically before building up again, e.g. state pension arrears were paid by 1 July 1997. On 8 July 1997 Yeltsin promised that wage arrears to the armed forces would be paid by 1 September 1997 and to all other state employees by the end of 1997. The former promise was kept but Yeltsin reckoned that the government failed to achieve the latter goal. The figures show that the authorities failed to pay back all budget sector wage arrears by the end of 1997, but they did manage to cut the stock by more than half by year-end. Most of these wages were due from regional governments, but the federal government loaned regional governments half of the sum needed to pay back the arrears. Regional governments were obliged to find the remaining funds themselves (*RET,* 1998, no. 1, p. 44). Total wage arrears reached 57 billion roubles ($9.51 billion) as of 1 March 1998, of which the federal and local governments owed 7.6 billion ($1.2 billion). As regards the 1 January 1998 deadline, the government claimed that it had pieced together the funds but that regional authorities were to blame when some workers remained unpaid. Wage arrears had begun to grow rapidly in mid-1995. The level of arrears in March 1997 reached 27.7 per cent of total state sector wages. Many workers were waiting six to eight months for their wages. More than half of employees in state enterprises were claiming at least two months' wages (*Transition*, 1998, vol. 9, no. 2, p. 6). Wage arrears remain a serious problem. (Chapter 9 on economic performance deals with the general problem of wage arrears.)

The consolidated budget refers to the total of three levels of government (federal, regional and local), less transfers among them. In 1997 total consolidated budget spending amounted to 33 per cent of GDP, which was split almost evenly between the federal budget (16 per cent of GDP, not including transfers) and regional and local budgets (17 per cent of GDP). In addition, a portion of government spending takes place in a large number of 'off-budget' funds at the federal and regional levels. The major federal off-budget funds (the only funds for which data are available) spent a further 8 per cent of GDP. Thus 'enlarged' government spending was over 41 per cent and probably somewhat larger. General government spending was 63 per cent in 1992. 'But relative to GDP the Russian general government spending remains quite large by international standards. The average ratio of spending to GDP for advanced countries in 1997 was 39 per cent and for countries in transition it was just 35 per cent, with the figure lower still for middle income countries. General government spending in OECD countries ranged from 15 per cent of GDP in South Korea to 66 per cent in Sweden. The United States general government spends roughly 35 per cent of GDP each year, and the United Kingdom roughly 42 per cent' (*RET*, Monthly Update, 2 July 1998, p. 1).

BANKRUPTCY

A credible threat of bankruptcy is necessary to turn 'soft budget constraints' into 'hard budget constraints', i.e. managers must be convinced that a stage will be reached when the state will no longer automatically bail out loss-making enterprises.

A bankruptcy law came into effect on 1 March 1993 (*CDSP*, 1993, vol. XLV, no. 5, p. 21; no. 12, p. 29). But bankruptcy is still relatively rare. Although direct state subsidies have been reduced loss-making enterprises have kept going by delaying the payment of taxes, bills, bank credits and wages. Richard Layard rejects the claim that Russia's factory managers have accumulated massive inter-factory debt while counting on the government to bail them out. The average delay in paying suppliers is rather less than in Western Europe. Most bail-outs go to agriculture, coal or defence and not to privatized industry (Richard Layard, *FT*, 14 March 1995, p. 20). Only a few industries, such as agriculture and coal, continue to receive big state subsidies (*The*

Economist, 18 February 1995, p. 90). (Workers have also accepted reduced real wages in order to remain with the enterprise and enjoy the social benefits associated with employment, such as health and housing.)

A decree 'On the sale of state debtor-enterprises' was signed on 2 June 1994. Insolvent enterprises ineligible for state assistance would be subject to sale under competitive conditions. The manager would be automatically replaced prior to the sale. The buyer would be responsible for the enterprise's debts and for undertaking a certain minimum investment (*CDSP*, 1994, vol. XLVI, no. 22, p. 11).

The following indicate the limited extent of bankruptcies:

1. Leyla Boulton (*FT*, 17 September 1993, p. 3) reported the first enterprise to be bankrupted under the new law (a cellulose plant in Archangel). According to Jill Barshay (*FT*, 29 December 1993, p. 2), only one small kitchen knife factory had filed successfully. Boris Fyodorov was quoted as saying, 'What kind of shock therapy is it if inflation runs at 20 per cent a month? If the whole nation had just five bankruptcies during a year?' (*IHT*, 2 February 1994, p. 4).

2. *The Economist* (19 March 1994, p. 83) reported that bankruptcy proceedings had begun against fewer than fifty industrial firms; all were small and not one had been forced into liquidation, according to the Federal Bankruptcy Agency.

In mid-July 1994 the agency declared the first three insolvencies (*RET*, 1994, vol. 3, no. 2, p. 34). By the end of September 1994 516 enterprises had been officially declared insolvent, fifty-six of which were auctioned off (*RET*, 1994, vol. 3, no. 3, p. 9). As of 23 January 1995 1,358 enterprises had been declared bankrupt out of 6,448 examined by the Federal Bankruptcy Agency. Sixty-one had been auctioned off during liquidation or privatization procedures (*RET*, 1995, vol. 3, no. 4, pp. 7, 99). A new bankruptcy law became effective on 1 March 1998 (*RET*, 1998, no. 1, p. 7). 'Even though insolvency procedures are becoming more commonplace, the number of bankruptcies today is not particularly high given the number of enterprises that use overdue debts to finance operations and cover losses' (p. 94). 'The main obstacles to implementing bankruptcy law in Russia are strong political resistance, the absence of a proper safety net, poorly staffed arbitration courts and poorly paid officials and, finally, a lengthy criminal prosecution procedure for non-compliance with the rulings of arbitration courts … Up to the end of 1997 the number of bankruptcies in Russia has been significantly lower than in other transition economies. The main reason for such slow progress are a pro-debtor bias in the bankruptcy law, low priority of private creditor claims, political opposition to the process of bankruptcy and an underdeveloped social safety net' (*RET*, 1998, no. 2, pp. 56–7).

In a late November 1994 speech Chernomyrdin referred to about fifty enterprises having been declared bankrupt (*CDSP*, 1994, vol. XLVI, no. 47, p. 2).

3. The agency reported that it had liquidated or sold 400 state enterprises (*The Economist*, 18 February 1995, p. 82). In the first two years after price liberalization in January 1992 not a single enterprise was allowed to go under. But the Federal Bankruptcy Agency was established in late 1993 and by January 1995 the agency had taken action against 400 state enterprises that had defaulted on their debts. Courts had placed over 500 privatized firms in receivership (*The Economist*, Survey, 8 April 1995, p. 13). Only one coal mine has been closed since the launch of radical reform (p. 19).

By the end of 1995 the federal bankruptcy agency (dealing with debtors with more than 25 per cent state ownership) had declared 3,343 enterprises insolvent. Only about 5 per cent of these cases were brought to court. 'Formal bankruptcy proceedings remain relatively rare' (EBRD 1996b: 170). By mid-1997 only about 1,000 enterprises had been declared bankrupt. The federal bankruptcy service has been unable to implement most of its decisions (EBRD 1997b: 195).

4. By September 1996 fewer than 1,000 enterprises had been declared bankrupt (*The Economist*, Survey, 12 July 1997, p. 12).

Problems of raising tax revenue

Russia's inability to raise sufficient tax revenue to finance the central (federal) government's essential activities is crucial to gaining an understanding of the financial crisis which hit Russia on 17 August 1998, as can be seen from the following dramatic comments:

1. On 23 June 1998 Sergei Kiriyenko (prime minister 23 March–23 August 1998) stated: 'If the state does not learn to collect taxes it will cease to exist.'

2. Anatoli Chubais had earlier (17 April 1997) thought likewise: 'Russia is experiencing a monstrous state budget crisis, whose parameters, if truth be told, call into question the ability of the state to perform its functions' (*FT*, 18 April 1997, p. 2).

3. 'The government is basically bankrupt. New York City collects more in municipal taxes than Russia collects federal taxes' (Boris Fyodorov, *FT*, 18 February 1999, p. 14).

4. '[Prime minister] Primakov ... announced that tax revenues in September [1998] were only half of what had been hoped for' (*IHT*, 30 September 1998, p. 5).

5. 'Deputy finance minister Mikhail Kasyanov said Wednesday [10 February] that the IMF wanted Russia to double its tax collection ... "The IMF considers that the revenues of the federal budget should be 17 per cent to 18 per cent of GDP", said Mr Kasyanov' (*IHT*, 11 February 1999, p. 13).

6. 'The federal government collects taxes equal to 10 per cent of GDP, one of the lowest tax collection levels in the world' (*FT*, 15 July 1998, p. 2).

7. 'Russia's inability to collect taxes is rapidly becoming the greatest threat to its economic and political stability. The current government cannot raise

the revenues needed to run a modern state. Since economic reforms began in 1992 *federal* tax revenues have fallen from about 18 per cent of Russia's GDP to less than 10 per cent in 1997 – compared with about 31 per cent in Austria, 27 per cent in Germany and 18 per cent in the USA' (Treisman 1998: 55).

8. 'A different model is now gaining currency among political and economic analysts, who say that Russia is in imminent danger of becoming a "failed state", not breaking into pieces as the Soviet Union did in December 1991, but simply ceasing to function as a cohesive federal government. Many Russian politicians and political analysts say the debasement of Moscow's authority... threatens to bring its own special dangers, opening the doors to even more corruption and lawlessness, weapons proliferation, health hazards and environmental pollution. If Russia becomes a failed state, the risks are that individual regions and parts of Russian society will go their own way – making it difficult, for example, for Russia to control factories making missile parts ... Hobbled by economic decline, the government has become dysfunctional in some of its core responsibilities, including such pillars of central authority as the military, the courts and tax collection' (David Hoffman, *IHT*, 27 February 1999, p. 1).

Tax revenues have fallen short of forecasts. There have been various estimates:

Federal revenues in 1996 were some 16 per cent below levels targeted in the budget, primarily due to increasing tax arrears (Ickes *et al.* 1997: 112).

According to the United Nations, only 70 per cent of planned revenue was realized in 1996 (*World Economic and Social Survey*, 1997, p. 27).

In 1996 about 60 per cent of expected tax revenue was collected (*IHT*, 2 October 1997, p. 7).

In 1997 the government collected little more than half its planned tax revenue (*FT*, Survey, 15 April 1998, p. viii). In 1997 65 per cent of planned tax revenue was raised (*FT*, 10 July 1998, p. 2).

Tax receipts have fallen to less than 20 per cent of GDP (Yavlinsky 1998: 71).

Budget revenues account for about 30 per cent of GDP, whereas in some East European countries the share is approximately 50 per cent (Yegor Gaidar, *CDSP*, 1998, vol. 50, no. 22, p. 4).

REASONS FOR TAX REVENUE PROBLEMS AND MEASURES TAKEN TO TACKLE THEM

High tax arrears are due to three factors: (1) low tax discipline; (2) excessive tax rates on many sectors (encouraging evasion) coupled with inadequate taxation of some goods (such as alcohol); and (3) a failure to prohibit barter (*RET*, Monthly Update, 17 March 1997, p. iv). Of total acknowledged tax debt 45 per cent is owed by only seventy-three enterprises and none of them have so far been bankrupted. According to Goskomstat, 'about 70 per cent of (industrial) shipments are exchanged through barter'. Another survey of 500 medium-sized manufacturing enterprises gives a figure of 40 per cent, compared with only 6 per cent in 1992 (p. vi). 'Tax rates remain very high in Russia. The combination of value-added taxes (standard rate 20 per cent), profit taxes (standard rate 35 per cent), social security payments (40 per cent) and personal income taxes (up to 30 per cent) is large ... With very high tax rates, it is no surprise that enterprises and households avoid taxes through under-reporting, or cannot pay the taxes due to financial problems ... One reason for the fall in revenues ... is the rapid growth of the untaxed shadow economy. The current GDP estimates include an estimate for the shadow economy of approximately 22 per cent of GDP... One of the most important means to widen the [tax] base is to reduce marginal tax rates, so that new enterprises and households are more willing to pay taxes and become part of the system' (*RET*, Monthly Update, 22 October 1996, pp. 5–6). ('The main structural distortion of the tax system by international comparison is the excessive role of profit taxation and the low share of taxes on individuals and the energy sector': EBRD 1996b: 171.)

'Until it is widely acknowledged that taxes have to be paid, I am afraid we are going to go on having problems with budget revenues. At present paying taxes is – to put it mildly – regarded as strange (or else as an obligation one does not have to meet in full) ... The irresponsibility of our government is the major cause of our low tax collection rate ... It was no accident that the federal default [of August 1998] was followed by a series of defaults by regional administrations – even by some that could easily have paid their debts. And if the government fails to meet its commitments to the people the people are not going to be in any hurry to pay their taxes either. Beside, what do they get for them? Free health care? Anyone who has ever had a relative in hospital ... knows exactly what they have to pay attendants and nurses under the table. Education? But who does not have to spend money to keep a kid at school? Law and order? I do not even want to say how much Alpha Bank has to spend on its private security service. All these services essentially amount to a second "shadow" system of taxation. So why bother with the first one, the legitimate one' (Pyotr Aven, president of Alpha Bank and former minister of foreign economic relations in Russia, *Kommersant*, 29 February 2000, p. 8: *CDSP*, 2000, vol. 52, no. 12, pp. 12–13).

'Russia has no actual tax system. In practice, taxation is a free negotiation between the ubiquitous tax inspectors and taxpayers, meaning that the strong win and small entrepreneurs are chased out of business. Hence Poland and Hungary, for example, have six times more enterprises in relation to their population than Russia. This means feeble competition, leading to substandard products and service, high prices and little economic growth. Russia needs radical tax reform before significant growth is possible' (Anders Åslund, *IHT*, 29 April 1998, p. 10). The IMF has been greatly concerned with Russia's failure to meet revenue targets and has demanded higher tax rates.

'The problem is an arbitrary tax system, with excessively high rates and ruthless government officials. Russia needs a new tax system, with lower – not higher – rates, which should defend the rights of honest taxpayers, so that it is meaningful to pay taxes. The present system is so arbitrary that you are more likely to be forced to pay a penalty if you pay your taxes than if you ignore them altogether. Moreover, excessive rates make it impossible to collect taxes. Until recently penalties have been extraordinarily high and big enterprises presume they can be negotiated away ... Apparently many big companies enjoy immunity... The main offenders should be compelled to pay up, sell off parts of their enterprises, face bankruptcy or go to jail' (Anders Åslund, *The World Today*, July 1998, vol. 54, no. 7, pp. 185–6).

'The central problem of the Russian economy is simple. The country has a large number of enterprises that are continuing to operate even though they are producing obsolete products of little value ... A complex web of barter transactions and subsidies keeps inefficient companies alive. Under current law many resource-producing companies are forced to continue supplying inputs to technically bankrupt enterprises ... Instead of payments the resource supplying companies are given a credit against their tax liability. As the magnitude of this credit is usually unclear, almost all of the large companies negotiate their tax liability with the government. This arrangement not only protects inefficient businesses, it is also a fertile field for political corruption ... The tax system must be simplified and tax rates reduced. The current system stifles growth, penalizes honesty and encourages evasion ... Employers supply the tax authorities with the salary information and handle the payment of both the payroll and income tax ... These arrangements lead to a dramatic understatement of wages and income. Given Russia's GDP, the income and wage tax bases are less than half the expected size. While non-compliance is rampant, everyone lives in fear that his or her tax fraud will be uncovered. Currently employers are required to pay a 41 per cent payroll tax on all wages and salaries. In addition, individuals with modest incomes confront marginal personal income tax rates of 20 per cent or more. If there were compliance with the law there would be an average tax wedge (that is, the cost of employing someone relative to the employee's net salary) of almost 45 per cent' (James Gwartney, *FT*, 9 May 2000, p. 27).

'Between 1995 and 1997 as federal tax revenues dropped by 1.4 per cent of GDP, regional and municipal tax revenues have increased relative to GDP by about 1 per cent' (Treisman 1998: 57). 'Available evidence suggests a kind of implicit or covert collusion between regional governments and big taxpayers to keep roubles from leaving their regions' (p. 59). 'The evidence suggests the growing importance of ... perverse incentives created by the way Russia's evolving federal system divides tax revenues and control over tax collectors between central and regional governments ... Federal, regional and local governments compete with one another to conceal and divert revenues that they would otherwise have to share. Yet commercial enterprises, such as

Gazprom and Yukos, which have divisions spread out across Russia, make billions of roubles at the government's expense by exploiting these rivalries' (p. 57). 'Tax-sharing rates [are] adjusted yearly by the Duma ... Regions that collected lower taxes in previous years are permitted to retain a larger share of VAT (or are allocated larger central transfers) to help cushion their losses. These regions, in turn, punish municipalities for their fiscal success. A study of thirty-five Russian cities found that ... in response to better collection regional governments adjusted downward the proportion of tax that cities could retain. Weaker incentives to support the growth of economic activities – and thus taxable revenue – are hard to imagine' (p. 63). The federal government is supposed to receive 75 per cent of most types of VAT in a typical year and about 35 per cent of profit tax, with the regions taking the rest (p. 59). Proposals to give the federal budget 100 per cent of VAT revenues (because of ease of collection) and give the regions 100 per cent of profit tax have so far failed because the regions would lose out in the absence of other tax amendments (pp. 64–5).

'On the revenue side the main purpose [of the June 1998 anti-crisis package] was to increase tax collections and shift the tax burden from big companies to consumers and to small enterprises that often operate in the shadow economy. The programme addressed the key problem in the tax system: high dependence on a handful of taxpayers and low contributions by individuals. At 2.2 per cent of GDP income tax revenues were ridiculously low by international standards; the average ratio is above 10 per cent in mature and about 8 per cent in transition economies' (Malleret *et al.* 1999: 109). 'Under the law on basic taxation principles new laws can be passed only by the legislature, while the president can issue decrees modifying existing laws. Therefore, Yeltsin could rule that VAT must be collected on an accrual basis, since the law was not specific in this particular, but he was powerless to introduce new taxes' (p. 126).

'Arbitrary tax demands and arbitrary tax exemptions need to be eliminated' (*RET,* Monthly Update, 16 December 1996, p. vii).

A decree of 23 May 1994 allowed the government to start bankruptcy proceedings against enterprises that were more than three months late in paying their taxes (*FT,* 24 May 1994, p. 2).

A 19 January 1996 decree stated that enterprises that made all current payments to the budget in full would be granted the right to defer their debts to the federal budget built up over previous years. The enterprises having the right to such deferments were to be identified by the end of March 1996, after which they would repay half their total debt over a period of two and a half years in 5 per cent quarterly instalments and the second half over the subsequent five-year period (*CDSP,* 1996, vol. XLVIII, no. 3, p. 22).

The 19 January 1996 decree established that enterprises which keep up with their current tax obligations after 1996 would be eligible for a deferral of past liabilities. Enterprises with arrears accrued prior to 1 January 1996 would pay 50 per cent of the total arrears during 1 April 1996 to October 1998 through quarterly instalments of 5 per cent of the total arrears. From 1 January 1996 a 30 per cent annual interest would be charged on the amounts paid. If the payments within this time period were to be implemented properly, a further deferral of the remaining 50 per cent for a period of five years would be authorized without any interest charges (*RET,* 1995, vol. 4, no. 4, p. 18).

Until August 1996 the tax authorities had first claim on all money flowing into company accounts. An amendment to the civil code has meant that since then the payment of wages has taken precedence over tax payments. 'However, the penalty for non-payment of taxes is far higher than any penalties incurred for non-payment of wages. Thus the amendment is hardly effective in discouraging the non-payment of wages and there is no sign that barter is in decline' (*Transition*, 1998, vol. 9, no. 2, p. 7).

'The main problem … lies not in the high profit tax, but rather in the moderate value-added tax. That tax is based on anticipated enterprise activity; it comes directly and automatically out of the enterprise bank account as soon as the account contains anything. Thus all monetary revenues are automatically confiscated until the full VAT is paid. This provides a tremendous incentive to expand barter relations and non-cash arrangements, accepting payment and profits only in the form of storable materials' (Ericson 1998: 4).

On 11 October 1996 an emergency tax committee was set up. One of the first steps it took was to threaten to liquidate six enterprises if they did not pay their tax arrears (*RET,* Monthly Update, 22 October 1996, p. 5).

On 26 December 1996, after a meeting of the emergency tax committee, it was announced that the government would restore the state alcohol monopoly in order to increase tax revenue. Pension arrears would be paid off and pensions were to be paid on time from 1 February 1997 onwards. Details would be given in a forthcoming presidential decree. But the aim was not to renationalize distilleries and liquor shops. Instead, the government would introduce tough controls on production, importing and distribution. Licensing would be centralized, so that local governments would lose the power to grant licences to produce and sell alcohol. President Yeltsin ordered the government to draw up a list before the end of January 1997 of the fifteen enterprises that owe most tax to the government.

The utilities are forced to subsidize households by charging them roughly one-quarter of the price paid by industrial users (*Transition*, 1997, vol. 8, no. 3, p. 15). On 28 April 1997 Yeltsin signed a decree shifting the cost of housing and municipal services to the public and away from government. Citizens' contributions were to rise from 27 per cent of the cost of housing and municipal services in 1996 to 35 per cent in 1997, 50 per cent in 1998, 70 per cent in 2000 and 100 per cent in 2003. The government would give subsidies to low income families rather than to cities and towns (*RET,* 1997, no. 2,

p. 119). There was a call to take away maintenance services from government and allow private companies to bid for them. About 40 per cent of apartments are still owned by municipal governments or by former Soviet enterprises that provide housing for their workers. Russians who privatized their apartments have captured about 25 per cent of housing. A further 10 per cent of apartments are co-operatives. The final 25 per cent of housing is the result of private construction and largely consists of wooden houses in the countryside. In general Russians pay about 6 per cent of their income for housing and utilities, with the subsidies going to municipal or private landlords and utility companies. Russia spends more than 3 per cent of GDP on housing and utility subsidies (Michael Gordon, *IHT*, 14 July 1997, pp. 1, 7).

On 25 June 1997 Gazprom announced that it had paid its debt to the state in full, having transferred 14.5 trillion roubles ($2.5 billion) to the budget in May and June 1997 (*RET*, 1997, no. 3, pp. 119–20). On 8 July 1997 a presidential decree required oil companies that owed taxes automatically to pay part of the proceeds from oil exports into the federal budget (p. 120).

'The government has been particularly ineffective in dealing with persistent non-payers ... The federal bankruptcy service ... has hardly produced any results. Its main activity has been to grant tax debtors extra time to pay ... A resolution introduced by the government in March [1997] enables an enterprise to restructure its debt over several years, while the state holds a controlling stake of the firm's shares or its bonds, collateralized by the firm's assets or guaranteed by a third party. The state has the right to sell these securities if the company misses its monthly payments two times in a row or more than twice a year ... However, the credibility of the punishment is again questionable ... The number of debtor companies which have been subjected to such a forced privatization is very small (eleven enterprises in the first half of this year)' (*RET*, 1997, no. 4, p. 94). On 2 October 1997 AvtoVaz agreed to a ten-year plan for paying back taxes and fines estimated at some 8 trillion roubles ($1.3 billion). A stake of 50 per cent plus one share in AvtoVaz would be transferred to the government and could be sold if the company breached the payments schedule (p. 106).

A presidential decree stated that as of 1 January 1998 all forms of offsets were suspended (*CDSP*, 1998, vol. 50, no. 2, p. 5). The 8 November 1997 decree stated that as of 1 January 1998 the government would be prohibited from cancelling mutual debts between the budget and enterprises, a practice known as 'offsetting' (*RET*, 1998, no. 1, p. 100). The government has stopped accepting tax 'offsets' (the practice of allowing enterprises to deduct from their tax bills money owed by the state) as a legitimate form of payment and is insisting on cash. In 1997 tax offsets accounted for a quarter of all revenues (*FT*, Survey, 15 April 1998, p. viii). 'At the IMF's request Russia eliminated all federal budget offset operations from January 1998. However, up to 20 per cent of taxes continued to come in the form of promissory notes or other surrogate payments' (Malleret *et al.* 1999: 115).

TAX REFORM IN THE PUTIN ERA

'The tax system was structured similarly to that of developed countries, but its drawbacks – including an enormous tax burden on enterprises – became more and more obvious ... The main aims of the tax reform include: lowering the overall tax burden; increasing equality in the tax system; simplifying the tax system by eliminating inefficient taxes and reducing the number of tax rates; increasing the tax base, and improving tax administration and tax collection ... The state Duma recently passed [on 7 June 2000], at the second reading, the chapters of Part II of the tax code introducing a 13 per cent flat personal income tax' (*RET*, Monthly Update, 10 July 2000, p. 4). 'It is clear that the reform of individual income tax and social security contributions is primarily intended to bring more transactions into the open, with the further intensions of simplifying tax collection and encouraging employers and employees to be tax compliant' (p. 7). The unified social tax passed its second reading in the State Duma on 9 June 2000. 'The tax is to replace payments to the pension fund, social insurance fund and medical insurance fund ... The system in which money was raised by separate social funds was inefficient and non-transparent and created incentives for fraud ... The [new] rates: 35.6 per cent for annual income less than 100,000 roubles; 20 per cent for annual income between 100,000 roubles and 300,000 roubles; 10 per cent for income between 300,000 and 600,000 roubles; 2 per cent for income higher than 600,000 roubles' (p. 9). The legislation on value-added tax was passed by the State Duma, at the second reading, on 23 June 2000. There is a 20 per cent VAT rate, with a 10 per cent rate for basic food and children's clothing (as before) and a zero rate for exported goods (with the exception of oil and gas exported to the CIS). The indexation of excises was passed by the State Duma, at the second reading, on 5 July 2000. In particular there is a 5 per cent rate for alcohol (10 per cent for beer) and 50 per cent for tobacco (p. 9).

The flat rate personal income tax of 13 per cent passed the third reading in the State Duma on 19 July 2000. It was approved by the Council of the Federation on 26 July 2000 and signed by the president on 7 August 2000. The unified social tax to replace payments to the pension fund, the social insurance fund and the medical insurance fund (with the standard rates for employers given above and the 1 per cent contribution to the pension fund by the employee being cancelled) was passed by the State Duma at its third reading on 19 July. It was approved by the Council of the Federation on 26 July 2000 and signed by the president on 7 August 2000. The same dates applied to the VAT and excise changes (*RET*, Monthly Update, 11 August 2000, pp. 3–6).

On 26 July 2000 the Council of the Federation voted by 115 to twenty-three to approve a package of tax reforms. (The State Duma approved a flat 13 per cent income tax rate in June 2000. 'Less than 5 per cent of Russian filed tax returns last year [1999]': *The Times*, 9 June 2000, p. 20.)

The top income tax rate will by cut from 35 per cent to a flat rate of 13 per cent. The tax on the cash flow of businesses, a tax on turnover (revenue), will be cut from 4 per cent to 1 per cent. Payroll taxes for pensions and other social programmes will be marginally reduced. The tax package, after approval by the president, will then go into effect in 2001 (*IHT,* 2 July 2000, p. 15, and 27 July 2000, p. 6; *FT,* 27 July 2000, p. 8).

'The bill abolishes a warren of special funds that had been created for various taxes, giving the federal tax service the power to collect and administer their receipts. The move is expected to reduce corruption and favouritism in government offices that had used the funds more or less as personal accounts … The changes are expected to reduce corporate taxes by about 20 per cent overall' (Michael Wines, *IHT,* 27 July 2000, p. 6).

'Christopher Granville … a strategist at … a Moscow-based investment bank, said the tax package should reduce the tax burden by 2.5 per cent of GDP … Mr Granville said a key measure was the introduction of a unified social tax paid by employers. At present employers are obliged to contribute to various off-budget funds such as the pensions fund, social security funds and health insurance funds. These payments account for half of the federal budget or 10 per cent of GDP but make many companies hide their payrolls' (*FT,* 27 July 2000, p. 8). '[There is] a flat rate personal income tax of 13 per cent, including 1 per cent in social security levies … The move is designed to increase substantially the number of taxpayers by reducing, through such a low rate, the temptation for tax evasion. It will be offset by additional revenues from increased duties on alcohol, tobacco and other products' (*FT,* 8 August 2000, p. 7). 'A flat rate income tax of 13 per cent is to be introduced from next year [2001], which is designed to entice the country's richer residents into the tax net … One percentage point of the total is to be paid into the national social fund to create a centralized and more transparent welfare system. A second package of laws is due to be completed in the autumn … Both measures are designed to increase the country's low rate of tax collection and to reduce the huge administrative uncertainty and leeway given to individual tax inspectors. This has encouraged tax evasion and created an uncertain climate for many local businesses' (*FT,* 9 August 2000, p. 16).

'The Federation Council confirmed new tax laws yesterday [26 July] … Back on 19 July the laws were adopted by the State Duma … [Finance minister] Alexei Kudrin spelled out the basic principles of the 2001 budget for the senators … [A] key provision is an improvement in interbudget relations and the creation of equal conditions for the regions. Today 66 per cent of the tax potential is formed in twelve regions of the country. The government proposed centralizing [the remaining] 15 per cent of the value-added tax [the percentage hitherto left to the regions] in the federal budget and putting it into a compensation fund for financial assistance to regions that need help. The 2001 budget calls for distributing revenue between the centre and the regions at a ratio of 57.5:42.5 in favour of the centre. Supposedly, the inclusion of support from the compensation fund makes the ratio 52.5: 47.5 and if all types of aid are counted the ration changes to 47.5: 52.5 in favour of the regions. A trilateral reconciliation commission on the budget will begin work today [27 July] ... The second part of the tax code got the votes of 115 senators' (*CDSP*, 2000, vol. 52, no. 30, p. 6). 'The centre is taking 15 per cent of the value-added tax away from them [the regions], but it is assuming all payments to disabled people and veterans. It will also pay child benefits, provide the money needed to build roads, and hand out at least 95 billion roubles from the transfer fund. According to Kudrin, the governors keep saying that 70 per cent of their revenue will go to the centre and the Federation members will get only 30 per cent. In fact, if the transfer fund and all compensatory payments are taken into account, the regions will be getting 56.6 per cent and the centre 43.4 per cent. "This is the first time that the Federation's members' spending will be higher than federal budget spending", Kudrin said' (*CDSP*, 2000, vol. 52, no. 32, p. 10).

'Yesterday [12 September 2000] the governors of the eighteen donor regions [those that put more money into the federal budget than they take out of it] asked the State Duma to send the budget to a conference committee instead of passing it on first reading ... [The] deputy finance minister ... acknowledged that under the new tax system and with [the remaining] 15 per cent of the value-added tax being transferred to the centre ... only the donor regions would suffer ... The seventy-one subsidized regions will end up in the black' (*CDSP*, 2000, vol. 52, no. 37, p. 7).

RUSSIA AND THE ASIAN FINANCIAL CRISIS

The Asian financial crisis started in July 1997 with a speculative attack on the currency of Thailand. Although at first it was Russia that suffered from the effects of the Asian financial crisis, after the dramatic events of 17 August 1998 it was Russia that became a major cause of uncertainty in emerging markets. (On 13 January 1999 Brazil devalued its currency.)

The Asian crisis hit Russia in October 1997 (*RET*, Monthly Update, 5 June 1998, p. 1). Russia has suffered from a financial crisis since late October 1997 (Anders Åslund, *The World Today*, July 1998, vol. 54, no. 7. pp. 185). 'The authorities in Russia successfully defended the exchange rate in late October/November 1997, and again in January 1998, by raising interest rates sharply' (John Odling-Smee, Director of the IMF's European II Department, *Finance and Development*, 1998, vol. 35, no. 3, p. 16). A combination of factors drove interest rates to dramatic heights in May 1998. Near the end of May they had risen to 150 per cent. ('The flight of non-residents from governments GKOs and the rouble could not be stopped despite a hike of the central bank interest rate to 150 per cent in June 1998: Desai 2000: 50.) Factors behind the rise in interest rates included the following:

1. The government's determination to defend the rouble on foreign exchange markets.

2. To discourage the withdrawal of funds from the bond market and the stock market.

3. Continuing fiscal problems, especially with raising tax revenue. (On 30 March 1999 Yeltsin said that: 'In July [1998] the government drafted its anti-crisis programme ... The State Duma rejected that programme ... The Duma sent a bad signal to investors, a signal telling them that Russia's authorities were unwilling to take responsibility for decisions that were difficult but that had to be made': *CDSP*, 1999, vol. 51, no. 13, p. 14.)

4. Political wrangling between the president and the State Duma over the appointment of a new prime minister. (See chronology of political events.)

5. Labour unrest over pay arrears, especially the blocking of railway lines by coal miners. (See chronology of political events.)

6. There were no bids on 26 May for a 75 per cent stake in Rosneft (the oil company), the starting price of which was set at $2.1 billion. Reasons included sharp falls in world oil prices and financial uncertainty in Russia.

7. The fall in world oil and other commodity prices.

'Commodities account for about 70 per cent of Russia's merchandise trade. Their prices started to decline in October 1997 due to lower demand from Asia ... On 16 June [1998] Brent oil fell to $10.6 a barrel, its all-time low in real terms. By the first half of August [1998] the Economist all-items commodity index was at its lowest level in real terms in over twenty-five years ... In the first half of 1998 Russia's .... current account position turned negative (minus 3 per cent of GDP) for the first time since the start of the reforms' (Malleret *et al.* 1999: 111).

'The decline in oil prices from $23 per barrel in mid-1997 to $11 per barrel a year later [was] accompanied by falling prices of non-ferrous metals' (Desai 2000: 50).

'Although oil prices have rebounded a bit in recent months the industry is still reeling from their collapse in 1998. Prices fell almost continuously through the year, averaging about $13 a barrel. That is a third below their average in 1997 and the lowest in real terms for twenty-five years' (*The Economist*, 3 July 1999, p. 128).

8. Continuing effects of the Asian financial crisis, especially political and economic turmoil in Indonesia.

9. Speculation.

10. IMF delays in releasing the latest tranche of its loan.

On 17 August 1998 the Russian government defaulted on its domestic debt and was forced to allow the rouble to float.

'The Russian government was forced to devalue the rouble on 17 August 1998; it also announced a unilateral rescheduling of most of its short-term debt into long-term securities and the imposition of a ninety-day moratorium on payments by Russian banks and enterprises on much of their foreign debt' (United Nations, *World Economic and Social Survey 1999*, p. 57).

'Russia's devaluation and default triggered a full-scale crisis in emerging markets. And spillovers have been felt in world stock markets as well as in the premium for emerging market risk' (*FT*, editorial, 1 October 1998, p. 23). 'The Russian financial crisis took a heavy toll on stock markets around the world Thursday [27 August 1998], pushing indexes in developed countries down by as much as 5 per cent, while emerging markets in Europe and the Americas saw prices fall 5 per cent to 7 per cent' (*IHT*, 28 August 1998, p. 1). These effects were felt despite the extraordinarily small contribution that Russia now makes to the world economy (as the figures below illustrate).

'Russia's economy ... is about the size of Switzerland's' (*The Economist*, 31 October 1998, p. 108). ('Russia's economy [is] smaller than that of the Netherlands': *The Economist*, 18 December 1999, p. 13.) 'It is easy to forget that Russia is a small economy, whose trade links with the West are tiny. Western Europe's exports to Russia, for example, account for well under 0.5 per cent of GDP. However, it is already clear that the impact of this crisis will be greatly disproportionate to Russia's size' (*FT*, 29 August 1998, p. 10). 'The country now accounts for less than 1 per cent of global GDP; its entire federal budget is dwarfed by the size of US military spending' (*FT*, 23 December 1998, p. 2). 'According to the IMF, Russia's GDP in 1999 was just 2 per cent of that of the USA' (*FT*, 3 June 2000, p. 14). 'GDP next year [1999] is expected to be about that of Belgium' (*The Independent*, 26 December 1998, p. 13). 'Russia's ... economy now accounts for little more than 1 per cent of world economic activity, compared with a US share of more than one-fifth' (*IHT*, 22 January 1999, p. 6). 'When trading ended [on 28 August] at the Tokyo stock exchange, Japanese stocks this week alone had dropped in value by $241 billion – a sum that exceeds the size of the entire Russian economy at present exchange rates' (*IHT*, 29 August 1998, p. 1).

The following chronology shows the dramatic developments of 17 August 1998 and the events immediately preceding them:

12 August 1998. The republic of Yakutia-Sakha becomes the first Russian region to go bankrupt as a result of the financial crisis. The Yakutsk government announces that it will be unable to pay off republic loan bonds (*CDSP*, 1998, vol. 50, no. 32, p. 10).

13 August 1998. 'Black Thursday.' The RTS index falls by 6.51 per cent to 101.17.

'Russian markets plunged ... as investors feared the government might soon be forced into devaluation or a domestic debt restructuring ... Yields on short-term Treasury bills also soared to more than 210 per cent at one point. They closed at 170 per cent, their highest level since before the 1996 presidential elections' (*FT*, 14 August 1998, p. 1).

'Russia's stock and bond markets plunged ... Demand for Russian debt vanished altogether, with yields on some short-term bonds exceeding an astounding 300 per cent' (Michael Wines, *IHT*, 14 August 1998, pp. 1, 17). 'The Thursday crisis was rooted in months of speculating by some banks in high-yield government bonds and currency "forwards" – contracts to buy or sell currencies at specified future dates' (Michael Wines, *IHT*, 15 August 1998, p. 13).

It was generally considered that a factor in the events of 'Black Thursday' was the following comment by George Soros: 'The best solution would be to introduce a currency board after a modest devaluation of 15 to 25 per cent' (George Soros, *FT*, 13 August 1998, p. 18).

14 August 1998. Yeltsin: 'I'll say it firmly and clearly. There will be no devaluation of the rouble in Russia.'

17 August 1998. A dramatic turnabout takes place.

The following measures are announced:

1. 'As of 17 August 1998 the Bank of Russia is switching to a policy of a floating rouble exchange rate within new exchange rate corridor limits, which have been set at a level of 6 to 9.5 roubles to the dollar' (official statement by the government and the central bank: *CDSP*, 1998, vol. 50, no. 33, p. 5).

The trading band for the rouble against the US dollar is widened (until the end of 1998) from 5.27/7.13 to 6.0/9.5. Although this amounted to a devaluation, prime minister Kiriyenko insisted otherwise: 'This does not mean the rouble is being devalued. It is simply a new approach to financial policy' (*The Times*, 18 August 1998, p. 10). (The rouble had traded at 6.36 to the US dollar on 13 August, 'Black Thursday'.)

'An effective float of the exchange rate' (*RET*, Monthly Update, 18 August 1998, p. 1).

On 19 August the central bank announced that since 20 July 1998 it had spent some $3.8 billion to support the rouble (*RET*, 1998, vol. 7, no. 3, p. 42). On 19 August the chairman of the central bank, Sergei Dubinin, admitted that some $3.8 billion of the $4.8 billion advanced by the IMF had been used since 20 July to shore up the rouble (*The Independent*, 20 August 1998, p. 13). The remainder was used to redeem short-term government debt (*FT*, 20 August 1998, p. 1). (There were allegations of impropriety made concerning the use of IMF aid. 'Three months [ago] Yuri Skuratov, the prosecutor-general, accused the central bank and Sergei Dubinin, its former chairman, of misusing the $4.8 billion first tranche of an IMF stabilization loan … Around the time of the national crash, when the central bank was simultaneously defending the rouble by selling dollars to Russian banks, and supporting Russian banks with liquidity problems by extending rouble loans to them with which they in turn bought dollars. "It was scandalous", said a Moscow-based Western economist. "After the banks had effectively collapsed, they were refusing to make payments to depositors, but the rouble was kept stable at seven roubles to the dollar while bankers closed their own accounts and shipped their money abroad, probably to Switzerland." The rouble has since plummeted to 20.62 to the dollar. During the collapse loans were being used with or without the central bank's knowledge, to bail out the accounts of the directors while the savings of the average depositor were wiped out ... Sergei Stepashin, interior minister, disclosed that the government was investigating allegations that central bank officials had fraudulently wasted "billions of dollars" ... Sergei Dubinin, former head of the central bank, hit back at allegations claiming that the allegations was a politically inspired attempt to discredit the previous government. Mr Dubinin said that reports that the central bank had salted $9 billion abroad were inaccurate and based on a misreading of statistics compiled to estimate illegal capital flight from Russia': *The Times*, 30 December 1998, p. 11. 'Police are investigating whether the Russian central bank illegally channelled $1 billion into its overseas accounts, interior minister Sergei Stepashin was quoted as saying': *IHT*, 30 December 1998, p. 11.)

'Russia's interior minister said yesterday [29 December 1998] it was widening its investigations into alleged wrongdoing at the central bank and suggested more than $1 billion could have gone missing ... Sergei Stepashin, interior minister, said: "We have been picking through the central bank's activities since 1992. We are talking about enormous losses" ... The auditing chamber, the government's financial watchdog, questioned how the central bank had used the $4.8 billion loan it received from the IMF in July as part of a last-ditch attempt to save the rouble. There were also allegations that the central bank had given soft loans to several politically influential commercial banks, which were facing big repayments on hard currency loans ... Sergei Dubinin, head of the central bank at the time of the August crisis, yesterday fiercely rejected suggestions he had been involved in any wrongdoing ... Mr Dubinin said the bank had been subject to emotional attacks, tarnishing its reputation and threatening its independence ... Other former government officials have suggested the investigation is politically motivated and is designed to blacken names, not to achieve prosecutions. Previous audits of central bank and finance ministry activities have not discovered evidence of fraud. The central bank has always said that it spent the IMF money on the purposes for which it was intended. Up to $3.8 billion was spent on the failed defence of the rouble, while the remaining $1 billion was used to retire a slab of government debt' (*FT*, 30 December 1998, p. 2).

2. 'Government securities (short-term bonds and federal loan bonds) due to mature by 31 December 1999, inclusive, will be converted into new securities ... As of 17 August 1998 there is a ninety-day moratorium on the repayment of loans received from non-residents of the Russian Federation, on insurance payments on loans collateralized by securities, and on payments on foreign currency futures' (official statement by the government and the central bank: *CDSP*, 1998, vol. 50, no. 33, pp. 5–6).

Details were revealed about the foreign debts affected on 18 August. It does not cover sovereign debt. Nor does it apply to interest on foreign credits and loans from the EBRD. Two areas will be affected: syndicated loans extended by Western banks to Russian banks and corporations; forward foreign exchange contracts taken out by foreign investors with Russian banks to protect their investments (and thus rouble exposures) in the domestic Treasury bill (GKO) market (*FT*, 19 August 1998, p. 2). The measures appear chiefly to affect repayment of principal of foreign syndicated loans, margin calls on repurchase transactions and settlements on foreign currency forward contracts (*FT*, 24 August 1998, p. 3).

(GKOs are short-maturity – less than one year – rouble-denominated Treasury bills, while OFZs are longer-dated coupon-bearing bonds: EBRD 1998b: 13. OFZs are medium-term fixed-rate government bonds: *FT*, 10 September 1998, p. 31.) (Margin calls are demands for additional funds to maintain an appropriate level of deposits which traders in futures contracts make to ensure their ability to meet their obligations.) ('Buying stock on margin [means] in effect borrowing to speculate': *IHT*, 6 April 2000, p. 10.)

The authorities announced a forced restructuring of the GKO/OFZ market and a ninety-day moratorium on principal payments by Russian commercial enterprises on their foreign currency debt (*RET*, 1998, vol. 7, no. 3, p. 16). There will be a ninety-day moratorium on repayment of debt to non-residents, which is a form of capital control. The moratorium does not include payments on the external debt of the Russian Federation (indeed, there are no sovereign debt payments due in the period). Instead, it covers all commercial activities, including forward contracts, margin calls and standard debt service. There will be a lengthening of the maturity of all GKO and OFZ instruments (short- and long-term rouble-denominated government bonds) maturing before the end of 1999. Trading on the GKO/OFZ markets is to be suspended. The government and the central bank have expressed their support for the formation of a pool of large banks to maintain the stability of interbank settlements and payments (*RET*, Monthly Update, 18 August 1998, p. 1).

The government declared a moratorium on debt principal payments to foreigners by Russian companies and banks (EBRD 1998b: 12). The government declared a ninety-day moratorium on principal repayments of private debts to non-residents (p. 187).

'The government declared a ninety-day moratorium on the repayment of foreign debt owed by Russian commercial banks and other private borrowers to avert a string of bank failures after the government rushed emergency loans to some institutions Friday [14 August] to help them meet their foreign-currency obligations' (David Hoffman, *IHT*, 18 August 1998, p. 1).

There will be an imposition of controls on capital account transactions.

'Russian banks held half of the Treasury bills affected by this week's restructuring, while the central bank and foreign investors each held about a quarter' (*FT*, 27 August 1998, p. 2). Of the $40 billion in short-term government paper, foreign investors, converting dollars to roubles, had bought about $10 billion (*IHT*, 27 August 1998, p. 10).

Details of the scheme to restructure $40 billion of short-term, rouble-denominated domestic government debt were released on 25 August 1998 (*IHT*, 26 August 1998, p. 15).

'The 281 billion roubles of Treasury bills and bonds are now worth $18.1 billion' (*IHT*, 7 November 1998, p. 13).

Bonds affected by the deal are GKOs and OFZs maturing before the end of December 1999 – or about 280 billion roubles (worth $17.9 billion at current exchange rates). About a third is held by foreigners (*FT*, 11 November 1998, p. 40).

'Western banks said yesterday [10 December] that they were unlikely to accept Russia's terms for restructuring the $15 billion of foreign-held domestic debt (GKOs/OFZs) which is in default' (*FT*, 11 December 1998, p. 3).

The Asian financial crisis has caused the greatest havoc in those economies with *fundamental weaknesses*. These weaknesses range from the incestuous links between government and companies and between banks and companies in some Asian countries ('crony capitalism') to the many affecting Russia itself. Russia's inability to raise sufficient tax revenue to finance the central (federal) government's essential activities is crucial to gaining an understanding of the crisis. 'If the state does not learn to collect taxes it will cease to exist', said Sergei Kiriyenko on 23 June 1998 (prime minister from 23 March to 23 August 1998). Although Russia succeeded admirably in bringing inflation (hyperinflation in 1992) down to single figures by gradually reducing reliance on the printing press to finance persistently high (though generally declining) budget deficits, the heavy dependence on short-term borrowing proved to be unsustainable. Investors became increasingly unwilling to roll over their loans.

Excellent analyses of the financial crisis and of Russia's fundamental weaknesses are to be found in the following:

'Although this latest crisis was confined to the financial markets, it does reflect a number of persistent and fundamental problems in the Russian economy and these seem to have been the main cause of the turmoil despite an apparent contagion effect from the Asian crisis. At the core of these problems is Russia's chronic fiscal imbalance and the manner in which it is being financed. Russia has been running large budget deficits for a number of years. Consequently, the Russian authorities have been forced to attract increasing amounts of foreign funds to finance the deficit: by selling Treasury bills to foreigners and by borrowing from the international financial markets. This has resulted in an increase in the exposure of Russia to volatile short-term foreign capital' (United Nations Economic Commission for Europe 1998b: 24–5). 'Given the nature and depth of the structural weaknesses of the Russian economy, a different policy mix, based on a more gradual disinflation but a more vigorous programme of institutional reform, would have probably been more effective with respect to macroeconomic stabilization in the long run' (United Nations Economic Commission for Europe 1998c: 12). 'Excessive emphasis on price stabilization implied monetary austerity and high interest rates; as a result economic activity was depressed and corporate profits fell; the tax base was eroded by lost incomes and growing corporate losses; and in addition perverse incentives and distorted markets led to demonetization of the economy and of fiscal relations' (p. 40). 'Key institutional foundations … [include] an effective judicial and law enforcement system, the creation of a healthy commercial banking system, and a coherent policy for changing the structure of incentives so as to encourage entrepreneurship and fixed investment rather than rent-seeking and asset stripping' (p. 10). 'Among the most damaging of the mistaken conclusions that were drawn early on in the transition process, both by Western advisers and by policy makers in Moscow, was that the Russian state remained too strong. The need to scale back inefficient spending, and to create room for private sector consumption is a necessary task for which a strong public administration is required; but this is a quite different task from *restructuring* the state so that it is strong enough and capable to perform the functions required to support a market economy' (p. 9). 'Russian public administration is infamous for its lack of transparency and corruption' (p. 34).

'The current crisis in Russia arose largely from a failure of the state – its inability to collect taxes, to enforce laws, to manage its employees and to pay them … [There has been a] failure of prudential regulation to contain banks' exposure to foreign exchange risk' (EBRD 1998b: iv, vii). 'The government's stabilization programme in 1995 managed to bring down inflation, but it did not address the underlying causes of macroeconomic imbalance. The government was not prepared to accept the consequences of enforcing hard budget constraints both in terms of the social and economic dislocation and the opposition of entrenched interest groups. Instead, it replaced monetary financing of the [budget] deficit with non-inflationary borrowing on a newly created Treasury bill market and on the international capital markets. It also used the exchange rate as an anchor to fight inflation' (p. 12). From 1995 the federal government financed much of its deficit by issuing short-term (less than one year) rouble-denominated Treasury bills (GKOs) and longer-dated coupon-bearing bonds (OFZs). Foreigners rushed into the high-yielding Russian debt market and, by the end of 1997, held an estimated 33 per cent of the total stock of GKOs and OFZs (p. 13). Foreign investors in the GKO market were at first obliged, and many later chose, to hedge themselves against the risk of devaluation by buying dollar forward contracts with Russian banks. The hedge contracts increased the exposure of the Russian banking system to declines in the rouble (p. 14). 'Russia's economy, having still achieved only modest progress in key structural reforms and with looming fiscal problems, looked particularly vulnerable' (p. 14). Falling commodity prices hit Russia's main sources of export earnings, sending the current account into deficit. 'At the root of Russia's macroeconomic problems have been persistently high federal budget deficits' (p. 14). 'The fundamental causes of the budget deficit were political: an inability to rein in government spending, weak tax discipline among politically influential firms and an excessive devolution of revenue to regional governments … Underlying Russia's fiscal problems has been a deeper set of difficulties afflicting the entire large corporate sector that has inhibited growth, encouraged capital flight, limited tax collection and reduced domestic savings. Politicians have been unwilling to draw sharp distinctions between public and private property or to impose hard budget constraints on large enterprises, both out of fear of the unemployment implications and to preserve rent-seeking opportunities for powerful vested interests' (pp. 14–15). In the absence of a credible bankruptcy threat, enterprises have increasingly resorted to financing themselves by accumulating arrears towards tax authorities, banks, suppliers and workers, as well as through non-monetary forms of payments, such as barter, monetary surrogates, offsets and payments in kind (p. 186).

'Since the introduction of the currency corridor in 1995 the strong rouble has served as a nominal anchor for the economy, helping bring down inflationary expectations and giving foreign investors the confidence to lend to the Russian government, banks and companies. Commitment to the rouble corridor limited the central bank's ability to print money and forced the government to finance its deficits in non-inflationary ways – by borrowing on the domestic and international bond markets' (*RET*, Monthly Update, 5 June 1998, p. 1). 'In May the rouble fell by its usual average of 0.5 per cent against the dollar. However ... the CBR used about $1.5 billion of reserves to defend its stability. This reduced reserves to $14.6 billion at the beginning of June' (p. 11). 'Foreigners' share of the government rouble debt market increased to roughly 30 per cent in the summer of 1997 ... Higher interest rates have turned out to be sufficient to stem the outflow of foreigners' (p. 4). 'In the ... first ten months of 1997 Russian banks took the opportunity to borrow heavily in the syndicated loan and eurobond markets ... The banks used these foreign funds to invest in Russian assets ... After the Asian crisis hit Russia in October 1997 the flow of foreign money came to a halt' (pp. 5–6). 'It is impossible to escape the conclusion that Russia's problems are largely home-made ... including an excessively large federal budget deficit, unsustainable build-up of rouble-denominated debt, poor tax collection, non-productive government expenditures, a weak and inefficient banking system, poor corporate governance and continued accumulation of payment arrears' (*RET*, 1998, no. 2, pp. 3–4). 'The balance of payments on current account moved from a $2.9 billion surplus in 1997 to a deficit of $1.5 billion in the first quarter of 1998' (*RET*, 1998, no. 2, p. 2).

Russia has suffered from a financial crisis since late October 1997. 'At first everybody blamed the Asian economic collapse, but by late January [1998] it became clear that this was a truly Russian crisis.' The budget deficit is too large (9 per cent of GDP in 1996 and 8.2 per cent in 1997). But the government undertook substantial cuts in February and May 1998, reducing the 1998 budget deficit target to 5 per cent of GDP. 'Russia's international reserves are low at some $14 billion. Russia's debt burden is not large in itself. As a share of GDP it is about 45 per cent. The external debt is about $130 billion (27 per cent of GDP) and the interest rates on that are reasonable. The problem is about $60 billion of short-term debt held in the form of Treasury bills. Although this is only 13 per cent of GDP, interest rates are very high (perhaps an average of 35 per cent in 1998), meaning that this part of the debt burden alone will cost 4.5 per cent of GDP (amounting to almost half federal revenues). The modest amount of domestic Treasury bills held by foreigners (some $20 billion) is the immediate threat to stability' (Anders Åslund, *The World Today*, July 1998, vol. 54, no. 7. pp. 185–7). 'Russia's most immediate problem is that it has too large a short-term government debt in comparison with international reserves. The critical issue is that about $25 billion of Treasury bills are held by Russian commercial banks and foreign investors, while the international reserves hover at around $15 billion' (Anders Åslund, *Transition*, 1998, vol. 9, no. 3, pp. 10–11).

'At about 30 per cent of GDP and some 150 per cent of exports the country's $141 billion foreign debt remained well under control: the Maastricht criteria for Emu countries fix the maximum debt-to-GDP ratio at 60 per cent' (Malleret *et al.* 1999: 109). 'Three aspects of Russia's debt policy made its debt position particularly vulnerable in 1998. First, the internal debt, which amounted to 15 per cent of GDP, was very short term. GKOs [Gosudarstvenniye Kratkosrochniye Obyazatelstva: Treasury bills with maturities of less than one year] constituted around 70 per cent of the market in early 1998. Second, the growth of the Treasury bill market is a measure of Russia's dependence on foreign capital for financing its budget deficit. Official figures put the non-residents' share of the domestic debt market at some 32 per cent in the first half of 1998, but several indirect schemes available to foreign investors brought their share closer to 50 per cent' (p. 115). 'The budget deficit ... was long financed by borrowing, which became increasingly burdensome. Whereas in 1993 debt servicing took up 26 roubles of each 100 roubles borrowed, in 1997 it consumed 85 roubles, while in 1998 all new borrowings went to repay old debts. The cost of borrowing started to grow in October 1997. In 1998 the fiscal situation became unsustainable. Debt servicing was beginning to crowd out other expenditures: in 1998 almost one in every three roubles (31 per cent) of public spending was going to debt servicing, compared with one in four in 1997' (p. 114). 'On 1 July [1998 prime minister] Kiriyenko urged the Duma to pass the anti-crisis package ... Before the end of the year Russia had to redeem $30 billion in GKOs, almost twice what it was collecting in cash taxes ($16 billion) ... The rationale for a $10–15 billion [IMF] package ran as follows: ... If foreign holders holders of GKOs refuse to roll over, the central bank's $15 billion reserves will melt away by the end of the year' (p. 123). 'Russian banks are not like banks elsewhere, institutions that mobilize savings and lend them for productive purposes. They are just conduits for channelling public funds to favoured firms. Before the crisis erupted the Russian banking system was saddled with forward contract liabilities while its involvement in industrial projects was ludicrously small. By mid-1998 the Russian banks had become extremely vulnerable to rouble devaluation. Their forward contract exposure increased dramatically in 1998 because of changes in Treasury bill regulation. Before 1998 banks sold forward contracts to non-resident holders of Russian domestic debt and were required to hedge the resulting risks (compensating deals) with the central bank of Russia. In January 1998 this requirement was dropped, which gave a strong boost to the Russian forward market but involved the entire banking sector in risk-taking as large banks hedged their risks with smaller ones. By August 1998 Russian entities held some $200 billion of foreign contracts, twice the amount of the banks' total assets. Russian banks had also feasted to surfeit on the international markets. Four of the largest banks issued eurobonds worth a total of $1 billion in 1997 and most took out foreign syndicated loans. The banks used these funds, which increased their hard currency liabilities, to build up domestic bond holdings' (p. 116).

'Interest earnings ... had had to be covered by growing GKO issues, as the Russian Treasury bill market degenerated into a pyramid scheme' (Hanson 1999: 1153). 'Russian sovereign debt levels were not particularly high by international standards (51 per cent of GDP in mid-1998), but the domestic GKO debt, especially, was rising very fast. Investors began to doubt the government's ability to reduce the deficit in future, and, therefore, to continue to roll over GKO debt at interest rates with which its revenue could cope' (p. 1155).

'After Russia's 1995 programme with the IMF brought inflation under control and the budget under control, the country embarked on a new programme with the IMF, with the goal of completing macroeconomic stabilization and moving ahead rapidly on structural reform. This did not happen because of Russia, nor the West: the framework of assistance was in place, but the Russian government failed to deliver for complex reasons, one of them the health of President Boris Yeltsin. The 1996–8 programme was an on-and-off affair, with the IMF repeatedly delaying payments while policies got back on track ... What went wrong with Russia? The basic problem was not the omission from the programme of some critical element, such as tax or legal reform. Rather, the problems arose from the Byzantine interaction of business and political interests in Russia, where the process of reform were often defeated by those seeking control over natural resources and the nascent market economy ... On the speed of reform there were two elements of shock therapy in Russia – price liberalization in 1992 and privatization in 1992–5. On both the decision to move fast was made by the Russian government ... In other respects reform has been too slow, not too fast. If Russia had implemented the 1996 reforms its economy would now be stronger, incomes would be higher and it would have avoided the 1998 collapse. Capital flight estimated at $10 billion to $20 billion a year, would be much smaller' (Stanley Fischer, first deputy managing director of the IMF, *FT*, 27 September 1999, p. 26).

Note that there is increasing stress on the 'primary' budget deficit or surplus, i.e. excluding interest payments. Interest payments made up a quarter of total federal spending in 1997. Debt service reached a third of federal spending in the first quarter of 1998 (*RET,* Monthly Update, 2 July 1998, p. 4). 'Over the years from 1994 onwards the amount of primary deficit financing performed by GKOs was about $15 billion. By the end of July [1998] the market was worth $70 billion in nominal terms. That difference of $55 billion was simply interest to investors, most of which went to the banking sector' (*RET,* Monthly Update, 4 September 1999, p. 2). The revised budget shows that about a third of total spending is needed just to cover interest payments on debt, compared with 14 per cent in the USA (*IHT,* 4 June 1998, p. 13). In 1997 25 per cent of the federal budget was spent on interest payments. In the first four months of 1998 the figure increased to 32 per cent (*IHT,* 8 June 1998, p. 10). In 1997 interest payments consumed 40 per cent of federal revenue and equalled 60 per cent of the consolidated budget deficit (Martin Wolf, *FT,* 23 June 1998, p. 24).

Such dramatic events have, not surprisingly, have produced widely differing opinions about, for example, the virtues of fixed (or, more accurately, adjustable peg) and floating exchange rate systems. Some of those broadly agreeing with government policy prior to 17 August 1998 were as follows:

1. 'Since the introduction of the currency corridor in 1995 the strong rouble has served as a nominal anchor for the economy, helping bring down inflationary expectations and giving foreign investors the confidence to lend to the Russian government, banks and companies. Commitment to the rouble corridor limited the central bank's ability to print money and forced the government to finance its deficits in non-inflationary ways – by borrowing on the domestic and international bond markets' (*RET,* Monthly Update, 5 June 1998, p. 1). 'A forced devaluation of the rouble ... would have very negative effects on the banking system, threaten a return of inflation, severely undermine confidence in the authorities and their policies and, in the end, lead to further social and political friction in a society that has already seen much grief' (*RET,* 1998, no. 2, pp. 3–4). 'The maintenance of a stable rouble exchange rate, in combination with other monetary measures, has been a central element in the fight against inflation. A forced devaluation of the rouble would trigger an immediate renewal of inflation, both because of higher import prices and because the chances are high that the central bank would resort to monetary expansion to finance maturing debt' (p. 14).

2. 'A devaluation in Russia would be catastrophic ... The greatest achievement of the reformers has been to bring low inflation and financial stability. If they cannot even do that they will lose all credibility ... A devaluation would lead to an immediate increase in inflation and, even worse, to bank failures. And bank failures would lead to bankruptcies of enterprise. Unemployment would rise on a massive scale ... Without the Asian debâcle, there would be no crisis now in Russia. The G7 nations need to put together a

stabilization fund of at least $10 billion which would be available for the Russian government' (Richard Layard, *The Independent*, 29 May 1998, p. 23).

3. 'Devaluation is not necessary because the rouble is not overvalued. Last year Russia had a huge trade surplus of $20 billion and it has had similar trade surpluses for years ... Russia's most immediate problem is that it has too large a short-term government debt in comparison with international reserves. The critical issue is that about $25 billion of Treasury bills are held by Russian commercial banks and foreign investors, while the international reserves hover at around $15 billion ... Devaluation would undermine what little remaining confidence there was in the rouble and the exchange rate would drop by 80 to 90 per cent' (Anders Åslund, *Transition*, 1998, vol. 9, no. 3, pp. 10–11). 'It is by no means obvious that the value [of the rouble] is too high ... If the rouble were devalued it could end up in free fall ... because the key issue is not valuation but confidence ... [In 1997 oil and oil products accounted for only 22 per cent of exports] ... A devaluation would eliminate all remaining confidence in the rouble among foreigners as well as Russians.' The budget deficit is too large (9 per cent of GDP in 1996 and 8.2 per cent in 1997). But the government undertook substantial cuts in February and May 1998, reducing the 1998 budget deficit target to 5 per cent of GDP. 'Russia's international reserves are low at some $14 billion and an international loan – on top of the ordinary IMF financing – is needed to calm markets.' Russia's debt burden is not large in itself. As a share of GDP it is about 45 per cent. The external debt is about $130 billion (27 per cent of GDP) and the interest rates on that are reasonable. The problem is about $60 billion of short-term debt held in the form of Treasury bills. Although this is only 13 per cent of GDP, interest rates are very high (perhaps an average of 35 per cent in 1998), meaning that this part of the debt burden alone will cost 4.5 per cent of GDP (amounting to almost half federal revenues). The modest amount of domestic Treasury bills held by foreigners (some $20 billion) is the immediate threat to stability. In the long term the budget deficit must be reduced. 'But further cuts are impossible. Instead, financing needs to be improved. Any privatization income would be welcome, but if Russia can launch international loans the cost of borrowing will be much less that the state currently pays. The latest Eurobond issue cost 12 per cent per annum. But Russia should preferably get a $10 billion international inter-governmental financing package to clear the hurdle and convince the market that it deserves lower interest rates. What Moscow needs is not a reduction of debt but a refinancing at more reasonable interest rates' (Anders Åslund, *The World Today*, July 1998, vol. 54, no. 7. pp. 185–7). ('Government debt prior to the crisis amounted to less than 60 per cent of GDP, of which roughly half was domestic debt. Even factoring in other commitments, overall indebtedness remains moderate': EBRD 1998b: 18.)

4. 'The exchange rate anchor has delivered some stability to the Russian economy and is the only credible monetary target. And the rouble is not overvalued' (editorial, *FT*, 28 May 1998, p. 19). 'Without substantial additional

support [a stabilization fund of perhaps as much as $20 billion] the currency is almost certain to collapse … The present pro-reform government is likely to go down with it … Devaluation is not a sensible short-term option: it would probably trigger a banking collapse and flight from the rouble' (editorial, *FT*, 6 July 1998, p. 21). 'Devaluation would almost certainly be uncontrollable; inflation would soar; and the government would fall … The new government consists of the most single-minded and determined group of reformers to hold office since 1992 … What is needed is an aid package capable of giving the needed breathing space' (editorial, *FT*, 13 July 1998, p. 19).

5. 'The argument for helping Russia now is that it would give its new government a chance of steadying market nerves, and thereby provide a long enough breathing space – a year or so – for reforms to bite and to start benefiting people. If no help is forthcoming, there is every chance that the ensuing economic chaos, in the wake of a rouble crash, will not only bring down the current government but may even bring down Russia's rough-and-ready democracy … Russia is politically at its most fragile since October 1993 … The inflation-driven mayhem following a rouble collapse could shift power into the hands of a new, more xenophobic, anti-reform parliament. Mr Yeltsin could fall. An anti-democratic strongman could emerge, whether or not by election. In short, Russia's future as a market-based, albeit rough-hewn, democracy hangs in the balance … Mr Kiriyenko's government … is the best-equipped to tackle the gargantuan tasks ahead of it since communism collapsed six-and-a-half years ago' (*The Economist*, 11 July 1998, p. 16).

Some of those broadly disagreeing with government policy prior to 17 August 1998 were as follows:

1. Jeffrey Sachs was an economic adviser to the Russian government from December 1991 to January 1994. In an article in *The Economist* (12 September 1998) comments on the financial crisis in general. 'Almost all observers now concede that premature liberalization of capital markets (often pushed by the IMF itself) was one cause of the current crisis … Developing countries should impose their own supervisory controls on short-term international borrowing by domestic financial institutions' (p. 24). 'The IMF worked mightily, and wrongheadily, to make the world safe for short-term money managers … exchange rate stability above all else … The IMF encouraged central banks from Moscow to Brasilia to raise interest rates to stratospheric levels to protect their currencies' (p. 24). Sachs believes that exchange rates should generally float. 'It is neither worthwhile nor feasible to twist monetary policy to soothe panicky investors, especially at the cost of internal depression. The only real exception to floating rates comes at the start of stabilization from extreme inflations, when exchange rate targeting is more efficient than monetary targeting' (p. 24). 'The IMF has become the Typhoid Mary of emerging markets, spreading recessions in country after country. It lends its client governments money to repay foreign investors, with the condition that the government jack up interest rates, cut the flow of credits to the banking

system and close weak banks. The measures kill the economies and further undermine investors' confidence. It would be more sensible to keep interest rates moderate and let the economies continue to grow. True, currencies would lose their value and speculators would lose their bets. But borrowers and lenders would be more cautious in the future' (Jeffrey Sachs, *IHT*, 5 June 1998, p. 8).

'To move away from the pegged exchange rate and to introduce a much more flexible exchange rate system ... is the path successfully taken by Israel after its 1985 stabilization and by Poland after 1990. Indeed, the basic stabilization strategy of an early pegged rate followed by a modest depreciation and subsequent flexibility had become part of the accepted professional lore of anti-inflation programmes ... Some governments, however, fall in love with the exchange rate peg since an overvalued currency generally means cheap consumer goods and high real wages in urban areas. Thus Mexico delayed a needed exchange rate exchange ... Brazil delayed needed exchange rate changes ... Any careful observer in 1998 could recognize the Mexico debâcle clearly. When Russia fell into the same currency trap in mid-year – for the same reason: an exchange-based stabilization programme held too long with IMF encouragement – Brazil was the subject of intense speculative attack once again ... Why has it [the IMF] been a party to such damaging and unsuccessful policies? There are, I think, four reasons. First, the IMF and the US Treasury have listened far too much to Wall Street importunings since the mid-1990s. US investors wanted to get their money out of Russia and Brazil without devaluation losses. Second, the IMF believes it can outsmart the market ... Third, as an anti-inflation zealot the IMF cooly accepts deep recessions if it thinks that the output collapse will save a few percentage points on the price level. Last, the IMF remains impervious to criticism' (Jeffrey Sachs, *FT*, 22 January 1999, p. 14).

'Every one of the major crises in recent years – Brazil (1999). Indonesia (1997), Korea (1997), Mexico (1994), Russia (1998), Thailand (1997) – went through similar stages. Each of the countries that succumbed to crisis started with a national currency pegged to the dollar. Each attracted large capital inflows, including short-term loans from international banks. In each country the currency became overvalued, leading investors to withdraw their money in anticipation of a devaluation. Each country defended the currency until it had depleted its foreign exchange reserves. And in each this was followed by a panic by foreign investors, in which the remaining short-term debts were abruptly recalled. The IMF then stepped in with a "rescue plan", but failed to stop the panic, and the downturn proceeded with ferocity. There are three lessons for the economic architect. First, emerging market currencies should be allowed to float, since countries with pegged currencies too often run out of foreign reserves. Second, these countries should abstain from taking short-term loans from international banks. Short-term inflows easily become short-term outflows. And third, these countries should not turn to the IMF for help. The IMF advice has often added to the economic destruction' (Jeffrey Sachs, *The Independent*, 1 February 1999, p. 11).

2. 'Trying to maintain an artificially high exchange rate will only deplete the country's remaining foreign reserves, use up its lines of credit to international financial institutions, and force it to stifle recovery with an exhorbitant interest rate' (Evan Scott, *Transition*, 1998, vol. 9, no. 3, p. 11).

3. Peter Oppenheimer (*FT*, 12 June 1998, p. 18). The rouble's nominal peg to the dollar is not the bedrock of stabilization policy. 'The bedrock has been the central bank restraint on growth of the monetary aggregates and government consolidation of the public finances. These policies were established in 1995 … in the presence of a freely floating exchange rate. In the summer of that year the "exchange rate corridor" was introduced as a pragmatic means of limiting exchange rate movements … [There is need] to secure a modest downward adjustment of the exchange rate path, which more than any other single measure will enhance tax revenues.'

Effects of the financial crisis

Foreign trade

There has been a sharp reversal of Russia's former heavy dependence on imports of consumer goods owing to the sharp depreciation of the rouble. (The share of imported goods in retail sales peaked at 53 per cent in 1995: *RET*, Monthly Update, 30 January 1998, p. 4.)

'Today … a remarkable 48 per cent of all consumer goods here are foreign made, according to the state statistics committee … Russian agriculture has so withered that the country imported 73 per cent of its sugar, 37 per cent of its fish and 35 per cent of its meat last year [1997], said Nikolai Kharitonov, leader of the Agarian Party' (Greg Myre, *IHT*, 2 October 1998, p. 15).

Yevgeni Primakov (6 October 1998): 'The rouble's autumn collapse has resulted in a sharp decline in food imports, which in recent years have accounted for half our food supplies' (*CDSP*, 1998, vol. 50, no. 40, p. 5).

Yuri Maslyukov (17 November 1998): 'In a country that depends on imports for 60 per cent of its food supplies, after the events of 17 August those imports had fallen by 86 per cent' (*CDSP*, 1998, vol. 50, no. 46, p. 9).

Food imports fell by 60 per cent in September 1998 (*CDSP*, 1998, vol. 50, no. 46, p. 7).

'Foreign producers provide 60 to 70 per cent of the goods in local stores' (*Transition*, 1998, vol. 9, no. 4, p. 8).

'Russia imported one-third of its food last year [1997]' (*IHT*, 19 October 1998, p. 5). 'Imports … account for a large percentage of Russian consumer goods, including more than half the food sold in stores' (*IHT*, 18 August 1998, p. 4).

'Officials admitted that imports to Russia fell by nearly 45 per cent in August' (*IHT*, 11 September 1998, p. 1). Imports fell by a third in August (*The Economist*, 12 September 1998, p. 41).

In September 1998 imports fell by 65 per cent compared with the previous month (*RET*, Monthly Update, 4 September 1998, p. 1).

'Imports have fallen about 25 per cent from a year earlier since ... August ... Imports in September were down 41 per cent from the previous month' (*IHT*, 29 December 1998, p. 11).

The proportion of imports in retail sales has fallen from 49 per cent to 30 per cent (*FT*, 9 July 1999, p. 15).

In 1997 exports totalled $87 billion: oil, $21.9 billion; gas, $16.4 billion; precious and base metals, $14 billion. The three together accounted for 60 per cent of exports (*IHT*, 11 December 1998, pp. 15, 18).

Inflation

Hyperinflation did not result. There was no massive increase in the money supply. IMF loans were sought (as is discussed in the section below).

In July 1998 prices grew only 0.2 per cent month-on-month. The monthly inflation rate was 15.3 per cent in August (year-on-year), 38.4 per cent in September, 4.5 per cent in October and 5.7 per cent in November (*RET*, Monthly Update, 4 September 1998, p. 1; Monthly Update, 11 September 1998, p. 10; 1998, vol. 7, no. 3, p. 10; Monthly Update, 8 December 1998, p. 7).

Inflation was 56.4 per cent in the year to October 1998, compared with 12.9 per cent in the year to October 1997 (*The Economist*, 14 November 1998, p. 178). Prices rose by 36 per cent in the first week of September alone (*The Economist*, 12 September 1998, p. 41). The annual inflation rate increased to 21.5 per cent in the year to August 1998, from 5.6 per cent in the year to June (p. 138).

'After a monthly inflation rate of 15 per cent in August, prices rose 43 per cent in the first two weeks of September, the state statistical office said' (*IHT*, 17 September 1998, p. 13).

Output

In July 1998 GDP was 4.5 per cent lower than in July 1997, while industrial output was 9.4 per cent lower (*RET*, Monthly Update, 4 September 1998, p. 1). In August 1998 GDP was 10 per cent lower than in December 1997, while industrial output was almost 14 per cent lower than in December 1997. Agricultural output was 23 per cent lower than in August 1997 (*RET*, Monthly Update 6 October 1998, p. 6). In September 1998 GDP was 11.4 per cent lower than in December 1997 and 9.9 per cent lower than in September 1997, while the respective figures for industrial output fell by 16.5 per cent and 14.5 per cent. Agricultural output was 15 per cent lower than in September 1997

(*RET*, Monthly Update, 11 September 1998, p. 9). In October 1998 industrial production increased by 4.8 per cent compared with the previous month, while the figure for agriculture was 1 per cent. But compared with October 1997 industrial output fell by 11.1 per cent, while agricultural output in the first ten months of 1998 was almost 9 per cent lower than the corresponding period of 1997 (*RET*, Monthly Update, 8 December 1998, p. 7).

In November 1998 industrial output fell by 5 per cent compared with November 1997. In October 1998 the fall had been 10.5 per cent (*IHT*, 23 December 1998, p. 13).

GDP fell by 8.2 per cent in the year to August 1998. In the year to July 1998 it had fallen by just 4.5 per cent (*The Economist*, 26 September 1998, p. 148).

The economics ministry predicted that GDP would shrink 5 per cent in 1999, after this year's decline of 3 per cent (*IHT*, 2 December 1998, p. 17).

On 21 December 1998 the IMF delivered a bleak assessment of the Russian economy, predicting output would contract by 8.3 per cent in 1999 following a 5.7 per cent decline in 1998 (*FT*, 23 December 1998, p. 2).

The IMF predicts that GDP in Russia will fall by 7 per cent in 1999 before stabilizing in 2000. The IMF report said: 'In the absence of coherent stabilization and reform policies, however, there would remain a risk of high inflation and continued economic contraction; access to international financial markets would be unlikely to resume; and much of the progress tentatively achieved in some areas during 1991–98 would be lost' (*FT*, 21 April 1999, p. 6). 'For 1999 the usually judicious IMF had forecast that Russian GDP would slump by 9 per cent' (Anders Åslund, *IHT*, 19 January 2000, p. 8).

Rapid recovery

'Gloomy forecasts predicting hyperinflation and a deep recession have not yet been realized. In spite of the collapse of Russia's banking system and the breakdown of its financial markets, the country appears to have started on the path of real growth by taking advantage of the rouble devaluation that has made Russian goods more competitive. Although output fell after August [1998] in the fourth quarter monthly industrial production grew 3 to 4 per cent month on month and this growth has continued in large part since then ... 1998 saw a return to negative growth figures. Official GDP fell by 4.6 per cent and industrial production by 5.2 per cent ... Initially after the August crisis output continued to fall, mainly as a result of the breakdown of the payments system, which led to disruption in deliveries. When the payment system was mostly restored in October [1998] production returned to levels observed immediately before the crisis and even surpassed them' (*RET*, Monthly Update, 14 May 1999, p. 1). 'At that time [August 1998] forecasts were made predicting hyperinflation and a rapid reduction in production ... This gloomy scenario [however] did not materialize. Instead the economy has been on a path of recovery with impressive growth rates in industrial production. Inflation has come down … [Central bank chairman] Gerashchenko's actions have been very different from that of 1992–4 … Emissions have been kept at a reasonable level … Two events in particular have provided the foundation for the industrial recovery and healthy export environment. These are the devaluation of the rouble in August 1998 and the agreement made by OPEC in March 1999 to limit world oil supply, bringing surging world market oil prices … The real exchange rate has depreciated 43 per cent since July 1998 … A devaluation of this magnitude … gives domestic producers and exporters a competitive edge. For Russia this has materialized in the form of strong growth in industrial production, driven mainly by import substitution and an improved situation for exporters, many of which have their costs in roubles and revenues in dollars … The devaluation has had a positive impact on Russia's current account and trade account, mainly due to the effect on imports, which in the first half of 1999 were down 45 per cent compared with the same period in 1998. However, exports … were down 12 per cent in the first half of 1999 … One consequence of the crisis was the disappearance of securities markets … Deprived of the main source of funding the government was finally faced with no other alternative than to come up with a much tighter budget for 1999, foreseeing a primary surplus of 1.6 per cent [of GDP] and a deficit after interest payments of 2.5 per cent … Not only has the government managed to collect its targeted revenues, but, more importantly, the bulk is now paid in cash … Monetary policy has remained relatively tight' (*RET*, Monthly Update, 10 September 1999, pp. 3–6). 'In the first nine months of the year [1999] the federal government exceeded its tax collection target by 27 per cent, while the expenditure target was more or less kept' (*RET*, 1999, vol. 8, no. 4, p. 4).

'GDP rose 3.2 per cent [in 1999] … thanks largely to a surge in industrial output [which rose by 8.1 per cent]. While a boost in world oil prices contributed usefully, the main gains came from import substitution prompted by the 80 per cent decline in the rouble's international value. Exports stayed roughly constant, but imports dropped by more than a third' (*FT*, Survey, 10 May 2000, p. ii).

'Even when economic growth is recognized it is dismissed as merely an effect of the large devaluation of the rouble in August 1998 and higher oil prices. But the EBRD reckons that Russia has done almost as much systemic reform as Latvia and Lithuania, and sooner or later the results are likely to emerge. The 1998 financial crash seems to have been a catalyst for more profound change. By imposing tough budget constraints the crash convinced many Russian businessmen that they could no longer live off the state but had to make real money in the market. Meanwhile the much-publicized barter economy is dwindling. From August 1998 to August 1999 barter dropped by one-third. Non-payments of most kinds have fallen by at least one-half … [Federal] revenue rose from 9 per cent of GDP in 1998 to 13 per cent in 1999, largely at the expense of the regional governments' (Anders Åslund, *IHT*, 19 January 2000, p. 8).

'Until the 1998 crash Russians could make easy money lending to the government or speculating against the rouble, so they stripped cash out of companies to do it. By destroying the government debt market and devaluing the rouble the crash has forced companies to look for investment opportunities' (*Business Central Europe*, May 2000, pp. 35–6).

But there are concerns about Russia's long-term prospects. 'What the country's current economic performance really suggests is that the window of opportunity opened by last year's crash is being wasted. For a start, investment is flat. Second, although output is up sharply compared with last year [1998], when it slumped, the crucial comparison is with the year before. For the nine months of this year [1999] industrial production is up only 2 per cent compared with the same period of 1997 – despite a huge (75 per cent) devaluation. All this hardly suggests dramatic restructuring. Third, the temporary stability in public finances may prove illusory' (*The Economist*, 23 October 1999, p. 144). 'Thanks to high oil and gas prices the value of Russian exports is soaring. In the first quarter of this year [2000] they were worth $23 billion, up from $16 billion a year ago. Oil and gas accounted for almost all that increase. Since the devaluation of the rouble in August 1998 imports have slumped ... The rouble is rising against the dollar. Coupled with [rising] inflation this erodes the competitiveness that Russian has enjoyed since devaluation. So the economy remains acutely vulnerable. Its fragility is a result of the lack of structural reform since the financial crisis. With some exceptions most Russian companies are still run inefficiently by crooked managers, using worn-out equipment to produce cheap, low-quality goods. Apart from raw materials, guns and vodka Russia has few things worth exporting ... Investment, though up a bit on the pitiful levels of last year [1999], is still paltry when set against Russia's modernization needs' (*The Economist*, 8 July 2000, p. 125). (In 1999 investment in fixed assets rose by 1 per cent: *CDSP*, 2000, vol. 52, no. 11, p. 17.)

Stanley Fischer, acting managing director of the IMF (6 April 2000): 'The good macroeconomic performance since early 1999 cannot be sustained without a broad-based acceleration of structural reforms ... The sustained growth that is needed will require an acceleration in economic reforms to spur investment and strengthen exports as well as comprehensive tax and expenditure reforms' (*FT*, 7 April 2000, p. 10; *IHT*, 7 April 2000, p. 15).

'The recovery in Russia has been underpinned by strong growth in industrial output, increased international competitiveness and the steep rise in commodity prices, especially the price of oil. Some of these developments are unlikely to persist. For sustainable growth to be achieved, Russia will have to make significant progress in improving the investment climate, in enterprise restructuring and in eliminating barter, non-payments and arrears. With the new government in place there is a window of opportunity to move forward on these fronts' (EBRD 2000a: 3). 'The higher profits due to lower competition from imports and lower real wages have helped to reduce the stock of arrears and the share of barter substantially, from 52 per cent of all transactions in 1998 to 34 per cent in 1999' (p. 5).

'The positive effects of the past year were almost guaranteed by the devaluation. They have also been substantially helped by the oil price rise. But there is no persuasive evidence that the devaluation has led to, or even been used for, reforming the Russian economy and improving its prospects in the longer term' (Clifford Gaddy, *Post-Soviet Affairs*, 2000, vol. 16, no. 1, p. 17). 'What real 1999 increment in production, in monetization and in fiscal balance has occurred is the result of massive devaluation coupled with a very fortuitous rise in energy and resource prices, and is unsustainable without massive investment and structural change' (Richard Ericson, ibid., p. 18).

President Vladimir Putin (8 July 2000): 'Russia's economic weaknesses continues to be another serious problem. The widening gap between the advanced countries and Russia is pushing us into the ranks of third-world countries. The figures showing current economic growth should not put our minds at ease ... The current growth has very little to do with the revamping of the economic mechanism. It is largely the result of favourable foreign economic conditions' (*CDSP*, 2000, vol. 52, no. 28, p. 5).

Prime minister Mikhail Kasyanov: 'While Russia's economic performance has improved significantly since the financial crisis of August 1998 much of the improvement is the result of one-off events. The challenge for Russia today is to implement extensive structural reforms that will ensure long-term economic growth and macroeconomic stability' (*FT*, 20 July 2000, p. 23).

'There is a strong consensus that in order to attain sustainable economic growth further progress must be made in the area of structural reforms' (*RET*, 2000, vol. 9, no. 1, p. 4).

'The new-found profitability of a number of industrial firms may be related not only to the weaker rouble and strong export prices, but also to severely repressed domestic prices for energy and transportation. This latter factor continues to raise questions about the quality and sustainability of current industrial growth' (OECD, *Economic Outlook*, June 2000, p. 146).

Further effects of the financial crisis

These are as follows:

1. Although there had been some ups and downs in the stock market, the trend was at first sharply downwards. The Russian Trading System (RTS) is an index of leading shares.

'The capital inflows led to a massive speculative asset bubble, with the stock market rising 142 per cent in 1996 and a further 184 per cent in the first eight months of 1997' (EBRD 1998b: 12). 'In 1996 and 1997 Russia was the darling of international investors. In 1996 its stock market, as measured by the RTS index, grew by 100 per cent. This was followed by an even more spectacular performance in 1997, when stock portfolios tripled in nine months' (Malleret *et al.* 1999: 107). 'Russian shares doubled in value in 1996 and 1997' (*FT*, 19 October 1998, p. 15). 'Shares have fallen 40 per cent since the start of the month [May] and have lost more than half their value since the beginning of the year [1998]' (*FT*, 28 May 1998, p. 1). The Russian stock market was down 40 per cent in May 1998 (*RET*, Monthly Update, 5 June 1998, p. 11). By the end of June 1998 the stock market was 75 per cent below its peak, 63 per cent below its level at the beginning of 1998 and 24 per cent below its level at the end of June 1996 (*RET*, Monthly Update, 2 July 1998, p. 13). 'Between March and August [1998] the Moscow stock exchange, which was the world's best-performing market in 1997, lost more than 80 per cent of its value' (*Transition*, 1998, vol. 9, no. 4, p. 7).

2 June 1998. The RTS ends the day 12 per cent higher at 192.75. The 1997 peak was 571.6, reached on 6 October (*IHT*, 3 June 1998, p. 1).

13 August 1998. 'Black Thursday.' The RTS index falls by 6.51 per cent to 101.17.

'Russian markets plunged ... as investors feared the government might soon be forced into devaluation or a domestic debt restructuring' (*FT*, 14 August 1998, p. 1).

'Russia's stock and bond markets plunged' (Michael Wines, *IHT*, 15 August 1998, p. 13).

31 August 1998. The RTS index falls by 1.16 per cent to 65.62.

16 September 1998. The benchmark RTS index closed down 3.17 points, more than 5 per cent, at 58.86, a record low (*IHT*, 17 September 1998, p. 13).

17 September 1998. The RTS index fell by 7.16 points to 51.70.

25 September 1998. 'Russia's stock market Friday [25 September] reached a new bottom, falling to the level at which it first opened in August 1995' (David Hoffman, *IHT*, 26 September 1998, p. 13).

16 October 1998. 'A wave of late selling Friday [16 October] halted trading three times on Friday and sent the market lower after a spectacular recovery from weeks of near paralysis and rock-bottom prices. The selling, which triggered computer-driven trading programmes, took the all-share RTS index down to 55.32 at the close, but still left the average share prices around 30 per cent higher than at the start of the week ... Prices soared on Friday trading before widespread profit-taking wiped out some of the earlier gains' (*FT*, 19 October 1998, p. 3).

January 1999. 'Moscow, which lost 85 per cent of its value in 1998, fell by a further 9.2 per cent ... in the week to 13 January [1999] ... Brazil devalued the real on 13 January' (*The Economist*, 16 January 1999, p. 116).

10 February 1999. The stock market index rose by 13.9 per cent in the week to 10 February, ending at 63 (*The Economist*, 13 February 1999, p. 146).

15 February 1999. The RTS-IF index has climbed 16 per cent this month (*FT*, 16 February 1999, p. 40).

Since October 1998 there has been a 68 per cent increase in the RTS index. 'The country's benchmark stock index was the world's worst performer last year [1998] after being the world's best in 1996 and 1997 ... A recent rally ... has pushed the index up 11 per cent so far this year' (*IHT*, 16 February 1999, p. 12).

The Moscow Times $ Share Index fell by 8.6 per cent in January 1999 (*RET*, Monthly Update, 10 February 1999, p. 11).

22 February 1999. 'The RTS stock index ... slid 85 per cent last year [1998], when it was the world's worst ... The Russian Trading Index rose 7.4 per cent Monday [22 February] to 74.53 points, its highest level since 26 August [1998], after rising 5.6 per cent Friday [19 February]. The index has gained about 28 per cent this year' (*IHT*, 23 February 1999, p. 13).

'Russia's stock market is rallying amid assumptions that holders of the frozen GKOs will be able to swap them for shares. In February the Moscow Times $ Index rose more than 40 per cent. Foreigners hold about $10 billion of GKOs/OFZs at face value, and the restructuring deal could mean that between $100–200 million will be spent on Russian shares' (*RET*, Monthly Update, 11 March 1999, p. 12).

24 February 1999. 75.5 (*The Economist*, 27 February, p. 124).

March 1999. *The Economist* (various issues: stockmarkets in dollar terms): 3 March, 73.3; 10 March, 76.5; 17 March, 90.0; 24 March (Nato attacks Serbia), 76.8; 30 March, 81.2.

'If Russia's stock market was labelled the worst performing stock market of 1998, the first three months of 1999 told a different story. The Moscow Times dollar index, which fell 87 per cent during the course of 1998, rose 58.9 per cent in the first three months of 1999, making Russia one of the world's best performing markets so far this year. A recent boost was given by expectations of part of the defaulted GKOs being swapped for equity (under the restructuring deal foreign holders of GKO Treasury bills will receive 10 per cent in cash which can then be invested in certain shares, decided by the ministry of finance, on the stock market) and by progress in the government's negotiations with the IMF. Equally the recent increase in the world market price of oil has aroused interest in the shares of oil companies' (*RET*, Monthly Update, 13 April 1999, pp. 15–16).

April 1999. *The Economist* (various issues: stockmarkets in dollar terms): 7 April, 73.0; 14 April, 73.6; 21 April, 76.9; 28 April, 81.5.

28 April 1999. An agreement is reached with the IMF. 'The Russian stock market rallied Thursday [29 April], with its main index rising to 85.90' (*IHT*, 30 April 1999, p. 16).

May 1999. *The Economist* (various issues: stockmarkets in dollar terms): 5 May, 102.7; 12 May, 81.4; 19 May, 98.2; 26 May, 99.9.

6 May 1999. 'The Moscow Times $ Index ... on 6 May stood at 79.4, the highest since mid-August last year [1998]' (*RET*, Monthly Update, 14 May 1999, p. 13).

12 May 1999. Yeltsin dismisses prime minister Yevgeni Primakov. 'The RTS share index fell 37.9 to 199.2, nearly 20 per cent' (*FT*, 13 May 1999, p. 3).

1 June 1999. The Moscow Times $ Index edged up another 9 per cent in May, standing at 78.9 at the beginning of June compared with 25 at the beginning of October 1998 (*RET*, Monthly Update, 10 June 1999, p. 11).

June 1999. *The Economist* (various issues: stockmarkets in dollar terms): 2 June, 94.2; 9 June, 107.5; 16 June, 117.7; 23 June, 125.5; 30 June, 125.7.

16 June 1999. The RTS index rises to 114.67, its highest level since 14 August 1998 (*IHT*, 17 June 1999, p. 15).

July 1999. *The Economist* (various issues: stockmarkets in dollar terms): 7 July, 144.3; 14 July, 141.3; 21 July, 127.1; 28 July, 125.2.

'The Moscow Times $ Index increased by 150 per cent in the first half of the year … Although foreign players have started to reenter the Russian market, the majority of transactions are still done by domestic players' (*RET*, 14 July 1999, p. 17).

8 July 1999. 'The equity market, which slumped by more than 90 per cent last year [1998], is up 145 per cent in 1999, making it the best performing stock market in the world' (*FT*, 9 July 1999, p. 15).

August 1999. *The Economist* (various issues: stockmarkets in dollar terms): 4 August, 105.5; 11 August, 102.8, 18 August, 104.9; 25 August, 115.4.

'The share market, which has seen very impressive growth so far this year [1999], started to falter in July, losing more than 8.2 per cent during the month. In the first week of August the market fell another 9.8 per cent despite IMF loan approval and continuing high oil prices' (*RET*, Monthly Update, 10 August 1999, p. 14).

9 August 1999. Yeltsin dismisses prime minister Sergei Stepashin (and thus the entire government).

'The [stock] market's initial reaction was negative, falling 11 per cent in the first hour of trading. However, it recovered later and was down only marginally at closing time' (*RET*, Monthly Update, 10 August 1999, p. 15).

September 1999. *The Economist* (various issues: stockmarkets in dollar terms): 1 September, 103.0; 8 September, 101.7; 15 September, 92.8; 22 September, 80.1; 29 September, 85.2.

October 1999. *The Economist* (various issues: stockmarkets in dollar terms): 6 October, 88.2; 13 October, 96.0; 20 October, 98.4; 27 October, 97.0.

November 1999. *The Economist* (various issues: stockmarkets in dollar terms): 3 November, 95.5; 10 November, 111.0; 17 November, 116.1; 24 November, 119.5.

December 1999. *The Economist* (various issues: stockmarkets in dollar terms): 1 December, 113.4; 8 December, 110.5; 14 December, 109.0.

31 December 1999. Yeltsin resigns as president. Prime minister Vladimir Putin becomes acting president.

January 2000. *The Economist* (various issues: stockmarkets in dollar terms): 5 January, 179.0; 12 January, 189.2; 19 January, 183.6.

February 2000. *The Economist* (various issues: stockmarkets in dollar terms): 2 February, 168.9; 9 February, 193.2; 16 February, 180.3; 23 February, 181.1.

March 2000. The Economist (various issues: stockmarkets in dollar terms): 1 March, 180.5; 8 March, 197.3; 15 March, 222.4; 22 March, 222.4; 29 March, 232.4.

April 2000. The Economist (various issues: stockmarkets in dollar terms): 5 April, 214.6; 12 April, 224.9; 18 April, 202.9; 26 April, 221.2.

May 2000. The Economist (various issues: stockmarkets in dollar terms): 3 May, 227.5; 10 May, 227.2; 17 May, 209.8; 24 May, 167.1; 31 May, 190.2.

June 2000. The Economist (various issues: stockmarkets in dollar terms): 7 June, 193.9; 14 June, 191.3; 21 June, 179.3; 28 June, 170.2.

July 2000. The Economist (various issues: stockmarkets in dollar terms): 5 July, 176.0; 12 July, 185.5; 19 July, 187.6; 26 July, 187.5.

August 2000. The Economist (various issues: stockmarkets in dollar terms): 2 August, 202.7; 9 August, 217.4; 16 August, 228.5; 23 August, 228.0; 30 August, 240.0.

September 2000. The Economist (various issues: stockmarkets in dollar terms): 6 September, 237.7; 13 September, 213.1; 20 September, 193.2; 27 September, 199.9.

October 2000. The Economist (various issues: stockmarkets in dollar terms): 4 October, 212.9; 11 October, 193.0; 18 October, 184.0; 25 October, 191.1.

November 2000. The Economist (various issues: stockmarkets in dollar terms): 1 November, 194.1; 8 November, 184.5; 15 November, 177.7; 22 November, 166.2.

2. Although there had been some ups and downs, at first the rouble plummeted in value against the US dollar.

17 August 1998. 'As of 17 August 1998 the Bank of Russia is switching to a policy of a floating rouble exchange rate within new exchange rate corridor limits, which have been set at a level of 6 to 9.5 roubles to the dollar' (official statement by the government and the central bank: *CDSP*, 1998, vol. 50, no. 33, p. 5).

The trading band for the rouble against the US dollar is widened (until the end of 1998) from 5.27/7.13 to 6.0/9.5 (*The Times*, 18 August 1998, p. 10). (The rouble had traded at 6.36 to the US dollar on 13 August, 'Black Thursday'.)

1 September 1998. The exchange rate is 9.33 roubles to the dollar (*IHT*, 6 October 1998, p. 15).

8 September 1998. 'Yesterday [8 September] the official rouble exchange rate dropped from 18.90 to 20.82 to the dollar, although the street value has fallen further' (*FT*, 9 September 1998, p. 24).

'The exchange rate slipped to twenty-three to the dollar' (*IHT*, 9 September 1998, p. 1).

14 September 1998. 'There were reports of banks squeezing the rouble to artificial levels ahead of the expiry of a number of forward currency contracts today [15 September]. The rouble surged to 8.5 to the dollar during electronic trading. The Emerging Market Traders Association estimated the rouble to be just below 9 roubles in morning Moscow trading' (*FT*, 15 September 1998, p. 43).

15 September 1998. 'Russian banks sold roubles Tuesday, after having bought the currency in the past four days to try to bolster its value before the contracts expired ... The central bank set a rouble rate for Wednesday [16 September] at 9.6 per dollar' (*IHT*, 16 September 1998, p. 15).

'The rouble yesterday [15 September] rose briefly to near its pre-collapse level of a month ago, pushed up by Russian banks who had to repay foreign investors in dollars on contracts that expired yesterday. It hit 7.5 roubles to the dollar ... However, as soon as the banks had paid up, it fell to about 12.5 roubles' (*FT*, 16 September 1998, p. 47).

17 September 1998. On the Moscow Interbank Currency Exchange the rouble fell from 12.4 to 15.8 against the dollar (p. 35).

22 September 1998. The official rate for the rouble is set at 16.22 to the US dollar (*FT*, 22 September 1998, p. 2).

19 October 1998. The rouble tumbles to 17.1 to the US dollar from 15.5 on 16 October.

23 October 1998. The rouble, which briefly fell to a rate where the dollar bought more than 20 roubles, has largely settled in the last week or so at sixteen or seventeen to the dollar.

12 November 1998. The dollar rose to 15.58 roubles on Thursday (12 November) from 15.56 the day before (*IHT*, 13 November 1998, p. 17).

16 November 1998. The dollar rose to 16.41 roubles on Monday from 15.93 roubles on 13 November (*IHT*, 17 November 1998, p. 17).

4 December 1998. 'The rouble tumbled Friday [4 December], trading near record low levels last seen immediately after Russia's economic crisis broke out in August. The rouble fell Friday to 20.61 to the dollar, compared with 18.56 to the dollar Thursday' (*IHT*, 5 December 1998, p. 13).

23 December 1998. 'The government's tough 1999 budget has its first reading tomorrow [24 December] ... The rouble will be kept to about its current rate at 21.5 to the US dollar' (*FT*, 23 December 1998, p. 2).

24 December 1998. A dollar is worth 19.87 roubles (*IHT*, 26 December 1998, p. 11).

28 December 1998. 'The rouble slumps by 7 per cent to a record low of 20.99 to the dollar' (*IHT*, 29 December 1998, p. 11).

6 January 1998. 'The dollar finished Wednesday at 22.9 roubles, up from 20.65 roubles Tuesday [5 January]' (*IHT*, 7 January 1999, p. 11).

10 January 1999. 'The value of the rouble has fallen about 10 per cent since 1 January [1999] ... Russia delayed introducing the euro on its currency markets Sunday [10 January], saying further technical preparations were needed; it scheduled the first day of trading for 19 January ... The central bank has assigned the euro an initial value of 25.89 roubles' (*IHT*, 11 January 1999, p. 11).

11 January 1999. The rouble is steady at 23.39 roubles (*IHT*, 12 January 1999, p. 12).

'The central bank, in order to influence the exchange rate, has banned some banks from the afternoon trading session. Furthermore, from 11 January, exporters are forced to sell 75 per cent of their export revenues on the market' (*RET*, Monthly Update, 20 January 1999, p. 13).

29 January 1999. 'The rouble is trading at twenty-three to the dollar' (*IHT*, 30 January 1999, p. 4).

4 February 1999. 'The rouble slipped Thursday [4 February], with the dollar quoted at 23.14 roubles on the Moscow interbank currency exchange, compared with 22.92 roubles on Wednesday [3 February]' (*IHT*, 5 February 1999, p. 13).

Inflation continues to lag behind the nominal depreciation of the rouble. It has depreciated 46 per cent in real terms since July 1998 (*RET*, Monthly Update, 10 February 1999, p. 12).

25 March 1999. The MICEX exchange rate reaches a record low of 27.4 roubles to the US dollar (*RET*, Monthly Update, 10 September 1999, p. 3).

The rouble fell seven points to the dollar Thursday [25 March]. The drop followed a similar slide Wednesday [24 March], when the rouble fell to about 26 to the dollar' (*IHT*, 26 March 1999, p. 13). (Nato attacked Serbia on 24 March.)

12 May 1999. President Yeltsin dismisses prime minister Yevgeni Primakov.

'The initial response of the rouble to the departure of Primakov and his government was more significant on the street, where it traded as high as 26 roubles to the US dollar, than on the trading on MICEX, where the rouble weakened 90 kopeks, closing at 25.14 roubles to the US dollar (the official CBR rate actually strengthened) (*RET*, Monthly Update, 14 May 1999, p. 15).

31 May 1999. The rouble appreciated in the second half of May, ending at 24.7 roubles to the US dollar (*RET*, Monthly Update, 10 June 1999, p. 11).

29 June 1999. The central bank ends the dual foreign exchange trading system where the central bank and limited other buyers purchase currency revenues from exporters required to sell during a special session (*IHT*, 12 June 1999, p. 11). 'The rouble emerged unscathed Tuesday [29 June] from its first open trading session since ... August [1998], with the dollar trading at 24.22 roubles' (*IHT*, 30 June 1999, p. 15).

'The exchange rate was unified at the end of June 1999. The special trading session for importers and exporters was scrapped and trading returned to a unified session for all agents ... Also the restriction of foreign banks' correspondent accounts has been lifted' (*RET*, Monthly Update, 10 September 1999, p. 3). 'At the end of June the CBR cancelled the special currency trading sessions for exporters and importers, unifying the exchange rate in accordance with IMF requirements' (*RET*, Monthly Update, 14 July 1999, p. 16). The restrictions on foreign banks buying hard currency using their rouble correspondent accounts were lifted on 29 June (*RET*, 1999, vol. 8, no. 2, p. 99).

5 July 1999. 'On 5 July the restriction on hard currency purchases via correspondent accounts of foreign banks was lifted ... On 6 July the rouble stood at 24.89 to the US dollar, down from 24.2 roubles a week earlier. The rouble then regained some strength and on 12 July the rate was 24.4 roubles' (*RET,* Monthly Update, 14 July 1999, p. 16).

9 August 1999. Yeltsin dismisses prime minister Sergei Stepashin (and thus the entire government).

The rouble fell from 24.55 to the US dollar to 25.29 (*FT,* 10 August 1999, p. 1).

'The official exchange rate reached 25.29 to the US dollar, which means that the first nine days of August have seen a [nominal] depreciation of 4.5 per cent ... The rouble decline started when the CBR withdrew its support at the end of July. The level of international reserves means that major interventions are not feasible ... The exchange rate is continuing to appreciate in real terms as the rate of inflation remains above the rate of depreciation' (*RET,* Monthly Update, 10 August 1999, pp. 13–14).

2 September 1999. 'The Russian rouble plunged 2.6 per cent against the dollar on Thursday [2 September] after the central bank said it would drop its defence of the currency and let it fall further this year. The rouble fell to 25.87 per dollar after weakening 1.6 per cent Wednesday. Viktor Gerashchenko, the central bank chairman, said Wednesday the rouble could fall to between twenty-seven and thirty to the dollar by the end of the year. The rouble has already dropped 74 per cent in the past year. With inflation running at an annual rate of about 50 per cent, the rouble has strengthened in real terms in recent months as the central bank kept it steady at between twenty-four and twenty-five to the dollar. The government has said it wants to keep the rouble's decline in line with inflation, and a fall to thirty roubles would accomplish that, said a [Western] analyst' (*IHT,* 3 September 1999, p. 15).

'The commotion surrounding suspect Russian accounts at the Bank of New York has also begun to unsettle the rouble in recent days causing it to slide more then 3 per cent so far this week as traders fear continued IMF financing could be jeopardized' (*FT,* Friday 3 September 1999, p. 2).

3 September 1999. 'The rouble slid further yesterday [3 September], with the central bank setting its official weekend rate at 25.82 to the dollar after ending its programme of intervention to support the exchange rate' (*FT,* 4 September 1999, p. 2).

January 2000. 'The rouble has slid 7 per cent since Christmas' (*IHT,* 14 January 2000, p. 5).

'The rouble has dipped, by nearly 7 per cent against the dollar, in the past month' (*The Economist,* 15 January 2000, p. 39).

What has happened to gold and foreign exchange reserves can be seen from the following:

7 August 1998. Central bank reserves stand at $17 billion (*IHT,* 22 August 1998, p. 4).

14 August 1998. The central bank's foreign exchange and gold reserves stand at $15.1 billion (*FT,* 27 August 1998, p. 2).

19 August 1998. The central bank announces that since 20 July 1998 it has spent some $3.8 billion to support the rouble (*RET*, 1998, vol. 7, no. 3, p. 42). The chairman of the central bank, Sergei Dubinin, admits that some $3.8 billion of the $4.8 billion advanced by the IMF has been used since 20 July to shore up the rouble (*The Independent*, 20 August 1998, p. 13). The remainder was used to redeem short-term government debt: *FT*, 20 August 1998, p. 1). (On 23 September 1998 Anatoli Chubais dismissed allegations that the central bank had misused the latest $4.8 billion tranche of the IMF loan as 'pure fantasy'. He said that $3.8 billion had been used, as specified, to bolster the central bank's reserves and defend the rouble, while the remaining $1 billion had been spent on legitimate budget needs. He claimed that the accusations against the central bank were 'politically motivated': *FT*, 24 September 1998, p. 2.)

27 August 1998. 'In the past two months alone the bank has spent $8.8 billion supporting the rouble' (*CDSP*, 1998, vol. 50, no. 35, p. 6).

8 September 1998. A government official says that the central bank's gold and foreign exchange reserves have fallen to $11 billion (*FT*, 9 September 1998, p. 24).

18 September 1998. A presidential decree from 18 September forces exporters to sell an additional 25 per cent of their export revenues to the central bank in addition to the 50 per cent which they are already required to sell on the MICEX (*RET*, 1998, vol. 7, no. 3, p. 13).

2 October 1998. 'Russia's central bank and state customs committee said they would tighten controls over repatriation of exporters' profits to prevent capital flight and to maintain a steady supply of dollars to prop up the rouble. Under the measures banks must deposit the roubles and the dollars they will sell for exporters and importers a day ahead of one-hour trading sessions, starting 6 October' (*IHT*, 3 October 1998, p. 13).

On 2 October the central bank introduced restrictions on hard currency trading by implementing a morning trading session at which exporters and importers sell and buy foreign currency, and from 15 October a second afternoon session for other actors. The central bank official rate is set as the weighted average rate from the morning session (*RET*, Monthly Update, 11 September 1998, p. 14). Commercial banks operate in the afternoon session (*RET*, Monthly Update, 8 December 1998, p. 11).

8 October 1998. The central bank says that its gold and foreign exchange reserves amounted to $12.8 on 2 October 1998, an increase from the $12.4 billion registered on 25 September (*IHT*, 9 October 1998, p. 17).

1 November 1998. A regulation becomes effective which attempts to reduce capital flight. The regulation limits purchases of foreign currency by Russian legal entities to that for business trips or imports (*RET*, Monthly Update, 11 September 1998, p. 14).

8 December 1998. Hard currency reserves fell by 8 per cent in November, shrinking from $13.6 billion at the start of the month to $12.5 billion at the end. Reserves have fallen by nearly 30 per cent since the start of 1998 (*IHT*, 9 December 1998, p. 19).

8 January 1999. International reserves fall to $12 billion, from $12.8 billion at the end of November 1998 and $12.2 billion at the end of December 1998 (*RET*, Monthly Update, 20 January 1999, p. 13).

10 January 1999. The central bank says that its gold and foreign currency reserves fell $77 million in the week that ended 1 January 1999, to $12.22 billion (*IHT*, 11 January 1999, p. 11).

11 January 1999. The central bank tightens currency controls, saying it will require exporters to repatriate 75 per cent of their hard currency revenues, up from the previous limit of 50 per cent (*IHT*, 12 January 1999, p. 12).

'The central bank, in order to influence the exchange rate, has banned some banks from the afternoon trading session. Furthermore, from 11 January, exporters are forced to sell 75 per cent of their export revenues on the market' (*RET*, Monthly Update, 20 January 1999, p. 13).

19 March 1999. Foreign currency and gold reserves have slipped to $11.2 billion (*IHT*, 26 March 1999, p. 13).

23 March 1999. Importers are ordered to guarantee contracts by depositing roubles in their banks until the goods reach Russia. The central banks introduced the new currency control in order to ensure that importers do not send dollars out of Russia under fake contracts (*IHT*, 24 March 1999, p. 13).

'A measure to prevent capital flight through false import contracts stipulates that importers paying for deliveries in advance now have to deposit the rouble equivalent with a commercial bank. The deposit is returned when the goods have been delivered. The measure effectively means that importers would have to double their working capital' (*RET*, Monthly Update, 13 April 1999, p. 13). 'Importers must deposit roubles at a commercial bank to an amount equal to the hard currency amount, bought to pay for imports, and they get back the roubles by proving receipt of the imports' (*RET*, Monthly Update, 14 July 1999, p. 16).

26 March 1999. The central bank announces that gold and foreign exchange reserves have fallen to a three-year low of $10.9 billion (*IHT*, 2 April 1999, p. 13).

7–8 April 1999. 'On 17 April the CBR introduced restrictions limiting commercial banks to buy dollars for redeeming deposits in the afternoon session only. On 8 April restrictions were imposed prohibiting foreign banks from buying dollars through their correspondent accounts in Russian banks' (*RET*, Monthly Update, 14 May 1999, pp. 14–15).

31 May 1999. International reserves stand at $11.9 billion (*RET*, Monthly Update, 10 June 1999, p. 11).

6 January 2000. 'Mr Putin's most significant move was to approve a central bank plan forcing exporters to sell 100 per cent of their hard currency earnings on authorized exchanges. The intention is to restrict capital flight and help bolster the value of the depressed rouble. At present Russia's biggest exporters, which include mainly gas, oil and mineral companies, are required to repatriate 75 per cent of their foreign earnings ... Mr Putin also signed an order unblocking exports of platinum after a delay of more than a year and scrapped tax breaks for tolling, a transfer pricing scheme used mainly by metal producers to reduce their stated profits' (*FT*, 7 January 2000, p. 6).

'Mr Putin approved a request from the Russian central bank to require Russian exporters to repatriate 100 per cent of their hard currency revenues, up from a previous requirement of 75 per cent ... A top Russian official said the government would also implement a separate requirement, long insisted on by the IMF, that will stop Russia's oil companies from exporting oil if they have not paid up delinquent tax bills' (*IHT*, 7 January 2000, p. 15). It is announced that access to the oil export pipeline in 2000 will be allowed only for companies with no arrears in its payments to the budget (*RET*, 1999, vol. 8, no. 4, p. 102).

April 2000. 'Russian gross gold and currency reserves have begun to increase, moving from roughly $11 billion in the first three quarters of 1999 to over $16 billion by April 2000' (OECD, *Economic Outlook*, June 2000, p. 146).

August 2000. 'International reserves rose sharply from $12.5 billion at the end of 1999 to $23 billion by August 2000' (EBRD 2000b: 202).

3. Food aid.

9 October 1998. 'Russia asked the EU for emergency aid yesterday [9 October] to stave off a massive humanitarian disaster in its northern and Arctic regions, where there are plans to evacuate people because of food and fuel shortages ... Rossiskaya Gazeta said this week [that] the grain and potato harvests are 40 per cent down on last year' (*The Guardian*, 10 October 1998, p. 16).

6 November 1998. The USA and Russia sign an agreement for 3.1 million tonnes of food aid to help Russia through the winter. Critics of food aid argue as follows: Western countries push food aid in order to reduce their farm surpluses; aid has a detrimental effect on domestic production; Russia has a problem with distribution rather than an overall food problem, e.g. providing areas in the far north in winter.

9 November 1998. The European Commission proposes a $480 million package of food aid (*IHT*, 10 November 1998, p. 5).

A tentative deal was reached on 10 November. Russia would buy up to $480 million of food and receive up to $14 million of EU humanitarian aid (*The Independent*, 11 November 1998, p. 14).

'The most recent idea, $500 million in food aid, has been a blatantly self-interested move by Europe's farm lobby ... Lobbying by Germany and Finland, among others, has delayed the food-aid package' (*The Economist*, 2 January 1999, p. 35).

'Russia and the EU should finally agree a pricing system this week for the first tranche of food aid for Russia under a package worth nearly $500 million

... Separately, an agricultural source at the US embassy in Moscow said negotiations on prices for a second tranche of US aid to Russia may start any day. Talks over the EU pricing have dragged on for months and have not been finalized even though half the food that the EU has agreed to send is either in Russia or on its way ... The stumbling block has been at what price the food should be sold. It is not to be given away, but sold with the proceeds paid into a special account at the finance ministry. This will then be paid into Russia's pension fund, which is seriously in arrears' (*FT*, 29 April 1999, p. 3).

The first shipment of EU food aid, which was scheduled for February, did not arrive until 25 March 1999 (*RET*, 1999, vol. 8, no. 2, p. 94).

The bulk of the EU's $500 million food aid package has been delivered (*FT*, 28 September 1999, p. 2).

4. The regions of Russia began to adopt policies which weakened central (federal) control and which in some cases were unconstitutional. Some examples, in chronological order, are as follows:

6 September 1998. '[There is] evidence that some of the eighty-nine republics, regions and territories are using the chaos to seize more power has been mounting since the crisis began last month.' Examples include regions no longer transferring any funds to Moscow, price freezes and 'import' taxes on goods from other regions (*The Independent*, 7 September 1998, p. 10).

8 September 1998. Regional leaders take measures deemed illegal by the federal authorities. The enclave of Kaliningrad on the Baltic Sea declares a 'state of emergency'. Other measures include the following: price controls; refusal to send payments to Moscow; bans on shipping foodstuffs out of particular regions. 'It turned out that banning the export of goods is inconsistent with Article 71 of the constitution and with provisions of the civil code and of Russian anti-monopoly legislation ... But a considerable number of governors have not toed the government's line' (*CDSP*, 1998, vol. 50, no. 41, p. 17).

16 October 1998. The Orenburg region of Russia defaulted Friday [16 October] on 40 million roubles ($2.6 million) in domestic debt and may miss payments on other bonds as it struggles to collect taxes (*IHT*, 17 October 1998, p. 13).

18 November 1998. Yeltsin instructs the 'security council' to hold an emergency meeting in response to comments made by Kalmykia's president. Kirsan Ilyumzhinov: 'Whereas Chechenia is still receiving certain sums of federal money, Kalmykia is not getting anything for paying student grants, or for vaccinating children, or for keeping maternity homes or for implementing a programme for combating plague. So, in fact, we are not a part of Russia. If this is so, we shall urge Moscow to give us the status of an associated member, or just secede.' When the economic crisis paralysed the banking system in August 1998 Ilyumzhinov refused to pay $200 million in taxes. Moscow retaliated by suspending credits to Kalmykia and shutting the central bank's local branch (*The Times*, 19 November 1998, p. 18).

On 17 November Ilyumzhinov said: 'Kalmykia might become an associate member of the Russian Federation or secede from it altogether.' He said that he made the statement because the Russian finance ministry had completely suspended transfer payments to Kalmykia. The following day a denial was issued that the statement was an act of separation (*CDSP*, 1998, vol. 50, no. 47, p. 11).

11 December 1998. The Moscow region (which does not include Moscow) says that it is seeking to restructure 1.2 billion roubles ($59.8 million) of bonds after it defaulted on a payment due today. About 90 per cent of the bonds sold by the Moscow region are held by foreign investors (*IHT*, 12 December 1998, p. 15).

29 September 1998. Primakov meets chief executives of the federation members. In September only half the tax revenues envisaged in the budget were collected. 'Primakov ... said that some regions were taking what he called a "fiefdom approach" ... "They have gotten to the point that they do not want to transfer tax revenues [to Moscow] and do not allow food products to be taken out of their regions." Yevgeni Primakov emphasized ... "It is time to be done with that kind of approach. Otherwise we will cease to have a unified state" ... In the prime minister's opinion, it would be a good idea to pass a law "making it possible to remove elected officials from office if their actions violate the constitution or existing legislation"' (*CDSP*, 1998, vol. 50, no. 40, p. 10). The thirteen member presidium includes deputy prime ministers, the central bank chairman, the president of the academy of sciences and heads of eight regional associations (p. 10). The eight includes authoritative governors who are not necessarily heads of regional associations (p. 11).

27 December 1998. 'Over the weekend [26–7 December] a trilateral commission, consisting of both houses of parliament and the government, agreed that Moscow would next year [1999] spend 33.7 billion roubles – or 14 per cent of all tax revenues – on supporting the regions but that the subsidies would be reallocated. Russia's thirty-nine worst-hit regions, including Dagestan in the north Caucasus and Kamchatka and Sakhalin in the far east, will receive additional support next year. But thirty-six better-off territories, such as the oil region of Tyumin and the industrial city of Novgorod, will lose some of their subsidies. Twelve regions will receive no financial support from Moscow ... The federal government would receive 49.5 per cent of all tax revenues with regional authorities receiving the rest' (John Thornhill, *FT*, 28 December 1998, p. 2).

(Many regions imposed price controls on basic goods, although in most cases these lasted only two or three months: EBRD 1999a: 20.)

5. The stirring up of antisemitism. On 4 November 1998 a motion censuring General Albert Makashov (a member of the Communist Party's central committee) for antisemitic comments was defeated in the State Duma by 121 votes to 107.

'The communists went looking last week for someone to blame for Russia's economic morass, and after an extraordinary discourse freighted with memories of the Soviet past they found a candidate: the Jews ... In a debate in the lower house of parliament communist legislators had pressed the argument that Jews in the government and the media were aligned with outsiders in a campaign to undermine Russian nationalism and sap the country's strength ... A communist legislator, Albert Makashov, proclaimed that Russia's economic woes were the fault of the *zhidy* [Yids] – a slur for Jews – and that certain of them should be found and jailed. Mr Makashov later expressed regret, saying he should have used the term "Zionists". But he also called for a debate about who really controls Russia' (Michael Wines, *IHT*, 9 November 1998, p. 5).

Albert Makashov (comments published on 11 November): 'There should be a clearly established percentage of Jews holding high-level positions ... I do not know [how many Jews there are in Russia] ... But it is less than 1 per cent' (*CDSP*, 1998, vol. 50, no. 45, p. 7). (Jews make up less than 0.5 per cent of the population. There are thought to be fewer than 500,000 Jews in the country: James meek, *The Guardian*, 5 November 1998, p. 16.)

'Albert Makashov, the communist member of parliament who has inveighed against the Jews as the source of Russia's economic malaise, set off a new uproar Wednesday [11 November] by calling for quotas on the number of Jews in Russia ... The exchanges in recent days underscore how Russia's economic hardships have spawned a bitter round of ethnic scapegoating. Such virulent antisemitism had been rare in post-Soviet Russian politics but appears to have taken on a new dimension with the country's difficulties since the 17 August devaluation of the rouble ... A subtext in the controversy is the communists' ire at the wealthy Russian business tycoons who have come to prominence in recent years, most of whom are Jewish, as are many of the free-market reformers. The tycoons also control two of Russia's biggest television channels. In his statement Mr Makashov has echoed the antisemitism of earlier generations, saying that Jewish moneymen were behind Russia's suffering. On Wednesday he attacked Boris Berezovsky, one of the magnates, who has control of the largest television network along with oil, aviation and industry holdings. "Don't behave as a yid", Mr Makashov said of Mr Berezovsky, using a slur for Jew. "Give this country, this nation" a billion or two "of your green money and this nation will calm down"' (David Hoffman, *IHT*, 12 November 1998, pp. 1, 10). 'Six of the seven oligarchs are Jewish' (David Hoffman, *IHT*, 9 April 1999, p. 5).

In late December 1998 Gennadi Zyuganov made public a letter in which he said members of the Communist Party had made 'insufficiently considered remarks directed against Jews' that were 'contrary to the directives' of the party. But he devoted most of the letter to an attack on Zionism, which he said was not a movement of Jews returning to their homeland. He believes there is a Zionist conspiracy to seize power in Russia and that 'Zionist capital' has wrecked the economy. The letter appeared to be aimed at the Russian business tycoons, known as the 'oligrachs'. Most of the small circle of tycoons are Jewish. He attacked the Jewish financiers without naming them (David Hoffman, *IHT*, 26 December 1998, p. 2).

Zyuganov: 'Zionism has in reality revealed itself as one of the varieties of the theory and practice of the most aggressive imperialistic circles striving for world supremacy. In this respect it is similar to fascism. The only difference between them is that Hitler's Nazism was performing under the guise of German nationalism and sought world supremacy openly. And Zionism, performing under the guise of Jewish nationalism, is operating stealthily, using other people's hands ... We have never put an equation mark between the notions of a Jew and a Zionist. The spread of Zionist ideology among the Jewish people is by far not the fault, but a misfortune of the Jewish people ... [While Jews were welcome to leave Russia or recognize it] as their only motherland [they could not be some kind of] inner emigrant in it, acting for the damage of her interests in favour of another state or an international corporation ... Our people are not blind. They cannot but see that Zionization of the government authorities of Russia was one of the reasons for the present catastrophic conditions of the country, mass impoverishment and dying out of its population. They cannot turn a blind eye to the aggressive, destructive role of Zionist capital in ruining Russia's economy and plundering her property owned by all.'

On 15 December 1998 the Duma's impeachment commission discussed the final charge against Boris Yeltsin, namely 'genocide against the Russian people'. Viktor Ilyukhin, security committee chairman, said that this 'large-scale genocide' would have had less serious consequences if 'members of the indigenous nationality instead of the Jewish nation alone, talented though that nation is, had predominated' in the president's inner circle (*CDSP*, 1999, vol. 50, no. 50, p. 9).

'A leading Russian Communist [Viktor Ilyukhin, head of the Duma's defence committee] told a parliamentary hearing [on 15 December 1998] that Jews were responsible for what he called the "genocide" of the Russian people' (*The Times*, 16 December 1998, p. 12).

('Russia is no longer considering the liberal goals of a year ago and the tycoons [oligarchs] have been humbled by huge losses in the downward economic spiral that followed devaluation of the rouble': David Hoffman, *IHT*, 2 November 1998, p. 5. But, in fact, most of the financial oligarchs have continued to prosper and Boris Berezovsky has made a remarkable political comeback.)

The IMF and Russia's fiscal and monetary policy.

The following provides some indication of the difficulties of raising sufficient tax revenue:

'Primakov ... announced that tax revenues in September were only half of what had been hoped for' (*IHT*, 30 September 1998, p. 5).

In September only half the tax revenues envisaged in the budget were collected (*CDSP*, 1998, vol. 50, no. 40, p. 10).

'Tax revenues in September came to only 9 billion roubles, 4 billion short of the monthly target drawn up before the collapse' (*The Economist*, 10 October 1998, p. 57).

Tax collection fell by 2 billion roubles in September, to 9.3 billion roubles. Only 70 per cent of all taxes are collected in cash, the rest being paid in offset arrangements with the government or in barter (*IHT*, 7 October 1998, pp. 4, 19).

The amount of taxes collected in the first half of 1998 was 12 per cent lower than in the first half of 1997 (*CDSP*, 1998, vol. 50, no. 32, p. 9).

Government revenues totalled $10.8 billion for the first ten months of 1998 or 59 per cent of target levels (*IHT*, 9 December 1998, p. 19).

Boris Fyodorov: 'Some 150 million people live in the country, but only 4 million filed [income] declarations last year' (*CDSP*, 1998, vol. 50, no. 22, p. 5). Another source claims that in 1997 the people with the highest incomes paid only 17 per cent of their tax liabilities, while those with the lowest incomes paid everything they owed: *CDSP*, 1998, vol. 50, no. 25, p. 5).

The problem of the government is to reconcile priorities such as payment of wage and pension arrears with avoiding hyperinflation through an over-reliance on printing money to finance the budget deficit (and so regain access to international aid and private finance). Under Kiriyenko's premiership the State Duma failed to pass critical aspects of government fiscal policy.

By law the central bank is not allowed to lend directly to the government, but it is allowed to buy government obligations from other holders (*RET*, Monthly Update, 6 October 1998, p. 10).

'The current government's stance on tax debtors has softed since the crisis and offset schemes to clear tax arrears remain widely used' (EBRD 1999a: 43).

23 June 1998. An anti-crisis programme is announced, comprising measures to reduce state expenditure and raise tax revenue.

The programme will seek to shift the tax burden from companies to individuals and from production to consumption (*FT*, 24 June 1998, p. 2). The package of revenue measures shifts much of the tax burden away from large manufacturing enterprises to consumers and small businesses, many of which operate in the shadow economy (*RET*, Monthly Update, 2 July 1998, p. 1). The idea is to introduce a uniform tax on imputed income in order to reduce the burden on law-abiding entrepreneurs and bring others out into the light. Another aim is to step up the collection of taxes from wealthy citizens (including targeting tax collection from Russians with money held offshore). Oil and gas companies are to be leaned on to pay taxes, e.g. using access to oil export pipelines.

'On the revenue side the main purpose [of the anti-crisis package] was to increase tax collections and shift the tax burden from big companies to consumers and to small enterprises that often operate in the shadow economy.

The programme addressed the key problem in the tax system: high dependence on a handful of taxpayers and low contributions by individuals. At 2.2 per cent of GDP income tax revenues were ridiculously low by international standards; the average ratio is above 10 per cent in mature and about 8 per cent in transition economies' (Malleret *et al.* 1999: 109).

25 June 1998. The IMF tranche is approved (*IHT,* 27 June 1998, p. 13).

13 July 1998. Negotiations between Russia and the IMF conclude with an agreement in principle to provide a $22.6 billion loan package covering the remainder of 1998 ($14.8 billion) and the whole of 1999 ($7.8 billion). The package comprises $17.1 billion in new loans and $5.5 billion in previously agreed loans. Of the total the IMF will provide $15.1 billion, the World Bank $6 billion and Japan $1.5 billion.

Among the conditions laid down was a reduction in the budget deficit to 5.6 per cent of GDP in 1998 and to 2.8 per cent of GDP in 1999. Current revenues had to exceed expenditures by 3 per cent; the deficit should come entirely from servicing the national debt. The IMF will release the loan in instalments and the aid will be cut off if the government fails to stay within the limits set (*CDSP,* 1998, vol. 50, no. 28, p. 1).

18 July 1998. Yeltsin vetoes two tax-cutting laws adopted by the State Duma. The Duma supported several government initiatives to reduce corporate tax rates but refused to endorse measures to shift more of the burden from the corporate to the personal sector (*FT,* 20 July 1998, p. 18, and 21 July 1998, p. 2).

Yeltsin vetoes two laws to lower taxes and also decrees land taxes (*IHT,* 20 July 1998, p. 11). The prime minister says that the decrees will raise even more revenue than the government sought (*IHT,* 22 July 1998, p. 1).

The Duma votes in favour of a reduction, for example, in the profit tax (from 35 per cent to 30 per cent) and in the excise tax on oil. But Yeltsin vetoes the reductions owing to the need to enact the tax package (including increases) in its entirety (*CDSP,* 1998, vol. 50, no. 29, p. 6). Yeltsin signs a decree increasing tax rates on land not being used for their designated purposes (p. 7).

20 July 1998. The IMF board releases the first tranche of the loan, but worth $4.8 billion rather than $5.6 billion because of the actions of the State Duma.

12 August 1998. The finance ministry announces that it has agreed with the IMF to amend its borrowing programme and use $1 billion of its initial $4.8 billion support loan to redeem a slice of domestic debt.

11 September 1998. Viktor Gerashchenko becomes chairman of the central bank for the second time. He says that Russia has no choice but to print more money (*FT,* 12 September 1998, p. 12). But he also says that he will not recklessly print money again (*IHT,* 12 September 1998, p. 7). Gerashchenko talks of the need for a 'small, controlled' increase in the money supply (*The Guardian,* 15 September 1998, p. 16). (Gerashchenko was chairman of the Soviet and later Russian central bank in the period 1988 to 1994: *The*

Economist, 19 September 1998, p. 51. 'Gerashchenko headed the central bank in the early 1990s. He is widely regarded as responsible for a bout of hyperinflation through a policy of printing roubles. Jeffrey Sachs ... once called him "the worst central banker in history"': Daniel Williams: *IHT*, 12 September 1998, p. 7. 'Gerashchenko was dismissed in 1994 and accused of undermining reform by printing roubles to bail out industry in defiance of government policy': *FT*, 12 September 1998, p. 1. Gerashchenko has said that inflation is a lesser evil than unemployment: Jeffries 1996a: 133. He offered his resignation to Yeltsin on 14 October 1994 and this was accepted: p. 138.)

14 September 1998. Primakov: 'We must not carry out reforms that have a bad effect on the people. If therapy stretches out for almost a decade and there is no sign of improvement, then of course it is not in the interests of the country or the people ... [Economic reforms must] make a lot of social sense ... We should make clear to the population that all inflationary turns, which are inevitable, and price increases, which will go ahead in a corresponding manner, will be duly compensated for the low-paid section of the population.'

15 September 1998. Alexander Shokhin (head of Our Home is Russia in parliament) is named as deputy prime minister in charge of finances (including negotiations with international institutions such as the IMF). He says that will stay in the government only if he is able to modify policies that, in his view, will lead to inflation. He believes that a mass printing of roubles will lead to hyperinflation (*IHT*, 17 September 1998, p. 13).

Gerashchenko says that he is in favour of printing more money to pay off unpaid wages: 'We cannot do without that' (*IHT*, 17 September 1998, p. 13).

'A group of academic economists leaded by Leonid Abalkin, prominent in the late Soviet era, yesterday [15 September] claimed the government intended to adopt all the main points of their programme set out in an open letter to the Russian media ... [which] include the "controlled" emission of roubles. This should allow the government to pay off mounting wage and pension arrears and inject liquidity into Russia's cash-strapped industries' (Arkady Ostrovsky and John Thornhill, *FT*, 16 September 1998, p. 1).

On 14 September members of the economics department of the Russian Academy of Science (Dmitri Lvov, Leonid Abalkin, Oleg Bogomolov, Nikolai Petrakov and Stepan Sitaryan) published an open letter to the president, the federal assembly and the government. Among other things, they advocated the following: regular cost-of-living increases in wages and salaries, pensions and other social support payments; the mandatory sale of 100 per cent of foreign currency earnings to the central bank; 'special exporters' of strategic goods; the 'possibility of non-payment of state obligations' should be eliminated by means of a 'controlled currency emission' (*CDSP*, 1998, vol. 50, no. 37, p. 7).

21 September 1998. 'Fears grew that the Russian government would increasingly resort to a large-scale printing of money after a bill was presented to the Duma threatening to reduce the central bank's independence. The proposed law would override current legislation that bars the central bank from printing money to cover the government's budget deficit. The central bank revealed that it had already printed 1 billion roubles to help free up the paralysed banking sector, and issued additional short-term credits' (*FT*, 22 September 1998, p. 24). 'On Monday [21 September] the central bank printed 1 billion roubles of new money and provided additional short-term credits to banks backed on frozen government debt (*FT*, 23 September 1998, p. 2).

22 September 1998. 'Michael Zadornov, acting finance minister, reiterated his position that the government would not resort to large-scale emissions in the next two to three months to finance its needs. "We will suggest tax reform", he said' (*FT*, 23 September 1998, p. 2).

24 September 1998. The government intends to establish an effective government monopoly on the production and sale of alcohol and of beverages with an alcohol content above 28 per cent. Primakov: 'What we are talking about here is not nationalization, but effective oversight of both production and wholesaling' (*CDSP*, 1998, vol. 50, no. 39, p. 1). As of 1 October 1998 there will once again be a state monopoly on alcoholic beverages. 'The first to suffer will be private producers of alcohol and wholesale marketers of beverages with an alcoholic content higher than 28 per cent. Their licences will be revoked if they do not transfer a controlling block of shares to state ownership, essentially without remuneration' (*CDSP*, 1998, vol. 50, no. 39, p. 3). 'Of the 160 distilleries 80 per cent either operate as wholly state-owned enterprises or are joint stock companies in which the state holds a controlling interest. The rest will have a choice: if they want to continue producing alcohol they will have to issue additional stock and transfer a controlling block of shares to the state' (p. 4).

'The new prime minister is preparing another vodka decree ... Details are scarce, but his aides said the government would effectively retake control of key parts of the vodka industry that were set free when Mr Yeltsin liquidated the state vodka monopoly in May 1992. Private vodka manufacturers – they are not distillers, just mixers of alcohol, water and flavours – would keep their licences if they let the government clear their major production decisions. The government would also decide who gets to sell the ... bottles of vodka ... Moscow already controls the 162 distilleries that make virtually all the alcohol used in legal vodka ... By the latest estimate, no more than 4 per cent of state revenue comes from vodka taxes or sales, a half to a third of what it should be ... Mr Primakov seeks to pay at least half of the total of back wages owed to state workers with proceeds from stricter enforcement of alcohol laws' (Michael Wines, *IHT*, 28 September 1998, p. 17).

(Yeltsin signed a decree imposing a state monopoly over the alcohol industry on 6 October: *IHT*, 7 October 1998, p. 4.)

22 October 1998. 'The government approved an emergency spending plan Thursday [22 October] that will require the central bank to print more than $1 billion in new money to help rescue banks, bring food to desperate regions and cover unpaid wages' (*IHT*, 23 October 1998, p. 17).

31 October 1998. 'IMF officials left Moscow last week after ten days of fruitless talks, refusing to release a $4.3 billion tranche of a $22.6 billion package agreed in July with the last government' (Arkady Ostrovsky, *FT*, 2 November 1998, p. 2).

November 1998. Russia has said that it will print at least 12 billion roubles before the end of 1998 to pay back wages (*IHT*, 5 November 1998, p. 17). The government has sent to parliament a spending plan for the final three months of the year calling for a 20 per cent increase in the money supply. By the end of 1998 that will add another 25.2 billion roubles to the money supply, which was 174.8 billion roubles at the start of October 1998 and 185.3 billion roubles on 2 November 1998 (*IHT*, 7 November 1998, p. 13). The government plans to print an additional 25 billion roubles ($1.52 billion) by the end of the year (*IHT*, 18 November 1998, p. 13).

In an interview given on 18 November Yuri Maslyukov said the government would print banknotes worth 15 to 20 billion roubles before the end of 1998 (*FT*, 19 November 1998, p. 2).

'Soon after the crisis the CBR started to print money when the decision was made to pay off some wage arrears and some banks received financial support ... Expectations of extensive money printing and high inflation following the devaluation of the rouble and the default on the domestic debt are still present. So far, however, these fears have not yet materialized ... The government and CBR continue to claim that emissions will be controlled and backed by an increase in international reserves ... The CBR can reduce the reserve-deposit ratio, enabling commercial banks to use additional funds for their purposes ... The reserve ratio was reduced from 11 per cent to 10 per cent at the outset of the crisis and to 5 per cent in mid-November ... The rhetoric with regards to emissions has been restrained, especially from the CBR's chairman, Viktor Gerashchenko' (*RET*, Monthly Update, 8 December 1998, pp. 3–6).

24 November 1998. 'Another delegation from the IMF left without releasing aid to the country' (*IHT*, 25 November 1998, p. 23).

10 December 1998. The government approves a draft budget for 1999. The budget calls for lower taxes on producers by lowering the value-added and corporate tax rates while raising regional sales and excise taxes on consumers (*IHT*, 11 December 1998, p. 17).

The Russian government approves the 1999 budget, which increases spending on the military and indexes wages while projecting a deficit cut down to 101 billion roubles (2.5 per cent of GDP). Planned revenues amount to 474 billion roubles and planned expenditures amount to 573 billion roubles. It incorporates payment of only $9.5 billion of the total $17.5 billion of foreign debt servicing owed during 1999. The revenue figure takes into account controversial modifications to the tax system, including a reduction in the rate of value-added tax from its current level of 20 per cent to 15 per cent from 1 March 1999. The proposal must be approved by the upper and lower houses of parliament (*FT*, 11 December 1998, p. 2).

The draft budget foresees expenditures of 575.1 billion roubles and revenues of 473.8 billion roubles. The deficit of 101.3 billion roubles is to be financed as follows: domestic sources, 22.7 billion roubles; foreign sources, 45.9 billion roubles; central bank loans (new money), 32.6 billion roubles (through the issuing of government bonds maturing in 2014). Optimistic forecasts include 30 per cent inflation and an exchange rate of 21.5 roubles to the dollar (*CDSP*, 1999, vol. 50, no. 50, p. 7).

'The draft budget 1999 budget provides for a deficit of just 2.75 per cent of GDP, with a primary surplus of 1.7 per cent. However, it makes a number of optimistic assumptions, including inflation of just 30 per cent, a rouble/dollar rate of 21.5 (average rate for 1999), and at least $7 billion in foreign financing' (*RET*, 1998, vol. 7, no. 4, p. 34). 'The budget is based on the ministry of economy's best case scenario including a 2 per cent fall in GDP' (p. 62). 'Expenditures are set at 575 billion roubles ... Revenues are projected at 474 billion roubles. The deficit of 101 billion roubles is to be financed by domestic borrowing (22.7 billion roubles), external borrowing (45.9 billion roubles) and central bank credits (32.6 billion roubles). Russia is due to pay back $17 billion of foreign debt next year [1999], $7.5 billion of which will hopefully be restructured. The budget draft assumes receipt of new foreign credits totalling $7.5 billion, which will leave $2 billion of debt repayments to be financed from domestic sources if restructuring can be achieved' (p. 38).

18 December 1998. The State Duma, in a first vote of three, approves part of a package of tax legislation aimed at shifting the tax burden from manufacturers to consumers. Deputies approved a gradual reduction of value-added tax from 20 per cent and cutting the corporate rate from 35 per cent to 30 per cent (*IHT*, 19 December 1998, p. 13).

23 December 1998. 'The government's tough 1999 budget has its first reading tomorrow [24 December] ... The finance ministry forecasts the budget deficit will be cut from 5.44 per cent of GDP this year [1998] to 2.53 per cent in 1999. Annual inflation will be no more than 30 per cent while the rouble will be kept to about its current rate at 21.5 to the US dollar ... The government's tax plans ... [include] reducing value-added tax from 25 per cent to 14 per cent' (*FT*, 23 December 1998, p. 2).

24 December 1998. The State Duma approves the budget for 1999 at its first reading by 303 votes to sixty-five. (Prime minister Primakov threatened to resign if the State Duma had not done so.)

'But it is a programme that critics say includes unrealistic economic assumptions as well as anticipation of continued financing from the IMF ... All the major parliamentary parties lined up to support the document except for the centrist Yabloko bloc, whose leader, Grigori Yavlinsky, complained that it did not cut taxes sufficiently ... The budget calls for the spending of 575 billion roubles ($27.5 billion), revenue of 473 billion roubles, and a deficit of 101 billion roubles. It envisions inflation next year at 30 per cent and the rouble trading at 21.5 to the dollar, although the rate already has come close to that level in recent weeks. A dollar was worth 19.87 roubles on Thursday [24 December]. Critics say the inflation and rouble-dollar assumptions are overly optimistic, especially if Russian leaders decide to increase the money supply and unleash still higher inflation' (David Hoffman, *IHT*, 26 December 1998, p. 11).

'The latest draft of the 1999 budget suggests a deficit of 105 billion roubles (2.75 per cent of GDP), more than 50 per cent of which is planned to be financed by external sources – a commitment which looks less than credible. The budget also assumes annual inflation of 30 per cent and a rouble/dollar rate of 21.5 ... These targets can be considered over-optimistic' (*RET*, Monthly Update, 8 December 1998, p. 5).

27 December 1998. 'Over the weekend [26–7 December] a trilateral commission, consisting of both houses of parliament and the government, agreed that Moscow would next year [1999] spend 33.7 billion roubles – or 14 per cent of all tax revenues – on supporting the regions but that the subsidies would be reallocated. Russia's thirty-nine worst-hit regions, including Dagestan in the north Caucasus and Kamchatka and Sakhalin in the far east, will receive additional support next year. But thirty-six better-off territories, such as the oil region of Tyumin and the industrial city of Novgorod, will lose some of their subsidies. Twelve regions will receive no financial support from Moscow... The federal government would receive 49.5 per cent of all tax revenues with regional authorities receiving the rest' (John Thornhill, *FT*, 28 December 1998, p. 2).

1 January 1999. The new tax code comes into effect. In addition, the reduction in the basic rate of VAT, which has been repeatedly postponed, is now scheduled for 1 July 1999 at a new rate of 15 per cent. Sales taxes have also been introduced in a majority of the regions (EBRD 1999a: 23). The new legislation codifies federal and regional taxes as well as the distribution of revenue from shared taxes. Separate tax legislation originally provided for the reduction of the VAT and profit tax rates and the introduction of a sales tax as a new source of regional revenue. But the government decided to postpone the reduction of VAT from 20 per cent to 15 per cent until 1 July 1999 (p. 43).

4 January 1999. A government resolution reinstates selective export duties for a period of six months. The duties apply to certain products immediately (e.g. various non-ferrous wastes and scrap), but oil and petroleum products may be affected later. 'Until 4 January ... Russia had been exacting only import duties for almost two years. The decision to lift duties on Russian exports, which went into effect on 1 April 1996, was ... considered one of the major achievements of Russian economic reforms and an important step toward Russia's joining the WTO ... [But there was a] 25 per cent decline in imports in 1998 as compared with 1997, [while] Russian exporters' revenues began rising as the rouble fell against the dollar' (*CDSP*, 1999, vol. 51, no. 2, pp. 12–13).

13 January 1999. Brazil devalues its currency and triggers another (limited) bout of financial turbulence around the world.

15 January 1999. 'The Russian government said Friday [15 January] that … pension arrears stand at 26.8 billion roubles, down from 35 billion in October [1998] … The ministry of finance said this week that it would pay off federal wage arrears by the end of the month, while 13.8 billion roubles in arrears remain to state employees of regional administrations. The government pledged to start paying all wages and pensions on time' (*IHT*, 16 January 1999, p. 11).

20 January 1999. 'The IMF … opened fresh talks with the government in Moscow yesterday [Wednesday 20 January]. The budget, which passed its second reading this week, is the toughest financial plan drawn up by any Russian government. But the IMF argues that it is not tough enough and is urging the government to aim for a primary budget surplus (before interest payments) of more than 3 per cent this year' (*FT*, 21 January 1999, p. 2). 'Russia … [is the IMF's] biggest recipient of funds – $19 billion to date … [Russia has a external debt of] $150 billion, including the $4.5 billion it must repay the IMF this year [1999] … Earlier this month [January] Stanley Fischer, the IMF's first deputy managing director, called on the Russian government to take immediate action to cut spending, raise revenues, and target a primary surplus (before debt servicing) of 3 per cent to 4 per cent of GDP this year' (*FT*, 29 January 1999, p. 16).

'IMF officials have said that any loans will hinge largely on Russia's ability to approve and put into effect a feasible budget. They have acknowledged that a $22.6 billion loan package that was frozen after the crisis last summer has since been scrapped. On Tuesday [19 January] the Duma … approved the draft 1999 budget in the second reading of the four required readings' (*IHT*, 21 January 1999, p. 13).

29 January 1999. The State Duma approves the draft 1999 budget at its third reading.

'Yuri Maslyukov … said the IMF wanted the cabinet to operate under the budget for three months to prove its feasibility and "only after that the IMF would be ready to give us money" … The agreement [with the IMF] could not be made until March or April … The draft 1999 budget already assumes the receipt of foreign loans that have not yet been granted. The government desperately needs the loans to pay off huge foreign loans. The budget also assumes that creditors will agree to restructure some loans that Russia cannot afford to pay even with the help of new loans … The budget proposal … calls for government spending of just 575 billion roubles ($25 billion) and revenues of only 474 billion roubles ($21 billion) for the whole year. By comparison the US government collects and spends more than $30 billion in an average week' (*IHT*, 30 January 1999, p. 4).

5 February 1999. The State Duma approves the budget at its fourth and final reading by 308 votes to fifty-eight. Spending on the presidential administration was finally cut by 20 per cent (instead of the proposed 40 per cent), while spending on Duma administration was cut by a mere 3.7 per cent. The 1999 budget envisages revenues of 473.8 billion roubles, expenditures of 575.1 billion roubles, and thus a deficit (after interest payments) of 101.3 billion roubles (2.53 per cent of GDP). Part of the deficit is to be financed by central bank credits (32.7 billion roubles) (*RET*, Monthly Update, 10 February 1999, p. 11). As regards external debt obligations, $9.5 billion is budgeted compared with $17.5 billion actually due (p. 12). Total federal revenues amount to 11.84 per cent of GDP (almost 10 per cent arising from taxes) and federal expenditures amount to 14.38 per cent of GDP. The planned federal budget deficit of 2.54 per cent of GDP arises despite a primary budget surplus of 1.64 per cent of GDP (*RET*, Monthly Update, 13 April 1999, p. 1).

10 February 1999. 'Deputy finance minister Mikhail Kasyanov said Wednesday [10 February] that the IMF wanted Russia to double its tax collection ... "The IMF considers that the revenues of the federal budget should be 17 per cent to 18 per cent of GDP", said Mr Kasyanov' (*IHT*, 11 February 1999, p. 13).

13 February 1999. 'He [Primakov] said the government was now targeting a primary budget surplus (before interest payments) of 2.3 per cent of GDP – compared with the 1.7 per cent pencilled into the draft budget – in an attempt to satisfy the IMF's demands. But he said it was impossible to run a 4 per cent primary surplus as recommended by the IMF' (*FT*, 15 February 1999, p. 2).

17 February 1999. 'The government is basically bankrupt. New York City collects more in municipal taxes than Russia collects federal taxes' (Boris Fyodorov, *FT*, 18 February 1999, p. 14).

22 March 1999. Russia announces that it will reduce its oil exports by 100,000 barrels per day in the second quarter of 1999 to support OPEC's supply reduction policy (*RET*, 1999, vol. 8, no. 2, p. 94).

25 March 1999. 'Finance minister Mikhail Zadornov said last week that the IMF had dropped one of its main demands – that the government increase revenues so that they exceed expenditures by 3.5 per cent of GDP after excluding debt service costs' (*IHT*, 26 March 1999, p. 13).

29 March 1999. Michel Camdessus, on a visit to Moscow, says that a framework agreement has been reached on an IMF loan. An IMF mission will visit Moscow to work out the details of the programme, which will then be submitted for approval to the board. The size of the loan is not revealed. A joint statement says: 'The parties have agreed on a primary budget surplus of 2 per cent of GDP to be realized in 1999 and most of the measures needed to achieve it.' Earlier the IMF had demanded a surplus of 3.5 per cent.

Russia agrees to raise new revenues, partly by postponing a cut in value-added tax (*IHT*, 31 March 1999, p. 12).

'Stanley Fischer ... [first deputy managing director of the IMF] insisted [on 31 March] that the IMF had agreed "neither dates nor amounts" with the Russian government, despite reports of a $4.8 billion package of loans agreed in Moscow this week. "There is a lot of detailed work to be done and there are undoubtedly prior actions to be taken. We have agreed on a framework, we have not agreed on measures." He added that the IMF had relaxed its negotiating stance on a Russian primary surplus of 3.5 per cent because it would have resulted in "unrealistically large cuts in pensions" and civil service salaries' (*FT*, 1 April 1999, p. 4).

Russia is facing more than $6 billion in foreign debt repayments through July and a total of $17.5 billion in 1999 as a whole, including $4.5 billion owed to the IMF. Since August 1998 Russia has missed about $1.5 billion in payments on foreign debt accumulated during Soviet times (*IHT*, 30 March 1999, pp. 1, 4).

'Russian officials said the government was likely to receive $4.8 billion in four tranches, starting at the end of April' (*FT*, 30 March 1999, p. 3).

'Russia owes the IMF $19 billion, making it one of the lender's largest debtors' (*IHT*, 8 April 1999, p. 13).

31 March 1999. Offsets at the federal budget level are discontinued (*RET*, 14 July 1999, p. 14).

3 April 1999. Yeltsin vetoes a law which would have introduced a lower VAT rate of 15 per cent as of 1 July 1999 (*RET*, 1999, vol. 8, no. 2, p. 95).

28 April 1999. 'The IMF has reached a preliminary agreement to lend Russia $4.5 billion over the next eighteen months ... But ... the money will never actually be sent to Moscow. Instead ... the loans will essentially be transferred from one of the Fund's accounts to another, allowing Russia to avoid default on money it owes the IMF this year and next. In addition, before the board of the IMF formally approves any accord, the Fund is insisting that the Russian parliament pass several bills to remake Russia's bankruptcy laws, strengthen the tax collection system and overhaul the banking system. Last year [1998] the IMF transferred money to Russia before parliament acted, only to discover that the Communist-led body failed to fulfil several commitments made by the government. After the IMF agreement the World Bank said it was also prepared to renew its lending programme to Russia, once its own executive directors approve the changes. New money would start flowing this summer [1999] "following implementation of agreed prior actions and approval by the IMF's board"' (*IHT*, 30 April 1999, p. 1). 'Russia owes more than $5 billion to the IMF over the next eighteen months, nearly $2.5 billion of it by the end of June [1999] ... In a statement released Wednesday night [28 April] about the loan agreement, the managing director of the IMF, Michel Camdessus, said Russia had agreed to provide the Fund with an explanation of how earlier loans had been used, a veiled reference to widespread suspicions that the loans had been funnelled to wealthy Russian oligarchs or secretly sent abroad ... In Mid-March [1999] ... [the US Treasury secretary] told a congressional panel that much of the $4.8 billion pumped into Moscow's foreign exchange reserves at that time "may have been siphoned off improperly". He was referring to investigations showing that when the IMF money briefly propped up the value of the rouble the country's richest oligarchs raced to convert their cash into dollars at a favourable exchange rate. More than $4 billion flowed out of Russia nearly immediately, much of it headed for Swiss bank accounts … The IMF's board has also demanded a report by Price Waterhouse on the operations of Financial Management Co. (Fimaco), a company based in the Channel Islands, where the Russian central bank was secretly sending a portion of its foreign exchange reserves' (p. 16).

'The Kremlin will struggle to implement the banking and taxation reforms that the IMF is demanding … Lending could begin after the next IMF executive board meeting in July [1999] and is likely to be part of a $7.8 billion package including funds from the World Bank and the Japanese government … The IMF is asking for legal action in five areas: passage of a new bank restructuring law; improvement of an existing law on bank bankruptcies; raising of excise taxes on alcohol; raising the value-added tax to 20 per cent [from 15 per cent]; and relaxing restrictions on foreign exchange … Michel Camdessus … on Wednesday [28 April] said the IMF would disburse about $3 billion over the first twelve months, which, combined with funds from other lenders, would be enough to cover Russia's payments obligations to the IMF of $4.9 billion for the twelve-month period beginning 1 July [1999]' (*FT*, 30 April 1999, p. 2).

16 June 1999. Representatives of more than fifty companies (including the railways, oil companies, UES and Gazprom) sign an agreement to limit price increases until the end of 1999 (*RET*, 1999, vol. 8, no. 2, p. 99).

The special price agreements involved limiting price increases to 50 per cent of the rate of producer price inflation until the end of 1999. 'In the energy sector obligatory deliveries to the domestic market or to selected customers have been reinstated. In some cases, such as fuel, oil and petrol, where the differentials between domestic and world market prices have been very high, significant shortages developed' (EBRD 1999b: 258).

1 July 1999. 'The IMF mission, which visited Moscow at the end of June–early July, expressed general satisfaction with a joint memorandum on economic policy issued by the government and the Central Bank of Russia. The fiscal part of the document is devoted to measures providing for an increase in revenues and a decrease in non-interest expenditures. Many of the measures set out in the document are already in place, including a programme of reduction of government expenditure, adopted in 1998, postponement of any decreases in VAT until at least 2000, part 1 of the tax code (aimed at improving tax administration), and some measures for reforming regional transfer policy. The government has also introduced a policy of cutting off access to export pipelines for oil companies with tax arrears' (*RET*, 14 July 1999, p. 15).

29 July 1999. The IMF executive board approves a loan of $4.5 billion.

'The money will be used for refinancing the country's debt to the Fund' (*RET*, Monthly Update, 10 August 1999, p. 13). The IMF plans to extend $4.5

billion in the course of 1999 and 2000. The first tranche of $640 million is to be disbursed on 1 August 1999 (*RET*, 1999, vol. 8, no. 3, p. 84).

'Approval of the loan by the IMF's board reflected Russia's geopolitical importance as a nuclear power rather than the belief that it has put its economy on a sound footing. The loan approval also paved the way for Moscow to pursue talks on restructuring billions of dollars in Soviet-era debt to bank and government creditors ... [The loan] enables Russia to continue repaying ... the IMF itself and to unlock loans from other lenders, such as the World Bank ... The money, rather than being handed over to Russia, will be used strictly for the repayment of existing loans to the IMF. In fact, beginning with an initial $640 million instalment, the $4.5 billion will simply be transferred from one IMF account to another over the next seventeen months as the debts owed the IMF come due during that period' (*IHT*, 30 July 1999, p. 15).

'The IMF has released a thirteen page economic policy statement agreed with the Russians earlier this month [July] ... alongside a series of detailed commitments by the government and central bank ... The IMF document contains a long list of detailed demands, including a new law forcing banks to issue annual financial statements; a reduction in the size of the federal civil service by the end of 1999 by 41,000 employees; and quarterly accounting according to international standards by the gas monopoly Gazprom, the utilities group UES, Russian railways and the oil pipeline operator Transneft ... The programme agreed with Russia includes an unusually high number of "prior actions" – initiatives that the Russian government had not only agreed to but had to implement before approval of the new loan ... The Russian central bank lied to the IMF in 1996 about the level of its foreign exchange reserves ... an auditor's report has concluded ... The report from Pricewaterhouse-Coopers concluded that the central bank channelled assets through Fimaco, based in the Channel Island tax haven of Jersey ... Central bank reserves had been overstated by $1.2 billion in the middle of 1996. But Stanley Fischer, deputy managing director of the IMF, said there was no evidence of "large-scale misappropriation of money" through Fimaco. He also said the auditors found no evidence of wrongdoing in the handling of $4.8 billion lent to Russia in July 1998 ... Apart from $1 billion that went, as agreed, to the budget, the rest went in foreign exchange intervention ... It [the central bank] would in future exclude any deposits from reserves' (*FT*, 29 July 1999, p. 2).

'The audit, by Pricewaterhouse-Coopers, concluded that Russia's central bank misreported its foreign currency reserves to the IMF by $1 billion in 1996. The auditors found that the central bank had lent the money to the Russian government and then dispatched the government's note to Financial Management Co. [Fimaco], a firm based in the Channel Islands that started with $1,000 in capital' (*IHT*, 15 July 1999, p. 13).

'Most attention has been focussed on Fimaco's 1996 operations, when the central bank used it as a backdoor conduit to invest in Russia's short-term

Treasury bills, known as GKOs, which were then just becoming available to foreigners ... The central bank shifted money through Fimaco, a subsidiary of Eurobank, a French bank in which the Russian central bank owns 78 per cent ... According to the central bank document, it directed $855 million onto the GKO market via Fimaco in 1996 ... In Russia the central bank, together with its affiliate Sberbank, were known to dominate 50 per cent of the GKO market ... From its start in 1991 Fimaco's operations have been highly secretive. By 1993, the year when the Jersey-based investment company was acquired by Eurobank, a directive had been issued by a Russian central bank official ordering that Fimaco's operations be kept off the books ... For months now central bank officials have said that they first began to use Fimaco in the early 1990s as a way to shelter Russian reserves from creditors looking to retrieve their Soviet debt ... This month [July] ... past and present bank officials announced that a three-month audit of the bank's relationship with Fimaco had found no "substantial" violations of normal procedure. They also produced a letter from the Russian prosecutor general's office, which first made public the charges involving Fimaco last February, saying that no evidence of "embezzlement or misappropriation" had been found ... This month the central bank's chairman, Viktor Gerashchenko, ... used the Pricewaterhouse-Coopers audit's findings to try to put the Fimaco matter to rest, promising to correct accounting practices by January 2000 to prevent inflation of foreign reserves' (Celestine Bohlen, *IHT*, 31 July 1999, p. ii).

'Russia's central bank used previous loan proceeds to invest in risky short-term government bonds, a new audit of the central bank's transactions shows ... It showed the central bank had improperly speculated with the IMF funds in the Russian government's own bond market, buying high-risk GKO bonds. It was previously known that the central bank had ploughed some of its hard currency into GKOs but not that it had used the IMF's money for that purpose. The audit shows that the central bank transferred $719 million of IMF funds it received in 1992 to two subsidiaries before the money ended up in the accounts of an offshore firm the bank indirectly controls. That firm, Financial Management Co., or Fimaco, invested the IMF funds in government bonds in 1996 in the months before President Boris Yeltsin's reelection. The audit does not spell out what happened to the profit from those transactions. In a review of the Russian economy released Monday [2 August] the IMF directors condemned the channelling of money through Fimaco and what they termed a "fictitious claim" involving the firm ... In 1996 the central bank left the IMF with the impression that $1.2 billion remained in its currency reserves when in fact the money had been rerouted elsewhere' (*IHT*, 6 August 1999, p. 13).

25 August 1999. The government submits a draft of the 2000 budget to the State Duma. Assumptions include an inflation rate in the range 18 to 22 per cent, an exchange rate of thirty-two roubles to the US dollar and a GDP growth rate of 1.5 per cent. The budget deficit is projected at 1.1 per cent of

GDP, with a primary surplus of 3.1 per cent of GDP (*RET*, Monthly Update, 10 September 1999, p. 14).

2 September 1999. Mikhail Zadornov resigns as the president's special representative for relations with international financial organizations. His place is taken by finance minister Mikhail Kasyanov (*CDSP*, 1999, vol. 51, no. 35, p. 16). (On 21 October 1999 first deputy prime minister Viktor Khristenko took over the post of special representative: *RET*, 1999, vol. 8, no. 4, p. 99.)

30 September 1999. 'The regular annual shareholders meeting of the IMF ended yesterday [30 September] in Washington ... The finance ministers of the G7 countries, followed by the IMF leadership, informed the Russian delegation ... of four additional conditions for the release of the next $640 million tranche of the standby credit. These conditions are as follows: arrange for quarterly audits of the management of foreign exchange reserves; draw up a timetable according to which the central bank and Russian commercial banks will adopt international accounting and financial reporting standards; submit a plan for the central bank's withdrawal from participation in Russian banks abroad; and, finally, subscribe to the codes of the best fiscal and monetary practice that the IMF is adopting' (*CDSP*, 1999, vol. 51, no. 39, p. 8).

7 December 1999. 'A decision [was made] this week by the IMF to further postpone delivery of a long-awaited $640 million credit ... Originally due to be delivered in September ... the loan was postponed after the fund, at the urging of leading industrial countries, pressed for new conditions, aimed largely at structural economic reforms, in part as a result of the Russian financial scandals. Failure to meet those conditions, which include measures setting higher standards of accountability and openness for Russian financial institutions, have been cited by IMF spokesmen as the reasons for the latest delay' (*IHT*, Wednesday 8 December 1999, p. 6).

'The IMF's decision to delay the next disbursement of a $640 million tranche [was] ostensibly for technical financial reasons' (*FT*, 9 December 1999, p. 8). 'The IMF said it would delay disbursement of further credits to Russia because Moscow had not implemented agreed structural reforms, including more effective bankruptcy legislation and improved banking regulations' (*FT*, 13 December 1999, p. 10).

'By no coincidence, the IMF is holding up, for "technical reasons", the release of a new $640 million package' (*The Independent*, 8 December 1999, p. 1).

(The tranche was delayed in the midst of Western criticism of the way Russia was conducting the war in Chechenia.)

27 December 1999. Prime minister Vladimir Putin says that the government has paid all its pension and wage debts to federal workers and will pay its remaining 1999 budgetary obligations by the end of 1999 despite the IMF delaying a $640 million loan disbursement (*IHT*, 28 December 1999, p. 15).

28 December 1999. The World Bank awards a $100 million loan, part of a package of more than $750 million destined for restructuring the coal sector (*FT*, 29 December 1999, p. 4).

'Russia completed its loan repayments for 1999 to the IMF and the World bank agreed to release $100 million in loans intended to help reform Russia's coal industry. Russia said its transfer of $62.9 billion to the IMF met its repayment commitments for the year' (*IHT*, 29 December 1999, p. 13).

'Mikhail Kasyanov, the finance minister, said Russia had paid off its debts to the IMF for 1999, but he warned that it would have difficulty in reimbursing the $3 billion due in the first quarter of next year [2000] if the delayed tranche was not paid out' (*FT*, 29 December 1999, p. 4).

6 January 2000. 'Viktor Khristenko, the first deputy prime said Mr Putin had approved a plan to pay off 4 billion roubles to 4.5 billion roubles ($145 million to $163 million) of wage arrears by 15 April' (*FT*, 7 January 2000, p. 6).

'The federal budget deficit, calculated on a cash basis, comprised 1.7 per cent of GDP in 1999 ... A very small part of the federal deficit was financed by foreign borrowing ... The bulk of the deficit was financed with credits from the central bank' (*RET*, 2000, vol. 9, no. 1, p. 66). The finance ministry says the primary budget surplus in 1999 was 2.2 per cent of GDP (p. 95). The federal budget deficit, according to the IMF definition, was 1.7 per cent in 1999 (*RET*, Monthly Update, 11 August 2000, p. 25). (IMF definition: 'Privatization receipts and net sales of state gold reserves are counted as deficit financing': *RET*, 10 February 1999, p. 24.)

August 2000. 'On 26 August [2000] the draft budget was submitted to the Duma ... For the first time a balanced budget is being proposed ... Interest payments (which exactly equal the primary surplus since the deficit is zero) are envisaged at ... 3.1 per cent of GDP. The first reading of the draft in the Duma is scheduled for 22 September' (*RET*, Monthly Update, 15 September 2000, p. 12).

'This is the first balanced budget in all the years of reform. Not counting debt service, revenues will exceed expenditures by 3.1 per cent of GDP. The extra revenue will go towards paying off our foreign debt, [finance minister] Kudrin said. Russia is supposed to pay back $14.5 billion next year [2001], but that is if the Paris Club does not agree to restructure Soviet debts. Right now the government is optimistic, so the budget reflects about $6 billion in debt service and $4.5 billion in payments on the principal. In other words, the government is planning to pay only about $10.5 billion altogether' (*Kommersant*, 10 August 2000, p. 2: *CDSP*, 2000, vol. 52, no. 32, p. 10).

Late summer 2000. 'In late summer 2000 the export quota system for oil was reinstated' (EBRD 2000b: 202).

6 October 2000. 'The lower house of parliament approved the country's first ever balanced budget ... The Duma approved the budget in the first reading' (*FT*, 7 October 2000, p. 8).

Political developments

Yeltsin personally went into steep decline during the financial crisis. In such a powerful presidential system this was potentially extremely destabilizing, but the practical running of the country was left largely in the hands of Yevgeni Primakov.

Yeltsin dismissed prime minister Chernomyrdin and the entire cabinet on 23 March 1998. He appointed Sergei Kiriyenko as acting prime minister. On 24 April, in its third vote, the State Duma approved Kiriyenko as prime minister. Members of the new cabinet (appointed 28–30 April 1998) included Boris Nemtsov, Mikhail Zadornov and Yevgeni Primakov. On 29 May 1998 Yeltsin dismissed the head of the tax service, replacing him with former finance minister Boris Fyodorov. On 17 June 1998 Yeltsin appointed Anatoli Chubais as a deputy prime minister, although with no seat in the cabinet, with special responsibility for co-ordinating relations with international financial institutions. Chubais was recommended by the 'financial oligarchy', who decided to bury their differences during the financial crisis. On 23 July Yuri Maslyukov became trade and industry minister. (He is a member of the Communist Party and was head of Gosplan between 1988 and 1991.) On 17 August Boris Fyodorov added to his duties by becoming deputy prime minister responsible for macroeconomic policy and the management of the state debt.

But on 23 August 1998 Yeltsin (who is still on holiday after about five weeks) dismissed prime minister Kiriyenko and the entire government. Viktor Chernomyrdin was named as acting prime minister. But Yeltsin failed to gain State Duma approval of Chernomyrdin as prime minister.

On 28 August 1998 Yeltsin dismissed Anatoli Chubais as deputy prime minister with special responsibility for co-ordinating relations with international financial institititions. The following day Boris Fyodorov was appointed acting deputy prime minister with responsibility for financial affairs and negotiations with international financial organizations.

On 7 September 1998 central bank governor Sergei Dubinin submitted his resignation, which was welcomed by Yeltsin.

Yevgeni Primakov commented on 8 September: 'I am grateful to all those who have suggested my candidacy. However, I must unequivocally state: I cannot consent to this … [I shall do] all that is possible in the interests of my country.' But on 10 September Yeltsin nominated acting foreign minister Yevgeni Primakov as prime minister, approval by the State Duma by 315 votes to sixty-three (with fifteen abstentions) following the very next day. Yuri Maslyukov became first deputy prime minister responsible for economic policy. Viktor Gerashchenko became chairman of the central bank for the second time.

On 15 September 1998 Alexander Shokhin (head of Our Home is Russia in parliament) was named as deputy prime minister in charge of finances (including negotiations with international institutions such as the IMF). He said that he would stay in the government only if he were able to modify policies that, in his view, would lead to inflation. He believes that a mass printing of roubles will lead to hyperinflation (*IHT*, 17 September 1998, p. 13).

'Summoned back from a decade of obscurity, a group of Gorbachev-era economists stood outside the headquarters building of the Russian government on Tuesday [15 September], waiting to give advice on how to rescue a floundering economy ... Among them were three top advisers to Mr Gorbachev – Leonid Abalkin [director of the Institute of Economics], Nikolai Petrakov and Oleg Bogomolov [director of the Institute for International Economic and Political Studies] ... Russia's new prime minister, a top economic aide and the new head of the central bank all served under Mr Gorbachev' (Celestine Bohlen, *IHT*, 16 September 1998, p. 6).

'A group of academic economists led by Leonid Abalkin, prominent in the late Soviet era, yesterday [15 September] claimed the government intended to adopt all the main points of their programme set out in an open letter to the Russian media ... [which] include the "controlled" emission of roubles. This should allow the government to pay off mounting wage and pension arrears and inject liquidity into Russia's cash-strapped industries' (Arkady Ostrovsky and John Thornhill, *FT*, 16 September 1998, p. 1).

On 14 September members of the economics department of the Russian Academy of Science (Dmitri Lvov, Leonid Abalkin, Oleg Bogomolov, Nikolai Petrakov and Stepan Sitaryan) published an open letter to the president, the federal assembly and the government. Among other things, they advocated the following: regular cost-of-living increases in wages and salaries, pensions and other social support payments; the mandatory sale of 100 per cent of foreign currency earnings to the central bank; 'special exporters' of strategic goods; the 'possibility of non-payment of state obligations' should be eliminated by means of a 'controlled currency emission' (*CDSP*, 1998, vol. 50, no. 37, p. 7).

On 25 September 1998 Alexander Shokhin resigned over the reappointment of Mikhail Zadornov as finance minister. It has been suggested that disagreement with the policies of Yuri Maslyukov was also a factor lying behind Shokhin's decision to resign (*CDSP*, 1998, vol. 50, no. 39, p. 6).

Boris Fyodorov was dismissed on 28 September 1998 (*IHT*, 29 September 1998, p. 2).

Primakov gained broad approval across the political spectrum and provided essential political stability. But an economic package was far slower in coming owing to such factors as a broad cabinet containing members with differing views. 'The first meeting of Mr Primakov's still-incomplete cabinet Thursday [24 September 1998] brought a welter of conflicting statements, suggesting that the government does not yet have a single economic plan and is torn between two ideological camps' (David Hoffman, *IHT*, 25 September 1998, p. 15). Primakov is not an economist, his speciality being foreign policy. He was critical of many aspects of economic policy before his premiership but was unsure where to draw the line as regards state intervention. He is essentially a pragmatist. As mentioned above, the dilemma of his government was to reconcile priorities such as payment of wage and pension arrears with avoiding hyperinflation through an over-reliance on printing money to finance the budget deficit (and so regain access to international aid and private finance).

(For later developments, see Chapter 12.)

Social unrest has continued to be very limited, despite effects such as sharp declines in real incomes and savings, a rise in the proportion of the population in poverty, continuing wage and pension arrears, increasing shortages and difficulties in gaining access to bank deposits. 'There were scattered reports Thursday [27 August] of panic buying of food, of stores shutting as they await new prices and of a spreading deadlock of payments from banks to their clients and from employers to their employees' (Celestine Bohlen, *IHT*, 28 August 1998, p. 1).

7 October 1998. A long-planned day of action aimed at wage and pension arrears and Yeltsin's resignation is supported by far less people than expected by the organizers. 'The demand for his [Yeltsin's] resignation was the dominant theme' (*CDSP*, 1998, vol. 50, no. 40, p. 6).

7 November 1998. The eighty-first anniversary of the Bolshevik revolution is quiet and uneventful.

Banks

Government action has taken the form of allowing some deposits to be transferred to Sberbank (which accounts for some 80 per cent of retail bank deposits and where deposits are effectively guaranteed), restructuring, withdrawing licences, encouraging mergers and conducting net clearing operations (offsetting bank debts and liabilities with the aim of unclogging the payments system). But bank restructuring has been very slow and large-scale asset-stripping took place after the financial crisis. The domestic banking system remains generally weak and inefficient and enjoys little confidence.

'Facing substantial margin calls and refusal of creditors to roll over their liabilities, Russian banks bought foreign exchange to repay debts, in the process drying up their liquidity and creating interbank loan defaults' (Desai 2000: 51).

'The banking crisis in principle would have provided an excellent opportunity to shake out and strengthen the Russian financial system in the medium term. The opportunity was completely lost. Worse, the manner in which the crisis was handled will worsen the already considerable damage for a long time. The authorities' lack of a clear strategy for how to deal with the banks, the non-transparency with which some well-connected banks were provided cash infusions by the central bank, and, worst of all, the ease with which assets could be stripped from insolvent banks without recourse from authorities have taught prospective bankers a lesson: you can rip off your credits (depositors and foreign investors) with impunity ... The only bank that commands a minimum of respect is Sberbank because of its ill-defined state deposit guarantee and because it honoured its commitments in the August 1998 crisis' (Knut Eggenberger, *RET*, 16 May 2000, p. 8).

'Sberbank ... controls about 90 per cent of the household deposit market and more than 25 per cent of the corporate clients market' (*RET*, Monthly Update, 11 August 2000, p. 10).

'Bank restructuring has advanced very slowly and the role of the bank restructuring agency, Arco, in the process has been minimal, as its financial resources and enforcement powers are still very weak. Very little has been done in reversing the previous large-scale stripping of assets. The much-improved liquidity situation has not led to a significant upsurge in lending to the real sector ... Foreign banks have increased their presence to about 11 per cent of the total capital of the sector' (EBRD 2000b: 203).

20 August 1998. Sergei Dubinin (chairman of the central bank) announced that the central bank would insure deposits at private commercial banks as long as they made special deals with Sberbank, which is already insured (*IHT*, 21 August 1998, p. 15). Total household deposits at the end of June 1998 stood at 165 billion roubles, including about 35 billion roubles of foreign currency deposits: three-quarters of these deposits are held by Sberbank (*RET*, Monthly Update, 18 August 1998, p. 2).

25 August 1998. 'The central bank announced after the rouble's decline that it had cut the mandatory reserve requirement for banks. This had the effect of immediately injecting 4 billion roubles into the banking system ... But instead of using the freed reserves for transactions, the banks almost immediately traded the roubles for dollars Tuesday [25 August]' (David Hoffman, *IHT*, 26 August 1998, p. 15).

It is announced that Oneximbank, Menatep and Most are to merge (*IHT*, 26 August 1998, pp. 1, 15). Bank mergers have produced some critical comments:

1. There is the argument that banks favour mergers in order to maximize the chances of a government bail-out.

2. Boris Nemtsov: 'This week we had planned to put a number of banks under government administration ... and to begin bankruptcy proceedings against major companies, including oil companies. They [the oligarchs] understood that the end was near, that there might be serious changes in ownership and that the current oligarchate might come to an end. Moreover, this fresh wind of bankruptcy ... could lead to a displacement of the current elite. Naturally, no acting elite wants to be replaced and so they decided to replace the government ... Of course, a significant role in the decision to sack the cabinet and nominate a new one was played by the well-known oligarch [Boris] Berezovsky' (*FT*, 25 August 1998, p. 2).

26 August 1998. 'Most analysts attributed the heavy trading on the Moscow currency exchange Tuesday [25 August] to the central bank's continued supply of credits to Russia's troubled banks and by its decision last week to lower the bank's minimum capital requirements' (*IHT*, 27 August 1998, p. 10).

3 September 1998. To stop the run on banks, depositors of six banks were allowed to transfer their accounts to Sberbank, which holds 80 per cent of all retail deposits. Foreign deposits were to be exchanged into roubles at the 1 September exchange rate (*RET*, Monthly Update, 11 November 1998, p. 2).

'The Russian government began enforcing a two-month freeze on withdrawals from six major commercial banks on Thursday [3 September] in an effort to prevent a wholesale collapse of the banking system ... The central bank said depositors would be able to take out their funds on 15 November ... Those with accounts in dollars ... would be paid at an exchange rate that collapsed Monday [31 August] – 9.3 roubles to the dollar, compared with 13.4 on Thursday [3 September] ... Clients of the six banks might transfer their accounts to the government-owned Sberbank' (*IHT*, 4 September 1998, p. 1). For savings held in foreign currencies Sberbank would pay out the deposits at the exchange rate that prevailed on 1 September 1998, namely 9.33 roubles to the dollar (*IHT*, 6 October 1998, p. 15). (On 25 September 1998 the Bank of Russia extended by two weeks a deadline for depositors to transfer their accounts from commercial banks Inkombank, Most Bank, Mosbusinessbank, Bank Menatep, Promstroibank and SBS-Agro to the state-controlled Sberbank. Depositors would have until 10 October to move their deposits. Sberbank would pay out deposits on 30 November instead of the originally scheduled 15 November: *IHT*, 26 September 1998, p. 15. Sberbank started paying out money on some of the deposits transfered to it from the six banks on 2 December 1998: *RET*, Monthly Update, 8 December 1998, p. 9.)

This week the central bank reduced the banks' minimum reserve requirement from 10 per cent to 7.5 per cent (*FT*, 4 September 1998, p. 2).

17 September 1998. 'The deputy head of the central bank said Thursday [17 September] that the bank intended to bail out many of the nation's bankrupt financial institutions by buying back their multibillion-rouble portfolios of government bonds and Treasury bills ... A decision to repay banks immediately would give preferential treatment over other bondholders inside and outside Russia' (Michael Wines, *IHT*, 18 September 1998, p. 13).

'The central bank said it would print money to pay off state debts and to bail out domestic banks, further raising fears of hyperinflation and discrimination against foreign creditors.' Foreigner creditors have threatened action to try to seize or freeze Russian assets abroad (Arkady Ostrovsky, *FT*, 18 September 1998, p. 2).

18 September 1998. 'This morning [18 September] banks are supposed to provide the central bank with a complete list of their own and their clients' overdue payments, including payments to the budget ... The central bank will take the debts in chronological order and pay them using money from the bank's correspondent account at the central bank. If there is not enough money there a one-day line of credit (overdraft) will be opened for the bank. When all the banks' payments are made the central bank will carry out a multilateral, mutual offsetting of debts between the banks and their clients. Once these operations are completed the overdrafts opened for banks on that day will be paid off with money from their mandatory reserve funds. In order to replenish the mandatory reserve funds on Monday [21 September] the central bank will begin buying government securities – short-term bonds and federal loan bonds maturing no later than 31 December 1998 – from banks participating in the account-clearing procedure. The bonds will be bought at face value' (*CDSP*, 1998, vol. 50, no. 38, p. 5). 'On Thursday [17 September] banks in the five most "financially advanced" regions – Moscow, Moscow Province, St Petersburg, Samara Province and Sverdlovsk Province – were asked to furnish the central bank with card files containing lists of their creditors … If a bank receives a payment order from a client and there is no money in that account, the bank in effect gives the client a number and has him wait in line until money appears … The debts are to be paid out of mandatory reserve funds, i.e. money belonging to the banks themselves that they are required by law to transfer to the central bank and thereafter cannot touch … It appears that the main instrument used in this operation [to replenish the reserve funds] will be frozen government short-term bonds … There is a risk that any roubles the banks get will be diverted to the currency market and serve to further drive down the rouble … Moreover, the action taken provides no guarantee that in a few weeks the banks won't be in the same trouble again' (p. 5). 'In order to get money from the central bank, starting today [22 September] banks can pledge their frozen short-term bonds as collateral. Those bonds will apparently then be exchanged for couponless Bank of Russia bonds, which will be paid off when they mature (remember these are two-week bonds). And the central bank can pay them off in only one way – by printing money' (p. 6).

'The new chairman and board of the central bank have been concentrating on unclogging the payment system. Three clearing operations have been conducted, whereby the banks pay and get paid overdue payments with any net difference being drawn from their required reserves held at the central bank. Getting the payment system working is a crucial priority, but it does not solve the underlying insolvency of the banking system' (*RET*, Monthly Update, 6 October 1998, p. 10). In order to help restore the payment system the central bank conducted three consecutive offsets of liabilities between banks on 18 September, 25 September and 2 October 1998, which allowed for 30 billion roubles of 40 billion roubles of stalled payments to go through. The central bank gave loans to banks and allowed them to draw on their obligatory reserves in order to make payments. To stop the run on bank deposits the central bank allowed depositors of banks which hold over 300 million roubles in retail accounts (about thirty banks) to transfer their savings to Sberbank (which holds 80 per cent of all retail deposits). The central bank gave a guarantee on these accounts. In return the depositors had to forgo the opportunity to withdraw their money before the end of November 1998.

Foreign currency deposits were to be exchanged into roubles at the 1 September exchange rate. The results of this operation, available for the six largest participating banks, showed that approximately 50 per cent of rouble deposits and 10 per cent of foreign currency deposits were transferred to Sberbank (*RET*, Monthly Update, 11 November 1998, p. 2). By law the central bank is not allowed to lend directly to the government. But it is allowed to buy government obligations from other holders (p. 13).

In October 1998 the government announced a programme involving the state-led restructuring and recapitalization of some troubled Moscow-based and regional banks and the liquidation of the remaining institutions (EBRD 1999a: 21). 'While the signing in February 1999 of the long-delayed law on the bankruptcy of credit organizations has increased the central bank's powers, the lack of an effective response to the crisis has enabled bank managers and shareholders to engage in extensive asset-stripping of insolvent institutions' (EBRD 1999a: 21). 'Very little progress has been made in implementing the banking restructuring programme announced in October 1998. Few licences have been revoked and many banks have been engaged in asset-stripping (p. 28).

6 October 1998. Primakov: 'On 18 September, 25 September and 2 October Russia's central bank took steps to break the logjam of payments between banks. Out of the total of approximately 40 billion roubles that are stuck in the banking system it freed up about 30 billion. Most of the money went into budgets at all levels or into non-budget funds' (*CDSP*, 1998, vol. 50, no. 40, pp. 5–6).

29 October 1998. The central bank revokes the licence of Inkombank.

30 December 1998. Tokobank, previously one of Russia's top twenty banks, says that a Moscow court has declared it bankrupt, four months after the central bank revoked its licence because it could no longer make its payments (*IHT*, 31 December 1998, p. 13).

10 January 1999. 'A survey by the interfax news agency said five of Russia's largest banks were insolvent – meaning they could neither pay creditors nor return deposits to savers' (*IHT*, 11 January 1999, p. 11).

9 July 1999. 'A new, tougher version of the law on the restructuring of credit organizations won quick approval from the Duma and was signed by Boris Yeltsin on 9 July thanks to pressure from the IMF and other donors. The new law obliges the central bank to either withdraw licences from large decapitalized banks or to refer those banks to Arco (the agency for restructuring of credit organizations), in which case shareholders are disenfranchised from the bank. In the process of bank restructuring Arco will have the right to question in court the validity of a bank's transactions over the last three years. This law finally gives the authorities powers to stop asset stripping in banks, though there is likely to be little that can now be rescued from the banks, which collapsed after August 1998. Still, the law is important for sustainability of the banking sector in the future. The central bank finally withdrew licences from Oneximbank, Mosbiznesbank, Promstroibank and Mezhkombank, which were the sixth, thirteenth, seventeenth and twenty-sixth largest in Russia before the crisis ... At the same time SBS-Agro, whose capital deficit is estimated to be even larger than that of the above-mentioned banks, received another stabilization credit from the CBR' (*RET*, 14 July 1999, p. 14).

Debt reschedulings

Russia's forced restructuring of domestic debt has been essentially confiscatory. But Russia has also at times effectively (though not formally) defaulted on its sovereign debt, disguised by payment delays and formal reschedulings. Defaults (in effect) have not only applied to Soviet-era debt. Rolled over IMF loans have on occasion avoided formal defaults (which the IMF is not permitted to condone) on loans the institution has made since 1992.

25 August 1998. Details of the scheme to restructure $40 billion (at the original exchange rate) of short-term, rouble-denominated domestic government debt are released, with debt being repaid over three to five years. Investors holding government bonds will be able to exchange them for three new types of rouble-denominated bonds, known as GKOs, to be issued by the government. The options are as follows for rouble-denominated bonds: a three-year bond with an annual rate of 30 per cent; a four-year paper with a 30 per cent interest rate for the first three years and 25 per cent for the fourth year; a five-year paper at 30 per cent for three years, 25 per cent in the fourth year and 20 per cent in the fifth year (*IHT*, 26 August 1998, p. 15; *FT*, 26 August 1998, p. 2). The plan also allows foreign investors to switch existing debt holdings into dollar-denominated bonds, which will pay interest at 5 per cent annually and will mature in 2006 (*FT*, 26 August 1998, p. 2). On 28 August the government said it would give investors in GKOs until 18 September 1998 to decide whether to accept its plan to convert them forcibly into longer-term debt. Investors would have to decide by that date what kind of securities to choose from a menu of either rouble-denominated debt or a mixture of rouble and dollar paper. Those choosing to swap up to 20 per cent of the nominal value of their GKOs into dollar bonds would convert them at market value as measured on 14 August. Foreign and other non-resident investors hold about $17 billion in GKOs; Russian banks and the central bank hold the rest (*FT*, 29 August 1998, p. 2).

As regards some of the details of the forced conversion of short-term domestic debt, the holders of rouble-denominated bonds maturing before the end of 1999 were, in essence, given two choices. In option one they could receive 5 per cent of principal in cash with the rest converted to three-, four- and five-year bonds with coupon rates of 30 per cent in the first three years, 25 4per cent in the fourth year and 20 per cent in the fifth year. Alternatively, in option two they could receive 20 per cent of the conversion in eight-year dollar bonds with 5 per cent coupons and the rest in the rouble bonds of the first option. 'On announcement the arithmetic of this package meant that it had a value of no more than twenty cents on the dollar of the pre-conversion value of the domestic debt. Subsequent events have now put the value of this conversion at below ten cents on the dollar' (Deutsche Bank Research, *Global Emerging Markets*, October 1998, vol. 1, no. 3, p. 72). 'The dynamics of the emerging market crisis turned Russia into a watershed country. Once the expropriation of foreign creditors commenced there was no way that any manager of emerging market funds could ignore the cross border problem' (p. 75). 'The drying well at the IMF meant that financing gaps might now be filled with forced conversion of domestic debt ... In any country with a Russia-like profile it might again be fair game to force the foreign investor into a conversion of domestic debt into worthless paper' (p. 81).

The basis of the plan is to convert the GKOs and OFZs into three to five year bonds as they fall due. The options for creditors are as follows: (1) three-year paper carrying an annual interest rate of 30 per cent; (2) four-year paper carrying an interest payment of 30 per cent for the first three years and 25 per cent in the fourth year; (3) five-year paper with a 30 per cent interest rate for the first three years, 25 per cent in the fourth and a yield of 20 per cent in the last year. (Investors were initially required to make their choice before 18 September, but the deadline was put off.) If the scheme goes ahead creditors who swap GKOs/OFZs for the new paper before the date of maturity will receive a cash payment equal to 5 per cent of the nominal value. Furthermore, investors have the option to convert 20 per cent of the nominal value into eight-year dollar-denominated paper, carrying an annual interest payment of 5 per cent. The dollar bond will be valued and converted according to the market value as of 14 August 1998 at the average MICEX rouble/dollar exchange rate between 17 and 26 August 1998 (*RET*, 1998, vol. 7, no. 3, p. 30).

10 September 1998. 'Hermes, the German export credit agency, said Russia had delayed payment for the first time on its sovereign debt obligations to Germany' (*FT*, 11 September 1998, p. 20). 'Russia has delayed payment of interest on debt to the German government for the first time since its escalating financial crisis erupted ... The delay is believed to be the first by Russia on its sovereign debt interest payments to an official creditor nation since the crisis began. Hermes, the export credit insurance company which acts as agent for the German government's debt receipts, said only part of a DM 800 million interest payment on rescheduled Soviet debt – so-called Paris Club debt – was received from the Russian government. The payment was due at the end of August' (p. 2). On 11 September the finance ministry said that Russia had defaulted on debt interest payments to several big Western creditor nations since the crisis began. The payments, due on 20 August, were on its $40 billion restructured Soviet-era debt – the so-called

Paris Club debt. Countries affected included Germany and the UK (*FT*, 12 September 1998, p. 6).

(Russia had still not paid any interest payments to Germany by 8 October 1998. Russia paid only DM 48.5 million – $30 million – of the DM 800 million in interest due on 20 August on Paris Club loans. Germany is Russia's largest creditor, with an estimated DM 100 billion in public and private loans outstanding: *IHT*, 9 October 1998, p. 17.)

24 September 1998. A US investment bank has won a court order in the UK freezing $113 million in two Russian banks ($87 million at Inkombank and $26 million at Oneximbank). The US bank was acting on behalf of clients whose forward foreign exchange contracts were in doubt (*FT*, 25 September 1998, p. 24). It is claimed that the Russian banks had defaulted on obligations due on 11 September (*IHT*, 25 September 1998, p. 15).

'[At] a meeting of the Paris Club on Thursday [24 September] … the creditors agreed to defer payments on the Russian Federation's current obligations to repay its debts … Russia was supposed to pay $600 million in interest on its $40 billion state debt, which was restructured for twenty-five years in 1996' (*CDSP*, 1998, vol. 50, no. 39, p. 5).

3 November 1998. 'First deputy prime minister Yuri Maslyukov said the government may have to reschedule some of its foreign debt … Russia has $17.5 billion in foreign debt payments due next year [1999] and $3.5 billion due this year [1998] (*IHT*, 5 November 1998, p. 17).

'Yuri Maslyukov … also said the country needed to restructure its huge foreign debt payments due this year and next, the first time the government admitted it would have problems making repayments. He said Russia would have to pay $3.5 billion this year and another $17.5 billion in 1999 … Russia has already failed to pay $685 million in interest to the Paris Club of sovereign lenders in August and September' (*FT*, 5 November 1998, p. 2).

16 November 1998. 'A ninety-day moratorium on the repayment of foreign debts held by Russian banks … expires Monday [16 November] (*IHT*, 16 November 1998, p. 19).

19 November 1998. Deutsche Bank (which chaired a meeting between Russia and its creditors) and the ministry of finance announce that they have reached agreement in principle on the terms of a voluntary restructuring of all GKO Treasury bonds and OFZ long-term obligations maturing between 19 August 1998 and 31 December 1999. The joint statement says: 'The arrangements contemplate a mechanism allowing for the periodic conversion and repatriation of roubles into dollars … [In addition, negotiations will be undertaken to reach agreement on a] consensual and constructive basis of the sums due to foreign creditors by Russian banks under foreign exchange contracts' (*FT*, 20 November 1998, p. 2). But time will still be needed to agree on final terms for restructuring 281 billion roubles ($16.5 billion) of defaulted Treasury debt. Foreign banks hold 85 billion roubles of the debt (*IHT*, 21 November 1998, p. 13).

20 November 1998. The government says it wants to reschedule more than $66 billion of restructured Soviet-era debt (*IHT,* 21 November 1998, p. 13). The government accepted that it could not pay more than $10 billion of the $17 billion of foreign debt repayments which fall due next year ... Russia has already missed $685 million of payments to Paris Club lenders and is due to repay a further $6.1 billion next year (*FT,* 21 November 1998, p. 2).

24 November 1998. 'Foreign banks could sign a restructuring deal on frozen Russian domestic debt, known as GKOs, by the end of the month [November] ... Under the terms of the proposal foreign banks, which have invested about $15 billion in GKOs, will only be able to repatriate about $550 million of their holdings ... Russia will provide $50 million a month at dollar auctions from February to December 1999. Those who decide not to take part in these auctions could put their money into special "transit" accounts for one year before other – still unspecified – mechanisms of repatriation were made available. Alternatively, foreign banks could use their money to buy more GKOs. Moscow has also agreed to hold two $100 million auctions in December and January which will be linked to forward contract payments owed to Western banks. Foreign bankers call the terms of the deal "confiscatory" but said that it was better than nothing ... Retreating from an earlier offer to pay investors 10 per cent in cash immediately, the Russian government would now pay 3.3 per cent cash straightaway and another two instalments of 3.3 per cent each in March and June. Mikhail Zadornov, finance minister, vowed that Russia would still honour all its post-1992 external debt, including $8.1 billion of eurobond payments and repayment of loans from the IMF and the World Bank' (*FT,* 25 November 1998, p. 2). 'Under the offer foreign investors will only be able to repatriate $550 million of the $15 billion they put into the GKO market, less than 4 cents on every dollar ... Unlike the original offer, which included a dollar component, this one almost entirely involves rouble-denominated securities. The complex structure, involving cash payments, a zero-coupon bond issued at par (effectively a non-interest-bearing IOU) and a series of securities with coupons reducing year by year, is almost beside the point, say opponents. A small component can be used for limited purposes such as paying for old tax liabilities or buying newly issued bank shares. The rest can only be recycled into new GKOs or placed for a year in a transit account. The money cannot be used for any other purpose ... The Russian central bank has agreed to put a total of $550 million up for auction in 1999 at a rate of $50 million a month' (*FT,* 26 November 1998, p. 23).

25 November 1998. 'Deputy finance minister Mikhail Kasyanov said Moscow would be able to pay less than $10 billion of the $17 billion of its foreign debt that came due next year [1999]' (*IHT,* 26 November 1998, p. 15). The London Club of bank creditors, representing holders of Russia's restructured Soviet-era debt, has agreed to let Russia pay $216 million of a $940 million debt payment due on 2 December 1998 in cash, with the remainder to be paid with new interest-arrears notes (p. 15).

26 November 1998. 'Russia has told Western bankers that it will not meet payment terms on $28 billion in Soviet-era debt to commercial creditors, effectively paving the way for a default on interest payments next month [December] ... Russia would not meet previously agreed terms to pay half of a $724 million interest payment due Wednesday [2 December] in cash and has offered instead to pay in bonds worth only some 13 per cent of their face value ... Separate negotiations on $10 billion in rouble-denominated domestic debt owed to foreigners had divided Western creditors over whether to accept new Russian terms ... Mikhail Kasyanov, the deputy finance minister, has signalled deepening troubles by saying Russia will be able to pay back less than $10 billion of the $17 billion in foreign debt that falls due in 1999. The negotiations with the London Club centred on terms agreed in 1997 setting out a schedule of repayments of debts from the former Soviet Union whose principal is denominated in so-called principal bonds. Under the 1997 agreement half of the interest due next Wednesday was to be paid in cash and half in bonds, called interest arrears notes. Instead, Russia now wants to pay the whole $724 million by issuing new interest arrears notes ... In separate discussions Russian officials have offered a complicated mix of repayments of some $10 billion on domestic debt that was part of the $40 billion Treasury debt frozen in August. Effectively, though, the Russian offer would permit foreign creditors to repatriate only $550 million staggered over a one-year period of monthly central bank auctions. The rest would be swapped for a variety of rouble securities useful only for transactions inside Russia' (*IHT*, 27 November 1998, p. 16).

30 November 1998. 'Negotiators representing Russia's domestic creditors yesterday [30 November] outlined details of an agreement reached with government officials over the restructuring of a number of financial instruments. The so-called "Moscow Club" unveiled a plan that would allow a theoretically higher rate of redemption for institutional investors who were forced to place money in the so-called GKOs and OFZs than the general terms offered to foreign creditors ... The basic scheme for restructuring debt offers 10 per cent in cash, 20 per cent in investment securities and 70 per cent in interest-bearing paper. The alternative "Moscow Club" proposals to cover pension funds and other institutions would allow 30 per cent cash, 20 per cent investment paper and 50 per cent interest-bearing paper. A group of about twenty outside experts met yesterday in Washington, where the IMF is based, for a brain-storming session designed to come up with proposals for dealing with Russia's continuing economic crisis and to further debate whether to extend further financial support' (*FT*, 1 December 1998, p. 2).

10 December 1998. 'Western banks said yesterday [10 December] that they were unlikely to accept Russia's terms for restructuring the $15 billion of foreign-held domestic debt (GKOs/OFZs) which is in default ... The only movement [by Russia], changing the allocation movement method of $550 million from an auction to a pro rata distribution, was unacceptable because of a 20 per cent discount on the exchange rate, bankers said' (*FT*, 11 December 1998, p. 3).

15 December 1998. 'Prime minister Yevgeni Primakov signed an order Tuesday [15 December] outlining the restructuring terms of frozen rouble debt that would allow investors to swap defaulted debt for new bonds and cash ... The finance ministry would provide more details Wednesday and announce the start of restructuring of 281 billion roubles ($13.98 billion) of defaulted domestic debt. Ministry officials said the swap could begin after that, though trading in the new bonds might not begin before next year. Under the proposed restructure programme investors will get 10 per cent in rouble cash, 20 per cent in interest-free rouble bonds and 70 per cent in rouble bonds with interest. In all creditors can expect to retrieve only a few cents on the dollar from their investment' (*IHT*, 16 December 1998, p. 17).

16 December 1998. 'The finance ministry said Wednesday [16 December] that it would swap 281 billion roubles in defaulted debt for new cash and bonds through 15 March, ending months of negotiations that resulted in investors securing a pledge for just a few cents on the dollar. The swap sets new terms for the cash portion of the deal, cutting the amount investors receive to 5 per cent of the value of their portfolio from the 10 per cent promised earlier ... Foreign bondholders, who hold about a third of the defaulted debt, have complained that Russia was imposing the restructuring deal unilaterally ... Altogether 70 per cent of each bondholder's portfolio will be swapped for bonds with maturities of four and five years that pay a fixed coupon that can be collected retroactively from 19 August. Another 20 per cent will be covered by a three-year bond that can be used to pay off tax arrears or swapped for equity in Russian banks. The remaining 10 per cent is covered in cash, but the government said it would pay that amount based on only half of the value of the portfolio on 19 August' (*IHT*, 17 December 1998, p. 17).

'Under the terms of the deal investors who held bonds bonds maturing before 31 December this year [1998] will be able to exchange them for 70 per cent by value in new securities with a four-to-five-year term, 20 per cent with zero-coupon bonds to be invested in Russian banks and the remaining 10 per cent in cash. Trading will begin in the securities in mid-January [1999]. The foreign banks have expressed frustration over plans that would prevent the securities being converted out of roubles for twelve months, with the exception of a small amount auctioned off each month starting in December [1998]' (*FT*, 17 December 1998, p. 3). 'Foreign creditors have been offered 10 per cent of the discounted value of their holdings in cash, 20 per cent in three-year zero-coupon bonds which can be used to pay taxes or exchanged for equity in near-bankrupt Russian banks, 70 per cent in four- and five-year securities bearing a 30 per cent coupon which would fall to 10 per cent in the last year. The whole package is worth about 4 cents on the dollar' (*FT*, 18 December 1998, p. 4).

Government short-term bonds (GKOs) maturing before 31 December 1999 and issued before 17 August 1998 are to be exchanged for new government securities during the period 15 December 1998 to 15 March 1999. The plan calls for 70 per cent of the debt will be exchanged for four- and five-year fixed-yield federal bonds (OFZs) and 20 per cent for so-called investment securities that, among other things, can be used to pay tax arrears. Only 10 per cent of the debt will be paid in 'hard cash' (in three instalments). The question of the repatriation of foreign exchange earnings remains unresolved. Discussions with London Club creditors will continue. The idea is for trading on the secondary market in the new government paper will begin in mid-January 1999 (*CDSP*, 1999, vol. 50, no. 50, pp. 16–17).

21 December 1998. 'Russia said Monday [21 December] that it would allow foreign investors to use a third of cash proceeds from the restructuring of its defaulted Treasury bonds to buy shares in Russian banks. Russia will continue talks Tuesday [22 December] with a working group of foreign bondholders in Moscow to work out terms that are "more attractive", said deputy finance minister Mikhail Kasyanov. The finance ministry will also begin swapping its defaulted debt for new bonds Tuesday … Mr Kasyanov said Monday that foreigners would not be allowed to use the new paper to invest in industrial concerns' (*IHT*, 22 December 1998, p. 15).

29 December 1998. 'Russia looks set to default on a $362 million payment on its Soviet-era debt to commercial banks, due Tuesday [29 December], after it failed to persuade enough holders of the debt to restructure the payment. Debt holders said they had expected Russia to miss the payment on bonds that were issued in late 1997 to restructure debt it inherited from the Soviet Union … Russia originally defaulted on what is now about $10 billion in domestic debt on 17 August. Last month [November] Russia asked creditors to accept new bonds in place of the $362 million interest payment. Not enough creditors agreed to that, so Russia was supposed to make the cash payment Tuesday. But Russia maintains that it will not be making any such payment. Bank of America, representing the creditors, said Tuesday that foreign banks were seeking legal clarification over what would be necessary to restructure the loans. Russia has said two-thirds of the creditors needed to agree on a restructuring for it to take force, while the London Club of commercial bank creditors said 95 per cent was necessary. By last week Russia had gained support from 72 per cent of its creditors for the debt-restructuring proposal. The IMF suspended payments in August on a $22.6 billion loan package after Russia defaulted on 281 billion roubles ($14.14 billion) of domestic debt' (*IHT*, 30 December 1998, p. 11). 'Russia … [failed] to make a $362 million payment on Soviet-era debt … [But] the commercial banks that are owed the money, led by Bank of America, stopped short of calling the failure to meet Tuesday's deadline a default, even though it appeared to be exactly that … Tuesday marked the first time it had failed to pay private creditors … Russia needed to reach agreement with 95 per cent of its creditors to restructure the debt, essentially allowing it to pay the money back over a far longer period of time. But only 72 per cent of those creditors approved a plan under which commercial banks would accept government-issued bonds as an alternative to cash. Russia insists that it needed to win the approval of only two-thirds of the creditors and therefore is not technically in default. "There is no legal basis for default", ... [according to] Vneshekonombank, the government's debt-paying agent ... [which argues that] at least half of the bank creditors must vote formally to declare the bank in default ... Bank of America said through a spokesman that it was seeking clarification of the Vneshekonombank position but that the 95 per cent approval requirement had not been changed' (*IHT*, 31 December 1998, p. 13).

'Russia yesterday [29 December] looked set to miss a $362 million cash payment on its private sector debt due by midnight ... Vneshekonombank, the government's agent, is now likely to issue interest arrear notes in place of the cash payment ... The government forecasts it will be able to service only $9.5 billion of the $17.5 billion of foreign debt payments due next year' (*FT*, 30 December 1998, p. 2). In 1999 Russia is due to pay the IMF $5 billion in principal and interest (*FT*, 31 December 1998, p. 19).

'Russia ... yesterday [29 December] failed to meet a $362 million payment due to creditor banks under a detailed restructuring agreement a year ago. The payment should have been made on 2 December but the deadline was moved to 29 December to allow the Russian government to renegotiate ... An estimated $9.5 billion or payments fall due in 1999 on post-Soviet debt, on top of the $8 billion due on pre-Soviet debts' (*The Telegraph*, 30 December 1998, p. 26).

'The Russian government claims that it has won the support of 70 per cent of the London Club of commercial creditors for a plan to restructure some $30 billion of debt inherited from the Soviet era (*The Times*, 30 December 1998, p. 11).

'In December 1997 London Club creditors accepted a swap of their claims of $22 billion for two tradable instruments, PRINs and IANs. The latter ones represented principal debt and the former were issued against overdue interest arrears. In December 1998 the Russian government breached the terms of of the restructuring agreement with the London Club by failing to make cash interest payment on PRINS' (*RET*, Monthly Update, 10 June 1999, p. 2).

'Mikhail Gorbachev ... said he lost his savings, about £48,000, in the Russian crash. "All my money is gone", he told *Bunte* magazine' (*The Times*, 30 December 1998, p. 11).

6 January 1999. 'Russia said Wednesday [6 January] that it had seen significant interest from domestic investors seeking to swap defaulted government debt for new bonds but that it expected foreigners to shun the offer until they receive more information on the terms. The government will resume talks with a group of foreign bondholders on 18 January to discuss concerns of foreign investors, including how they can invest roubles they receive. So far only domestic investors have applied to swap the defaulted debt … Foreign investors hold about a third of the 281 billion roubles ($13.6 billion) in Treasury bonds on which the government defaulted in August. The securities, originally valued at about $40 billion, have lost value with the rouble's plunge … The Bank of Russia … said the rouble's exchange rate, which the bank forecasts will average 21.5 to the dollar this year [1999], would depend on the government's ability to restructure its foreign debt. The dollar finished Wednesday at 22.9 roubles, up from 20.65 roubles Tuesday [5 January]' (*IHT*, 7 January 1999, p. 11).

10 January 1999. 'Russia marked the end of its long New Year's holiday with renewed warnings that it will be able to pay only a little more than half of its foreign debt obligations without outside help … The declaration acknowledged that the government had only budgeted $9.5 billion for debt payments and $17.5 billion is due. As for the rest, either payments will have to be delayed or Russia will default' (*IHT*, 11 January 1999, p. 11).

11 January 1999. 'Russia will resume trading its frozen domestic debt Friday [15 January] … The central bank said it would start trading new rouble bonds that were being swapped for the defaulted debt. In addition, it will resume trading in so-called OFZ bonds maturing after 31 December 1999 … The defaulted debt was worth around $40 billion at the time of the freeze, but with the resulting plunge in the value of the rouble, it is valued at about $12 billion' (*IHT*, 12 January 1999, p. 12).

13 January 1999. Brazil devalues its currency and triggers a (limited) bout of financial turbulence around the world.

15 January 1999. 'Russian bonds were traded Friday [15 January] for the first time since the government defaulted in August, as the central bank limited yields to 120 per cent – about their level of five months ago – to prevent prices from plummeting. About 948,000 roubles ($43,000) in Treasury bonds known as OFZs traded in the first hour. Prior to August [1998] when short-term securities known as GKOs traded along with the longer-term OFZs, daily levels topped 4 billion roubles. What investors had been expecting – the start of trading in new government securities being swapped for defaulted bonds – never happened … Although the government said it had received applications from many domestic holders of the defaulted bonds, officials have indicated that no swap has taken place … The planned restructuring returns investors just a few cents on the dollar for their investment. Foreigners have said they are not satisfied with the government's proposals' (*IHT*, 16 January 1999, p. 11).

'Nearly six months after the suspension of Russia's domestic debt market, on 15 January the central bank relaunched trading. However, so far interest has been limited despite yields of 120 per cent, twice the size of the refinancing rate. The new securities are to be used in the restructuring of frozen GKOs and OFZs, standing at 108 billion roubles for domestic creditors' (*RET*, Monthly Update, 10 February 1999, p. 11).

20 January 1999. 'Finance minister Mikhail Zadornov said that Russia would meet its scheduled debt repayments in the first quarter of the year while it continued talks on rescheduling the rest of its foreign debts ... Russia must pay $493 million in the first quarter of this year. The government has promised to honour this debt' (*IHT,* 21 January 1999, p. 13).

26 February 1999. The Deutsche Bank says that it has accepted restructuring terms for part of its share of the $15 billion of GKOs and OFZs held by foreigners. Credit Suisse First Boston is not accepting the terms and is considering unilateral action (*FT,* 27 February 1999, p. 2).

(Foreigners hold about $10 billion of GKOs/OFZs at face value: *RET,* 11 March 1999, p. 12.)

'Arguing that Russia's package was worth as little as 2.5 per cent of face value before devaluation last August [1998], the GKO committee had been seeking a six-week deadline to 30 April in the hope of getting more details about the mechanics and legal backing of the offer. The committee officially made that request on Thursday [25 February] ... Other banks were less concerned about Chase Manhattan's decision to accept the GKO offer on behalf of its proprietary holding, but not those of its clients' (*FT,* 1 March 1999, p. 1).

Deutsche Bank says it has agreed to restructure some of its own and its clients' rouble debt (*IHT,* 2 March 1999, p. 13).

1 March 1999. Chase Manhattan becomes the second foreign bank to agree to restructure some of the frozen rouble bonds (*IHT,* 2 March 1999, p. 13).

'Deutsche Bank, which was chairing the creditors' nineteen-strong committee, announced that it would accept unilaterally the terms offered – worth at best six cents in the dollar (and probably much less) – on its own behalf, though not on its clients.' The other banks, outraged, sacked Deutsche on 1 March, and then voted to continue without a chairman. Two banks, including Japan's Nomura, are thought likely to sue ... Only 3 billion roubles ($125 million) will be immediately payable in cash. The rest – amounting to around 70 billion roubles by the end of the year – will be paid in new rouble bonds, with predictably unattractive coupons and maturities. These can be traded, but almost all the proceeds must be kept inside Russia, where they can be used to buy more bonds, or equities, or deposited in local banks' (*The Economist,* 6 March 1999, p. 77).

2 March 1999. Finance minister Mikhail Zadornov says that the deadline for foreign investors to accept a proposed restructuring of the government's frozen domestic GKO debt is to be extended until the end of April 1999 (*FT,* 3 March 1999, p. 2).

8 March 1999. Three Western banks, Credit Lyonnais, Deutsche Bank and Chase Manhattan, accept the plan for restructuring GKOs and OFZs. The plan will give them 10 per cent in cash, 20 per cent in zero coupon bands and 70 per cent in four-to-five-year paper (*RET,* 1999, vol. 8, no. 1, p. 97).

15 March 1999. Credit Suisse First Boston, the largest creditor bank, announces a plan for a new rouble-based investment fund designed to recover debt. Its seven-year Nikitsky Recovery Fund provides an alternative to the Russian restructuring terms, enabling creditors to invest in infrastructure projects at the face value of the debt (*IHT*, 16 March 1999, p. 13).

The nominal rouble amount of the domestic securities on which Russia defaulted would be recycled into infrastructure investments and other projects. The plan requires 35 billion roubles of GKO and OFZ securities (or about 40 per cent of that held by foreigners) to be committed to Nikitsky. CSFB and its clients hold about that much (*FT*, 16 March 1999, p. 3).

'The ministry's current derisory, restructuring offer would leave debt-holders with about five cents in the dollar. On 15 March CSFB suggested an alternative. This would involve a pooling of foreigners' Russian bond holdings into what would be called the Nikitsky fund. The full nominal value of the bonds would be repaid into the fund, for investment in infrastructure and other projects in Russia. Returns would go to the investors, shifting the obligation to repay from the government to the fund ... Together with its clients it [CSFB] owns some 40 per cent of outstanding GKOs and OFZs' (*The Economist*, 20 March 1999, p. 109).

29 March 1999. Russia is facing more than $6 billion in foreign debt repayments through July and a total of $17.5 billion in 1999 as a whole, including $4.5 billion owed to the IMF. Since August 1998 Russia has missed about $1.5 billion in payments on foreign debt accumulated during Soviet times (*IHT*, 30 March 1999, pp. 1, 4).

2 April 1999. Nizhny Novgorod fails to pay a $4.4 million Eurobond coupon (*RET*, 1999, vol. 8, no. 2, p. 95).

15 April 1999. The World Bank says it has promised $2.3 billion in new loans over the next two years once Russia has reached agreement with the IMF. The loans will be used for industrial restructuring, banking reforms, improved tax collection, utility regulation and and social reforms. The World Bank will also help arrange a Japanese credit of over $1 billion (*IHT*, 16 April 1999, p. 16; *FT*, 16 April 1999, p. 2).

20 April 1999. 'Russia is set to default for the first time on its Soviet-era foreign currency bonds in a move aimed at husbanding resources to help it avoid reneging on post-Soviet debt ... Russia plans to miss the repayment of a $1.3 billion tranche of Soviet-era bonds, known as Minfin bonds, due next month [May], in order to avoid defaulting on dollar international bonds issued since the collapse of the Soviet Union. It plans to pay $330 million in interest falling due at the same time, but the default could still trigger cross-defaulty on $11 billion total outstanding paper ... The default on Minfins, held mainly by banks and other private investors, would form part of a deal under negotiation with the Paris Club of sovereign debtors' (*FT*, 21 April 1999, p. 3).

'Minfins are dollar-denominated domestic debt that was issued in 1993 to compensate Russian entities whose hard currency accounts in the state-owned Vneshekonombank were frozen when Moscow defaulted on Soviet debt in 1991' (*IHT*, 21 April 1999, p. 15).

'Minfins [are] bonds offered by the Russian government as compensation for those ... [who] held hard currency deposits in Soviet banks' (*The Economist*, 24 April 1999, p. 99).

21 April 1999. 'Ignoring the protests of several international banks, Russia has held foreign investors to a plan that restructures ... defaulted government debt at a fraction of its face value ... Under the government's restructuring plan foreigners would get a package of new Russian securities and between 3 cents and 8 cents on the dollar' (*IHT*, 22 April 1999, p. 13).

'The government defaulted in August [1998] on ... GKOs, domestic rouble debt, once worth $40 billion ... Bondholders are now contemplating a restructuring deal worth – at best – one solitary cent in the dollar' (*The Economist*, 24 April 1999, p. 99). 'Holders of GKOs ... took the bone they were tossed – a confiscatory restructuring scheme giving them a couple of cents in the dollar' (*The Economist*, 5 June 1999, p. 106).

'By late last week nearly all of them [foreigners who had been lured by the high interest rates on government bonds] had agreed to the stringent terms of the Russian government's debt restructuring plan. The trouble is that no one really knows exactly what it is they have agreed to and how much, if anything, the government's plan will give them in the end ... The broad terms of the restructuring plans are clear. In return for the nearly $17 billion in rouble-denominated Treasury securities they held at the time of the default, foreigners will get about 10 per cent of their investments in "cash" – dollars purchased at special currency auctions using some rouble proceeds from the Treasury bills. Twenty per cent of the restructuring package comes in the form of tax write-offs, which most foreigners do not need but can sell to Russian investors. But the bulk of their investments will be swapped for new government securities that mature over four to five years. All proceeds from trading in these new securities will be in roubles and foreigners will not be able to convert those roubles to dollars and repatriate them for an unspecified period. The government agreed to let non-residents use those roubles to buy stocks and bonds. But it has yet to disclose an official, complete list of the Russian companies involved and the mechanism by which foreigners may invest in them' (*IHT*, 7 May 1999, p. 15).

27 April 1999. 'The City of Moscow is seeking to restructure $100 million of a foreign currency loan, the first time the city has signalled it cannot meet its foreign debt obligations since the financial crisis lat year [1998]. Moscow is perceived to be the best credit risk in Russia but it has now succumbed to the pressures of its foreign debt burden, which includes $1.1 billion of international bonds. The city ... said it will not be able to repay in June [1999] $100 million of a $200 million syndicated loan that it negotiated in 1997 ... The three-year loan of $200 million was arranged by Deutsche bank, WestLB and Société Générale ... Mr Luzhkov's government has pledged it would continue to service the city's international bonds. But some syndicated loan holders said they would demand that international bond holders share the pain of any restructuring ... Moscow's total foreign debt is estimated at $1.8 billion, including $1.1 billion of bonds' (*FT,* 28 April 1999, p. 44).

'The city has acknowledged that it may not be able to meet all the demands of its foreign creditors this year [1998]. The deputy mayor announced last week that the city would soon begin talks about restructuring a $100 million debt remaining on a $200 million syndicated loan ... The city borrowed heavily, including the $200 million syndicated loan arranged ... in 1997. The city paid off $100 million last year [1998], but the loan agreement includes a "put option" allowing the lenders to demand early payment. In anticipation that they would shortly exercise this right ... [the deputy mayor] announced that the city would have to restructure the debt ... Overall the city has $2 billion in outstanding foreign currency debt ... The Leningrad region last week defaulted on a $50 million loan, called in early by nervous creditors, and has begun restructuring talks. A host of agriculture bonds issued by regions have also been put in default. AO Tatneft, an oil company in the Russian autonomous region of Tatarstan, is also expected to default soon on a Eurobond ... Russia's sovereign credit rating has fallen to the worst in the world' (David Hoffman, *IHT,* 10 May 1999, p. 6).

14 May 1999. 'Russia skipped a $1.3 billion payment on its Soviet-era debt Friday [14 May], transferring only interest payments on a raft of obligations to its debt agent ... With $1.6 billion of liabilities maturing, May is a busy month for debt repayments. A further $2.5 billion is due in June' (*IHT,* 15 May 1999, p. 11).

'Against expectations the authorities last month [May] paid $333 million to service hard currency debt, known as MinFins, to the benefit of the wealthy Russian individuals and institutions that hold it ... IANs are bonds representing $6 billion worth of unpaid interest on $22 billion of Soviet-era debt which was restructured in 1997 by the London Club of private commercial creditors. Russia wants to delay by six months a $855 million combined debt-service payment due on 2 June' (*The Economist,* 5 June 1999, p. 108).

'In December 1997 London Club creditors accepted a swap of their claims of $22 billion for two tradable instruments, PRINs and IANs. The latter ones represented principal debt and the former were issued against overdue interest arrears ... In May [1999] London Club creditors decided to postpone further discussions on whether to declare Russia bankrupt until a formal request on debt restructuring was made by the Russian side. By 31 May 1999 total debt to the London Club members was $26.4 billion, of which $200 million was overdue interest' (*RET,* Monthly Update, 10 June 1999, p. 2).

'[There is] internal foreign currency denominated debt. The last significant part of the debt restructured in 1991 was the foreign currency denominated accounts of Soviet enterprises and individuals at Vneshekonombank. These obligations were restructured into five tranches of tradable securities called OVVZs (MinFins or Taiga bonds). OVVZs are considered to be part of the internal debt and disputes arising in connection with MinFins are under the jurisdiction of Russian courts. In 1996 Russia issued its own OVVZ bonds, By 1 May 1999 the face value of MinFins in circulation was around $8.7 billion. It is clear that the government assigns relatively low priority to OVVZ debt and its failure to redeem the third tranche due in May 1999 did not come as a surprise. However, up to now all interest payments have been made on time' (*RET*, Monthly Update, 10 June 1999, p. 2).

17 May 1999. Lukoil has been given permission to issue four-year bonds in return for the rouble proceeds of restructured GKOs. The bonds will be denominated in roubles but linked in yet undisclosed terms to the rouble-dollar exchange rate. Gazprom and the Tyumen Oil Company have also applied for permission. 'The bonds are likely to prove popular with foreign investors unable to repatriate the rouble proceeds of their restructured GKOs ... After many months of bargaining more than 80 per cent of foreign investors last month [April] accepted a punitive restructuring deal requiring them to hold most of their proceeds in cash roubles and rouble bonds' (*FT*, 18 May 1999, p. 36).

26 May 1999. Russia asks the London Club to allow deferral for six months of a $850 million payment, due on 2 June (*RET*, 1999, vol. 8, no. 2, p. 98).

2 June 1999. Russia misses a $850 million payment due to London Club creditors (*RET*, 1999, vol. 8, no. 2, p. 98). The deadline of 16 June for the London Club to declare Russia in default passed without event (p. 99).

'In June Russia failed to make a payment of $216 million to the London Club, but the club did not declare Russia in default' (*RET*, 14 July 1999, p. 17).

12 July 1999. 'The finance ministry has ventured into the bond market again. On Tuesday it announced the results of Monday's auction [12 July] of state savings bonds ... Holders of this type of bond, unlike the holders of GKOs, were not hurt by the events of last August [1998]; the finance ministry continued to service its savings bond debt on time and in full ... Floating the savings bonds was a dress rehearsal for the state's full-scale return to the bond market' (*CDSP*, 1999, vol. 51, no. 28, p. 13).

23 July 1999. The World Bank approves a plan to restructure $650 million in loans to help retrain coal miners and support other social programmes. The World Bank halted payments of the loans in August 1998 (*IHT*, 26 July 1999, p. 15).

1 August 1999. 'Russia has reached an agreement with the Paris Club that postpones payments on Soviet debt until the end of next year [2000]. Over that period Russia will have to service a mere $600 million instead of a scheduled $8.1 billion' (*RET*, Monthly Update, 10 August 1999, p. 14).

'Russia won a temporary reprieve on $8 billion of foreign debt ... and signalled it would seek further concessions from its Paris Club of sovereign creditors ... The Paris Club agreed to reschedule roughly $8 billion of arrears and Soviet-era debt falling due between August 1998 and the end of 2000. Russia stopped servicing this debt after the crisis in August last year [1998] ...

The $8 billion would be repaid over fifteen to twenty years. Discussions about the final fate of this debt would start in autumn 2000 … Russia agreed to pay $620 million until the end of 2000 in interest arrears and $880 million between 2001 and 2005. The rest of the debt payments, which fall due in 1999 and 2000, as well as some interest arrears accumulated since August last year, have been consolidated and restructured for twenty years, consisting of a five-year grace period, when Russia will pay only interest on the debt, and a fifteen-year repayment period of the principal' (*FT*, 2 August 1999, p. 3).

'Russia struck a deal with the Paris Club of country creditors to reschedule Soviet-era debts falling due this year [1999] and next [2000] … Russia would now pay about $600 million in 1999 and 2000 instead of $8 billion … An overall settlement on the total Soviet-era debt would be discussed at talks in autumn 2000 … The discussion concerned sovereign debts falling due between 1 July this year [1999] and the end of 2000, plus arrears accumulated since Russia stopped payment on some debt last August [1998]' (*IHT*, 2 August 1999, p. 13).

'Russia and its creditors will meet late next year [2000] to find a solution to the rest [of the debt]' (*The Economist*, 7 August 1999, p. 78).

20 August 1999. The EBRD agrees to raise the annual ceiling on its lending to Russia to Euro 1 billion (from Euro 0.5 billion) over the medium term, provided that Russia restructures its banking sector and introduces further measures to improve the investment climate. The EBRD has been dealing with projects on a strict case-by-case basis since August 1998. The EBRD says that the medium term means a gradual increase over three or four years. Measures required to improve the investment climate means clear bankruptcy laws, and legislation to improve transparency, as well as banking reform (*FT*, 21 August 1999, p. 2).

20 August 1999. 'World Bank loans to Russian totalling $200 million have been scrapped after a damning assessment of the investment projects. World Bank officials said a review showed that only about a third of the projects were on track' (*IHT*, 21 August 1999, p. 11).

31 August 1999. 'Nizhny Novgorod … yesterday [31 August] added to the woes of emerging market investors by saying it would seek to postpone the next interest payment on its outstanding international bond … Nizhny Novgorod … has requested a meeting with bondholders on 22 September to reschedule its payments' (*FT*, 1 September 1999, p. 30).

10 February 2000. Agreement is reached between Russia (represented by first deputy prime minister Mikhail Kasyanov) and the London Club of commercial creditors to restructure $31.8 billion of foreign debt. Under the agreement $22.2 billion in Soviet-era debt and $6.8 billion in Russian state debt will be exchanged for new Russian Federation eurobonds. But the new bonds for Soviet debt will be offered at a 37.5 per cent discount and the Russian debt at a 33 per cent discount, e.g. rather than getting 100 per cent of the value of the Soviet debt creditors will get 62.5 per cent. 'The agreement … would basically write off about half of Russia's foreign commercial debt, analysts said.' Later in 2000 Russia will resume talks with the Paris Club about $42 billion owed to foreign governments (*IHT*, 14 February 2000, p. 19). The agreement involves nearly $32 billion of Soviet-era debt (*IHT*, 29 March 2000, p. 6).

As a result of the agreement 36.5 per cent of the total outstanding debt of $32 billion was written off, with the balance being converted into two types of Eurobonds. Payments on most of the restructured debt will be spread over thirty years, including a seven-year grace period, and will bear below-market interest rates (EBRD 2000a: 16).

'[The deal] effectively writes off half of Russia's commercial foreign debts ... A third of the debt is to be written off, with repayment of the rest rescheduled over the next thirty years, easing Russia's overall debt burden to the London Club by 50 per cent' (*The Times*, 14 February 2000, p. 10).

'The deal ... to forgive more than one-third of its $32 billion private sector debts ... comes after eighteen months of negotiations ... The banks agreed to write off about 36.5 per cent of the $32 billion debt ... and restructure the remainder into thirty-year eurobonds, with a seven-year grace period ... Paper issued by the partially state-owned Vneshekonombank ... [has been converted] into eurobonds backed by the Russian Federation' (*FT*, 14 February 2000, p. 1).

Prime minister Mikhail Kasyanov: 'This week Russia offered to exchange new Russian eurobonds for $31.8 billion of debt of the former Soviet Union owed to the London Club of private sector financial institutions. This voluntary exchange will provide much needed debt relief, reducing the principal amount of London Club debt by, on average, 36.5 per cent' (*FT*, 20 July 2000, p. 23).

'As a result of the February negotiations $10.6 billion of the total $31.8 billion was written off. In addition the repayment of the majority of the remaining $21.2 billion was postponed to begin in 2008' (*RET*, Monthly Update, 13 April 2000, p. 3).

'Russia closed a landmark debt restructuring deal with the London Club of commercial lenders Friday [25 August], issuing $21 billion of new Eurobonds to replace $32 billion of the debt it inherited from the Soviet Union' (*IHT*, 26 August 2000, p. 11).

(On the table is some $22 billion in Prins, representing principal, and $6 billion in Ians or interest arrear notes, as well as debt servicing charges some of which have been unpaid since the default in autumn 1998. Prins and Ians are the fruit of a previous round of restructuring with the Russian government completed in December 1997: *FT*, 3 August 1999, p. 2. 'Negotiations concern $31 billion in Soviet-era debt. At issue is $24 billion in Prins and $6.8 billion in Ians': *FT*, 6 August 1999, p. 28. See the entries for 29 December 1998 and 14 May 1999. 'The London Club debt was scheduled for the first time in 1995, after which it was divided into the Principal Loans [Prins] and Interest Arrears Notes [Ians]': *RET*, Monthly Update, 13 April 2000, p. 3.)

'Russia made a return to the domestic debt market in February as the government issued a modest 2.5 billion roubles in new short-term GKOs. This is the first issue since the August 1998 crisis' (*RET,* Monthly Update, 10 March 2000, p. 16).

'Russia moved Wednesday [23 February] to restore its battered bond market to life, raising 3.43 billion roubles ($119.3 million) in the first regular auction of Treasury bills since the government's default in August 1998 … Still, foreign investors remain wary of Russian debt. Domestic investors were the main buyers at the auctions' (*IHT,* 24 February 2000, p. 15).

'After the default foreign investors were given mere cents back on the dollar and even this was trapped in special "S" accounts at the central bank. Special rules allowed profits from the first GKO auction to be repatriated. It raised about 3 billion roubles – not very much. Since then the central bank has been issuing new tranches of between 3 billion roubles and 5 billion roubles every two months or so. And while foreigners have been staying away, strong demand from domestic investors has driven down yields … Foreigners are put off by investment restrictions, which mean they can only buy GKOs [the initials stand for "short-term bonds"] through an "S" account' (*Business Central Europe*, September 2000, p. 40).

CHAPTER EIGHT

FOREIGN DEBT AND AID BEFORE THE AUGUST 1998 FINANCIAL CRISIS

FOREIGN DEBT

Russia's foreign debt is relatively small given the size and endowment of its economy. Russia is actually a net international creditor, being owed more than it owes. But the problem is that most of the debt owed to Russia by poor and current/former communist countries will never be repaid. On 17 September 1997 Russia became a member (the nineteenth) of the Paris Club of creditor nations. (The London Club comprises creditor banks.)

In reality Russia has, on occasion, defaulted on its sovereign debt. Although the term has never formally been used by Western creditors, commentators have been less constrained. For example, 'Russia went into default in January 1992' (Jeffrey Sachs, *FT*, 31 March 1994, p. 21). Formal default on Russia's foreign debt has been avoided by a series of payment delays and rescheduling agreements.

Estimates of the size of Russia's debt

Estimates of the size of Russia's debt are as follows:

1. On 1 January 1992 the total external debt of the Soviet Union was $107.7 billion (*RET*, Monthly Update, June 1999, p. 1).

Russia's foreign debt consists of two parts: (1) the debts of the former Soviet Union, which were inherited by Russia in exchange for sole Russian entitlement to all assets abroad formerly owned by the republics of the USSR (around $80 billion by the end of 1993, of which about $40 billion was owed to Paris Club governments, nearly $26 billion to the London Club banks and the rest to 'non-organized' creditors, mainly Western exporters to the former Soviet Union); and (2) the purely 'Russian' debts, accumulated over 1992–93 and totalling approximately $18 billion. In 1993 the total amount due was almost $40 billion, which was comparable to total annual exports. But only $3 billion was actually repaid. In 1994 total debt service due was $32.5 billion. Russia is actually a net international creditor and is owed $150 billion by debtors to the Soviet Union. But the largest debtors (such as Cuba, Vietnam and Mongolia, which account for 38 per cent of total debt) are insolvent (*RET*, 1994, vol. 3, no. 2, pp. 70–1). (See below for revised figures.)

2. Russia's foreign debt at the end of 1994 was estimated at $91 billion (later put at $93.6 billion), but the figure rose to $120 billion (later put at $121.6 billion) if debts to former Comecon countries were included (these will probably never be settled in cash). Purely Russian debt, accumulated after 1992, was estimated at $11.2 billion (later put at $11.3 billion). In 1993 only $3.6 billion was actually paid out of the $31 billion due in debt servicing. In 1994 total debt service due was $32.5 billion, but only $3.7 billion had been paid by the end of September (*RET*, 1995, vol. 3, no. 4, pp. 79–80; vol. 4, no. 1, p. 84).

3. At the beginning of 1995 Russia's external debt (including debt of the former Soviet Union) was $122 billion (38.7 per cent of 1994 GDP). This figure includes $28 billion in debts to former Comecon countries and $94 billion due to other countries. Of the $122 billion, $11 billion had been built up by the Russian government since 1992 (*RET*, 1995, vol. 4, no. 4, p. 87).

4. At the end of 1995 Russia's foreign debt was $120.4 billion, broken down into $103 billion inherited from the Soviet Union and $17.4 billion dating from 1992 (*RET*, Monthly Update, 17 May 1996, p. 6).

5. Russia's total foreign debt (as of 1 January) was as follows, broken down (in brackets) into that owed to official creditors, to commercial banks and firms, and to international financial organizations: 1994, $112.7 billion ($73.1 billion, $36.1 billion and $3.5 billion); 1995, $121.6 billion ($76.2 billion, $40 billion and $5.4 billion); 1996, $120.5 billion ($68.7 billion, $40.4 billion and $11.4 billion); 1997, $125 billion ($69.8 billion, $39.9 billion and $15.3 billion); 1998 (estimate), $130.8 billion ($68.2 billion, $42.7 billion and $19.9 billion). The stock of debt at the end of 1997 will represent about 30 per cent of annual GDP (*RET*, 1997, no. 4. p. 80).

The Russian government's external debt (end of year) was as follows, broken down into the external debt of the former Soviet Union (for which the Russian government has agreed to be responsible) and the external debt of the Russian government: 1993, $112.7 billion ($103.7 billion and $9.0 billion); 1994, $119.9 billion ($108.6 billion and $11.3 billion); 1995, $120.4 billion ($103.0 billion and $17.4 billion); 1996, $125.0 billion ($100.8 billion and $24.2 billion); 1997, $123.5 billion ($91.4 billion and $32.1 billion) (*RET*, 1998, no. 3, p. 65).

As of 31 May 1999 Russia's external debt was $134 billion. This was broken down as follows:

1. Soviet-era debt $87.1 billion, subdivided into $39.4 billion (Paris Club bilateral creditors), $21.3 billion (other bilateral creditors) and $26.4 billion (London Club creditors).

2. Russian debt $47.1 billion, subdivided into $23.3 billion (multilateral creditors: IBRD and IMF), $7.9 billion (bilateral creditors) and $15.9 billion (eurobonds) (*RET*, Monthly Update, June 1999, p. 4).

Russia's total external debt amounts to about $150 billion, close to 90 per cent of GDP (*RET*, Monthly Update, 10 September 1999, p. 7).

The foreign debt is about $150 billion. 'Following the 1998 crisis the total value has leapt to more than 100 per cent of GDP' (*FT*, Survey, 10 May 2000, p. ii).

(At the end of 1998 the total external debt was $150.8 billion – not including indebtedness to foreign holders of government short-term bonds, known as GKOs, and federal bonds, known as OFZs. The total debt was broken down into Soviet-era debt, amounting to $91.4 billion, and Russian debt, amounting to $59.4 billion: *CDSP*, 1999, vol. 51, no. 11, p. 9.)

As of 1 January 2000 Russia's external debt was $158.8 billion. This was divided into the following:

1. Commercial creditors $56.8 billion: Eurobonds (Russia), $16.0 billion; Eurobonds (former London Club Soviet debt), $31.8 billion; MinFin bonds tranche 4–7, $7.4 billion; MinFin bonds tranche 3, $1.3 billion.

2. Multilateral loans $21.8 billion: IMF, $14.9 billion; World Bank, $6.9 billion.

3. Bilateral loans $64.1 billion: Paris Club (post Soviet). $9.2 billion; Paris Club (Soviet), $40.2 billion; Comecon, $14.7 billion.

4. Other $16.1 billion (*RET*, 13 April 2000, p. 3).

FOREIGN AID

Although Russia's record of fulfilling the conditions laid down for aid has generally been poor, the IMF has continued to provide further aid (though tranches have frequently been delayed). The IMF has been the subject of considerable controversy, including the accusation that Western countries (especially the USA) have leaned on it to continue supporting Russia for broader political reasons (not least Russia's large number of nuclear weapons).

Prime minister Mikhail Kasyanov: 'After the Second World War the USA provided an estimated $88 billion of aid – in current dollars – under the Marshall Plan to promote postwar European economic recovery' (*FT*, 20 July 2000, p. 23).

A chronology of major aid agreements, including debt rescheduling

1 April 1992. An international aid package is announced to be financed by the G7 and other Western countries (in part via institutions like the IMF). It was not clear how much was new or what each country was to contribute. There is still a dispute about how much of the $24 billion aid package was actually spent. The aid package was conditional (including targets for reducing the budget deficit and inflation rates) and the main monitoring agency was to be the IMF. On 5 August 1992 the IMF agreed to release $1 billion in spite of considerable concern about Russia's progress in meeting its commitments.

In 1992 Russia received $14.1 billion in loans and grants disbursed by the West. All but $1.6 billion were in loans, mostly trade credits. Russia paid the West $1.6 billion in debt service, nearly all of it interest (*RET*, 1993, vol. 2, no. 1, p. 43).

2 April 1993. The Paris Club of creditor countries formally reschedules over ten years $15 billion due to be paid by Russia in 1993 (most of it would not have been paid had the agreement not been made). There will be a six-month grace period and $3.5 billion will be repaid over the following twelve months ($1.95 billion in 1993). The governments hope that Western banks will grant relief on 'comparable terms'.

15–16 April 1993. A G7 meeting in Tokyo agreed on a $43.4 billion aid package, which was larger than expected. There was more old than new, but the exact proportion was not clear. Included was a $3 billion 'systemic transformation facility' from the IMF. Not only was this new, but some of the conditions laid down were also new. The first instalment of $1.5 billion was to be disbursed simply when a commitment to economic change was made (the IMF actually approved the first tranche on 30 June 1993), although the second depended on the curbing of inflation and the budget deficit. The second tranche, due in September, was delayed because of the IMF's concern that its conditions were not being met (*IHT*, 21 September 1993, p. 13). It was not until 22 March 1994 that Michel Camdessus, the managing director of the IMF, agreed in principle to the second tranche; formal IMF approval had to wait until 20 April 1994. The agreed conditions included cutting planned expenditure programmes in the event of tax deficiencies and/or spending overruns and a target monthly inflation rate of 7 per cent by the end of 1994.

Bilateral commitments were also made, although the exact amount of additional aid was uncertain. Germany did not announce additional bilateral aid because of the large commitments already made.

3 August 1993. The London Club of Western bank creditors agrees to accept $0.5 billion of the $3.5 billion in interest owed in 1993, with the repayment of the remaining $3 billion postponed for five years. (It was estimated that in 1993 Russia would have to make only about 8 per cent of payments due in 1992 and 1993 to the London Club and to the Paris Club: *IHT*, 4 August 1993, p. 11.) Towards the end of December 1993 a new roll-over replaced the old one, expiring on 31 March 1994 (Leyla Boulton, *FT*, 31 December 1993, p. 2).

4 June 1994. Western creditor governments agree to reschedule $7 billion of the debt due in 1994 (Russia allocated $4.1 billion for debt servicing in that year) (Leyla Boulton, *FT*, 6 June 1994, p. 3).

5 October 1994. Preliminary agreement is reached with the London Club of creditors to reschedule Russia's commercial bank debt (there is a five-year grace period and the following ten years will be allowed to pay off the debt). Russia agrees to pay $500 million in interest before the end of the year.

16 November 1995. Russia reaches an agreement with commercial bank creditors to reschedule $32.5 billion, $25.5 billion of principal and $7 billion of interest. The principal will be restructured over twenty-five years, with the right to defer payments for seven years. An interest payment of $1.5 billion will be made by the end of 1996. The balance of the interest will be repaid over a twenty-year period, with the right to defer payments for seven years (*CDSP*, 1995, vol. XLVII, no. 46, pp. 5–6).

29 April 1996. The Paris Club rescheduled Russia's $40.4 billion of sovereign debt inherited from the Soviet Union and owed to eighteen creditor countries. The repayment period was to be twenty-five years. There would be a grace period for the repayment of principal until 2002. Until then only interest would be paid. Russia would pay only $2 billion in 1996 instead of the $8 billion it owed. The amounts paid back would increase over time. The rescheduling accord would depend on Russia fulfilling its commitments under the IMF agreement of 26 March 1996.

6 October and 2 December 1997. The London Club agreement was signed on 6 October and completed on 2 December 1997. The $33 billion of Soviet-era debt to commercial banks was rescheduled. The deal rescheduled the $24 billion of principal repayments over twenty-five years from the end of 1995, with a seven-year grace period (i.e. payments would start at the beginning of 2003). Repayment of $8 billion of overdue interest was rescheduled over twenty years, starting after 2002. Russia made a down-payment of $3 billion on 2 December 1997 when the deal had been completed (*RET*, 1997, no. 4, pp. 79, 106).

The $31 billion of Soviet-era debt to commercial banks was rescheduled: principal transformed into $22 billion worth of new, long-term loans; $6 billion in long-term notes for interest due; $3 billion paid in cash for interest due (*IHT*, 4 December 1997, p. 15; *FT*, 3 December 1997, p. 2).

(Further details of the role of the IMF are to be found in Chapter 7 dealing with macroeconomic stabilization and the financial crisis of August 1998.)

The merits and demerits of aid

Views on aid vary. Opponents of large-scale (non-humanitarian) aid to Russia argue that aid would be wasted and would deter the necessary and painful changes that only Russia itself can undertake. Aid critics point to the size of capital flight (especially the illegal element). Even supporters of aid to Russia are aware of the potential for abuse. Former (late) US president Richard Nixon (1994): 'I found no one who had a good word to say for the US aid programme. The issue is not the amount but how it is administered. Rip-offs, shakedowns and corruption among recipients, along with incompetence among administrators, have created enormous disillusionment.' Proponents stress the missed opportunity for early, substantial aid.

'Moscow is being asked to reduce its budget deficit by collecting more taxes and cutting spending. International financial organizations and Western countries in July [1998] pledged an emergency loan package of $17 billion to stabilize the immediate financial crisis and restructure the short-term debt. These measures, it is argued, will allow the government to get back to the business of market reform. But such measures cannot remedy Russia's economic problems ... Most of the Russian economy has not been making progress toward the market or even marking time. It is actively moving in the other direction. Over the past six years Russian companies, especially in the manufacturing sector, have indeed changed the way they operate, but to protect themselves against the market rather than join it. What has emerged is a new kind of economic system with its own rules and its own criteria for success and failure. The new system can be called Russia's virtual economy [see Chapter 1] ... The principal motivation for providing bailout funds is a belief not only that more money is required to preserve social and political stability but that strings can be attached to induce more reform. The opposite, however, is true: a bailout will prop up the virtual economy, which is fundamentally not market-based and whose inefficiency will ensure continued economic decline and further crises. A bailout will merely postpone the day of reckoning' (Gaddy and Ickes 1998b: 53–4). 'The virtual economy ... could not have developed to the extent it has, and arguably might not have become as corrupt and inefficient as it has, unless over $70 billion had been infused from the outside since 1992' (p. 65).

Boris Fyodorov: 'For the past ten years I have been of the view that foreign money has only helped incompetent people to buy time to do nothing. Giving this [Primakov's] government more money will not solve a single economic problem in Russia' (*FT*, 23 March 1999, p. 25). 'For the past six years Russia's governments have been living from one IMF infusion to the next ... We forget our promises, get into trouble and ask for money again ... They give us money for reforms and we immediately lose motivation to conduct these reforms ... The Russian authorities have learned the craft of pulling the wool over the eyes of the West and the West has learned to pretend not to notice it. For political reasons the West periodically tosses money at us. The main idea is to keep us quiet and non-threatening. The West does not believe that any economic reforms are under way in Russia and so it simply aims at producing the appearance of decency with the help of the IMF missions and negotiations. It should be recognized honestly that we have lost six years, increased out debts by $20 billion to the international financial organizations alone and completely failed to conduct reforms. And now we ask to write off part of the debts. We want to get new credits, but in fact we are not planning to reform anything. Yet another gift of charity from the West does not solve a single problem apart from producing the overall image of something positive going on ... It becomes increasingly obvious that the state is falling apart and is not coping normally with its most elementary functions. Periodic financial injections from the West delay only slightly the need to make decisions that are a matter of principle ... The new [Stepashin] government has been in charge for two months now and it has still has no economic programme of its own. We hear nothing apart from the continuation of the course of Yevgeni Primakov, who did not have a programme either ... Prime minister Sergei Stepashin should address the IMF and reject any new credits until the moment when Russia has a real plan of action and has started carrying it out' (Boris Fyodorov, *IHT*, 28 July 1999, p. 9). (See below for a somewhat more positive view of aid.)

'To say "no" to Russia now and then does not mean that we want to cut Russia off from the world and force it to resume a hostile arms buildup ... The time has come for [Western] policymakers to ask themselves whether saying "no" occasionally might not facilitate the reforms they seek more effectively than always saying "yes" ... Almost no responsible officials in the USA and Russia governments, nor those in international lending organizations, will admit publicly that their funds or foreign aid have been misused ... [But] there are responsible voices in Russia, including the former minister of finance, Boris Fyodorov, who have urged the IMF to stop lending money to Russia. Not only is Russia unable to repay such loans, Mr Fyodorov warns, but continued borrowing only nourishes destructive habits ... Russian economists have complained that in 1993 US food aid was diverted and then reexported, which was contrary to the agreement. Roskhlebprodukt, the Russian agency chosen to distribute the grain in Russia, profited at the expense of the intended recipients. Yet the same firm was selected to process the US food aid provided this year [1999] ... Former prime minister Sergei Stepashin has complained that "30 per cent of our humanitarian aid is invariably stolen" ... According to the audit committee of the Russian Duma, the $600 million [World Bank] loan provided in 1996 for the coal mines seems to have disappeared with little evident restructuring ... IMF officials have not addressed the claim that senior [Russian] central bank officials took [IMF] funds and invested them in high-yielding government securities back in Russia and kept the proceeds for their personal use. The central bank also has a long history of taking dollars borrowed from the IMF. Instead of selling them all at auction to prop up the rouble, as it is supposed to do, it sets aside a substantial portion at a lower rate for a few selected banks owned by a few favoured oligarchs. Moreover, these transfers have a habit of taking place immediately before a sharp devaluation of the rouble. Many of those dollars then quickly find their way back to the West' (Marshall Goldman, *IHT*, 15 October 1999, p. 10).

Before discussing the arguments in favour of aid, it is important to note the time dimension to aid. 'The West should offer a hand by facilitating Russia's accession to the World Trade Organization. But Russia no longer needs Western aid. Instead, private investors can look at Russia with new interest' (Anders Åslund, *IHT*, 19 March 1997, p. 8). 'Foreign assistance could have benefited the reform efforts early on. For example, if small amounts of assistance were directed to the budget, and ideally if this assistance was in the form of grants rather than credit, then it might have strengthened the hands of the reformers to fight off pressures from the groups fighting against reform.

But this could only have played a small role in the political battle, and it would not have dealt with many of the other problems plaguing the Gaidar team, such as the rapid alienation of the parliament. These benefits must be contrasted with the reality that very often foreign assistance has slowed reforms – because it allowed Gorbachev and sometimes Yeltsin to temporarily postpone making needed policy changes. On balance, the outcome of the early debate over foreign assistance was probably more harmful than helpful to reform. Gorbachev, Yeltsin, Yavlinsky and Gaidar all helped encourage public expectations that foreign assistance could solve Russia's economic problems ... The history of foreign aid to Russia is riddled with mismanagement on both sides and enormous false hopes ... Foreign assistance continued to be misused and wasted ... Today assistance from the IMF does play an important role in the stabilization programme ... Foreign assistance is essential ... to reschedule external debt obligations which can no longer be rolled over in private markets ... This is one area where Western assistance could have been helpful early on, but both the London Club and Paris Club were reluctant to make agreements' (Boone and Fedorov [Fyodorov] 1997: 185–6).

Arguments in favour of substantial aid to Russia and criticisms of the Western response include the following:

1. Jacques Attali (the former chairman of the EBRD) thinks it 'folly' to ask Russia to repay any of the Soviet debt and proposes that Western governments should compensate Western banks for debts incurred by the former Soviet Union (*FT*, 31 March 1993, p. 22). But he believes that Russia must repay its own debts, albeit restructured (*Moscow News*, 23 April 1993, p. 9).

2. Writing in 1993, Stanley Fischer (*IHT*, 7 April 1993, p. 8) offered the following advice. To stabilize the economy Russia would need direct financial assistance of $12 billion a year for the following two years, plus even further debt relief, from the West. The large sums, mainly export credits, that had flowed into Russia in the previous year were not tied to economic reform and were totally ineffective. Fischer recommended looser conditions than the IMF normally imposed for macroeconomic stabilization in order to escape from a Catch–22 situation. After the initial $12 billion a year for two years, Western aid could decline. The West should relieve Russia of the need to repay the remainder of its $85 billion debt for five years. When the time is right to stabilize the exchange rate of the rouble, Russia should also have access to the $6 billion stabilization fund. The essential requirement was to rein in the growth of credit, and Russia also needed to agree on a budget deficit target and on the need to adhere to a single rate of exchange. ('The West rightly fears that economic assistance would simply be wasted. But without Western financial assistance the Russians will not be able to balance the budget and bring inflation down to a level that will allow other reforms to succeed': Fischer, cited in *FT*, 5 April 1993, p. 4.) (Fischer is now first deputy managing director of the IMF.) (*The Economist*, 27 March 1993, p. 14, noted that the Russian government could use dollar aid to buy roubles on the Moscow

market. This would increase the value of the rouble and help finance the budget deficit without printing money.)

3. *The Financial Times* thought that the West 'should decide that $24 billion a year in long-term assistance (a mere 0.2 per cent of its aggregate gross domestic product) is a price well worth paying for the chances of successful Russian reform … all assistance must be conditional, but the conditions should be neither over-detailed nor excessively unrealistic' (4 March 1993, p. 19). 'What is needed … is true stabilization. That could be achieved through a programme to peg the exchange rate, combined with elimination of inflationary financing of the budget deficit. More funding would be needed than is now available. Much of it could be raised domestically, some in higher domestic revenue and some in domestic borrowing, but a precondition would be more Western finance. Some 4–5 per cent of Russian gross domestic product in external assistance, for two or three years, might do the trick. The bill for the West would be perhaps $14 billion a year' (20 June 1994, p. 17).

4. A Clinton-Yeltsin summit was held in Vancouver on 3–4 April 1993. It was the first between the USA and Russia (and the former Soviet Union) to concentrate on economic rather than military matters. Prior to the summit President Clinton had stressed the urgency of aid to Russia and the need for an emergency meeting of the G7 countries. On 1 April 1993 he said that: 'Nothing could contribute more to global freedom, security and prosperity than the peaceful progression of Russia's rebirth. It is not an act of charity. It is an investment in our own future. While our efforts will entail new costs, we can reap even larger dividends for our safety and prosperity. The danger is clear if Russia's reforms turn sour, if it reverts to authoritarianism or disintegrates into chaos. The world cannot afford the strife of the former Yugoslavia replicated in a nation spanning eleven time zones and armed with a vast arsenal of nuclear weapons.' President Clinton (26 February 1999): 'We must confront the risk of Russia weakened by the legacy of communism and also by its inability at the moment to maintain prosperity at home or control the flow of its money, weapons and technology across its borders. The dimensions of this problem are truly enormous. If Russia does what it must to make its economy work, I am ready to do everything I can to mobilize international support for them.'

5. 'Due to a complex of reasons – the start of a presidential campaign in the United States … the fact that Germany was overburdened with the incorporation of East Germany etc. – the main Western powers proved to be incapable of providing such leadership … Instead there appeared the simplest, deliberately inadequate solution of shifting the burden of responsibility to the IMF. The scale of the problems brought to life by the disintegration of a superpower, political in nature, were beyond the competence of the IMF … the IMF took nearly half a year to admit Russia to IMF membership … The most serious technical mistake made by the IMF … [was] the attempts to maintain the rouble zone on the post-Soviet territory.

It was clear to the Russian government that any agreements about co-ordination of fiscal and monetary policy would not be effective. That is why the Russian government wanted … to introduce its own national currency as soon as possible. The IMF, wanting to maintain a common post-Soviet economic space, obviously underestimated the difficulties of co-ordinating fiscal and monetary policies … Only in summer 1992 was a decision made to support national currencies; by this time there were no readily available political solutions' (Gaidar 1997: 14).

6. 'Its [the World Bank's] chief economist suggests that the early emphasis should have been on building institutions – a working court system, for example – rather than the traditional set of monetary guidelines favoured by the IMF' (Michael Dobbs and Paul Blustein, *IHT*, 13 September 1999, p. 2).

7. 'The IMF's first big mistake was its failure to support the reformers of the early 1990s with something akin to a Marshall Plan. Had the reformers been able to avoid hyperinflation and create a semblance of widely shared prosperity the move to a market economy might have taken a different path. Instead of mass poverty, destitution and an obscene oligarchy more equitable economic progress might have engendered strong centrist democratic parties like those of eastern Europe … Of course, blaming the IMF for this historic failure misses the point: the USA had no vision. Neither did its partners in Europe … It is not obvious whether large-scale support would have brought about a different outcome in Russia. But, with hindsight, there is no question that not to try was a big mistake … The West must make a bold bid to support the next president of Russia with a very large and extended financial programme. The support must be unconditional and far removed from IMF bean counting' (Rudiger Dornbusch, *FT*, 23 September 1999, p. 30).

8. Jeffrey Sachs says that Russia started its reforms in January 1992 in 'dire financial conditions'. '[But] it took the West nearly eighteen months to grant Russia a debt standstill in the Paris Club and to grant it its first $600 million from the World Bank … The long delay of the G7 was nearly fatal. By failing to move early on, the West left the Russian reformers confused and anxious to find political allies among the old guard. In the middle of 1992 they vainly tried to compromise with so-called centrist forces representing parts of the old *nomenklatura* … To date, the Western world in its entirety has provided less grant aid to Russia in two years than the US alone provides to Egypt each year' (*The Independent*, 11 October 1993, p. 18). ('Western governments and international aid institutions missed their greatest chance for influence in 1992, when they failed to provide financial backing to the inexperienced and largely honest reformers led by prime minister Yegor Gaidar. Because of the lack of outside support and poor economic conditions, Boris Yeltsin felt he had to compromise with the corrupt old guard. Most of the reformers were pushed from power and by the end of 1992 the apparatchiks had seized control of the central bank and much of the government': Jeffrey Sachs, *IHT*, 6 December 1995, p. 10.)

Jeffrey Sachs and Charles Wyplosz argue that foreign aid can be crucial for stabilization. It helps the government pay the bills (such as for social programmes) in a non-inflationary way, while it also fosters government unity, increases public confidence in the reforms and signals that the government has staying power. The reformers did badly in the election of 12 December 1993. 'They were undone by government inconsistencies and inaction – not by too much reform.' The West had failed to help push through basic improvements in the economy and to help finance an adequate social safety net. Sachs and Wyplosz suggest that Western governments should provide about 4 per cent of Russian GNP ($14 billion) in quick-disbursing funds for socially orientated projects such as housing for the military, support for targeted social relief and funds to close coal mines and compensate miners and their families. The programmes should be monitored by G7 governments rather than the IMF. Another $8 billion – from the World Bank, the EBRD and the export credit agencies – could support long-term industrial restructuring, with investment funds and programmes for promoting small businesses. The IMF would make available $6 billion in loans subject to normal conditions, but it would not have the overall lead or be able to block disbursement of other funds. 'Payment of less than one-tenth of 1 per cent of Western GNP, or $14 billion, is surely the most important investment in Russia's democratic future and, thus, in Western security' (*FT*, 11 January 1994, p. 17).

Sachs (1995: 60) returned to the attack later on, claiming that 'Not only the Russian economy, but also Russian democracy has been put recklessly at risk by Western neglect.' The Western effort has failed at three levels:

a. 'The Marshall Plan architects had one brilliant insight that is missing today: the purpose of economic assistance is *political*, to support fragile democratic regimes attempting to implement more basic reforms' (p. 60). 'Fragile regimes are likely to collapse before they can implement needed market reforms if aid is not present as a *temporary* support' (p. 61). One of the basic principles of aid-giving in general is that it should be limited in time to no more than five consecutive years, since the goal is to bolster fragile governments and not to finance economic development. Some cases where serious reversals occur may merit throwing out another aid lifeline, however, if a new reformist government takes power at a later date (p. 61).

b. The sums have been derisory. In the fiscal year 1995 Russia would receive roughly $380 million in US aid. This was about one-sixth of US aid to Egypt or roughly 0.005 per cent of US GDP (compared with Marshall Plan commitments to Europe in fiscal year 1949 of 2 per cent of GDP).

c. The USA has failed almost entirely in leading a co-ordinated Western effort to aid Russia. Virtually all Western 'aid' has come in the form of export credits to Russian enterprises, with short periods for repayment, rather than in the form of grants and long-term loans to the Russian budget (almost all the Marshall Plan support was in the form of grants). Repayments of these loans have been straining the Russian budget. Overall support from Western governments for the budget, vitally needed for stabilization, has been essentially nil. Very little co-ordination of the G7 aid packages ($24 billion announced in 1992 and $28 billion in 1993) was ever undertaken to bring those packages to fruition. In 1994 there was essentially a complete collapse in US attempts to mobilize international assistance, and the IMF and World Bank have proved to be hugely inefficient (pp. 60–1).

Jeffrey Sachs and Charles Wyplosz (*FT,* 11 January 1994, p. 17) are very critical of the Western aid effort and of the IMF in particular. 'The Western aid effort for Russia has been a debâcle. Over the past two years much aid has been promised but very little has been delivered. Technical assistance and food aid aside, almost no programmes have taken off.' Reformers consequently suffered at the polls. As early as 1991 Western governments sought to avoid budgetary responsibility for Russia's reforms by assigning the lead role to the IMF, 'a cautious, narrowly focused bureaucracy ill-suited for a task needing breadth of vision and risk-taking'. The West promised a $28 billion package for 1993, of which about $5 billion was actually delivered. Some $13 billion was to come from the IMF, of which $1.5 billion arrived; $3 billion was to come from the World Bank, of which $600 million arrived. Most of what actually came was in the form of export credits, which were of very limited use for the reforms.

In an article in the *IHT* (24 January 1994, p. 4) Sachs continued his attack on the IMF and the World Bank. 'The financial crisis left behind by the communist regime was too deep. The reformers could not win without outside help, but help never arrived, and the reformers paid the price, losing badly in the December elections.' Sachs estimates that of the roughly $18 billion that the IMF and the World Bank were to lend to Russia in 1993, only $2 billion was handed over. The main goals of financial policy, he maintains, should have been to reduce the budget deficit, to float new government debt on the domestic market in order to cover the budget deficit without printing new money, to staunch the flow of cheap government loans to weak industries and to establish a separate Russian currency so that Russia could pursue a monetary policy independent of its neighbours. At the same time international grants and loans should have been provided to help the government pay its bills. 'The IMF failed miserably in advising the Group of Seven countries and the Yeltsin administration on Russia's financial reconstruction. It discouraged Russia from rapidly introducing a separate national currency. For two years it downplayed Russia's need and ability to issue domestic Treasury bonds, focusing nearly all its efforts on pressuring the Russians to make politically impossible cuts in the budget deficit. It advised Russia against the stabilization of the rouble exchange rate and held back a rouble stabilization fund designed to support such a policy. Most remarkably, it never acknowledged the urgency of mobilizing international assistance to help Russia finance its deficit. The IMF's relentless advice was to cut the deficit, not to find acceptable and non-inflationary ways to finance part of it.'

Sachs believes that the World Bank also failed in its most important task, namely to help finance a viable social support system.

In an article in the *FT* (31 March 1994, p. 21) Sachs continued in the same vein. 'IMF incantations of budget cutting and tight monetary policy are insufficient. Almost no stabilization programme in history has worked the way the IMF recommends in Russia. Real stabilization programmes ... start from the proposition that a country needs a stable convertible currency as the *first* step towards ending high inflation, not the last. After currency stability is achieved, and inflation is lowered as a direct result, then cuts in the budget become politically and economically more likely.' To achieve such a stable currency typically requires large-scale help from the outside world to back the currency and to help finance the budget deficit, as well as immediate relief on debt servicing. 'The foreign help should surely come together with significant deficit cutting, but well before the fundamental budgetary problems are fully resolved.' Sachs considers that the IMF blundered badly on these points. It delayed the introduction of a separate Russian currency in 1992, with the result that Russia was bombarded with inflation from the other states. 'The IMF has argued constantly against pegging the exchange rate until several months *after* inflation is ended, so guaranteeing a vicious circle of currency depreciation and rising deficits, not a virtuous circle of currency stability and falling budget deficits. The IMF has failed to mobilize international assistance to help Russia fund its budget deficit. Russia went into default in January 1992, but the Russian government did not receive its first working capital loan, from the World Bank (for $600 million), until nearly eighteen months later. Even debt service relief is not fully in place.'

CHAPTER NINE

ECONOMIC PERFORMANCE, HEALTH AND THE ENVIRONMENT

ECONOMIC PERFORMANCE

GDP growth rates were negative from 1990 to 1996 inclusive. There were a number of false dawns before 1997, the year when (modest) positive growth returned. The Asian financial crisis (which began in July 1997) in general and the Russian financial crisis of August 1998 in particular sent the economy into reverse in 1998. The hyperinflation of 1992 was conquered and by 1997 the inflation rate was not much into double figures. The 1998 inflation rate was not too bad since increases in the money supply were held in reasonable check. The typical surplus on the balance of payments on current account has been a bright spot in a generally bleak overall economic performance. (See Table 9.1.)

There was a return to negative growth in 1998, but in 1999 (in contrast to early forecasts) GDP growth turned decidedly positive owing to such factors as the large depreciation of the rouble and rapidly rising world oil prices.[1] Inflation did not take off. (See Chapter 7.)

In 1999 GDP was an estimated 57 per cent of the 1989 level (EBRD 2000b: 65).

'Russia ... has fallen from fourth place in terms of GDP in 1913 to fifteenth place in 1999; in terms of GDP *per capita* we currently rank 101st' (Pyotr Aven, *Kommersant*, 29 February 2000, p. 8; *CDSP*, 2000, vol. 52, no. 12, p. 13).

Inflation

By way of comparison with Russia's record on inflation, during the German inflation of 1922–23 the average inflation rate was 322 per cent a month or 40 per cent a week (*RET*, 1992, vol. 1, no. 3, p. 16). The monthly peak in Germany was 45,213 per cent in October 1923.

The annual rate of inflation in Russia peaked in 1992, at around 1,500 per cent. In the year to December 1992 it was even higher at 2,500 per cent (*FT*, Survey, 9 April 1997, p. ii). The highest monthly inflation rate was 245.3 per cent in January 1992. (See Tables 9.1 and 9.2.)

Table 9.1 Russia: selected economic indicators 1990–1999

Economic indicator	1990	1991	1992	1993	1994	1995	1996	1997	1998	1999
Rate of growth of GDP (%)	−4.0	−5.0	−14.5	−8.7	−12.7	−4.1	−3.5	0.8	−4.6	3.2
Rate of growth of industrial output (%)	−0.1	−8.0	−18.0	−14.1	−20.9	−3.3	−4.0	1.9	−5.2	8.1
Rate of growth of agricultural output (%)	−3.6	−3.7	−9.0	−4.4	−12.0	−7.6	−5.1	0.1	−12.3	2.4
Inflation rate (consumer) (%)	5.3	100.3	1,526.0	875.0	311.4	197.7	47.8	14.7	27.6	86.1
Budget surplus or deficit (% GDO)[1]			−18.9	−7.3	−10.4	−6.0	−8.9	−7.6	−8.0	−1.0
Unemployment rate (end of year, %)[2]			4.7	5.5	7.5	8.9	10.0	11.2	13.3	12.3
Balance of payments (current account, $ billion)		4.100	−1.200	12.800	5.882	5.026	7.001	0.440	2.094	24.730
Foreign direct investment (net, $ billion)		0.100	0.800	0.682	0.500	1.663	1.665	4.036	1.734	0.746
Gross fixed investment			−41.5	−25.8	−26.0	−7.5	−19.3	−5.7	−8.6	1.4
Natural gas output (billion cubic metres)	641	643	641	619	607					
Oil output (million tonnes)	516	462	399	354	316				302	
Grain output (million tonnes)	116.7	89.1	106.9	99.1	81.3	63.5	76.0	89.0	47.9	54.7
Population (million) (Data as of 1 January of the following year)			148.7	148.4	148.3	148.0	147.5	147.1	146.4	145.7

1 General government balance: includes the federal, regional and local budgets and extrabudgetary funds and excludes transfers (EBRD)
2 United Nations Economic Commission for Europe: based on ILO definition, i.e. including all persons not having employment but actively seeking work

Sources: Various issues of *Russian Economic Trends*; European Bank for Reconstruction and Development, *Transition Report*; United Nations Economic Commission for Europe, *Economic Survey of Europe*; United Nations, *World Economic and Social Survey*; IMF, *World Economic Outlook*.

Table 9.2 Russia: monthly rate of inflation (%)

Month	1991	1992	1993	1994	1995	1996	1997	1998
January	6.2	245.3	25.8	17.9	17.8	4.1	2.3	
February	4.9	38.0	24.7	10.8	11.0	2.8	1.6	
March	6.3	29.9	20.1	7.4	8.9	2.8	1.4	
April	63.5	21.7	18.8	8.5	8.5	2.2	0.9	
May	3.0	12.0	18.1	6.9	7.9	1.6	0.9	
June	1.2	18.6	19.9	6.0	6.7	1.1	1.1	
July	0.6	10.6	22.4	5.3	5.4	0.8	0.9	
August	0.5	8.6	25.8	4.6	4.6	−0.3	−0.1	
September	1.1	11.5	23.1	7.7	4.5	0.3	−0.3	
October	3.5	22.9	19.5	15.0	4.7	1.2	0.2	
November	8.9	26.1	16.4	15.0	4.5	1.9		
December	12.1	25.4	12.5	16.4	3.2	1.4		

Source: Russian Economic Trends (various issues)

Output

There is considerable debate about the output figures, but Table 9.1 indicates that GDP growth was negative through 1996. 'Over the past three years Russia's output has declined by 38 per cent. The USA's fell by a mere 30 per cent in the Great Depression between 1930 and 1933' (*The Economist*, 15 January 1994, p. 71).

But there is considerable debate about what has happened to output once the 'black' economy is fully taken into account. (There is no standard term and 'black economy', 'grey economy', 'unrecorded economy', 'informal economy' and 'shadow economy' seem to be used interchangeably.) There are various estimates of the importance of the black economy:

1. A flourishing private economy in services and trade is under-reported and virtually untaxed. As a result, up to 40 per cent of the economy may not be taxed at all and GDP may be underestimated by as much as 15 per cent (Leyla Boulton, *FT*, Survey, 27 June 1994, p. ii).

2. 'Half of it [the economy] is a shadow economy' (Yuri Afanasyev, *Moscow News*, 30 December 1994–5 January 1995, p. 3).

3. According to the Washington-based Bureau of National Affairs, the 'black' economy accounts for 20 per cent of GDP (*Business Europa*, February–March 1995, p. 45).

4. Managers today have a strong incentive to under-report production to avoid paying taxes, while official GDP figures do not reflect what is happening in the new private sector. Guesses at how big the unrecorded economy may be begin at 25 per cent of official GDP and rise from there (*The Economist*, Survey, 8 April 1995, p. 14). The unrecorded economy may be at least half the size of the recorded economy (*The Economist*, 1 June 1996, p. 39). The black economy is

equivalent to perhaps 40 to 50 per cent of GDP (*The Economist*, 25 October 1997, p. 125).

5. 'The private sector is growing rapidly and the overall economy may be as much as 50 per cent larger than official statistics indicate' (Thane Gustavson and Daniel Yergin, *IHT*, 8 May 1995, p. 10).

6. Various estimates put the shadow economy in the range 20 per cent to 40 per cent of GDP (*Moscow News*, 26 May–1 June 1995, p. 9).

7. 'About 90 per cent of private sector income and about 40 per cent of all wages are never reported to Goskomstat and are therefore not reflected in the official reports of Russia's GDP… These unreported earnings are part of the informal economy, an economy that by now may be larger than the formal economy' (Sharma 1996: 112).

8. The current GDP calculations include an estimate for the shadow economy of approximately 22 per cent of GDP (*RET*, Monthly Update, 22 October 1996, p. 6).

9. It has been estimated that the shadow economy is 20 to 40 per cent as large as the 'open economy' (*CDSP*, 1996, vol. XLVIII, no. 44, p. 1).

10. 'The shadow economy is at least equal to the legal one' (Boris Fyodorov, *IHT*, 28 July 1999, p. 9).

Trends in total and industrial output

There have been a number of false dawns as regards the sustained recovery of total output and industrial output:

1. 'After four years of sharp fall in GDP, the decline in output appears to have bottomed out' (Anders Åslund, *IHT*, 24 April 1995, p. 8). 'The Russian recession apparently levelled off in the first quarter of 1995' (OECD, *Economic Outlook*, June 1995, p. 111). 'Overall, and despite a poor harvest, the decline in GDP in 1995 will be much less pronounced than in recent years. Recorded output should grow slowly during 1996 and continue to rise in 1997, provided the momentum of progress with financial stabilization is maintained and in the absence of major adverse political shocks' (OECD, *Economic Outlook*, December 1995, pp. 109–111). 'The great Russian depression … appears to be bottoming out (Thane Gustavson and Daniel Yergin, *IHT*, 8 May 1995, p. 10).

2. Industrial production ceased to fall during the summer of 1994 (*RET*, Monthly Update, 17 November 1994, p. 3). Real industrial production has been fairly steady since October 1994 (on a seasonally adjusted basis) (*RET*, Monthly Update, 14 April 1995, p. 9). Industrial production (seasonally adjusted) improved slightly in October 1995. But in general it has remained roughly stable since June 1994, fluctuating around 55 per cent of the December 1991 level (*RET*, Monthly Update, 15 December 1995, p. 9). The decrease in industrial production stopped in June 1994 (Deutsche Bank, *Focus: Eastern Europe*, 1994, no. 112, p. 3). Industrial output was more or less stable from the middle of 1994 until the autumn of 1995. After rising in May–August

1995, however, industrial production started to fall again in the fourth quarter of 1995 and for the whole year it fell by some 3 per cent (United Nations Economic Commission for Europe 1996: 65).

Electricity consumption and national income

There is a debate about the extent to which electricity consumption is a better guide to what is happening to output as a whole than official estimates of GDP:

Åslund (1994b: 66) says that electricity consumption is universally closely correlated with real GDP. In 1992 official GDP in Russia fell by 19 per cent, but electricity consumption declined by only 6 per cent. In 1993 the respective decreases were 12 per cent and 5 per cent. 'The latter figures probably reflect the development of the economy more accurately, indicating that the depression of the Russian economy is wildly exaggerated' (p. 66). This becomes all the more evident when consumption is considered. 'Private consumption has started rising as a share of GDP from a paltry 40 per cent ... real income rose by no less than 9 per cent [in 1993]' (p. 66).

Critics of this line of argument include the following:

1. '[Åslund makes] no mention is made of the possibility that high electricity consumption may merely reflect waste. Estonia ... has managed to reduce electricity consumption by considerably more than the corresponding decline in GDP, an indication of the results that a true success story would have to generate.' Moreover, 'at least some of the output decline is real, most importantly the decline in oil production ... Aggregate investment in 1994 may be a full 70 per cent below the 1990 level. It is hard not to call that a collapse' (DIW, *Economic Bulletin*, December 1994, vol. 31, no. 12, p. 1).

2. Valeri Markov and Alexander Bulatov dismiss electricity statistics as indicators of aggregate industrial production because most electricity is used for household and municipal consumption and prices remain controlled (cited in *Comparative Economic Studies*, 1994, vol. XXXVI, no. 4, p. 42).

3. The weaker the statistical system the more useful electricity consumption as a measure of economic activity becomes. But it assumes constant ratios between electricity use and value added, and these may have changed a lot, in either direction, during the transition. In Eastern Europe the efficiency of electricity use may have risen, but this is perhaps less intuitively clear in the case of the CIS countries, where the payment discipline for electricity is weak (Kasper Bartholdy, *Transition*, 1995, vol. 6, no. 4, p. 3).

4. 'In some countries there may be solid grounds for refuting the assumption that the relationship between electricity use and value added has remained constant. In particular, certain countries, including Kazakhstan and Kyrgyzstan, have pursued a relative price policy which has led to substitution of electricity for other sources of energy' (EBRD 1995b: 181, 183).

5. 'The remarkably small fall in electricity generation has elicited a variety of speculative interpretations: from a relative increase in unrecorded

production activity using electricity to suspicions that electricity output figures have been inflated. A reasonable guess, perhaps, is that the efficiency of energy use has in any case declined drastically as factories have been kept open (heated and lighted, and machinery maintained) while producing nothing or almost nothing' (Sutherland and Hanson 1996: 372–3).

Investment

There were massive falls in the volume of real investment even before the financial crisis of August 1998. A positive figure for the rate of growth of gross fixed investment was achieved only in 1999. (See Table 9.1.)

Aggregate investment in 1994 may be a full 70 per cent below the 1990 level. It is hard not to call that a collapse' (DIW, *Economic Bulletin*, December 1994, vol. 31, no. 12, p. 1).

Real investment is low and in 1994 it was a quarter down on the previous year. It would not appear to be due to an absolute shortage of funds. The problem is that investment is so risky that investors require an extremely high expected return (*RET,* Monthly Update, 21 March 1995, p. 3). Capital investment fell by 26 per cent in 1994 (*RET,* 1995, vol. 3, no. 4, p. 67). Investment in fixed capital fell by 18 per cent in 1996 and by 5 per cent in 1997 (*RET,* Monthly Update, 30 January 1998, p. 8).

In 1994 Russians saved an amount equal to 33 per cent of GDP, but in Russia an amount equal to only 16 per cent of GDP was invested (*The Economist*, Survey, 8 April 1995, p. 15).

In real terms gross fixed investment in 1997 was a mere quarter of its 1991 level (United Nations Economic Commission for Europe 1998c: 36).

'Since 1991 investment has run at about one third of replacement levels' (*FT,* 30 August 2000, p. 18).

'We contend that the present stabilization in Russia is not sufficient for a resumption of growth. Economic recovery requires that enterprises *invest* in such growth-orientated as restructuring and entry into new activities. The problem is that uncertainty over the durability of financial stabilization and other macroeconomic conditions in Russia might cause investors to postpone such activity until some of this uncertainty is resolved … When sunk (or irreversible) costs are associated with uncertainty over future outcomes there is an option value to waiting … In transition investment in restructuring and new activities is typically associated with high levels of sunk costs … This is especially the case in Russia. Institutions that are key to the market system remain underdeveloped … in particular the legal system … The costs that new firms incur in trying to establish new relationships are typically "sunk"; that is, they cannot be recovered should the new relationship prove unsuitable … Firms find informal profit-seeking more advantageous … activities that produce wealth for management without generating official profits … they typically involve trade of traditional products with traditional trading partners and not the development of new activities' (Ickes *et al.* 1997: 106–7).

'Last year [1999] investment rose for the first time since the transition began, albeit by a modest 2 per cent. Not much when you consider it has plunged by 75 per cent over the past decade. But remarkable, given that Russian firms have plenty of overcapacity, and some big foreign debt repayments drained money from the economy last year... There are certainly signs of restructuring ... Even outside big money areas like oil and telecoms, there are tentative signs that companies are restructuring' (*Business Central Europe*, March 2000, p. 15).

In 1999 investment in fixed assets rose by 1 per cent (*CDSP*, 2000, vol. 52, no. 11, p. 17).

'The financial condition of the enterprise sector has been improving ... Investment increased by 12 per cent in the first half of 2000, up from 4.5 per cent in 1999' (EBRD 2000b: 203).

Structural change

Services have increased in importance at the expense of manufacturing industry. In 1994 services accounted for half of GDP, compared with one-third in 1990 (*Transition*, January–February 1995, p. 20). In 1995 services accounted for about 53 per cent of GDP, compared with 43 per cent in 1993 (*RET*, Monthly Update, 15 December 1995, p. 9). The service sector now accounts for half of officially recorded GDP (*The Economist*, Survey, 8 April 1995, p. 14).

The Russian economy has undergone considerable structural change with little net investment. The investment share of output has fallen steeply and there has been a shift in favour of services, farm output and primary or extractive industries (and against the branches of manufacturing that involve more extensive processing) (Sutherland and Hanson 1996: 378).

The share of imported goods in retail sales peaked at 53 per cent in 1995. The figure was 49 per cent in the third quarter of 1997 (*RET*, Monthly Update, 30 January 1998, p. 4). In 1995 domestic production of consumer goods fell to 48 per cent of its 1991 level and was still shrinking at the start of 1996. The market share of imports has soared from an average of 12 per cent in 1991 to 56 per cent in 1995, by official reckonings. When smuggled goods and 'personal imports' are added the true proportion of foreign consumer goods is probably higher still (*The Economist*, 13 April 1996, pp. 71–2).

Unemployment

Several figures appear in Table 9.3, including one column calculated according to the definition used by the International Labour Organization (ILO). Unemployment is a mainly urban phenomenon and women fare much

Table 9.3 Russia: unemployment

Date		*'Out of employment'*		*'Registered'*		*ILO concept*
		No.	*%*	*No.*	*%*	*%*
1991	July	351,000		16,000		
	December	469,000	0.6	62,000	0.1	
1992	January	485,000		69,000		
	July	843,000		248,000	0.4	
	December	982,000	1.4	578,000	0.8	
1993	January	1,029,000	1.5	628,000	0.9	4.9
	July	989,000		717,000	1.0	5.2
	December	1,085,000	1.5	836,000	1.1	5.7
1994	January	1,165,000	1.6	894,000		5.9
	July	1,581,000		1,324,000		7.2
	December	1,878,000	2.5	1,637,000	2.2	7.5
1995	January	1,963,000	2.6	1,710,000		7.7
	July	2,394,000	3.0	2,048,000		8.3
	December	2,642,000	3.2			8.9
1996	January				3.3	10.1
	July				3.5	9.3
	December				3.4	9.3
1997	January				3.5	10.1
	July				3.1	10.9
	December				2.8	11.2
1998	January				2.7	11.4
	July				2.5	11.3
	December				2.7	12.4

Source: Russian Economic Trends (various issues)

worse than men. At the end of 1992, for example, 72 per cent of the unemployed were female (*RET*, 1993, vol. 2, no. 1, pp. 45, 48; no. 4, pp. 60–1). Women and young people accounted for two-thirds of the unemployed in 1994 (*Transition*, January–February 1995, p. 21). Long-term unemployment is a growing problem. In March 1993 2 per cent of the unemployed had been out of work for more than a year and 42 per cent for more than four months. As of December 1994 the respective figures had reached 17 per cent and 50 per cent (*RET*, 1995, vol. 3, no. 4, p. 87).

Unemployment benefit for redundant workers lasts for fifteen months on a sliding scale: for three months they get 100 per cent of their former money wage (from their employers); then (from the Employment Service) 75 per cent for the next three months, 60 per cent for the next four months and 45 per cent for the next five months. After that they can get 'material assistance' of not more than the minimum wage. With high inflation the real value of benefit fell rapidly. Consequently, most unemployed people receive the minimum wage, which is the minimum guaranteed level of unemployment benefit. All unemployed people not made redundant by a former employer are entitled to the minimum wage, which has fluctuated around 10 per cent of the average wage (*RET*, 1994, vol. 3, no. 2, pp. 48–9).

Those 'out of employment' must be registered with a local office of the Federal Employment Service to receive benefit. From September 1992 onwards redundant workers were automatically included in the more restrictive 'registered unemployment' category as long as they registered with the FES, but they do not receive benefit during the first three months of unemployment because they are still being paid by their former employers (*RET*, 1993, vol. 2, no. 1, pp. 45, 48; no. 4, pp. 60–1).

The figures for 'out of employment' and 'registered' unemployment are considered to be too low to be meaningful. The unemployment numbers may be biased downward. Firstly, those who do not register with the FES are not counted. (The advantages of registration are generally quite low, since the average level of benefit for those eligible is poor. On the other hand, workers may be reluctant to dissociate themselves from their enterprises because of non-cash benefits such as housing, subsidized meals and health services.) Secondly, an estimated 9 per cent of the industrial work force at the end of 1992 were working (often involuntarily) reduced hours (*RET*, 1993, vol. 2, no. 1, pp. 45, 48; no. 4, pp. 60–1). Some examples of other estimates of unemployment using different definitions are as follows:

1. According to the methodology used by the International Labour Organization (those out of work and actively seeking employment), 3.8 million were unemployed (5 per cent of the active population). If the 'partially' ('potentially') unemployed had been included (i.e. people who would have been laid off in other countries), the figure would have gone up to 7.8 million or 10.4 per cent (*Izvestiya*, 21 December 1993, p. 1).

2. As of June 1994 4.5 million people or 6 per cent of the labour force were unemployed using ILO methodology. Another 6 per cent were employed part-time or 'on leave' without pay or with partial pay. Thus the 'total potential unemployment' was 12 per cent of the economically active population (*CDSP*, 1994, vol. XLVI, no. 32, p. 13).

3. The unemployment rate is 7.1 per cent, but if the partially unemployed are taken into account the rate rises to 13.5 per cent (*Transition*, January–February 1995, p. 21).

4. At the end of 1996 the unemployment rate calculated in accordance with ILO norms was 9.3 per cent. According to Goskomstat, hidden unemployment at the beginning of January 1997 (i.e. those on short-time work and administrative leave) was 8 per cent of the labour force (*RET*, Monthly Update, 17 March 1997, p. 9).

5. Guy Standing of the ILO has recalculated the figures, recording all those on short working hours and unpaid leave as unemployed, and comes up with a rate (excluding agriculture) of 35 per cent (*The Economist*, 18 February 1995, p. 90). According to Standing, more than a third of the industrial work force is 'suppressed' unemployed (*FT*, 6 February 1997, p. 2).

The consequences of closing down loss-making enterprises would be serious indeed. According to official calculations, 25 million Russians would be thrown out of work if subsidies to loss-making enterprises were eliminated (*Newsbrief*, January 1994, vol. 14, no. 1, p. 2). If all the unprofitable enterprises were to shut down at once, at least 50 per cent of the adult population would be thrown out of work (Deutsche Bank, *Focus: Eastern Europe*, 1994, no. 104, p. 6).

Wage arrears and industrial unrest

In March 1994 accumulated wage arrears amounted to some 40 per cent of the monthly wage bill in industry, construction and agriculture (*RET*, Monthly Update, 30 April 1994, p. 3). In the first quarter of 1994 wage arrears roughly equalled two weeks' wages (*RET*, 1994, vol. 3, no. 1, p. 37). At the end of the third quarter of 1994 arrears as a percentage of the wage bill were 44 per cent in industry, 85 per cent in agriculture and 26 per cent in construction (*RET*, 1994, vol. 3, no. 3, p. 50). In 1995 an average of 28 per cent of all firms were experiencing wage arrears at any one time, compared with 48 per cent in 1994 (*RET*, 1995, vol. 4, no. 4, p. 53). Wage arrears rose during 1996 and by the end of the year were the equivalent of about one month's total wage bill. The arrears remained concentrated in coal mining and education but seemed to be spreading more widely in manufacturing (*RET*, 1997, no. 1, pp. 4, 71).

At the beginning of 1994 the total amount of overdue pay was almost 800 billion roubles; employees of 24,000 enterprises had not received their pay by the established dates (*CDSP*, 1994, vol. XLVI, no. 29, p. 7). As of 1 August 1994 the sum had risen to 3,800 billion roubles: more than 20 million people at 34,000 enterprises were involved (*CDSP*, 1994, vol. XLVI, no. 33, p. 22).

A survey was published in December 1996. Only 30 per cent of wages were paid in full and on time in 1996, some 31 per cent of wages were delayed and 39 per cent of workers were not paid at all. (The respective figures for 1995 were 45 per cent, 38 per cent and 17 per cent.) High-ranking officials and managers, white-collar workers and the inhabitants of Moscow, St Petersburg and the European North were more likely to get paid on time, while manual workers and those living in rural areas, the far east and Siberia had their salaries delayed (*Transition*, 1996, vol. 7, nos 11–12, p. 28).

'The wages arrears of central and local governments are now 20 per cent of all wage arrears' (*RET*, Monthly Update, 16 December 1996, p. vii).

Some arrears have been paid off periodically before building up again, e.g. state pension arrears were paid by 1 July 1997. On 8 July 1997 Yeltsin promised that wage arrears to the armed forces would be paid by 1 September 1997 and to all other state employees by the end of 1997. The former promise was kept but Yeltsin reckoned that the government failed to achieve the latter goal. The figures show that the authorities failed to pay back all budget sector wage arrears by the end of 1997, but they did manage to cut the stock by more than half by year-end. Most of these wages were due from regional governments, but the federal government loaned regional governments half of the sum needed to pay back the arrears. Regional governments were obliged to find the remaining funds themselves (*RET*, 1998, no. 1, p. 44). Total wage arrears reached 57 billion roubles ($9.51 billion) as of 1 March 1998, of which the federal and local governments owed 7.6 billion ($1.2 billion). As regards the 1 January 1998 deadline, the government claimed that it had pieced together the funds but that regional authorities were to blame when some workers remained unpaid. Wage arrears had begun to grow rapidly in mid-1995. The level of arrears in March 1997 reached 27.7 per cent of total state sector wages. Many workers were waiting six to eight months for their wages. More than half of employees in state enterprises were claiming at least two months' wages (*Transition*, 1998, vol. 9, no. 2, p. 6).

Åslund says that in August 1993 only 56 per cent of workers polled had received their latest monthly wage in full and on time. Nevertheless, apart from coal miners, Russian workers rarely strike, even when they have not been paid for months. Nor are workers likely to strike, because they lack both organization and leaders. Real wages seem perfectly flexible. Workers are kept on the payroll for these reasons and because they are a useful pawn in negotiations with the authorities over subsidies (1994b: 67).

Industrial action remains negligible by Western standards, with 1,366,300 man days lost through strikes in 1995 compared with 94,375 in 1994 (*RET*, Monthly Update, 13 February 1996, p. 12; *RET*, 1995, vol. 4, no. 4, p. 95). But the number of strikes, mostly in response to wage arrears, was higher in December 1996 than in the whole of 1995. These strikes were concentrated in coal mining and education (*RET*, 1997, no. 1, pp. 4, 71). Although over 40 per cent of workers were not receiving wages on time by late 1996, less than 1 per cent of workers went on strike in that year (*RET*, Monthly Update, 24 October 1997, p. viii).

Unemployment and wage flexibility

The figures are for unemployment are relatively low considering what has happened to output and explanations have been given:

1. Real wages seem perfectly flexible. Workers are kept on the payroll for these reasons and because they are a useful pawn in negotiations with the authorities over subsidies (Anders Åslund 1994b: 67). 'The labour market remains highly flexible, with one-quarter of workers changing jobs each year' (Anders Åslund, *IHT*, 24 April 1995, p. 8).

2. Richard Layard argues that the labour market is both very buoyant and remarkably flexible. Its buoyancy is reflected in the large number of new jobs being created, while its flexibility stems from the fact that employees are willing to accept much lower real wages rather than lose their jobs. Even in declining sectors enterprises are paying their workers less and sending them

on unpaid leave rather than sacking them. Because unemployment benefit is so low and social services (such as schools and clinics) are often attached to enterprises, it makes sense for the worker to stay. The enterprise gains by not having to pay redundancy money and by the fact that cheap labour helps mitigate the effects of the excess wage tax (*The Economist*, 18 February 1995, p. 90).

Living standards

Apart from falls in living standards there has been increasing inequality in the distribution of income and wealth.

A study conducted by the International Labour Organization in 1996 concluded that 'There should be no pretence. The Russian economy and the living standards of the Russian population have suffered the worst peacetime setbacks of any industrialized nation in history' (*FT*, 26 March 1997, p. 2). Nevertheless, there is considerable controversy about what has happened to living standards:

1. Lipton and Sachs (1992: 220–2) dispute the common assertion that real living standards fell by around 50 per cent. They argue that price liberalization basically restored wage-price relations that had prevailed before the 1987 changes in enterprise autonomy, without representing an actual fall in living standards. Over the period 1985 to December 1991 average industrial real wages increased by 79 per cent. But because the supply of consumer goods grew little if at all, and certainly not commensurately with the increase in rouble wages, excess demand developed. There were price controls and, therefore, intensifying shortages and lengthening queues in official markets and inflation in black markets. The statistical real wage was thereby disconnected from actual living standards. If anything an inverse relationship occurred; higher real wages resulted in longer queues and thereby a loss of work and leisure time. The costs in terms of lower living standards are exaggerated (p. 246). Even if the reforms *per se* do not reduce living standards sharply, the backdrop is still one of a falling trend in such key sectors as energy. An income squeeze resulting from trends that preceded the reforms might be widely blamed on the reforms themselves. Also it is likely to be the case that income inequality has risen as a result of the reforms, with pensioners probably being squeezed relative to younger workers (pp. 247–8).
2. The United Nations (*World Economic Survey 1993*, p. 33) adds that surveys indicate that nearly half the working population now hold more than one job, often in the growing non-state and informal sectors which are not reported in the official data. Thus the officially measured 50 per cent fall in average real wages in the year to December 1992 is an overstatement.
3. *The Economist* (6 February 1993, pp. 35–6) notes that the average wage buys only 60 per cent of what it could buy before the January 1992 price liberalization and is lower in real terms than the average wage in 1985. But

this ignores the previous shortages. The average standard of living may not have fallen by as much as is claimed, but fallen it has, especially for the old and unemployed' (p. 35). There has been a halving of living standards over the past year (*The Economist*, 1 May 1993, p. 13).

4. 'While the big boys ... fight over an ever larger piece of the Russian economic pie, the government has been unable to create economic conditions in which the majority of Russians can thrive. The problem is not only that the majority of Russians remain worse off than before the economic transition began, but that they cannot become better off. The economy is stagnating at half its 1989 level. Real incomes have fallen by a third and living standards in most regions have deteriorated to levels not seen in decades ... The current Russian market economy has created a handful of super-wealthy individuals while leaving the rest behind to struggle ... The current level of consumption ... for the majority of the population means semi-pauperhood' (Yavlinsky 1998: 70–1).

5. Since the reform began there has been a severe fall in living standards. The measured after-tax real wage is now roughly three-quarters of its level in 1985 and about half its unsustainably high level in 1991. Compared with 1985 the average pension has fallen by a quarter relative to the average wage. In November 1992 about 30 per cent of the population had incomes below the 'physiological minimum' level of living (*RET*, 1993, vol. 2, no. 1, pp. 5, 32). Taking all factors into account living standards fell by roughly 20 per cent in 1991–93 (although living standards actually rose slightly in 1993) (*RET*, 1993, vol. 2, no. 4, p. 32).

6. The real income of the population during the first half of 1994 was 10 per cent higher than one year earlier. A new class of 'super rich' is emerging in Russia, but the share of the population below the minimum subsistence level has been falling (from an average of 31 per cent in the first half of 1993 to 17 per cent in the first half of 1994) (*RET*, 1994, vol. 3, no. 2, p. 41). Real incomes grew by 16 per cent during 1994 (compared with 10 per cent in 1993), although real incomes were still some 30 per cent below pre-reform levels. Over the year 24 per cent of the population received incomes below an official subsistence level of income, compared with 31 per cent in 1993 (*RET*, 1995, vol. 3, no. 4, p. 46). During 1995 measured real wages were 27 per cent lower than in 1994. But this ignores factors such as understatements to avoid tax and inadequate account of the private sector. The fall in real incomes was only 13 per cent owing to the increasing importance of non-wage sources of income such as dividends and returns from small-scale retail activity (*RET*, 1995, vol. 4, no. 4, p. 49). Some 27 per cent of the population fell below the poverty line (a 'minimum subsistence' basket of goods), compared with 26 per cent in 1996 (p. 53). The degree of measured inequality has declined. People in the bottom 20 per cent of the income distribution received 6.5 per cent of total incomes in 1996, up from 5.5 per cent in 1995. In addition, the percentage of people below the poverty line continued its steady decline and now stands at 18 per

cent (*RET*, 1997, no. 1, p. 4). According to Goskomstat statistics, the share of the population living below subsistence level was 21 per cent in both 1996 and 1997 (*RET*, 1998, no. 1, p. 46). In the first quarter of 1999 37 per cent of 1999 lived in families with a *per capita* income below the official subsistence level (*RET*, 1999, vol. 8, no. 2, p. 40).

7. 'Its [Russia's] economy and standard of living are almost twice as high as officially reported, and they have been growing since 1994 ... Most Russians have been experiencing an improved standard of living since 1994' (Sharma 1996: 111–13).

8. In 1994 about 23 per cent of the population had money incomes below the minimum subsistence level. Russians with the highest incomes had fifteen times as much as the lowest. In 1993 the ratio was 11:1 and in 1991 it was 4.5:1 (*Transition*, January–February 1995, p. 21).

9. The top 10 per cent of the population now earn fourteen times the income of the poorest 10 per cent, compared with 5.4 times three years ago (*FT*, 31 December 1995, p. 2).

10. According to the OECD, about 35 per cent of the population now live below the official poverty line compared with 21 per cent in 1997 (*FT*, Survey, 10 May 2000, p. ii).

HEALTH

The population of Russia has fallen in recent years. At the end of 1992 the population was 148.6 million, while at the end of 1995 it was 148.0 million (EBRD 1997b: 233). In 1997 the population was 147 million. '[There was a] natural decrease of 4.2 million between 1992 and 1997' (*CDSP*, 1999, vol. 50, no. 49, p. 16). The population in October 1998 was 146.4 million (*Transition*, 1998, vol. 9, no. 6, p. 27). On 1 January 1999 the population was 146.3 million (*IHT*, 5 February 1999, p. 13). On 1 July 1999 the population was 145.9 million (*CDSP*, 1999, vol. 51, no. 35, p. 20). By the end of 1999 the total had fallen to 145.5 million (*Transition*, 2000, vol. 11, no. 1, p. 32).

Between 1989 and 1994 Russia's crude death rate rose from 10.7 to 15.5 per thousand (Chen *et al.* 1996: 518). The death rate was 14.6 per thousand in 1993, a rise compared with the 1992 figure of 12.2. The birth rate, on the other hand, fell from 10.7 per thousand in 1992 to 9.2 in 1993 (*RET*, 1993, vol. 2, no. 4, p. 41). 'In today's Russia the death rate for men of working age (sixteen to fifty-nine) is higher than it was 100 years ago. If the death rate for men continues at its present level, no more than half of today's sixteen-year-olds will survive to the age of sixty. But 100 years ago and earlier (in 1889–97) the probability that males who had reached the age of sixteen would live to be sixty was 56 per cent' (*Sevodnya*, 13 May 1997, p. 2; reprinted in *CDSP*, 1997, vol. XLIX, no. 19, p. 8). The infant mortality rate increased from 17.4 per thousand in 1990 to 19.1 per thousand in 1993 (*FT*, 14 February 1994, p. 1).

The figures for life expectancy are also startling:

1. By the end of 1993 male life expectancy had fallen to just fifty-nine years, putting Russia on a par with India and Egypt (*The Economist*, 9 July 1994, p. 40).

2. The figure of fifty-nine years in 1993 compares with the 1980s peak of sixty-five in 1987 (61.45 in 1979–80): 'This steep and rapid decline is a remarkable demographic phenomenon. By 1993 male life expectancy at birth in Russia had fallen below the level of the medium income countries and had probably fallen to a level about that of Indonesia in the second half of the 1980s' (Ellman 1994: 334, 351–2).

3. Between 1990 and 1994 life expectancy for men fell from sixty-four to fifty-eight years and for women from seventy-four to seventy-one years. In 1995 men's life expectancy remained static, while women's actually rose by a year (Nicholas Barr, *Finance and Development*, 1996, vol. 33, no. 3, p. 26).

4. In 1994 male life expectancy was 58.3 years (Alexei Yablokov, *The Economist*, 29 April 1995, p. 10).

5. Average life expectancy in Russia has fallen to levels lower than those found in many developing countries with relatively high mortality, such as Bangladesh. 'Other than the dramatic losses of life due to famine or war, contemporary history offers no precedents for this type of crisis.' Over the period 1990 to 1994 the number of 'excess deaths' (the number of deaths above what would have occurred had the pre-crisis level of mortality remained unchanged) totalled 1.3 million in the former Soviet Union (no separate estimate is provided for Russia alone) (Chen *et al.* 1996: 517). Between 1989 and 1994 life expectancy at birth fell from 64.2 to 57.7 years for men and from 74.5 to 71.3 years for women. (By 1965 Soviet life expectancy had approximated that of Japan and the USA: p. 519.) Hardest hit have been adult men between twenty-five and fifty-nine years of age. The predominant causes of the excess deaths are cardiovascular diseases (heart attacks and strokes) and injuries (homicide, suicide and alcohol poisoning) (p. 518).

6. Life expectancy reached a low of 64.1 years in 1994, with a huge differential between that of women (71) men (57.4) (*FT*, Survey, 10 May 2000, p. vii).

7. In 1995 life expectancy increased by one year to sixty-five (*The Economist*, 3 August 1996, p. 40).

8. Male life expectancy decreased from 64.2 years in 1989 to 57.6 years in 1994, partially recovering to 60.9 years in 1997 (EBRD 1999b: 7).

9. Average life expectancy for men was 57.7 years in 1994. In 1998 the figure was 61.8 years (Anders Åslund, *IHT*, 19 January 2000, p. 8).

10. The Russian Academy of Medical Sciences says that overall life expectancy fell by one year in 1999 to 65.5 years (59.8 for men and seventy-two for women). The death rate was 14.7 per thousand, while the birth rate stood at 8.4 per thousand (the official figures for 1998 being, respectively, 13.6 and 8.8) (*The Guardian*, 25 October 2000, p. 20).

'Life expectancy at birth has been on the decline in Russia since the beginning of transition. The decline in life expectancy reflects the overall worsening of the health of the Russian population. Since the early 1990s there has been an increase in the incidence of almost all major illnesses, with the exception of respiratory illnesses. The number of people suffering from tuberculosis has almost doubled in all age groups ... Changes in life expectancy and health indicators depend both on changes in the quality of the health care system and on changes in lifestyle and ecology. In Russia GDP has been declining throughout the 1990s and the ecological situation has worsened. A substantial share of the population has been unable to support its previous lifestyle, and the spread of such diseases as tuberculosis and dysentery can be blamed on more lax hygiene controls following liberalization and privatization of food processing and trade ... The direct effects of changes in health care are best calculated by looking at infant and child mortality rates, which are reckoned to correlate more closely than other health indicators with the quality of health care. The pattern of changes in infant and child mortality rates in Russia was completely different from the countries of Central and Eastern Europe. At the end of the 1980s the child and infant mortality rate in Russia was comparable to the rate in Poland and Hungary. But in the 1990s child and infant mortality in Russia increased, while it almost halved in several Central and Eastern European countries ... In Russia ... there were no major, country-wide improvements of the health care system. On the contrary, some observers talk of a complete collapse of the Russian health care system in the 1990s ... The reform of the health care system was not limited to the creation of a compulsory and voluntary insurance system. It also legalized private health care institutions, both in the form of new private facilities and provision of paid services in otherwise public institutions. Private institutions, while being relatively expensive, are usually better equipped and provide higher quality services ... However ... the demand for private health care is quite low and is concentrated in rich areas, such as the city of Moscow. The share of the private sector in Russian health has remained very small ... Public expenditure on health care has declined by about 30 per cent in real terms since the beginning of transition and now constitutes a fairly modest amount by international standards both in *per capita* terms and as a percentage of GDP' (*RET*, Monthly Update, 14 July 1999, pp. 3–8).

THE ENVIRONMENT

The Russian environment minister revealed that about 15 per cent of Russia could be considered an environmental disaster zone. Some 100,000 people lived on land where radiation levels were too high. Half of Russia's 222 million ha of arable land was unsuitable for farming and only 20 per cent of industrial waste was adequately treated (*The Independent*, 28 December 1993, p. 7).

The chief environmental adviser to the president has said that between 14 per cent and 16 per cent of the Russian land mass can be considered environmental disaster zones, an area inhabited by roughly 40 million people. Some 40 per cent of the ground water supply is now heavily polluted. The official data show that 1.2 per cent to 1.3 per cent of oil going through pipelines is lost every year, but unofficial data suggest that the figure may be 2 per cent or even 3 per cent (Erik Ipsen, *IHT*, 24 April 1995, p. 6).

There have been disturbing reports about oil spills. For example, major environmental damage was caused by a leaking pipeline in the Komi republic, near Usinsk (300 km from the Arctic Ocean). It came to world attention in September 1994, but it looked as though the pipeline had been leaking badly since February 1994 (*CDSP*, 1994, vol. XLVI, no. 43, pp. 18–19). Losses due to broken pipes and defective plant are high. The Russian environment ministry cites an annual loss of 20 million tonnes of crude oil (Deutsche Bank, *Focus: Eastern Europe*, 1995, no. 126, p. 3).

A presidential decree of 17 May 2000 abolished the state committee for environmental protection and the federal forestry service. Both were incorporated into the ministry of natural resources. Critics claim that ministry of natural resources is more concerned with economic development than the environment.

NOTE

1 One source puts GDP growth at 5.4 per cent in 1999 and 8.3 per cent in 2000 (*RET*, Monthly Update, 30 July 2001, p. 2).

PART TWO

POLITICAL DEVELOPMENTS

CHAPTER TEN

THE DISSOLUTION OF THE SOVIET UNION

EVENTS PRIOR TO THE 19–21 AUGUST 1991 ABORTIVE COUP

The Gorbachev era saw moves towards political democracy, reflected, for example, in the following two state bodies:

1. *The Congress of People's Deputies* (CPD) (2,250 members). Although the initial vote (first round March 1989) was only partially free (two-thirds of seats directly elected and one-third reserved for social organizations such as the communist party and trade unions – these reserved seats were to go next time), a surprising number of independent and radical deputies were elected. Sessions were lively and open.

2. *The Supreme Soviet* (542 members). This was the standing body of the Congress of People's Deputies, divided into the Soviet (Council) of Nationalities and the Soviet of the Union. Gorbachev (unopposed) was elected 'President' (Chairman of the Supreme Soviet) on 25 May 1989.

Gorbachev's political strategy was to separate party and state and to increase the powers of state bodies at the expense of party ones. This process was taken a stage further under the new presidency, including the establishment of two presidential councils. The new presidency was approved by the Supreme Soviet on 27 February and by the CPD on 13 March 1990. The new-style president was to be popularly elected for five years, with a two-term limit. The exception to the popular vote was the first election: Gorbachev (unopposed) was actually elected President (until March 1995) by the CPD on 15 March 1990. The president could propose both the appointment and the sacking of key people, such as the premier, to the Supreme Soviet and the CPD. After considerable debate it was decided that if the Supreme Soviet overrode a presidential veto on legislation by a two-thirds majority then the president would be unable to appeal to the CPD. The issuing of presidential decrees had to be done on the basis of existing laws and had to be consistent with the constitution. The president could introduce a state of emergency in specific localities, with immediate submission to the Supreme Soviet for approval. Note that on 24 September 1990 the Supreme

Soviet granted Gorbachev powers to implement economic reform by presidential decree until 31 March 1992; he was able 'to give instructions on matters of property relations, organization of the management of the economy, the budget and financial system, pay and price formation, and the strengthening of law and order'. Two new councils were formed:

1. *The Presidential Council.* The Presidential Council played an advisory and policy presentational role, to the detriment of the party Politburo, in order to help implement Gorbachev's reform programme: its role was to 'work out measures to implement the cardinal planks of the domestic and foreign policy of the Soviet Union and to ensure the country's security'.

2. *The Council of the Federation.* The council comprised the presidents and prime ministers of the republics. The critical question here was the relationship between the republics and the federal state.

It is ironic that the swing to the right in the autumn of 1990 took place just as Gorbachev reached the pinnacle of international acclaim. On 15 October 1990 he was awarded the Nobel Peace Prize: 'For his leading role in the peace process which today characterizes important parts of the international community. During the last few years dramatic changes have taken place in the relationship between East and West. Confrontation has been replaced by negotiations. Old European nation states had regained their freedom. The arms race was slowing down and we [the Nobel Committee] see a definite and active process in the direction of arms control and disarmament. Several regional conflicts have been solved or have at least come closer to a solution. The UN is beginning to play the role which was originally planned for it.'

On the international level Gorbachev, by this time, had long become a household name. The urgent need to solve the country's domestic problems was an important explanation of his outstanding international achievements. The December 1987 INF treaty involved the scrapping of land-based, intermediate nuclear missiles, while the START 1 treaty, signed at the Moscow summit 30–1 July 1991, *reduced* (for the first time) long-range nuclear weapons by some 30 per cent on average (35 per cent in the case of the Soviet Union and 25 per cent in that of the USA). Nuclear disarmament was given a massive boost by Presidents Bush (27 September 1991) and Gorbachev (5 October 1991) by proposals for further, large reductions in weapons; what was of historical importance was the inclusion of dramatic, competing *unilateral* gestures. For example, ground-launched theatre nuclear weapons were to be removed from Europe. Soviet troops were withdrawn from Afghanistan by 15 February 1989 as promised, while Soviet influence helped secure the withdrawal of Cuban troops from Angola and of Vietnamese troops from Cambodia. Gorbachev went to Beijing in May 1989. The countries of Eastern Europe were freed after Gorbachev's refusal to use Soviet troops in 1956 Hungarian or 1968 Czechoslovak style. At the Paris November 1990 meeting of the Conference on Security and Co-operation in Europe (CSCE) Nato and the Warsaw Pact declared that they were 'no longer adversaries'. The Warsaw

Pact (formed 1955), already dead in reality, lost its formal military role on 1 April and its political role on 1 July 1991. Nato, formed in July 1948, is still a thriving organization and, indeed, has decided to expand into Eastern Europe (More recent events relating to Nato expansion are dealt with later on.)

The 7–8 November 1991 meeting decided to set up the North Atlantic Co-operation Council to consult more formally with the former members of the Warsaw Pact. On 20 December 1991 Russia (which replaced the old Soviet Union in international negotiations) astounded all by requesting that references in the final communiqué to the 'Soviet Union' be erased and by requesting membership of Nato in the long run. On 7 January 1992 it was announced that the post-Soviet Union states were formally to be admitted to the council. Ten more states joined on 10 March 1992 (Georgia was the one missing; admission was delayed until 15 April 1992). The 5 June 1992 meeting saw the signing of a protocol to the CFE treaty. (Note that Yeltsin continued the nuclear dismantling process. In visits to the USA, the UK and France in late January–early February 1992 Yeltsin announced that he no longer saw these countries as potential adversaries and that their cities would no longer be targeted. The USA and Russia made unilateral gestures and conditional proposals as regards nuclear reductions, Yeltsin proposing a reduction of long-range nuclear warheads to 2,000–2,500 each – there were then at least 27,000 in the ex-Soviet Union – and President Bush proposing 4,500. On 1 February 1992 Bush proposed the setting up of a joint centre to employ both US and ex-Soviet nuclear scientists.)

At home, however, the political climate in the later stages of the Gorbachev era continued to deteriorate. Economic reform took a back-seat to trying to preserve the union, the very country itself. Although there was a formal procedure for secession, the impatience of republics such as Lithuania, Latvia and Estonia for early independence played a major role in the rightward swing; the line was finally drawn at the chaotic disintegration of the Soviet Union. One reason why Gorbachev finally opted for a less radical economic programme than the Shatalin scheme was to limit the powers of the republics. Personnel changes confirmed the drift, e.g. on 14 January 1991 Valentin Pavlov (appointed finance minister in 1989) became the new prime minister (Ryzhkov having had a heart attack on 26 December 1990). Also in January 1991 Gorbachev lost the services of advisers of the stature of Nikolai Petrakov and Stanislav Shatalin. Petrakov's open letter of resignation said, among other things, that: 'We are in trouble not because we are creating a market. We are not creating it, but destroying it.' Gorbachev began to rely increasingly on the army, the KGB and a resuscitated communist party.

The political situation took a very ugly turn when lives were lost in the Baltic republics. On 11 January 1991 Soviet troops took over the printing works and defence headquarters in Vilnius (the capital of Lithuania), and two days later the radio and television station (with loss of life). In Riga (the capital of Latvia) deaths also resulted from the 20 January attack on the

Latvian interior ministry building by members of the Soviet Interior Ministry's special unit (OMON, more popularly called the 'black berets'). So-called 'National Salvation Committees' popped up, claiming readiness to take control away from the democratically elected parliaments. (Most nationalists in the Baltic States are convinced of Gorbachev's complicity, but I am not.)

On 25 January 1991 it was announced (although the order was actually signed by interior minister Boris Pugo and defence minister Dmitri Yazov) that, as of 1 February, there would be joint police-army patrols in Moscow, all the republican capitals, and large industrial and military centres; they were formally to be used for 'certain demonstrations, major political events, or weekends and holidays if necessary'. The 26 January 1991 decree (rescinded 21 October) allowed KGB and interior ministry officials to enter any enterprise in the Soviet Union 'without hindrance' and demand documents, confidential commercial information and samples of goods. Full information could also be demanded about bank accounts (although the confidentiality of this and all other information was supposed to be respected once obtained). The alleged target was 'economic sabotage' and economic crime in general. The 29 January 1991 decree set up a committee to co-ordinate the activities of law enforcement bodies.

On 20 December 1990 foreign minister Eduard Shevardnadze unexpectedly announced his retirement. (He resigned from the communist party on 4 July 1991.) He warned against the movement to dictatorship.

Gorbachev set up new state structures, receiving CPD approval on 25 December 1990. The new bodies were answerable to the president and the new powers were meant to bring order to an increasingly chaotic situation before reforms were introduced. The new bodies were as follows:

1. *The Federation Council.* This became the chief decision-making body, comprising the president, the vice-president and the presidents of the union (fifteen maximum) and autonomous republics (twenty). The main function was 'to co-ordinate the efforts of the centre and the republics'. The council was to meet every two months, and fundamental issues needed a two-thirds majority (there being no presidential veto). An inter-republican economic committee was to co-ordinate the economic relations between centre and republics.

2. *The National Security Council.* This replaced the Presidential Council and was headed by the vice-president. The council was in charge of 'implementing the country's all-union policy in the field of defence … and guaranteeing stability, law and order'. In other words, the council co-ordinated the law-enforcement agencies within the framework of presidential rule. Membership included the heads of the military, the KGB, the interior ministry and the foreign ministry.

3. *The Cabinet of Ministers.* This replaced the Council of Ministers and was subordinate to the president, not the Supreme Soviet. Membership included

the Soviet prime minister, deputy prime ministers, ministers, and republican prime ministers. The president could propose the appointment and dismissal of the prime minister and other ministries, but Supreme Soviet approval was needed. (The Supreme Soviet could, in fact, pass a vote of no confidence in the president, but a two-thirds majority was needed.)

As regards the republics, Gorbachev, although he was in favour of preserving the union, introduced a Law on Secession. In an 8 October 1990 speech to the Central Committee he warned of the danger of 'Lebanonization'; on 17 November he pronounced himself 'resolutely' opposed to dissolution, while on 23 November he said that the break-up of the union could lead to 'bloodshed and civil war'. On 12 December 1990 he said: 'We must beware of falling from one extreme to the other; instead of strong republics and a strong centre, instead of a strong central government, to have something that resembles an amoeba.' In his new year message for 1991 Gorbachev stated that: 'For all of us Soviet people there is no more sacred cause than the preservation and renewal of the union in which all our peoples can live well and freely.' Ethnic clashes became numerous, such as those between Armenians and Azerbaizanis (especially over Nagorno-Karabakh), between Georgians and both Abkhazians and Ossetians, between Uzbeks and the Meskhetian minority (Meskhetian Turks transported from Georgia by Stalin), and between Uzbeks and Kyrgyz. The brutal suppression of demonstrators in Georgia in April 1989, with loss of life, left an indelible mark. (Most Georgians are convinced of Gorbachev's complicity, but, as with the Baltic States, I am not.)

By the end of 1990 all fifteen republics had declared their sovereignty or independence. But the Baltic republics of Estonia, Latvia and Lithuania, Armenia, Georgia and Moldavia expressed a wish to secede from the union; independence referenda were strongly supported (e.g. Lithuania 90.5 per cent in February 1991; Estonia 77.8 per cent in March 1991; Latvia 73.6 per cent in March 1991; Georgia 98.9 per cent in March 1991). Boris Yeltsin was elected president of the Russian Federation on 12 June 1991 with 57.3 per cent of the popular vote; on 29 May 1990 he had been elected chairman of the Russian CPD (the first session of which had begun on 16 May) and resigned from the communist party in July.

The draft bill on the Law of Secession was presented on 21 March 1990 and contained the following elements (*CDSP*, 1990, vol. XLII, no. 15, pp. 20–1):

1. The decision to hold a referendum was to be made by the republican Supreme Soviet at its own initiative or on the basis of a request signed by one-tenth of the citizens permanently residing in the republic and entitled to vote.

2. The referendum was to be conducted by secret ballot no sooner than six months and no later than nine months after the adoption of the decision to raise the question of secession. A republican decision to secede from the USSR should be considered adopted by referendum if it wins the votes of at least two-thirds of the citizens who were residing permanently on the republic's territory at the time the question of secession was raised.

3. The USSR Congress of People's Deputies was to establish a transitional period not to exceed five years, during which questions arising could be resolved. In the final year of the transitional period a repeat referendum could be held to confirm a decision to secede at the initiative of the republican Supreme Soviet or was obligatory if demanded by one-tenth of the citizens. If fewer than two-thirds of the resident citizens voted to confirm the decision to secede, the decision to secede should be considered rescinded. At the end of the transitional period the approval of the USSR Congress of People's Deputies was needed.

The Supreme Soviet passed emergency legislation on 24 October 1990 reasserting the supremacy of federal over republican law until the signing of a new union treaty. The 17 March 1991 referendum posed the question: 'Do you consider it necessary to preserve the Union of Soviet Socialist Republics as a renewed federation of equal sovereign republics, in which the rights and freedoms of all nationalities will be fully guaranteed?' The overall 'yes' vote was 76.4 per cent, but Estonia, Latvia, Lithuania, Armenia, Georgia and Moldavia did not take part. In April 1991 Gorbachev swung back to the centre ground of politics by signing an agreement with nine republican leaders. (The Baltic Republics, Armenia, Georgia and Moldavia did not take part.) Essentially the 'anti-crisis' economic programme was supported, although concessions included a 'radical' increase in the role of the republics and allowing them 'independently to decide on the question of accession to the union treaty'.

THE 19–21 AUGUST 1991 ABORTIVE COUP

The coup caught most people by surprise, although there were many earlier signs and warnings of deep dissatisfaction among 'hard liners'. In his December 1990 resignation speech the liberal foreign minister Eduard Shevardnadze warned of a slide towards dictatorship, while on Friday 16 August 1991 Alexander Yakovlev (who had resigned as adviser to Gorbachev the previous month) resigned from the communist party with the extraordinarily prescient comment that a 'Stalinist' core of the party was preparing a coup. Yakovlev resumed his role as adviser on 24 September, while Shevardnadze resumed his role as foreign minister on 19 November (albeit as head of the new ministry of foreign relations). (Earlier in the month the foreign ministry and the ministry of external economic relations had merged to form the new body.)

On a more democratic note, a statement announcing the setting up of the Movement for Democratic Reform was signed on 1 July 1991. A conference was later fixed for October. Leading figures included Shevardnadze, Yakovlev, Ivan Silayev (prime minister of the Russian republic), Gavril Popov (mayor of Moscow), Anatoly Sobchak (mayor of Leningrad), Alexander Rutskoi (vice-president of the Russian republic), Nikolai Petrakov, Arkady Volsky (president of the Scientific and Industrial Association, which represented a number of important enterprises), and Stanislav Shatalin (who became chairman of the new Union of Democratic Parties on 17 July). On 20 July Boris Yeltsin signed a decree (operational from 4 August, although fully effective only by the end of 1991) allowing workplace political activity in the Russian republic only 'during non-working hours and outside the limits of state organs, institutions, organizations and enterprises'. Gorbachev disagreed and the Constitutional Review Commission was asked to examine the decree.

On 19 August 1991 Gorbachev was ousted by the 'State Committee for the State of Emergency'. Known popularly as the 'Gang of Eight', they were Gennadi Yanayev (vice-president), Valentin Pavlov (prime minister), Boris Pugo (interior minister; he subsequently shot himself), Vladimir Kryuchkov (chairman, KGB), Dimitri Yazov (defence minister), Oleg Baklanov (first deputy chairman of the Defence Council), Vasily Starodubtsev (chairman of the Farmers' Union), and Alexei Tizyakov (president of the Association of State Enterprises). Others acting behind the scenes included Anatoly Lukyanov, the chairman of the Supreme Soviet, who was subsequently arrested and charged with treason. A veneer of legitimacy was attempted by claiming that Gorbachev (who had been on holiday in the Crimea since 4 August) was unable to carry out his duties as president 'owing to the state of his health'. In fact, Gorbachev was presented with the option of signing a decree proclaiming a state of emergency or resigning; he was placed under house arrest.

The immediate cause of the attempted coup was the proposed signing of the Union Treaty on 20 August 1991 by Russia, Kazakhstan and Uzbekistan. The State Committee acted to stop, as they saw it, political and economic chaos, to prevent the disintegration of the country, and to preserve the power exercised by the federal institutions of the communist party, the KGB and the armed forces. The plotters subsequently revealed that they feared increasing dependence on the USA. They relied on the assumed political passivity of most of the population, enhanced, so they hoped, by economic dissatisfaction.

A statement laying out the reasons for the coup was released by the State Committee (*CDSP*, 1991, vol. XLIII, no. 33, pp. 1–4): 'The aim of overcoming the profound and comprehensive crisis, political, ethnic and civil strife, chaos and anarchy that threaten the lives and security of the Soviet Union's citizens and the sovereignty, territorial integrity, freedom and independence of our fatherland ... to adopt the most decisive measures to prevent society from sliding into national catastrophe and ensure law and order, to declare a state of emergency in some parts of the Soviet Union for six months from 0400 Moscow time on 19 August 1991 ... with a view to protecting the vital interests of the peoples and citizens of the Soviet Union and the country's independence and territorial integrity, restoring law and order, stabilizing the situation, overcoming the gravest crisis, and preventing chaos, anarchy and a fratricidal civil war.'

Although the State Committee promised to adhere to the reform process, the radio appeal made much of the grave economic situation: 'The crisis of power has had a catastrophic effect on the economy. The chaotic and uncontrolled slide towards the market has aroused egoism [self-interest] – regional, departmental, group and individual. The war of laws [federal versus republican] and the encouragement of centrifugal trends has meant the destruction of the unified machinery of the national economy which has taken decades to evolve. The result has been a sharp decline in the standard of living of the great majority of the Soviet people and the flourishing of speculation and the black economy.'

The decrees issued on the first day of the coup suspended political parties, social organizations and movements 'that prevent normalization'. Demonstrations and strikes were banned and censorship was imposed. Federal laws were given 'unconditional priority'. On the economic front administrative measures were decreed and populist measures taken: 'strict fulfilment of measures to preserve and restore vertical and horizontal economic ties between economic-management entities … and unfailing achievement of planned targets regarding production and supplies of raw materials and components'; 'a decisive struggle against the shadow economy'; laws against 'corruption, theft, profiteering, bungled management and other economic wrongdoing' to be enforced; 'moonlighting' by state employees to be eliminated; 'emergency measures' were to be employed to bring in the harvest, including drafting factory and office workers, students and soldiers; urban dwellers were to receive allotments (up to 0.15 ha each) to grow fruit and vegetables; control was to be exercised over food distribution, with priority for children and pensioners; there were to be price freezes or reductions for certain consumer goods and foodstuffs, and increases in some wages and pensions. A 20 August decree banned the purchase of foreign currency by private individuals for travel purposes. (A decree issued by Yanayev on the same day overrode all of Yeltsin's decrees.)

Nato stressed that Eastern Europe's security was 'inseparably linked' with that of Nato's. The West responded on the economic front by suspending much of its promised aid (EC humanitarian aid continued, for example). The EC promised to speed up negotiations on associate status with Czechoslovakia, Hungary and Poland and to strengthen co-operation with Albania, Bulgaria and Romania.

The coup failed and the plotters were put on treason charges. (Note, however, that when most of them were formally charged on 14 January 1992 they were accused of attempting to seize power illegally. It was difficult to charge them with betraying a country which by then no longer existed and which they had tried to preserve. How they fared is dealt with later on.) There was very little loss of life, e.g. three civilians were killed in Moscow. Although there was much talk of 'people's power', the bulk of the population (even in Moscow and Leningrad) remained passive: one source cited an estimate by

Yeltsin's aides of 1 per cent of the population of Moscow and some other cities taking part in demonstrations (*IHT*, 9 September 1991, p. 4). *The Telegraph* (28 October 1991, p. 10) suggested an upper figure of 100,000 taking an active part in resisting the coup. Yeltsin's call for a general strike was also not heeded, with very few actually striking (although there was strong support for Yeltsin among coal miners). There was sufficient *active* popular support, however, to swing the balance. Popular support as a whole was for Yeltsin personally and for constitutionality/legitimacy in general. Gorbachev had long been much more popular abroad than at home, largely because of the dire economic situation. In this context, the plotters relied on general economic discontent to ensure passivity (or even positive support from particularly disadvantaged sections of society). The West could and, in my opinion, should have promised large-scale aid to the Soviet Union at the July 1991 G7 conference in London, since the plotters would have been less likely to assume passivity from a population at least perceiving the prospects of betterment. The odds against the plotters' chances of success would have lengthened. Gorbachev returned from the London conference largely 'empty-handed' and thus weakened politically after so many concessions to the West.

The consequences of the failure of the August 1991 coup were, without any exaggeration, of truly historical dimension. Ironically, it put the final nail in the coffin of the Soviet Union. The coup collapsed on 21 August and Gorbachev proclaimed he was back in control. He initially defended the party as a whole; the very next day he said that 'We shall do everything we can to undertake reform in the party in order to give it a sort of kiss of life'. But on 24 August Gorbachev resigned as General Secretary of the Communist Party of the Soviet Union (CPSU) and recommended the Central Committee to dissolve itself and local bodies to form a new party of 'renewal'. Party property was to be taken over by local authorities, pending a final decision on the role of the party in the coup. There was to be a ban on all political parties in the interior ministry and in all security agencies (including the armed forces and the KGB). On 29 August 1991 the Supreme Soviet suspended the operations of the CPSU, pending a judicial enquiry into its role in the coup; its bank accounts were frozen and financial operations halted. In the Russian republic the following actions were taken: a ban on communist party cells in the army and nationalization of party printing presses and publishing houses (23 August 1991); on the same day Yeltsin signed a decree suspending the party 'pending a court determination of its involvement' in the coup (Gorbachev was present in the Russian parliament at the time and protested; it was seen as a personal humiliation for Gorbachev); on 6 November 1991, the eve of the first anniversary of the Revolution not to be celebrated, Yeltsin banned all communist party activities in the Russian federation and nationalized its property. (In May 1992 the legality of Yeltsin's decrees was formally challenged, but the tables were turned when the Russian constitutional court was asked to look into the charge that the communist party had acted illegally and unconstitutionally while in office, e.g. usurping state power, violating human rights and supplying arms to international terrorist organizations.)

The new Union Treaty

On 2 September 1991 a joint statement was presented to the emergency session of the Congress of People's Deputies (CPD) (held 2–5 September) by President Nursultan Nazarbayev of Kazakhstan. All republics signed the statement except the Baltic states, Moldova and Georgia (although Georgia was an observer at the negotiations). It was popularly known as the 'ten-plus-one' agreement (ten republics plus Gorbachev). The measures outlined were meant to prevent a further collapse of the structures of power, pending the creation of a new political state system of relations between the republics and the formation of new inter-republican union structures. The temporary arrangements were as follows.

1. All the consenting republics should work out and sign a Treaty of the Union of Sovereign States (USS) in which each of them would be able to determine independently the form of its participation. This was popularly known as the 'à-la-carte' principle. The final resolution, passed on 5 September, said that the new union had to be based on the principles of independence and territorial integrity of states, the observance of the rights of the nations and of the individual, social justice and democracy.

2. An appeal was made to all republics, irrespective of the status they had declared, to conclude right away an economic agreement to co-operate within the framework of a free common economic space to secure the normal functioning of the economy, supply of the population and accelerated implementation of radical economic reform.

3. The creation, for the transitional period, of the following institutions:

(a) *Council of Representatives of People's Deputies.* Each republic to have equal representation (twenty deputies delegated by each republican Supreme Soviet). The council was to decide upon matters of general principle.

(b) *State Council.* This would comprise the Soviet president and top state officials from the republics. Its role was to co-ordinate foreign and domestic issues that concerned common republican interests. This was to be the most powerful body. In the finally agreed version, Gorbachev shared responsibility for the armed forces, KGB and interior ministry with the republican presidents. There was no vice-president. If Gorbachev fell ill, his powers were to revert to the Council.

(c) *Interim Inter-republican Economic Committee.* This committee would comprise representatives of all the republics on a parity basis. Its role was to co-ordinate both the management of the economy and economic reform. It was to be accountable to the president, the State Council and the Supreme Soviet. It would replace the Committee for the Control of the National Economy.

The draft constitution, when ready, was to be considered and approved by republican parliaments and finally approved at a congress of plenipotentiary representatives of union republics. The status of all elected people's deputies of the Soviet Union was to be preserved during their elected term.

4. An agreement on defence, on the principle of collective security, to preserve united armed forces and military-strategic space, to carry out radical military reforms in the armed forces, KGB, interior ministry and prosecutor's office of the USSR. (The 5 September resolution referred to the principle of 'collective security and defence while preserving a single armed forces and single control of nuclear and other arsenals of the means of mass destruction'.)

5. Strict observation of all international agreements and obligations of the Soviet Union.

6. The rights and freedoms of citizens and the rights of national minorities.

7. Support for applications of the individual republics to the United Nations. Note that Ukraine and Belorussia already had UN status, although until then they had not had independent voices. The Baltic states, as mentioned previously, were admitted to the UN on 18 September 1991, while the others (with the exception of Georgia) became members on 28 February 1992.

On 3 September 1991, however, Gorbachev (with the agreement of the ten republics) decided to withdraw support for the Council of Representatives of People's Deputies. There had been adverse reaction to the proposals on various grounds (constitutional problems, the overwhelming shift of power to the republics at the expense of the centre and the disproportionately low weight given to Russia). Instead, it was proposed to revamp the Supreme Soviet along the lines suggested in the previous Union Treaty. The Supreme Soviet was to comprise two bodies:

1. *The Council of the Republics*, with members nominated by the parliaments of the individual republics as an interim measure. The finally agreed distribution of the 332 seats was as follows, although each republic still only had one vote: each republic had twenty representatives plus one for each of its autonomous republics or regions; Russia, for example, had fifty-two. This council had veto power over the decisions of the Council of the Union.

2. *The Council of the Union*, with representatives appointed by the republics on the basis of districts with an equal number of people (thus weighting republican representation according to population size). Members of the current Supreme Soviet were eligible for consideration.

The Supreme Soviet would deal with changes in the constitution, accept states into the new union, receive presidential reports on the most important domestic and foreign issues, confirm the union budget, declare war and conclude peace. But decisions still had to be ratified by republican parliaments.

The final vote by the Congress of People's Deputies was taken on 5 September 1991, with the new arrangements approved by 1,682 votes for to forty-three against and sixty-three abstentions. These arrangements were, of course, temporary and no fixed time scale was announced for a more permanent Union of Sovereign States. The CPD did not vote itself out of existence in principle (its life extended to 1994), but there seemed no reason to call another emergency session.

On 26 September 1991 the names of the members of a new (federal) Presidential Consultative Council were announced; they included Eduard Shevardnadze, Alexander Yakovlev, Gavriil Popov and Anatoly Sobchak. Gorbachev himself temporarily found a new role as arbitrator between the republics, especially since the other republics feared a dominant Russia.

The role of Boris Yeltsin and the Russian republic

Boris Yeltsin, elected president of the Russian republic by popular vote, played a crucial role in defeating the coup. He epitomized legitimacy/constitutionality and displayed immense personal courage. He provided leadership and focused resistance to the coup on the Russian parliament building (the 'White House'). Yeltsin and the Russian parliament also moved quickly once the coup began to founder to fill the power vacuum left by the crumbling of central authority. Some of Yeltsin's actions were of dubious legality, however, and aroused fears among some of the other republics of possible Russian domination (the republic accounting for over 51 per cent of the population and over 76 per cent of the land area of the Soviet Union). Yeltsin's actions included the following:

22 August 1991. To transfer by 1 January 1992 control of Union-level enterprises and organizations on Russian territory apart from specified exceptions. (Gorbachev subsequently described the early decrees as 'necessary at the time.' A 12 September decree specifically confirmed Russian control over oil, gas and coal.)

23 August 1991. Gorbachev and Yeltsin agreed to take over each other's presidency if one fell ill. Yeltsin suspended six newspapers, including *Pravda*, and dismissed the heads of the state media. (*Pravda* was set up by Lenin in 1912 and became the communist party's official newspaper. It was not published on 24 August 1991 for the first time since the 1917 Revolution and only reappeared on 31 August as an 'independent' paper. Publication was suspended for economic reasons on 14 February 1992, but it reappeared on 7 April although only three times a week.) The whole Soviet Cabinet of Ministers was forced to resign. Key appointments were Yeltsin nominees, e.g. defence, Yevgenny Shaposhnikov; KGB, Vadim Bakatin; interior, Viktor Barannikov (Russia's interior minister.)

24 August 1991. It was announced that Russia was to take over the Soviet government, the economy ministry, the KGB and the interior ministry as far as its territory was concerned until a new Soviet government was formed. The Russian prime minister, Ivan Silayev, was named as head of a temporary four-man (subsequently expanded) Committee for Control of the National Economy. The others were Grigori Yavlinsky, Arkadi Volsky (head of the Scientific-Industrial League, an organization representing state and private employers) and Yuri Luzhkov (chairman of the Moscow City Council). In effect, the committee took over the role of the Soviet cabinet of ministers (government).

26 August 1991. Anxiety was caused by talk among Yeltsin's spokesmen of republics which left the union (except the Baltic States) having to discuss borders and the minorities question with Russia. By way of example, the Crimea was included in the Ukraine as recently as 1954.

28 August 1991. Announcement that from 15 September onwards Russia would temporarily take over the institutions of the Soviet ministry of finance, Gosbank and Vneshekonombank on Russian territory. Russian control was claimed over foreign exchange and precious metals operations, but ceded back to the centre later the same day. Gorbachev warned Yeltsin not to act unconstitutionally (the previous day Gorbachev had announced he was against border changes). (Note that on 28 August the head of Gosbank, Viktor Gerashchenko, and of Vneshekonombank, Yuri Moskovsky, were reinstated, partly to mollify Western anxiety.)

A Russian delegation went to Ukraine and agreed on an economic and military union. Borders were to remain. Other republics were invited to join without the involvement of the centre (temporary inter-state structures were deemed necessary).

30 August 1991. A similar agreement was drawn up between Russia and Kazakhstan in order to prevent the 'uncontrolled disintegration' of the Soviet Union.

Note that of the sixteen autonomous republics within Russia, only ten had by then agreed that a new union treaty should be signed by Russia on their behalf. There were also five autonomous regions and ten autonomous areas. Around 20 per cent of the republic's population is non-Russian. On 25 December 1991 the name was formally changed from the Russian Soviet Federative Republic to the Russian Federation; on 17 April 1992 an alternative of simply 'Russia' was added. Resistance to the Russian federal authorities was led by Tatarstan and Chechenia. A Russian federation treaty was signed by most representatives on 31 March 1992 (for details see *CDSP*, 1992, vol. XLIV, no. 13, pp. 15–16). The autonomous republics of Tatarstan and Chechenia did not sign, preferring to deal bilaterally with the Russian federal authorities. The federation treaty granted increased powers to the autonomous republics, but many crucial areas of decision-making were left vague, e.g. control over natural resources. The treaty was approved by the Russian Congress of People's Deputies on 10 April 1992.

There was, however, been political disarray in the Russian parliament over such matters as political drift, delays in implementing economic reform and Yeltsin's decree-making powers and authoritarian traits (e.g. the sending of interim unelected 'governor generals' to inforce policies in the regions). Vice-president Alexander Rutskoi became increasingly critical, talking of chaos (decrees were largely ignored, for example), a lack of democracy, the danger of Russia splitting up (into 'hundreds of banana republics' he said on 30 January 1992), and mistaken economic reforms. (Rutskoi believed, for instance, that price increases should *follow* privatization, the relative saturation of markets, the introduction of competitive conditions, land reform and financial reform, and that there was a need for some planning.) He deplored (30 January 1992) the 'impoverishment of the people', referring to the 'inept and often essentially experimental attempts' of the government, and talked (8 February 1992) of 'economic genocide', proposing a state of emergency for at least a year. Following the swingeing price increases on 2 January 1992, the chairman of the Russian parliament, Ruslan Khasbulatov argued that the government should resign and that Yeltsin ought to give up his second post as prime minister. Georgi Matyukin, chairman of the Russian central bank, attacked price rises before a competitive production and distribution environment was established. He also opposed the notion of a freely convertible rouble in prevailing conditions, since its value had been reduced to such an extent that property could be bought up too cheaply and Russian enterprises would be unable to import. On 28 October 1991 Yeltsin announced a radical economic reform package to the Russian Congress of People's Deputies.

The control of the economy in the immediate aftermath of the coup attempt

Yeltsin's call for a general strike against the coup was not generally heeded. Although there was some response (e.g. from coal miners in Siberia, the Ukraine and Belarus) it was not widespread. As has already been discussed, Yeltsin and the Russian parliament stepped in to fill the power vacuum as central authority crumbled (sometimes on dubious grounds constitutionally).

The union Supreme Soviet met on 26–9 August 1991. Gorbachev, in his 26 August speech, stressed the need for the union treaty to be signed. Those republics unwilling to sign had to be given the right of 'independent choice', but all fifteen republics had vital economic ties and so work on an economic agreement had to begin right away. He argued that gradual reform had to be reconsidered and proposed the following measures:

1. The removal of all obstacles on the way to the market. There should be full freedom for entrepreneurship and the removal of monopoly, dictates from above and forcible methods. Market institutions should be created.
2. There should be a decisive shift of emphasis in the governing of the economy to the republics, with the union retaining legislative control for regulating a single economic space.
3. Macroeconomic stabilization.

4. The removal of all obstacles to putting land in the hands of those who wanted to work it.

5. The removal of 'economic populism', concentrating on basic issues of social protection during the transition to the market.

On 27 August 1991 Gorbachev threatened to resign if the union ceased to exist: 'The Soviet Union must be preserved as a union of sovereign states with a united army and a common economic treaty.' He announced agreement with Russia, Kazakhstan and Kyrgyzstan to begin negotiations on an economics accord, with the other republics eligible to join.

On 28 August 1991 the union Supreme Soviet ratified the dismissal of the cabinet of ministers. The allocation of duties was announced for the Committee for Control of the National Economy; this was expanded to include representatives from eleven other republics, besides Russia, with even the Baltic states sending 'active observers'. (In mid-November the body was renamed the Inter-state Economic Committee.) The individuals and their portfolios included the following: Ivan Silayev (defence, security, media, internal and external affairs, natural resources, ministry of finance and chairman of the Inter-republican Economic Committee); Grigori Yavlinsky (overall economic strategy, drawing up the new reform programme); Arkadi Volsky (industry, transport and communications); Yuri Luzhkov (agro-industrial sector, trade, including urban food supplies during winter, and social affairs).

On 29 August 1991 the Supreme Soviet removed Gorbachev's powers to rule by decree. On 30 August the deputy heads of Soviet ministries and economic experts from all the republics began a meeting in Moscow to work out an economic accord. On 1 September Gorbachev discussed economic measures (such as reductions in both wages and the money supply) with ten republics.

The Economic Community

The title 'economic union' was rejected in favour of 'economic community' or 'commonwealth'. The treaty was signed on 18 October 1991 by only eight of the remaining twelve republics (the Baltic states having been recognized as fully independent); Azerbaijan, Georgia, Moldova and Ukraine declined at that time (Moldova and Ukraine initialling the treaty on 6 November). The treaty was only in draft form, the details having to be worked out in following detailed negotiations (hopefully only lasting until the end of the year) and ratified by the parliaments of the individual republics. An initial three-year duration was envisaged. Pressures to sign included the high degree of economic interdependence, aggravated by the highly monopolistic position of many suppliers. (In 1989 the volume of inter-republic exchanges of Soviet-made output was more than 20 per cent of the USSR's GNP, the corresponding figure for the EC being only 16 per cent: *CDSP*, 1991, vol. XLIII, no. 41, p. 3). There was also pressure from Western countries concerned with issues like foreign debt. The main features of the draft treaty were as follows (*CDSP*, 1991, vol. XLIII, no. 42, pp. 4–9):

1. Free trade within a united market (a 'common economic space'). Co-ordinated policies in transport, energy, the monetary and banking system, finances, taxation and prices, customs rules and tariffs, and foreign economic relations.

2. It was recognised that 'concerted monetary and credit policies are of priority importance to find a way out of the crisis and controlling inflation'. There was also a need 'to preserve and strengthen the rouble as the common currency of a single monetary system', but this did not rule out national currencies, provided they did not harm the community's monetary system. The immediate aim was an internally convertible rouble.

3. There was to be set up 'on the principles of a reserve system, a banking union including the central banks of member states' and an inter-state bank for issuing money, as well as a banking inspectorate with equal representation for republics to monitor the banking union's implementation of the charter. Pending the adoption of the charter, a provisional board of Gosbank USSR and republican central banks was to run the central banking system.

4. Limits were to be set on member states' budget deficits. Sums in excess would be considered a debt to other members. A community budget, to be formed by fixed payments from members, was not allowed to be in deficit.

5. 'Private ownership, free enterprise and competition form the basis of economic recovery.'

6. There was to be free movement of labour (coupled with a common social security system), the same legal conditions for business as for states' own nationals. Restrictions on the movement of goods and services were to be removed within an 'agreed period of time'. If contractual deliveries were not fulfilled, the offending republic had to compensate the others with the hard currency value of the goods.

7. The foreign economic commitments of the USSR would be honoured. The foreign debt burden was to be shared out. (The remaining twelve republics actually agreed to do this 'jointly and severally' on 28 October 1991, after two days of talks with the G7 countries, i.e. others will assume the debts of defaulting republics.) A bank was to be set up as a successor to Vneshekonombank to handle debt repayments; members recognized the need for a 'single procedure for accumulating hard currency receipts to service the foreign debt'. Assets, including gold and foreign currency reserves, were to be divided up. The G7 talks (19–21 November 1991) resulted in a memorandum of understanding on foreign debt, signed by eight republics there and then (i.e. excluding Azerbaijan, Georgia, Ukraine and Uzbekistan). A specific allocation of debt burden was to ensue, and the republics promised macroeconomic stabilization measures, price and exchange rate liberalization and free inter-republican trade (in agreement with the IMF). In return the G7 countries

stood ready to support the following: a deferral of payments on the principal of medium and long-term official debt until the end of 1992 (worth about $3.6 billion); other creditors were to be urged to follow suit, bringing the total to $6 billion; G7 export agencies were to be asked to continue extending short-term lines and guarantees as an inducement for banks and suppliers to renew credit lines; and possible emergency financing of up to $1 billion, using gold as collateral. As of 5 December 1991 Vneshekonombank suspended payments on the principal of medium and long-term debt incurred before 1 January 1991 to commercial banks until 1 January 1993, in line with the G7 agreement. On 17 December the Western banks agreed to a postponement on the principal owed from 5 December 1991 to 30 March 1992 worth $5.4 billion; this was later extended to 30 June 1992 and then to 30 September.

The early debt-sharing arrangement gradually fell apart, however, and on 8 February 1992 it was formally agreed that each country should, if possible, pay its own debt. Ukraine had prior to this made it clear that it would itself pay 16.37 per cent of the debt and in mid-January had set up a foreign exchange organization to deal with this. (On 19 February 1992 Ukraine said it would take responsibility for some of the debt owed by the smaller republics, bringing its share up to a possible 21.13 per cent. On 13 March 1992 Russia and Ukraine agreed to pay for 61.34 per cent and 16.37 per cent of the debt respectively.) Moldova said it was unable to pay its share, but would forgo a claim on ex-Soviet assets if Russia paid on its behalf.

8. Customs policy towards third countries was to be co-ordinated, but member states were independently to regulate foreign economic activity and establish licences and quotas within the limits of overall quotas.

9. There was agreement on joint membership of the IMF, but individual membership was permitted.

Twenty-five detailed agreements were to be negotiated, including the following: the status and powers of community institutions (these were to include a council of heads of government, an executive inter-state economic committee, whose chairman was to be appointed by heads of government, and a court of arbitration); banking union regulations and monetary policy, and principles and mechanisms for servicing the foreign debt; the community budget; co-ordinated price reform and a list of those goods whose prices were to remain fixed at agreed levels during a transitional period.

The treaty provided for the possibility of new full or associate members, but the unanimous consent of existing ones was needed. Those republics not prepared to join the community would be penalized by, for example, having to pay world market prices and in hard currency for energy and raw materials.

THE COMMONWEALTH OF INDEPENDENT STATES (CIS)

For some time it looked as though Gorbachev might be able to form a Union of Sovereign States (USS), but Ukraine's reluctance and ultimate refusal (after the 1 December 1991 referendum) in particular to join proved to be decisive in the end. The State Council met on 14 November 1991, but only seven republics agreed in principle to form a union (Russia, Azerbaijan, Belarus, Kazakhstan, Kyrgyzstan, Tajikistan and Turkmenistan). Uzbekistan had intended to join the talks, but the president was indisposed. The meeting on 25 November saw a somewhat different seven (Uzbekistan was represented, but not Azerbaijan) fail to initial the treaty, agreeing only to send a draft text to the individual republican parliaments.

The USS draft text was hazy on detail, but, although the centre would only have powers delegated by the republics, there were to be significant central authorities. The following were envisaged: a USS president, popularly elected for a five-year term; a Ministry of Foreign Relations, supervised by a Council of Foreign Ministers of the republics; a Ministry of Defence, co-ordinated by the republics; joint responsibility for fighting crime; a joint energy policy; and defence of human rights.

The presidents of Russia (Boris Yeltsin), Ukraine (Leonid Kravchuk) and Belarus (Stanislav Shushkevic: strictly, speaker of the parliament) met on 7–8 December 1991 in Minsk, the capital of Byelorussia (to avoid the impression of Russian dominance). Gorbachev was not invited. This historic meeting rejected the idea of the Union of Sovereign States and instead decided to form a Commonwealth of Independent States (CIS). It was declared that: 'The Union of Soviet Socialist Republics as a subject of international law and a geopolitical reality is ceasing its existence … activity of organs of the former USSR on the territory of the members of the commonwealth ceases.' The 'Minsk accords' (Belovezh; Belovezhskaya Forest; Belevezhsky Pusche agreement) pronounced the 1922 treaty founding the USSR dead. Minsk was declared the 'capital' ('headquarters' or 'co-ordinating centre') of the CIS, membership of which is open to former republics or indeed any other state meeting the requirements.

The details of the commonwealth remained to be worked out, but certain broad concepts were agreed. For instance, there was to be joint control of nuclear weapons and economic policy was to be co-ordinated within a single economic space. There were to be no central authorities as envisaged in the Union of Sovereign States, no federal president and no federal parliament. The 'co-ordinating bodies' were to play a minimal role, with members of the CIS regarded as subjects of international law.

Most of the remaining twelve republics expressed interest in joining, the five Asiatic republics, on 13 December, going so far as to 'declare their readiness to become equal co-founders of the Commonwealth of Independent States, taking into account the interests of all their subjects'.

Gorbachev's initial reaction was generally hostile, describing certain aspects as 'illegal' and 'dangerous'. But he soon came round to accepting the idea and concentrated his concern on an orderly and constitutional transition. On 17 December 1991 Gorbachev and Yeltsin met and agreed that the Soviet Union would formally come to an end when the new year arrived. Decrees issued by Yeltsin on 19 December 1991 stated that: 'All the buildings, including the Kremlin, as well as the property, assets and foreign currency of the Soviet president and the Inter-republican Economic Committee are transferred to the management of the Russian administration.' The foreign and interior ministries and the domestic intelligence wing of the KGB were taken over by Russia, with the intention of creating a new Russian Ministry of Security and Internal Affairs; the Foreign Intelligence Service of the KGB was taken over the following day (the idea of a new ministry being later scuppered by the constitutional court after unrest in the Russian parliament about the apparent re-emergence of a 'Stalinist' organization). The creation of a Russian Law and Order Ministry was also decreed. Only the Soviet Ministry of Defence and Ministry of Atomic Energy remained.

The CIS agreement was signed on 21 December 1991 in Alma-Ata, the capital of Kazakhstan, by eleven of the remaining twelve republics. Georgia sent only observers, although its president requested admittance on 26 December. (This was amid serious fighting with the opposition that had started in Georgia started four days earlier. The CIS would only consider entry when the conflict was resolved.) The Soviet Union was declared dead: 'With the formation of the CIS, the USSR ceases to exist.' Gorbachev was not invited to attend and his suggestion of a final session of the Supreme Soviet to transfer power constitutionally was not taken up. (The Supreme Soviet did vote for its own dissolution on 26 December 1991, but there were so few deputies there that the end was farcical.) The main features of the CIS were as follows.

1. The states were independent and disputes would be resolved peacefully. Existing borders were inviolable. There was to be no common citizenship (as Gorbachev suggested for a transitional period), but visa-free travel would be permitted.

2. 'Allegiance to co-operation in the formation and development of a common economic space, and all-European and Eurasian markets, is confirmed.' There would be no central budget, but the aim was to keep republican budget deficits to 3 per cent of national income at most. The more distant future of the rouble as a common currency was not decided upon. (Note that the question of intra-CIS trade prices was not decided upon, but the 8 February 1992 meeting talked of 'world prices', although at a rouble exchange rate of twenty to thirty to the US dollar; this was the rate which Russia then thought appropriate for defence of the rouble by a Western stabilization fund.) The 14–15 February 1992 meeting of the CIS in Minsk did not see much progress made, but the principle of free trade between republics was confirmed and there was agreement to allow the reexport of goods subject to licensing and quotas only with the consent of the republic which produced the goods. On 17 February 1992 Russia and Ukraine agreed on the terms for the issuing of a new currency, e.g. Ukraine would remit all roubles to the Russian central bank.

3. The supreme co-ordinating body of the CIS would be a Council of the Heads of State (the presidents). There would be a parallel Council of Heads of Government (prime ministers). These councils would 'co-ordinate the activities of the states of the new commonwealth in the sphere of common interests'. Meetings were to held at least twice a year and at least once every three months respectively. There were also to be ministerial committees on foreign affairs, economics and finance, transport and communications, social security and internal affairs; at least four meetings per year were envisaged.

4. The CIS was open to any other state which shared its goals and principles and provided all members agreed.

5. Russia would take over USSR membership of the UN, including the seat on the Security Council. Ukraine and Belarus (already UN members) and Russia would help the others to become members of the UN and other international organizations. (Note that Gorbachev had suggested common international representation and a CIS seat on the UN Security Council.)

6. The defence issue was far from resolved. The Soviet defence minister, Yevgeni Shaposhnikov, was named as temporary commander of the military. (Note that Gorbachev was formally commander-in-chief until his resignation on 25 December 1991.) Further discussions produced broad agreement: the Russian president and the commander-in-chief were to control nuclear weapons, but Ukraine, Belarus, and Kazakhstan would have to agree to their use, and the other CIS members would have to be consulted. Ukraine would remove or destroy tactical nuclear weapons by 1 July 1992 (actually achieved ahead of time after many objections) and destroy or dismantle strategic weapons by the end of 1994. Belarus's nuclear weapons would be removed or destroyed by mid-1992. At the 14 February 1992 Minsk meeting it was agreed that a council comprising the presidents of Russia, Ukraine, Belarus and Kazakhstan would command strategic nuclear weapons. Kazakhstan's attitude towards strategic nuclear weapons was very unclear for a long time. A protocol to the 1991 Start Treaty was signed by the USA, Russia, Ukraine, Belarus and Kazakhstan on 24 May 1992, pledging to implement it. The last three countries agreed to give up nuclear weapons by the end of the decade. On 16 June 1992, during Yeltsin's visit to the USA, further drastic reductions in strategic nuclear weapons were announced; the target numbers agreed in the 1991 Start Treaty were approximately halved. (See later for details.)

As regards conventional defence, each republic could choose to have its own forces or join a single command structure. Subsequently, Ukraine, Azerbaijan, Armenia (announced 27 February 1992), Moldova, Belarus and Uzbekistan expressed interest in the former. Yeltsin announced plans to form a Russian National Guard. On 2 January 1992 Ukraine announced that, with the exception of strategic nuclear forces, it was assuming control of the armed forces on its territory (a ceiling of 220,000 being fixed later on). Belarus assumed control on 12 January 1992 and Moldova of certain forces in March. The Black Sea Fleet became a real bone of contention between Russia and

Ukraine. On 7 April 1992 Ukraine issued a decree assuming control over all forces on its territory, including the fleet. Yeltsin issued a counter-decree, but a potentially dangerous situation was calmed by the mutual suspension of the decrees and the setting up of a joint commission. On 26 May it was announced that the fleet was to be divided up. Indeed the only area to be left to CIS joint military command was strategic nuclear weapons.

The 14 February 1992 meeting of the CIS in Minsk led to a clear assertion that Ukraine, Moldova and Azerbaijan would form their own armies and not join a unified command. The other eight republics (Georgia sent only an observer) agreed to a unified command for a transitional period of two years, although Belarus and Uzbekistan made clear their intention to opt out then. During the transitional period individual members were permitted to form their own armies, which 'may or may not join the unified force'. On 16 March 1992 Yeltsin announced the intention to form a separate Russian ministry of defence with himself as acting minister. A definite commitment to an army was made on 7 April 1992. A decree followed on 7 May, with Yeltsin as commander-in-chief; Russian personnel were estimated at 2.63 million out of the 3.7 million former Soviet armed forces, and the intention was to bring the former down to 1.5 million by 1996 (later put back to the year 2000). Pavel Grachev was appointed Russian defence minister on 19 May. On 16 March Kazakhstan proclaimed the setting up of a republican guard. A poorly attended CIS meeting in Tashkent produced a defence pact signed on 15 May 1992 by Russia, Armenia, Kazakhstan, Tajikistan, Turkmenistan and Uzbekistan. The signatories promised not to attack each other and to come to one another's assistance if a member were attacked by another country. On 4 June 1992 Russia announced that formal border controls would be established with Ukraine, the Baltic states and Azerbaijan. The meeting of the CIS on 6 July 1992 produced agreement on the setting up of a peacekeeping force to be employed in areas of ethnic strife; Moldova was mentioned as the probable first use. On 15 June 1993 defence ministers announced that they would recommend to their governments the disbandment of the Supreme Command of the Commonwealth Joint Armed Forces and its replacement by a 'united headquarters for co-ordinating military co-operation' (i.e. the end of joint forces). Marshal Yevgeni Shaposhnikov would be replaced by a lower ranking individual. At the CIS meeting in Almaty on 10 February 1995 Russia's proposal for the joint defence of external borders was rejected. Ukraine and Azerbaijan were categorically opposed, while Russia, Kazakhstan, Kyrgyzstan and Tajikistan were strongly in favour. A non-binding (fully supported) 'Memorandum on Peace and Accord' urged members to refrain from putting military, political and economic pressure on each other. Members pledged to oppose any actions that undermined the stability of existing borders.

International recognition of the CIS members was patchy. For example, China and Vietnam recognized all the republics, but the main Western countries discriminated. The USA recognized Russia, Ukraine, Belarus,

Kazakhstan and Uzbekistan on 26 December 1991, but, while the others were acknowledged to be independent states, diplomatic relations would be established with them only when it was confirmed that they followed 'responsible security policies and democratic principles' (President George Bush). The upheaval in Georgia following allegations of undemocratic practices by President Gamsakhurdia gave rise to the gravest doubts. (The EC and the USA did not recognize Georgia until 23 and 24 March 1992 respectively, after the return of Shevardnadze.) The EC recognized Russia as the successor to the Soviet Union on 25 December 1991 and recognition was extended to Ukraine and Armenia the next day; eight republics were mentioned on 31 December 1991 as fulfilling EC conditions (Ukraine, Armenia, Azerbaijan, Belarus, Kazakhstan, Moldova, Turkmenistan and Uzbekistan).

Gorbachev's anticipated resignation came on 25 December 1991. He was the first leader of the Soviet Union to resign. The changeover was remarkably peaceful. His speech confirmed that he would have preferred a union of sovereign states, but he promised to help all he could: 'I firmly came out in favour of the independence of nations and sovereignty for the republics. At the same time I support the preservation of the union state and the integrity of the country ... I shall do all I can to ensure that the agreements that were signed there lead towards real concord in society and facilitate a way out of the crisis.' (His first new role was to become chairman of the International Foundation for Social, Economic and Political Research, a body set up soon after the abortive August coup.)

ECONOMIC RELATIONS BETWEEN RUSSIA AND THE OTHER COUNTRIES OF THE FORMER SOVIET UNION (THE 'NEAR ABROAD')

The payments mechanism

Although Russia alone controlled the printing of rouble notes (widespread shortages of cash roubles developed), before 1 July 1992 the central bank of each country in the rouble zone had the ability to create rouble credits acceptable as a means of payment throughout. Since Russia had a large trade surplus, the enterprises of the other republics receiving credits from their own central banks made net payments to Russia (especially for fuels and energy). These swelled bank deposits and thus the money supply in Russia. The lack of monetary control and co-ordination was exacerbated by the introduction of currency in the form of coupons in some countries. In the words of the IMF (*World Economic Outlook*, May 1993, p. 65), the Russian central bank had the sole power to issue rouble currency, but the other banks could extend credit themselves by creating new commercial bank reserves, borrowing from the Russian central bank and, in many cases, issuing coupons. (*RET*, 1993, vol. 2, no. 4, pp. 18, 96–7; Lipton and Sachs 1992: 226, 237–8; Michalopoulos and Tarr 1993: 22–5; and United Nations, *World Economic Survey 1993*, p. 119.)

In order to staunch the outflow of goods (Russia's trade surplus was expanding) and control the provision of credit to other states, in July 1992 Russia established a network of bilateral correspondent accounts for the other central banks. (More strictly, according to Eichengreen, correspondent banks existed from the beginning of 1992, but the credit ceilings were not enforced in the first half of the year: 1993: 315.) A halt was called to the automatic crediting of other countries running trade deficits with Russia and it was laid down that Russian goods could be purchased only with rouble deposits in Russian banks (gained through exports to Russia or permitted credit limits). The Russian central bank thus constrained the movement of non-cash roubles in settlements between enterprises. It forbade direct settlements, shifting them to a state-to-state basis through these correspondent accounts held by the various national banks (Noren 1993: 437). The system did not work smoothly because of Russia's large trade surplus. The correspondent accounts began to serve as mechanisms for bilateral barter in which energy-exporting states, including Kazakhstan, tended to run substantial trade surpluses without there being any obvious mechanism to encourage them to increase their imports from 'weak rouble' states. The idea of an inter-state bank, discussed below, is meant to facilitate mutual account settlement so that surpluses earned with one trading partner can be used to offset deficits with another (United Nations, *World Economic Survey 1993*, p. 119).

The United Nations Economic Commission for Europe (1993: 171) points to the emergence not only of national cash surrogates but also of 'national roubles' used in non-cash settlements. This was due chiefly to large imbalances in trade between the republics. The central banks of Russia and the Baltic States were increasingly reluctant to accept non-cash roubles in payment for exports to deficit countries such as Ukraine. Towards the end of 1992 Latvia introduced differentiated exchange rates for non-cash roubles originating in various states and the practice was quickly adopted by the central banks of some other countries (Russia and Belarus).

The Russian authorities even tried to limit monetary growth in the rouble area by restricting deliveries of cash roubles. But several republics responded by introducing parallel currencies or coupons (Havrylyshyn *et al.* 1994: 357).

A distinctive feature of 1993 and 1994 is that the majority of payments between Russia and the other countries of the former Soviet Union now go directly through commercial banks rather than via the central banks (*RET*, 1994, vol. 3, no. 1, p. 28).

The question of subsidies

Sachs is reported as saying that Russia continued to subsidize the other countries through cheap resources and credits, to the tune of 10 per cent of national output (*IHT*, 20 March 1993, p. 11). The Deutsche Bank (*Focus: Eastern Europe*, 1993, no. 67, p. 4) quotes the World Bank's estimate that Russian subsidies (the supply of commodities at bargain prices) to the other countries of the former Soviet Union amounted to $20 billion in the first half of 1992. According to Boris Fyodorov, in 1992 Russia provided $17 billion in aid (21.4 per cent of GDP) to CIS countries in the form of cash transfers, credits and low prices (*CDSP*, 1993, vol. XLV, no. 28, p. 30). The $17 billion constituted, for example, soft credits and goods sold at below market prices. In 1992 Russian subsidies in cash and kind accounted for 69 per cent of Uzbekistan's GDP and 67 per cent of Turkmenistan's GDP (*The Economist*, 20 November 1993, p. 115). The IMF/World Bank calculate that the loss of cheap credits and subsidized energy would cost Ukraine, Armenia, Azerbaijan, Georgia, Moldova, Kazakhstan, Kyrgyzstan, Tajikistan and Uzbekistan together $15.5 billion or almost 15 per cent of Russia's GNP (*FT*, 12 November 1993, p. 2).

Orlowski (1993: 1005–6) has calculated the value of 'indirect transfers' between the Soviet republics in 1990 through underpriced oil and natural gas and overpriced other goods (compared with world market prices). Two republics made net transfers (as a percentage of their own GDP) to the other republics, namely Turkmenistan (10.8 per cent) and Russia (3.7 per cent). The others were net recipients (in descending order as a percentage of their GDP): Moldavia, 24.05 per cent; Lithuania, 17.09 per cent; Georgia, 16.02 per cent; Estonia, 12.08 per cent; Latvia, 10.43 per cent; Azerbaijan, 10.09 per cent; Armenia, 9.16 per cent; Belorussia, 8.91 per cent; Tajikistan, 6.08 per cent; Ukraine, 3.61 per cent; Kirghizia, 2.72 per cent; Uzbekistan, 1.26 per cent; Kazakhstan, 0.50 per cent.

Tarr (1994: 1–24) estimated the impact on the fifteen countries of the former Soviet Union of shifting to world prices in their trade had that been accomplished in 1990 or 1989. He concluded that energy and raw material exporters, especially Russia, Turkmenistan and Kazakhstan would be the gainers, while countries that concentrated on food and machinery exports (notably Belarus, Estonia, Latvia, Lithuania and, in particular, Moldova) would be the biggest losers.

In the first quarter of 1993 Russian supplies under bilateral intergovernmental agreements to other rouble zone countries were priced at about half the world market price for oil and one-third for gas. But other deliveries were priced close to world market levels (Bartholdy and Szegvari 1993: 285). By mid-1993 Russia's energy export prices stood at about half the world market level, up from one-third in the first quarter of the year. Price subsidies to other CIS countries were to be almost entirely phased out by the start of 1994 (Bartholdy and Flemming, *Economics of Transition*, 1993, vol. 1, no. 3, p. 369).

CIS countries continued to benefit from low Russian domestic oil prices immediately after the collapse of the Soviet Union, but the price they paid rose to much higher world market levels calculated in US dollars when they left the rouble zone and created their own currencies. Their oil purchases were still in fact heavily subsidized, although no longer to the previous extent, as the price was calculated at an exchange rate considerably lower than in official trading. Some portions were guaranteed at even lower prices under bilateral agreements (Deutsche Bank, *Focus: Eastern Europe*, 28 February 1995, no. 126, p. 7).

The rouble zone

There was considerable controversy about whether to retain or abandon the rouble zone. For example, the EBRD advised the former Soviet republics to abandon it. Separate national currencies or smaller currency zones could improve the prospects for production and trade. The rouble zone was undermined by unco-ordinated credit policy. The argument was that outside the rouble zone countries would adopt more prudent fiscal and monetary policies (*FT*, 12 February 1993, p. 3).

At first the IMF advised the countries of the former Soviet Union to remain in the rouble zone, but later favoured independent currencies. The IMF has been criticized:

1. Jeffrey Sachs has criticized the IMF for its early stance on the rouble zone and is still very critical of the IMF for advising each of the countries of the former Soviet Union to adopt a floating exchange rate regime (*FT*, 29 July 1994, p. 13). 'The most urgent question facing the IMF – whether in Ukraine, Russia, Kazakhstan or elsewhere – is how to help a bankrupt government trying to end high inflation. The IMF's approach is straightforward – sharp cuts in the budget deficit, a low target growth of the money supply, high real interest rates, and a floating exchange rate. But while these policies will end high inflation in the long run, they almost invariably lead to an unnecessarily deep recession; indeed, often to a reversal of the policies themselves, as recent history in Ukraine and other former Soviet Union countries confirms. The IMF has always blamed the governments for not following through, not recognizing that its advice has played a significant role in these failures.' Sachs argues that there is a better way. Stabilization policies in Israel in 1985, Bolivia in 1986, Mexico in 1987, Poland in 1990, Argentina in 1991 and Estonia in 1992 were based on a different principle. The governments of these countries recognized that low money growth was insufficient. It was also necessary to bolster expectations of low inflation and to increase confidence in the money in order to build up money holdings and to reverse capital flight. This was accomplished by a strong government commitment to a stable exchange rate, at least for several months, together with other fiscal, monetary and privatization measures along normal IMF lines. Sachs argues that exchange rate stabilization serves several key functions in ending high inflation. It directly limits price increases in tradable goods (thereby providing a 'nominal anchor' to the price level), it ties the government to a highly visible target, it co-ordinates future

price expectations around a common standard and it raises confidence in the currency (especially when the pegged exchange rate is backed by international resources or gold, as in the case of the most highly successful programmes). 'The situation [in Kyrgyzstan] cries out for a defence of the currency, backed by an international stabilization fund. Instead, the IMF plan calls for more budget cuts and a further decline in the ratio of money to GDP.' (See also Sachs's attack on the IMF in Chapter 8 on aid to Russia.)

2. *The Economist* (30 July 1994, p. 77) also recommended a fixed exchange rate regime. 'Following the advice of the IMF, most ex-Soviet republics allowed their new currencies to float freely ... If the governments concerned had instead pegged their exchange rates to a stable currency, they would have had a more visible anchor against inflation ... If the exchange rate is pegged, prices of traded goods stabilize quickly, because they are subject to competition from abroad at the fixed exchange rate. With a pegged rate, the goal of monetary policy becomes that of defending the exchange rate ... Pegging the exchange rate is not a substitute for cutting budget deficits and keeping monetary policy tight, but – if these things are done – it can make it easier to bring down inflation.' The exchange rate stabilization school thinks it 'far more efficient ... to give a clear signal of confidence through a pegged exchange rate early on'.

On 7 September 1993 Russia, Belarus, Armenia, Kazakhstan, Tajikistan and Uzbekistan agreed (subject to ratification) to form a rouble zone. The others would synchronize their fiscal and monetary policies with Russia, whose central bank would be the only authority allowed to issue roubles. In the meantime the others would use their own currencies or receive new rouble notes with special markings to invalidate their use within Russia.

But Russia began to impose more stringent conditions soon after the dissolution of its parliament on 21 September 1993: (1) the supply of new rouble notes to other countries would be in the form of a credit for a term of half a year at the central bank's interest rate (then 210 per cent); the credit would not be repayable by those countries which, at the end of the period, showed 'readiness for joint functioning' and promised not to introduce national currencies for five years (to prevent new roubles flooding back into Russia); (2) security (collateral) in the form of the gold and hard currency reserves of the other countries (*Moscow News*, 12 November 1993, p. 5; 19 November 1993, p. 4). President Nazarbayev of Kazakhstan replied that 'We have made all possible concessions, but now Moscow has asked us to do the impossible, to hand over to them billions of dollars.' Kazakhstan then introduced its own currency. (A new rouble zone has not been set up.)

Trade

The average share of intra-regional trade in the total trade of the republics of the former Soviet Union (71.8 per cent in 1988) was higher than that of the

EU (59.2 per cent) (Kaser and Mehrotra 1992: 5). Trade between the republics of the former Soviet Union fell sharply:

1. Trade between the states of the former Soviet Union fell by over 30 per cent in 1991 (Michalopoulos and Tarr 1993: 22). In 1993 total trade among the fifteen countries of the former Soviet Union declined to a third of its 1990 level, while trade with the rest of the world fell to 46 per cent compared with 1990. By late 1993 all countries except Tajikistan had introduced their own currencies. The new currencies, with the exception of the Baltic currencies (and possible the Russian rouble) were not convertible and could not be used in trade. Denominating trade in roubles, however, was risky because of the rouble's instability. Barter continued to be the favoured instrument of trade among most of the new states. For countries other than the Baltic States, annually renegotiated intergovernmental barter agreements provide the framework for allocating goods through state ministries or agencies. This mandatory trade leads to widespread distortions, even though prices fixed in the agreements are getting closer to world market levels and the goods included in the agreements have narrowed to a few commodities (Constantine Michalopoulos and David Tarr, *Transition*, 1994, vol. 5, no. 9, pp. 1–4).

2. The United Nations Economic Commission for Europe (1993: 76, 139) puts the falls in trade at 5 per cent in 1990, more than 25–35 per cent in 1991 and 25 per cent in 1992. According to official Russian statistics, Russia's trade with the 'near abroad' in 1993 was 50 per cent in volume terms below the level of 1991 (United Nations Economic Commission for Europe 1994: 105).

3. According to Russian reports, trade with the 'near abroad' fell by 21 per cent in 1993. From 1991 to 1993 Russian exports to the CIS fell as follows: oil, 60 per cent; natural gas, 8 per cent; coal, 68 per cent; petrol, 60 per cent (Deutsche Bank, *Focus: Eastern Europe*, 1994, no. 118, p. 4).

4. Trade among the former Comecon partners and among the republics of the former Soviet Union shrank by half or more between 1989 and 1993. Over 70 per cent of intra-CIS trade in 1992–93 was conducted on the basis of bilateral agreements on strategic supplies at regulated prices, which often diverged widely from world prices (EBRD 1994: 104).

5. In a February 1995 speech Yeltsin stated that the CIS countries accounted for only 20 per cent of Russia's foreign trade, compared with 56 per cent in 1991 (*CDSP*, 1995, vol. XLVII, no. 8, p. 13).

6. In 1994 Russia established a free-trade regime with nearly all CIS states. Some Russian exports to the CIS (fuels, metals, timber and chemicals) still remain subject to export taxes. Export quotas now apply only to the fourteen most important raw materials (*RET*, 1994, vol. 3, no. 2, p. 71).

7. The volume of intra-CIS trade has probably continued to fall (United Nations Economic Commission for Europe 1996: 6). 'The dollar value of intra-CIS trade probably stagnated in 1995, after a fall in 1991–93 and perhaps also in 1994, and the volume of this trade almost certainly continued to fall' (p. 122).

8. In 1997 trade among CIS states fell by about 10 per cent (*IHT*, 29 April 1998, p. 6).

9. 'Whereas in 1991 trade between the current members of the CIS constituted 21 per cent of their combined GDP, today this has fallen to around 6 per cent' (Sakwa and Webber 1999: 407).

Demographic aspects of the CIS

A United Nations study analyses what it considers 'the largest, most complex and potentially most destabilizing' population movements in any region since the Second World War (Frances Williams, *FT*, 23 May 1996, p. 3). Nearly 9 million people have moved within or between the twelve countries of the CIS since 1989, one in thirty of the total CIS population (in the five Central Asian republics one in twelve of the population). Factors include armed conflicts, the breakup of the Soviet Union, Stalin's forced deportations and environmental degradation. About 3 million people have fled seven conflicts since 1988 (when Armenia and Azerbaijan went to war over Nagorno-Karabakh). (Ethnic disputes in Georgia, Armenia and Azerbaijan have led to 1.5 million people leaving their homes: *The Guardian*, 23 May 1996, p. 13. At least 2 million people have fled regional conflicts like those in Tajikistan and Georgia: *IHT*, 27 May 1996, p. 6.) In Chechenia about 500,000 people have been displaced. The breakup of the Soviet Union left between 54 million and 64 million people outside their 'home' territories. More than 3 million of these people have 'returned', mostly to Russia. Between 1936 and 1952 Stalin deported more than 3 million people, including entire populations. Among them were Volga Germans, Crimean Tatars and Meskhetians from Georgia. Some 850,000 Germans have since left for Germany and another 330,000 (the bulk of them Crimean Tatars) have returned to their homeland. Nearly 700,000 people are 'ecological' migrants from areas such as the Chernobyl district, the Aral Sea basin and the former nuclear test site at Semipalatinsk in Kazakhstan. About 450,000 illegal immigrants are in Russia, many trying to reach the West.

According to the 1989 census, 26.3 million ethnic Russians in the Soviet Union lived outside the Russian republic. Together with people of other nationalities indigenous to Russia, the total came to more than 28 million. As of 1 January 1995 the population of Russia was 148,306,000. In 1992, despite the numbers added by migration, Russia's population fell (by 309,000) for the first time in postwar history. The number of Russians who moved to Russia from various republics/countries in the period 1989–95 was as follows: Kazakhstan, 652,600; Uzbekistan, 359,200; Kyrgyzstan, 199,500; Tajikistan, 187,500; Azerbaijan, 164,300; Ukraine, 151,900; Georgia, 134,100; Latvia, 80,200; Turkmenistan, 54,800; Estonia, 51,000; Lithuania, 42,700; Moldova, 36,800; Armenia, 28,300; Belarus, 16,300 (*CDSP*, 1997, vol. XLVIX, no. 1, p. 12).

Later developments in the CIS

At first the CIS seemed to be merely a way of allowing a 'peaceful divorce'. It remains a weak organization, but after 1993 Russia's military and economic dominance (especially its supplies of energy and raw materials) gave it a temporary boost. Political and economic desperation drove reluctant countries to become members and today only the Baltic States have refused to join. Azerbaijan joined on 24 September 1993. On 8 October 1993 Shevardnadze announced that Georgia would seek to join the CIS. He signed a decree on 24 October and parliament ratified a bill on 1 March 1994.

The 22 January 1993 meeting of the CIS was held in Minsk. Azerbaijan was then only an observer and Estonia, Latvia, Lithuania and Georgia were not members of the CIS, either. Seven members signed a charter on closer political and economic integration. Ukraine, Moldova and Turkmenistan signed only the memorandum, allowing them more time to reflect. The idea was that the other seven would ratify the charter during the course of the year, which would also allow time for suggested changes to and amplification of the charter.

All ten members of the CIS accepted the idea of an inter-state bank. This would act as multilateral clearing house for inter-state trade, but not as a central bank in charge of the money supply. The rouble would be the clearing bank's unit of account and the intention was that monetary policy should be co-ordinated. Russia would have 50 per cent of the shares and votes, while the allocation of the remaining percentages would depend on the share of each country in inter-state trade in 1990. But decisions would require a two-thirds majority.

On 17 March 1993 Yeltsin pessimistically concluded that the CIS to date had been 'unable to fulfil the hopes vested in it'. But he proposed closer integration.

At the CIS meeting in Moscow on 14 May 1993 nine of the ten members signed the following declaration of intent: 'Heads of state of the Commonwealth announce their determination to proceed along the path of in-depth integration, the creation of a common market for the free movement of goods, services, capital and labour within the common "economic space" of the states, and to move by phases toward an economic union.' Yeltsin (optimistically) said that an inter-state bank would be set up by 1 October 1993. Turkmenistan did not sign and asked for further time to consider. (Turkmenistan was concerned to protect the price of its natural gas, but it signed during the 23–4 December 1993 meeting: *CDSP*, 1993, vol. XLV, no. 52, p. 16.) Ukraine stressed that it was only a declaration of intent.

There was a declaration regarding economic integration on 10 July 1993. In Moscow Russia, Belarus and Ukraine signed a surprise 'declaration on economic integration', which envisaged the drawing up of a full treaty by 1 September 1993. The declaration called for the following: (1) the creation of a customs union and a single market in goods and services, labour and capital: 'the interests of our states dictate the need to maintain a single economic space'; (2) the unification of monetary, fiscal, price and tax policies; (3) respect for territorial integrity: 'The governments proceed from the fact that economic integration cannot be effective without wider, multilateral joint action in the political, defence and legislative spheres'; (4) the economic union is open to all the countries of the former Soviet Union, but only on condition that they do not belong to another economic grouping that would prevent them carrying out the foreign economic policies of the new union.

On 24 September 1993 there was a meeting to discuss the CIS Treaty of Economic Union. Of the republics of the former Soviet Union only the Baltic States were totally absent from the Moscow meeting, Azerbaijan joining the CIS and (non-member) Georgia sending an observer. Not all members of the CIS signed the framework agreement (individual countries needed to agree on the details), Turkmenistan and Ukraine remaining associate members pending discussion and possible ratification by their parliaments. (The former affiliated as a full member at the 23–4 December 1994 CIS meeting.) The treaty aimed 'gradually to build a common economic space on the basis of market relations' by means of the following: (1) the gradual reduction and eventual abolition of trade barriers (the aim was the free movement of goods, capital and manpower, and unified customs regimes were eventually to be established); (2) equal legal status for all enterprises in the economic union to encourage joint ventures (partly to enable Russia to exchange energy supplies for shares in partners' enterprises); (3) payments union or multi-currency clearing system operated via an inter-state bank (ten CIS states formed the bank on 16 December 1993: *RET*, 1993, vol. 2, no. 4, p. 102) (it would eventually be transformed into a currency union under which members' currencies would float against the rouble within agreed limits; those countries retaining the rouble would allow their fiscal and monetary policy to be synchronized with that of Russia).

A CIS meeting was held in Moscow on 15 April 1994. There was agreement on the setting up of an Inter-state Economic Commission, aimed at integrating the economies and eventually creating a customs union. Ukraine joined the economic union as an associate member. There was also agreement in principle to co-ordinate border policing and peacekeeping duties.

A CIS meeting was held in Moscow on 9 September 1994. There was agreement on the formation of a payments union and an Inter-state Economic Commission. But Azerbaijan and Turkmenistan did not sign and requested more time to consider. The commission is sited in Moscow, its purpose being to implement decisions. It undertakes administrative functions of common concern delegated by members (e.g. the co-ordination of power, oil and gas pipelines, transport and communications; analysis of the economies and the progress of economic reforms; the drawing up of joint economic programmes). Russia has 50 per cent of the votes (Ukraine 14 per cent; Belarus, Kazakhstan and Uzbekistan 5 per cent each; and the other members 3 per cent each). Some major decisions need a 75 per cent vote, e.g. quotas, currency reserves and new funds. (Ukraine was still only an associate member of the CIS economic union and, therefore, could not sign up for the payments union and could be only an associate member of the commission.)

A CIS meeting was held on 21 October 1994. Although the Inter-state Economic Commission, a payments union and a customs union were again on the agenda, it seems that countries would be able to opt out.

At the CIS meeting held in Almaty on 10 February 1995 (the seventeenth) very little was achieved. Yeltsin complained about the 'unsatisfactory work during the past year ... there have been lots of agreements, but no sign of their implementation'. He called on heads of state to 'make a breakthrough, first and foremost, in the area of economics' (*CDSP*, 1995, vol. XLVII, no. 6, p. 23). The meeting confirmed the appointment of Alexei Bolshakov as chairman of the Inter-state Economic Commission.

At the CIS meeting held in Minsk on 26 May 1995 one of the few concrete results was the signing by Russia and Belarus of a customs union agreement, border posts being removed. The summit almost unanimously (Turkmenistan abstained from the voting) agreed to create the inter-state currency committee to promote the mutual conversion of national currencies and to ease mutual payments (*Moscow News*, 2–8 June 1995, p. 2).

Subsequent meetings of the CIS (e.g. 28 March 1997) have achieved very little in practical terms.

A CIS meeting was held in Moscow on 29 April 1998. The controversial Russian businessman Boris Berezovsky was appointed executive secretary. 'The summit meeting this week represents a desperate effort by Moscow to preserve the CIS ... A summit meeting last fall [1997] broke up in confusion. This time officials hope to focus on economics and give its members concrete incentives to integrate. Although President Boris Yeltsin of Russia has declared 1998 "the year of the CIS", most observers consider the organization virtually expired ... Since the founding of the group in December 1991 more than 800 decisions have been issued on topics ranging from military co-operation to liquor sales, but no one knows how many have been signed by whom and ratified by which parliaments. The 2,000-worker bureaucracy in Moscow is launching a study to find out' (Daniel Williams, *IHT*, 29 April 1998, pp. 1, 6). 'The summit meeting was the second in succession to end without a major policy directive or any clear indication of how the organization intends to develop' (Daniel Williams, *IHT*, 30 April 1998, p. 5).

'The CIS [is] a talking-shop dedicated nominally to reintegration. But the CIS has achieved nothing, as was confirmed by yet another purposeless summit in Moscow last week' (*The Economist*, 9 May 1998, p. 28).

'The CIS has failed to integrate the Soviet successor states in any meaningful sense. Although on paper it has been a forum for several ambitious projects of co-operation, in reality the CIS has been gradually emptied of responsibility and has been witness to a diminishing base of collaborative activities' (Sakwa and Webber 1999: 379). 'The CIS provides a forum for diplomacy, informal discussions and the voicing of grievances ... Yet it is clear that the achievements of the CIS are few in number' (p. 408).

'The presidents of Russia, Belarus, Kazahstan, Kyrgyzstan and Tajikistan – the countries of the customs union – have held a meeting in Minsk [23 May 2000]. An attempt was made at the meeting to accelerate the establishment of a free trade zone, which is being held back by the Russian position ... Russia is the only one that has not ratified the free trade treaty. This is because if the treaty takes effect the Russian Treasury will lose millions in revenue from transporting energy resources abroad' (*Kommersant*, 24 May 2000, p. 11: *CDSP*, 2000, vol. 52, no. 21, p. 21).

'We are becoming economic strangers to one another. The customs union has been in an embryonic state for more than four years now, its five members [Russia, Belaus, Kazakhstan, Kyrgyzstan and Tajikistan] in no hurry to fully co-ordinate their trade legislation. Furthermore, all of these countries are trying to gain admission to the WTO, and Kyrgyzstan has already joined it. Yet the WTO has completely different rules. Restoring all production relations within the framework of the Soviet division of labour is not realistic. And the hard currency the post-Soviet republics need so desperately cannot be earned by trading with one another – everyone in the CIS is poor' (Semyon Novoprudsky, *Izvestia*, 17 June 2000, p. 1: *CDSP*, 2000, vol. 52, no. 25, p. 16).

'The new Russian government will not have a ministry for CIS affairs, which has been abolished by presidential decree [24 May 2000]. The ministry's functions will be transferred to the foreign ministry and the ministry of economics ... This is the second time the commonwealth ministry has been abolished. The first time was in April 1998 ... Six months later, however, the commonwealth ministry was reestablished ... True, economic ties with the CIS countries were none the better for it ... Overall management will be the [Russian] security council's job. Putin's new plan accords priority to bilateral ties, with all integration efforts to be based on security' (*Kommersant*, 25 May 2000, p. 11: *CDSP*, 2000, vol. 52, no. 21, p. 22).

At a CIS meeting held in Moscow on 6–7 June 2000 it was decided to terminate the 1992 Bishkek agreement on visa-free travel. Henceforth terms governing travel throughout the former USSR would be established by bilateral and multilateral agreements among CIS countries. Turkmenistan withdrew from the visa-free travel agreement in 1999. Turkmenistan is the only CIS country with which Russia requires visas (*CDSP*, 2000, vol. 52, no. 23, pp. 16–17).

On 30 August 2000 Russian announced that it was to scrap the visa-free travel regime with other CIS states. 'Igor Ivanov, Russia's foreign minister, said the Russian step was motivated by concerns over terrorism, organized crime, drug trafficking and illegal immigration. Analysts said Russia may seek to extract political concession in exchange for non visa travel' (*FT*, 31 August 2000, p. 7). 'Russian foreign minister Igor Ivanov has announced that Russia is withdrawing from the 1992 Bishkek agreement on visa-free travel for CIS citizens … Yesterday [30 August] the government adopted a resolution on pulling out of the accord … In setting forth the reasons for the Russian government's decision Igor Ivanov put "national security interests" at the top of the list … It appears that the only exceptions will be made for … [Russia's] customs union partners (Belarus, Kazakhstan, Kyrgyzstan and Tajikistan), and also for Armenia, Russia's closest ally in the Caucasus … Today [31 August] Russia will inform the CIS executive secretary in Minsk of its decision, after which notes will be sent to all the Commonwealth capitals proposing bilateral talks on entry and exit regulations. Countries … that fail to hold talks within the ninety-day period allotted for this purpose will run the risk of putting their citizens in an awkward position as of 1 December [2000], when Russia will introduce visa requirements unilaterally' (*CDSP*, 2000, vol. 52, no. 35, p. 16).

'At a summit meeting in Astana of the leaders of the CIS customs union (Belarus, Kazakhstan, Kyrgyzstan, Russia and Tajikistan) the Five will proclaim their transformation into a Eurasian Economic Community [EurAsEc]. Weary of charges that Russia was refusing to give the "green light" to a free trade zone in the CIS, Moscow decided to create one within the framework of the Customs Five. Attempts will be made to resolve the main problem involved in establishing a free trade zone – abolishing the assessment of indirect taxes at the place from which goods are shipped – through bilateral agreements, as Russia and Kazakhstan did yesterday [9 October 2000]. The creators of EurAsEc say the community will be modelled on the European Economic Community. The five countries' financial contributions and the number of votes each will have for decision-making purposes will be proportional to each country's economic potential: Russia, 40 per cent; Belarus and Kazakhstan, 20 per cent each; and Kyrgyzstan and Tajikistan, 10 per cent each … If a country fails to keep the financial commitments its voting rights can be temporarily suspended … [Problems include differences in] market reforms … the degree of dependence on foreign ties … and the excessive customs duties that Russia charges for transit across its territory' (*CDSP*, 2000, vol. 52, no. 41, p. 21). 'The treaty founding a Eurasian Community became a reality yesterday [10 October] … The document signed by the presidents of the five customs union countries still has to be ratified by their parliaments. The excessively high transit fees that Moscow has instituted for rail shipments by third countries is another sensitive issue that shapes the climate for real co-operation in Eurasia and remains unsolved … In Astana yesterday Russia and Kyrgyzstan signed an agreement on procedures for collecting indirect taxes' (p. 22).

CHAPTER ELEVEN

THE FEDERAL STATE AND THE CHECHEN CRISIS

THE FEDERAL STATE

Political features of the federal state

The Russian Federation consists of republics, territories, provinces, federal cities, an autonomous province and autonomous regions, all of which are equal members of the Russian Federation. There are eighty-nine 'members' or 'subjects' of the federation, twenty-one republics, six territories, forty-nine provinces, two federal cities (Moscow and St Petersburg), one autonomous province (the Jewish Autonomous Province) and ten autonomous regions.

Demographic features of the federal state

The population of Russia (end of year) was 148.6 million in 1992, 148.3 million in 1993, 148.2 in 1994, 148.0 in 1995 and an estimated 147.5 million 1996 (EBRD 1997b: 233).

There are more than 100 nationalities, the main ones being Russians (81.3 per cent), Tatars (3.6 per cent), Ukrainians (2.7 per cent), Chuvash (1.2 per cent), Dagestanis (1.0 per cent) and Baskirs (0.9 per cent) (*The Independent*, 24 April 1993, p. 11).

The percentage of ethnic Russians in the population of each of the twenty-one republics (in 1989 in descending order) was as follows: Khakassia, 79.5; Karelia, 73.6; Buryatia, 69.9; Adygeya, 68.0; Mordovia, 60.8; Altai, 60.4; Udmurtia, 58.9; Komi, 57.7; Yakutia (Sakha), 50.3; Mari-El, 47.5; Tatarstan, 43.3; Karachevo-Balkaria (Karachai-Cherkessia), 42.4; Bashkortostan, 39.3; Kalmykia, 37.7; Kalbardino-Balkaria, 31.9; Tuva, 32.0; North Ossetia, 29.9; Chuvashia, 26.7; Ingushetia, 23.0; Chechenia, 22.0; Dagestan, 9.2 (*The Economist*, 14 January 1995, p. 33; *Business Central Europe*, September 1996, p. 79).

In the republics the titular population is a majority of the population in only five (Tuva, Chechenia, Ingushetia, North Ossetia and Chuvashia). Even in these republics, as well as Tatarstan, ethnic Russians are a significant minority (Kempton 1996: 586–7).

Economics of the federal state

As the economy disintegrated in the late Soviet and early post-Soviet periods the regions of Russia came to play a more important economic role. Indeed, in a more general sense it can be argued that local government assumes greater importance in conditions of economic and political instability. Not only is central authority weakened, but the local population finds it easier to identify with and has greater confidence in local administration.

The Russian economy is now highly differentiated in economic terms. Affluent Moscow stands out like a beacon. Reformist Nizhny Novgorod contrasts starkly with traditionalist Ulyanovsk.

Since the collapse of communism economic differences amongst the regions have apparently increased (Sutherland and Hanson 1996: 367).

'While the Soviet state was highly autarkic and self-sufficient in most goods, its lower-level components were not' (Kempton 1996: 588).

Nine of the eighty-nine members are net donors, while eighty are net receivers (*The Times*, 9 September 1998, p. 1).

'Under the system of so-called budget federalism the ten richest regions are net contributors to federal coffers. Moscow redistributes this and other cash to the rest, many of which are incapable of fending from themselves. In the poorest regions, such as Ingushetia, Dagestan and Tuva, federal handouts can account for up to two-thirds of total revenues' (*Business Central Europe*, November 1998, p. 46).

The shelling of parliament on 4 October 1993 was a turning point for the nature of the federal state in Russia. The danger of Russia disintegrating through 'members' ('subjects') of the federation breaking away seemed to be over. (Note that Yeltsin had previously tried to curry favour with regional leaders in his dispute with parliament by offering greater autonomy.) Åslund argues that 'Since most economic powers have devolved from Moscow to regional governments, there is little incentive to claim independence' (1994b: 61–2). The example of Chechenia is 'unlikely to be emulated if only because it has won its freedom at such cost'. 'Few regions are anyway tempted to try to win outright independence. Most – seventy-nine of the eighty-nine – receive more from the federal treasury than they pay in. And all know that, even if oil or gold or diamonds made them economically viable, independence in the middle of a huge Russian land mass would be largely illusory' (*The Economist*, Survey, 12 July 1997, p. 16). 'Those regions or republics that put more into the central coffers in taxes than they take out [number] a dozen or so out of Russia's eighty-nine' (*The Economist*, 12 September 1998, p. 42).

Twenty-three of the eighty-nine 'members' of the federation collect sufficient taxes to meet their own needs; the others need federal subsidies (*Moscow News*, 14–20 October 1994, p. 8). A presidential decree of 22 December 1993 allowed the members of the federation to vary the tax rate on profits in the range from 13 per cent to 25 per cent (of which 13 percentage points were to go to the federal budget and the remainder was to go to the local budget) (*CDSP*, 1994, vol. XLVI, no. 19, p. 10).

'Russia has been transformed from the most decentralized state in Europe to a decentralized federation, with roughly half of public spending going through local governments' (*The Economist*, 15 June 1996, p. 23). 'The regions need friends in the Kremlin: most rely heavily on transfers from the federal budget. True, such transfers fell from 3.4 per cent of GDP in 1994 to 1.8 per cent in 1995' (*The Economist*, 31 August 1996, p. 35).

The share of the 'territories' in total tax revenue was 44.1 per cent in 1992 and 58.8 per cent in 1993, while the respective shares of budgetary expenditure were 38.6 per cent and 50.1 per cent (Tesche 1994: 116–17).

An October 1991 law established the independence of budgets at all levels of government, thus breaking the previous unitary fiscal system. Fiscal independence of regional and local governments was to be ensured by the availability of their own revenue sources and by their right to decide how to spend their revenues. The share of regional revenues in the consolidated 'official' budget (which excludes off-budget operations) was 50.7 per cent in 1992, 65.7 per cent in 1994 and 54.6 per cent in 1995 (Le Houerou and Rutkowski 1996: 22–3). Regional governments' share of the consolidated 'official' general government budget was 36 per cent in 1992, about 50 per cent in both 1993 and 1994 and 47 per cent in 1995. The regions' share of social sector spending (mainly education and health) increased from 66.3 per cent in 1992 to more than 80 per cent in 1993–95. The regional share of expenditures under 'national economy' also increased, from 46.8 per cent in 1992 to 70.6 per cent in 1994, reflecting the sharp rise in the regions' subsidies and capital transfers to the productive sectors. A number of central functions were shifted to the regional budgets in early 1992, e.g. consumer price subsidies (such as for milk, bread, meat and baby food), cash subsidies for vulnerable groups, welfare programmes for pensioners and the disabled, family and child allowances, and support for the homeless. Initially these subsidies were financed by the central government through transfers. Budget-financed investments were also decentralized in 1992. Up until then regional governments had borne responsibility only for capital expenditures relating to housing. The federal government has progressively cut its subsidies to the 'productive' sector, including agriculture. In 1994 responsibility for financing vocational technical schools was shifted to sub-national governments. The growing share of regional spending has been accompanied by an increasing deficit in pre-transfer regional budget deficits and by an increase in federal budget transfers to regional government. The consolidated pre-transfer regional budget balance shifted from a small surplus in 1992 to a deficit that widened from 2 per cent of GDP in 1993 to 3.5 per cent in 1994. The establishment of the formula-based federal fund for financial support to regional governments in July 1994 represented a change toward more transparent mechanisms for grant allocation. The fund accounted for 22 per cent of federal budget transfers in 1994 and about 50 per cent in 1995, with specific transfers and short-term credits accounting for the rest. Federal transfers also take place off-budget through the national extrabudgetary funds (e.g. for roads, employment, ecology and medical insurance) (pp. 25–7). 'The findings suggest that the effects of transfers on regional revenue and regional income moved from equalizing to counter-equalizing in the period 1991–95 ... The equalizing role of *explicit* transfers in Russia, such as equalizing subventions, partial funding of federal spending mandates, grants for particular purposes or short-term credits, is minor, and the equalization fund does not play any meaningful role in promoting equalization' (p. 39).

'Over two-thirds of local government revenues comes from their share in taxes collected by the central government. Moreover, while this share is in theory fixed, in practice it is negotiated. Regional government negotiate with Moscow, and local governments negotiate with regions. The effects of such fiscal federalism ... are perverse. Governors have little incentive to broaden their tax bases, and instead devote their efforts to negotiations with Moscow ... Under these circumstances it is not surprising that local governments in Russia do not feel pressured to promote small business' (Shleifer 1997: 403). 'Rather than encourage local business and profit when it does, local officials in Russia often destroy local business through excessive up-front corruption and regulation ... The likely reason is that many of the local officials in Russia see a rather short and insecure future for themselves in politics' (p. 404). 'Perhaps the most critical one [of essential public sector reforms] is to accelerate elections at the sub-regional or local levels. Such elections would increase accountability of the local politicians to the public and, therefore, through such channels as the need for public revenue and for political contributions, make local government friendlier to business ... Fiscal federalism – and more generally the tax system – in Russia needs to be reformed as well. If local government are to be responsive to the needs of their constituents, they must tax their constituents themselves and spend the money to a large extent from these proceeds' (pp. 406–7).

The Economist (25 January 1997, p. 37) comments as follows: 'The regions have learned to seek strength in numbers. All save Chechenia have joined "economic associations" ... The Far East and Siberian associations speak for the regions richest in natural resources. The Greater Volga and Urals associations embrace many quite prosperous industrial cities. The Black Earth and the North-West associations include harder-up cities and swathes of farmland. Central Russia makes an uneasy marriage between Moscow and the poorer industrial belt around it. North Caucasus includes some of Russia's poorest places, which are correspondingly dependent on federal handouts. A ninth, informal association, which took shape in November, may prove the most influential of the lot. Led by Yuri Luzhkov, the mayor of Moscow, it brings together the rich regions ... which put more money into the federal kitty than they get out of it.' (The 'community of donor regions' involves twelve of the eighty-nine members: *The World Today*, 1997, vol. 53, no. 2, p. 33.) The economic associations are as follows:

1. Central Russia: Bryansk, Vladimir, Ivanovo, Kaluga, Kostroma, Moscow, Ryazan, Smolensk, Tver, Tula, Yaroslavl and Moscow city.
2. Black Earth: Voronezh, Belgorod, Kursk, Lipetsk, Orel and Tambov.
3. Greater Volga: Tatarstan, Mordovia, Mari-El, Astrakhan, Volgograd, Nizhni Novgorod, Penza, Samara, Saratov and Ulyanovsk.
4. North-West: Karelia, Komi, Arkhangelsk, Vologda, Kaliningrad, Kirov, Leningrad, Murmansk, Novgorod, Pskov, Nenets and St Petersburg city.
5. Urals: Bashkortostan, Udmurtia, Kurgan, Orenburg, Perm, Sverdlovsk, Chelyabinsk and Komi-Permyak.
6. North Caucasus: Adygeya, Dagestan, Ingushetia, Kalbadino-Balkaria, Karachai-Cherkessia, North Ossetia, Kalmykia, Krasnodar, Stavropol and Rostov.
7. Siberia: Buryat, Altai, Khakass and Krasnoyarsk, Irkutsk, Novosibirsk, Omsk, Tomsk, Tyumen, Kemerovo, Agin Buryat, Taimyr, Urst-Orda Buryat, Khanty-Mansi, Yevensk and Yamal-Nenets.
8. Far East: Sakha, Primorski, Khabarovsk, Amur, Kamchatka, Magadan, Chita, Sakhalin, Jewish autonomous province, Koryak and Chukotka (*The Economist*, 25 January 1997, p. 37).

'So thinly is its [the federal government's] authority spread that, save in defence and foreign policy, what happens today owes much more to the sum of regional-government action than to government at the federal centre in Moscow ... Elected governors quickly found they were as unsackable as the republics' presidents. Witness, last summer [1997], Mr Yeltsin's futile attempt to boot out Yevgeni Nazdratenko, the ... elected governor of Russia's far-eastern Primorski ("maritime") territory ... The balance of power may be even tilting further towards the regions – partly because many local leaders are still gaining in experience, partly because governments are fast bolstering political with financial autonomy ... Local governments have also been learning to borrow, and so run explicit budget deficits. Most were dabbling in the issuing of unregulated promissary notes until this was banned by law in February 1997. Since then more respectable borrowing has become the rule. Some regions have even managed to borrow abroad' (*The Economist*, 3 January 1997, pp. 31–2).

As late as 1993 social benefits accounted for a third of Russia's total wage bill and more than 10 per cent of industrial employment. Since then there has been a general redistribution of enterprise responsibilities to individuals and local and national governments. Over half of enterprise-owned housing stock has been privatized since 1992. Many kindergartens have either been shut down or transferred to local authorities. Holiday camps have been closed or sold to private enterprises. Houses of culture have often been turned into casinos. Hospitals and clinics have mostly stayed open, but are run by local government and financed through health insurance premiums. Fewer than a quarter of private enterprises started since 1991 provide child care, whereas two-thirds of state-owned smoke-stack industries do (*The Economist*, 10 January 1998, p. 79).

'Over the weekend [26–7 December 1998] a trilateral commission, consisting of both houses of parliament and the government, agreed that Moscow would next year [1999] spend 33.7 billion roubles – or 14 per cent of all tax revenues – on supporting the regions but that the subsidies would be reallocated. Russia's thirty-nine worst-hit regions, including Dagestan in the north Caucasus and Kamchatka and Sakhalin in the far east, will receive additional support next year. But thirty-six better-off territories, such as the oil region of Tyumin and the industrial city of Novgorod, will lose some of their subsidies. Twelve regions will receive no financial support from Moscow ... The federal government would receive 49.5 per cent of all tax revenues with regional authorities receiving the rest' (John Thornhill, *FT*, 28 December 1998, p. 2).

'There are only ten "donor" regions – that is, regions that contribute more to the federal budget than they receive from it' (Andrei Nesterenko, *Finance and Development*, September 2000, vol. 37, no. 3, p. 22).

'Vladimir Mau [in a personal interview conducted in Moscow on 17 October 1999] estimates that in 1992 the centre accounted for 60 per cent of total expenditures in Russia and the subjects 40 per cent. His best estimate is that by 1998 these figures had been reversed' (Stepan 2000: 169).

(For later developments, see the section on 'tax reform in the Putin era' in Chapter 7.)

Bilateral agreements

Bilateral, power-sharing agreements ('treaties') had been drawn up between the centre and the 'members'.

Agreements with Tatarstan, Bashkortostan and Sakha (Yakutia)

These were as follows:

1. *Tatarstan.* In 1991 Tatarstan had a population of 3.8 million (48 per cent Tatar and 42 per cent Russian). It is an important oil producer. A referendum was held on 21 March 1991. The turnout was 81.7 per cent and 61.4 per cent said 'yes' to a 'sovereign state'. In December 1991 Tatarstan was granted increased economic autonomy, over oil for example.

A bilateral power-sharing treaty with the autonomous republic of Tatarstan was signed on 15 February 1994 by President Yeltsin and President Mintimir Shaimiyev. Tatartstan agreed to drop the terms 'sovereign state' and 'subject of international law' from its constitution and to pay federal taxes (*CDSP*, 1994, vol. XVLI, no. 7, p. 11). Tatarstan would retain its own constitution, have its own police force and have substantial freedom in economic affairs. It would not be allowed to decide for itself the share of tax revenue to remit to the centre, but it actually transfers to Moscow only 10 per cent of the taxes it collects (ordinary provinces transfer up to 80 per cent) (*Business Central Europe*, October 1994, p. 24). Tatars who do not wish to serve in the federal army may opt to perform some other service specified by the Tatar authorities.

'The 1994 treaty with Moscow gave Tatarstan extensive responsibility. While Russia kept control of the military factories and higher education and agreed to pay for half of the police costs, Tatarstan got virtually everything else, including the lucrative oil and petrochemical industries, the sole right to collect taxes and control of key appointments' (David Hoffman, *IHT*, 17 June 1997, p. 10).

Tatarstan has introduced a three-year tax holiday for foreign companies and joint ventures. In addition local property and profit tax exemptions are available for all manufacturing and service companies with at least 30 per cent foreign ownership and assets worth at least $1 million (*IHT*, Survey, 2 December 1994, p. 12).

In the February 1994 treaty Tatarstan won full ownership rights over its large oil reserves and industrial enterprises, the right to retain the bulk of tax revenues and to conduct an independent foreign economic policy. President Mintimer Shaimiyev was a fierce critic of the economic policy adopted by Russia in 1992: 'I think Russia could have fashioned its economic reforms along the Chinese way and avoided many of the social problems it has today ... Shock therapy affected a large proportion of the population and resulted in a landslide of impoverishment. We therefore decided to change things more gradually in Tatarstan.' But Thornhill says that Tatarstan is now determined to forge ahead with its own brand of market reforms. It is looking to speed up privatization, reduce bureaucracy, promote small businesses and attract foreign investment. Tatarstan accounts for 10 per cent of Russia's oil output and has some of Russia's largest industrial plants, e.g. the Kamaz truck enterprise. General Motors of the US has already signed a contract to produce annually 50,000 of its own vehicles (John Thornhill, *FT*, 20 February 1996, p. 2).

'Some representatives of the centre believe that Shaimiyev manipulates the democrats and the nationalists, not allowing either to gain any real strength. These same methods – the combination of compromise and force – are used by the president in his dealings with Muslim leaders, who actively strive for more political influence. Shaimiyev believes that religion should play no part in politics ... Another trusted method Shaimiyev uses is transposing national problems onto the economic plane: not changing Russian schools into Tatar schools, but building new Tatar ones as the need arises' (Sanobar Shermatova, *Moscow News*, 28 March–3 April 1996, p. 3). Tatarstan draws up its own budget, has won the right of ownership of its subsoil resources and land, and has the right to do as it wishes with a third of the oil it produces. Shaimiyev tries 'to put nationality-related problems in an economic perspective. Do not change Russian schools to Tatar ones; build new schools as needed. Do not force people to study the Tatar language; create a system (by publishing textbooks and leaning aids) to promote its study' (Sanobar Shermatova, *CDSP*, 1996, vol. XLVIII, no. 12, pp. 15–16).

'Whereas ethnic nationalism contributed to a devastating war in the Russian Republic of Chechnya, economic nationalism has been one of the driving forces behind the peaceful devolution of power from the federal government in Moscow to the Republic of Tatarstan. Avoiding the emotionally charged rhetoric of self-determination and of Tatars' ethnic and historical claims to sovereignty, the republic's leaders have instead used their vast oil resources and their industrial base as levers to secure political and economic concessions from Moscow. Few of Russia's eighty-nine administrative units are rich in petroleum or other valuable resources, however, and so few can negotiate from positions of such strength' (Hanauer 1996: 63). Ethnic nationalism has played a minor role in Tatarstan's attempts to claim greater autonomy due to factors such as the following: (1) the high degree of urbanization (and therefore cultural assimilation) of ethnic Tatars; (2) long historical links; (3) the fact that only 48 per cent of Tatarstan's population is ethnically Tatar (ethnic Russian constitute 43 per cent), while only 32 per cent of Russia's 5.5 million ethnic Tatars live in the Republic of Tatarstan; (4) the high degree of economic interdependence between the regions of the former Soviet Union; (5) geographically Tatarstan is completely surrounded by Russian territory (pp. 69, 70, 78). The 15 February 1994 bilateral treaty gives ownership of the land, mineral wealth and other resources to Tatarstan. Tatarstan has the authority to impose taxes, to draft the republic's budget, to conclude treaties and 'independently to conduct foreign economic activity'. The agreement also calls for Russia and Tatarstan to negotiate export quotas for certain products, including oil. 'Its greatest gain … has been the ability to establish foreign economic relations' (p. 73).

On 24 March 1996 Shaimiyev ran unopposed in the presidential election. He was reelected with 97.3 per cent of the vote in a turnout of about 80 per cent.

'Aspects of the agreements that accompanied Tatarstan's 1994 bilateral treaty were up for renewal in 1999. Tatarstan made no effort to significantly expand its prerogatives. It was a status quo power seeking to preserve what it has won in 1994. But in the newly negotiated April 1999 bilateral treaty the federal centre was successful in "clawing back" some resources they had lost in 1994. Moscow won back the "right" to have a federal tax collection authority located in Tatarstan to collect federal taxes. Moscow also received shares in Russia's largest truck company, Kamaz, which is located in Tatarstan and was a federally owned factory that had in essence been expropriated by Tatarstan. As part of the 1999 bilateral treaty the minister of economics of the Federation will be, *ex officio*, the chairman of the board of directors of Kamaz' (Stepan 2000: 171).

2. *Bashkortostan.* The power-sharing agreement with this oil-producing (6 per cent of total output) autonomous republic was signed on 3 August 1994. The republic had already adopted its own constitution, but there would be a federal constitutional and macroeconomic policy framework and the federal government would be responsible for foreign affairs and defence. The republic would have significant powers, e.g. its own judiciary, certain tax-raising authority and the right to conclude foreign economic agreements.

All the republic's natural resources, including oil, were put under its exclusive 'ownership'. As regards industrial facilities the republic retained, among other things, all oil refineries and petrochemical enterprises. The federal government was allocated the defence and coal industries. The republic renounced the system whereby taxes are paid only to the republic government, which then decides how much to give the federal government. The division of taxes going to the federal government was as follows: VAT, 75 per cent; revenue from foreign-economic activity (i.e. duties), 100 per cent; the 38 per cent tax on profits, 13 percentage points (*CDSP*, 1995, vol. XLVII, no. 6, p. 8).

John Lloyd (*FT*, 25 February 1995, p. 7) argues that these sorts of arrangements are 'likely to be available only to relatively wealthy regions and republics that pay more into the federal budget than they receive. Moscow is unlikely to be so generous with parts of the federation that rely on the centre for finance.'

3. *Sakha* (*Yakutia*). Sakha comprises 20 per cent of Russia's land area and is one of Russia's most richly endowed components. It produces, for example, 98 per cent of Russia's rough diamonds and 21 per cent of its gold. But it is sparsely populated (just over 1 million in 1989). The titular population, the Sakha (Yakuts, of Turkic origin) comprise about 38 per cent and ethnic Russians about 50 per cent (Kempton 1996: 589).

The bilateral agreement was signed on 29 June 1995. Under the 1991 agreement the sovereignty of the Republic of Sakha-Yakutia was recognized and Moscow undertook to finance Yakutia's social sphere in exchange for 100 per cent ownership of the republic's minerals. But Moscow's failure to meet its commitments led to the 1995 agreement. Under this the republic (1) has the right to diplomatic representation in the world and (2) finances its own social sphere (such as education and health) in return for ownership of 26 per cent of diamond output, 30 per cent of gold output and a slightly smaller percentage of oil and gas output (*Moscow News*, 30 June–6 July 1995, p. 1; *CDSP*, 1995, vol. XLVII, no. 26, pp. 14–15).

Other agreements

By November 1995 thirteen republics, including North Ossetia, Sakha (Yakutia) and Buryatia, had signed treaties with Moscow (Hanauer 1996: 74).

Tyumen accounts for roughly two-thirds of oil output and is now permitted to sell up to 10 per cent of its production on its own account. Other regions are also allowed to sell some oil on their own account (Deutsche Bank, *Focus: Eastern Europe*, 1995, no. 126, pp. 4–5).

James Meek (*The Guardian*, 31 January 1996, p. 9) reports on four separate regional agreements signed in January 1996 with Sverdlovsk, Kaliningrad, Orenburg (30 January) and Krasnodar (30 January). 'The four treaties mark a dramatic departure for Mr Yeltsin's administration, which had previously struck agreements with the federation's twenty-one ethnically-based autonomous republics ... Instead of giving all the regions the same degree of self-determination, Moscow appears intent on handing out tailored packages of privileges and powers to each in turn.' The governor of Orenburg said that his treaty meant that the regional legislature would be able to pass vital laws which the Russian parliament had failed to draft, especially one to control flows of migrants and refugees from Central Asia. In addition, he claimed that Orenburg had received little in return for its contribution to the federal treasury.

In mid-January 1996 agreements were signed with Kaliningrad and Sverdlovsk provinces. The special status of Kaliningrad province has to do with its detachment geographically from the rest of Russia (and thus its dependence on transport and communications links running across the Baltic States) and the heavy concentration of military installations. Hence the need to grant the province both additional powers in the foreign-economic shere and the status of a duty-free zone. Sverdlovsk province is distinguished by the fact that it has virtually no food supply of its own and is replete with enterprises of the military-industrial complex. A good many enterprises were to switch from federal ownership to provincial jurisdiction. Joint jurisdiction was also provided for, including agro-industrial enterprises and enterprises in the defence complex (and programmes for their conversion to civilian production). The province was granted the right to deduct 10 per cent of receipts from the extraction of rare metals and gems. Federal taxes earmarked for the funding of federal programmes were to remain in the province and sent to their proper destinations through local authorized commercial banks. Pacts could be concluded in foreign economic relations, although within the framework of the federal constitution (*CDSP*, 1996, vol. XLVIII, no. 3, p. 21).

Of Russia's twenty-one 'autonomous republics', eight have signed special treaties. Komi (signed on 20 March 1996) now has 'unparalled powers over its oil-filthy environment'. Ethnically homogeneous Tuva, abutting Mongolia, has insisted on a right to secede. Ingushetia has a special tax status, enjoying 'offshore' tax status within the Russian Federation and destined to become an international tax haven. In March 1996 the Karachaev-Cherkess republic gave itself a new constitution. In 1991 there were contested elections for the heads of the twenty-one republics. 'The first elections for governors of Russia's regions followed hesistantly, the winners still confirmed (and sometimes dismissed) by presidential decree, until Eduard Rossel, voted in as governor of Sverdlovsk province a year ago, became the first to owe his office solely to the ballot box. December saw the election of a dozen more governors, including Yevgeni Nazdratenko, the autocratic boss of gangster-ridden Primorski Krai on Russia's Pacific coast, and Boris Nemtsov, reformist boss of Nizhny Novgorod. It was striking that, whereas the federal "party of government" performed dismally at the polls, most of these incumbent governors won handily' (*The Economist*, 23 March 1996, pp. 37–8).

Twenty-four of the eighty-nine members of the Russian Federation have negotiated power-sharing deals (David Hoffman, *IHT*, 17 June 1997, p. 10).

On 4 July 1997 Yeltsin signed power-demarcation pacts with the provinces of Bryansk, Volgda, Magadan, Saratov and Chelyabinsk. 'Despite the diverse and distinctive features of the federation members ... virtually all of the treaty texts assign to joint jurisdiction such matters as drafting and implementing economic restructuring programmes, converting defence-complex enterprises (for civilian production), ensuring the stable functioning of industry and of the fuel and power complex, inter-budgetary relations, and a co-ordinated personnel policy ... It is indicative that it was work on the treaties that gradually gave rise to a practice whereby the regions ... channel part of the taxes that are collected into federal expenditures in their areas ... As a result, federal taxes are not sent off to Moscow but are used on the spot for their intended purposes' (*CDSP*, 1997, vol. XLIX, no. 27, p. 8).

On 9 July 1997 Yeltsin signed a decree by which presidential representatives in the regions were to oversee federal personnel and funds and to co-ordinate federal agencies (*CDSP*, 1997, vol. XLIX, no. 28, pp. 10–11). Presidential representatives in the regions would be responsible for co-ordinating the activities of regional branches of all federal agencies and would monitor the use of federal funds in the regions (*RET*, 1997, no. 3, p. 120).

Although Moscow's 8.6 million officially registered residents made up only 6 per cent of the population of Russia in 1996, the capital accounted for 10.9 per cent of GDP and provided 24 per cent of total tax revenue. Moscow was the only one of Russia's eighty-nine regions that ran a budget surplus as well as being (along with nine other regions) a net contributor to the federal budget. In 1996 Moscow's average income per person was $6,122, compared with a Russian average of $1,797. Moscow has attracted two-thirds of foreign investment in Russia. 'Moscow's mayor, Yuri Luzhkov, has managed to retain rules that force out-of-towners to register for residence, despite the constitutional court's ruling that they should not have to' (*The Economist*, 6 September 1997, p. 38).

In June 1998 an agreement was signed with Chelyabinsk province whereby the federal government would provide support only if various obligations were assumed. The federal government would monitor these commitments on a quarterly basis and non-compliance could mean a reduction or even discontinuation of financial assistance. This was seen as the first of a series of agreements with the regions (*CDSP*, 1998, vol. 50, no. 24, pp. 8–9).

Local politics

'Although Russia held local elections for a variety of positions in 1990, President Yeltsin has subsequently assumed control over local governments. In 1991 he signed a decree giving himself power to appoint governors and mayors without elections in most regions, and in 1993 he sharply curtailed the power of the local legislatures' (Shleifer 1997: 402).

On 4 October 1994 a presidential decree made regional administrators ('governors') subject to presidential appointment instead of being elected (*IHT*, 5 October 1994, p. 2). The decree banned all elections for governors (*FT*, 6 October 1994, p. 2).

'Whereas up until now chief administrators have generally been appointed by the President of the Federation, now the regions will be governed by leaders who are elected by the local population and whom the President will not be able to dismiss by decree from Moscow' (*Izvestia*, 27 August 1996, p. 1; *CDSP*, 1996, vol. XLVIII, no. 34, p. 18).

On 4 September 1997 North Ossetia and Ingushetia signed a treaty normalizing relations (*IHT*, 5 September 1997, p. 6).

The 1996–97 provincial (regional) and local elections

Some notable results were as follows:

1 September 1996. Dmitri Ayatskov (reformer) wins Saratov.

20 October 1996. Alexander Rutskoi wins Kursk with 78.9 per cent of the vote, compared with 18 per cent for his pro-Yeltsin opponent. (Rutskoi was only reinstated as a candidate thirty-six hours before polling, being initially disqualified because he no longer lives in Kursk.)

Nizhny Novgorod is won by Boris Nemtsov.

Sverdlovsk is won by Eduard Rossel. (In August 1995 he won a famous victory over the incumbent head of the province, Alexei Strakhov of Our Home is Russia: *CDSP*, 1996, vol. XLVIII, no. 34, p. 19.)

22 December 1996. Khakassia is won by Alexei Lebed (brother of Alexander Lebed).

23 March 1997. Tula is won by Vasily Starodubtsev, a member of the 'Gang of Eight' in the abortive coup of August 1991.

13 July 1997. The governorship of Nizhny Novgorod is won by a reformer, the successor to Boris Nemtsov (who gave his support). (On 29 March 1998 Andrei Klimentyev, although charged with corruption and extortion, won the election for mayor of Nizhny Novgorod. He campaigned on a populist platform, capitalizing on the anxieties of the poor and unemployed by making extravagant promises. But the local electoral commission declared the election invalid. A local judge ruled that Klimentyev had violated the terms of his bail and so had to return to prison. Klimentyev and former governor Boris Nemtsov were friends before the former was accused of misappropriating credits. 'The political establishment was unable to rally around a common candidate ... Virtually nobody around here believes the confluence of events was a coincidence ... The heavy-handed intervention has stirred local resentment against Moscow': Michael Gordon, *IHT*, 16 April 1998, p. 4. An appeal against the annulment was turned down on the grounds of numerous infractions by all candidates, e.g. empty promises and libel: *CDSP*, 1998, vol. 50 no. 20, p. 14.)

On 11 October 1998 Yuri Lebedev was elected mayor. He had been acting governor of Nizhny Novgorod province for three months after Boris Nemtsov went to Moscow in the spring of 1997 (*CDSP*, 1998, vol. 50, no. 41, p. 17).

17 May 1998. Alexander Lebed is elected governor of Krasnoyarsk.

In the first round, held on 26 April 1998, he won 45.1 per cent of the vote. He was backed by the industrial tycoons Boris Berezovsky and Vladimir Gusinsky. The incumbent governor, Valeri Zubov (backed by Yeltsin and Moscow's mayor Yuri Luzhkov), was second with 35.4 per cent of the vote. In the second round Lebed won 57.1 per cent of the vote, compared with Zubov's 38.1 per cent.

Some comments on the 1996–97 elections are as follows:

1. By late December 1996 three regions still had to hold second round elections and elections in three other regions were to take place no earlier than January 1997. But Gleb Cherkasov and Vladimir Shpak (*Sevodnya*, 26 December 1996, p. 2; *CDSP*, 1996, vol. XLVIII, no. 52, pp. 4–6) argue that it was still possible to draw general conclusions. The results of the gubernatorial elections have been assessed in differing ways. The Kremlin has assessed them 'as an unqualified victory for itself: in addition to twenty reelected governors, there are now seventeen new ones with whom ... the "party of power" will have no problems ... the PPUR (Popular-Patriotic Union of Russia) can count on only eight new consistent oppositionist votes in the Council of the Federation'. The opposition, however, considers that the Kremlin lost these elections. 'Starting with the fourteen new governors who were nominated by the PPUR, the opposition adds in all the "independents" who received any degree of opposition support during the election campaign, leaving on the authorities' side of the ledger only the reelected "Moscow appointees", of whom there are twenty ... the Communists give themselves a victory ... with a score of twenty-five to twenty.' But Cherkasov and Shpak consider there that was no 'Red Shift'. 'If one starts from the premise that the regional elections were a struggle between the "party of power" and the popular-patriotic opposition, the Kremlin definitely won the campaign.' On the other hand, 'if one regards the regional elections as a struggle to keep incumbent governors in office, the Kremlin lost the elections'. But the authors believe that the degree to which the new governors who ran as independent economic managers will be willing to support Kremlin policies in the future is another question. 'A "third force" that can provisionally be called "the party of strong economic managers", with Moscow mayor Yuri Luzhkov as its leader, has

already been virtually rounded into shape in the Council of the Federation, even though it has not yet been legally formalized … leaders of the donor regions [those who put more money into the federal budget than they take back from it] … are actively establishing contacts with the leaders of both neighbouring and more distant regions where the newly elected governors are not yet fully aware of what it means to be elected rather than appointed.' The authors estimate that at least seventeen new members of the Council of the Federation are ready to join the 'party of strong economic managers' (PSEM). This number includes not only independent candidates but also governors from the ranks of 'Moscow appointees', and even some who were until recently active members of the opposition bloc. 'PSEM supporters are united chiefly by the fact that they head fairly strong and financially sound regions where the local elite … sees further federalization of society as an opportunity to realize its own financial and political ambitions … On the other hand, opposition figures, most of whom came into power in regions that are heavily dependent on subsidies, will objectively resist the development of federalism … and this … will unite them with supporters of the "party of power" … If one sums up the results of the regional elections from this standpoint … both … the Communist opposition and the "party of power" lost the elections. They lost simply by virtue of the fact that they allowed the emergence in the established system of counterbalances of a "third force" – federalist regional leaders who are capable of deliberately or inadvertently destroying that entire system … it is entirely possible that, with the RFCP moving into the position of a "constructive opposition", the centre of the political struggle will shift from the State Duma to the Council of the Federation.'

2. 'The new regional order followed Russia's adoption of a new constitution in 1993 and subsequently of a law obliging local leaders to be elected by the end of 1996. That left forty-seven … oblasts, krais and autonomous okrugs … scrambling to hold last-minute polls … In all but one region the incumbent governor has sought another term; just twenty have so far succeeded and twenty-one have lost. The communists backed most of the successful challenges and called the results a slap in the Mr Yeltsin's face, which they were. But all save eight or nine of the newcomers have been independent candidates for whom communist endorsement was merely a nice bonus … So few regions have gone truly "red"' (*The Economist*, 25 January 1997, p. 37).

3. Between June 1996 and the end of March 1997 fifty-five regions held elections for the post of 'head of administration', generally known as 'governor'. 'The 1996–97 gubernatorial elections brought to a close a fifteen-month electoral season that produced, for the first time in Russian history, elected governments at the national and subnational levels throughout the country' (Solnick 1998: 72). 'Neither side [the Yeltsin administration and Zyuganov's Communist Party] could claim victory from the regional election marathon. Roughly half the incumbents who faced the voters were defeated … On the other hand, many of the "opposition" candidates who did win quickly

expressed their eagerness to work with rather than against the presidential administration. ['Many of the victorious challengers ... rushed to strike deals with the Kremlin to gain some economic benefits for their region ... Even some of Yeltsin's most partisan opponents – Alexander Rutskoi in Kursk and Nikolai Kondratenko in Krasnodar – indicated their intention to withdraw from partisan politics to focus on regional problems': p. 73.] A closer examination of the voting fails to support a portrayal of the gubernatorial elections as an extension of the national partisan contest between the "party of power" and the communists. The correlation between gubernatorial outcomes and votes for presidential candidates or Duma parties in the oblasts and krais is weak at best; the association with economic conditions in the regions is almost non-existent. Local issues and personalities predominated in the regional races, suggesting that the three major election campaigns since 1995 have failed to produce any coherent political party structures operating at the regional level. Instead ... this latest round of elections is likely to perpetuate the syndrome of regional leaders negotiating with central authorities for economic concessions for particular regions' (pp. 48–9). 'The regional elections did not prove to be continuations of the 1995–96 national electoral confrontations. Local issues and personalities played important roles, and the national coalitions exerted only selective influence over outcomes' (p. 73). 'The new governors sitting in the Federation Council are unlikely to organize along the same lines as their counterparts in the Duma' (p. 74).

4. About half of the fifty-odd [fifty-two] incumbent regional governors up for election from September 1996 were voted out of office. 'Almost all went quietly, demonstrating that the electoral process in Russia is beginning to gain some bit' (Richard Sakwa, *The World Today*, June 1997, vol. 53, no. 6, p. 167).

5. Only twenty-three of the fifty regional governors appointed by Yeltsin were returned to office (John Thornhill, *FT*, Survey, 9 April 1997, p. ii).

Other local political events

7 June 1998. Larisa Yudina, the editor of an independent newspaper critical of President Kirsan Ilyumzhinov of Kalmykia, disappears. She was later found murdered (*CDSP*, 1998, vol. 50, no. 24, p. 14).

16 June 1998. Incumbent Murtaza Rakhimov is reelected president of the republic of Bashkortostan.

He won 70.2 per cent of the vote, with the only other candidate winning less than 9 per cent. A large number of people voted 'against all candidates'. There was considerable unease about aspects of the election, including the way other candidates were disqualified, intimidation and manipulation of the media (*CDSP*, 1998, vol. 50, no. 24, p. 12).

October 1998. 'The eighty-nine regions ... have assiduously created autonomous space ... Regions habitually ignore federal legislation and so act unconstitutionally. For example, Tatarstan's state council passed a law this year [1998] on citizenship which contradicts Russian law – a resident of Tatarstan can hold the republic's citizenship without retaining that of Russia ... In the June 1998 presidential election in Bashkortostan, the incumbent, Rakhimov, barred three other candidates from standing against him. He was following the example of Tatarstan's President Mintimir Shaimiyev ... The federal budget has been unable to pay for basic provisions such as food, accommodation and energy and [so] federal troops have become dependent for survival upon regional handouts ... In the Russian far east ... governor Nazdratenko is paying wage arrears for the Russian Pacific fleet from regional budgets in return for ensuring that only those officers born in the region serve in it ... Regions [are] becoming foreign policy actors, signing agreements with foreign countries – Tatarstan with Ukraine, for example ... Japan has been increasingly enthusiastic about establishing direct links with neighbouring regions – the Russian far east receives the largest share of Japanese aid' (Herd 1998: 251–2).

THE PUTIN ERA

13 May 2000. President Putin issues a decree organizing Russia into seven administrative districts, each to be overseen by a presidential representative.

The seven districts, their representatives and the base of operations are as follows: Central Federal Disrict (Georgi Poltavchenko, based in Moscow); North-west Federal District (Lieutenant General Viktor Cherkesov, based in St Petersburg); North Caucasus Federal District (General Viktor Kazantsev, based in Rostov-on-Don); Volga Federal District (Sergei Kiriyenko, based in Nizhny Novgorod); Urals Federal District (Colonel General Pyotr Latyshev, based in Yekaterinburg); Siberian Federal District (Leonid Drachevsky, based in Novosibirsk); and Far East Federal District (Lieutenant General Konstantin Pulikovsky, based in Khabarovsk).

'[The decree says that its aims are] to facilitate the Russian Federation president's exercise of his constitutional powers, increase the effectiveness of federal bodies of state power and improve the system for monitoring compliance with their decisions ... The institution of authorized representatives of the president of the Russian Federation president in the regions of the Russian Federation shall be transformed into the institution of authorized representatives ... in federal districts' (*CDSP*, 2000, vol. 52, no. 20, p. 1).

Putin: 'The activity of the presidential representatives is not aimed at replacing the powers of the local authorities ... [but to produce] uniform understanding of the laws [across Russia]' (*IHT*, 31 May 2000, p. 4).

'Putin's ... 13 May decree replaced the presidential representatives to the eighty-nine regions of the Russian Federation with seven plenipotentiary representatives (polpredy). They will oversee new federal districts of between six and seventeen regions each ... The polpredy were not given additional powers, although the language used to describe their role was tougher than that defining the functions of their predecessors. However, it was clear that the decree was intended to create the basis for a much broader recentralization of power. A few days later Putin addressed the nation on the subject and the Kremlin submitted four bills to the State Duma … The new polpredy … have already been made members of the national "security council"' (Tompson 2000a: 14–16). 'The authority leakage of the 1990s was largely a consequence of the Kremlin's weakness – of Boris Yeltsin's unpopularity and his need for regional support in battles with parliament. The situation is now reversed … His successor is now acting with the Duma to bring the regions to heel' (p. 16). (See below.)

'Mostly it [the decree] modifies the current Kremlin arrangements that places a presidential envoy in every province in favour of a handful of administrators who oversee federal affairs … The order grants the representatives considerable authority … to carry out Kremlin decisions … The representatives answer only to Mr Putin, who has the sole power to appoint and dismiss the envoys, to finance their local operations and to determine how patronage is dispensed. The envoys' main task, the decree states, is "the realization of the organs of state power of the main policy of the state, as determined by the president of the Russian Federation". Among their other powers, the decree states, is "the right to enter any organizations on the territory of this federal district". Television news programmes on Saturday evening [13 May] called the decree an outgrowth of Mr Putin's pledge in his presidential campaign this spring to strengthen central control over the regions … [Existing] envoys rely on local leaders for housing, favours and even jobs for family members … [Putin's] decree explicitly shifts to his office the responsibility for housing and supporting the [new] envoys … The new order establishes regional capitals in the seven districts and gives Mr Putin authority to set up staffs in each one … On Wednesday [10 May] in the provinces of Ingushetia, in the Caucasus, and Amur, in eastern Siberia, he [Putin] suspended local laws that conflicted with federation law and sent a letter to the legislature of Bashkortostan, in the Urals, to urge it to bring the province's constitution in line with federal constitutional law. Mr Putin also announced that he was considering legislation to restrict the governors' powers' (Michael Wines, *IHT*, 15 May 2000, p. 7). 'Under Mr Yeltsin both the envoys and many federal agencies became willing captives of the governors, who supplied the favours the Kremlin could or would not provide. The federal officials depended on the provinces for much, from office space and telephones to jobs for their families and summer camps for their children. That will change under Mr Putin. The seven envoys will work from regional capitals with budgets, housing and offices supplied by the Kremlin, as well as power to bestow perks on federal officials in their districts' (Michael Wines, *IHT*, 22 May 2000, p. 7).

'The eighty-plus presidential representatives in the regions appointed by Boris Yeltsin in an attempt to reestablish his authority have usually become little more than figureheads' (*The Economist*, 20 May 2000, p. 67).

'The seven new envoys will report exclusively to Mr Putin and will be responsible for enforcing federal law and for hiring and firing federal employees ... They will have broad rights to enter and search other government offices as well as serving as the sole regional conduit for presidential thanks and patronage ... *Izvestia* noted that the seven "super districts" correspond almost exactly to Russia's seven military regions, with headquarters in the same cities as military commands ... Regional military commandants will consolidate their power over uniformed units from the border guards, the interior ministry and the Federal Security Service' (Giles Whittell, *The Times*, 16 May 2000, p. 18).

'These governors-general, as the Russian media call them, are to manage the local operations of the "power ministries" – those for defence, the interior, security and justice' (*The Economist*, 20 May 2000, p. 67).

'Last week Mr Putin ordered Bashkortostan to rewrite its constitution, to make it conform with Russia's basic law ... Among the constitutional articles Russia objects to is the stipulation that the Bashkir president must speak the the Bashkir language, effectively disqualifying four out of five citizens. Bashkortostan [population 4.5 million] is only 20 per cent Bashkir, a Turkic people; ethnic Russians account for 40 per cent and Tatars almost 30 per cent' (Ian Traynor, *The Guardian*, 15 May 2000, p. 13).

17 May 2000. President Vladimir Putin proposes to revise the composition of the Council of the Federation.

Putin (in a television address): 'The bills being submitted to the Duma continue the line that was begun by my 13 May decree establishing federal districts. This line is aimed at strengthening the unity of the state ... First is a proposal to change the principles for forming the Federation Council ... [which] is made up of representatives of the executive and legislative branches of government. But the constitution does not say that these representatives necessarily have to be the top officials of a region – the governors, republic presidents and heads of regional governments. Yet that is precisely how things are today. I believe that regional leaders should focus their energy on the specific problems of their own regions ... And they should have representatives who engage in lawmaking, but on a regular and professional basis, not once a month, the way things are now ... The second significant proposal involves introducing procedures for removing regional leaders from office and dissolving legislative assemblies that adopt acts that conflict with federal laws ... The third proposal ... [is that] if, under certain conditions, the head of a region can be removed by the country's president, then the regional leader should have a similar right with respect to lower-ranking authorities ... The proposed laws are not directed against regional leaders. On the contrary, I firmly believe that the leaders of the regions are a very important base of support for the president and will continue to do so during the process of strengthening our state ... [But] a fifth of the legal acts adopted in the regions contradict the country's Basic Law, when the republic constitutions and province charters are at odds with the Russian constitution, and when trade barriers or, even worse, border demarcation posts are set up between Russia's territories and provinces' (*CDSP*, 2000, vol. 52, no. 20, p. 5).

'The Kremlin submitted four bills to the State Duma. The first would change the mechanism for forming the Federation Council. The constitution says only that each member of the federation has two representatives, one each from its executive and legislative branches. An ordinary federal law has made the chamber an assembly of governors and speakers of regional legislatures … The law before the Duma would require the regions to appoint individuals to represent the executive and legislature in the council. This would reduce the governors; power and status – and deprive them of parliamentary immunity … The second bill would empower the president to ask the supreme court to remove a governor guilty of two or more violations of federal law or the constitution. He would be able to ask the State Duma to dissolve the legislature of a federation member on the same grounds … The bill would allow him to suspend those under investigation for legal violations even without the supreme court's approval. Governors suspended by the president or removed by the court would be replaced by "temporary" presidential appointees … A third bill would extend similar powers to the governors over the municipal and other lower-level authorities … The president would be given analogous powers over sub-regional governments. Local authorities in border areas, large cities, closed administrative-territorial formations and regional capitals would in any case be regulated by the Federation. A fourth bill would curtail regional authorities' voice in the appointment and removal of key officials. Putin's removal of Moscow's police chief was recently overturned in court … Moscow is also determined to eliminate entirely the role of local administrations in financing the courts and the police … The new federal districts, not coincidentally, correspond with the country's major military districts' (Tompson 2000a: 14–15).

'Mr Putin unexpectedly went on nationwide television Wednesday evening [17 May] to announce that and other initiatives he said were aimed at "strengthening and cementing Russian statehood … These submitted bills are not directed against regional leaders, who should remain pillars of the president". Some, such as a plan to permit citizens to recall local leaders and dissolve regional assemblies, would clearly make provincial leaders more accountable to voters' (*IHT*, 18 May 2000, p. 5). 'Mr Putin on Wednesday night proposed to strip the governors of their seats in the upper chamber of parliament, the Federation Council, and impose new rules that would allow the Kremlin to dismiss regional leaders who defy Moscow' (*IHT*, 19 May 2000, p. 7). 'On Wednesday he proposed to evict all eighty-nine governors and the leaders of their legislators from their guaranteed seats in the Federation Council. The move would wipe out the current membership of the 188-seat upper house, replacing it with less senior regional officials … Mr Putin apparently intends to replace the council members with provincial officials elected by their peers ... He also said that he would seek the legal authority to suspend or dismiss any governor who flouted federal law or defied the Russian constitution ... Mr Putin claims that a fifth of provincial laws run counter to federal legislation' (*IHT*, 22 May 2000, p. 7). 'Mr Putin proposed that the members be elected by regional legislatures and that the governors lose their seats' (*IHT*, 1 June 2000, p. 1). 'Mr Putin's plan would remove the governors and other regional leaders from the Federation Council and replace them with regional representatives of lesser prestige and power. Half would be chosen by the regional parliaments and half would be chosen by the governor or regional executive. The governors would lose their immunity from prosecution as well as their parliamentary seats' (*IHT*, 24 June 2000, p. 2).

'Right now governors and chairman of province legislative assemblies automatically become deputies to the upper house of parliament. The president has proposed that instead the governors and province deputies choose the senators ... The governors would lose their deputy's immunity. Another bill has been proposed under which the president would be able to remove governors from office if they break the law. The governors, in turn, would have the power to remove mayors for the same reason. To prevent governors from abusing this power, mayors would be able to appeal to the president's representatives, who would have, if not the power, at least the ability to uphold the law' (*CDSP*, 2000, vol. 52, no. 20, p. 6).

'Mr Putin called for radical changes to Russia's federal relations. The president said he wanted greater powers to remove incompetent governors and questioned whether regional leaders should have the automatic right to sit in the Federation Council' (*FT*, 19 May 2000, p. 9).

'Mr Putin ... is calling for more power to sack regional bosses and wants to end their automatic right to seats in Russia's upper house of parliament' (*The Economist*, 20 May 2000, p. 67).

18 May 2000. 'In a further step Thursday [18 May] Mr Putin appointed seven new super-governors who will make up a fresh command structure over the regions ... Mr Putin named four military men, as well as a liberal former prime minister, Sergei Kiriyenko, to be the seven administrators' (*IHT*, 19 May 2000, p. 7).

'Five of the seven "super governors" are military, police or security service officers ... Sergei Kiriyenko ... [is the president's representative] in the Volga region ... General Viktor Kazantsev, the commander of Russian forces in Chechenia, [is] to supervise the new North Caucasus Federal District, which includes [Chechenia] ... Viktor Cherkesov, the first deputy director of the Federal Security Service, [is] to oversee the north-west regions ... Men who built their careers in the services were also sent to the Central Urals and Far Eastern Federal Districts. That left Leonid Drachevsky as the only civilian besides Mr Kiriyenko ... The role of the president's men will be to make sure the elected governors in all Russia's eight-nine regions obey federal law' (*The Independent*, 20 May 2000, p. 16).

'Mr Putin has tapped the military and security services for five of the seven super-administrators … For the St Petersburg region Mr Putin has tapped Lieutenent General Viktor Cherkesov, deputy director of the Federal Security Service … For the Moscow region Mr Putin chose … Georgi Poltavchenko, a former deputy mayor of St Petersburg. Earlier he was the director of the tax police in the city. [He later became the president's representative in Leningrad province: *CDSP*, 2000, vol. 52, no. 20, p. 3.] In the southern district, headquartered Rostov-on-Don Mr Putin chose General Viktor Kazantsev, commmander of the [North] Caucasus Military District and a leading general in the Chechen war. In the Urals, headquartered in Yekaterinburg, he chose another military man, Colonel General Pyotr Latyshev, a deputy interior minister… In the Far East, with headquarters in Khabarovsk, Mr Putin named Lieutenent General Konstantin Pulikovsky, who had earlier been a presidential envoy in the region. The general was a leader of Russian forces during the first Chechen war. Two other appointments were not from the military or security services. Sergei Kiriyenko … was named chief of the Trans-Volga zone, based in Nizhy Novgorod. And Mr Putin chose Leonid Drachevsky for the huge Siberian zone. A onetime athlete and diplomat, last summer [1999] he became Russia's minister for the CIS' (*IHT*, 20 May 2000, p. 1).

31 May 2000. In its first vote the State Duma approves three of Putin's measures. The votes were as follows: reform of the Council of the Federation (362 to thirty-four with eight abstentions); allowing the Kremlin to fire regional governors (357 to twenty-eight); allowing governors to remove local leaders (319 to thirty-eight). The seven new super-districts were ordered by presidential decree (*IHT*, 1 June 2000, p. 1; *CDSP*, 2000, vol. 52, no. 22, p. 1).

21 June 2000. Lawmakers approved a measure granting the interior ministry the right to sack local police chiefs. The State Duma passed an amendment to a police bill that strips governors of a say in police appointments (*IHT*, 22 June 2000, p. 5).

23 June 2000. 'The State Duma passed the bill on new procedures for forming the Federation Council on second and third (final) readings. The governors suffered defeat in almost all key areas; the deputies rejected the majority of their amendments … Regional leaders will have to clear their protégés [i.e. their nominees for executive branch representative in the Federation Council] with their regional legislatures (a procedure similar to the State Duma's confirmation of the prime minister). The second senator from a region will be elected by the local legislators on the basis of a nomination by the chairman of the house. In addition, an alternative senate candidate may be nominated by one-third of the deputies to a legislative assembly or province Duma … Under the law the election of all members of the Fedration Council must be completed by 1 February 2001' (*CDSP*, 2000, vol. 52, no. 26, p. 1).

The third and final vote was 308 to eighty-six.

28 June 2000. The Council of the Federation votes by 129 to thirteen with one abstention to reject the proposal to reform the Council of the Federation. The State Duma needs at least a two-third majority in the lower house (i.e. at least 300 of its 450 members) to override the upper house.

30 June 2000. The State Duma votes by 399 to nine in favour of the president being able to dismiss regional governors if the supreme court agrees on appeal (*IHT,* 30 June 2000, p. 2; *CDSP,* 2000, vol. 52, no. 27, p. 5).

19 July 2000. 'The State Duma and the Federation Council worked out a compromise version of the bill after a week of often bitter negotiations. The compromise, which contains mostly cosmetic changes, was approved by the Duma on Wednesday [19 July] by a vote of 308 to eighty-eight, with five abstentions' (*IHT,* 20 July 2000, p. 5).

'[On 19 July] the State Duma voted for the conference committee's version of the embattled law on forming the Federation Council – a law the upper house had rejected earlier. Three hundred and seven State Duma deputies voted for the law ... and five abstained. As a result of a difficult conciliation process ... the deputies managed to reach a compromise with the senators, even on the point of contention, the procedure for appointing and recalling the regional leaders' representatives to the reconstituted upper house. The toned-down version of the law now reads: "The executive leader of a federation member appoints a Federation Council representative by resolution and forwards his resolution to the legislative body within three days." The resolution goes into effect if it is approved by the legislative assembly by a majority vote, and it does not go into effect if it is rejected by a two-thirds majority. The same procedure is to be used for recalling representatives from their posts ahead of schedule. In addition, the governors won't be leaving the upper house all at once; the law provides for so-called "natural rotation", which should be complete by 1 January 2002' (*CDSP,* vol. 52, no. 29, p. 12).

26 July 2000. The Council of the Federation approves plans to reform the upper house by 119 votes to eighteen.

'Under the legislation ... [existing members] will leave by January 2002 ... The council members assented to their own ouster after persuading the Duma and the Kremlin to accept a compromise that holds out the prospect of a new constitutional convention to set a final form for the Russian government. The compromise also allowed members to remain in the council until their terms expire, and gave the governors the right to appoint and remove their successors. Council members from the provincial legislatures, who had been named in the past by the governors, will now be elected by their peers' (*IHT,* 27 July 2000, p. 6).

'The only serious concession the senators won from the Kremlin was postponement. The date by which the senators are to leave the Federation Council has been pushed back from early next year [2000] to 1 January 2001 ... The senators ... voted overwhelmingly to defeat the law [on local self-government] ... and the Council moved to establish a conference committee to modify it ... The Kremlin has already promised to stipulate in the law the right of governors to remove mayors from office' (*CDSP*, 2000, vol. 52, no. 30, p. 4).

27 July 2000. President Putin signs a directive soliciting proposals for the creation of a 'state council'. By the end of August all proposals are to be drawn up and the president will sign a decree to establish the new body (*CDSP*, 2000, vol. 52, no. 31, p. 11).

3 August 2000. 'Vladimir Putin continued his campaign to recentralize federal power this week as he stripped local governors of control over special police units ... This week Russia's interior ministry and tax police created new jurisdictions that coincide with the seven federal districts, and centralized control over their units from Moscow ... A new project is being developed to compensate the governors for the loss of the Federation Council by naming them to a "state council" with access to the president' (*FT*, Friday 4 August 2000, p. 8). 'Debate continues around an amendment to the Russian constitution which would create a new institution, the "state council"' (*FT*, 8 August 2000, p. 7).

31 August 2000. 'President Vladimir Putin said Thursday [31 August] that he would include regional officials in a new council as consolation for losing their seats in the Federation Council ... but stressed that it would only be an advisory body ... saying: "Today these powers can only be consultative. What will happen in the future we will think over and decide with regional leaders"' (*IHT*, 1 September 2000, p. 7).

22 November 2000. 'President Vladimir Putin inaugurated Russia's new "state council" on Wednesday [22 November] and warned the long-powerful regional bosses who sit on the advisory body not to challenge the authority of his government ... Mr Putin created the council on 1 September ... The council has eighty-nine members plus the president ... The new body's first task was to debate Russia's economic future and a [replacement] national anthem ... The council's members ... discussed a 100-page development plan for the decade overseen by Viktor Ishayev, head of the far eastern Khabarovsk region ... [Putin]: "The state council can set the direction of the country, but it must not replace parliament or the government ... The most important part of our joint work is reinforcing the chain of command. That means control from the federal centre and effective feedback. I believe the state council could be an excellent instrument in such a relationship ... It is important for us not just to work out solutions together, but to implement them altogether" ... Political analysts say the new "state council" is a toothless body whose main role is to reconcile regional chiefs to their loss of influence by giving the appearance of having the president's ear four times a year' (*IHT*, 23 November 2000, p. 2).

THE CHECHEN WARS

Chechenia (Chechnya) has always had a fearsome reputation as a warrior nation. It took years of fighting before Russia finally conquered the Chechens. Chechenia formally became part of Russia in 1859, but the Caucasian wars lasted from 1817 to 1864. According to *The Independent* (18 January 1996, p. 13), the name comes from a village where a famous battle took place between the Chechens and the Russians in 1732. The Chechens converted to Islam in the seventeenth century. The last nineteenth-century Chechen rebellion was in 1877.

In 1922–24 the Chechens and Ingushes formed two autonomous regions and in December 1936 the two united as an autonomous republic (Chechen-Ingushetia). Stalin banished the Chechens to the Central Asian republics in February 1944, because of the alleged danger of collaboration with the Nazi invaders. The move led to massive loss of life. According to *The Economist* (10 June 1995, p. 43), perhaps 240,000 out of a population of 800,000 died in the process. But some estimates go up to half the population. Khrushchev allowed them to return in 1957, when the republic was reconstituted as Chechenia-Ingushetia. ('Today [23 February 2000] marks the fifty-sixth anniversary of the start of the mass deportation of Chechens under Stalin ... About 650,000 Chechens were deported to central Asia and Siberia': *The Guardian*, 23 February 2000, p. 17.)

Chechenia had a population of about 1.2 million, about three-quarters of whom were Chechens. The 900,000 Chechens were Sunni Moslems; there were a further 400,000 scattered throughout the world (Deutsche Bank, *Focus: Eastern Europe*, 1994, no. 117, p. 3). Before 1991 about one-third of the population of 1.2 million were ethnic Russians. By autumn 1994 around 150,000 remained (*The Times*, 30 December 1994, p. 12). As of January 1995 the population was 1,006,000, of which 22 per cent were Russians (*The Economist*, 14 January 1995, p. 33). Some 380,000 Russians lived in Chechenia, but by December 1994 only 100,000–110,000 remained (*CDSP*, 1995, vol. XLVI, no. 51, p. 4).

'Along with Chuvashia and Tuva, it is the only one of the three dozen republics where the titular group forms a majority' (Jonathan Steele, *The Guardian*, 18 March 1995, p. 24). 'In only ... the neighbouring smaller Caucasian one of North Ossetia, even tinier Tuva (on the Siberian border with Mongolia) and the Chuvash republic (... in central Russia), does the local ethnic group hold an outright majority' (*The Economist*, 10 June 1995, p. 16).

In 1973 the northern Caucasus region produced over 23 million tonnes of oil (about 5.7 per cent of the Russian total), a little over half of which came from Chechenia. But the region produced only 5.5 million tonnes in 1992 (1.4 per cent of the Russian total), with Chechenia's contribution slightly over 3 million tonnes. Russia has imposed economic sanctions since 1991. Unemployment is supposed to have topped 50 per cent. Average incomes were 30 per cent of those in Moscow in 1991 and only 3.6 per cent in March 1994 (Deutsche Bank, *Focus: Eastern Europe*, 1994, no. 117, p. 4).

In 1992 oil production was 3 million tonnes and in 1993 2.5 million tonnes (*CDSP*, 1995, vol. XLVI, no. 51, p. 7). Oil production was 4.5 million tonnes in 1992, 2.6 million tonnes in 1993 and 1.2 million tonnes in 1994 (*Moscow News*, 20–26 January 1995, p. 8). According to the Russian government, oil production in 1994 was 2 million tonnes (*IHT*, 30 January 1995, p. 13).

'[There has been a] collapse in Chechenia of the institutions of modern statehood – law enforcement, schools, hospitals, courts – since the national revolution of 1991. This disintegration was caused in large part by war, but it also owes a great deal to the Chechens' historical resistance to any superior authority and their traditional tolerance for what we would now regard as banditry... Most of the dozens of Chechen refugees I have interviewed at the region's border with Ingushetia in the last week ... furiously denounced the Russian military ... On the other hand they lamented the anarchy that has gripped Chechenia since it broke free from Russia eight years ago. The overwhelming majority were bitterly critical of leading Chechen and Islamic militia commanders... Almost unanimously, the refugees I spoke to expressed special hatred for the Chechens who are fighting alongside militias led by foreign Islamic extremists, who most Chechens believe are threatening their own religious traditions. Indeed, the tragedy of the Russians' ham-fisted brutality is that they might have attracted the support of most Chechens had they tried to work peacefully with Mr Maskhadov to expel the extremist groups' (Anatol Lieven, *IHT*, 1 December 1999, p. 8).

'Chechen bands have taken about 1,300 hostages since 1996 and about 700 have been released' (*The Times*, 27 November 1999, p. 16).

The toll in the first Chechen war, 1994–6

Parliament's human rights commissioner Sergei Kovalyov issued a report on 21 February 1995. His team's estimate was that between 25 November 1994 and 25 January 1995 24,400 civilians were killed in Chechenia, including 3,700 children under the age of fifteen, 4,650 women over fifteen, 2,650 men over fifty and 13,350 unarmed men between fifteen and fifty. The number of armed Chechen men killed was put at 650. No figure was given for Russian military losses, but Russian military officials had put the number of Russian troops dead and missing at more than 1,000. Most of the civilian casualties were believed to have been ethnic Russians who were unable to leave Grozny because, unlike Chechens, they could not go to the countryside to join relatives. The number of refugees was put at 400,000. (Reports in *IHT*, *The Independent*, *The Times* and *The Guardian* of 22 February 1995. See also *CDSP*, 1995, vol. XLVII, no. 8, p. 10.)

On 9 February 1995 the Russian army put the number of Chechen militants killed in the period 11 December 1994 to 8 February 1995 at 6,690. Russian army losses (excluding interior ministry troops) were put at over 1,100. There were also several hundred missing and unidentified corpses (*CDSP*, 1995 vol. XLVII, no. 6, p. 4).

Russian officials put the number of Russian servicemen killed as of 24 February 1995 at 1,146, those missing at 374, the number wounded or ill at 5,000 and the number of unidentified bodies in morgues at about 100 (reports in *IHT* and *The Guardian* of 25 February 1995; see also *CDSP*, 1995, vol. XLVII, no. 8, p. 11). The Russian ministry of defence reported that Russian troops had killed about 7,000 Chechen fighters (*The Times* and *IHT* of 1 March 1995).

On 23 March 1995 Anatoli Kulikov, the commander of Russian forces in Chechenia, said that Russian forces had included as many as 58,000 men; 1,385 troops had been killed and 4,439 wounded. Russian forces initially faced 15,000 'well prepared, well trained and excellently armed men' and an additional 30,000 'semi-trained' local militia. 'They are considerably less now' (*IHT*, 24 March 1995, p. 5).

General Kulikov talked of 1,426 Russian soldiers killed, 4,630 wounded and ninety-six taken prisoner (*The Telegraph*, 31 March 1995, p. 18), while on 19 April 1995 he estimated that some 9,500 Chechen militia had been killed (*CDSP*, 1995, vol. XLVII, no. 16, p. 5).

Official Russian figures show that between 11 December 1994 and 10 April 1995 1,721 Russian servicemen were killed, 6,301 wounded and 336 declared missing (*CDSP*, 1995, vol. XLVII, no. 15, p. 10).

On 30 July 1995 Anatoli Kulikov (now interior minister) revealed that 1,800 Russian troops had been killed, 6,500 wounded and 250 classified as missing (*The Times*, 31 July 1995, p. 11).

The war has claimed at least 40,000 lives (*FT*, 11 December 1995, p. 2). A conservative estimate would be 20,000 dead, most of them civilians (*IHT*, 13 December 1995, p. 2).

According a spokesman for the Russian 'security council', the number of civilians dead range between 20,000 and 30,000 (*The Telegraph*, 8 January 1996, p. 10).

Most estimates now put the number of Chechen dead at close to 40,000, while more than half the population has been displaced. The toll among Russian soldiers, many of them virtually untrained teenagers, is also high (*IHT*, 9 March 1996, p. 6). An estimated 30,000–40,000 people have died, including some 3,000 Russian servicemen. At least half of the 1 million population has been displaced (*IHT*, 29 March 1996, p. 6). Only about 30,000 refugees fled to Ingushetia (*IHT*, 11 November 1999, p. 4).

The US State Department estimates that 35,000 civilians have been killed (*The Independent*, 10 August 1996, p. 11). An estimated 35,000 have been killed (*IHT*, 30 August 1996, p. 6). 'The most careful scholarly analysis to date puts the number of actual deaths at roughly 35,000' (Lapidus 1998: 6).

On 2 September 1996 General Igor Rodionov, the defence minister, said that at least 2,837 Russian soldiers had been killed, 13,270 had been wounded and 337 were listed as missing (*The Times*, 4 September 1996, p. 13).

On 3 September 1996 Alexander Lebed made the following starting statement about total casualty figures since December 1994: 'There are conflicting data, but one can speak about 80,000 killed, give or take 10,000, and probably about three times as many wounded and maimed.' (According to the interior ministry, losses total 18,500 people: *CDSP*, 1996, vol. XLVIII, no. 40, p. 5.)

The Chechen president, Aslan Maskhadov, stated the following in an interview on 14 May 2000: 'During the eight months of the current war civilian deaths are more than 40,000. Military losses are more than 1,500. In the first war, from 1994 to 1996, about 120,000 civilians were killed and 2,870 fighters' (*IHT*, 15 May 2000, p. 7).

About 500,000 people have been displaced (*FT*, 23 May 1996, p. 3).

By mid-February 1995 Grozny had no more than 60,000 residents left, compared with over 300,000 two months before (*CDSP*, 1995, vol. XLVII, no. 7, p. 7). Grozny was devastated by the heavy bombardment, which turned it into a wasteland. Steven Erlanger (*IHT*, 30 March 1995, p. 5) described 'a city of 400,000 only four months ago, but now a blasted landscape in which 120,000 dazed people try to live ... Even those Chechens who hate Mr Dudayev, and there are many, are outraged by the seemingly wanton destruction of Grozny and the civilian deaths there, which number at least 10,000, aid agencies estimate.' Some 250,000 Chechens have been displaced (Steven Erlanger, *IHT*, 10 April 1995, p. 5). There are an estimated 250,000 people now living in Grozny, well below the pre-war total of 400,000. Across Chechenia about 400,000 have been displaced (*The Economist*, 10 June 1995, p. 43).

'According to official figures, 3,826 people were killed over a period of twenty months (from December 1994 through August 1996). In other words, the federal forces lost an average of 190 men a month' (*CDSP*, 2000, vol. 52, no. 31, p. 6).

Nineteen journalists have been killed (*IHT*, 14 August 1996, p. 6).

The toll in the second Chechen war (which started in 1999)

'The losses brought the total Russian toll so far to forty dead and 160 wounded, according a [Russian] deputy interior minister' (*IHT*, 20 August 1999, p. 1).

'Casualty reports continued to be conflicting. A Russian military spokesman put the number of federal losses at fifty-nine and 210 wounded, while claiming that more than 1,000 rebels had been killed. A rebel spokesman said the insurgents had lost thirty-seven men, while claiming that federal losses were over 1,000' (*IHT*, 26 August 1999, p. i).

The official Russian death toll for federal forces during the hostilities in Dagestan is 230 (*CDSP*, 1999, vol. 51, no. 38, p. 4).

The Chechen authorities claim that two weeks of Russian bombing has killed 298 people and led to 300,000 people fleeing their homes (*IHT*, 25 September 1999, p. 2).

'The bombing campaign, according to official Chechen sources, has claimed 384 lives, left more than a thousand wounded and caused tens of thousands of Chechens to leave … An estimated 65,000 Chechen refugees have been streaming across the border into neighbouring Ingushetia' (*IHT*, 29 September 1999, pp. 1, 4).

President Ruslan Aushev of Ingushetia estimates that the number of refugees is approaching 60,000. Ingushetia's own population is just over 300,000 (*CDSP*, 1999, vol. 51, no. 39, p. 4).

'At least 70,000 refugees have flooded into Ingushetia … and many are camped out near the border in makeshift shelters' (*IHT*, 30 September 1999, p. 7). Russia says that 62,000 refugees have fled to Ingushetia (*The Times*, 30 September 1999, p. 16).

'The authorities in Ingushetia … said 80,000 refugees had fled the bombing and settled in rudimentary camps along the frontier' (*IHT*, 1 October 1999, p. 5).

Approximately 88,000 refugees have fled the bombing (*IHT*, 2 October 1999, p. 2). Almost 100,000 Chechens have now crossed into Ingushetia (*The Guardian*, 2 October 1999, p. 21).

'More than a week of air strikes and the fear of a full-scale ground invasion have displaced 100,000 Chechens, a tenth of the republic's population. Russian officials estimate over 88,000 have fled to Ingushetia' (*FT*, 4 October 1999, p. 9).

'An Ingush official … [said] that about 8,000 new refugees had crossed … Sunday, bringing the overall number to over 100,000 … President Aslan Maskhadov was quoted … as saying that more than 400 people had died in the bombing and 1,000 had been wounded' (*IHT*, 4 October 1999, p. 1).

'In Ingushetia officials said that about 23,000 refugees had arrived … bringing the number of refugees to more than 100,000' (*The Guardian*, 4 October 1999, p. 11).

The Russian emergency committee says that more than 120,000 people have left Chechenia (*The Times*, 7 October 1999, p. 17).

Some 105,000 refugees are in Ingushetia (*IHT*, 7 October 1999, p. 4).

'Russian air raids and artillery bombardment have prompted at least 125,000 civilians to flee, with most of them heading to the neighbouring republic of Ingushetia' (*IHT*, 8 October 1999, p. 4).

Aslan Maskhadov says that twenty Chechen fighters and 100 Russian soldiers have died so far in the conflict. A Chechen leader says that 450 civilians have died in the past two weeks. Some 133,000 Chechen refugees have fled to Ingushetia (*The Independent*, 9 October 1999, p. 14).

'Some reports suggest that more than 150,000 refugees have fled the conflict zone.' The normal population of Ingushetia is about 240,000 (*FT*, 11 October 1999, p. 12).

The ministry for emergency situations in Moscow says that more than 166,000 Chechen civilians have so far fled to neighbouring republics, mainly to Ingushetia (*FT*, 13 October 1999, p. 8).

'The Russians admit to losing forty-seven soldiers killed since 25 October and claim to have killed 2,000 Chechen fighters ... President Aslan Maskhadov ... said his forces had lost thirty-two men and killed 1,500 Russians' (*The Independent*, 18 October 1999, p. 11).

Russia says that 180 Russian soldiers have been killed so far, while 'terrorist' losses amount to 3,500 (2,000 in Dagestan and 1,500 in Chechenia) (*The Independent*, 19 October 1999, p. 17).

'The general staff says that Russian forces have suffered 350 dead in two months of fighting, a figure ridiculed by the Chechen guerrillas' (*IHT*, 21 October 1999, p. 17).

'The [Russian] defence ministry said 196 soldiers had been killed in North Caucasus conflicts since August ... The number of refugees has now topped 170,000, more than a third of Chechenia's already diminished population' (*IHT*, 22 October 1999, pp. 1, 4).

More than 160,000 people have already fled Chechenia into Ingushetia (*IHT*, 26 October 1999, p. 9).

There are up to 200,000 refugees. 'Russia's military command ... yesterday [29 October] put its own losses at 222 killed' (*The Times*, 30 October 1999, p. 15).

'Almost 200,000 people have fled Chechenia since late September, most of them seeking refuge in Ingushetia' (*IHT*, 1 November 1999, p. 5).

'Some 193,000 [refugees] have reached Ingushetia' (*The Independent*, 3 November 1999, p. 1).

'The Ingush president, Ruslan Aushev, said last night [3 November] that the refugees now number 188,166, most of them staying in private Ingush homes' (*The Guardian*, 4 November 1999, p. 3). ('About 10,000 refugees are housed in tent cities set up by the Russians: the rest ... shelter in private homes, abandoned factories and farms, on construction sites, inside vacant railway cars, at bus stations and in the open: *IHT*, 5 November 1999, p. 7. 'In Ingushetia an estimated 50,000 people ... are living in often miserable conditions in camps and trains: *IHT*, 24 November 1999, p. 1. 'According to Russian sources, 30,000 [Chechen refugees] are sleeping rough in tents and disused railway carriages in Ingushetia': *The Independent*, 25 November 1999, p. 15.)

'Official figures have suggested nearly 500 deaths among Russian troops' (*FT*, 22 November 1999, p. 7).

'General Valeri Manilov, deputy chief of staff ... claimed 4,000 Chechen militants had died since the campaign began, against 187 soldiers killed' (*FT*, 27 November 1999, p. 5).

'About 80 per cent of the capital's buildings are in ruins' (*IHT*, 1 December 1999, p. 6). 'Grozny was home to almost 400,000 people in the 1980s' (*IHT*, 13 December 1999, p. 6).

'More than 250,000 Chechens have fled the territory since the fighting began, emergency situations ministry officials said Friday [17 December]...

The Russians have lost 533 soldiers in the campaign, the military said Friday' (*IHT*, 18 December 1999, pp. 1, 5).

'Mr Putin said Saturday [18 December] that civilian casualties "could be counted on one's fingers" ... Spokesmen for the Chechen rebels assert that several thousand civilians have been killed ... Official [Russian] figures state that 404 Russian soldiers and 129 interior ministry troops have been killed ... The figures for Russian military casualties do not include soldiers who are "missing in action"' (*IHT*, 20 December 1999, pp. 1, 9).

'Russian commanders maintain that they have lost a total of only 347 troops since entering Chechenia' (*The Times*, 28 December 1999, p. 13).

'Russian defence officials made the rare admission that they were suffering heavy losses ... The officials said that a total of 544 Russian soldiers had been killed ... since the offensive began four months ago' (*The Times*, 7 January 2000, p. 20).

'The Soldiers' Mothers Committee ... has claimed that 3,000 [Russian] troops have been killed in the war in Chechenia ... Official figures stand at around 600 dead' (*The Times*, 18 January 2000, p. 13).

'The Union of Committees of Soldiers' Mothers ... tries to help soldiers' families negotiate the military bureaucracy. The internationally funded committee says that Russia has lost 3,000 soldiers since the start of ground combat, compared with an official count of 712' (*IHT*, 19 January 2000, pp. 1, 6).

'[There have been] allegations that Russia's military is concealing the extent of its casualties in Chechenia ... New figures attributed to "informed sources" in the defence establishment identified the number of soldiers killed and wounded since the start of fighting in the north Caucasus in August [1999] as 1,152 and 3,246 respectively. Nearly half of those losses have been sustained since the beginning of the attack on Grozny, said the Interfax newsagency ... Of the overall total 529 had been killed and 1,515 wounded since 27 December, soon after Moscow's forces first attacked Grozny ... There was no official confirmation of the report ... Differences over the number of casualties have worsened the rivalry between the interior ministry and the army. The ministry is inclined to put the figures much higher ... The defence and interior ministries have always released figures separately. Experts say the [official] numbers include only those confirmed killed on the battlefield, not soldiers who die of wounds or are listed as missing' (*The Telegraph*, 25 January 2000, p. 17).

'Interfax reported that 1,152 military servicemen and interior ministry troops have been killed since fighting erupted in Dagestan in August [1999]. Those figures are roughly consistent with other independent estimates. An analysis prepared by a former defence ministry press secretary and published in the newspaper Komsomolskaya Pravda estimated the number of soldiers killed at around 1,300 – almost twice a many as reported officially. General Anatoli Kulikov, the former commander of federal troops during the 1994–6 war, has also said that losses are substantially higher than officially reported' (*IHT*, 25 January 2000, p. 5). 'The Interfax news agency said the Russian toll in Chechenia had reached 926, a third more than official tallies. Of those, more than 500 died in December, when the Russian attacks on Grozny began. Russian observers attribute the disparity to deception and bureaucratic accounting methods, which do not list deaths that occur in hospitals or fatalities among so-called "contract" soldiers who have signed up solely for the duration of the war' (*IHT*, 26 January 2000, p. 6).

'Interfax says that 1,152 soldiers and police have been killed and 3,246 wounded since Shamil Basayev advanced into Dagestan in August [1999]. Some 926 of these have died since the Russian army crossed into Chechenia on 1 October [1999]. The real figures may be even higher since it is not clear if the present estimate includes soldiers missing or who died later in hospital' (*The Independent*, 25 January 2000, p. 15).

'Russian officials said Tuesday [25 January] that 1,055 troops had died since the Chechenia ground operation began in September [1999]' (*IHT*, 27 January 2000, p. 4). The defence ministry releases its official casualty figures: 1,173 dead and 3,487 wounded. The Union of Committees of Soldiers' Mothers of Russia estimates that some 3,500 servicemen have been killed in action or died of their wounds, the casualty figures including all the various services (the defence ministry, the interior ministry, the civil defence troops, construction battalions and so on). Including the military actions in Dagestan, the number of wounded is at least 6,000. The bodies of interior ministry soldiers and policemen are sent to civilian morgues and death certificates are written there. There are soldiers who are missing and unaccounted for. Servicemen who may be dead are listed as deserters (*CDSP*, 2000, vol. 52, no. 5, pp. 2–3).

'Russian sources claimed to have killed 1,500 Chechens in the operation ... A rebel spokesman ... put the figure at 400' (*The Times*, 5 February 2000, p. 9).

'General Manilov said that 1,290 Russian servicemen had been killed since ... last summer' (*The Independent*, 5 February 2000, p. 18).

'Sergei Yastrzhembsky, chief war spokesman, said that from 1 October [1999] until Friday [3 March 2000] the Russian forces had lost 1,420 soldiers and 3,869 wounded. However, these figures do not include 227 killed and 792 wounded in the Dagestan conflict in August and September [1999]. Critics have also said the Russian statistics do not include soldiers who died later of their wounds in hospital ... The secretary of the Soldiers' Mothers Committee ... said Friday ... that some losses were simply classified as desertions' (*IHT*, 4 March 2000, pp. 1, 4).

'Soldiers' Mothers ... said yesterday [22 March] that at least 4,000 men and officers had been killed in combat and about 8,000 wounded since ... 1 October [1999]' (*The Times*, 23 March 2000, p. 18).

'The number of Russian dead has risen to 2,119' (*The Guardian*, 14 April 2000, p. 14).

'The Russian general staff said its total losses since the fighting began last summer have been 2,144 dead and 6,325 wounded' (*The Telegraph*, 21 April 2000, p. 14).

On 27 April 2000 Russia announced its military losses to date. Since the August 1999 incursion by rebels into Dagestan 2,181 had been killed and 6,388 had been wounded. Of these 1,901 had been killed since Russian forces moved into Chechenia (*IHT*, 28 April 2000, p. i).

Russia claims that 13,500 Chechen fighters have been killed. The Chechens admit to only 1,300 (*The Economist*, 29 April 2000, p. 42).

The Chechen president, Aslan Maskhadov, stated the following in an interview on 14 May 2000: 'During the eight months of the current war civilian deaths are more than 40,000. Military losses are more than 1,500. In the first war, from 1994 to 1996, about 120,000 civilians were killed and 2,870 fighters' (*IHT*, 15 May 2000, p. 7).

According to official figures, Russia has lost 2,127 soldiers killed and 6,021 wounded (*The Independent*, 24 June 2000, p. 16).

Since 1 October 1999 more than 2,100 Russian troops have been killed and more than 6,000 wounded (*IHT*, 26 June 2000, p. 1).

'Russia says it has killed up to 20,000 rebels ... Chechen guerrillas still number up to 3,500, according to official Russian estimates' (*The Economist*, 1 July 2000, p. 50).

'First deputy chief of staff Valeri Manilov yesterday [3 August] made public figures on Russian Army losses in the North Caucasus in the year since the war began ... He claimed that 14,000 rebels had been exterminated ... According to Manilov, 11,000 had been destroyed as of 18 February and 14,000 as of 17 March. But on 24 March ... total rebel losses fell to 13,000. Figures for the total number of fighting rebels have behaved just as strangely ... On 2 August 1999 units led by Basayev and Khattab crossed the Chechen-Dagestani border, triggering the second Chechen war. According to Colonel General Valeri Manilov, 2,485 Russian servicemen have been killed and 7,505 wounded since then ... [The Committee of Soldiers' Mothers continues to maintain that the numbers of men killed or wounded are at least double the figures cited by military officials]' (*Kommersant*, 4 August 2000, p. 1: *CDSP*, 2000, vol. 52, no. 31, p. 6).

There are 200,000 Chechen refugees (*Kommersant*, 29 July 2000, p. 3: *CDSP*, 2000, vol. 52, no. 31, p. 6)

'Some 155,000 people are still refugees' (*IHT*, 1 September 2000, p. 7).

'The other day the United Nations High Commissioner for Refugees warned that about 170,000 Chechens are facing the prospect of a second winter in tents and other makeshift shelters outside their home province in Russia' (*IHT*, 9 September 2000, p. 6).

'In all about 3,200 Russians [soldiers] have died since Moscow began an offensive last year [1999], according to the official count ... Russian now maintains about 25,000 troops and military policemen in Chechenia, down from about 90,000 at the beginning of the year [2000]' (*IHT*, 22 September 2000, p. 2).

'Yesterday [5 October] General Valeri Manilov, the deputy chief of staff, said 2,479 soldiers had been lost in the year-long war' (*The Times*, 6 October 2000, p. 20).

Public opinion in Russia during the first Chechen war, 1994–6

There have been a number of public opinion polls:

1. January 1995: 66 per cent against sending Russian troops into Chechenia and only 21 per cent in favour (*CDSP*, 1995, vol. XLVII, no. 3, p. 17).
2. January 1995: 71 per cent against sending Russian troops (*CDSP*, 1995, vol. XLVII, no. 4, p. 12).
3. January 1995: 46 per cent want a cessation of the Russian army's military action in Chechenia, while 31 per cent wanted more decisive use of force to eliminate the rule of Dudayev (*CDSP*, 1995 vol. XLVII, no. 6, p. 19).
4. Polls suggest that two-thirds of Russians oppose the war (*The Economist*, 25 February 1995, p. 43).

Public opinion in Russia during the second Chechen war

Steady losses among Russian troops have taken their toll on the initially very strong public support. But the second Chechen war is arguably the most important single factor explaining the meteoretic rise of Vladimir Putin from relative obscurity to president. Russians overwhelmingly accept the official explanation that Chechen rebels were responsible for the September 1999 bombings on Russian soil which led to the loss of many civilian lives.

International opinion during the first Chechen war

The international community generally saw the crisis as an internal Russian one, but criticism mounted, especially regarding the effects on civilians. Concern was also expressed about unannounced Russian troop movements in the light of treaties on conventional forces.

On 5 January 1995 the EU delayed signing an interim trade agreement with Russia (until 17 July 1995) as a form of protest.

On 6 January 1995 President Clinton sent a letter to Yeltsin calling for a halt to the assault because of the number of civilian casualties.

On 10 January 1995 the Council of Europe suspended Russia's application for entry.

On 23 January 1995 a meeting of EU foreign ministers concluded by saying that the group 'deplores the serious violations of human rights and international humanitarian law which are still occurring there'.

On 30 January 1995 an OSCE fact-finding mission reported on its visit to Grozny: 'disproportionate and indiscriminate force' used by Russian forces; 'unbelievable devastation'; violations of human rights on both sides; a cease-fire recommended, to enable aid to get through, civilians to be evacuated and corpses to be cleared from the streets.

On 6 March 1995 the EU delayed signing an interim trade accord with Russia until progress was made on settling the Chechen crisis, e.g. moves towards political dialogue with Chechen leaders, access for humanitarian aid for refugees and continuing co-operation with OSCE.

On 29 March 1995 US secretary of state Warren Christopher described the assault on Chechenia as 'tragically wrong'. He warned that 'the evaluation of Russia's participation in Western institutions will be affected by the world's judgement' of the military campaign.

International opinion during the second Chechen war

'The USA and others have criticised what they have described as indiscriminate bombing of civilians and the creation of a large number of refugees' (*FT*, 18 November 1999, p. 1).

An OSCE summit meeting was held in Istanbul on 18 November 1999. Russia came under attack for its indiscriminate bombing and the creation of large numbers of refugees.

Yeltsin: 'You have no right to criticise Russia for Chechenia. We do not accept the advice of the so-called objective critics of Russia. Those people do not understand that we simply must stop the spread of this cancer and prevent its growth spreading across the world. We are for peace and for a political settlement in Chechenia. That is exactly why we need the total elimination of armed gangs and terrorists. When dealing with terrorists, questions of proportionality and humaneness do not apply. There will be no negotiations with bandits and murderers ... We simply are obliged to put an end to the threat of terrorism ... As a result of the bloody wave of terrorist acts that have swept over Moscow and other cities of our country, 1,580 peaceful inhabitants of our country have suffered. Nobody should have any illusions on this score ... [I reject] the new idea of humanitarian interference in the affairs of another state, even under the pretext of defending human rights ... Suffice it to recall the aggression of Nato headed by the United States that was mounted against Yugoslavia.' Yeltsin left the meeting two hours earlier than planned.

'The final Istanbul declaration [19 November] called for the organization [OSCE] to have both a political role and a humanitarian role in Chechenia' (*IHT*, 20 November 1999, p. 1). 'The Istanbul summit declaration said a political solution to the Chechen crisis was essential, and international aid for refugees was important' (*FT*, 20 November 1999, p. 5). The final declaration included the following: 'We fully acknowledge the territorial integrity of the Russian Federation and condemn terrorism in all its of forms ... We agree that a political solution is essential and that the assistance of OSCE would contribute to achieving that goal ... We welcome the agreement of the Russian Federation to a visit by the chairman in office [Knut Vollebaek] to the region.'

'A decision [was made] this week by the IMF to further postpone delivery of a long-awaited $640 million credit ... Originally due to be delivered in September ... the loan was postponed after the fund, at the urging of leading industrial countries, pressed for new conditions, aimed largely at structural economic reforms, in part as a result of the Russian financial scandals. Failure to meet those conditions, which include measures setting higher standards of accountability and openness for Russian financial institutions, have been cited by IMF spokesmen as the reasons for the latest delay' (*IHT*, Wednesday 8 December 1999, p. 6). 'The IMF's decision to delay the next disbursement of a $640 million tranche [was] ostensibly for technical financial reasons' (*FT*, 9 December 1999, p. 8). 'The IMF said it would delay disbursement of further credits to Russia because Moscow had not implemented agreed structural reforms, including more effective bankruptcy legislation and improved banking regulations' (*FT*, 13 December 1999, p. 10). 'By no coincidence, the IMF is holding up, for "technical reasons", the release of a new $640 million package' (*The Independent*, 8 December 1999, p. 1). (In the West the IMF's move was generally seen as a punishment for Russia's conduct of the war in Chechenia.)

Yeltsin (on 9 December 1999 in Beijing on a visit to China): 'President Clinton permitted himself to put pressure on Russia ... It seems he has for a minute, for a second, for a half minute, forgotten that Russia has a full arsenal of nuclear weapons.'

'Leaders of the EU strongly condemned [on 10 December] Russia's behaviour in Chechenia as "in contradiction with the basic principles of humanitarian law" ... They called for ... an end to "The disproportionate use of force against the Chechen population". The heads ordered an immediate review of their common strategy with Russia, which includes all aspects of political co-operation. They also announced the partial suspension of their partnership and co-operation agreement with Moscow' (*FT*, 11 December 1999, p. 1). 'The EU ... switched aid for the Russian economy to humanitarian assistance ... The EU leaders, meeting in Helsinki, also agreed to tighten trade terms, to suspend parts of a co-operation agreement and to review the bloc's entire strategy on Russia' (*The Independent*, 11 December 1999, p. 1). 'In Helsinki EU leaders shifted some technical aid funds to humanitarian assistance' (*The Guardian*, 11 December 1999, p. 2).

'Returning from a three-day visit to Chechenia [on 17 December 1999], Knut Vollebaek, the Norwegian foreign minister who is also serving as chairman of OSCE, gave a bleak assessment of the military lines of battle to his G7 colleagues. "We urgently need a ceasefire, otherwise there will be a bloodbath [Grozny will not fall easily]", Mr Vollebaek said' (*IHT*, 18 December 1999, p. 1). Joschka Fischer (German foreign minister): 'Nobody is questioning Russia's right to combat terrorism. But present actions by the

Russians are often in contradiction with international law. We see things only getting worse unless they work for a political solution as quickly as possible. They must realise they cannot fight terrorism by indiscriminately bombing a whole population' (p. 5).

'Strobe Talbott, the US deputy secretary of state, accused Russia on Thursday [23 December] of violating international standards during its military offensive in Chechenia ... Mr Talbott ... during his three-day visit to Moscow ... said the United States wanted to see Russia deal with what is a global problem of "extremism and terrorism" but it also wanted Russian to deal with that problem "in a fashion that meets international norms. And the feeling is that this standard has not been met"' (*IHT*, 24 December 1999, p. 1).

'The EU yesterday [24 January 2000] decided to impose sanctions on Russia to register its continuing concern over Moscow's military campaign in Chechenia. Taking the lead from last month's EU summit in Helsinki, foreign ministers decided to suspend some for some months the EU's Tacis programme of economic support for Russia ... They asked the European Commission to divert unspent Tacis money for humanitarian purposes. Some of these funds are expected to benefit refugees from Chechenia ... They decided to pursue Russia for breaches in its partnership and co-operation agreement with the EU. Russia has been exporting about 20 per cent more scrap than allowed under the accord. The ministers also agreed to suspend consideration of further trade concessions to Russia under the EU's generalized system of preferences. In addition, they confirmed the suspension of an economic dialogue and a scientific and technical agreement with Russia, which had been halted to register disapproval at Russia's actions in Chechenia' (*FT*, 25 January 2000, p. 8).

On 17 February 2000 Vladimir Kalamanov (head of the federal immigration service) was appointed as the special presidential representative in Chechenia 'for safeguarding safeguarding human rights and liberties'. (There had been growing complaints in the West about the behaviour of marauding Russian troops, allegedly including executions, rape and looting. Criticism had also been aimed at so-called 'filtration' camps, detention centres or internment camps meant to filter rebels from civilians. Allegations included torture, rape and killings in the 'filtration' camps.)

'The Council of Europe, a forty-one-nation human rights assemblage, on Thursday [6 April 2000] became the first foreign organization to threaten Russia with sanctions over the war in Chechenia when it started procedures to suspend Moscow from its ranks. The council, which met in Strasbourg, demanded that Russia stop the war immediately and begin talks with elected Chechen officials ... It also urged member governments to take Russia to the European Court of Human Rights for atrocities committed against civilians ... Preliminary suspension cannot be finalized before June [2000] ... Russia joined the Council of Europe in 1996' (*IHT*, 7 April 2000, p. 5). 'The parliamentary assembly of the Council of Europe voted in Strasbourg yesterday to suspend Russia from the organization unless it improved its human rights record in Chechenia ... Members of the assembly supported an appeal by Sergei Kovalyov, Russia's leading human rights activist, to impose sanctions on his country. They approved a motion calling on the other forty governments in the Council of Europe ... to begin proceedings towards suspending Russia unless there was "substantial, accelerating and demonstrable progress ... made immediately" to stop human rights abuses in Chechenia' (*FT*, 7 April 2000, p. 10). 'The assembly has lifted Russia's voting rights and proposed the suspension of Russian membership of the forty-one member council, over human rights violations during the Chechenia war. The suspension of a country depends on the approval of ministers from the countries concerned' (*The Independent*, 8 April 2000, p. 15).

David Russell-Johnson (president of the Parliamentary Assembly of the Council of Europe): 'The civilian population has suffered from the disproportionate and indiscriminate use of force by Russian troops. Grozny ... has been reduced to rubble. There is evidence of torture, rape and murder. Certainly, the Chechen fighters have been responsible for many, often most brutal human rights violations themselves ... Russia must respect human rights, ensure that the alleged abuses are investigated in a transparent manner, and make a genuine commitment to a peaceful solution to the conflict. If they fail to achieve demonstrable and accelerated progress in this regard in the immediate future, the governments of the Council of Europe would be expected to suspend Russia's membership. Member states were also asked to lodge an interstate complaint at the European Court of Human Rights, for Russia's alleged violations of the European Convention on Human Rights. In the meantime the assembly voted to deprive our Russian colleagues of their voting rights' (*IHT*, 14 April 2000, p. 6).

15 April 2000. 'A London lawyer ... is taking Russia to the European Court of Human Rights on behalf of a Chechen nurse ... who alleges five of her patients were killed in front of her and sixty-one others vanished' (*The Guardian*, 17 April 2000, p. 2).

25 April 2000. 'The top United Nations human rights body Tuesday [25 April] accused Russia of widespread violations in Chechenia. The EU-sponsored resolution attacked "disproportionate and indiscriminate use of Russian military force, including attacks on civilians", while also expressing concern over "serious crimes and abuses" committed by Chechen forces. The fifty-three-nation Human Rights Commission called on the Russian government to establish a national commission of inquiry and agreed to send a series of human rights experts to the region to report on the situation. The resolution was approved by twenty-five votes to seven, with nineteen abstentions. Joining Russia in voting against the resolution were China, Cuba, Republic of Congo, India, Madagascar and Sri Lanka ... The vote came after negotiations between the EU and the Russian delegation failed to come up with an agreed statement' (*IHT*, 26 April 2000, p. 6). 'The United States and

Europe decided not to press for an international investigation through the United Nations Commission of Human Rights … Rather the EU submitted a draft resolution that merely calls on Russia to set up its own ostensibly independent national commission and to allow foreign monitors unfettered access to the province' (p. 8).

'The resolution was presented by the EU and co-sponsored by countries including Canada and the USA … Two delegations were absent' (*FT*, 26 April 2000, p. 8).

'[Russia] suffered … a vote of censure at the United Nations yesterday [25 April] over "gross, widespread and flagrant violations" of human rights in Chechenia … The vote … came after lengthy talks between Russian and EU diplomats … Moscow … was intransigent on two key EU demands outlined in the UN resolution: that it establish an independent [national] commission of inquiry to investigate alleged abuses and to grant international organizations "free and effective" access to the republic' (*The Times*, 26 April 2000, p. 17).

A chronology of developments

27 October 1991. Dzhokhar Dudayev is elected president. (He was previously a Soviet air force general.)

2 November 1991. 'Independence' is declared (as 'Chechenia', not as Chechen-Ingushetia). (Russian forces soon beat a hasty retreat after some resistance and the refusal of the Russian parliament to ratify the move.)

June 1992. Russia declares Ingushetia a semi-autonomous republic.

2 April 1993. Dudayev dissolves parliament after an attempt at impeachment and rule by presidential decree begins. (Fighting with opposition forces begins in mid-1993.)

13 June 1994. There is open fighting in Grozny with a rival clan led by Ruslan Labazanov.

29 July 1994. The Russian government (which supports the opposition) issues a statement attacking the Dudayev regime as 'illegitimate' and promises Russian 'intervention' (Yeltsin ruled out the use of troops) to ensure the rule of law and protection of Russian citizens. (Chechenia was considered a hive of criminality in general, but a series of hi-jackings in southern Russia particularly angered the Russian government.)

2 August 1994. The opposition Provisional Council of Chechenia (led by Umar Avturkhanov) claims to have assumed power, but this is denied by the Dudayev regime and proves not to be the case.

10 August 1994. Russia imposes an air blockade.

2 September 1994. Heavy fighting breaks out.

15 October 1994. Opposition forces attack Grozny.

25 November 1994. Opposition forces attack Grozny once again (and fail once again). Some of the Russians aiding the opposition are captured (the Russian government claiming that they are mercenaries).

29 November 1994. Yeltsin issues an ultimatum. If there is no ceasefire within forty-eight hours Russia will intervene militarily and impose a state of emergency.

Unidentified planes (later admitted to be Russian) bomb Grozny airport and a military airport in the capital.

9 December 1994. Yeltsin issues a decree entitled 'On measures to bring an end to the activities of illegal armed formations on the territory of the Chechen republic and in the zone of the Ossetian-Ingush conflict'. 'Activity aimed at violating the integrity of the Russian Federation, undermining the security of the state, creating armed formations or stirring up national or religious discord is prohibited and unlawful ... The Russian Federation government ... is instructed to use all means at the state's disposal ... to disarm all illegal armed formations.'

11 December 1994. Russian forces invade Chechenia, but stop short of Grozny (negotiations were to take place the following day). They meet resistance in both Ingushetia and Dagestan.

Yeltsin: 'The government's actions were prompted by the threat to the integrity of Russia and to the safety of its citizens both in Chechenia and elsewhere, and by the destabilization of the political and economic situation. Our goal is to find a political solution to the problems of a member of the Russian Federation, the Chechen republic, and to protect its citizens from armed extremism ... I order all officials responsible for conducting measures to restore constitutional order in the Chechen republic not to use violence against the civilian population.'

The initial political reaction in Russia itself was split in ways which made strange bedfellows. Yegor Gaidar, Grigori Yavlinsky and Gennadi Zyuganov (the leader of the Communist Party) opposed the move. Sergei Kovalyov, member of the State Duma and human rights commissioner, was an especially vocal critic from the start. Supporters of the move included Vladimir Zhirinovsky, foreign minister Andrei Kozyrev (who resigned from his party, Russia's Choice, over the issue) and Boris Fyodorov (who later called for the dismissal of the government for incompetence; he opposed the use of violence against civilians and the use of conscripted servicemen). Alexander Solzhenytsin thinks that only a third of Chechenia, the northern part, should remain within Russia.

McFaul argues that 'Yeltsin did not order his troops into Chechenia to save the Russian Federation. He moved against Chechenia to save his presidency' (McFaul 1995: 151). The December 1993 election, for example, convinced Yeltsin of the need to tap the nationalist and law-and-order vote (p. 151). Another factor was the personal interest of members of the 'party of war' exercising increasing influence over the president, e.g. defence minister Pavel Grachev (to deflect attention from corruption in the army) and Alexander Korzhakov (a nationalist and 'law and order' man in charge of Yeltsin's personal security and totally dependent on Yeltsin for his political power) (pp. 153–6).

23 December 1994. Moscow claims that Grozny has been surrounded. (This proves to be untrue. Moscow has engaged in disinformation, e.g. the claim that the Chechens themselves, for propaganda purposes, have engaged in self-inflicted bombing.)

The State Duma passes a resolution (by 228 votes to thirty-eight with three abstentions) calling for an end to hostilities and a resumption of peace talks. Efforts to call for a vote of no confidence in the president fail. (Note that critics among military personnel include General Boris Gromov, a deputy defence minister and former commander of Soviet forces in Afghanistan, and General Alexander Lebed, commander of the Fourteenth Army in the Dniestre region. They both oppose a military solution.)

27 December 1994. In a television address Yeltsin says that: 'Russian soldiers are defending the unity of Russia ... The Chechen republic is a part of the Russian Federation ... Not a single territory has the right to secede from Russia ... The regime in Grozny is illegal ... there are neither authorities nor law there today ... The regime set up in the republic has become a source of great criminal danger, above all for Russia ... the longer the situation in the Chechen republic goes on the greater the destructive impact on Russia's stability. It has become one of the main internal threats to our state's security ... the explosion of banditry on Chechen soil threatens our entire country.'

1 January 1995. Russian forces reach the centre of Grozny.

2 January 1995. Russian forces incur heavy losses in men and equipment as they are forced to withdraw from the centre of Grozny. (Prior to the invasion defence minister Grachev thought that a regiment of Soviet paratroops could take Grozny in 'two hours'. Military observers severely criticized the sending in of tanks unaccompanied by ground troops. The tanks were easily surrounded and destroyed. Moreover, the Russian troops were mainly inexperienced conscripts.)

6 January 1995. The 'security council' (currently comprising twelve members, excluding Yeltsin) resolves to carry on with the assault on Grozny. (There has been increasing concern about how Yeltsin, the security chiefs and a small number of presidential advisers have dominated policy-making. Among the main individuals were defence minister Pavel Grachev, interior minister Viktor Yerin, head of counter-intelligence Sergei Stepashin, nationalities minister Nikolai Yegorov and the head of the 'security council', Oleg Lobov. The influence of the chief of presidential security and Yeltsin's bodyguard since 1985, General Alexander Korzhakov, has caused particular disquiet in a more general sense, e.g. his attempts to prevent the liberalization of oil exports. The term 'party of war' was coined by the critics of the attack on the Chechen republic.)

10 January 1995. Yeltsin creates a five-strong inner circle (permanent members) of the 'security council', only these having voting rights (note, however, that the council is only a consultative body): existing 'security council' members Yeltsin (chairman), Chernomyrdin and Oleg Lobov (secretary) are joined by two new ones, Ivan Rybkin (speaker of the State Duma) and Vladimir Shumeiko (speaker of the Council of the Federation).

The other members of the 'security council' are Sergei Shakhrai (deputy prime minister), Pavel Grachev (defence minister), Viktor Yerin (minister of internal affairs), Andrei Kozyrev (foreign minister), Sergei Stepashin (director of the counter-intelligence service), Yevgeni Primakov (director of the Foreign Intelligence Service), Sergei Shoigu (minister of civil defence affairs, emergency situations and the elimination of the consequences of natural disasters) and Andrei Nikolayev (director of the Federal Border Service).

16 February 1995. Yeltsin comments on the Chechen crisis in his 'state of the nation' speech to a joint session of parliament: 'Abcesses like the Medellin cartel in Colombia, the 'golden triangle' of South East Asia and the criminal dictatorship of Chechenia do not heal themselves ... The state can and must use the force of its authority to preserve sovereignty, independence and integrity.'

10 March 1995. The State Duma sacks the parliamentary human rights commissioner Sergei Kovalyov. (He has been criticized in particular for advocating foreign observers in Chechenia; he still retains the presidential position.)

14 March 1995. Dzhokhar Dudayev, in a published article, calls for (1) a real and unconditional cease-fire monitored by international observers, (2) direct negotiations at any mutually agreed level under the auspices of international mediators and (3) the holding of presidential and parliamentary elections in 1995 under international supervision. 'We are not secessionists. We are not demanding complete independence. We are not criminals. Nor did we start this war' (*IHT*, 14 March 1995, p. 8).

14 June 1995. Chechen forces led by Shamil Basayev attack the town of Budyonnovsk, north of the Chechen border in the Stavropol region of Russia. There is significant loss of life and many hostages are held in a hospital. The Chechens demand the withdrawal of Russian forces from Chechenia.

19 June 1995. The Chechens are allowed to leave accompanied by Russian 'volunteers' to ensure their safe passage to Chechenia.

31 July 1995. The constitutional court rules that the 9 December 1994 presidential decree authorizing the use of force against 'illegal armed units' was constitutional (despite the fact that no state of emergency had been declared).

9 January 1996. Chechen fighters hold a large number of hostages in a hospital in Kizlyar (Dagestan) after failing to seize a military airfield. The Chechens are led by Salman Raduyev, a son-in-law of Dudayev. Two of the hostages are killed.

6 March 1996. Chechens fighters launch a large-scale attack on Grozny. (The Chechens made sweeping early gains, occupying perhaps a third of the city. The Russian forces claimed victory by the fourth day, but sporadic clashes continued: *IHT*, 12 March 1996, p. 5.)

31 March 1996. Yeltsin announces a unilateral ceasefire as of midnight. He proposes a partial and gradual withdrawal of Russian troops ('special operations' are allowed within Chechenia), indirect talks with Dudayav via intermediaries, local elections and a level of autonomy 'very close to independence' (*IHT*, 1 April 1996, p. 1). (Localized fighting continued.)

7 April 1996. Yeltsin sends a telegram to Dudayav declaring offensive operations by Russian forces to be at an end.

14 April 1996. The first Russian troops pull out of Chechenia.

21 April 1996. Dzhokhar Dudayev is killed in a rocket attack by the Russian airforce (allegedly made after monitoring a call he was making in a field, using a portable satellite telephone). He is replaced as leader by his deputy Zelimkhan Yandarbiyev.

4 May 1996. There is heavy fighting in Grozny.

16 May 1996. Yeltsin decrees that, with immediate effect, only volunteers will be sent to 'conflict areas'.

27 May 1996. The talks in Moscow produce rapid agreement on a halt to all hostilities (as of midnight 31 May) and an exchange of prisoners within two weeks.

10 June 1996. The following is agreed after the talks resumed: (1) Russian troops will withdraw from Chechenia by the end of August 1996 (apart from two brigades: *The Times*, 26 June 1996, p. 13) and dismantle their fortified checkpoints around towns and cities by 7 July 1996, (2) Chechen fighters will disarm (Chechenia will be 'demilitarized') and (3) local elections, due to be held on 16 June 1996, will be postponed until after the withdrawal of Russian troops.

28 June 1996. Russian troops begin their withdrawal.

9 July 1996. There takes place the worst fighting since the 10 June agreement, with Russian forces pounding Gekhi (south-west of Grozny). (The siege was ended on 14 July.)

6 August 1996. The Chechens launch major offensives in Grozny (led by Shamil Basayev), Argun and Gudermes.

(Chechen forces went to occupy large parts of Grozny, a humiliating setback for Russian forces.)

10 August 1996. Alexander Lebed replaces Oleg Lobov as Yeltsin's special representative on Chechenia.

12 August 1996. Lebed visits Chechenia and meets the Chechen military commander Aslan Maskhadov.

13 August 1996. A ceasefire is agreed, starting noon the following day.

14 August 1996. Confusion surrounds the status of the ceasefire. Lebed is given the power to coordinate the operation of all federal agencies in Chechenia.

15 August 1996. Lebed meets Yandarbiyev and they agree to set up a joint commission to monitor the ceasefire.

21 August 1996. Lebed announces a new ceasefire after talks with Aslan Maskhadov.

22 August 1996. Lebed signs a ceasefire to come into force the following day. There will be a withdrawal of forces from Grozny and the city will be come under joint military police control to ensure law and order. Russian forces will be withdrawn from the mountainous southern districts.

23 August 1996. The ceasefire comes into force and seems to be generally holding.

27 August 1996. Lebed is still not granted a meeting with Yeltsin.

General Vyacheslav Tikhomirov, commander of Russian forces in Chechenia, and his Chechen counterpart Aslan Maskhadov sign the ceasefire agreement.

31 August 1996. Lebed declares that 'the war is over' after a peace agreement is negotiated with Aslan Maskhadov. No details are given but the agreement is thought to contain the following: (1) the 'final constitutional status' of Chechenia is to be deferred until a referendum in Chechenia in December 2001; (2) an interim government is to be set up with at least two representatives of the previous, Moscow-backed government; (3) a joint commission is to be set up on 1 October to monitor the withdrawal of Russian forces and oversee economic and social recovery. In an article published in *The Times* (10 October 1996, p. 20) Lebed said: 'The republic's status is thus far defined by the Russian constitution, according to which Chechenia is a member of the Russian Federation. Under the Khasavyurt agreements its permanent status is to be determined by the year 2001.'

3 September 1996. Lebed also says that 'I am in permanent touch with the president through writing and by telephone. I think the fuss about this is out of place'. During recent telephone conversations Yeltsin 'did not say anything. But silence is a sign of agreement'. Nevertheless, 'I must say I could do with an expression of sincere support from the president'.

Gennadi Zyguganov says that the agreements signed by Lebed and Maskhadov on 31 August in Khasavyurt 'violate the constitution of the Russian Federation'. Zyuganov 'welcomes a peaceful resolution of the Chechen crisis' but expresses concern about the 'imminent threat to Russia's territorial integrity'. 'Either we manage to settle the situation peacefully while preserving the state's integrity … or the splitting apart and destruction of Russia will begin' (*CDSP*, 1996, vol. XLVIII, no. 36, p. 11).

5 September 1996. In a television interview, in which he announces that he is to have a heart operation, Yeltsin says that he supports Lebed's efforts 'except for one question: the withdrawal of troops. I believe there is no need to hurry with this. Everything else I supported and approved.' But he adds that the documents signed by Lebed and Maskhadov are not legally binding.

8 September 1996. Russian troops begin leaving Chechenia.

17 October 1996. Yeltsin dismisses Lebed (see entry for that date in Chapter 12).

23 November 1996. Yeltsin orders the last two Russian brigades to be withdrawn by 27 January 1997 (when Chechenia is to hold elections for a president and legislature).

Russian prime minister Viktor Chernomyrdin and Aslan Maskhadov sign an interim agreement on relations until 27 January 1997. A final decision on the status of Chechenia will not be made until the end of 2001. The economic co-operation agreement calls for restoring trade, communications and road links by December 1996. Customs regulations are to be established. By December 1996 a new agreement will be concluded on refining and transporting oil and gas. (The Chechen negotiators promise to guarantee the security of the oil pipelines and refineries.) Pensions and wages are to be paid, as is compensation to victims of the war (*IHT*, 25 November 1996, p. 5).

29 December 1996. The last Russian combat unit withdraws from Chechenia. (Russia tried unsuccessfully in negotiations to keep two divisions there.)

5 January 1997. The interior ministry announces that the last Russian troops have left Chechenia.

23 January 1997. Yandarbiyev announces that Grozny is to change its name to Dzhokar-Ghala (City of Dzhokar) after the late Dzhokar Dudayev.

27 January 1997. Presidential and parliamentary elections take place in Chechenia. There are over a hundred international observers, including seventy-two from OSCE. The OSCE observers reported that there were no serious irregularities: 'These elections reflect the true will of the voters and create a legitimate basis for the new authorities.' There is a high turnout.

Thirteen candidates contest the presidential election. The turnout is 79.4 per cent. Aslan Maskhadov wins comfortably in the first round with 59.32 per cent of the vote. 'In 1991 … we declared our sovereignty … Chechenia is already an independent country. What is important for us now is to achieve international recognition, including that of Moscow.'

Shamil Basayev comes second with 23.5 per cent of the vote. Zelimkhan Yandarbayev comes third with 10.1 per cent.

12 February 1997. Aslan Maskhadov is sworn in as president. He talks, among other things, of 'the right to live freely and independently' and 'to strengthen the Moslem religion, to free the nation from the violence and mockery of the criminal elements'. The inauguration ceremony is attended by Ivan Rybkin (secretary of the 'security council', representing Yeltsin) and Alexander Lebed.

Late April 1997. The Chechen government introduces a new currency, which is against Russian federal law (*IHT*, 2 May 1997, p. 6).

12 May 1997. Boris Yeltsin and Aslan Maskhadov sign a treaty 'on peace and the principles of Russian-Chechen relations' in Moscow. Yeltsin: 'Our firm intention is never to use force or threaten to use it in relations between the Russian Federation and the Republic of Ichkeria.' Maskhadov: 'There will be no room for terrorists and abductors of people on our land … Today we have really cut the ground from under those people who order terrorist acts and kidnappings.' (Maskhadov has threatened hostage-takers with the death penalty: *FT*, 7 July 1997, p. 2.)

The treaty between Russian and Chechenia, 'wishing to end their centuries-long antagonism', includes the following:

1. 'To renounce forever the use of force and the threat of its use in resolving all disputed questions.'

2. 'To build their relations in accordance with generally recognized principles and norms of international law.'

The national bank of Chechenia will have a single correspondent account with the central bank of Russia, through which all financial transactions between Russia and Chechenia will be handled. Chechenia's banking system is not part of the central bank of Russia's system. The agreement will remain in effect for one year (*CDSP*, 1997, vol. XLIX, no. 19, pp. 110–11).

'Chechenia will keep the Russian rouble and will have no power to issue roubles of its own. But its national bank will be free to run the local banking system and to borrow money' (*The Economist*, 17 May 1997, p. 44).

10 July 1997. Shamil Basayev resigns as deputy prime minister of Chechenia.

18 August 1997. Yeltsin and Maskhadov meet in Moscow. Yeltsin announces that a joint commission will be established to come up with a political settlement.

3 September 1997. The first public executions takes place (by firing squad) of a husband and wife convicted of murder. Russia protests at the use of the Sharia (Islamic law), calling the executions barbaric and illegal.

9 September 1997. Russia and Chechenia agree to repair the pipeline to allow the transport of oil from Azerbaijan (planned to begin in October/November 1997).

(On 15 September Boris Nemtsov announced that a pipeline bypassing Chechenia was to be built to export oil from Azerbaijan: *RET*, 1997, no. 4, p. 105.)

10 September 1997. The public execution of two more people is delayed.

18 September 1997. Two men are executed in public after being found guilty of murder.

10 November 1997. It is announced that women in state employment are to observe the Islamic dress code.

1 January 1998. President Maskhadov dismisses the government and asks Shamil Basayev to form a new government. (One of Basayev's first moves was to start dividing up state farms among former fighters and anyone else who wishes to work the land: *FT*, Survey, 15 April 1998, p. xii.)

6 January 1998. General Anatoli Kulikov (interior minister) calls for air strikes against 'bandit targets' in Chechenia. His call is unheeded.

1 May 1998. Yeltsin's personal envoy, Valentin Vlasov, is kidnapped in Chechenia by gangsters. (He was freed on 13 November 1998.)

23 June 1998. President Maskhadov announces a state of emergency and a curfew, saying he needs three weeks to reimpose order (*The Economist*, 4 July 1998, p. 43).

8 July 1998. Shamil Basayev resigns as prime minister.

13 July 1998. There is a violent clash (with loss of life) between Wahhabis and a national guard battalion.

15 July 1998. There is another clash (with even greater loss of life). Maskhadov declares Wahhabism and Wahhabi organizations illegal. Wahhabis are Islamic fundamentalists, adherents of the strict, orthodox Saudi version of Islam (*CDSP*, 1998, vol. 50, no. 28, p. 15, and vol. 50, no. 29, p. 15).

18 July 1998. The state of emergency is prolonged for another ten days.

20 July 1998. Shamil Basayev is made commander of Chechenia's armed forces. President Maskhadov also calls up 5,000 army reservists.

23 July 1998. Maskhadov survives an assassination attempt (by car bomb). (This was the fourth attempt on his life but the first since he became president: *IHT*, 24 July 1998, p. 5.)

1 August 1998. Maskadov meets Russian prime minister Kiriyenko.

4 September 1998. A bomb blast in Makhachkala (capital of Dagestan) kills sixteen people and injures eighty-three (*FT*, 7 September 1998, p. 2).

25 October 1998. The Chechen general in charge of the campaign to counter kidnappings is assassinated.

10 November 1998. Salman Raduyev is demoted from brigadier to private after he was convicted of attempting a coup (*The Times*, 11 November 1998, p. 14).

8 December 1998. 'Chechenia has experienced lawlessness and banditry since the end of a 1994–96 war with Russian troops ... On Tuesday [8 December] the severed heads of four Western hostages seized in Grozny in October were discovered in a sack on a Chechen highway' (*IHT*, 12 December 1998, p. 2).

12 December 1998. 'Officials in ... Chechenia have accused a renegade guerrilla commander of leading the kidnap ring that murdered four Western hostages last week. They also called for a mobilization of armed forces to help protect the government ... The Chechen deputy prime minister ... said Arbi Barayev had led the band that killed three Britons and a New Zealander' (*IHT*, 14 December 1998, p. 5).

'Chechenia began recruiting veterans of its independence war with Russia for a crackdown on hostage-taking and organized crime. President Maskhadov signed a decree mobilizing a force of 1,500 army militia and veterans' (*The Times*, 14 December 1998, p. 10).

15 December 1998. President Maskhadov declares a thirty-day state of emergency. His decision to call up army reservists is declared unconstitutional by the Chechen parliament (*The Times*, 16 December 1998, p. 15).

19 March 1999. There is a bomb explosion in a market in Vladikavkaz in North Ossetia. Estimates of the number of dead range between fifty-six and sixty-two.

21 March 1999. Aslan Maskhadov survives another assassination attempt when a bomb explodes near his car.

28 May 1999. 'Russian troops carried out combat operations on Chechen territory for the first time since the end of the Chechen war. Several helicopters inflicted heavy missile strikes on positions held by [terrorist leader] Khattab's fighters on the Terek River. This act of retribution followed an attempt by the fighters to take over a post manned by internal troops on the Dagestani-Chechen border' (*CDSP*, 1999, vol. 51, no. 22, p. 14). 'Yesterday [2 June] … Chechen raiders attacked a guard post manned by Russian internal affairs ministry troops at the Grebenskaya Bridge across the Terek River. They also attacked a police detachment in … Dagestan' (p. 15).

14 June 1999. 'The Russian fuel and power minister… has announced that it will be necessary to close the Baku-Novorossisk pipeline, which is used to transport Azerbaijani oil … And so something long apparent has been acknowledged at the official level: Russia is incapable of guaranteeing oil transport through Chechenia … Openings that are constantly being made in the Chechen section of the pipeline have created a situation in which the pipeline is down about as often as it is up and running. The latest shutdown occurred after a 14 June explosion along a raised portion of the pipeline over a river in Dagestan … When the oil will start flowing again remains unclear. Officials at Transneft … [say] that the Chechens are failing to meet their commitments to protect the pipeline … Illegal tap-ins are made … In the past Grozneft [Grozny Petroleum] compensated for siphoned-off Azerbaijani oil by adding its own oil to the pipeline. But it has not done so this year [1999] … Transneft … said yesterday [16 June] that transporting crude oil by rail through Dagestan could offer an alternative … Another alternative would be to bypass Chechenia by building a section of pipeline through Dagestan … A few days ago [President] Aliev [of Azerbaijan] said that the Azerbaijani Republic State Oil Company has been preparing to phase out the Baku-Novorossisk pipeline for more than two months now' (*CDSP*, 1999, vol. 51, no. 24, p. 16).

16 July 1999. '[The] Chechen minister of state security … who was arrested at Moscow's Vnukovo airport on Friday [16 July], spent about twenty-four hours in Moscow's … pretrial detention facility. He was detained in connection with … the case of the Chechen militants' attack on the Dagestani town of Kizlar in January 1996 … [But he] was released … Immediately after the arrest was reported by news agencies an extraordinary session of the shura [a state council made up of influential field commanders], which is led by Maskhadov opponent Shamil Basayev, opened in Grozny. Members … vowed to take "countermeasures"' (*CDSP*, 1999, vol. 51, no. 29, p. 11).

18 June 1999. 'Yesterday [18 June] Moscow decided to essentially seal off Chechenia. Virtually all checkpoints on the administrative border with Ichkeria [Chechenia] have been closed. Moreover, 2 million roubles have been allocated for border fortifications … All these measures have been taken in response to Chechen guerrilla attacks Thursday night [17 June] on posts in Dagestan manned by Russian internal affairs ministry troops. Three policemen were killed and sixteen were wounded. At the same time a Cossack patrol clashed with Chechen guerrillas on Chechenia's border with Stavropol territory. Four Cossacks were killed' (*CDSP*, 1999, vol. 51, no. 25, pp. 15–16).

2–3 August 1999. 'Russian security forces and a band of attackers waged two furious gun battles near Chechenia, leaving four officers and at least ten militants dead ... About forty gunmen started the initial attack Monday [2 August] near the village of Gagatl, on the Chechen border ... The shooting resumed before dawn Tuesday [3 August] in the village of Dacha ... inside the Russian province of Dagestan' (*IHT*, 4 August 1999, p. 3).

4 August 1999. 'Russia announced last night [4 August] that it was rushing troops to its border with ... Chechenia after weeks of border skirmishes and two days of gun battles ... The Chechen first deputy secretary security minister said that none of its forces had been involved in what they said was fighting between armed groups in Dagestan ... The Russian reinforcements have been sent in response to a plea by the pro-Moscow government of Dagestan ... The attacks in border areas have been blamed on fundamentalist Wahhabi Moslems who are fighting to create an independent Islamic republic made up of Chechenia and Dagestan ... The Wahhabis are thought to be beyond the control of the moderate but embattled Chechen president, Aslan Maskhadov, who has been trying for weeks to arrange a personal meeting with Mr Yeltsin ... The regime in Grozny has been unable to quell clashes between autonomous field commanders and continual hostage-taking of Russians and foreigners ... The trade in human lives has become Chechenia's only source of hard currency' (David Hearst, *The Guardian*, 5 August 1999, p. 15).

7 August 1999. 'Hundreds – some reports say up to 2,000 – of gunmen ... crossed into Dagestan early on Saturday [7 August]' (*The Guardian*, 9 August 1999, p. 10).

'On Saturday [7 August] in Dagestan's Tsumada and Botlikh districts ... leaders of the Shura [council] of Moslems of Chechenia and Dagestan announced the establishment of the independent state of Dagestan' (*CDSP*, 1999, vol. 51, no. 32, p. 9).

'In August Shamil Basayev led 400 Dagestanis and Chechens into Dagestan to fight Russian forces that had surrounded a Dagestani nationalist leader known as Bagaouddin and his men in his home village high in the mountains near the Chechen border ... When the Russian forces turned their firepower on two other villages that had been overtaken by Islamic militants, Mr Basayev and Mr Khattab burst back into Dagestan on 5 September' (Carlotta Gall, *IHT*, 18 October 1999, p. 6).

8 August 1999. 'Federal forces, including army units, opened fire from the ground and the air on Islamic militants who late last week occupied four villages along the Dagestani border with Chechenia ... Federal forces on Sunday [8 August] redoubled their artillery and rocket attacks on the militants' strongholds after more than 2,000 residents – mostly women and children – had fled the area ... The refugees said the militants were led by two well-known Chechen field commanders, Shamil Basayev and a shadowy Jordanian-born figure known as Khattab who reportedly runs commando training centres in Chechenia. Both men have been waging an undeclared war against ... President Aslan Maskhadov ... Terrorist attacks along the Chechen border with neighbouring Russian regions have stepped up in recent months, as armed commandos clash with interior ministry troops. About fifty interior ministry personnel have been killed in almost eighty such incidents this year [1999] ... Wahhabis, a militant Islamic sect, have set as their goal the establishment of an Islamic state in Dagestan' (Celestine Bohlen, *IHT*, 9 August 1999, p. 5).

'Unrest has been simmering in Dagestan for more than a year, with occasional clashes between federal troops and local guerrillas. But Russian news agencies quoted security sources as saying a Moslem group was now intent on exploiting the turmoil in Dagestan to turn the republic into an independent Islamic state' (John Thornhill, *FT*, 9 August 1999, p. 3). 'Russian officials have said many gunmen in Dagestan are from the Moslem Wahhabi sect, which Moscow claims is funded by Saudi Arabia and Kuwait' (*FT*, 16 August 1999, p. 2).

9 August 1999. Yeltsin dismisses Sergei Stepashin as prime minister and nominates Vladimir Putin (who was approved by the State Duma on 16 August).

Georgia protests that Russian planes have bombed a Georgian village near the border with Dagestan (*CDSP*, 1999, vol. 51, no. 32, p. 9).

10 August 1999. '[Acting prime minister] Vladimir Putin stressed that the period of establishing order, which he estimates will last a week and a half to two weeks, will be followed by a "period of stabilization of local authority", which "will take more time". "We know it will be possible to do", Vladimir Putin said, "since we are relying on the local population ... All our actions, ... not only have been cleared with the Dagestani authorities but are being carried out at the request of those authorities"' (*CDSP*, 1999, vol. 51, no. 11).

The Shura declares a jihad (holy war) to liberate Dagestan (*CDSP*, 1999, vol. 51, no. 32, p. 10).

'On Tuesday [10 August] Islamic militants who late last week [7 August] set off the most recent crisis by crossing the Chechen border into the neighbouring republic of Dagestan and seizing several mountain villages, issued a statement declaring Dagestan's independence as an Islamic state and vowing to drive "infidels" from its territory' (*IHT*, 11 August 1999, p. 1).

'Radicals yesterday [10 August] declared Dagestan an independent Islamic state after a secret meeting of the Shura of Dagestan, an Islamic council not recognized by Moscow: "We, the Moslems of Dagestan, officially declare the return of independence to the Islamic state of Dagestan"' (*The Guardian*, 11 August 1999, p. 13).

'[Dagestan has] an impoverished population of just 2 million split into some thirty-two distinct ethnic groups ... [It is in a] strategic location along the oil-rich Caspian Sea ... Lawlessness in the neighbouring breakaway republic of Chechenia has helped destabilize the region, and provided a base for local warlords to send their militias into Dagestan' (*FT*, 11 August 1999, p. 2).

'Dagestan ... boasts some thirty-four different nationalities, every one with a different language and different leadership. It barely exists as a unified republic, except that each group tolerates its neighbours, and power has traditionally rotated between the main ethnic groups. The republic is strategically important because of the oil pipeline which runs through it from the Caspian oilfields, via Grozny, to the Black Sea. But the pipeline runs along the Caspian coasts, many miles from the fighting in the mountains ... His {Shamil Basayev's] force may well include foreign fighters in its ranks, as the Russian government claims. Mr Basayev is seeking to proclaim an Islamic republic in Dagestan, but seems driven by little more than personal ambition and frustration. His chances of uniting Dagestan around a motley force of Wahhabi militants and Chechen warlords seem remote' (*FT*, 18 August 1999, p. 17).

11 August 1999. 'Russia launched a new offensive Wednesday [11 August] against Islamic insurgents ... A council of Moslem leaders, called Shura, named Shamil Basayev, a Chechen fighter who played a key role in deadly attacks against Russia during the 1994–6 war, as their commander ... Mr Basayev said he had given control of the rebel army to Khattab, a Jordanian known by one name who has become a prominent warlord in Chechenia. The presence of Mr Khattab and Mr Basayev would appear to verify Russian government claims that the rebels are members of the fundamentalist Wahhabi sect of Moslems, who support independence for mostly Moslem neighbours. Mr Khattab has long been described as a Wahhabi, while Mr Basayev considers the Wahhabis his allies. Both Mr Basayev and the authorities in Chechenia denied the fighters were connected in any way to the Chechen government led by Aslan Maskhadov. Mr Basayev, once prime minister of Chechenia, split with Mr Maskhadov this year [1999]' (*IHT*, 12 August 1999, p. 6).

'The guerrillas' positions are being bombarded by frontline aircraft, rocket launchers and artillery guns ... The [Russian] command has chosen ... to rely on bombing to force the guerrillas out of the occupied territory and then "mop up" whoever is left. The military men say they have been given two days, three at most, to complete the operation' (*CDSP*, 1999, vol. 51, no. 32, pp. 11–12).

12 August 1999. 'The head of the Dagestani legislature ... told a news conference in Moscow that Dagestanis remained loyal to Russia and that local residents were being armed to resist' (*IHT*, 13 August 1999, p. 5).

13 August 1999. Russian acting prime minister Vladimir Putin: 'Strikes will be delivered on the militants' bases. Chechenia is Russian territory and strikes will be delivered wherever militants are located, Chechenia or no Chechenia' (*IHT*, 14 August 1999, p. 6).

'The head of the [Russian] regional border guard said five armoured vehicles and troops crossed briefly into Chechenia yesterday [13 August], according to Russian press agencies. They moved into areas where the rebels appear to have been based ... The [Russian] interior ministry claimed that the rebels were occupying seven villages in the Botlikh district ...The Russian authorities estimated this week that up to 1,200 rebels had been involved in the campaign' (*FT,* 14 August 1999, p. 3).

15 August 1999. President Aslan Maskhadov signs a decree introducing a month long state of emergency in Chechenia as of midnight. This includes curfews, a mobilization of veterans of the 1994–6 war with Russia, placing military units, especially border guards, on high alert and suspending the licences of private television companies.

'In response to the incursion Russia launched an aerial bombardment of the guerrilla positions and over the weekend also bombed inside Chechenia' (*IHT,* Monday 16 August 1999, p. 1).

17 August 1999. The Chechen president says that Russian troops and armoured personnel carriers have entered the north-western region of Chechenia (*IHT,* 18 August 1999, p. 4).

Russia says that the army has formally taken command of the operation from the interior ministry, although the latter's troops are to remain involved (*IHT,* 18 August 1999, p. 4).

18 August 1999. 'Russian forces suffered their biggest one-day loss on Wednesday [18 August] in the remote frontier region of Dagestan. Eight soldiers trying to storm a village held by Islamic guerrillas ... On Wednesday defence minister Igor Sergeyev dismissed ... the interior ministry police troop commander in Dagestan ... He failed to organize his troops when the war broke out, the defence ministry said ... Moscow officials are beginning to prepare the Russian public for a drawn out conflict rather than the two-week affair promised by the new prime minister, Vladimir Putin' (*IHT,* 19 August 1999, p. 1).

19 August 1999. 'Russian troops have suffered the worst loss yet in an attempt to storm a Dagestani mountain village controlled by Islamic militants, and troop commanders said Thursday [19 August] that they would not attempt another direct assault because they fear heavy casualties. In the previous twenty-four hours Russian troops lost eighteen soldiers during an unsuccessful attack ... The losses brought the total Russian toll so far to forty dead and 160 wounded, according to a [Russian] deputy interior minister ... The battle for [the village of] Tando came after the village had been heavily bombed and shelled in recent days ... [The deputy interior minister] said that artillery and air strikes, which have been the basic tactic of the Russian troops in the outbreak had failed to dislodge the insurgents ... Instead of storming the villages where the fighters are entrenched ... [he said] that the troops would try to cut off the insurgents from their retreat routes back into Chechenia and also destroy their communications and supply lines. Russia has sent not only troops and interior ministry police units to the battle region but also local Dagestani volunteers, who are being organized and armed to fight the insurgents' (*IHT,* 20 August 1999, p. 1).

20 August 1999. 'Russian forces bombed two villages in Chechenia yesterday [20 August], in what they described as a strike against rear bases of the Islamic militants' (*The Guardian*, 21 August 1999, p. 12).

23 August 1999. Islamic militants claim to have quit the Botlikh region of Dagestan in order to 'redeploy'.

'Mr Basayev [issued a] statement on Monday [23 August] that he was switching from military to "military-political" tactics' (*FT*, 25 August 1999, p. 2).

'At the time of his inauguration Vladimir Putin, Russia's new prime minister, promised the conflict would be over by today [23 August] ... Mr Basayev ... has met considerable resistance from the local Dagestani population' (*FT*, 24 August 1999, p. 2).

24 August 1999. 'A military assault by Russian troops appeared Tuesday [24 August] to be driving Islamic militants from several villages in the Caucasian republic in Dagestan they seized more than two week ago. Conflicting claims by the rebels and the Russian military forces made it difficult to determine the exact status of the villages' (*IHT*, 25 August 1999, p. 6).

25 August 1999. 'The fighting in Dagestan appeared to be over Wednesday [25 August] ... But even the [Russian] defence minister, Marshal Igor Sergeyev ... said Wednesday that while federal forces ... had driven the rebels from the Botlikh district of Dagestan, the threat posed by the Islamic rebels ... remained ... Unlike the brutal war in Chechenia that ended in a humiliating defeat for Russian forces, the operation in Dagestan had broad political support in Russia as a whole, but also in Dagestan' (Celestine Bohlen, *IHT*, 26 August 1999, p. i).

26 August 1999. 'Prime minister Vladimir Putin of Russia hailed Russia's operation to flush out armed Islamic guerrillas in the Dagestani region as a success' (*IHT*, 27 August 1999, p. 5).

'The Russian defence minister said yesterday [26 August] that his forces had halted all offensive action in Dagestan and begun mopping-up operations' (*The Times*, 27 August 1999, p. 14).

'Russian planes were said to have bombed rebel camps Thursday [26 August] in "border areas" near Chechenia. But Chechen officials said the bombs struck villages in their republic ... Russian officials say more than 2,000 guerrillas were involved in the Dagestani incursion ... before retreating' (*IHT*, 28 August 1999, p. 3).

27 August 1999. Prime minister Vladimir Putin visits Dagestan.

30 August 1999. 'Russian troops on Monday [30 August] pressed on with efforts to flush out rebels holding out in a remote area of Dagestan ... The gunmen ... are holed up in two villages ... and have refused to surrender their weapons ... On Sunday [29 August] the Russian attacked the villages with helicopter gunships and artillery' (*IHT*, 31 August 1999, p. 5).

31 August 1999. 'Russia has opened a new offensive against Islamic forces in Dagestan, shifting the conflict to a new area as officials said Tuesday [31 August] that three days of fighting had brought fresh casualties, with eight Russian soldiers killed ... Starting Sunday [29 August] and continuing through Tuesday [31 August] Russian interior ministry forces have besieged [two] villages ... in the Buinaksk district of Dagestan, just south-west of the capital, Makhachkala' (*IHT*, 1 September 1999, p. 5).

There is a bomb explosion in a Moscow shopping centre in Manege Square near the Kremlin. One died.

2 September 1999. 'Russian forces on Thursday [2 September] entered the last bastion of Islamic insurgency in Dagestan, seizing control of the village of Chabanmakhy, said ... the [Russian] deputy interior minister. But fierce fighting continued in the area surrounding the village ... The village of Chankurbe ... no longer poses a military threat, officials said. Russian forces on Wednesday [1 September] reclaimed control of Kadar and Karmakhi ... [The deputy interior minister] said that twenty-five Russian troops died in the latest offensive, which was launched on Sunday [29 August] ... More than 100 area residents who are alleged to have supported the insurgents in battles last month have been arrested' (*IHT*, 3 September 1999, p. 5).

4 September 1999. A block of flats used by Russian troops and their families in Buinaksk (Dagestan) is destroyed by a bomb explosion. Sixty-four were killed (including twenty-five children).

5 September 1999. Islamic insurgents cross into Dagestan from Chechenia. Estimates range from around 500 to around 2,000. They seize several villages.

'The economically impoverished western border region of Dagestan contains over 60,000 ethnic Chechens who were forcibly removed by Stalin to Central Asia in 1944 and resettled in the late 1950s' (*FT*, 6 September 1999, p. 2).

6 September 1999. 'Russia was engaged in a full-scale war on Monday [6 September] against hundreds of Chechen fighters who have seized control of six villages and a town in western Dagestan in the most intense fighting since the end of the Chechenia-Russia war ... On the second day of fighting the Chechen rebels extended their hold inside Dagestan ... An estimated 2,000 fighters entered Dagestan from Chechenia on Sunday [5 September] ... On Sunday night, Chechens say, Russian planes bombed the village of Zamai-Yurt inside Chechenia' (*IHT*, 7 September 1999, pp. 1, 4).

7 September 1999. 'The force of about 2,000 rebels advanced to within 5 kilometres of Khasavyurt, a key provincial town, by nightfall ... The rebels held firm to six villages and another town, Novolakskoye, that they had captured ... Russia has lost twenty-four soldiers since the latest combat began, compared with forty-nine killed the previous month. the death toll among the rebels is not known' (*IHT*, 8 September 1999, pp. 1, 5).

Yeltsin: 'How did it happen we lost a whole village? A whole district to be precise ... This is sloppiness of the military [referring to the bombing of the block of flats] ... These bandits are wrongly called Islamists. They fight against the Moslem peoples in Dagestan ... They are degenerates and murderers.'

'The president said "carelessness on the part of the military" was the cause of the terrorism in Buinaksk. "Why does more terrorism occur at our closed military compounds than anywhere else?"' (*CDSP*, 1999, vol. 51, no. 36, p. 4).

9 September 1999. A massive explosion destroys the middle section of a large apartment block in Moscow. A bomb is suspected rather than gas. Ninety-two died.

12 September 1999. 'Chechens have been urged by President Maskhadov to arm themselves … Mr Maskhadov extended the state of emergency and asked all men to mobilize themselves after a week in which Russian troops have repeatedly pounded suspected rebel bases west of Grozny. He claimed 150 people have been killed and accused Russia of violating the peace agreement with Chechenia. Mr Maskhadov said Russian aircraft had bombed three villages … According to Mr Maskhadov, the only solution would be a personal meeting with President Yeltsin … Russia has denied the allegations, saying it only bombed military bases and not civilians in Chechenia' (*The Times*, 13 September 1999, p. 14).

13 September 1999. A bomb demolishes another apartment block in Moscow. The death toll was 121.

Yeltsin: 'This enemy has no conscience, pity or honour. It has no face, ethnicity or religion. I emphasize in particular: no ethnicity or religion.'

A reregistration requirement for out-of-town citizens is imposed in Moscow. On 16 September a constitutional court judge called the requirement unconstitutional in the absence of the declaration of a state of emergency (*CDSP*, 1999, vol. 51, no. 38, p. 7).

'Russian troops … [have] expelled a second, separate group of Islamic fighters from two villages deeper inside Dagestan (*IHT*, 14 September 1999, p. 4).

14 September 1999. Vladimir Putin: 'Today many people are speaking of a "Chechen connection" in the recent acts of terrorism. And there are unquestionably grounds for doing so … However, this is no excuse for calls to exterminate the Chechen people. The ones who must be exterminated are the terrorists, marauders and aggressors, who have neither home, nor tribe, nor nationality nor religion … Today Chechenia, while remaining part of Russian territory, is a kind of "international anomaly", a huge terrorist camp that supposedly enjoys legal status. But if Chechenia's authorities are unable to gain control of the situation and yet decline assistance from the centre, that means they must be content with the current state of affairs … We must carry out an impartial analysis of the way the Khasavyurt accords have been implemented and of the accords' actual content … I am convinced that extremist forces are taking advantage of the 1996 agreements in a bid to unilaterally solve the problem of the republic's status in a separatist spirit and solely in the interests of one party … A special economic status must finally be imposed on the [Chechen] republic. It must include severe sanctions' (*CDSP*, 1999, vol. 51, no. 37, pp. 5–7).

'The agreement reached at Khasavyurt, imperfect though it may have been, put an end to the bloodshed and provided time to reach a final settlement between the sides. But that time was essentially wasted. The only constructive actions since Khasavyurt have been the presidential and parliamentary elections in Chechenia under international observation and with Russia's consent. Those elections demonstrated the good sense and prudence of the bulk of the population, which elected its most moderate leader, Aslan Maskhadov, as president. The popularly elected parliament was also inclined to look for a mutually acceptable formula for relations between Chechenia and Russia, and it opposed outbursts of both religious and political extremism. Unfortunately, the Russian leadership' slack of a definite, constructive and consistent policy towards Chechenia ... weakened the position of the ... republic's lawfully elected president ... and played into the hands of extremists ... More and more segments of the population ... found themselves in poverty with no employment or means of subsistence and fell prey to homegrown extremists, and they in turn became easy prey for the many-headed hydra of international terrorism ... Maskhadov has stated repeatedly that official Grozny has nothing to do with the intentions and actions of the militants. Not long ago he knocked on the Kremlin's doors asking for a top-level meeting' (Boris Pankin, *Rossiiskaya Gazeta*, 17 September 1999, p. 4: *CDSP*, 1999, vol. 51, no. 37, p. 10).

15 September 1999. 'Prime minister Vladimir Putin accused the separatist republic of Chechenia on Wednesday [15 September] of harbouring and supporting terrorists who have bombed three Russian apartment buildings in recent weeks, killing 276 people ... "We have identified the people who carried out the explosion", said ... the Moscow deputy police chief. "It is now an established fact the terrorist attacks were carried out by Chechen fighters. The used people with Slav appearances." Mr Putin said: "It is perfectly obvious for us now that terrorists hide on the territory of the Chechen republic and they are backed by extremist forces in Chechenia" ... Mr Putin also reiterated an earlier accusation that the Chechens were being helped by international terrorists' (*IHT*, 16 September 1999, p. 6).

'The Russian defence minister, Igor Sergeyev ... said that 2,000 to 3,000 fighters were massing along the border [between Dagestan and Chechenia]. However, the Chechen fighters appear to have retreated from villages they seized earlier near the town of Novolakskoye' (*IHT*, 16 September 1999, p. 6).

16 September 1999. An apartment building in Volgodonsk suffers extensive damage from what seems to have been a truck bomb. Eighteen were killed.

'The parliament of the mainly Moslem republic of Tatarstan voted to suspend its military draft. The Tatar leadership said it would not send any more ill-trained, young conscripts to die in the civil war ... in Dagestan' (*FT*, 17 September 1999, p. 2).

17 September 1999. There is an explosion in a St Petersburg apartment block, but it is considered to be the work of common criminals rather than terrorists. Two people were killed.

19 September 1999. There is a gas explosion in a Moscow apartment block.

'Russia claimed yesterday [19 September] to have killed more than 140 rebels in bombing raids over ... Chechenia, striking out against those it holds responsible for a wave of terrorist rebels bombings around Moscow ... There were also reports of strong Russian troop build-ups on the Chechen borders ... The arrival of additional troops appears to reflect Mr Putin's stated objective last week of sealing off Chechenia from Russia ... Mr Putin reiterated ... his disregard for the fragile peace accords reached at the end of the 1994–6 Russian-Chechen war, stating that the agreement had no legal force' (*FT,* Monday 20 September 1999, p. 2).

'Russian warplanes launched fresh military attacks over the weekend against suspected Islamic guerrilla bases in Chechenia ... The attacks are also apparently retaliation for the apartment bombings that have killed nearly 300 Russians during the last two weeks. Russian officials have attributed the blasts to the Chechen rebels, who have denied responsibility. The rebels hold no positions in Dagestan, but Russian military officials said they were bracing for the third major offensive since the hostilities began in early August. Rather than send in troops, Russian commanders have decided to try to pound the guerrillas from the air ... [Russia] said Sunday [19 September] that 140 guerrillas had been killed in the past twenty-four hours ... [and] four federal soldiers had been killed ... Russian military officers announced that they were sending ... [extra troops and equipment] to the combat zone, in part to set up a cordon along the border with Chechenia ... Chechen officials said Saturday [18 September] that Russian troops had crossed into their republic, but Moscow dismissed the report ... [The Chechen officials] said Russian troops had crossed from the neighbouring region of Ingushetia ... and started to dig in' (*IHT,* Monday 20 September 1999, p. 5).

22 September 1999. 'Russia has formally sealed its border with Chechenia' (*IHT,* 23 September 1999, p. 6).

23 September 1999. 'Russian aircraft yesterday [23 September] bombed the airport of the Chechen capital Grozny... They also hit fuel depots and a radar installation in Grozny's suburbs ... Russian officials claimed the rebels had been using the Grozny airport facilities ... [Chechenia claimed that] Russian bombers had targeted objects ... such as gas supply lines' (*FT,* 24 September 1999, p. 3).

'Russian warplanes pounded central Chechenia on Thursday [23 September] with bombs and missiles, targeting aviation and oil supplies ... Russian jets fired missiles at the main airport [fifteen miles] north of Grozny and dozens of other locations ... The missile attack destroyed radar equipment at the airport ... [and] another radar in a village north of Grozny ... The airport raid was followed by other targets across Chechenia, including a power station, gas line and oil depot' (*IHT,* 24 September 1999, p. 1, 12).

24 September 1999. 'The raids over the last twenty-four hours took out Grozny's oil refinery ... and paralyzed the Grozny gas distribution plant ...

Airstrikes Friday [24 September] targeted a television tower, a cellular communication centre and the city district where the Chechen president lives (*IHT*, 25 September 1999, p. 2).

25 September 1999. Air attacks continue, targets including television transmitters and oil installations.

26 September 1999. Igor Sergeyev (defence minister): 'There are several variants for a land operation, which will be carried out depending on the developing situation. The main aim is to destroy the bandits and to create a sufficiently broad zone of safety around Chechenia.'

'More than 10,000 refugees have fled from Chechenia into neighbouring Ingushetia, causing the Ingush interior ministry to close its border with Chechenia' (*FT*, 27 September 1999, p. 2).

Air strikes continue.

'Although Moscow maintains that the Chechens are Russian citizens, it has just announced that anyone living in Chechenia will no longer qualify for a Russian pension. In the three years since it lost the war Moscow has done nothing to rebuild [Chechenia]' (Ian Traynor, *The Guardian*, 27 September 1999, p. 3).

27 September 1999. Air strikes continue, targets in Chechenia including oil refineries, bridges and communications facilities.

'At least 50,000 refugees were reported streaming from Chechenia into other Caucasus republics. Most have entered Ingushetia, which flanks Chechenia's western border ... Some travellers complained that that if their identification cards bore only Chechen nationality they were turned back ... Russians ... believe – and the [Russian] government has insisted – that Chechens are responsible for a series of deadly bombings of apartment buildings in Moscow and other cities ... Target selection included oil refineries which the Russians say funnel money to Mr Basayev's private army. The jets also hit a shop where workers disguised trucks as army and police vehicles for use in infiltration, said a Russian interior ministry spokesman ... On Monday the Chechen president, Aslan Maskhadov requested an urgent meeting with Russian president Boris Yeltsin. Mr Maskhadov said that 300 civilians had been killed in Russian air strikes. "I need to save my people", Mr Maskhadov said. Mr Putin quickly dismissed Mr Maskhdov's appeal. "We will not hold meetings for the sake of meetings", he said' (*IHT*, 28 September 1999, pp. 1, 6). Maskhadov: 'I need to save my people and will do anything to prevent a new war' (*The Independent*, 28 September 1999, p. 14). (Maskhadov has repeatedly requested a meeting with Yeltsin.)

'The Chechen leader's office said that 420 people had been killed and 1,000 wounded since the beginning of the month [September], including 300 dead since the beginning of bombing last Thursday [23 September]' (*The Guardian*, 28 September 1999, p. 13).

'"These tactics are almost fully identical to what Nato did in Yugoslavia", said the newspaper Izvestia' (*IHT*, 28 September 1999, p. 6).

Vladimir Putin: 'The difference this time is that we will not thoughtlessly send our boys to absorb hostile fire. We will act with the help of modern forces and means to destroy the terrorists from a distance. There will be no frontal attacks. We will destroy the infrastructure. This will require time and patience ... We will patiently and methodically destroy the militants from the air ... Highly trained troops [might be required for] mopping up operations.'

28 September 1999. The bombing campaign continues.

'The Russian military says it is attacking economic and military targets controlled by Islamic militants who have set up training bases inside Chechenia ... There are lingering doubts about whether the [Russian] government has hard evidence linking the wave of terror in Russia to Chechen militants ... The Chechen government has disclaimed responsibility for the Islamic militants' (*IHT*, 29 September 1999, pp. 1, 4).

29 September 1999. The bombing campaign continues, targets including oil depots, roads and bridges.

Vladimir Putin: 'We are expecting the Chechen leadership to finally condemn terrorism in explicit and definite terms ... [The Chechen leaders should] extradite the criminals for whom a search has been declared.'

'Mr Putin sent Magomedali Magomedov, who heads the Dagestani parliament, to meet Chechen president, Aslan Maskhadov. Talks were supposed to take place inside Dagestan, but the trip ended in disarray. Angry Dagestanis blocked the convoys of both officials, protesting that the pair should have met before all the fighting' (*IHT*, 30 September 1999, p. 7). 'Mr Magomedov was not inclined to see President Maskhadov until he apologized for two incursions, this month and last, by militants beyond the control of the Grozny government. The Russian prime minister Vladimir Putin instructed that the meeting should go ahead. Only when Russia started bombing Chechenia did President Maskhadov show an interest in negotiations ... [furious Dagestanis] said' (*The Independent*, 30 September 1999, p. 15).

'President Maskhadov defiantly enlisted the warlords' help in defending his country. Shamil Basayev and ... Khattab ... received formal instructions from President Maskhadov for defending Grozny yesterday' (*The Times*, 30 September 1999, p. 16).

'On Wednesday [29 September] the newspaper Sevodnya published an elaborate account of a plan to conquer half of Chechenia and set up a puppet government ... to take the relatively easy to hold northern plains' (*IHT*, 30 September 1999, p. 7). 'Sevodnya claimed that the military had a plan to take the low-lying parts of Chechenia and to set up a pro-Moscow government there. The army was just waiting for a green light from the politicians' (*The Independent*, 30 September 1999, p. 15).

30 September 1999. 'Russian troops invaded Chechenia on Thursday [30 September], apparently with the goal of setting up a no-man's-land inside the region and shrinking Chechenia's territorial control by about half ... "Military operations are already underway in Chechenia", Mr Putin said. "Chechenia is

Russian territory and our troops can move anywhere. The military is going to choose its positions" ... For the eighth day Russian war planes struck villages, factories, bridges and oil depots inside Chechenia' (*IHT*, 1 October 1999, p. 5).

On 30 September Gazprom halted natural gas deliveries to Chechenia 'because of unpaid debts'. The Russian Unified Power System has announced decreased electricity supplies. The head of the pension fund has vowed not to transfer any pension money (*Sevodnia*, 6 October 1999, p. 2: *CDSP*, 1999, vol. 51, no. 40, p. 4). 'Starting this June, one after the other, the heads of ministries began making radical decisions: the Chechen section of the oil pipeline was shut down, Gazprom announced that of 30 September Chechenia would not be receiving natural gas, and a few days later the Russian Unified Power System Joint Stock Company virtually ceased supplying the republic with electricity' (*CDSP*, 1999, vol. 51, no. 41, p. 6).

1 October 1999. The bombing campaign continues.

'Russian troops have seized high ground in northern Chechenia' (*IHT*, 2 October 1999, p. 2). 'Russian tanks and troops were reported to have penetrated seven miles into Chechenia on three fronts, seizing strategic heights in the north, east and west' (*The Guardian*, 2 October 1999, p. 21).

'Ten Russian soldiers were killed yesterday [1 October] in the first clash of ground troops inside Chechenia since the 1994–6 war there ... The Russian defence ministry said a buffer zone was being created "sufficient to guarantee security" in neighbouring Russian territories' (*The Times*, 2 October 1999, p. 17).

'The only legitimate order of power in Chechenia is a parliament in exile in Moscow set up during the war three years ago, Mr Putin said ... "All other organs of power are, to say the least, only partially legitimate' (*The Times*, 2 October 1999, p. 17). 'Vladimir Putin threw his support behind an exile group who declared they were establishing a new Chechen government loyal to Russia ... The exile group has been formed by the forty-eight surviving members of a Chechen parliament elected in June 1996 ... They have been living in Moscow since a peace agreement was signed in August 1996 ... "According to Russian law, this is the most legitimate body", Mr Putin said. "We will give then full support" ... One of the Moscow loyalists announced after the meeting with the prime minister that his parliament was being reconstituted ... The exiles sent a letter to the president, Boris Yeltsin, "requesting" Russia's help in Chechenia' (*The Guardian*, 2 October 1999, p. 21).

2–3 October 1999. The bombing campaign continues.

'Russian troops took the Chechen town of Borozdinovskoe, 3 kilometres from the border with Dagestan, on Saturday [2 October] ... "Chechenia will not give up a single metre of its land", he [Aslan Maskhadov] told reporters in Grozny yesterday [3 October]' (*FT*, 4 October 1999, p. 9).

'Russian forces pressed Chechenia from all sides Sunday [3 October], although Moscow denied it was planning a full-scale assault ... "I would welcome inspections by representatives of the international organizations,

Western countries and Russia", Mr Maskhadov said … "Let them show us where the terrorist bases are and we will destroy them ourselves. We would also welcome sending a peacekeeping force to Chechenia" … Russian officials confirmed that their troops had entered Chechenia and skirmished with rebels there' (*IHT*, 4 October 1999, p. 1).

'The Russian military and Chechen guerrillas engaged in their first ground clashes inside Chechenia over the weekend [2–3 October] as … Aslan Maskhadov declared that Chechenia was now at war' (*The Guardian*, 4 October 1999, p. 11).

'Aslan Maskhadov issued a call to arms to his people at the weekend [3 October] … [to] "take up arms in defence of their country"' (*The Times*, 4 October 1999, p. 14).

'Refugees were also building up on the eastern side. But the region of Dagestan … refused to let them in' (*The Independent*, 4 October 1999, p. 12).

Russia later admitted that two Russian soldiers were killed on 3 October.

5 October 1999. 'Prime minister Vladimir Putin declared Tuesday [5 October] that Russian troops had occupied the northernmost [relatively flat] third of Chechenia, in some places reaching the Terek River that bisects the secessionist republic, and he said the military operation was not over yet … The military's advance into Chechenia was far deeper than the goal announced two weeks ago of creating a cordon around – and outside – the republic. Now, Mr Putin said, the Russian troops are trying to establish a "security zone" within Chechenia. "The operation to create a security zone has not yet been completed", Mr Putin said. "This is just one stage in this operation. But the ultimate aim is to fully destroy terrorists and their bases throughout Chechen territory" … According to Mr Putin, the Russian troops have suffered only light casualties as they advanced, with four soldiers killed and twenty-two wounded … On Tuesday [5 October] Russia reported the loss of two fighter-bombers … Mr Maskhadov responded to the Russian advance by declaring martial law … due to come into effect at midnight Tuesday [5 October] … Prime minister Putin said Tuesday that Russia intended to resettle the tens of thousands displaced by the conflict to parts of the republic now controlled by Russian troops' (*IHT*, 6 October 1999, pp. 1, 5).

'The plan was … to resettle there many of the refugees who have fled … "The Chechen republic was, and remains, a part of the Russian Federation", Mr Putin declared … "We're dealing with an exclusively domestic problem and we'll solve the problem ourselves"' (*The Guardian*, 6 October 1999, p. 15).

Two men (the crew of one of the planes) are believed to have been killed.

6 October 1999. Russia has already cut off gas supplies to Chechenia (*IHT*, 7 October 1999, p. 4).

7 October 1999. 'The Russian army admitted yesterday [7 October] that it had suffered 125 dead in the recent fighting in Chechenia' (*The Independent*, 8 October 1999, p. 15).

8 October 1999. Aslan Maskhadov: 'Russia has launched a full-scale war against Chechenia, breaking the peace treaty signed by the Chechen and Russian presidents. In this situation I had no other choice but to declare war.'

10 October 1999. Aslan Maskhadov: 'They blow up apartments and attribute it to us. Only the Russian secret service could do a thing like that' (*The Independent*, 11 October 1999, p. 12). 'Russian politicians deliberately say Chechens blew up their houses so they could start this bloody war here' (*FT*, 13 October 1999, p. 8).

11 October 1999. 'Mr Putin, responding to Mr Maskhadov's calls over the weekend [10 October] for peace talks, told reporters that Chechenia must first "extradite" the militant commander Shamil Basayev ... Mr Maskhadov had offered a peace plan under which he said he would crack down on warlords ... after Russian troops pulled out, and he suggested reviving negotiations on a Russian-Chechen peace treaty. "I view it in a positive light, but I would change the priorities", Mr Putin said in response, insisting that Mr Basayev must be handed over first' (*IHT*, 12 October 1999, p. 5).

'On Sunday [10 October] Aslan Maskhadov ... reiterated his call for peace talks with Russia, adding for the first time that if Russian halted combat operations "illegal militias" would be disbanded and Chechenia would co-operate with Moscow in "fighting terrorism" ... Malik Saidullayev emerged in Moscow yesterday [11 October] as the head of a "Chechen state council" created in exile, loyal to the Kremlin and intended to supplant the Maskhadov government' (*The Guardian*, 12 October 1999, p. 13).

Vladimir Putin: 'First the terrorists guilty of attacking peaceful villages ... and bomb attacks on blocks of flats ... must be extradited. Give us the men whose hands and arms are stained with blood and we will be prepared for full-scale talks.'

'Russia yesterday [11 October] claimed it had seized control of a new district south of the Terek river' (*FT*, 12 October 1999, p. 8).

12 October 1999. Igor Sergeyev (Russian defence minister): 'The troops will not stop. They will fulfil their task of liquidating armed groups and terrorist bands. They will improve their position so as to control the entire situation.'

15 October 1999. 'The commander of Russian forces in the North Caucasus ... said his troops had finished setting up a security zone that now covered a third of Chechenia ... [He] said federal forces were moving to a second stage from which they would strike at rebels trapped inside Chechenia ... The Kremlin said Mr Yeltsin had promoted Nikolai Koshman, a deputy minister for railways, to the posts of deputy prime minister and envoy to Chechenia ... Mr Koshman would be in charge of rebuilding the local economy and ensuring the region's return to normal life ... Mr Koshman was prime minister in a failed pro-Moscow government Russia set up in occupied parts of Chechenia in 1996' (*IHT*, 16 October 1999, p. 2).

16 October 1999. Yeltsin appoints Nikolai Koshman to the post of deputy prime minister and puts him in charge of administering Chechenia (*RET*, 1999, vol. 8, no. 4, p. 99).

17 October 1999. 'Russian artillery pounded villages just outside the Chechen capital overnight ... news reports said Sunday [17 October]. Russian tanks and artillery were in place atop a hill just outside the capital, Grozny ... Vladimir Putin reiterated Sunday that Moscow did not plan a big military operation in Chechenia but would continue its air strikes against the rebel region. "We will not undertake the tactics of a large-scale military action with tank attacks and the storming of towns", Mr Putin said ... The number of Chechens seeking refuge has risen to more than 150,000, Ingushetia's president, Ruslan Aushev, said' (*IHT*, 18 October 1999, p. 6).

'"We do not know if we will take Grozny. We have the capacity to take it. We do know that we will occupy the heights around Grozny", said ... the commander of Russian forces in the north Caucasus' (*The Independent*, 18 October 1999, p. 11).

20 October 1999. 'Russian artillery pounded the outskirts of Chechenia's capital on Wednesday [20 October] ... Russia has been slowly advancing on Grozny from three directions but has not entered the capital' (*IHT*, 21 October 1999, p. 7).

21 October 1999. 'Rockets slammed into the centre of Grozny on Thursday [21 October], killing and wounding dozens of people as Russian officials continued to give mixed signals over whether troops would try to storm the city ... Three rockets hit the central market ... A Chechen spokesman ... said at least sixty people had been killed in the attack on the crowded market ... With their troops only ten to fifteen kilometres (seven to ten miles) from the capital, Russian leaders gave mixed signals as to their next move' (*IHT*, 22 October 1999, pp. 1, 4).

22 October 1999. 'Russia was in a state of confusion yesterday [22 October] over whether to claim or deny responsibility for a rocket attack on an open market in Grozny ... Vladimir Putin ... flatly denied involvement in the rocket attack. Chechen officials have said that 143 people died. "It [the market] is one of the headquarters of the armed bandits and the explosion was the result of a clash between rival gangs", Mr Putin said. However ... the spokesman for the Russian military said: "A special [Russian] military operation destroyed the arms market together with all weapons, explosives and arms peddlers." He denied there were any civilians in the market at the time' (*FT*, 23 October 1999, p. 6). The spokesman said: 'If there were victims they were those who sell arms and ammunition to gangsters ... Civilians do not go at night to markets where arms are sold to gangsters; they stay at home' (*The Independent*. 23 October 1999, p. 6; *The Guardian*, 23 October 1999, p. 17).

'Chechen officials said ten missiles hit Grozny on Thursday evening [21 October], damaging a maternity hospital, a mosque and a food market ... Yet another Russian explanation was provided by ... [a member] of the federal security service. He admitted a food market had been destroyed, but claimed arms and ammunition was stored there and suggested there had been "a spontaneous explosion of ammunition which led to loss of life"' (*The Independent*, 23 October 1999, p. 6).

'Reuters correspondents ... said teenagers and children were among the dead ... The market is [only] in part an arms bazaar [it is also a food market]' (*IHT*, 23 October 1999, pp. 1, 4).

'News agency reports put the number of dead at 118 ... One report stated that a maternity hospital had been hit ... and said that thirteen women and fifteen newborns were among the victims ... Although arms were discreetly on sale in the market, most of the produce on offer was routine – food, clothes, CDs' (*The Guardian*, 23 October 1999, p. 17).

'Witnesses say that at least 137 people, including dozens of women and children, were killed when as many as ten surface-to-surface missiles slammed into a cluster of targets at the heart of the Chechen capital on Thursday evening [21 October]' (*The Times*, 23 October 1999, p. 13).

'The Chechen president, Aslan Maskhadov, said a missile attack on Thursday [21 October] had been aimed at his presidential residence ... and said 282 people had died in the attack' (*IHT*, 28 October 1999, p. 6).

24 October 1999. 'Russian officials continued to give differing explanations for the powerful explosion in Grozny on Thursday [21 October] ... The deputy army chief of staff said that as a result of a Russian "special operation" two gangs of Chechen gunmen were induced to open fire on one another at the central market. A bullet hit a nearby arms cache, where, among other things, rockets were hidden. The shot "caused a powerful explosion", he said. But Izvetia, the first Russian newspaper to take issue with official accounts since the war began, said the Russians had fired a missile from North Ossetia, another neighbouring republic. The targets were government offices, where Chechen commanders were thought to be meeting ... Russian artillery and jet bombers pounded more towns in Chechenia on Sunday [24 October] and witnesses reported dozens of civilian deaths from the onslaught ... On Sunday Russian forces also continued to block major roads to and from Grozny, cutting the Chechen capital's main highway link to the west ... Russian artillery and aircraft have indiscriminately bombed numerous towns and hamlets ... Russian troops continued to block the main highway west from Grozny to the neighbouring republic of Ingushetia, making it impossible for hundreds of stranded refugees to flee' (*IHT*, 25 October 1999, pp. 1, 8).

'Russia was accused yesterday of waging war on refugees by sealing their last escape route from Chechenia ... Russia closed the road [into Ingushetia] on Saturday [23 October], saying terrorists may be escaping among the civilians' (*The Times*, 25 October 1999, p. 15).

'Russia's intelligence service, the FSB, yesterday [24 October] sought to justify the road's closure. A spokesman insisted that the route had been used by rebels to smuggle fuel into Ingushetia where it was being used to help finance the Chechen guerrilla forces' (*The Guardian*, 25 October 1999, p. 11).

25 October 1999. Yeltsin meets Putin, calling the prime minister's policy in Chechenia 'useful work'.

'The Ingush leader, Ruslan Aushev, was quoted by Interfax as criticising the army's decision to shut the remaining road for refugees from Chechenia … "The way army officials are behaving is like a military dictatorship", he said. They feel there is no control over them and they can do anything they want"' (*IHT*, 26 October 1999, p. 9).

26 October 1999. 'Russian troops [have] moved within a few miles of Grozny … On Tuesday [26 October] Russian forces moved closer to the north-western edge of Grozny, within sight of the city's airport … A decision had been taken recently to post a $1 million bounty … for the capture of Shamil Basayev … The money would not come from the Russian government, but from "patriotically minded businessmen"' (*IHT*, 26 October 1999, p. 1).

'The Russian government said Russian and foreign businessmen, backed by law enforcement agencies, had contributed the $1 million … The reward was for information leading to his capture' (*The Independent*, 27 October 1999, p. 17).

27 October 1999. 'Fighter bombers struck central Grozny on Wednesday [27 October] in some of the heaviest air strikes … since Russian troops invaded … Russian tanks and soldiers closed in on Grozny from the north' (*IHT*, 28 October 1999, p. 6).

President Maskhadov's representative in Moscow is charged with 'illegal possession of weapons' and is to be kept in custody (*CDSP*, 1999, vol. 51, no. 45, p. 4).

29 October 1999. 'Refugees fleeing Russia's bombing campaign said Friday [29 October] that they had seen warplanes hit a convoy of people trying to escape … A spokesman for President Aslan Maskhadov said that about fifty refugees had been killed … Separately, the UN secretary-general, Kofi Annan, said Friday that the UN would send a humanitarian mission to the area around Chechenia to help civilians caught in the conflict. A UN spokesman had said Thursday [28 October] that the mission would go to Chechenia itself to assess the needs of refugees, but later said it would go only to neighbouring areas' (*IHT*, 30 October 1999, p. 2).

'The International Committee of the Red Cross in Geneva said at least twenty-five people were killed … when a Russian air strike hit a clearly marked Red Cross convoy of five vehicles on Friday [29 October] … Two Red Cross workers were killed in the attack. The Chechen government said forty people died' (*The Guardian*, 1 November 1999, p. 11).

'The Geneva-based International Committee for the Red Cross said two of its local workers had been killed … Friday when a convoy of refugees came under air attack … The head of local administration in Urus-Martan district said forty refugees died' (*IHT*, 1 November 1999, p. 5). 'The International

Committee of the Red Cross said trucks bearing Red Cross emblems and carrying civilians were bombed Friday. Twenty-five people, including two Chechen Red Cross workers, were killed' (*IHT*, 2 November 1999, p. 7).

31 October 1999. 'Russian jets and artillery continued to bombard Chechenia on Sunday [31 October] while routes for Chechens seeking to flee the attacks remained closed ... The Russian authorities had promised to reopen the crossing between Chechenia and Ingushetia on Sunday [and previously promised to reopen the crossing on Friday 29 October]' (*IHT*, 1 November 1999, p. 5)

1 November 1999. 'Russia ... opened the frontier to a token few on Monday [1 November]' (*IHT*, 3 November 1999, p. 7). 'Russian guards briefly reopened Chechenia's borders Monday [1 November] but allowed only a small fraction of the thousands blocked there for more than a week. The [Chechen-Ingushetia] border was shut only a few hours after it was opened. The police ... told huge crowds waiting to cross in either direction that they should come back Tuesday [2 November]. Refugees [were trying to leave Chechenia while] ... there were large numbers of people trying to reenter Chechenia to find lost relatives. The border was reopened a day after prime minister Vladimir Putin acknowledged that there "might have been some mistakes" during Russia's relentless bombing of Chechenia, but dismissed the charge that Russian forces deliberately targeted civilians ... Officials said another corridor had been opened on Chechenia's eastern border to allow refugees to cross into Dagestan ... Mr Putin ... assured the West on Monday [1 November] that Russia will reduce its military might in Chechenia to levels envisaged in a European arms control treaty it breached with the recent push into the rebel region. "The Russian government will restore the tenets of the agreement in this area as soon as necessary conditions are fulfilled", he said in a statement. Mr Putin told reporters that Russia wanted to abide by the 1990 Conventional Forces in Europe treaty, and would underline its commitment by providing more information about its forces to the West' (*IHT*, 2 November 1999, p. 7).

2 November 1999. 'Thousands of refugees want to leave Chechenia ... while hundreds more want to return to the region from neighbouring Ingushetia to rescue family members trapped by the conflict. But Russia has opened only a tiny crossing point, denying passage to nearly all the thousands of people ... A handful of people managed to cross ... on Tuesday [2 November] ... The Norwegian foreign ministry said the Russian foreign minister ... gave Moscow's approval on Tuesday for an observer mission to visit Chechenia and Dagestan to inspect the humanitarian situation ... But it remained unclear whether the mission from the OSCE would travel to Chechenia itself or just the surrounding areas' (*IHT*, 3 November 1999, p. 7).

3 November 1999. Igor Sergeyev (Russian defence minister): 'We plan to free not only the city of Grozny from terrorists but the whole of Chechenia. The support of the president and the government is guaranteed ... [But] no storming of Grozny will take place … Reconnaissance, artillery and the air force [will be used] to destroy gangs, their camps and their bases.'

'On Wednesday [3 November], as in the past several days, Russia let in a few score refugees, but has refused to reopen the frontier to a major influx' (*IHT*, 4 November 1999, p. 5).

'Six weeks ago a presidential edict banned conscripts with less than six months service from combat zones, but that requirement has been quietly dropped' (*The Times*, 4 November 1999, p. 23).

'A UN mission flew to Ingushetia yesterday [3 November]' (*The Independent*, 4 November 1999, p. 1).

4 November 1999. 'Russian troops permitted large numbers of refugees to move across the border Thursday [4 November] … The Ingush president, Ruslan Aushev, said that 3,000 Chechens crossed the frontier… After weeks of muted commentary Western governments have stepped up criticism of Russia's bombing of civilian targets and treatment of refugees' (*IHT*, 5 November 1999, p. 7).

'Russia yesterday [4 November] allowed large numbers of refugees … to cross into neighbouring Ingushetia … as a UN mission arrived in the region' (*FT*, 5 November 1999, p. 10).

5 November 1999. Refugees continue to move into Ingushetia.

'Beslan Gantemirov, the former mayor of Grozny and deputy prime minister of the Chechen government, who was sentenced to six years imprisonment for embezzling funds from the budget that had been allocated for the reconstruction of Grozny, has been pardoned by Yeltsin and released. The Kremlin's plan is for him to head up the Chechen opposition, scrape together a military detachment of supporters and help the federal troops' (*CDSP*, 1999, vol. 51, no. 43, p. 6).

7 November 1999. 'Mr Maskhadov appealed to President Bill Clinton to help end the "genocide of the Chechen people" as Russian guns shelled the outskirts of Grozny … A western suburb came under artillery fire' (*IHT*, 8 November 1999, p. 5).

9 November 1999. 'Strong domestic political support for Russia's offensive in Chechenia cracked Tuesday [9 November] for the first time as Grigori Yavlinsky… called for peace talks and a halt to the bombing… Mr Yavlinsky… issued an appeal to the government, saying the Russian troops had already gone far enough and created the necessary conditions for talks with the Chechen president, Aslan Maskhadov. His appeal marked the first time that a major figure has called for a halt in military operations … Mr Yavlinsky demanded that Russia "stop the massive bombing of the territory of the Chechen republic" and "suspend broad-scale ground offensive operations". He suggested negotiations be held with Mr Maskhadov, who has also appealed for talks. But Mr Yavlinsky said he would insist that Chechenia release hostages, halt kidnappings and slave trade, extradite to Russia or elsewhere those responsible for a series of terrorist attacks in Russia and take "decisive" measures to disarm

Chechen warlords. He further said that if Chechenia refused to talk, after thirty days he would allow civilians to leave Chechenia and the Russian forces would be free to open fire again' (*IHT*, 10 November 1999, pp. 1, 7).

Yavlinsky: 'Russia's armed forces fulfilled their task in the north Caucasus from August to November and for the first time in five years have created sound preconditions for the start of the political process' (*FT*, 10 November 1999, p. 14).

'Prime minister Valdimir Putin rejected suggestions from the United States that the bombing campaign was in violation of international conventions on warfare ... After a cabinet meeting Tuesday the Russian government decided to impose a blockade on transport to and from Chechenia, closing off airports, roads and docks that link Russia and overseas points with Chechenia. The Russian government said the measures were an effort to stop contraband and reinforcements from reaching the Chechen fighters' (*IHT*, 10 November 1999, pp. 1, 7). 'Western criticism ... [concerns] the refugee tide fleeing the war ... and charges that Russian forces have used indiscriminate force against civilians' (*IHT*, 12 November 1999, p. 8).

'Prime minister Vladimir Putin ... ordered a curb on road and air traffic between southern Russia and most of the Middle East ... closing six airports in southern Russia to traffic from ten Middle Eastern countries ... The government also announced that it was closing Russia's southern borders with Georgia and Azerbaijan to foreigners and prohibiting all road freight heading for Chechenia ... Georgia and Azerbaijan [were included] in yesterday's suspension of air links with southern Russia' (*The Guardian*, 10 November 1999, p. 15).

'Prime minister Vladimir Putin said the measures were needed to stop arms smuggling and also to prevent Islamic terrorists from entering the north Caucasus region ... Under the new controls Russia banned the import of all foreign goods to Chechenia. To enforce this restriction it ordered that all ships entering Makhachkala, the Caspian Sea port of Dagestan, be searched. Russia also suspended flights between cities in southern Russia and nations in the Caucasus and Middle east ... Russia is halting flights between southern Russia and Saudi Arabia, Jordan, Afghanistan, Pakistan, Turkey, the United Arab Emirates, Iran, Syria, Qatar, Cyprus, Azerbaijan and Georgia ... Russia ordered that all foreigners visiting Chechenia and the nearby republics of Dagestan, Ingushetia and North Ossetia be scrutinized by the security services. The number of visas granted to foregners to visit the region will be reduced' (*IHT*, 11 November 1999, p. 11).

'Russia ... closed its borders to Georgia and Azerbaijan to all foreigners other than citizens of the CIS' (*FT*, 10 November 1999, p. 14).

'Mr Putin's new resolution means the the FSB ... will search every plane, ship and lorry entering the region. It also gives the FSB broad powers to control foreigners' movements in Ingushetia, North Ossetia and Dagestan' (*The Times*, 10 November 1999, p. 22).

'In order to keep out "members of foreign terrorist organizations" and prevent "arms and equipment intended for subversive purposes from entering the North Caucasus region", the government has all but closed the North Caucasus to the outside world. From now on only citizens and vehicles from the CIS countries will be permitted to cross Russia's borders with Azerbaijan and Georgia. All foreign vessels in the seaport of Makhachkala will be inspected ... Air traffic to and from ... Azerbaijan, Georgia, Saudi Arabia, Jordan, Afghanistan, Pakistan, Turkey, the United Arab Emirates, Iran, Syria, Qatar and Cyprus ... via the airports [in the designated region] has been halted' (*CDSP*, 1999, vol. 51, no. 43, p. 7).

'Mr Yavlinsky's remarks may aggravate Russian commanders, who have warned in recent days against any political order to pull back, or any negotiation with the Chechens' (*IHT*, 10 November 1999, pp. 1, 7). 'Major general Valdimir Shamanov, who commands the Russian forces on the western front with Chechenia, said last week that any effort to stop the military operations would result in a military revolt' (*IHT*, Friday 12 November 1999, p. 8). 'Generals have talked of massive resignations and even civil war if the politicians interfere with their campaign, an ominous note in the disintegration of Russian governance after a strong tradition of the military keeping out of politics' (Flora Lewis, *IHT*, 13 November 1999, p. 6).

10 November 1999. An OSCE mission arrives in Ingushetia. Members of the mission toured refugee camps and called for urgent steps to ease the plight of the refugees (*IHT*, 12 November 1999, p. 8).

11 November 1999. 'Officials of OSCE yesterday [11 November] cut short a visit to the conflict zone after the authorities refused them access to the northern part of Chechenia ... The head of the OSCE mission described the situation facing Chechen refugees as "serious" but said he was prevented from travelling into Chechenia to assess the humanitarian situation of those living within Russia's "security zone" ... In a first admission that Russia's bombardment had brought civilian casualties, Igor Shabdurasulov, deputy Kremlin chief of staff, said: "There have been some tragic errors during the operation in Chechenia. We regret these errors and we carry the moral responsibility"' (*FT*, 12 November 1999, p. 9).

Prime minister Vladimir Putin: 'In the midst of war even the most carefully planned military operations occasionally cause civilian casualties, and we deeply regret that' (*IHT*, 15 November 1999, p. 8).

12 November 1999. 'Prime minister Vladimir Putin said Friday [12 November] that ... "The Russian flag has been raised over the town" ... Gudermes, Chechenia's second biggest city ...The Russian foreign minister, Igor Ivanov ... rejected an offer of mediation by OSCE ... to help end the fighting ... Defence minister Igor Sergeyev ... [said] "It is in the national interests of the United States that a guided, armed conflict smolder constantly on the territory of the north Caucasus" ... He was speaking after a military meeting also attended by Mr Putin, who pledged to make Russia's armed forces more powerful ... Mr Putin vowed to increase military spending and the Russian Air Force suggested it might fly nuclear-capable bombers to Cuba and Vietnam. Moscow also ruled out unfreezing ties with Nato for now... Interfax quoted the Chechen president, Aslan Maskhadov, as calling for "a joint struggle" with Russia against bandits and terrorists' (*IHT*, 13 November 1999, p. 2).

Russia ruled out the imminent return of a Nato presence in Moscow, i.e. the opening of the Nato communications mission (*FT*, 13 November 1999, p. 6).

'Moscow ... said Gudermes would become the new Chechen capital' (*The Guardian*, 13 November 1999, p. 1).

14 November 1999. 'President Boris Yeltsin yesterday [14 November] issued a striking endorsement of Vladimir Putin as his prime minister and chosen heir ... Mr Yeltsin said his prime minister remained the "only choice for Russia" in next year's presidential elections. "My personal support for him remains and my conviction is growing with every day", Mr Yeltsin said' (*FT*, 15 November 1999, p. 9).

15 November 1999. 'President Boris Yeltsin ... said Western leaders "had no right to blame Russia for destroying bandits and terrorists on its territory. We will not stop [the offensive] as long as there is even one terrorist there"' (*FT*, 16 November 1999, p. 13).

17 November 1999. Russia says that it will allow the UNHCR, Sadako Ogata, to visit Chechenia.

'Russian helicopters ventured across the border into Georgia last Wednesday [17 November] and dropped mines near the town of Shatili in an apparent effort to seal a route from Georgia into Chechenia. Russia has charged that Chechen militants continue to receive arms shipments across the 80 kilometre-long (50 mile) Chechen-Russian frontier, something Georgia has denied. And Georgia has rejected Moscow's proposal to send Russian troops to the Georgian side of the border' (*IHT*, 25 November 1999, p. 7).

18 November 1999. UNHCR Sadako Ogata begins her four-day visit.

Russia agrees to a visit to Chechenia by the OSCE chairman Knut Vollebaek.

22 November 1999. 'The military planned to surround Grozny by mid-December ... Russian forces already had the city 80 per cent surrounded' (*IHT*, 23 November 1999, p. 5).

Russian says that the number of refugees who have left Chechenia now number some 222,000. 'Meanwhile Georgia has protested that on 17 November three Russian helicopters attacked two Georgian villages ... ten miles from the border' (*The Independent*, 23 November 1999, p. 14).

23 November 1999. 'Igor Sergeyev, Russia's defence minister, yesterday [23 November] said federal troops would not storm ... Grozny and predicted the inhabitants would co-operate in driving out rebel forces, as they had in other towns in the last few days ... Russia claims to have almost sealed off Grozny and has nominated a shadow government under Beslan Gantemirov, a former mayor of the city and an opponent of President Maskhadov' (*FT*, 24 November 1999, p. 9).

'Defence minister Igor Sergeyev said Tuesday [23 November] that he believed Russian forces ... could capture ... Grozny without a bloody fight, and ruled out any storming of the city ... Mr Sergeyev said the local Chechen population wanted to co-operate with the Russian forces to drive out the rebels ... Despite offering relatively low-level resistance so far to the advancing Russian troops, the Chechen forces are expected to fight hard for Grozny, where Aslan Maskhadov ... is reportedly directing the defence plans' (*IHT*, 24 November 1999, p. 7).

24 November 1999. 'Mr Putin ... announced that Russia would offer an amnesty to fighters who lay down their arms and who "do not have blood of Russian citizens on their hands"' (*IHT*, 25 November 1999, p. 7).

26 November 1999. 'Russia yesterday [26 November] said it had begun a new phase in its conflict in Chechenia with an offensive to clear out rebels from the mountainous south ... which it claimed should be largely completed before the end of the year ... The latest step in the Russian military operations ... follows the establishment of a "security zone" in the northern third of Chechenia and the advance of troops towards Grozny ... Media reports suggested yesterday that the city was coming under its most intense bombardment since the Russian attacks began' (*FT*, 27 November 1999, p. 5).

'Russian commanders said Friday [26 November] that their troops would soon begin pursuing guerrilla forces directly into their mountain hideouts, a new phase in the three-month war ... Military spokesmen said their newest strategy would be to send soldiers into the mountainous southern part of Chechenia to find rebel strongholds and arms caches ... Russia has repeatedly complained that the Islamic militants are being resupplied from the south, particularly through Chechenia's southern border with Georgia. Officials charged Friday that a rebel hospital and major communications centre were operating in Georgia near the Chechen border. In Moscow a senior Russian officer said the forays into the mountains could be completed by the end of the year ... Airplanes and cannons hit Grozny and some seventeen surrounding villages. The attack was said to be the fiercest of the war ... Hundreds of civilian refugees waving white flags streamed out of the city' (*IHT*, 27 November 1999, pp. 1, 2).

'Five hostages were freed yesterday [26 November] ... Chechen bands have taken about 1,300 hostages since 1996 and about 700 have been released' (*The Times*, 27 November 1999, p. 16).

27 November 1999. Chechen rebels claim to have retaken most of the town of Novogroznensky, about forty kilometres east of Grozny.

28 November 1999. Russia says that a 'humanitarian corridor' has been offered to civilians wishing to leave Grozny. Leaflets have been dropped on Grozny.

29 November 1999. '[Russian] paratroopers surrounded Novogroznensky ... forcing out several hundred rebels' (*The Times*, 30 November 1999, p. 16).

'Chechen forces captured Noibyora, a second village they had taken back after the seizure of the nearby settlement of Novogroznensky' (*FT*, 30 November 1999, p. 10).

30 November 1999. 'After two months of steady advances into Chechenia's heartland, the Russian military has admitted that it is beginning to encounter serious resistance from Islamic militants ... After retreating from the Russian onslaught ... Islamic fighters are fortifying their positions in Grozny and the towns of Urus-Martan, Shali and Argun. And Salman Raduyev ... is commanding a band of militants in Novogroznensky ... Chechen defence officials reported that clashes continued at the foothills of the rebel republic's southern mountains ... as well as Novogroznensky ... About 80 per cent of the capital's buildings are in ruins ... On Monday [29 November] the Russian government acknowledged a firefight on 17 November that decimated a Russian reconnaissance patrol ... As of Friday [26 November] 305 Russian soldiers and interior ministry troops were reported by the [Russian] government to have been killed since ... August' (*IHT*, 1 December 1999, p. 6).

3 December 1999. 'Russian officials declared the near-capture of Argun, Chechenia's third largest town, a major step in a "third phase" of their two-month ground offensive. This phase is intended to drive Chechen defenders from cities and into the mountains, establish a government loyal to Moscow and begin a permanent occupation of Chechenia ... Officers said troops had surrounded Argun and said police units would enter it Saturday [4 December] ... On Friday [3 December] ... troops stayed in the suburbs ... Chechen representatives in Georgia ... confirmed that most defenders had abandoned the town ... An official in Ingushetia said Chechen fighters had attacked an armoured Russian column near Urus-Martan and slaughtered more than 200 soldiers. Russian officials called the claim "lies and slander" ... Chechen officials said about forty Russian soldiers died in an attack two days ago ... Reports from Chechenia said that forty refugees had been killed by Russians who had fired on a bus ... Russia sealed the main road from Chechenia into Ingushetia again Friday [3 December]' (*IHT*, 4 December 1999, p. 2).

The deputy interior minister of Ingushetia claimed that up to 250 Russian soldiers had been killed near Urus-Martan (*FT*, 4 December 1999, p. 6). He said that Russian officers admitted that 200 troops had been killed and a further fifty had been taken prisoner and executed. The Russian armed forces denied the claim (*The Times*, 4 December 1999, p. 13; *The Guardian*, 4 December 1999, p. 2).

4 December 1999. Russian forces claim to have largely surrounded Grozny.

Russian forces in Chechenia number nearly 100,000 compared with a peak of 40,000 in 1994–6 (and often not more than 30,000). The size of Chechen forces is unknown, with estimates ranging from 5,000 to 15,000 (*IHT*, 6 December 1999, p. 4).

6 December 1999. Russian planes drop leaflets on Grozny containing the following: 'For the sake of avoiding victims within the peaceful population, we ask you to leave Grozny before 11 December... You are surrounded. All roads out of Grozny are blocked. You have no chance of winning. The United Troop Command gives you a last chance. Until 11 December there will be a safe corridor through the village of Pervomaiskaya ... [Those who choose to leave] will be offered housing food and medicine and – most important – life. Those who remain will be treated like terrorists and bandits. They will be destroyed by artillery and air power. There will be no more negotiations. Everyone who does not leave the city will be destroyed.'

'Up to 20,000 civilians remain in the city, the Russians say. Chechen officials put the number at 40,000. The Russian say about 5,000 guerrillas are defending the city' (*IHT,* 7 December 1999, p. 4).

7 December 1999. 'Russia appeared to soften the deadline for the evacuation of Grozny. The interior minister, Vladimir Rushailo, said the checkpoints for the residents would remain open beyond Saturday ... General Viktor Kazantsev, the commander of the forces in the north Caucasus, said it should not be viewed as a final ultimatum' (*The Independent*, 8 December 1999, p. 1). 'Russia's military commander in Chechenia, General Viktor Kazantsev, said the ultimatum had been issued to the rebels and not to Grozny's civilian population' (*The Guardian*, 9 December 1999, p. 2). 'The Russian interior minister, Vladimir Rushailo, was quoted as saying that checkpoints leading to safe corridors outside Grozny would not be closed on Saturday [11 December] ... General Viktor Kazantsev of Russia claimed the ultimatum was not aimed at civilians but rather at making Islamic militants lay down their arms ... The Russian foreign minister, Igor Ivanov, assured the EU on Wednesday [8 December] that Russian forces would not bomb civilians in Grozny' (*IHT,* 9 December 1999, p. 4). Vyacheslav Ovchennikov (commander of Russian interior ministry troops, on 9 December 1999): 'The guerrillas will not be able to hold out for long without light, heat or food ... There is nothing to capture in a blockaded city' (*The Independent*, 10 December 1999, p. 15).

'Residents in Grozny were reported by Russian news media to be refusing to use a "safe corridor" ... As of Tuesday [7 December] none had passed through' (*IHT,* 8 December 1999, p. 6).

'Prime minister Vladimir Putin ... made an unexpected announcement that ... Aslan Maskhadov had sent his family out of the war-ravaged republic and that Mr Maskhadov's family was now under the "protection" of the Russian security service. The Chechen leadership "indeed have long ago taken all their relatives beyond the territory which is still under their control", Mr Putin said. "They took them to safe places", he said. "Even the person who calls himself the president of the republic, he has long ago sent his family to a different region of the Russian Federation." Interfax reported that the Maskhadov family first went to neighbouring Ingushetia at the invitation of the president there, Ruslan Aushev, and that they later fled elsewhere.

Mr Putin said they were "under the control and protection" of the Russian security forces' (*IHT*, 8 December 1999, pp. 1, 6).

8 December 1999. 'Urus-Martan becomes the fourth major town in Russian hands. Apart from Grozny, which Russian troops have completely surrounded, only one large lowland town, Shali in the south-east, remains under rebel control' (*IHT*, 9 December 1999, p. 4).

10 December 1999. Vladimir Putin: 'We have been keeping ongoing contacts with Maskhadov since eight days ago and I have had a personal meeting with one of the representatives of his government' (*FT*, 11 December 1999, p. 10). 'Yesterday we had another meeting with one of Maskhadov's deputies in Moscow. He was charged personally by Maskhadov to come and explain his position once more and we explained our position. But that representative disappeared without explaining whether our position was acceptable to them' (p. 1).

'Mr Putin said Russia would insist on the Chechen leadership fulfilling harsh conditions before opening formal talks' (*FT*, 11 December 1999, p. 1). 'First, Mr Maskhadov must publicly denounce terrorism. Second, he must secure the release of Russian and foreign hostages seized by Chechen bandits. Third, the Chechen authorities should hand over the terrorists who are accused of the raids into Dagestan and the bomb explosions in Moscow and other Russian cities' (p. 10).

'Mr Putin said Mr Maskhadov's representatives "appear in Moscow regularly". He said he met eight or nine days ago with "one of his deputy prime ministers", who came from Grozny ... "We have received no concrete answer up until now", Mr Putin said. "Over and over again new people turn up, and there are no replies to questions put by us." Mr Putin repeated the conditions that Mr Maskhadov had set earlier, including that Mr Maskhadov "condemn terrorism in all its forms", that the Chechen government "immediately hand over all hostages", both Russian and foreign citizens, and "hand over those criminals" involved in the apartment house bombings in Moscow and other cities' (*IHT*, 11 December 1999, p. 2).

('The head of information and analysis at the Chechen foreign ministry ... denied that there had been negotiations with Moscow since the start of the war ... She said that Russia ... had been in contact with a former Chechen minister ... in Moscow, but he had no mandate from Maskhadov. On the contrary ... the Russian security services were harrying Chechen officials and their families. They were holding President Maskhadov's wife under house arrest at Nalchik in southern Russia': *The Independent*, 13 December 1999, p. 11.)

'The interior ministry announced it would extend its ... deadline to the residents of Grozny ... Vladimir Rushailo, the interior ministry, said every person wanting to leave Grozny would be allowed to do so. "We do not foresee the bombing of the city in the days ahead if things go like this", he said' (*FT*, 11 December 1999, p. 1).

'Sergei Shoigu, the minister of emergency affairs ... said he was ready to meet Chechen leaders to organize an evacuation of civilians ... The Saturday [11 December] deadline "is not a deadline after which the corridors for civilians to leave Grozny will be closed"' (*IHT*, 11 December 1999, p. 2).

'Sergei Shoigu ... said civilians could leave safely by six routes and that troops would stop operations while they did so. "There is no deadline" ... Almost no refugees have left since 2 December, when Grozny was surrounded by Russian troops' (*The Independent*, 11 December 1999, p. 1).

'Since the Russians tabled their ultimatum on Monday [6 December] only a couple of hundred civilians have braved the trek out of the city through the northwestern corridor proposed by the Russians' (*The Guardian*, 11 December 1999, p. 2).

'Aslan Maskhadov ... left Grozny ... yesterday [10 December]' (*The Times*, 11 December 1999, p. 20).

'Moscow's mayor, Yuri Luzhkov ... denounced the ultimatum as an effort to wipe out a whole people. "Why have we started a war against people again?", Mr Luzhkov asked at a conference on ethnic movements. "The war against people has absolutely no prospect ... It will undoubtedly be lost"' (*IHT*, 11 December 1999, p. 1).

11 December 1999. The deadline is extended to midnight 12 December. A new corridor is opened that leads south to Alkhan-Yurt.

12 December 1999. 'Russian commanders ordered a pause in the bombardment of Grozny on Sunday [12 December], dropping instead thousands of leaflets urging fighters to surrender and civilians to leave the city ... leaflets showing two safe corridors set up to allow civilians to get out ... Sergei Shoigu said an 8 a.m. to 2 p.m. daily ceasefire would allow civilians to continue leaving the city unharmed ... Russian troops have taken control of Khankala military airport on the eastern outskirts of Grozny ... General Vladimir Shamanov, who commands the Western Group of Russian forces ... estimated that there were up to 7,000 civilians in the city, but Nikolai Koshman, Russia's deputy prime minister for Chechenia, has said there may be as many as 50,000. Grozny was home to almost 400,000 people in the 1980s. A large but unknown number of its residents have left since 1994' (*IHT*, 13 December 1999, p. 6).

'Civilians [from Grozny] were reported to be leaving in numbers for the first time since the easing of the ultimatum' (*The Times*, 13 December 1999, p. 12).

13 December 1999. 'Few refugees arrived from Grozny on Monday [13 December]'. Increasing numbers of refugees are returning to areas of Chechenia under Russian control. 'The Chechens say that they are tired of wintry life in tent camps, abandoned buildings and as guests of friends and relatives ... Moscow has moved quickly to restore utilities and schools in the northern section of Chechenia already under its control. Most military units are stationed outside towns, although riot police usually occupy a central building.' 'On Monday [Russian] troops occupied Khankala, a small village that abuts Grozny on the east side.' The State Duma issues an amnesty for anyone who has committed 'public-threatening actions' during the war (*IHT*, 14 December 1999, p. 7).

'Chechen forces denied that the Russians had captured the military airport east of Grozny ... An amnesty for Chechen rebels who wanted to turn their backs on the struggle by 1 February [2000 was] voted by the Duma' (*The Independent*, 14 December 1999, p. 11).

'Russian forces ... were reported to be clashing with Chechen fighters over control of a military airport' (*The Guardian*, 14 December 1999, p. 12).

14 December 1999. 'Small Russian units made probes into Grozny ... Russian reconnaissance units entered Grozny ... [Sources] disagreed about the intensity of fighting' (*IHT*, 15 December 1999, p. 4).

'The army said yesterday [14 December] that its troops had cleared the guerrillas from Shali, the last town held by Chechen fighters on the plains' (*The Independent*, 15 December 1999, p. 12).

'Russian infantry and tanks ... entered Shali ... after a three-day blockade. Moscow now controls the entire lowland portion of Chechenia' (*The Times*, 15 December 1999, p. 14).

Kurt Vollebaek, head of OSCE, arrives in Dagestan (*The Telegraph*, 15 December 1999, p. 12).

'Mr Vollebaek is expected to visit Chechenia today [15 December], but will be allowed to see only parts occupied by the Russians' (*The Guardian*, 15 December 1999, p. 1).

15 December 1999. There are reports that over 100 Russian soldiers were killed in Grozny.

'In Moscow officials denied that anything happened, but ... AVN, an unofficial military news agency, said officials in Mozdok [North Ossetia], the staging area for the war, acknowledged that fifty soldiers died overnight in central Grozny. They had entered the city in fifteen armoured vehicles [seven tanks and eight armoured personnel carriers] ... The Interfax news agency said that an "intelligence unit" was ambushed in Grozny's downtown Minutka Square. Twenty-five servicemen were killed ... The three-hour battle occurred in and around Minutka Square, an open traffic circle in central Grozny, according to accounts from the city' (*IHT*, 17 December 1999, pp. 1, 9). An Associated Press reporter saw part of the fighting and afterward counted the bodies of 115 Russian soldiers near Grozny's Minutka Square. Other reporters have provided similar eyewitness accounts, but the Russians claim no such battle ever took place' (*IHT*, 18 December 1999, p. 1).

'The local correspondent of US-based Associated Press reported that 115 Russian troops had died in clashes in Grozny on Wednesday evening [15 December]. Separately, AVN, an independent Russian military press agency, said fifty troops had died and seven vehicles were destroyed in what was it said was a reconnaissance mission into the centre of Grozny' (*FT*, 17 December 1999, p. 1).

'The Chechen president, Aslan Maskhadov, renewed his appeals on Wednesday [15 December] for negotiations to end the conflict with Russia, but Moscow rejected any talks ... Thousands of civilians remain in the city [Grozny], hiding in cellars and refusing to come out despite Russia's promises of safe passage ... The ministry for emergency affairs said that 2,973 civilians had left the city since Saturday [11 December] ... But reporters said they had seen only small numbers of people straggling out ... Knut Vollebaek is in the region and is expected to go to Russian-controlled parts of Chechenia on Thursday [16 December] ... General Valeri Manilov ... estimated [Chechen fighters to] number 12,000 to 15,000 ... Russian forces now control 60 per cent of Chechenia, Russian officers said' (*IHT*, 16 December 1999, p. 8).

'Reports yesterday [15 December] suggested that these routes [safe corridors] remained under Russian military bombardment and that few people have used them' (*FT*, 16 December 1999, p. 8).

17 December 1999. 'In one of the heaviest attacks yet on the Chechen capital, Russian tanks advanced on Grozny from three directions on Friday [17 December], probing for weaknesses in Chechen rebel positions ... Russian artillery and ground forces also struck at targets in mountainous southern Chechenia ... The rebels have used routes from Georgia to move supplies into Chechenia ... Georgia claimed Friday that Russian helicopters dropped bombs near a village in Georgia' (*IHT*, 18 December 1999, pp. 1, 5).

'Returning from a three-day visit to Chechenia, Knut Vollebaek, the Norwegian foreign minister who is also serving as chairman of OSCE, gave a bleak assessment of the military lines of battle to his G7 colleagues. "We urgently need a ceasefire, otherwise there will be a bloodbath [Grozny will not fall easily]", Mr Vollebaek said' (*IHT*, 18 December 1999, p. 1).

'Knut Vollebaek ... [said] the so-called "humanitarian corridors" ... were unsafe and inadequate ... There were 45,000 civilians trapped' (*The Independent*, 18 December 1999, p. 16).

'Paratoopers were dropped yesterday near a key pass on the republic's southern border to cut off the rebels' main supply line. The paratroopers ... clearly hope to block the Argun Gorge road which Moscow claims rebels have use to supply Grozny ... The Georgian government has denied that any arms are getting through to Chechenia from the south, but its border ... is the only one Russia does not control' (*The Times*, 18 December 1999, p. 12).

18 December 1999. 'Russian generals ... on Saturday [18 December] reported that they had taken virtual control of the city's Chernorechnie district. They said they would not order a frontal blitz against the capital, where Moscow estimates the number of civilians still in the city as 10,000 to 50,000 ... In an effort to block the southern escape routes for Islamic rebels in Chechenia, Russian paratroopers have cut the road between the breakaway republic and Georgia ... Georgian officials reported that Russian helicopters had dropped bombs on the Georgian side of the frontier… The Russians initially sought to persuade Georgia to let Russian troops use its territory. Georgia refused' (*IHT*, 20 December 1999, pp. 1, 9).

20 December 1999. 'Russia's generals opened a new front in the Chechen war yesterday [20 December], sending marines into the … rugged south-eastern corner to cut off possible supply routes to rebel fighters from Azerbaijan' (*The Times*, 21 December 1999, p. 13).

Russian forces claim to have captured Grozny's (civilian) Severny airport.

There are still an estimated 8,000 to 35,000 civilians inside Grozny (*IHT*, 21 December 1999, p. 6).

It is reported that residents of Alkhan-Yurt witnessed a massacre of forty-one civilians by Russian troops on a looting spree (*The Independent*, 21 December 1999, p. 10). 'The Russian military denied Tuesday [21 December] reports that its forces shot forty civilians in the village of Alkhan-Yurt, south-west of Grozny' (*IHT*, 22 December 1999, p. 4). 'The killings were said to have taken place between 1 December and 15 December. Towards the end of this period refugees began telling the Human Rights Watch organization that something terrible had happened in Alkhan-Yurt. The first reports from the village itself were carried by the BBC on Monday [20 December] – prompting the Russian defence ministry to issue a flat denial that any incident had taken place … The Russian deputy prime minister with responsibility for Chechenia, Nikolai Koshman, made a secret visit to Alkhan-Yurt at the weekend, promising that justice would be done. In contradiction to earlier blank denials, military sources said an inquiry into the allegations of a massacre was now expected' (*The Independent*, 23 December 1999, p. 12).

'Interfax said the armed forces chief of staff had ordered an inquiry into reports that Russian troops massacred civilians in the Chechen village of Alkhan-Yurt' (*IHT*, 24 December 1999, p. 7).

There are reports that fifteen Russian soldiers and two generals have been arrested by the Russian army (*The Telegraph*, 24 December 1999, p. 13).

'At the south-west edge of Grozny is the devastated town of Alkhan-Yurt, taken by the Russians on 1 December… A human rights report released on Tuesday [28 December] said that seventeen civilians in the town were murdered by soldiers and that many civilians had been killed by shelling. Several of the victims, though unarmed, had been trying to defend their homes from the booty hunters, the report said' (*IHT*, 29 December 1999, p. 8).

'The allegations that Russian soldiers plundered Alkhan-Yurt have stirred up a political storm here [in Moscow]. They were documented on a videotape prepared by Malik Saidullayev, an affluent Chechen businessman from Alkha-Yurt who supports the three-month-old war … Ten kilometres (six miles) south-west of Grozny, Alkhan-Yurt was the scene of a bloody battle. Hundreds of Russian troops laid siege last month [November] when, residents say, the town was occupied by about fifty rebels who refused the residents' appeals to leave. The Russian approached the village believing the militants had fled, only to be drawn into an ambush. When they seized Alkhan-Yurt on 1 December, Human Rights Watch has reported, the Russains plundered the town over a two-week period and killed seventeen civilians ... Nikolai Koshman, a deputy prime minister who administers the Moscow-controlled area of Chechenia ... and General Anatoli Kvashnin, chief of the the Russian general staff ... flew by helicopter to Chechenia [from the Russian military base at Mozdok in North Ossetia] ... On 17 December Mr Saidullayev ventured to Alkhan-Yurt, joined by his cameraman ... The troops were from the Fifteenth Battalion, part of the Western Group of forces under the command of Major General Vladimir Shamanov. General Shamanov has denied that his soldiers committed any crimes. On Tuesday [28 December] he was one of several commanders awarded a high military honour, Hero of Russia ... Mr Koshman ... promised to supply food and medicine. He also promised a thorough investigation. Civilian and military prosecutors have since begun an investigation' (*IHT*, 31 December 1999, pp. 1, 7).

21 December 1999. 'Russian troops battled hundreds [an estimated 500] of militants Tuesday [21 December] on the edge of Chechenia's southern mountains, trying to knock out rebel supply routes as jets and ground forces kept up their action against Grozny ... An estimated 4,000 Chechen rebels remain in the city [according to Russia] ... There are still civilians in Grozny, with estimates ranging from 8,000 to 35,000 ... Shelling of the roads out of town has continued despite the military's pledge that there would be safe corridors for refugees fleeing Grozny ... Both sides reported heavy fighting on Tuesday at Serzhen-Yurt, at the entrance to the Vedeno Gorge, one of the two main routes into the Caucasus mountains ... Russia said Monday [20 December] that it had seized the main civilian airport in Grozny's north, but on Tuesday [21 December] state television said that, although the rebels had been pushed out, Russian troops had yet to roll in to the airport because of the danger of land mines' (*IHT*, 22 December 1999, p. 4).

The UNHCR says that it will send foreign workers back into the north Caucasus this week after Russia provide new security guarantees. UN refugee workers should arrive in Ingushetia in mid-week (*IHT*, Wednesday 22 December 1999, p. 4).

22 December 1999. 'The war is raging in the mountainous south of Chechenia ... Russian paratroopers are trying to gain control of the main road south into Georgia, which Moscow asserts is a major supply and infiltration route ... Estimates of the numbers of civilians in Grozny range as high as 40,000 ... Few civilians have left, in part because heavy shelling has made them afraid of leaving their basement shelters' (*IHT*, 23 December 1999, p. 5).

'Up to 1,000 paratroopers who were dropped into the High Caucasus last week to cut off a key Chechen supply line were surrounded ... according to a Chechen spokesman. Near Duba Yurt, at the foot of the mountains, the

Chechens claimed to have inflicted heavy losses on Russian paratroopers' (*The Times*, 23 December 1999, p. 11).

23 December 1999. 'Opening a cabinet meeting in Moscow on Thursday [23 December], Mr Putin said that "almost all the territory of Chechenia is now controlled by the federal forces"' (*IHT*, 24 December 1999, p. 7).

'Vladimir Putin, the prime minister, said that 90 per cent of the population of Chechenia now lived in areas "liberated" by Russian forces' (*FT*, 24 December 1999, p. 6).

'Some 3,500 civilians had managed to escape along the army's "humanitarian corridors" in the past twenty-four hours and others had fled over the past few days ... according to Russia's independent NTV channel ... Its earlier estimate [was] that 40,000 civilians were trapped in the city ... [Those who] have stayed lack transport to the corridors or, in the case of men, fear they would automatically be arrested as "terrorists"' (*The Independent*, 24 December 1999, p. 9).

'The foreign ministry of Georgia denied on Thursday [24 December] that Georgia was aiding rebels in Chechenia' (*IHT*, 24 December 1999, p. 7).

'Russia's commander in the north Caucasus, General Viktor Kazantsev, has alleged that the rebels established a camp just inside Georgia to move men and matériel into Chechenia. The Georgian parliament accused Moscow of violating Georgian sovereignty and the Georgian foreign ministry issued a protest over alleged Russian bullying tactics' (*The Guardian*, 24 December 1999, p. 9).

24–6 December 1999. 'The long-awaited attack, reportedly headed by pro-Russian Chechens, was launched at midnight on Friday [24 December] ... Russian television said that pro-Moscow troops had reached the strategic Minutka Square crossroads, five minutes' drive from the city centre by late yesterday [26 December] ... Russian forces probed from four directions behind a huge artillery barrage' (*The Times*, 27 December 1999, p. 12).

'The Russian launched the "main stage of the operation to cleanse Grozny" ... at midnight on Friday [24 December] .... advancing slowly from four directions ... Up to 40,000 civilians ... remained penned in the city ... There are believed to be some 2,000 highly mobile Chechen guerrillas fighting to retain control of the city, though yesterday [26 December] Russian officials said the resistance appeared to be smaller than previously assumed' (*The Guardian*, 27 December 1999, p. 20. ('The Russian military reduced its estimates of the size of the guerrilla force still in the city from around 2,000 to several hundred': *The Telegraph*, 27 December 1999, p. 15.)

'Continuing their sector-by-sector "cleansing" of Grozny yesterday [26 December], federal ground troops were pushing into suburbs until they met resistance, then pulling back again to allow long-range guns to hit the areas where they had discovered rebels ... Caught in the middle of the fighting were up to 50,000 civilians, according to deputy prime minister Nikolai Koshman ... But Mr Koshman said now it was safer for them to stay put in their basements until the city was "liberated" ... Fighting was also raging south of the city, in the foothills of the Caucasus mountains' (*The Independent*, 27 December 1999, p. 1).

'Russian commanders said Saturday [25 December] that they had launched a "special operation" to take control of the city ... Thousands of Russian soldiers died in street battles in Grozny in the 1994–6 war in Chechenia. Moscow has vowed not to repeat the mistakes of that war, in which Russian soldiers stormed the centre of Grozny at the outset ... This time the military says it will move cautiously to take back the city ... Between 1,500 and 5,000 guerrillas are thought to still be defending Grozny in fighting that has trapped up to 40,000 civilians in basements with little food or firewood ... Now even Russian officials say the fighting is too dangerous for civilians to attempt to leave ... Most of the information about the assault came from the Russian military or officials, or Russian news media. Few Western reporters have permission to visit Chechenia' (*IHT*, 27 December 1999, pp. 1, 7).

27 December 1999. 'The already sluggish advance of Russian troops towards the heart of Grozny slowed yesterday [27 December] ... Russian losses in the mountains continued ... in the mountains of eastern Chechenia, close to the republic's borders with Dagestan' (*The Times*, 28 December 1999, p. 13).

'The Russians published figures showing that 397 federal troops had been killed and 917 injured in Chechenia since October [1999] ... Emergencies minister Sergei Shoigu was holding talks in Ingushetia with ... a representative of the Chechen president, Aslan Maskhadov, about ways of releasing the estimated 50,000 civilians entrapped in Grozny' (*The Independent*, 28 December 1999, p. 9). 'Russia's emergency situations minister, Sergei Shoigu, met Mr Maskhadov's senior negotiator ... in the neighbouring republic of Ingushetia on Sunday [27 December]. The official purpose was to negotiate the safe passage of civilians out of Grozny, but the possibility of a peace deal was also discussed, a source close to the Chechen side said yesterday [28 December]. The source said ... [they] talked behind closed doors but failed to agree on a peace deal' (*The Times*, 29 December 1999, p. 13).

'In Grozny, as the ground battle entered its fourth day, there were conflicting reports of advances and setbacks ... The Russians admitted they were meeting stiff resistance' (*The Guardian*, 28 December 1999, p. 2).

'Russia's hopes of a quick victory in the battle for Grozny were dashed yesterday [27 December] by a fierce defence of their capital by Chechen guerrillas ... President Maskhadov vowed to defend the city to the last man' (*The Telegraph*, 28 December 1999, p. 16).

'Aslan Maskhadov ... pledged to hold Grozny "until the end" ... Grigori Yavlinsky ... criticized the advance on Grozny as "unacceptable" and part of a "war of revenge"' (*FT*, 28 December 1999, p. 5).

'Russian commanders announced yesterday that they had ordered the bombardment of Chechenia's southern mountains with fuel-air bombs' (*The Times*, 28 December 1999, p. 13).

'The Russians said they had begun dropping so-called fuel-air bombs over the mountains ... The bombs release a large cloud of inflammable gas and cause massive explosions that penetrate bunkers and caves ... The Russian say they were using them only over sparsely populated areas' (*IHT*, 28 December 1999, p. 4).

28 December 1999. There are conflicting claims about the progress of Russian forces in Grozny.

Yeltsin presents medals (Hero of Russia gold stars) to the three generals commanding the war in Chechenia (General Viktor Kazantsev and his two deputies. General Vladimir Shamanov and General Gennadi Troshev): 'Before there were little mistakes which turned into big mistakes. There has been nothing of the sort this time. The army is faultlessly carrying out the instructions of the president and the government. That is why we have so many hero generals.'

A medal was presented to General Vladimir Shamanov, 'some of whose soldiers were implicated in recent killings of civilians on the town of Alkhan-Yurt' (*The Independent*, 29 December 1999, p. 11).

'General Vladimir Shamanov ... [is] a controversial figure who in recent days had been rumoured to have been sacked. The ostensible reason for the supposed firing was said to be an alleged massacre of up to forty-one civilians by drunk and rampaging Russian troops in the destroyed village of Alkhan-Yurt under general Shamanov's command. General Shamanov has also upset Moscow politicians with his outspoken comments, suggesting that the army would defy its political superiors. Several weeks ago he declared that the army's officer corps would not heed any moves to negotiate with the Chechens. He also blamed the lost war of 1994–6 on a Russian government that "betrayed" the military, and he threatened to tear off his epaulettes and resign, along with many other officers, should the politicians meddle in Chechenia ... The daily newspaper Izvestia said yesteday [27 December] that Mr Yeltsin had complained about General Shamanov on Monday [27 December]' (*The Guardian*, 29 December 1999, p. 10).

'The troops [allegedly involved in Alkhan-Yurt] were from the Fifteenth Battalion, part of the Western Group of forces under the command of Major General Vladimir Shamanov. General Shamanov has denied that his soldiers committed any crimes. On Tuesday [28 December] he was one of several commanders awarded a high military honour, Hero of Russia' (*IHT*, 31 December 1999, pp. 1, 7).

Vladimir Putin: 'Without combating terrorism we cannot realize a single socio-economic goal' (*The Guardian*, 29 December 1999, p. 10).

29 December 1999. 'Chechen rebels said Wednesday [29 December] that they had retreated slightly from mountain positions in the south ... and on key heights in Grozny ... a rebel spokesman said guerrilla fighters had retreated from two key hills in the capital ... Between 10,000 and 40,000 [civilians] remain trapped [in Grozny] ... Russian forces arrested six Western journalists in Chechenia on Wednesday' (*IHT*, 30 December 1999, pp. 1, 4). (The journalists were released the following day. Russian officials said they lacked proper accreditation to visit the region: *IHT*, 31 December 1999, p. 7.)

'Russian police and secret service agents have arrested eight people in connection with four apartment bombings in Russia that killed about 300 people, the Federal Security Service said Wednesday [29 December]. A spokesman refused to give any other details or say when they had been arrested' (*IHT*, 30 December 1999, p. 4).

'Explosives of an identical type to those used in a wave of apartment bombings in Russia were found in a Chechen "school for terrorism", officials said yesterday [29 December]. The Federal Security Service [FSB] said it found the bombers' college in ... Urus Martan and concluded that Chechens must have been responsible for the bombings which killed nearly 300 people in September ... Vladimir Kozlov [of the FSB] said: "We have no doubt that the main authors of these acts were Khattab and Basayev" ... The Chechen government denied responsibility but Khattab ... hinted that the bombings had been in revenge for Russia's expulsion of Islamic fundamentalists from Dagestan in August ... The FSB said eight people suspected of involvement in the bombings had been arrested, although it was not clear whether that had happened recently or whether they were referring to Chechens picked up immediately after the blasts. Nine more suspects were on international wanted lists' (*The Independent*, 30 December 1999, p. 10).

30 December 1999. 'Russian forces launched fresh attacks Thursday [30 December] on the Chechen capital and on rebel bases in the south, ignoring warnings by the Chechen president, Aslan Maskhadov, who said they could not win the war ... President Maskhadov told the Interfax news agency that the real war in Chechenia would start only when the Russian had moved further into the mountains ... "Even if the war goes on for ten years Russia will not be able to conquer Chechenia and its people", he said. "That is why I remind the Kremlin that its actions will lead nowhere ... Even if after a while the Russian Army manages to conquer Grozny, the price it will have to pay for it will be very high", he said' (*IHT*, 31 December 1999, p. 7).

31 December 1999. Boris Yeltsin resigns as president and Vladimir Putin becomes acting president.

1–2 January 2000. On 1 January 2000 Putin attended a military awards ceremony in Chechenia: '[The campaign] is not simply about restoring honour and dignity to the country ... This is how to bring about the end of the breakup of Russia.'

'While the acting president ... was in Chechenia civilians in Grozny said that they had experienced the worst bombing of the war ... The Chechen resistance yesterday [2 January] was as fierce as ever ... The Russians crowed that the Chechens had scored an "own goal" in Grozny by blowing up stocks of chemicals from the local petrochemical industry, the green fumes from which blew back in their own direction ... The Russian military claimed to have made inroads into rebel-controlled territory in southern Chechenia, capturing strategic heights overlooking their opponents' key stronghold of Vedeno ... The Pentagon said on Friday [31 December] that Russia had fired three conventional Scud missiles, the heaviest weapons used in the conflict so far' (*The Independent*, 3 January 2000, p. 8).

'Heavy fighting flared in several parts of the Chechen capital on Sunday [2 January] as the Russians again accused rebel fighters of using homemade bombs filled with chlorine and ammonia against them ... This was the third time the accusation was made' (*IHT*, 3 January 2000, p. 4).

'Russian troops are intensifying their campaign to seize Grozny with a bombardment that is said to be one of the heaviest yet ... The Russians are avoiding storming the city with ground troops ... [Russian] military commanders admitted at the weekend [1–2 January] that they were losing ten men each day ... At the same time jets intensified their bombardment of the mountainous south ... The bombings come after the first reported use of Scud missiles in the war. Three were detected on Friday [31 December] by US systems looking out for millennium bug problems ... Yesterday [2 January] Russia reported a third chemical attack by the rebels and a green cloud was seen over Grozny' (*The Times*, 3 January 2000, p. 12).

'Arbi Barbayev, a warlord allegedly linked to the beheading of three British telecommunications engineers and a New Zealander in December 1998, was yesterday [2 January] reported to have been killed in the fighting, tough Chechen sources denied this' (*The Telegraph*, 3 January 1999, p. 11).

3 January 2000. 'In an unusual day ... Chechen rebels moved on the offensive and Russian troops were pressed to contain them ... The rebels have put up stiff resistance in the capital, blocking their foes at the city's edge ... On Monday [2 January], for the first time, the Chechens launched an attack westward from Grozny to an area occupied by the Russians for more than a month: the towns of Alkhan-Kala and Alkhan-Yurt ... Chechen officials ... said fighters had reclaimed three towns: Alkhan-Kala, Alkhan-Yurt and Kurali. The three form a triangle to the south-west of Grozny. A spokesman ... said attackers had destroyed the headquarters of General Vladimir Shamanov, the western front commander ... The Russians denied [the spokesman's claim]. A thrust westwards indicates not an attempt to flee Grozny and head south to the mountains but a strategy of inflicting casualties and causing havoc behind Russian lines. Chechens have mounted small ambushes in Russia-occupied Chechenia, but nothing that the Russians previously characterized as co-ordinated combat ... On Monday the rebels also attacked Russian forces along the Argun Gorge road, which leads south to Georgia' (*IHT*, 4 January 1999, p. 7).

A Palestinian fires four rocket-propelled grenades at the Russian embassy in the Lebanese capital of Beirut. No Russian were hurt, but a Lebanese policemen was killed. A note in the pocket of the Palestinian, who was shot dead by Lebanese forces, said: 'I martyred myself for Grozny.'

4 January 2000. 'Russian forces have been claiming for days that their forces were making steady progress, but reports from Grozny indicate that the federal troops are pinned down by rebel fire ... A rebel field commander said Chechen fighters were mounting a fierce attempt to take Alkhan-Yurt, a Russian-occupied town just south-west of Grozny ... Refugees also reported firefights in nearby Alkhan-Kala between Russian forces and rebels' (*IHT*, 5 January 2000, p. 6).

5 January 2000. 'Rebels defending Grozny ... are carrying out surprise raids in and around the city that appears to have Russian forces off balance. Reports from Grozny and from refugees who have recently left suburban areas say that rebels have broken the Russian armoured ring and occupied at least two towns that abut the city. In the west Alkhan-Kala was said to be under rebel control as late as Wednesday morning [5 January], and Alkhan-Yurt, until Tuesday [4 January]. In the east the guerrillas made inroads into Khankala on Wednesday, according to unconfirmed reports. All three towns were taken by the Russians more than three weeks ago ... It appears certain that the rebels have gone on a limited offensive... The Associated Press reported the capture of sixty Russian soldiers and the occupation of buildings in Khankala, just outside western Grozny, by rebel snipers ... On Wednesday ... Vladimir Putin continued to label Chechenia a high priority ... "I am absolutely convinced that we won't be able to solve economic or social problems if the state disintegrates", he said. On Wednesday representatives of ... Aslan Maskhadov issued a statement in Georgia calling for a three-day ceasefire in Grozny beginning Saturday [8 January]. The statement also asserted that Russia had used chemical weapons in the capital on 29 December' (*IHT*, 6 January 1999, pp. 1, 6). (Putin: 'I am absolutely convinced that we will not be able to solve any economic or social problem if the state disintegrates. So there is nothing unusual about us now paying such attention to combating terrorism. We must bring it to an end': *FT*, 7 January 2000, p. 6.)

'Rebel fighters retook part of the northern Grozny suburb of Khankala, which Russian forces claimed to have occupied days ago' (*The Telegraph*, 6 January 2000, p. 20).

6 January 2000. 'Chechen rebel fighters abandoned a key village south-west of Grozny that they claimed to have seized from Russian forces earlier this week, witnesses said. The Chechen fighters at Alkhan-Kala retreated back to Grozny on orders from commanders, according to ... refugees ... About 600 Chechen fighters said they had taken contol of Alkhan-Kala and two other neighbouring villages on Monday [3 January]. The next day they abandoned the two villages and regrouped in Alkhan-Kala ... Refugees reported Thursday [6 January] that all but two dozen rebels had retreated from Alkhan-Kala ... and that the rest had slipped through Russian lines. Military sources said Thursday that casualties among Russian forces were increasing, in a rare admission that rebel resistance was taking a heavy toll' (*IHT*, 7 January 2000, p. 1).

'General Vladimir Shamanov ... confirmed what official Russian sources had previously denied: that Chechen rebels recently broke out of Grozny and overran the village of Alkhan-Yurt, first taken by the Russians on 1 December ... "Cleaning up" operations ... would soon have to be repeated in Alkhan-Yurt and other towns' (*The Telegraph*, 7 January 2000, p. 17).

7 January 2000. The Russian military announces that it is suspending air strikes. Russia says there are 211,600 refugees (*The Independent*, 18 November 1999, p. 16). The Russian military announces that it is suspending its bombardment of Grozny, allegedly on the grounds that the rebels are using civilians as human shields and are blowing up containers of toxic chemicals (chlorine and ammonia). (The military has also complained about the bad weather, including thick fog.)

General Gennadi Troshev: 'We have been forced to suspend military operations all around Grozny for one single reason. There are still civilians there who fighters kept behind deliberately to use as human shields ... Grozny has today been officially declared a risk area, an ecological danger zone. That chiefly affects civilians, children. Therefore the military command decided to suspend operations. Suspend does not mean discontinuing military operations. Military operations are conducted around the clock.' The Tass news agency: 'The military is continuing to force fighters out of areas of the city where there are no civilians.'

General Gennadi Troshev is replaced by his deputy, General Sergei Makarov, as commander of the eastern front in Chechenia. General Vladimir Shamanov is replaced by his deputy, General Alexei Verbitsky, as commander of the western front in Chechenia. A defence ministry spokesman says that the changes were 'not a consequence of any professional errors in the counter-terrorist operation', merely a rotation so that 'other commanders can gain combat experience'. (Both Shamanov and Troyev were presented with medals on 28 December 1999.)

(*The Times*, 8 January 2000, p. 15; *The Independent*, 8 January 2000, p. 16; *The Guardian*, 8 January 2000, p. 15; *The Telgraph*, 8 January 2000, p. 1; *IHT*, 8 January 2000, pp. 1, 5.)

'General Shamanov has been a particularly outspoken general. When reports surfaced in October [1999] that the Kremlin might be considering peace talks with the Chechens, general Shamanov openly warned that he would strip off his shoulder boards and quit the army and that others would follow him' (*IHT*, 8 January 2000, p. 1). 'Asked what he would do if ordered to stop the advance, General Vladimir Shamanov, the commander of the western group of forces in the Caucasus, replied: "I would tear off my stars. I would no longer serve in such an army." General Shamanov, one of several military chiefs with scores to settle from the last war, is the most outspoken of the commanders but his sentiments are shared by many in the army. General Viktor Kavantsev, the overall commander of Russian forces in the Caucasus, and General Gennadi Troshev, who is in charge of the eastern group, have said they would regard any order to suspend their advance as "treason". Behind them is the figure of General Anatoli Kvashnin, the chief of the general staff, who is believed to be the most energetic supporter of a purely military solution to Moscow's Chechen programme ... The general is rumoured to have threatened to resign if the more conciliatory line to Chechenia favoured by the diplomats, worried by the mounting condemnation of the war in the west, won the day. General Kvashnin ... masterminded the operation to seize Pristina airport [in Kosovo] before Nato forces in June [1999]. But if that was one of the Russian army's most glorious victories in recent years, its most humiliating defeat was also commanded by General Kvashnin, the slaughter of a brigade and several regiments in the storming of Grozny five years ago': Marcus Warren, *The Telegraph*, 9 November 1999, p. 14.)

8–9 January 2000. 'Russia's acting president, Vladimir Putin, may have suspended air and artillery strikes on Grozny to mark the Orthodox Christmas and the end of Ramadan, the Moslem holiday. But ... fighting raged in Chechenia's mountains and lowlands Sunday [9 January] ... Several hundred Islamic rebels were reported to have surrounded the headquarters of the Russian commandant in Argun, a town east of Grozny, which the Russians had assumed they had under control. Fierce fighting was raging in Shali, south-east of the capital. And clashes were also reported near Gudermes, Chechenia's second-largest city, which the Russian have used as an administrative capital for the Chechen territory under its control. There were shootings and attempted infiltrations at checkpoints elsewhere in Chechenia ... On Saturday [8 January] militants left their hideout in the mountains and tried to break through the Russian lines here [Duba-Yurt]. They were repelled ... Russian helicopter gunships rocketed rebel positions in Grozny on Sunday as heavy street fighting resumed after a brief lull ... The gunships supported ground attacks by rocketing rebel positions in a north-western district. The military said it was still refraining from bombardment of central Grozny, where many civilians are hiding – and where federal troops are trying to overrun rebel positions. But artillery continued to support ground units, and the ban on air bombardment did not appear to extend beyond the centre of the city. Commanders had announced a pause in bombardment of Grozny on Friday [7 January], saying it was meant to mark the Orhodox Christmas and to allow civilians to flee' (*IHT*, 10 January 2000, pp. 1, 4).

'Defence officials are covering up staggering losses in Chechenia, according to Russian troops ... The reports coincide with a new wave of media criticism [in Russia] of the war ... On Sunday [9 January] Russian forces admitted that 300 Chechen rebels had surrounded the town of Argun nine miles east of Grozny ... Rebels exploited the lull in fighting to storm Shali, twelve miles south-east of Grozny, but it was unclear whether the rebels had now withdrawn' (*The Times*, 10 January 2000, p. 12).

'Vladimir putin said [Saturday 8 January] the decision to suspend artillery and air strikes, taken as Orthodox Christians celebrated Christmas and Moslems marked the Eid al-Fitr feast at the end of Ramadan, was taken because civilian safety was paramount' (*The Independent*, 10 January 2000, p. 12).

10 January 2000. 'The Russian defence ministry announced that it was cancelling their moratorium on artillery and air strikes on Grozny. An evening curfew was imposed on the entire territory. Russian officials also vowed to take a tough line of the refugees returning to Chechenia. From now on every male under the age of sixty-five [the correct figure was sixty] will be questioned and checked. Only women, children and the elderly will be beyond suspicion ... The rebels have now demonstrated that virtually no part of Chechenia is secure, because there is no longer a clear front line. The Russians are looking over their shoulder as the militants have fought to create a corridor between their forces in the Chechen mountains and their comrades in Grozny ... The Russian media reported that ... the Russian army's toll [on 10 January] was twenty-six dead and thirty wounded ... That would be the highest one-day loss in the three-month campaign ... The figure did not include the interior ministry troops, who have had the main responsibility for finding and destroying the rebels inside Grozny and other Chechen cities ... Viktor Kazantsev, commander of Russian forces in the north Caucasus region told reporters that the limited ceasefire would now be lifted and a full-scale offensive resumed' (*IHT*, 11 January 2000, pp. 1, 7).

'An interior ministry spokesman said that rebels killed twenty-six soldiers and wounded thirty during the previous twenty-four hours. Russia has claimed for weeks that its losses are no more than one or two a day' (*The Independent*, 11 January 2000, p. 13).

'Russian officials reported yesterday's death toll of twenty-six men after months of reporting one or two deaths a day' (*The Times*, 11 January 2000, p. 14).

'The ministry of defence said that General Gennadi Troshev ... and General Vladimir Shamanov ... were both retaining their roles as "strategic leaders" of the military operation in the north Caucasus, while their deputies were taking on roles as "tactical leaders"' (*FT*, 11 January 2000, p. 8).

'According to reports from Russia's eastern command, twenty-six soldiers were killed and thirty injured in an ambush of a column carrying drinking water to Gudermes on Sunday [9 January] ... Monitoring the progress of the war is almost impossible for outsiders as foreign journalists are rarely allowed into Chechenia. Their Russian colleagues are often grounded in military bases and promised trips to the front fail to materialize ... Orders from Viktor Kazantsev ... [state that] only women, children and men over the age of sixty should be regarded as refugees. "Everyone else is to be detained and inquiries to be made", he said' (*The Telegraph*, 11 January 2000, p. 13).

'The military said that Chechen males aged between ten and sixty would now automatically be treated as rebels and detained for "thorough" checks' (*The Guardian*, 12 January 2000, p. 17).

'General Viktor Kazantsev ... announced that the two senior generals commanding the eastern and western fronts in the war had been reinstated and remained his deputies... "Nobody has dismissed anybody. Generals Troshev and Shamanov are simply loaded with additional work", General Kazantsev insisted yesterday [10 January] ... Fierce fighting was reported yesterday from Argun and Gudermes, from the capital itself and from the region of Urus-Martan ... The Russian setbacks are triggering unusually adverse comment in the 'Russian media' (*The Guardian*, 11 January 2000, p. 12).

11 January 2000. 'Russian troops reclaimed control of the town [Shali] on Tuesday [11 January] ... The rebel offensive began Sunday morning [9 January] when hundreds of militants made a series of co-ordinated attacks on Shali and Argun ... The series of co-ordinated attacks that began in Shali and Argun on Sunday included the outskirts of Gudermes, Chechenia's second largest city' (*IHT*, 12 January 2000, pp. 1, 5).

'Details are emerging of a two-pronged raid that could mark a turning point in the war... The bold operation at the weekend [8–9 January] ... for the first time led to critical reports in the Russian media ... A rebel spokesman said that the weekend raids signalled a switch in Chechen tactics to a partisan war, avoiding frontal clashes with Russian troops' (*The Times*, 12 January 2000, p. 14).

12 January 2000. 'Russian officials said Wednesday [12 January] that they have secured Argun and a nearby town of Shali and that rebels turned back before they reached a third town of Gudermes. But Interfax reported intense fighting and air strikes in Argun and Shali as late as Tuesday [11 January]' (*IHT*, 13 January 2000, p. 4).

13 January 2000. 'At the Ingush-Chechenia border ... Russian troops demanded that all males between the age of ten and sixty be checked. The move effectively reversed the Russian policy of encouraging refugees to return' (*IHT*, 14 January 2000, p. 1).

14 January 2000. 'Moscow appeared to have eased a ban on Chechen males aged ten to sixty crossing the border into Ingsushetia after criticism by the UN refugee agency and the leader of Ingushetia, although there were conflicting accounts ... An NTV reporter said he understood Moscow had raised the age limit to fifteen from ten. President Ruslan Aushev of Ingushetia ... [said] a total ban was still in force ... General Gennadi Troshev, the deputy commander of the Russian forces in the northern Caucasus, said Friday [14 January] that the assault on Grozny had come to a "standstill" ... The Russian Orthodox Church ... has backed the Kremlin's hard line in Chechenia. Several Russian priests were abducted before the war ... "We are bringing order to our own country and struggling with international terrorists who have invaded our motherland", Patriarch Alexei II said in November [1999]' (*IHT*, 15 January 2000, p. 5).

'Russia said yesterday [14 January] it had dropped its blanket ban on them [those between ten and sixty] leaving Chechenia, but is still "closely questioning" those within [Chechenia]' (*The Independent*, 15 January 2000, p. 16).

16 January 2000. The Taliban administration in Afghanistan recognizes Chechenia as an independent state.

'Russia increased its onslaught on ... Grozny at the weekend [15–16 January] ... Russian aircraft and artillery subjected Grozny to one of the severest poundings of the four-month war and Russian commanders said the Russian ground campaign to capture Grozny ... had entered a "new phase"' (*The Guardian*, 17 January 2000, p. 12).

17 January 2000. 'The Russian military renewed its assault on Grozny on Monday [17 January] ... With clearing skies, Russian aircraft and artillery bombarded the city ... This is the second major Russian offensive' (*IHT*, 18 January 2000, p. 4).

18 January 2000. 'Russian soldiers battled their way toward the centre of Grozny on Tuesday [18 January] as the struggle for control of Chechenia's capital reached a critical phase. After a thunderous bombardment Russian troops began moving through Grozny's streets at dawn Tuesday. It was the most intense ground attack in Grozny during the nearly four-month-long war. Russian forces moved from the north, the east and the west in an effort to fracture the heart of the city ... There was no way to verify the Russian claims of success. The Russian military kept most reporters well away from the fighting raging in Grozny ... A group representing soldiers' mothers sent an open letter to ... Vladimir Putin, warning that the air and ground assault were needlessly endangering civilians. "The military actions launched by the state's military authorities in Chechenia are not helping to solve the conflict and are using methods outlawed by the Geneva convention of 1949 and 1977", the Union of Committees of Soldiers' Mothers said, referring to the international accords intended to protect the rights of civilians ... The Committee of Soldiers' Mothers tries to help soldiers' families negotiate the military bureaucracy ... In another development, a powerful explosion shook the supreme court building in ... Ingushetia ... It was not known if the blast was related to the war' (*IHT*, 19 January 2000, pp. 1, 6).

19 January 2000. 'Russian generals plan to conclude their military campaign by 26 February, one month before the presidential election, the deputy commander of Russian forces in the north Caucasus ... Lieutenant General Gennadi Troshev ... said Wednesday [19 January] ... "Nobody is giving the force any firm deadline for ending the operation", he declared. But he did not hesitate to publicize the goal: an end to the military campaign by 26 February ... Since Russian forces renewed their assault on the Chechen capital two days ago ... Russian troops have fought their way toward the centre of the city, advancing from the north, east and west. Still, reports ... suggested the Russian troops were advancing slowly ... Wednesday was the second day of the ground attack ... Vyacheslav Ovchinnikov, the commander of Russia's interior troops, said that there were an estimated 2,500 militants in the city ... From the start the war in Chechenia has been inextricably bound to Kremlin politics. Acting President Vladimir Putin emerged as Russia's most popular politician by serving as a powerful and visible proponent ... The Russian government had hoped to evacuate the city by establishing two "humanitarian corridors", or escape routes, that Grozny's residents could use to flee. According to statistics made public Wednesday [19 January], however, only 7,820 people used the corridors since they were established in mid-December [1999]. And a mere fifty-nine used it over a recent twenty-four-hour period, Russian officials say. In contrast, as many as 40,000 civilians may still inhabit the city ... A Chechen businessman [Malik Saiddullayev] who is supporting Moscow's side in the war said Wednesday that discussions were under way between Russian officials and a group of rebel commanders ... The Russian media, which served mostly as a cheerleader for Russian generals at the start of the war, have begun to ask more searching questions' (Michael Gordon, *IHT*, 20 January 2000, pp. 1, 5).

'Several top Chechen field commanders flew to Moscow this week for talks with the Russian government ... Malik Saidullayev ... said that talks began on Monday [17 January] between four Chechen field commanders and several Russian deputy ministers and representatives of Russian law enforcement. A representative of the Chechen government was also involved in the talks ... Mr Saidullayev was the head of the Chechen State Council, the basis of the pro-Moscow puppet government, until last November [1999], when he left, apparently because the defence ministry persistently ignored his calls to stop the fighting. Beslan Gantemirov, his replacement ... was released from prison, where he had been serving a six-year sentence for embezzling billions of roubles reserved for rebuilding Chechenia after the last war' (*The Times*, 20 January 2000, p. 21).

20 January 2000. It is announced that on 18 January General Mikhail Molofeyev (deputy commander of the northern group of Russian forces in Chechenia) went missing in Grozny. There are conflicting reports about when he was shot dead or captured by Chechen fighters. (His body was found on 23 January.)

23 January 2000. Russian forces claim to have taken control of Vedeno.

General Vyacheslav Ovchinnikov, commander of interior ministry troops, is replaced by General Vyacheslav Tikhomiriv (who led Russian troops in the final year of the last war in Chechenia).

26 January 2000. There are about 2,500 rebels in Grozny and an estimated 6,000 in the southern mountains. 'A pro-Moscow Chechen leader, Malik Saidullayev, claimed to have made progress in unofficial talks in Moscow with rebels and to have travelled on Wednesday [26 January] to discuss the talks with Aslan Maskhadov' (*IHT*, 27 January 2000, p. 4).

27 January 2000. 'Acting President Vladimir Putin approved plans Thursday [27 January] to sharply increase the purchase of new weapons and equipment to modernize the Russian military. Mr Putin ... also said that the defence budget would be reallocated so that more money goes to develop high-technical conventional weapons ... "The army has been underfinanced for several years, which has entailed negative consequences for the nation's defence potential", Mr Putin said ... Mr Putin insisted that the new policy was not linked to Russia's stalled military campaign in Chechenia ... While the new policy announced by Mr Putin does not call for an increase in the military budget of 146.35 billion roubles ($5.06 billion) for 2000, it authorizes a shift in spending priorities. Deputy prime minister Ilya Klebanov said the plan called for an increase in spending on weapons and development by up to 80 per cent in some categories. He said that spending on military supplies overall would increase by 50 per cent' (*IHT*, 28 January 2000, p. 5).

'Since being appointed prime minister last August [1999], Mr Putin has ... promised to increase the defence budget by 57 per cent' (*The Guardian*, 28 January 2000, p. 13).

'Between 10,000 and 40,000 civilians are believed to be hiding [in Grozny] ... Speaking in Moscow on Thursday [27 January] the UN secretary-general, Kofi Annan, said: "Whilst we all support attempts to root out terrorists, we should take every step to protect the rights of the civilians and ensure that they do not suffer undue hardships" (*IHT*, 28 January 2000, p. 5).

'Sergei Yastrzhembsky [the newly appointed Russian spokesman on Chechenia] yesterday [27 January] revealed the number and a detailed breakdown of Russian forces in the north Caucasus for the first time. There were 93,000 troops serving in the region overall, 57,000 from the regular army and 36,000 paramilitary soldiers from the interior ministry, he disclosed. Russian estimates of rebel strength put the number of guerrillas at around 11,000' (*The Telegraph*, 28 January 2000, p. 19).

28 January 2000. 'After five days of saying that they had no information, Russian authorities acknowledged Friday [28 January] that five days ago they detained a Radio Liberty correspondent ... The military has allowed extremely limited access to the combat zone, under heavily controlled circumstances, for the few correspondents it is willing to give accreditation' (*IHT*, 29 January 2000, p. 2).

'A senior Russian leader says that Russia made its plans to invade Chechenia six months before the bombing of civilian targets in Russia and the Chechen attack on Dagestan which were the official pretext for launching the war ... Sergei Stepashin [former Russian interior minister and prime minister] ... in recent interiews ... says that as early as last March [1999] Russian intended to invade Chechenia as far as the Terek river north of Grozny ... He says the inner cabinet held a closed meeting with army and security chiefs in March [1999] to discuss the operation against Chechenia' (*The Independent*, 29 January 2000, p. 15).

'Mr Stepashin firmly contradicted the official line that the campaign began in September [1999] was a response to the invasion of Dagestan by Chechen rebels last August [1999] and to four subsequent apartment explosions that the government also blamed on them. When he was still interior minister in March

1999 … Mr Stepashin says there was a already a plan to create a "buffer zone" occupied by federal troops in the northern third of Chechenia, as far as the Terek river. "It was Russian territory from time immemorial", he says. "It was a dangerous thing for Khrushchev to hand it to Ingushetia-Chechenia in 1957." He says active preparations for an invasion … continued throughout his period as prime minister, from May until August 1999' (*FT*, 31 January 2000, p. 8).

'On 5 March 1999 at Grozny airport General Gennadi Shpigun, the Russian interior ministry's representative in the republic, boarded a TU–134 passenger plane for Moscow. Masked gunmen grabbed General Shpigun and bundled him off the plane and into a waiting car. The abduction outraged officials in Moscow … Mr Stepashin said he started planning to cordon off the region after the Shpigun abduction, a plan that envisioned Russian troops taking northern Chechenia all the way to the Terek river north of Grozny. The plan … would allow Russia to launch strikes from the north deeper into Chechenia to destroy the rebels' bases' (*IHT*, 21 March 2000, p. 2).

31 January 2000. Russian forces claim to have taken control of Minutka Square.

'Russian officials said that 250 rebels had surrendered in Grozny, although a pro-Russian Chechen parliamentary deputy said the reports were false' (*IHT*, 1 February 2000, p. 5).

'Shamil Basayev had surgery yesterday [31 January] at the hospital in Alkhan-Kala, outside Grozny, after slipping out with more than 2,000 rebels [2,100 men] … Interfax news agency quoted the military as saying 40 per cent of the city was under the control of Russian troops' (*The Independent*, 1 February 2000, p. 15).

'They had left at dawn, a group of rebels and civilians several hundred strong … A woman fighter … says she received the order from her commander to leave Grozny … She says there are still several thousand Chechen fighters inside the city centre, as well as 40,000 civilians, mainly ethnic Russians' (*The Times*, 1 February 2000, p. 14).

1 February 2000. 'The war in Chechenia appeared to reach a dramatic turning point on Tuesday [1 February] when rebels began to flee Grozny … taking heavy casualties and opening the way to Russia's conquest of the city. Chechen officials and witnesses in Chechenia said the guerrillas began pulling out overnight … A spokesman for the Chechen government of President Aslan Maskhadov said that rebel fighters "have been completely withdrawn from the city. The withdrawal has been carried out in an orderly fashion" … One report said that several top Chechen commanders were wounded or killed in action in recent days. Shamil Basayev … lost a leg to a mine when he led hundreds of fighters out of Grozny, Chechen officials said … Other reports said that along with Mr Basayev a large contingent had arrived in Alkhan-Kala. The town is nominally under Russian control … Fighting continued at several locations [in Grozny] … Holding Grozny has been costly for the guerrillas. Some reports Tuesday said a Chechen commander, Aslanbek

Ismailov, and the mayor of Grozny, Lecha Dudayev, were killed in the capital ... Mr Ismailov ... had masterminded Grozny's defence. Mr Dudayev was the son of Dzokhar Dudayev, Chechenia's first president ... The cost of restoring the city will be immense and all the while Moscow's occupation forces may be vulnerable to attack. This might account for the lack of triumphal pronouncements Tuesday; if large numbers of guerrillas simply escaped the city it would undermine a main objective, which was to "liquidate terrorist bands"' (*IHT*, 2 February 2000, p. 4).

'The Russian say 600 rebels ... are still in Grozny and sporadic fighting is going on ... The Chechens have always said they would fight for Grozny to cause maximum casualties to the Russian army but would then leave the city at a moment of their own choosing ... Nevertheless, the loss of Grozny will be a blow to Chechen morale' (*The Independent*, 2 February 2000, p. 14).

2 February 2000. 'Reports were confused from Alkhan-Kala ... where hundreds of rebels ended up after they fled the capital early Monday [31 January]. Some residents there who arrived in Ingushetia on Wednesday [2 February] said the rebels had slipped away overnight ... The fighters left numerous wounded comrades in the town, they said. All refugee informants concurred that the guerrillas had suffered high casualties in their flight from Grozny, mostly from land mines laid by the Russians ... Still, Chechen officials insisted that up to 2,000 rebels have escaped Grozny as part of the withdrawal ... The Russians ... rejected reports that hundreds of rebels had escaped Grozny ... General Viktor Kazantsev, the Russian commander in Chechenia, declared victory ... The Russian were reordering their math to explain why, after months of bombing and after issuing consistently high enemy body counts, there were any rebels left alive. General Kazantsev said 2,000 remained in Grozny out of 7,000 to 10,000 at the beginning of the war. Previously, the Russian said only 3,500 were defending Grozny. At stake in the duelling assessments is just who will be declared the victor when Grozny falls to the Russians' (Daniel Williams, *IHT*, 3 February 2000, p. 5).

'Igor Sergeyev, the Russian defence minister, claimed that ... 586 rebels were killed on Tuesday [2 February] ... A spokesman for Aslan Maskhadov said that some rebel units had remained behind in the capital ... "There are some areas, some objectives in Grozny which we will have to keep until the end of February"' (*The Times*, 3 February 2000, p. 21).

'Chechen officials said that some 2,000 of their guerrillas had broken through Russian lines ... Shamil Basayev ... has confirmed that he was wounded in the leg when he left Grozny ... but denies that his leg has been amputated' (*The Independent*, 3 February 2000, p. 14). (It was later revealed that he had had a foot amputated.)

3 February 2000. 'The Chechens now admit that at least forty-three of their fighters have been killed, including top commanders, since they began fleeing the Russian lines and minefields around Grozny on Monday [31 January]. But they insist that the bulk of their forces got away, their weapons intact, as they head for the southern mountains ... The Russian army was moving through the shattered Chechen capital yesterday [3 February] without meeting any serious resistance ... But as the soldiers close in on the centre of Grozny there is growing controversy in Russian about how some 4,000 Chechen rebels managed to escape the besieged city ... The ability of the Chechens ... to escape Grozny shows that the Russian army is short of combat-ready infantry. This may explain why Vladimir Putin ... has called up 20,000 reserve officers who are expected to replace officers who can then be sent on duty to Chechenia' (*The Independent*, 4 February 2000, p. 15).

'A large group holed up in a village outside Grozny ... escaped, heading for the mountains, on 3 February' (*The Economist*, 5 February 2000, p. 45).

'Russian authorities handed over a Radio Liberty correspondent to Chechen rebels on Thursday in exchange for two captured Russian soldiers. Russian authorities had detained Andrei Babitsky, the correspondent [since 1989] for the US-funded Radio Liberty, as he was leaving Grozny on 16 January and later charged him with "participating in an illegal, armed group" ... Russian authorities have long viewed Mr Babitsky as a thorn in their side. His reports from Grozny have irritated Russian authorities, who have sharply restricted access to the battlefield and sought to discourage reporting from the Chechen side ... Mr Babitsky was a human rights activist during Soviet times ... When Chechen rebels seized a hospital and hostages in Budyonnovsk during the first war in Chechenia Mr Babitsky was there to cover the episode. He later agreed to take the place of some of the hostages' (Michael Gordon, *IHT*, 4 February 2000, p. 4).

4 February 2000. 'Grozny appeared to be in Russian hands Friday [4 February], but combat continued in towns and hamlets to the west as large groups of rebels fled the city for mountain and forest hideouts. Russian forces in Grozny claimed to control much of the city but were still wary of snipers ... "It was decided to prepare for a withdrawal of a considerable part of the troops engaged here", the first deputy chief of staff, General Valeri Manilov, told a news briefing. Russia has at least 93,000 troops in Chechenia. Russian military officials said resistance was drying up, suggesting that thousands of rebels had succeeded in escaping ... The cost of the exodus was high, Chechen officials acknowledged, as mines in particular inflicted heavy losses on guerrilla units ... Hundreds took shelter [in Alkhan-Kala] ... General Vladimir Shamanov ... said that the rebels had been tricked by secret agents from the intelligence service. Undercover operatives offered to open safe corridors for the rebels in return for $100,000, he said ... General Shamanov said that more than 580 guerrillas were killed leaving Grozny and another hundred in a Russian mop-up campaign ... A Chechen spokesman acknowledged that the rebels had suffered heavy casualties. A Chechen commander said 3,000 guerrillas had fled Grozny and would regroup in the mountainous south ... Russia said it had pinned down about 1,000 Chechen rebels who fled Grozny into a trap' (*IHT*, 5 February 2000, p. 5).

'Russian officials said that a total of 93,000 army and interior ministry troops had been posted to Chechenia, but thousands of troops would soon be sent home, leaving a permanent garrison of 15,000 troops' (*FT*, 7 February 2000, p. 6).

'A group of rebel fighters said to be 1,000 strong was still locked in a battle to break out of Alkhan Kala' (*The Times*, 5 February 2000, p. 9).

6 February 2000. Vladimir Putin: 'A short time ago the last bastion of resistance of the terrorists was seized, the Zavodskoi district of Grozny. A Russian flag has been raise on one of the administrative buildings, so we can say that the operation to liberate Grozny is over.'

7 February 2000. 'Combat flared in towns and hamlets west and south of Grozny ... Rebels were navigating paths to mountain strongholds and the Russians tried to stop them ... Russian officials say they will need another few weeks to complete the Chechenia-wide destruction of the rebel force, estimated to number between 2,000 and 7,000 ... The Russian claimed to have inflicted heavy casualties during the past day – 450 dead' (*IHT*, 8 February 2000, p. 7).

Defence minister Igor Sergeyev estimates the remaining rebel force at 5,000 to 7,000 (*The Independent*, 10 February 2000, p. 14).

According to Russia, the Chechens 'lost some 1,500 in their retreat' (*The Independent*, 8 February 2000, p. 15).

Russia claims to have killed 300 Chechen rebels on 6–7 February (*The Guardian*, 8 February 2000, p. 15).

8 February 2000. Russia estimates that up to 300 rebels and around 10,000 civilians are still in Grozny (*IHT*, 9 February 2000, p. 7).

There is an explosion in an apartment block in Khabarovsk in the far east. (A gas explosion seems the most likely cause.)

17 February 2000. Vladimir Kalamanov (head of the federal immigration service) is appointed as the special presidential representative in Chechenia 'for safeguarding human rights and liberties'.

18 February 2000. The Russian prosecutor opens criminal proceedings against Chechen president Aslan Maskhadov, charging him with 'armed insurrection ... with the aim of forcibly changing the constitutional order and territorial integrity of the Russian Federation'. He is also to be investigated for complicity in 'genocide' against ethnic Russians.

18 February 2000. A Russian helicopter is shot down in the mountain region of Shatoi.

20 February 2000. Russian forces claim to have captured Duba Yurt, the main entrance to the Argun Gorge.

22 February 2000. '[Human Rights Watch] claimed yesterday [22 February] that Russian troops summarily executed at least sixty-two people earlier this month in the worst massacre to date in the Chechen war. Survivors have described how around 100 soldiers systematically robbed and shot civilians on the southern outskirts of Grozny [the district of Aldi] in a two-day rampage that began on 5 February ... Researchers ... say the final figure could be as high as eighty-two' (*The Guardian*, 23 February 2000, p. 17). (On 2 June 2000 Human Rights Watch issued a report which claimed that sixty-two civilians were confirmed killed in the Aldi suburb of Grozny on 5 February. A further nineteen deaths were unconfirmed: *The Guardian*, 3 June 2000, p. 17.)

'The New York-based organization Human Rights Watch has complied what it calls a credible list of thirty victims in Aldi. Other survivors have circulated a list of eighty-two dead' (*IHT*, 23 February 2000, p. 1).

'Human Rights Watch says that sixty-two civilians were murdered in the Aldi district on 5 February' (*The Independent*, 24 February 2000, p. 17).

Peter Bouckaert: 'For months the international community's response to Russia's abusive campaign in Chechenia has been all talk and no action. In recent weeks, as allegations of summary executions emerged, even the rhetorical condemnations ceased ... I have been documenting these atrocities for Human Rights Watch during the last three months. I have evidence of more than 100 summary executions committed by Russian troops during the takeover of Grozny, acts of murder by Russian soldiers plain and simple, and I am investigating more. Most of the victims have been elderly men and women, who emerged from their cellars after months of bombing and shelling only to be shot down by Russian soldiers "liberating" Grozny. The Russian have detained hundreds of Chechen men in "filtration camps", where they are at risk of torture' (*IHT*, 26 February 2000, p. 8).

23 February 2000. 'Today marks the fifty-sixth anniversary of the start of the mass deportation of Chechens under Stalin ... About 650,000 Chechens were deported to central Asia and Siberia' (*The Guardian*, 23 February 2000, p. 17).

25 February 2000. A German television station makes public a videotape (made by a Russian journalist) showing Russian soldiers dumping bodies into two mass graves (some corpses with their hands tied behind their backs with wire and tied at the ankles). Some corpses showed signs of mutilation. There are differences of opinion as to the significance of the videotape.

The wife of the missing Russian reporter Andrei Babitsky says that her husband had telephoned her from Dagestan. (Babitsky was detained on 25 February for trying to cross into Azerbaijan on a false Azerbaijani passport. On 27 February he was formally arrested. But he was released and flown to Moscow on condition that he stayed there. He said he was personally beaten in the 'filtration' camp at Chernokozovo and heard others being tortured.)

27 February 2000. The Council of Europe's human rights commissioner, Alvaro Gil-Robles visits a refugee camp in Ingushetia. He hopes to visit the 'filtration' camp at Chernokozovo in Chechenia. The State Duma's human rights commissioner, Oleg Mironov, complains that he has been prevented from accompanying him. (Gil-Robles was allowed only a one-day visit to Grozny.)

29 February 2000. 'Igor Sergeyev, the Russian defence minister, told Mr Putin in Moscow yesterday [29 February] that "full scale operations in

Chechenia are over". Russian forces have taken the last rebel stronghold at the town of Shatoi. But Russian officers on the ground said the 2,000 Chechen guerrillas in Shatoi had simply disbursed into the surrounding region' (*The Independent*, 1 March 2000, p. 17). (Shatoi controls the Argun Gorge.)

Russian officials arrange a visit for journalists around the 'filtration' camp at Chernokozovo.

2 March 2000. A Russian column (mostly made up of the elite Omon riot police) is ambushed on the north-eastern outskirts of Grozny. The number of Russians reported dead was given as either twenty or thirty-seven.

'The Russian military believes that there are still about 2,500 rebels at large ... while independent observers put the number closer to 6,000' (*The Telegraph*, 4 March 2000, p. 7).

Vladimir Kalamanov says that a human rights office will soon be opened in northern Chechenia and that Russia has agreed to allow two representatives from the Council of Europe to be stationed there. But they will report to Vladimir Kalamanov and not to the council (*IHT*, 4 March 2000, p. 4).

5 March 2000. General Gennadi Troshev says that thirty-one Russian paratroopers have been killed in the fighting in the Argun Gorge since 3 March (*IHT*, 6 March 2000, p. 8). 'Russian leaders had said the Argun Gorge was under its control, but on Friday [3 March] rebels killed thirty-one Russian paratroopers in fierce battles near the villages of Ulus-Kert and Selmentausen as they tied to break out of the gorge into Chechenia's flatland. On Thursday [2 March] rebels killed at least twenty Russian police troops in an ambush near Grozny' (*IHT*, 7 March 2000, p. 7). 'Russia said Tuesday [7 March] that it had suffered "heavy" losses in fierce fighting in Chechenia in recent days, confirming that an earlier death toll of thirty-one was an understatement ... Sergei Yastrzhembsky said that an earlier statement that thirty-one paratroopers had been killed in recent fighting in southern Chechenia was now outdated. "The number of losses have increased because fierce fighting is continuing in this region", he said. But Mr Yastrzhembsky would neither confirm nor deny a report Tuesday [7 March] by the AVN press agency that quoted Russian military sources as saying eighty-six paratroopers were killed in fighting a week ago in the southern Argun Gorge' (*IHT*, 8 March 1000, p. 5). 'Russia on Thursday [9 March] acknowledged ... that eighty-four paratroopers died in four days of clashes last week near Ulus-Kert ... Only one soldier in an airborne detachment survived when it took on a much larger rebel group breaking out of Ulus-Kert on 29 February' (*IHT*, 10 March 2000, p. 1).

'Reports yesterday [6 March] from the north-western Russian town of Pskov – home to the elite seventy-sixth airborne guards division – said that between sixty and eighty paratroops were killed fighting in the Argun Gorge ... The governor of the Pskov region ... said he had been told that sixty to eighty paratroops had been killed in the mountains ... Moscow has estimated that 5,000 Chechen guerrillas are trapped in the mountains' (*The Guardian*, 7 March 2000, p. 15).

6 March 2000. 'The threat posed by the rebel hit-and-run tactics caused the government yesterday [6 March] to call off two trips to Chechenia by Russian and international human rights monitors' (*The Guardian*, 7 March 2000, p. 15).

10 March 2000. 'After days of denial the Russian authorities reported Friday [10 March] that their forces suffered heavy losses in Chechenia in the last ten days, in a war they all but declared won just a week ago. In all, 156 Russians were killed since the beginning of the month ... Officials confirmed in particular a report from a regional governor of numerous combat deaths in a single company from the town of Pskov in western Russia. The unit lost eighty-four soldiers between 29 February and 3 March in fighting in and around the Argun Gorge in south-central Chechenia, said General Valeri Manilov, a deputy chief of staff' (*IHT*, 11 March 2000, p. 4). Eighty-five paratroops were killed then (*The Independent*, 15 March 2000, p. 15).

12 March 2000. Russian forces capture the Chechen field commander Salman Raduyev.

'The Chechen rebels ... remain ... in numbers estimated anywhere from 1,500 to 7,000' (*IHT*, 15 March 2000, p. 1).

14 March 2000. 'Russian troops have finally seized the strategic village of Komsomolskoye in South Chechenia after nine days of fierce battles ... Russian troops finally took control ... late on Tuesday [14 March]. Chechens seized Komsomolskoye on 6 March' (*IHT*, 16 March 2000, p. 4).

19 March 2000. 'Russian forces pulled out of the southern Chechen village of Komsomolskoye on Sunday [19 March] while artillery units prepared to shell the town to flush out rebel holdouts, the military command said. The military had claimed to have retaken Komsomolskoye earlier this week' (*IHT*, 20 March 2000, p. 6).

20 March 2000. Putin flies into an airport outside Gronzy to meet Russian troops.

21 March 2000. Russia claims that Komsomolskoye is now under its control (*The Times*, 22 March 2000, p. 16).

22 March 2000. The Russians are still trying to capture Komsomolskoye (*The Independent*, 23 March 2000, p. 16).

26 March 2000. Chechen fighters claim to have captured the village of Nozhai-Yurt, near the border with Dagestan. Russia dismisses the claim.

29 March 2000. Thirty-two Russian servicemen are killed in an ambush in Chechenia. Others are missing.

'As many as forty-three Russian soldiers and police died' (*IHT*, 4 April 2000, p. 4). A forty-nine-strong column was ambushed, resulting in the death of as many as thirty-six policemen from the Perm region (*IHT*, 17 April 2000, p. 4). (On 1 May 2000 Russian troops found the bodies of nine missing combat policemen. The men were in a unit of forty-one paramilitary fighters from the city of Perm who were ambushed on 29 March: *IHT*, 2 May 2000, p. 1.)

'Chechen rebels said yesterday [5 April] that they had killed nine Russian paramilitary police captured in an ambush after Moscow refused to hand over a colonel accused of raping and murdering a Chechen woman. The men were captured when a special-forces unit was wiped out in an attack by guerrillas near Zhani-Vedeno, in the mountains of southern Chechenia. Forty-three of those killed came from Perm, in the Urals' (*The Independent*, 6 April 2000, p. 16).

30 March 2000. It is announced that the Red Cross will be allowed into Chechenia. Visits to 'filtration camps' will be permitted.

'The gesture was the second in two days ... On Wednesday [29 March] officials said that an officer suspected of raping and murdering Chechen woman would be prosecuted ... the first time Moscow has taken steps to prosecute any of its soldiers for abusing civilians' (*IHT*, 31 March 2000, p. 4).

31 March 2000. Mary Robinson, the United Nations High Commissioner for Human Rights, arrives for a five-day visit.

2 April 2000. Mary Robinson travels to Chechenia but her request to visit five 'infiltration camps' is refused.

3 April 2000. '[Mary Robinson] returned to Moscow on Monday [3 April] from Chechenia after the Russian authorities barred access to a detention centre and towns where atrocities against civilians allegedly took place ... A spokesman for Mary Robinson ... said she requested a visit to a "filtration camp" in the town of Urus-Martan ... and three hamlets near Grozny' (*IHT*, 4 April 2000, p. 4).

'Vladimir Putin ... yesterday [3 April] refused to meet Mary Robinson ... for discussions about Chechenia' (*FT*, 4 April 2000, p. 12).

'Her Russian hosts added insult to injury by cancelling meetings with senior government officials in Moscow yesterday after her return from the north Caucasus was delayed by a day, officially because inclement weather kept her grounded in Dagestan' (*The Guardian*, 4 April 2000, p. 15).

4 April 2000. Mary Robinson ends her visit to Russia with a meeting with foreign minister Igor Ivanov.

Mary Robinson: '"I do believe that there have been serious human rights violations" in Chechenia, Mrs Robinson told reporters after a five-day visit to Russian that included a trip to Chechenia' (*IHT*, 5 April 2000, p. 4).

'In Moscow yesterday ... Mary Robinson stressed the need for an "independent, national investigation" of human rights violations in Chechenia, a significant shift from the earlier call for an international inquiry' (*The Guardian*, 5 April 2000, p. 18).

(See the 6 April 2000 decision by the Council of Europe, above.)

5 April 2000. Mary Robinson reports on her 31 March to 4 April visit: 'During my visit to the region I heard allegations of mass killings, summary executions, rape, torture and pillage ... I focussed in my discussions in Moscow yesterday [4 April] with foreign minister Ivanov and with other ministers and officials on encouraging the establishment, according to recognized international standards, of a national, broad-based independent commission of inquiry into the serious allegations ... I met with President

Aushev [of Ingushetia] and heard from him about the efforts his government is making to cope with the flood of IDPs [internally displaced persons] fom Chechenia – whose number totals, according to the best estimates, 213,000' (*The New York Review of Books*, vol. XLVII, no. 9, pp. 12–13).

13 April 2000. 'Russia's foreign minister said Thursday [13 April] that Russia was actively seeking a political settlement to the war in Chechenia ... But the minister, Igor Ivanov, declined to spell out just with whom the Russians were talking ... Other officials said this week that the Kremlin had opened contacts with the Chechen president, Aslan Maskhadov' (*IHT*, Friday 14 April 2000, p. 4).

'The Russian government said yesterday [13 April] that it was talking directly to rebel representatives in Chechenia ... Mr Ivanov said the government was conducting a "direct dialogue" with the Chechens and was "confident that this would lead to concrete results". His comments were interpreted as an indication that talks were being held with ... Aslan Maskhadov. Chechen sources confirmed yesterday that talks had been under way with Mr Maskhadov since the beginning of April through local intermediaries – the president of Ingushetia, Ruslan Aushev, and the president of North Ossetia, Alexander Dzasokhov. Mr Ivanov said the "Russian leadership has always advocated a political settlement in Chechenia, been prepared for dialogue and never closed the door on anybody". It was only this week that the Kremlin spokesman on Chechenia, Sergei Yastrzhemsky, began to hint at a change, commenting: "We have repeatedly made Moscow's point of view known to Maskhadov – in an attempt to launch some kind of political process." Mr Maskhadov ... on Monday [10 April] publicly distanced himself from the two leading warlords. He said they were responsible for starting the war' (*The Guardian*, 14 April 2000, p. 14).

14 April 2000. It is announced that Brigadier General Apti Batalov, Aslan Maskhadov's military chief of staff, has been captured by Russian forces.

17 April 2000. Putin (on a visit to the UK): 'The actions of Russia are a struggle against extremism. They are directed entirely against extremism and terrorism. For Russia it is completely unacceptable there should be a situation in which one of its republics is used as a launching pad for undermining Russian statehood and Russian sovereignty.'

Russia announces that an independent, domestic commission of inquiry into alleged human rights abuses in Chechenia will be set up.

'Russian government officials said the commission of inquiry into alleged human rights atrocities would be independent. But the commission's members are individuals who have taken a broadly sympathetic line towards Mr Putin. They include Pavel Krasheninikov (a former justice minister), Ella Pamfilova (a presidential candidate); Pavel Polayok (a writer) and Mikhail Kozhokhin (chief editor of the Izvestia newspaper) (*FT*, 18 April 2000, p. 2).

20 April 2000. In an interview in *Kommersant* Aslan Maskhadov says he has ordered his forces to stop fighting Russian troops in Chechenia as a step to start peace talks. He also says that he has ordered the release of Russian prisoners and that he is in control of rebel forces fighting in the Chechenia. He says that he has criticized the Dagestan invasions by Shamil Basayev and Khattab as 'a provocation against the Chechen people'. Maskhadov: 'I gave the order unilaterally to suspend military action. This was part of a plan for a peaceful settlement I proposed to Moscow.' (*The Independent*, 21 April 2000, p. 15; *IHT*, 21 April 2000, p. 1, and 22 April 2000, p. 2.)

Russia's reaction was negative. 'Mr Putin said Russia regarded Mr Maskhadov as a criminal. Moscow was not interested in anything less than the release of all hostages in Chechenia and the surrender of warlords responsible for raids on Russia' (*The Independent*, 22 April 2000, p. 15).

21 April 2000. 'The Kremlin is willing to grant amnesty to the Chechen leader … if he accepts Moscow's conditions … "Moscow's conditions for initiating political talks remain unchanged: the unconditional and immediate release of all hostages, and the surrender of all rebels. We know their names very well … If Maskhadov wants to hold talks but cannot deliver the rebels, we are prepared to help him. Let him enter into the talks and catch the bandits in conjunction with us", Putin said' (*Kommersant*, 22 April 2000, p. 3; *CDSP*, 2000, vol. 52, no. 17, p. 8).

'In a sign that Russia is looking for a political solution to its war in Chechenia, President-elect Putin acknowledged for the first time Friday [21 April] that Moscow had exchanged peace plans with the Chechen president, Aslan Maskhadov. Mr Putin, speaking to reporters, said he still regarded Mr Maskhadov as a "criminal" but one who could be amnestied … Russia … this week again opened the way for European observers to travel to Chechenia … Russian authorities have this week begun to allow residents back into Grozny' (*IHT*, 22 April 2000, p. 2).

23 April 2000. 'Russian troops have finished a two-month operation to clear … [Grozny] of land mines … A delegation from the European Committee for the Prevention of Torture visited a huge detention camp at Chernokozovo' (*IHT*, 24 April 2000, p. 5).

24 April 2000. 'Russia said Monday [24 April] that fifteen of it soldiers had been killed in a Chechen rebel ambush of a supply convoy [on Sunday 23 April], but the guerrillas claimed that the Russian death toll was eighty … More than fifty Russian soldiers and police officers had already been killed in Chechen ambushes over the last two months. The latest fighting has undermined talk of a truce in the region. The Chechen president, Aslan Maskhadov, denied that he ordered a unilateral ceasefire last week. Mr Maskhadov was quoted by the newspaper Kommersant last Friday [21 April] as saying he had ordered his men to stop firing as part of a proposed peace deal. The US-funded Radio Liberty quoted him Sunday [23 April] as saying: 'They did not understand me properly" and adding that he was ready only for a bilateral ceasefire, and then only if negotiations were started. The Russian president-elect, Vladimir Putin, had in any case scorned Mr Maskhadov's ability to arrange a ceasefire, saying he did not control all the guerrillas and could not guarantee that the terms of any peace deal would be respected ... President Ruslan Aushev of Ingushetia ... estimates there are still 17,000 active rebels' (*IHT*, 25 April 2000, p. 5). (In mid-March 2000 the Russian authorities put the number of Chechen rebels at about 5,000: *CDSP*, 2000, vol. 52, no. 12, p. 9.)

25 April 2000. 'Rebel snipers have resumed shooting in Grozny, Russia said Tuesday [25 April], warning that 500 well-armed Chechen fighters remained [in Grozny]' (*IHT*, 26 April 2000, p. 6).

27 April 2000. Russia says that ten Russian soldiers were killed, including a senior officer, in an ambush the previous day, while seventeen rebels died (*IHT*, 28 April 2000, p. i).

A Russian military spokesman says that ten of its soldiers were killed and that the bodies of twenty-five Chechens were found. The Chechens say that only one Chechen was killed while twenty Russian soldiers were killed. The Chechens also claim that thirty Russians were killed on 23 April' (*The Independent*, 28 April 2000, p. 17).

'On Thursday [27 April], in an interview published by the newspaper *Novaya Gazeta*, Mr Maskhadov said he was prepared to work with Russia ... "I am 100 per cent sure that I would be able to find a mutually acceptable solution with any politician", he said. Mr Maskhadov also claimed in the interview that the latest conflict was started by the Russian as well as "some of our short-sighted, radically minded people ... I was categorically against the actions which they undertook ... I was trying to prevent them at any cost. I even got in touch with the leadership of Russia and Dagestan. Alas, I failed" ... The Russian leadership on Thursday immediately dismissed the interview and the possibility of talks with Mr Maskhadov' (*IHT*, 28 April 2000, p. i).

10 May 2000. 'The head of a Russian commission investigating the wars in Chechenia [Pavel Krasheninnikov] met Wednesday [10 May] with a former Chechen interior minister [Kazbek Makhashev] who is close to the Chechen president' (*IHT*, 11 May 2000, p. 4). 'Pavel Krasheninnikov, the head of an independent Russian commission looking into wartime abuses, had met in Ingushetia with a top representative of the Chechen president' (*IHT*, 12 May 2000, p. 5).

11 May 2000. Russia says that eighteen of its troops were killed on Thursday 11 May in a Chechen ambush in Ingushetia.

'With Thursday's deaths, General Valeri Manilov [first deputy chief of the Russian general staff] said, 2,251 Russian servicemen have died in the Chechen conflict ... Rebel leaders had threatened Tuesday [9 May] to carry the war for Chechen independence into nearby provinces unless Russian troops withdraw by the end of May' (*IHT*, 12 May 2000, p. 5).

'The Council of Europe ... dropped the threat Thursday [11 May] at a meeting in Strasbourg after foreign minister Igor Ivanov argued that Russia has established its own agency to investigate allegations of crimes and human rights abuses by its troops' (*IHT,* 12 May 2000, p. 5). 'After hearing a conciliatory statement by Igor Ivanov ... a ministerial meeting in Strasbourg concluded that Russia was "taking steps towards meeting the concerns" of the Council of Europe ... Ministers will therefore tell the next session in June of the Council of Europe's parliamentary assembly, which has only consultative powers, that there is at present no case for suspending Russia. In its fifty-one-year history the Council has never totally suspended any member, though it came close with Greece and Turkey. Ministers said they were "encouraged" by Mr Ivanov's statement on holding a political dialogue and negotiations with peaceful elements in Chechen, as well as his commitment to speed arrangements for the Council of Europe representatives to join the newly-appointed Russian human rights commissioner in Chechenia' (*FT,* 12 May 2000, p. 8).

14 May 2000. 'About 130 rebels have surrendered with their weapons and have been released ... Russian officials said. But most rebels were said to scorn the [amnesty] offer, which expires Monday [15 May]' (*IHT,* 15 May 2000, p. 7).

29 May 2000. Putin (meeting a delegation from the EU): 'All violations of law in Chechenia, whoever has committed them, will be resolutely stamped out' (*IHT,* 30 May 2000, p. 4).

30 May 2000. An ambush on the outskirts of Grozny results in the death of Colonel Sergei Zverev, the deputy civilian representative of the Russian government in Chechenia (i.e. deputy to Nikolai Koshman, the chief envoy in Chechenia). The deputy mayor of Grozny was also killed. The mayor of Grozny, the Supyan Makhchayev (an ethnic Chechen), was wounded and there was speculation that he was the intended victim. Offensive operations in the southern mountains and near the border with Dagestan against Chechen rebels continued. (*IHT,* 1 June 2000, p. 5; *The Times,* 1 June 2000, p. 17; *The Guardian,* 1 June 2000, p. 16.)

Two Russian soldiers are killed in a bomb explosion near a military base in the southern city of Volgograd. It was unclear whether the incident was connected with Chechenia (*IHT,* 1 June 2000, p. 5).

Bislan Gantemirov, the leader of the a pro-Moscow Chechen militia force, has been dismissed for 'systematic absenteeism' (*The Times,* 1 June 2000, p. 17). 'Mr Koshman sacked Bislan Gantemirov ... on Tuesday [30 May]. Mr Gantemirov is a convicted embezzler and former mayor of Grozny recruited by the Russians months ago as head of a pro-Russian Chechen militia ... Hostility between the Russian forces and the Gantemiriv men has been soaring for the past month. Mt Koshman admitted that the militiamen were "uncontrollable" and said almost 300 of them had been sacked for "absenteeism"'(*The Guardian,* 1 June 2000, p. 16).

31 May 2000. Customs officials at Moscow's Sheremetyevo airport confiscate a report by Amnesty International on human rights violations in Chechenia.

2 June 2000. Chechen rebels undertook a rocket attack on Russian army headquarters in Grozny and claim to have killed fifteen Russian soldiers (*The Guardian*, 3 June 2000, p. 17).

7 June 2000. Chechen rebels claim that at least seventeen Russian soldiers died during a suicide bomb attack on a Russian army base. This was the first suicide attack (*The Times*, 8 June 2000, p. 17).

Russia says that two Russian police officers were killed (*IHT*, 8 June 2000, p. 5).

8 June 2000. Putin imposes direct presidential rule over Chechenia 'for what his aides said would be a period of up to three years' (*The Guardian*, 9 June 2000, p. 18).

'It is stipulated that the law [On Organizing a Temporary System of Executive Agencies in the Chechen Republic] will be in effect for a "transitional period", until a legislative body is elected and Chechen republic executive agencies and bodies of local self-government are formed. Federal or, in effect, presidential rule is being introduced in Chechenia' (*CDSP*, 2000, vol. 52, no. 24, p. 10).

11 June 2000. A Chechen suicide bomber kills two Russian soldiers, according to Russia. The Chechen rebels say that four were killed (*The Telegraph*, 13 June 2000, p. 20).

12 June 2000. President Putin appoints Akhmad Kadyrov to head the administration in Chechenia.

Kadyrov will work under the supervision of Viktor Kazantsev, former commander of the joint group of federal forces in Chechenia and now the president's representative in the North Caucasus Federal District (*CDSP*, 2000, vol. 52, no. 24, p. 9).

'The [Moslem] cleric once favoured independence for Chechenia, but fell out with President Aslan Maskhadov and supported the September ground invasion ... Already this year Mr Kadyrov was the target of two assassination attempts' (*IHT*, 13 June 2000, p. 5). 'Mufti [chief Moslem cleric] Akhmad Kadyrov, the official Islamic leader in Chechenia, is to become chief administrator of the republic ... Mr Kadyrov fought in the first Chechen war from 1994 to 1996 but has criticised both Aslan Maskhadov and the brutality of Russia' (*FT*, 13 June 2000, p. 10. (The inauguration of Mufti Akhmad Kadyrov took place on 20 June.)

Russia denies the claim of Chechen rebels that five Russian soldiers were killed in the third suicide bomb attack (*IHT*, 14 June 2000, p. 11).

23 June 2000. Russia has reduced its forces in Chechenia to 48,958, compared with a peak of almost 100,000 during the battle for Grozny earlier in the year (*The Independent*, 24 June 2000, p. 16).

25 June 2000. 'The Russian military said Sunday [25 June] that it had suspended major offensive operations in Chechenia, a move intended to build support for the new Kremlin-appointed administrator ... Colonel General Gennadi Troshev, the senior commander of Russian forces in the region, made the announcement after meeting with Akhmad Kadyrov ... 'An agreement was reached that the Unified Army Group is not conducting offensive operations and not carrying out aviation or artillery strikes' [said General Troshev] ... A former Moslem religious leader, Mr Kadyrov recently resigned his religious post as Mufti of Chechenia' (*IHT*, 26 June 2000, p. 1).

26 June 2000. 'One day after a top Russian military commander announced a halt to artillery and air strikes in Chechenia, the Kremlin said Monday [26 June] that the attacks would continue' (*IHT*, 27 June 2000, p. 1).

28 June 2000. Russia admits that twelve Russian soldiers have been killed in fighting which has already lasted three days (*IHT*, 29 June 2000, p. 6).

2–3 July 2000. Chechen rebels undertake a co-ordinated series of five suicide missions using lorries packed with explosives. Early Russian estimates put the number killed at fifty-four, thirty-seven of them Russian servicemen (and others missing). The attack on 2 July on a military dormitory in Argun alone accounted for at least thirty-six killed (at least twenty-five of them Russian servicemen).

On 4 July Russia said that thirty-three Russian servicemen had been killed (twenty-two at Argun) and three were missing.

9 July 2000. There are two bomb explosions in areas near Chechenia. A bomb explosion in a central market in Vladikavkaz in North Ossetia kills five (another died later) and another outside a shop in Rostov-on-Don kills two.

'This week EU foreign ministers released $55 million in aid to Russia that they had frozen last December to protest the war [in Chechenia]' (*IHT*, Thursday 13 July 2999, p. 6).

28 July 2000. There are reports of talks between Russia and Aslan Maskhadov (*The Times*, 29 July 2000, p. 14; *The Independent*, 29 July 2000, p. 14).

8 August 2000. A bomb explosion in a Moscow pedestrian underpass kills twelve people.

There was widespread speculation that Chechen rebels were to blame, but the following day Putin said: 'A crime was perpetrated, either the result of a criminal feud or an act of terrorism. Discussing the terrorist version I have to state that it is not right to look for an ethnic connection, a Chechen connection to this or any other crime. It is wrong to brand a whole people. Criminals and terrorists are not confined to any one nationality or religion.'

'Federal prosecutors say that the bomb ... was probably planted by somebody settling a business dispute ... The deputy head of the interior ministry's department for economic crimes was quoted as saying that evidence was accumulating against businessmen "whose interests are concentrated at Pushkin Square". He was presumably referring to gang wars between the different groups that control stallholders selling cheap goods in the underpasses' (*The Independent*, 13 September 2000, p. 13).

12 September 2000. The head of Ukraine's security service announced that an attempt to assassinate Putin during a conference of nine CIS members in the Crimea had been foiled. Information had been provided by foreign (non-CIS) secret services. Putin attended the summit for only one day (18 August) because he had to return to Russian to deal with the sinking of the Kursk nuclear submarine. Four people from Chechenia and several others from the Middle East had been arrested and expelled from Ukraine.

21 September 2000. 'Up to four masked men took several people hostage in the Black Sea resort of Lazarevskoye on Thursday [21 September] and Russian news agencies said they were demanding $30 million and the release of Chechen prisoners. But an aide to Viktor Kazantsev, the presidential representative in southern Russia, was quoted as saying the hostage drama – near the main resort centre of Sochi ... had no link to Moscow's military campaign [in Chechenia]' (*IHT,* 22 September 2000, p. 5). 'They initially demanded $30 million or the release of all Chechen prisoners in Russian jails, as well as talks with President Vladimir Putin. Later they also demanded a helicopter and dropped the demand for releasing Chechens. By Friday [22 September] they were no longer asking for ransom and surrendered at midday ... [Russian] officials suggested that the incident might have been a fake hostage-taking started on a drunken whim' (*IHT,* 23 September 2000, p. 2).

6 October 2000. There are (unattributed) bomb explosions in the two southern Russian towns of Pyatigorsk and Nevinnomyssk.

Andrei Babitsky is convicted of using false documents. A small fine is imposed but even that will not be paid because it is covered by the May 2000 amnesty.

28 November 2000. 'A two-day [OSCE] conference [in Vienna] ended ... Russia refused to accept a specific deadline for the return of an organization observation mission to Chechenia. Russia agreed at the organization summit meeting last year [1999] in Istanbul to accept such a mission, but the members have been unable to reach [Chechenia]' (*IHT,* 29 November 2000, p. 6).

'President Putin created a cabinet post to oversee the rebuilding of Chechenia. He appointed Vladimir Yelagin ... minister for "socio-economic development" in the region' (*The Telegraph*, 29 November 2000, p. 16).

CHAPTER TWELVE

A CHRONOLOGY OF POLITICAL DEVELOPMENTS, 1992–2000

The vagueness of the (much amended) 1977 constitution and the general lack of clarity about decision-making powers left the status of presidential decrees in the air. The conflict between president and parliament was to lead to a violent dénouement.

A CHRONOLOGY OF EVENTS PRIOR TO THE DISSOLUTION OF PARLIAMENT ON 21 SEPTEMBER 1993

In the run-up to the seventh session of the Russian Congress of People's Deputies (1–14 December 1992) Yeltsin tried to mollify the industrial lobby, but at the same time sought new powers to push the main elements of the reforms along. On 29 July 1992 he expressed a wish that in 1993 he should have powers to rule by decree and to appoint top executives for a transitional period. He also thought that the Congress of People's Deputies should be scrapped. Earlier, in a 7 July 1992 decree, Yeltsin had given wide powers to the 'security council' to help determine and implement policy; the four permanent members were Yeltsin, Rutskoi, Gaidar and Yuri Skokov. Yeltsin also set up a Council of the Leaders of the Republics of the Russian Federation, which first met on 15 October 1992. Skokov was appointed secretary of the former council and head of the latter council. In a 6 October 1992 speech to parliament Yeltsin talked of the need to modify the economic reform programme to some extent. On the same day Gaidar stressed the need to tighten fiscal and monetary policy and ruled out the Chinese economic model on the grounds that China was not a democracy with political opposition: 'Russia is not China ... China has retained a powerful structure of authoritarian management; all attempts by the opposition to destabilize the situation have been cruelly suppressed ... in order to follow the Chinese path it would have been necessary to work out a political strategy different from the one that the Russian parliament voted for in 1990.' (Note that on 18 December 1992 Yeltsin, during a visit to China, commented on that country's economic system. China began their economic reform fourteen years ago, while Russia only started in January 1992. 'The Chinese tactics of reform is not to hurry, not to force, without revolutions, without cataclysms, which is very important, and I think that for us has a certain significance. Russia does not need revolutions or cataclysms either': *IHT*, 19 December 1992, p. 5.)

October 1992 brought forth claims of a possible 'constitutional coup', to be carried out by those opposed to the government's reform process. On 21 October Yeltsin tried, unsuccessfully, to persuade parliament to postpone the opening of the new session of the Congress of People's Deputies from 1 December 1992 (when his power to issue decrees without legislative approval would come to an end) to March 1993. On 28 October 1992 Yeltsin banned the National Salvation Front (established only three days earlier by communists and nationalists opposed to Yeltsin and the government) for calling for 'the overthrow of the legally constituted authorities' and for 'destabilizing society'. Yeltsin also banned the 5,000-strong parliamentary guard, which had been formed in October 1991 and which had become directly answerable to the speaker of parliament, Ruslan Khasbulatov.

On 29 October 1992 Yeltsin announced that he would halt the troop withdrawal from the Baltic States (although the process actually continued). He claimed the need to protect Russian civilians and to come to an agreement about the social rights of Russian soldiers and their families. Yeltsin sent extra troops to the Russian autonomous republic of North Ossetia on 1 November 1992 to intervene in the fighting between Ossetian and Ingush forces. The Ingush claim the right to land in North Ossetia taken from them in 1944. On 2 November 1992 Yeltsin declared a state of emergency in North Ossetia and Ingushetia to last until 2 December 1992.

A chronology of events is as follows:

14 November 1992. Yeltsin attended a congress of the Union of Industrialists and Entrepreneurs. The union and the government were to try to reach agreement before the start of the next and crucial session of the Congress of People's Deputies on 1 December 1992. Yeltsin, however, ruled out 1 trillion roubles in fresh credits, the restoration of state orders and price and wage freezes.

25 November 1992. Deputy prime minister and information minister, Mikhail Poltoranin, resigned. This was seen as a concession to the industrial lobby, as was the abolition the next day of the post of state secretary, which was created for Gennadi Burbulis. (Note that Burbulis was immediately reappointed as head of a presidential advisory council. On 26 December 1992 Poltoranin was put in charge of the Federal Information Centre, a newly created body designed 'to increase the role of the press, news agencies, television and radio in elucidating state policy … to secure through print and the mass media, the distribution of timely and wide information about the progress of reforms in Russia and to clarify government policy'.)

26 November 1992. In a speech to parliament Gaidar committed the government to the main principles of the reform programme; there could be 'no retreat from the strategic course of changes … we are not ready to combine incompatible approaches'. Specifically, Gaidar ruled out a return to a centralized distribution of resources, a price and wage freeze, a 'limitless' money supply and intervention to support the rouble at an artificial rate. The acting prime minister was prepared, however, to provide extra support during the transition period for those enterprises with a long-term future.

29 November 1992. Yeltsin declared that: 'Radical reforms need a strong social base and an appropriate structure, maybe a party, maybe a political movement.'

30 November 1992. The Russian constitutional court decided that Yeltsin was correct in banning the CPSU and the Russian Communist Party at the national level. (The court avoided a ruling on the question of whether the party had acted unconstitutionally or in criminal fashion. The court simply said that by the time of the ban the former had effectively ceased to exist and the latter had not been officially registered.) But the court also decided that Yeltsin had been wrong to ban the local branches of the communist party (the primary organizations), since their members had been elected and had paid for local property out of dues. The court drew a distinction between state property, which should not be returned, and party property which should. (Local property should be returned, for example, but the vagueness of the distinction meant that disputes would have to be resolved on a case-by-case basis.)

1–14 December 1992. The seventh session of the Russian Congress of People's Deputies is held.

In his speech to the 1,041 deputies of the Congress of People's Deputies Yeltsin stressed the need for a breathing space of between a year and eighteen months to consolidate the reforms: 'We favour a strict and coherent state and industrial policy that would lead us along the golden path between the freedoms of the market and a regulatory role for the state … In the period of building a market economy, we need a well-considered protectionism.' Yeltsin proposed the indexing of savings.

Ruslan Khasbulatov pleaded for a 'Scandinavian' rather than an 'American' type of economic system. Gaidar argued that there was little room to manoeuvre as regards economic reform. He criticized the alternatives put forward by Khasbulatov: 'At the moment the choice is more crucial. It is between pursuing reforms or giving in to criminal delays which are pulling our country down … the real dilemma facing our society is far more dramatic than a choice between these two models.' If the reforms are not pursued 'then we will develop not according to the American or Swedish pattern, but according to African or Latin American patterns … [leading to] the chronic poverty and political instability, the populist politicians and dictatorships so common in Third World states.' Arms sales would continue to 'reliable' partners, but not to zones of conflict. (Recent deals included the export of arms to China, India, Iran and Syria.) On 1 January 1993 proper border posts would be set up, for export control for example. On the following day, however, Gaidar made a more conciliatory speech: 'Our friends and colleagues from the centrist factions underestimate the opportunities for compromise and flexibility in co-operation to build a normal, civilized economy.' A slower rise in the price of oil to the world level was promised.

On 4 December congress voted 668 to 210 (with thirty-four abstentions) in favour of a resolution expressing dissatisfaction with a government economic reform programme deemed 'contrary to the interests of the majority of citizens'. The following day a resolution giving the Supreme Soviet and the CPD the right to approve all top government posts failed to achieve the required two-thirds majority (694), but the shortfall was only four votes. (Note that the Supreme Soviet already had the power to approve a 'full-time' prime minister, Gaidar being only an 'acting' premier; Yeltsin could keep Gaidar in that role for three months before submitting a name for approval.) On 5 December congress approved an amendment to the constitution allowing land sales subject to restrictions (albeit reduced, e.g. sales would be allowed after five rather than ten years). Deputy prime minister Chubais revealed that the government would like a voucher scheme to apply to land privatization.

Yeltsin offered to allow the Supreme Soviet the right of veto over the defence, security, interior and foreign ministers in return for approving Gaidar as prime minister. The CPD accepted this offer the next day, but still rejected Gaidar as prime minister by 486 to 467 (a simple majority of 521 being needed for approval).

Yeltsin savagely attacked the congress on 10 December: 'Congress is a bulwark of conservative forces and reaction. The reforms which have been carried out for a year in Russia are in serious jeopardy. A high-powered offensive has been launched at the congress against the course pursued by the president and the government, against those real changes that have kept the country from economic disaster throughout the past months. What they failed to do in August 1991, they have decided to repeat now by means of a creeping coup. We are being pushed towards a dangerous brink beyond which there is nothing but destabilization and economic chaos. We are being pushed towards civil war. I see only one way out of the most profound crisis of power, a nationwide referendum ... I am proposing that the congress schedule a referendum for January 1993 with the following wording: "Who should be given the task of taking the country out of the economic and political crisis, of reviving the Russian Federation? The President of the Russian Federation or the presently constituted Congress of People's Deputies and Supreme Soviet?" Yeltsin said he would resign if he lost the referendum to be held on 24 January 1993 and a fresh presidential election would follow. If Yeltsin won, parliamentary elections would be held on 27 March 1993. Yeltsin asked his supporters to start collecting the one million signatures needed for a referendum in the absence of support from one-third of the deputies in the CPD. He also called upon reformist deputies to follow him out of the congress hall, but only around 150 did so. The CPD reacted by adopting a resolution which would ask people whether they support early elections for the presidency (whose mandate expired in June 1996) and for the CPD (elected for the period March 1990–March 1995). The congress also adopted a constitutional amendment providing for the impeachment of the president if he tried to introduce a state of emergency without its consent. The chairman of the constitutional court, Valery Zorkin, called on Yeltsin and Khasbulatov to meet under his auspices to seek a compromise.

On 11 December 1992 congress voted to amend the law to preclude a referendum that would result in the dissolution of any high state body before the end of its term. The opposing camps met only briefly and issued a statement agreeing to settle problems by 'constitutional means'. The following day a compromise was reached. Gennadi Burbulis was dismissed as Yeltsin's adviser and a nine-point accord was agreed. The accord included the following elements:

1. Yeltsin would present to congress a list of candidates for prime minister. The president would be able to choose one of the three candidates receiving the highest congressional votes. If Yeltsin's choice was not endorsed by congress, he could appoint an acting premier until the next session of congress in April 1993.

2. A referendum was to be held on 11 April 1993 on the basic principles of a new constitution.

3. Before the referendum congress would abstain from considering any laws changing the balance of power between the executive, the legislature and the judiciary.

4. Congress would have the right of veto over the defence, security, interior and foreign ministers.

The final day of the December session of the congress produced a shock result. Yeltsin (reluctantly) chose Viktor Chernomyrdin as prime minister and congress (enthusiastically) endorsed him by 721 votes to 172. Yeltsin had produced a list of five candidates for congress to consider, but Gaidar only came a poor third with 400 votes, behind Yuri Skokov (637) and Chernomyrdin (621). Gaidar resigned as acting premier and announced that he would not join the new government. Nevertheless, he was convinced that the changes 'have a great momentum of their own and it is very difficult to reverse them'; 'the main lines [of the reforms] have been set down and they will continue' (although he later expressed concern that the privatization programme might be amended to increase the proportion of shares going to workers and managers). (On 17 December 1992 Yeltsin announced that Gaidar was to become his personal adviser on economic policy. Gaidar had just taken up the post of director of the Institute for Economic Problems in the Transitional Period.)

Viktor Chernomyrdin had been made energy minister and a deputy prime minister on 30 May 1992, one of a number of more interventionist-minded industrialists appointed around that time as a concession to the industrial lobby. (He had become gas industry minister in February 1985 and head of Gasprom in 1989.) A flavour of his ideas can be detected in some of Chernomyrdin's comments after his appointment: 'I am for reforms, in favour of deepening reforms, but without impoverishing the people'; 'the reforms should now take a somewhat different tone ... First of all, the decline of production must be stopped. No reform can proceed if industry is in ruins ... We are going to give priority to basic industries ... A country like ours, with its great wealth and powerful infrastructure, should not turn into a nation of shopkeepers'; 'I am for a market economy, but not for a bazaar. I am for a real market'; 'I have never given anyone reason to say that the course of reform would be changed under my leadership. I am for deepening reforms. There is no way back.' Chernomyrdin repeated, however, that the priority was to stop the fall in industrial production. He also saw the need for controls on energy prices and he quickly increased credits to the energy sector. While he supported privatization, he did not favour 'landslide privatization'. (Chernomyrdin proved to be a pragmatic personality. He remained prime minister until 23 March 1998.)

Yeltsin visited China 17–19 December 1992 (a number of political, military and economic agreements being signed and the two countries pledging 'to regard each other as friends'). He returned to Russia earlier than planned, saying that 'they have begun to fight for portfolios too early, to pull apart the cabinet, so the master must return and restore order there'. On 20 December it was announced that the 'core' of the reform team was to be retained, that the 'basic current team' was to be preserved. This proved to be the case when the actual list of cabinet ministers was revealed on 23 December. The reformist casualty was Pyotr Aven, the minister of foreign economic relations (he was in charge of negotiations with the West about debt rescheduling), who had resigned the previous day in anticipation. He was replaced by his deputy, Sergei Glazyev. Boris Fyodorov was appointed as a deputy prime minister with the role of co-ordinating overall financial and economic policy. (He had resigned as Russian finance minister in 1990 over the slow pace of reform in the then republic of the former Soviet Union. He subsequently took positions in the EBRD and the World Bank. In late March 1993 he gained the finance ministry as well.) The other new deputy prime minister to be appointed was Yuri Yarov, the deputy speaker of the Supreme Soviet. (Note that on 22 December the Supreme Soviet confirmed that the president had the power to dismiss the prime minister.)

As head of economic policy Fyodorov quickly pitched a pro-reform tone. He put control of inflation as the number one priority and vowed to continue the reform programme. He even attacked Gaidar's record on inflation: 'The Gaidar government was repeatedly accused of having a rigid monetary policy, but it did not. Billions of roubles of worthless money were poured into the economy' (*IHT*, 19 January 1993, p. 14; *FT*, 19 January 1993, p. 2). Although reform needed to take the 'social factor' into account, 'market-orientated relations will ultimately help our country out of a difficult situation. These envisage that the state will no longer support enterprises which cannot withstand competition.' Enterprises should be reorganized and less able managers dismissed. Fyodorov's criticism of the 5 January 1993 decree on price controls (which restricted the profits of enterprises producing basic goods) led to a major climbdown by Chernomyrdin. On 18 January 1993 the controls were lifted on all prices except those charged by monopoly suppliers. Fyodorov outlined the government's stabilization proposals on 20 January 1993, with the aim of reducing inflation to 5 per cent a month by the end of 1993 and reducing the budget deficit to 5 per cent of GNP.

12 February 1993. The constitutional court rules that the 28 October 1992 presidential decree outlawing the National Salvation Front was unconstitutional. (On 14 February a congress was held in Moscow to reconstitute the Communist Party, with some of the coup leaders in attendance.)

16 February 1993. Yeltsin and Khasbulatov (speaker of parliament) agree to call a special session of the Congress of People's Deputies to ratify a 'constitutional agreement' (defining the powers of the executive and the legislature) that teams appointed by the government and parliament will attempt to draw up within ten days.

20 March 1993. In a television address to the nation Yeltsin announces that he has that day signed a Decree on Special Rule pending the Resolution of the Crisis of Power. On 25 April 1993 there will a popular 'vote of confidence' in the president and vice-president. (The published version confined the vote to the president, Rutskoi having refused to sign the decree.) The nation will also vote on the draft of a new constitution and a draft law on elections to a new federal parliament (followed by fresh parliamentary elections if it is passed). The Congress and the Supreme Soviet may still operate but may not overturn presidential decrees. Yeltsin later issues a decree renaming the Kremlin guard as the presidential guard and puts it under presidential control.

21 March 1993. The Supreme Soviet votes to ask the constitutional court for a ruling on the president's actions. Vice-president Alexander Rutskoi and 'security council' secretary Yuri Skokov refuse to sign the decree and the chairman of the constitutional court, Valery Zorkin, blunders by speaking of an 'attempted coup' before even consulting the other twelve members of the court. But Yeltsin is supported by the government, whose statement speaks of 'the efforts of the democratically elected president to prevent anarchy, chaos, political confrontation, separatism, nationalism and crime'. The government's statement is signed by the ministers of defence (Pavel Grachev, who constantly stresses the neutrality of the army), security (Viktor Barannikov) and the interior (Viktor Yerin), who pledge loyalty to the 'principles of the constitution'. Western governments back Yeltsin.

22 March 1993. Yeltsin says that he is placing television, radio and the newspapers under presidential protection in order to ensure their freedom, thwarting any attempt by parliament to subject the mass media to its control.

Yeltsin asks the interior ministry to guarantee the security of the premises. Justice minister Nikolai Fyodorov resigns, but prime minister Chernomyrdin says that 'no reforms, not even the normal functioning of the economy, is possible unless the political crisis is halted'.

23 March 1993. Yeltsin signs another decree threatening to dismiss local officials who do not carry out decrees.

The constitutional court (established by parliament in November 1991), although it had not actually seen the presidential decrees, decided by nine votes to three that Yeltsin had violated a number of provisions of the constitution and the federal treaty. But there was no ruling on impeachment. (It was reported that a phrase explicitly calling Yeltsin's actions impeachable had been removed before the findings were published.) The court also conceded that the president could ask for a popular vote, but only on the question of trust in himself (and not, for example, on the question of where power should lie). The preamble to the findings also accepted the need to end the crisis over the division of power, to continue political and economic reform and to safeguard the unity and integrity of the country.

Khasbulatov said that 'there is every ground for impeachment ... We face a direct attempt at a *coup d'état*.' (Yeltsin had already indicated that he would ignore an impeachment vote; a successful one requires a two-thirds majority vote of the 1,033 deputies of the Congress of People's Deputies; the vice-president would take over for three months, after which a fresh election would be held.)

24 March 1993. Yeltsin causes a stir when he actually publishes the final version of his decree. It contains no reference to 'special rule' and accepts the constitutional court as arbiter of the constitutionality of presidential decrees. The decree refers to 'urgent measures ... aimed at stabilizing the situation and providing conditions for economic reform'. There are brief talks between the two sides, but no agreement is reached. (Khasbulatov suggested things like early elections and cabinet changes, but rejected a national vote.) The Supreme Soviet approves another extraordinary session of the Congress of People's Deputies.

25 March 1993. Khasbulatov: 'I am not a supporter of impeachment.' (By then it was clear that the required 689 votes were not attainable.) He suggests a coalition government and simultaneous presidential and parliamentary elections.

26–9 March 1993. The ninth (and special) session of the Congress of People's Deputies takes place.

On 27 March, the second day of the Congress, not enough votes were cast even to get impeachment on the agenda. But the compromise proposals presented to the Congress by Yeltsin and Khasbulatov the following day provoked a violent reaction from a Congress generally unwilling to bring about its own dissolution. The proposals were as follows: there would be no popular vote in April and early elections would be held in November 1993 for both the presidency and a new two-chamber parliament (although deputies would receive their salaries and privileges until their mandate expired in 1995). In angry response the Congress agreed to vote not only on the impeachment of the president but also on the dismissal of the speaker. But the impeachment motion was defeated, with 617 votes for (689 were needed) and 268 against. The vote of no confidence in Khasbulatov was also defeated; only a simple majority was needed (517), but there were just 339 votes in favour and 558 against.

The final day of the Congress saw bitter denunciations of Yeltsin (who did not attend) and no resolution of the crisis. An approved resolution accused the president of 'serious violations' of the constitution and said that he 'bore personal responsibility for the increasing confrontation between the branches of authority and different sections of society'. The Congress called for a coalition government and the dismissal of the president's representatives in the regions. The constitutional court was asked to judge the legality of the president's recent decrees and declared them null and void pending a decision. Congress also asked the court to investigate whether a speech made by Yeltsin at a public rally constituted grounds for impeachment (saying, for example, that he would ignore the decisions of Congress). The Congress did accept a referendum on 25 April, but four questions were to be put to the people:

1. 'Do you have confidence in the President of the Russian Federation, B. N. Yeltsin?'
2. 'Do you approve of the socio-economic policy carried out by the President of the Russian Federation and the government of the Russian Federation since 1992?'
3. 'Do you consider it necessary to hold an early election for the presidency of the Russian Federation?'
4. 'Do you consider it necessary to hold early elections for the People's Deputies of the Russian Federation?'

No specific date was set for either election, but it was laid down that to be accepted each of the four questions had to gain 50 per cent of the votes of all eligible voters (i.e. not just 50 per cent of those who actually cast ballots).

1 April 1993. Yeltsin accepts the Congress's referendum but challenges the 50 per cent of eligible voters' rule in the Constitutional Court.

6 April 1993. Vice-president Alexander Rutskoi: 'If the situation is not changed in the next two or three months, we shall get something between civil war and dictatorship.' He advocates a government reshuffle and says that there is a need to revive the centrally planned economy in the next six months in order to avert total collapse.

14 April 1993. The trial of twelve of the leaders of the August 1991 coup attempt begins. They are all charged with 'treason against the motherland' ('betraying the native land in the form of a conspiracy to seize power') and five are also charged with exceeding their legal authority. Alexei Tizyakov falls ill and two days later the trial is suspended. On 19 May 1993 the three presiding (military) judges of the Supreme Court rule that the prosecuting team should be dismissed and the matter referred to the Supreme Soviet. The prosecutor-general and his deputy (although not actually part of the prosecuting team) had earlier written and published a book (*The Kremlin Conspiracy*) in which they described the defendants as 'criminal'. On 7 September 1993 the constitutional court ruled that Tizyakov could be tried separately and the prosecuting team should remain in place.

15 April 1993. Yeltsin reduces Rutskoi's perquisites, such as depriving him of his personal doctor and most of his bodyguards and replacing his Mercedes with a Volga. Yeltsin also intends to deprive Rutskoi of his agriculture portfolio. (Rutskoi is against an overhasty dismemberment of collective farms.)

21 April 1993. The constitutional court rules that the first two questions in the referendum need gain only 50 per cent of votes actually cast in order to win acceptance, but the minimum 50 per cent turnout condition still applies.

23 April 1993. Yeltsin strips Rutskoi of his agriculture portfolio.

25 April 1993. There is a surprisingly high turn-out of 64.6 per cent of the 107.3 million registered voters and an unexpectedly strong show of support for Yeltsin and, to a lesser extent, for his economic policy. (Note that the number of registered voters was given as 106.2 million for the 12 December 1993 general election.) Question 1 receives a 'yes' vote of 58.7 per cent of those who voted and question 2 a 'yes' vote of 53.0 per cent. Question 3 receives 31.7 per cent of eligible voters and question 4 43.1 per cent, indicating a much stronger desire for early parliamentary elections than for an early presidential election.

Support was stronger in the towns than in the countryside, although the gap was not as wide as anticipated. There were considerable regional variations. For example, Yeltsin scored especially well in cities like Moscow (75.2 per cent) and St Petersburg (a 72.8 per cent 'yes' vote). Chechenia did not take part at all and in Tatarstan the turnout was so low (22 per cent) that the result was declared invalid. In Ingushetia question 1 received a 'yes' vote of only 2.4 per cent and in Dagestan it was 14.28 per cent.

During the election campaign Yeltsin made some costly promises, some of which were honoured. For example, on 1 April 1993 the minimum monthly wage was doubled to 4,500 roubles and on 1 May 1993 the minimum monthly pension was raised from 4,275 roubles to 8,122 roubles. Yeltsin did promise to postpone an increase in petrol prices, but changed his mind on 24 May.

28 April 1993. Yeltsin dismisses Rutskoi from his position as head of the Interdepartmental Committee on Crime and Corruption and takes over the role himself.

1 September 1993. Yeltsin issues a decree suspending vice-president Alexander Rutskoi and first deputy prime minister Vladimir Shumeiko. 'The situation that has come about as a result of reciprocal accusations of corruption and legal claims against one another by officials in the system of executive power is seriously undermining the state authority of the Russian Federation ... Rutskoi ... and ... Shumeiko ... are temporarily suspended from the performance of their duties.' (The period will depend on the results of an official investigation.) (Rutskoi considers that Yeltsin is acting unconstitutionally, while Shumeiko claims that he asked to be relieved of his duties in order to concentrate on clearing his name. Both have been accused of misuse of state funds earmarked for essential imports, Shumeiko allegedly authorizing the transfer of state funds to a company in Switzerland which failed to deliver the whole consignment.)

3 September 1993. The Supreme Soviet refers Yeltsin's suspension of Rutskoi to the constitutional court.

16 September 1993. It is announced that Yegor Gaidar is to return to the government on 18 September as a first deputy prime minister in charge of the economy (there being three first deputy premiers altogether). (Gaidar had been elected president of the All-Russia Association of Private Enterprises and Enterprises undergoing Privatization at its founding congress held on 2–3 April 1993.) Oleg Lobov is to be moved to another post.

18 September 1993. A decree issued by Yeltsin formally appoints Gaidar and also appoints Oleg Lobov as secretary of the 'security council' and Nikolai Golushko as security minister. Rutskoi is deprived of his last role, namely as stand-in for the president when he is abroad.

THE DISSOLUTION OF PARLIAMENT ON 21 SEPTEMBER 1993

On 21 September 1993, in a television and radio address, Yeltsin announced the dissolution of parliament and elections on 11–12 December for the lower house (the State Duma) of a new bicameral Federal Assembly (with a presidential election to follow; on 23 September the date was set for 12 June 1994 and Yeltsin said that he would stand). (Deputies were to receive a year's pay and to go on enjoying other benefits, such as apartments. But later it was announced that only those who left the building before 3 October and who did not participate in the disturbances were still eligible.) The president was to rule by decree until the new parliament began its work.

'Parliament has been seized by a group of people who have turned it into the headquarters of irreconcilable opposition. Hiding behind deputies, this group is pushing Russia towards the abyss. My duty as president is to state that the current corps of deputies has lost its right to be in control of crucial levers of state power. The security of Russia and its peoples is more precious than formal obedience to contradictory norms created by the legislature, which has finally discredited itself. The measures that I have to take as president are the only way to protect democracy and freedom in Russia, to defend reform and the still weak Russian market. There will not be fresh elections to the

Congress or the Supreme Soviet. There will be no more sessions of the Congress. According to a presidential decree signed today, the Congress of People's Deputies and the Supreme Soviet cease to perform their legislative functions. The authority and powers of the people's deputies of the Russian Federation are regarded as void ... every one of them has the right to be nominated a candidate to stand in the elections to the Federal Assembly. Russia needs deputies who do not play political games at the expense of the people. We need people who are more professional, more civilized and more democratic, and I believe there are such people in Russia. The already weak legal foundation of the already weak Russian state is being deliberately eroded. Laws are being approved for the sake of momentary political goals. The only way to overcome the paralysis of state power is to renovate it fundamentally on the basis of the rule of the people and constitutionality. The current situation does not allow that; neither does it allow of the passage of a new constitution. Being the guarantor of the security of the state, I must offer a way out of the stalemate and to break this disastrous, vicious circle. These measures are necessary in order to protect Russia and the whole world against the catastrophic effects of the disintegration of Russian statehood, against the triumph of anarchy in a country with a huge nuclear arsenal. This is my only aim.'

Rutskoi denounced the move as an 'overt *coup d'état*' and announced that he had assumed the presidency. Khasbulatov talked of a 'state coup', called for a general strike and called upon the army not to obey Yeltsin. In a defiant emergency session the Supreme Soviet approved Rutskoi's presidency (and appointed an alternative government, including ministers of security, defence and the interior) and denounced Yeltsin's actions as unconstitutional. The constitutional court ruled (by nine votes to four) that Yeltsin had violated the constitution and so this provided grounds for impeachment. (The court was advised not to convene again until a new parliament had been elected.) The Congress of People's Deputies could muster only 638 deputies (689 were needed for a quorum; deputies' travel allowance and foreign passports had been taken away). But this was deemed enough for the Congress to be quorate when Yeltsin supporters were dismissed and Yeltsin was impeached on 23 September. The next day Congress voted in favour of simultaneous elections for a new parliament and the presidency in March 1994. But the parliament was more or less ignored. Yeltsin had its finances terminated, telephones disconnected, electricity and heating cut off, water flow reduced, assets seized and its newspaper (*Rossiskaya Gazeta*) closed down; the special radio and television programmes devoted to parliament were taken off the air. The country remained quiet and the number of people actively participating in the events was tiny, much smaller than in August 1991, when the participation rate was already low. (One source puts the number taking part in the revolt on 3–4 October, according to 'modest calculations', at some 4,000: *Moscow News*, 8 October 1993, p. 4.)

Prime minister Chernomyrdin (and the rest of the government, with the exception of the minister of foreign economic relations, Sergei Glazyev, who resigned) backed Yeltsin (as did the central bank and the prosecutor general, Valentin Stepankov) and said that the heads of the ministries of the interior, security and defence had also expressed support. Yeltsin received generally strong support internationally (including the republics of the former Soviet Union; a supportive CIS meeting was held in Moscow on 24 September). The picture among the regions of Russia itself was more mixed; most of the administrators (governors or chiefs of administration) appointed by Yeltsin supported the President (although the Bryansk governor was dismissed for his opposition), but Yeltsin himself estimated that the (elected) regional councils were split more or less evenly. (Yeltsin's actions were not supported by twenty-nine of the fifty-eight provincial and territorial soviets: *CDSP*, 1993, vol. XLV, no. 38, p. 11.) A gathering in St Petersburg of thirty-nine regional representatives on 26 September suggested simultaneous elections for parliament and president and the cancellation of the decrees issued by both sides since the crisis began. (Jonathan Steele reported the following: the Interfax news agency said that only 52.6 per cent of the elected regional councils and 80 per cent of the regional governors, most of whom had been appointed by Yeltsin, backed the President's declaration of a state of emergency: *The Guardian*, 6 October 1993, p. 10.) (The idea of regional representatives being 'for' or 'against' Yeltsin was an oversimplification. There was also a desire to remain above the fray.)

(The radio and television were biased in favour of Yeltsin and most newspapers were supportive too.)

23 September 1993. A policeman and an elderly onlooker are killed in an attack by opponents of Yeltsin on the headquarters of the CIS military command.

24 September 1993. Yeltsin orders interior ministry troops and riot police to surround parliament (the 'White House') and orders those defending the building to disarm.

2 October 1993. Police and demonstrators clash and some people are hurt.

3 October 1993. Armed demonstrators (some put the number at around 10,000) break through the cordon around parliament to join those inside and then move on to attack other buildings, including that of the mayor, the Ostankino television station and Itar-Tass. There is loss of life in heavy fighting. Yeltsin dismisses Rutskoi (who, together with Khasbulatov, called on the crowd to attack the mayor's office and the television centre) as vice-president (and names prime minister Chernomyrdin as his replacement), declares a seven-day state of emergency in Moscow and calls in the army.

4 October 1993. The 'second October revolution' comes to a rapid end when the army (around 1,300 troops) blasts the White House into submission with the aid of tanks (subsequently becoming known as the 'Black House'). (It was subsequently revealed that defence minister Grachev was reluctant to use force.)

(The prosecutor-general's report, published on 6 September 1995, put the number of dead at 123; 'both sides were found responsible' for the conflict.)

Yeltsin addresses the nation: 'All that was and still is going on in Moscow was an armed revolt planned in advance. It was organized by communists seeking revenge, by fascist leaders and some of the former deputies. The armed fascist-communist revolt in Moscow will be suppressed in the shortest possible time.' Both Rutskoi and Khasbulatov are arrested (they sought international mediation to ensure their safety on surrendering). Some publications are suspended, including *Pravda* (Communist Party) and *Den* (neo-fascist). Also suspended are a range of opposition parties and organizations, including the Russian Communist Workers' Party (founded in November 1991, one of whose leaders, Viktor Antipov, was arrested on 7 October for helping to organize armed resistance at the White House), Working Russia (founded in October 1992), the National Salvation Front (an umbrella communist-extreme nationalist organization, i.e. a 'far left-far right' or 'red-brown' organization; it was set up in October 1993), Pamyat ('Remembrance', founded in 1986; neo-fascist, virulently antisemitic) and the Officers' Union (founded in 1992 by servicemen, led by Stanislav Terekhov and openly opposed to Yeltsin's reforms). A curfew is imposed in Moscow from 11 p.m. to 5 a.m. (The curfew was later renewed.)

6 October 1993. Yeltsin addresses the nation: 'What happened in Moscow last Sunday was not spontaneous action of some sort. All of it has another name – an armed rebellion, planned and prepared by the leaders of the former Supreme Soviet, the former vice-president and the leaders of a number of parties and public organizations ... Fascists and communists, the swastika and the hammer and sickle, came together in this dark deed.'

Opposition publications remain suspended, but general press censorship is lifted.

The chairman of the constitutional court, Valery Zorkin, resigns. (The court was created by a 12 July 1991 decree and parliamentary approval was obtained in October.) He remains a member of the court, since the appointment is supposed to be for life, but the deputy chairman Nikolai Vitruk assumes the top position. (In fact, following a newspaper interview given on 1 December 1993 in which Zorkin criticized the constitution, six of his fellow judges dismissed him.)

The guards attending Lenin's mausoleum in Red Square are removed for the first time since August 1924. (The present mausoleum was opened in 1929.)

7 October 1993. The constitutional court is suspended until a new constitution is adopted. On the day the dead are buried Yeltsin promises to banish the spectre of 'communist fascism'.

8 October 1993. The Communist Party, led by Gennadi Zyuganov is suspended.

9 October 1993. Yeltsin issues a decree suspending all councils in cities, towns and villages (their functions to be taken over by mayors). The republic and regional councils are to be subordinate to local governors. Local council elections are to be held in December and the republics are advised to do the same. A special commission will look into local government reform.

The state of emergency in Moscow is extended for a week, although the curfew is to last from midnight to five in the morning.

14 October 1993. Fifteen newspapers are closed down permanently. Those such as *Den*, *Pravda* and *Sovietskaya Rossiya* are allowed to reregister under different titles and with new editors. (The editor of *Pravda* resigned on 28 October, but the paper reappeared under its own name on 2 November.)

15 October 1993. Rutskoi and Khasbulatov are charged with 'organizing mass disorder'.

18 October 1993. The state of emergency in Moscow is not renewed.

19 October 1993. The following six organizations are suspended and barred from participating in the election: National Salvation Front; Russian Communist Workers' Party; Union of Officers; Russian Communist Youth League; Russian National Unity; Union for the Defence of the Social Rights of Servicemen. But the Communist Party of Russia and the People's Party of Free Russia (formerly led by Rutskoi) are allowed to participate in the election. (Note that individual members of banned organizations are still to take part in the election unless they are in prison.)

9 November 1993. The draft constitution is published.

THE SEARCH FOR A NEW CONSTITUTION

Formally the Congress of People's Deputies was the only body that had the authority (with a two-thirds majority) to amend the 1970s constitution (already subjected to hundreds of amendments) or to adopt a new one. In order to bypass the Congress (and its standing representative, the Supreme Soviet) Yeltsin appointed a constituent assembly which initially sat on 5–16 June 1993. The assembly comprised a wide range of interests, including the president, parliament, political parties, the constitutional commission, the various regional authorities in the Russian Federation (including Moscow and St Petersburg), trade unions, the Russian Orthodox Church and the business community. The aim was to draw up a new constitution laying out the division of power between the president and parliament and between the federal and regional authorities.

The summer of 1993 saw much wrangling over many of the president's proposals. The draft constitution was published on 9 November 1993 (*CDSP*, 1993, vol. XLV, no. 45, pp. 4–16). It was to be subject to a referendum (formally a 'national vote': 'Do you agree with the constitution of the Russian Federation?') on 12 December, a simple majority being required for acceptance with a turnout of at least 50 per cent. The draft reflected Yeltsin's strengthened position following the dissolution of parliament. A powerful presidency was the key feature, i.e. the executive gained at the expense of the legislature.

Procedures are laid down for changes in the constitution. 'A federal law is considered to have been adopted if it is approved by a majority of at least three-quarters of the total number of members of the Council of the Federation and at least two-thirds of the number of deputies to the State Duma. The President of the Russian Federation has fourteen days to sign and promulgate an adopted federal constitutional law' (see below for procedures where there is disagreement). 'If a proposal to revise chapters 1, 2 or 9 of the constitution of the Russian Federation is supported by a three-fifths vote of the total number of members of the Council of the Federation and of deputies to the State Duma, a Constitutional Assembly is convened in accordance with federal constitutional law. The Constitutional Assembly either confirms the immutability of the constitution of the Russian Federation or works out the draft of a new Russian Federation constitution, which may be adopted by the Constitutional Assembly by a two-thirds vote of the total number of its members or may be submitted to a nationwide vote. When a nationwide vote is conducted, the constitution of the Russian Federation is considered to have been adopted if more than half the voters who took part in the balloting voted in favour of it, provided that more than half of all eligible voters took part.'

The main clauses of the constitution are as follows:

1. 'The Russian Federation/Russia is a democratic and federal state based on the rule of law, with a republican form of government.' 'Basic human rights and liberties are inalienable and belong to everyone from birth.' 'A citizen of the Russian Federation may hold citizenship in a foreign state (thus dual citizenship).' 'Private, state, municipal and other forms of ownership enjoy equal recognition and protection under the Russian Federation … The right of private property is protected by law.' An ombudsman is to be appointed by the State Duma.

'The Russian Federation consists of republics, territories, provinces, federal cities, an autonomous province and autonomous regions, all of which are equal members of the Russian Federation.' There are eighty-nine 'members' or 'subjects' of the federation, twenty-one republics, six territories, forty-nine provinces, two federal cities (Moscow and St Petersburg), one autonomous province (the Jewish Autonomous Province) and ten autonomous regions.

Many of the concessions granted to 'members' or 'subjects' during the negotiations prior to the dissolution of parliament were withdrawn. All subjects have equality of rights and responsibilities. An earlier draft referred to the republics as 'sovereign states within the Russian Federation', but the term 'sovereignty' was omitted in the final draft. Subjects do not have the right to secede. Relevant clauses include the following. 'If there is a contradiction between a federal law and another Act issued under the Russian Federation, the federal law prevails.' 'The status of a member of the Russian Federation may be changed on the basis of mutual consent by the Russian Federation and the member of the Russian Federation, in accordance with federal constitutional law.' 'The borders between members of the Russian Federation may be changed with their mutual consent.' 'The following matters fall within the jurisdiction of the Russian Federation ... the federal structure and territory of the Russian Federation ... determining the status and protecting the border ... of the Russian Federation.'

(On 9 November 1993 Yeltsin cancelled Sverdlovsk Province's declaration of itself as 'the Urals Republic'. The fifteen Soviet republics, based on the most populous nationalities, were supposed to give a semblance of statehood, a reflection domestically of 'internationalism'. Although it was constitutionally feasible, in reality there was no possibility of secession. The sixteen autonomous republics of Russia became full republics when the Soviet Union disintegrated. Four new republics were created in the early 1990s and Chechenia split away from Ingushetia in 1992. Thus there were twenty-one republics in total. The Chechen crisis is dealt with separately.)

2. *The president.* 'The President of the Russian Federation is head of state.' (Note that there is no vice-president.) 'In accordance with the constitution of the Russian Federation and federal laws, the President of the Russian Federation determines the basic guidelines of the state's domestic and foreign policy ... exercises leadership in Russian Federation foreign policy ... conducts negotiations and signs international treaties of the Russian Federation.' 'The same person may not hold the position of President of the Russian Federation for more than two consecutive terms.' Each term lasts for four years. (The problem subsequently arose as to whether Yeltsin's first term counted, since he was first elected while Russia was still part of the Soviet Union.) The President of the Russian Federation:

'Appoints the chairman of the government of the Russian Federation [the prime minister], with the consent of the State Duma ... makes decisions on dismissing the government ... acting on a proposal by the chairman of the government of the Russian Federation, appoints vice-chairmen [deputy prime ministers] of the Russian Federation and federal ministers to their posts and relieves them of their duties.' (See below when there is disagreement.)

'Presents to the Council of the Federation for appointment to positions as judges of the Constitutional Court of the Russian Federation, the Supreme Court of the Russian Federation and the Higher Court of Arbitration of the Russian Federation [economic disputes are dealt with by this court], and also a candidate for the post of Prosecutor General of the Russian Federation ... submits a proposal to the Council of the Federation on relieving the Russian Federation prosecutor-general of his duties ... appoints judges of other federal courts.' 'Judges are not subject to removal from office.' ('The powers of a judge may be terminated or suspended only on grounds and according to procedures established by federal law.')

'Appoints the Supreme Commander of the Russian Federation Armed Forces and relieves members of their duties ... The President of the Russian Federation is the Supreme Commander in Chief of the Russian Federation Armed Forces ... in the event of aggression against the Russian Federation, or a direct threat of aggression, the President of the Russian Federation may introduce martial law throughout the Russian Federation or in specific localities, giving immediate notification of his action to the Council of the Federation and the State Duma ... Under circumstances and in accordance with procedures stipulated by federal constitutional law, the president may introduce a state of emergency throughout the Russian Federation or in specific localities, giving immediate notification to the Council of the Federation and the State Duma.'

'The President of the Russian Federation issues decrees and directives ... [which] ... are binding throughout the Russian Federation ... [but which] ... may not be at variance with the constitution of the Russian Federation or with federal laws.'

'The President ceases to exercise his powers before his term expires if he resigns, if he is totally unable to exercise his powers for reasons of health, or if he is removed from office.' 'In all cases in which the President of the Russian Federation is unable to perform his duties, those duties are temporarily performed by the chairman of the government of the Russian Federation. The acting president of the Russian Federation has no power to dissolve the State Duma, to schedule referendums, or to propose amendments of the constitution of the Russian Federation or the revision of its provisions.' (Note that Yeltsin's later recurring illnesses exposed the vagueness of some of the provisions. In the event of the president's death the prime minister assumes responsibility for three months, when a new presidential election has to be held.)

'The President of the Russian Federation may be removed from office by the Council of the Federation only on the basis of an accusation that charges the president with high treason or the commission of another grave crime, an accusation brought by the State Duma and confirmed by a finding of the Russian Federation Supreme Court on the presence of the elements of the crime in the actions of the President of the Russian Federation and by a finding of the Russian Federation Constitutional Court on compliance with the established procedure for bringing the accusation ... A decision by the State Duma on bringing an accusation and a decision by the Council of the Federation on removing the president from office must be adopted by a two-thirds vote of the total number of members of each chamber and on the initiative of at least one-third of the deputies of the State Duma, and there must be a finding by a special commission formed by the State Duma ... A decision by the Council of the Federation on removing the President of the Russian Federation from office must be adopted no later than three months after the State Duma has brought an accusation against the President.'

3. *The Federal Assembly*. This consists of two chambers, the Council of the Federation (the upper house) and the State Duma (the lower house):

The members of the Council of the Federation (CF) consist of two representatives of each member of the Russian Federation, one from the representative body of state power and one from the executive body of state power. (CF representatives were, in reality, to be elected for the first term of office: see 12 December 1993 general election.) The following matters fall under the jurisdiction of the Council of the Federation: confirming border changes between members of the Russian Federation; confirming presidential decrees on the introduction of martial law or on the declaration of a state of emergency; deciding the question of using Russian armed forces outside the territory of the Russian Federation; scheduling presidential elections; removing the president from office; approving nominations for judges of the Constitutional Court, the Supreme Court and the Higher Court of Arbitration; approving the nomination for prosecutor-general or relieving him of his duties.

The following matters fall under the jurisdiction of the State Duma: approving the nomination for prime minister; deciding on the question of confidence in the government; approving the presidential nomination for the chairman of the central bank of Russia and relieving him of his duties; bringing accusations against the president with the aim of removing him from office.

Legislation can be initiated by the president, the Council of the Federation, the State Duma, the government and the legislative (representative) bodies of the members (subjects) of the federation. Draft laws are submitted to the State Duma. Draft laws relating to fiscal matters may be submitted only 'if there is a finding by the government of the Russian Federation ... The government of the Russian Federation works out the federal budget, presents it to the State Duma and ensures its fulfilment.' Federal laws are adopted by the State Duma (by simple majority unless otherwise stipulated by the constitution). Federal laws adopted by the State Duma are forwarded to the CF for its consideration (simple majority voting applies). If the CF rejects a federal law there is a conciliation process. If it fails the State Duma can vote again, albeit requiring a two-thirds majority this time. Federal laws adopted by the State Duma are subject to mandatory consideration by the CF if they concern the federal budget, taxes, monetary policy, customs regulations, international treaties, the state border, or war and peace. A federal law must be submitted to the president. If he rejects the law the State Duma and the CF must reconsider. But the two chambers can overrule the president: 'If, when the federal law is reconsidered, it is approved, in the words previously adopted, by a majority of at least two-thirds of the total number of members of the Council of the Federation and deputies to the State Duma, it must be signed by the President of the Russian Federation within seven days and promulgated.'

'Where nominations for chairman of the government of the Russian Federation have been rejected three times by the State Duma, the President of the Russian Federation appoints a chairman of the government of the Russian Federation, dissolves the State Duma and schedules new elections.' 'The State Duma may express lack of confidence in the government of the Russian

Federation. A resolution of no confidence in the government of the Russian Federation is adopted by a majority vote of the total number of deputies to the State Duma ... [if this takes place] ... the president has the right to announce the dismissal of the government of the Russian Federation or to disagree with the decision of the State Duma. If the State Duma, within three months' time, again expresses no confidence in the government of the Russian Federation, the President of the Russian Federation announces the dismissal of the government or dissolves the State Duma.' (Note that the president cannot dissolve the State Duma within a year of a general election.)

Comments. 'The Russian constitution is based on the French system, and it contains the latter's major inherent flaw: the premier and his government are responsible to both the president and the legislature' (Hough 1994: 21).

'The Russian constitution gives the president political dominance, leaving parliament with little power. One power that the Duma does possess is that it has to approve the budget and the country's taxation system. Virtually the only way that the Duma can express its opposition to presidential and government policy, therefore, is to wield its budgetary and taxation powers. This explains why the adoption of the budget is frequently a lengthy and conflictual process ... The weakness of the constitution is not just that it makes it impossible for parliament to counterbalance the power of the executive and hold the government to account. By giving the Duma too little legislative power and insufficient responsibility, deputies have little incentive to compromise, or to learn to balance between their obligations to their constituents and their duties to the interests of the country. On the contrary, deputies are encouraged to oppose for the sake of opposition and to put their own short-term interests before those of their constituents or the country. A further potentially serious weakness becomes more evident as the country moves to the next presidential election. Since it is extremely difficult to either amend the constitution or to impeach the president, it would be virtually impossible to remove him even if he lost his commitment to democratic change ... A major weakness of Russia's political system and its political culture is the absence of strong national political parties. Without such parties little aggregation of interests take place. Numerous small parties lead to fragmented parliaments in which unstable coalitions are formed. This can make it difficult to pass coherent legislation, or to offer concerted opposition to the government ... Two curious features of the Russian political system are particularly significant in fostering conflict. First, Russia has no reformed communist party with a social democratic programme, and this absence of centrist parties encourages a polarization of politics. Second, reform-minded politicians have found it impossible to unite in a coalition party in favour of reform. Their divisions deprive the president of solid and dependable parliamentary support' (Light 1998: 90–1).

THE GENERAL ELECTION OF 12 DECEMBER 1993

Of the twenty-one parties and blocs that had registered by the deadline of midnight 6 November 1993 (thirty-five were in the running), eight were subsequently disqualified for not meeting one or more of the conditions (e.g. the Russian National Union, the National Republican Party of Russia, the Constitutional Democratic Party and the New Russia Bloc). Each party or bloc had to collect at least 100,000 signatures from eligible voters in order to be registered. In addition, since no more than 15,000 signatures could come from any one of the eighty-nine 'federation subjects', the support of at least seven subjects was required. Polls were considered valid in any constituency if 25 per cent or more of the electorate voted (compared with 50 per cent previously). There was a 5 per cent threshold for any party or bloc to be allocated those seats in parliament to be decided on a proportional representation basis. (There had been earlier efforts to form an overtly pro-Yeltsin party, but Yeltsin was reluctant to attach his name to any particular one. Prime minister Chernomyrdin, too, did not overtly support any particular party or bloc, although apparently he favoured the Party of Russian Unity and Accord.)

The two representatives from each of the eighty-nine federation 'members' or 'subjects' were to be elected under a first-past-the-post system (rather than appointed, as originally conceived), although for one term of office only (thereafter the representatives having to be to be nominated by the members). There were to be 450 deputies in the State Duma, half elected by proportional representation from national party lists (to encourage the growth of parties) and half by single-member constituencies under a first-past-the-post system (no party affiliation to accompany any candidate's name on the ballot paper). (Originally 400 deputies were mooted, elected on a 130 and 270 split respectively.) The first term of office for both houses was reduced to two years (as opposed to the four years proposed earlier). (Note that Chechenia boycotted the election.)

The parties, leading personalities and platforms

Russia's Choice. Yegor Gaidar, Anatoly Chubais, Andrei Kozyrev, Boris Fyodorov, Sergei Filatov, Mikhail Poltoranin, Gennadi Burbulis, Sergei Kovalev and Ella Pamfilova (i.e. many members of the pre-election cabinet and presidential advisers). Founded 16–17 October 1993 in Moscow, the bloc comprises several parties and movements, such as Democratic Russia, the Peasants' Party of Russia, the Association of Privatized and the Private Entrepreneurs and the Party of Democratic Initiative. Its motto is 'Freedom, property and legality' and its symbol is Peter the Great. The draft constitution is supported. The bloc advocates radical economic reform, although promising protection for the poorest members of society. The inflation target is set at 4–5 per cent a month by the end of 1994. (During the election campaign more populist measures were promised, such as greater protection for industry from foreign competition and greater stress on reorganizing enterprises than on closing them down.)

Liberal Democratic Party of Russia. Vladimir Zhirinovsky. (Zhirinovsky never joined the Communist Party. He came third out of five behind Yeltsin and Nikolai Ryzhkov in the Russian presidential election of June 1991 with 6.2 million votes, or 7.8 per cent of those cast.) He was born in Kazakhstan and his father was apparently from a Jewish family, referred to by Zhirinovsky simply as 'a lawyer'. It is alleged that he changed his name from Eidelshtein to Zhirinovsky in June 1964, the latter being the name of his mother's first husband.

Founded in June 1989 and reregistered in December 1992, the party is extreme right-wing, ultra-nationalistic and antisemitic. There was a promise to 'raise Russia off its knees'. The draft constitution is supported. (But greater centralization is advocated. Russia should be divided into territorial units 'without any nationality-based overtones', according to Zhirinovsky.) Populist economic and anti-crime measures are advocated. Economic promises include the following: restoration of 'lost' savings; increased pensions; a halt to the run-down of the military and of the defence industry (including conversion to civilian output) as well as more housing for military personnel; arms exports to be encouraged; no aid to be given to other countries, including the countries of the former Soviet Union; cheap vodka; lower business taxes; and a ban on trading within Russia by non-Russians. There should be state ownership of land, but renting and inheritance should be allowed. (After the election Zhirinovsky talked of a 'mixed economy' with equal rights for the state and private sectors. There should be reform, but it should not mean the destruction of the state sector and collective farms.) (The Liberal Democratic Party has in mind a form of state capitalism, with the state remaining in control of strategic sectors such as defence and the railways. The state would control the privatization process, with only Russian citizens allowed to hold certificates paying an annual dividend. The state would ensure that Russia does not become simply a supplier of raw materials to the West: Kipp 1994: 79–81.)

Zhirinovsky has been associated with some very wild ideas, although during and especially after the campaign a more moderate style was adopted. The following are taken from *The Financial Times* (14 December 1993, p. 2), *The Guardian* (14 December 1993, p. 12), *The Telegraph* (14 December 1993, p. 1) and *The Times* (15 December 1993, pp. 1, 13):

1. *Antisemitism.* 'Although we are not antisemitic we won't tolerate an increase in the strength of the Jews.' 'It is certain that representatives of Zionism have also made their contribution to the decay of the Russian media.' 'Zionists who control international banks.'

2. *Crime.* 'We'll set up courts on the spot and shoot the leaders of criminal bands.'

3. *Foreign policy.* Against the 'Westernization' of Russia. The protection of Russians in the 'near abroad' would include dumping nuclear waste along the borders of the Baltic States if they mistreated their ethnic Russian citizens (although after the election Zhirinovsky said that economic sanctions could be employed). (Within Russia itself ethnically based autonomous republics would be abolished.)

Strong support was given to Serbia and Iraq (volunteers have been sent to fight on the side of Iraq).

The Kuril Islands dispute. 'I would bomb the Japanese. I would sail our large navy around their small island and if they so much as cheeped I would nuke them.' 'Not a single foreign ship will enter the sea between the Russian mainland and the Kurils, so that all the seafood will get on to the tables of the Russian people.'

Germany and Japan. 'When I am sitting in the Kremlin if a German so much as challenges Russia you will pay for everything ... the third time will be the last time if you meddle again ... [I will not hesitate] ... to create new Hiroshimas and Nagasakis ... You will get your own Chernobyl in Germany.'

4. *Territorial ambitions.* Advocates a return to Russia's 'natural historic borders', i.e. a return to the old Tsarist empire, including parts of Poland and Finland (although during the campaign it was stressed that force would not be used and economic forces in particular would be instrumental in inducing countries to rejoin the empire). 'Russia should not permit its borders to shrink. The only possible version is to move the border farther, to Russia's former borders.' 'How I dream of our Russian soldiers washing their boots in the warm waters of the Indian ocean.' (Zhirinovsky's solution to the North-South problem is for the former to take over the latter: Russia – Central Asia and the Middle East; Europe – Africa; USA/Canada – Latin America; China/Japan – East and South East Asia). 'It is difficult to establish borders today. We need to provoke wars between native tribes. To do this we do not even need to wage war actively, we simply need to avoid interfering. They will simply slaughter each other (Armenians against Azerbaijanis ... Tajiks against Uzbeks and so on) ... They ... will come rushing to ask Russia to accept them as districts or provinces' (*The Times*, 17 December 1993, p. 13). (After the election Zhirinovsky talked of the need to withdraw Russian troops from all foreign countries. He also said that the former Soviet republics would soon 'beg with tears in their eyes to be taken back into the Russian state. On 28 December 1993 Zhirinovsky was ordered to leave Bulgaria after insulting the Bulgarian president; he said the president should be 'pensioned off' and introduced a Bulgarian colleague and adviser as the future president. The following day Zhirinovsky was refused entry into Germany. The Romanian parliament condemned his portrayal of Romania as an 'artificial state' – made up of territory seized from Russia, Bulgaria and Hungary – peopled by 'Italian Gypsies'. On 26 January 1994 the public prosecutor's office instigated criminal proceedings against Zhirinovsky, charging him with spreading war propa-

ganda. On 14 June 1994 the state prosecutor asked the Duma to withdraw Zhirinovsky's immunity from prosecution in order to face charges of 'incitement to war' and stirring up national hatred. On 15 September 1994 Zhirinovsky won a libel action against Yegor Gaidar and *Izvestia* for calling him a fascist; both had to pay 500,000 roubles. 'The situation is made confusing for outsiders by the lack of an assumed link in Russia between fascism and antisemitism. The word "fascist" is an insult to men like Zhirinovsky – who has won libel cases after being called that – because it is linked specifically with Nazi Germany': James Meek, *The Guardian*, 14 March 1995, p. 11.)

The Communist Party of the Russian Federation. Gennadi Zyuganov. (The party list includes Vladimir Khryuchkov and Anatoly Lukyanov.) A membership of 600,000 is claimed, but disputed. The party advocates a 'planned market economy', with a powerful role for the state, e.g. generous social protection, wages indexed to inflation and protection of industry. 'Big bang'/'shock therapy' would be abandoned. The party does not oppose a wider spread of ownership; 'destatization' cannot be achieved overnight. Neither is it opposed to private farming, but it does reject the buying and selling of land. Zyuganov talks in terms of reforms with 'a human face' and being more 'socially orientated' (Jonathan Steele, *The Guardian*, 25 November 1993, p. 12). Yeltsin's draft constitution is opposed.

Agrarian Party of Russia. Mikhail Lapshin, Valentin Rasputin, Viktor Shcherbak and Alexander Zaveryukha. (Vasily Starodubtsev is on the list of candidates.) Founded in February 1993. The draft constitution can be adopted 'as a basis'. There should be a state-regulated change-over to a socially orientated market economy. The state should manage the economy, provide easy credits for domestic producers and offer social protection. The programme acknowledges diversity of ownership and accepts 'sensible destatization'. Domestic producers should be protected, especially farmers. It opposes the 'reckless' buying and selling of land (although not private farming as such) and offers strong protection for collective and state farms in particular.

The Yavlinsky-Boldyrev-Lukin bloc. Subsequently nicknamed Yabloko, or 'Apple', an acronym loosely derived from the surnames of the three leaders, Grigori Yavlinsky, Yuri Boldyrev and Vladimir Lukin. Formed in October 1993. The bloc is supported by parties such as the Republican Party of the Russian Federation, the Social Democratic Party and the Russian Christian Democratic Party. Generally seen as 'centrist' in terms of policy, a more gradual process of market reform is espoused along with a strong federal state. (There seem to be differences of attitude within the bloc towards the draft constitution.) The bloc is critical of the government's policy of stressing financial stabilization before the creation of a competitive market economy. Financial stabilization cannot be achieved overnight. As Yavlinsky puts it, 'Gaidar ... simply made state monopolists into private monopolists. My programme is to demonopolize, to privatize much further, and only then can you stabilize the currency' (quoted in *FT*, 11 December 1993, p. 10). Yavlinsky also criticizes 'big bang' price liberalization at the start of 1992 on these grounds. Yavlinsky stresses the need for economic and monetary co-ordination between CIS members. (In a later article he spelt out his idea of an economic union in order to encourage trade, economic growth and social stability. There should be a customs union, a payments union and co-ordinated economic policies and legislation: *IHT*, 12 October 1994, p. 4.)

Women of Russia Bloc. Alevtina Fedulova, Yekaterina Lakhova and Natalya Gundareva. Formed in October 1993. Main platform is a strengthening of the role of women in society by providing the conditions enabling women to have a choice of whether to work or not, e.g. a generous child benefit scheme. Improved health care is stressed. Slogan: 'There is no real democracy without women.' There should be less social tension on the way to the market; social policy is a priority and there should be less spending on defence. There is support for (inherited) land leasing but not sales. No stand is taken on the constitution.

Party of Russian Unity and Accord. Sergei Shakhrai, Alexander Shokhin, Oleg Soskovets and Konstantin Zatulin (head of Entrepreneurs for a New Russia). Founded 16 October 1993 in Novgorod (genuine regional devolution is advocated), the bloc comprises important members of the pre-election administration. Motto: 'Stability, family, property and motherland.' The draft constitution is supported on the whole. The party is concerned about 'big bang'/'shock therapy' and thus advocates a more gradual process of market reform, with greater protection offered to industry and the poorest members of society. Shakhrai recommends 'an active industrial policy, directed to the support of branches and enterprises able to become the locomotives of economic growth' (cited in *FT*, 17 November 1993, p. 25). Strong links with the other CIS countries are advocated.

Democratic Party of Russia. Nikolai Travkin, Oleg Bogomolov and Stanislav Govorukhin. Policies include moderate, evolutionary reform, restrictions on land sales, protection for domestic industry, strengthened Russian statehood and a strong political centre. The draft constitution is not supported.

Russian Democratic Reform Movement. Anatoly Sobchak, Gavriil Popov, Alexander Yakovlev, Yevgeni Shaposhnikov and Sviatoslav Fyodorov. Founded in October 1993. Advocates a genuine federation with meaningful decentralization. (The draft constitution is supported on the whole.) There is support for 'realistic' economic reform (with greater support for production and entrepreneurship) but stress is put on the party's independence from Yeltsin. Policies include wider access to higher education, greater protection for pensioners and the low-paid, and wider ownership of private land.

Dignity and Compassion Alliance. Mikhail Trunov and Vyacheslav Grishin. Founded in 1992. Represents vulnerable groups, such as invalids, pensioners, war veterans, Chernobyl victims and cultural figures. Broadly in favour of reform, but concerned to protect those most in need, i.e. reforms should be for people and not at their expense.

Civic Union for Stability, Justice and Progress. Arkady Volsky (head of the Russian Union of Industrialists and Entrepreneurs), Nikolai Bekh, Alexander Vladislavlev. Founded 26 October 1993, it has the support of the Social Democratic Centre (headed by Oleg Rumyantsev) and the Russian Union of Youth. The draft constitution is not supported. A centrist party of 'reasonable realists', it rejects 'big bang'/'shock therapy' and advocates more gradual market reform, greater state regulation of the economy, increased state investment in industry and greater protection of industry. Economic reform, it argues, should not mean the destruction of the country's scientific and technological potential. The government should control the export of raw materials and privatization is not an end in itself. Specific policies include higher taxes on the wealthy, subsidies aimed at consumers rather than producers and an incentive system to ensure the effective use of land. Active participation in the CIS is recommended.

The Future of Russia – New Names. Vyacheslav Lashchevsky. Established in October 1993. Most leaders in this youth movement come from the Russian Union of Youth (successor to the Komsomol). Policies include a gradual adoption of the market system ('a market economy in the interests of broad strata of society'), a reasonable and equitable tax system, a reduction in the government apparatus (there is recognition of the supremacy of the 'rights, liberties and vitally important values of the individual and society over the state'), a truly federal state and higher domestic and foreign investment. The referendum on the draft constitution should be postponed since it is too early to vote.

The result of the elections

The turnout was 54.8 per cent (58.2 million of the 106.2 million registered voters took part; note that the 25 April 1993 referendum gave a figure of 107.3 million registered voters). (On 5 May 1994 a commission, set up by the president and headed by Alexander Sobyanin, reported massive fraud during the election; the commission's figures were 49 million or 46.1 per cent. The findings were not accepted by the president's office and the electoral commission.) The constitution was approved by 58.4 per cent of those who cast their votes.

Eight of the thirteen participating parties or blocs passed the 5 per cent threshold. Table 12.1 shows the distribution of seats in the State Duma. The election was declared illegal in six constituencies. The picture of the total distribution of seats became muddled later on as factions developed and changed.

Overall the election produced no decisive result. Although Russia's Choice gained most seats in the State Duma, Zhirinovsky's (misleadingly named)

Table 12.1 Russia: the general election of 12 December 1993: the State Duma

Party or bloc	*Party list*		*Constituency seats*	*Total seats*
	% vote	*Seats*		
Russia's Choice	15.38	40	30	70
Liberal Democratic Party	22.79	59	5	64
Communist Party	12.35	32	16	48
Agrarian Party	7.90	21	12	33
Yabloko	7.83	20	3	23
Women of Russia	8.10	21	2	23
Russian Unity and Accord	6.76	18	1	19
Democratic Party	5.50	14	1	15
Russian Democratic Reform Movement	4.06	0	4	4
Dignity and Compassion	0.70	0	2	2
Civic Union	1.92	0	1	1
The Future of Russia – New Names	1.25	0	1	1
Independents	–	–	141	141
Total				444*

* Election declared illegal in six constituencies.
Source: Jeffries (1996: 126); White (1998: 265).

Liberal Democratic Party (LDP) did surprisingly well in the party list section. This came as a bombshell at home and abroad. The initial panic subsequently turned into a generally held opinion that the LDP's success was largely a protest vote against the dire economic circumstances of a large section of the population (associated in people's minds with radical economic reform), the very high level of crime, national humiliation at the decline of a great power and foreign 'meddling'. Zhirinovsky did well among the armed forces. (Yeltsin thinks Zhirinovsky gained about one-third of the votes.) On a more positive note, Zhirinovsky (treated by many as something of a clown) ran a very effective (and well-financed) campaign. His simple messages took full advantage of people's misery and prejudices. The reformist parties were deeply divided, unable to unite through policy differences and personal rivalries.

Comments on the 12 December 1993 election and public opinion polls

Hough (1994) describes the results of a major public opinion poll undertaken during the three weeks preceding the 12 December 1993 election. 'One fact is abundantly clear from our survey data: the Russian population does not see the choice as one between radical economic reform and a return to the past … The great bulk of the population takes a centrist position on economic change' (pp. 5–6). 'The support either for very radical reform or for a return to the past … has become quite small … the centre is still strong in the Duma' (p. 34). 'Perhaps the most consistent political fact about Russia is the much stronger support for the radicals in the large cities than in the countryside and small towns' (p. 24).

Sakwa (1995: 220–1) concludes that: 'If the elections had been held only on a proportional system, the LDPR would have been the single largest group in the Duma; but if the old two-stage first-past-the-post system had been retained, the LDPR would hardly have figured. The confused results reflect genuine confusion in the Russian political scene. A large number were seduced by the promises of easy solutions and the restoration of Russia's great power status; but a solid bloc at the same time voted for the continuation of reforms. The population had sent two mutually exclusive signals: in apparently accepting the constitution they were voting for stability; but in voting for the opposition they were rejecting the existing basis for order. In the constituency elections the personal factor was generally more important than programmes, and conjunctural factors (like the non-payment of wages in many sectors since September) amplified the protest vote. The elections revealed not so much "support" for nationalist or neo-communist parties as disenchantment with the democrats ... the protest vote was less against a centre that barely existed than a mark of dissatisfaction with the venality of post-communist politics and the persistence of elite structures across the August divide ... The strong showing for Zhirinovsky reflected the insurgency of outsider groups against the embryonic post-communist "new class". The results suggest a highly discerning and sophisticated pattern of voter behaviour ... the party list vote was used as a classic instance of the "protest" vote ... whereas in the single-member constituencies the electorate voted *for* rather than *against* particular candidates and programmes.'

'The end result was a parliament that was roughly equally divided between liberals, centrists and a third group of communists and nationalists (the so-called "red-brown coalition")' (Boone and Fedorov [Fyodorov] 1997: 170).

Prime minister Chernomyrdin (18 December 1993): 'We should face the truth and admit that many people voted against the hardships and mistakes of the current reforms, rather than for a particular programme ... As many as 35 million Russians live below the poverty line, which means that some 30 per cent of the electorate were potentially "against". Naturally, any "shock" methods must be precluded in the future ... I said it a year and a half ago and I am ready to repeat it now; it is wrong to jump in the river without testing the water first ... The election defeat is a personal evaluation of Gaidar's work, not as a representative of the whole government but as the person responsible for the economics ministry. The same goes for Chubais. It is their personal defeat. They should think it over hard. They have a lot to think about now.' The focus, the prime minister says, should be less on monetary and spending controls and more on social protection and on investment in efficient state and private enterprises in order to create jobs.

On 19 December 1993 Gaidar and others called for an 'anti-fascist front'.

On 21 December 1993 Yeltsin described the election success of Zhirinovsky as 'a protest against poverty'. 'Do not forget the poor. There are many of them. It was they who voted for the Liberal Democratic Party. They were not voting for its leader or its programme, but against poverty.' The following day Yeltsin said that 'no matter whom the voters cast their ballots for, they were agreed on one point: Russia needs strong rule, Russia needs order ... and they are exasperated by the rise in crime ... to a considerable extent people's patience has been exhausted. For two years they have tightened their belts and put up with difficulties. Now they want results.' But 'Gaidar remains, which means the course he is pursuing with the president and the government also remains ... basic foreign policy remains in place.' The rate of inflation has started to slow down, however, and 'if the trend continues we shall seriously change our social policy'.

DEVELOPMENTS BETWEEN THE DECEMBER 1993 GENERAL ELECTION AND THE DECEMBER 1995 GENERAL ELECTION

21 December 1993. Yeltsin abolishes the Security Ministry (successor to the KGB, although it had been made progressively much weaker than its predecessor). It is to be replaced by the Federal Counter-intelligence Service (the Foreign Intelligence Service dealing with security matters abroad).

10 January 1994. A decree issued by Yeltsin makes the defence, interior and foreign ministries accountable to the president as well as the committees responsible for espionage, frontier troops, information, television and radio.

11 January 1994. The Federal Assembly convenes. Yeltsin personally addresses the Council of the Federation, calling for co-operation and on deputies not to 'stop half-way' on the path to economic reform: 'Now is the time we need our second wind.' In contrast, prime minister Chernomyrdin informs the State Duma that 'the government will not allow ill-considered leaps forward and unreasonable shock actions ... The limit of the people's patience is nearly exhausted.' He calls for 'a new stage of economic reforms, a stage of stabilization during which we should provide the right conditions for producers'. (On 13 January Vladimir Shumeiko was elected speaker of the Council of the Federation; the following day Ivan Rybkin of the Agrarian Party was elected speaker of the State Duma.)

16 January 1994. Gaidar resigns from the government: 'I cannot work without having the necessary levers at my command ... where decisions I have taken are not approved and at the same time decisions I regard as dangerous are adopted by the government ... I cannot serve in the government and at the same time be in opposition to it ... I would stay in the government if I had the least hope of improving things, but I have not.' Gaidar cited his opposition to the decisions to form a monetary union with Belarus (which he considers inflationary) and to spend $500 million on a new building for parliament:

'those things were examples of contributing factors, of which a great many had accumulated'. There was 'a much more serious problem ... stay ... but at the same time serve more and more as a cover for a policy I do not agree with' (*CDSP*, 1994, vol. XLVI, no. 3, p. 7). The social security minister, Ella Pamfilova, also announces her intention to resign: 'this is not an ultimatum – it is an act of despair': 'when your advice is ignored it is simply pointless.' (Pamfilova complained about the amount of money spent on refurbishing the White House when social services urgently needed resources. Her final and irrevocable intention to resign was not actually announced until 16 February: 'my departure is a protest against the discrediting of the idea of the current reforms ... I consider it dishonest to participate in conducting a policy that I do not agree with and cannot bear responsibility for': *CDSP*, 1994, vol. XLVI, no. 7, p. 18.)

17 January 1994. Yeltsin issues a statement on Gaidar: 'Accepting his resignation, I would particularly like to stress the unchangeability of the president's course towards deep and democratic reform of Russian society, its economy and political institutions. The policy of reforms will be continued.' Russia's Choice's parliamentary faction also issues a statement: 'The economic and political situation in Russia has changed considerably. The leadership of the Russian government regularly departs from the course of stabilization and reform while declaring it is true to it. In this situation the departure of Russia's Choice representatives responsible for economic and social policy is the only possible decision.'

18 January 1994. Boris Fyodorov refuses the post of finance minister (without the rank of deputy prime minister). (The conditions he laid down were not accepted, e.g. that Viktor Gerashchenko, chairman of the central bank, and Alexander Zaveryukha, deputy prime minister in charge of agriculture, should be dismissed and that he should be in charge of monetary policy.) Fyodorov also leaves Russia's Choice and joins the 'Union of 12 December', an alliance of liberal independents formed after the election and led by Irina Khakamada. (Andrei Makarov also joins.)

20 January 1994. Prime minister Chernomyrdin announces the new government: first deputy prime minister, Oleg Soskovets; deputy prime ministers, Anatoli Chubais (privatization), Alexander Zaveryukha (agriculture) and Yuri Yarov (social issues); economics, Alexander Shokhin (the government would try to 'cling to a narrow corridor between hyperinflation and a stop in industrial production'; he became deputy prime minister in charge of the economy on 24 March 1994); foreign affairs, Andrei Kozyrev; nationalities and regional policy, Sergei Shakhrai.

Chernomyrdin (whose position has strengthened): 'The government will not retreat from the course of continuing and deepening reform ... The course adopted by the government in 1993 remains unchanged ... [but the new government must] ... correct the course of reforms ... The period of market romanticism is now over. But we will not permit its replacement by a fetishism of production ... The current government considers the fight against inflation its utmost aim. But in fighting inflation we will switch from mainly monetarist methods to mostly non-monetarist methods widely tested abroad.' (He seemed to have in mind such measures as demonopolization and price and wage controls.)

The new more 'centrist' government (more in tune with parliament) was generally expected to pay greater attention to production, adopt a more selective approach to the allocation of credit (e.g. to encourage exports) and lay greater emphasis on demonopolization. Fyodorov is of the opinion that inflation will increase and that 'the government will evidently be one that is incapable of advancing reform'.

21 January 1994. Prime minister Chernomyrdin: 'The mechanical transfer of Western economic methods to Russian soil has caused more harm than good.' A government spokesman talks in terms of using only 'elements of Western market economics.'

Izvestiya: 'The government of reformers has ceased to exist in Russia. It is replaced by directors and apparatchiks who know only how to administer and issue credits' (cited in *The Independent*, 22 January 1994, p. 10).

Western advisers Jeffrey Sachs and Anders Åslund resign, saying that 'the aims and policies announced by the prime minister are strongly contrary to our views'. Sachs: 'This is a massive failure of Western efforts. There was nothing inevitable about this result. We had a lot of ability to affect things and failed to do it. But the IMF, which held back $15 billion in Western aid this year, always claimed that everything was going fine and fails to see the consequences of its failure to deliver aid.' (For further comments by Sachs see Chapter 8 on aid.)

26 January 1994. Fyodorov's resignation is formally accepted after a further period of negotiations. (Sergei Dubinin, a deputy finance minister in charge of legal and insurance issues, becomes acting finance minister.) Fyodorov warns of an 'economic coup' and a 'social explosion': 'the presence in the cabinet of the lifeless and illiterate ideology of Gosplan red industrialists, in the conditions of a market economy, would inevitably bring the country to ruin and the peoples of this country to a dreadful decline in their living standards. Ukrainianization has crossed over the border into Russia ... It is inadmissible that people who have inflicted colossal economic and political damage on the state, who are resolute and open opponents of the course of reforms, should keep their posts in government.'

8 February 1994. Andrei Illarionov resigns as chief economic adviser to the prime minister: 'I entered the government to conduct economic reforms, not to bury them.'

23 February 1994. The State Duma passes by 253 votes to sixty-seven (with twenty-eight abstentions; note that Russia's Choice voted against) the following resolution: there will be an amnesty for those involved in 'crimes in the sphere of political and economic activity'. Those concerned include

(1) those involved in the events of 19–21 August 1991 and 3–4 October 1993; (2) elderly and ill criminals; (3) first-time petty offenders; (4) people convicted of economic crimes in the Soviet era. (Note that the president cannot veto this amnesty.) The State Duma also cancels a previous decision to investigate the events of 3–4 October 1993.

24 February 1994. Yeltsin delivers his state-of-the-nation speech to a joint session of parliament. The theme was the need to strengthen Russian statehood (1) at home, e.g. to tackle crime and to regulate the market: 'without a strong, effective state we cannot overcome the economic crisis or set up a true market system'; and (2) in foreign affairs, e.g. to defend the interests of ethnic Russians in the 'near abroad'. 'The main task of our foreign policy is the consistent advancement of Russia's national interests.' 'Russia is against widening Nato by admitting various countries on the European continent and not Russia'. 'I shall defend and uphold the course of economic transformation ... As long as inflation is not curbed, the crisis will be insurmountable ... [but] ... The task is to find a reasonable balance between the pace of reform and its social cost ... [but] ... The past two years have shown that reform is not the only thing that exacts social costs. Even greater harm is being caused by delaying urgently needed changes in the economic mechanism. It is time to establish effective state regulation that is compatible with market mechanisms ... The year 1994 must be the year in which the effective structural reorganization of the Russian economy begins.'

26 February 1994. Among those released from prison are Rutskoi and Khasbulatov. (The latter vows to retire from politics and concentrate on academic studies of economic policy. The prosecutor-general, Alexei Kazannik, resigns, saying that he cannot carry out Yeltsin's request to suspend the amnesty. (Yeltsin's argument is that parliament has in effect pardoned men not actually convicted.) (Kazannik later said that 'my resignation is connected with the fact that demands were being made on me to break the law, but I am unable to break the law': *CDSP*, 1994, vol. XLVI, no. 9, p. 1. On 7 April 1994 the Council of the Federation refused to accept his resignation.)

4 March 1994. Prime minister Chernomyrdin: 'Our choice is fairly limited. If we let inflation rip we shall end up in a spiral fall from which we will not be able to extract ourselves. But if we stop production we shall end up with a seething country, collapse and chaos. Today's most important task is to walk along the edge of a razor blade without falling to one side or the other.' In reply to central bank chairman Gerashchenko's view that inflation was a lesser evil than mass unemployment he says: 'if you want to have a weak state then go and give out money. If not, do not. Future Russian generations will never forgive us if we leave them a weak country.' (Later in the month he told the upper house of parliament that 'many, perhaps everybody, wants to be kind. But either we come to grips with the problem of financial discipline or we shall never extricate ourselves from this crisis.')

Gaidar's comment on the razor's edge analogy: 'There is no such dilemma. Economic decline is by and large caused by our failure to adhere to tough monetary policies.'

11 March 1994. The Supreme Court rules that the August 1991 coup leaders must stand trial, albeit with new judges.

16 March 1994. The 'Accord for Russia' is formed by communists, agrarians and nationalists (although not by the Liberal Democrats) in order 'to prevent the final collapse of historic Russia'.

27 May 1994. Alexander Solzhenitsyn returns to Russia. (He was deported on 14 February 1974. He undertook a staged train journey from Vladivostok to Moscow in order to acquaint himself with the new Russia and ordinary people; he arrived in Moscow on 21 July.)

12 June 1994. Yegor Gaidar forms a new party called Democratic Choice of Russia. (He was elected leader the following day.)

10 July 1994. Yeltsin joins the G7 meeting (8–10 July) as a full and formal participant in the political (but not economic) talks. (Informally the new grouping became known as the 'political G8'.)

11 August 1994. The verdict on the trial of General Varennikov is delivered. (The trial began on 7 July. Varennikov was the former commander of Soviet ground forces; his troops suppressed the democracy demonstrations in Vilnius in January 1991, when fourteen people lost their lives. Varennikov turned down the pardon granted by parliament to those involved in the August 1991 coup attempt and insisted on a trial – although a jail sentence was automatically ruled out whatever the verdict.) The Military Collegium of the Russian Supreme Court found that Varennikov was not guilty of treason for his participation in the abortive coup of August 1991: 'In Varennikov's actions there was no plan to impair the defence capacity and security of the Soviet Union. He was guided exclusively by the state interests of the USSR.'

21 September 1994. President Clinton ends the need for an annual waiver of the Jackson-Vanik amendment (which links 'most favoured nation' status with emigration policy), but every six months a report must be submitted to Congress on the state of Russia's emigration policy.

7 October 1994. The Council of Europe turns down Russia's application for membership on two grounds:

1. Constitutional guarantees of human rights 'seem to be more theory than practice. In many important fields the essential legal codifications have not yet been reformed as planned ... traditional authoritarian thinking still seems to be dominant ... the concept that it should ... be for the judiciary to protect the individual has not yet become a reality in Russia'. The concerns of the Council of Europe included the difficulty of ensuring fair trials and the poor pre-trial conditions for remand prisoners.

2. The difficulty of actually implementing laws, e.g. enforcing property rights.

11 October 1994. 'Black Tuesday', so named because of the dramatic fall (21.5 per cent) in the exchange value of the rouble against the US dollar. (The rouble quickly recovered.)

14 October 1994. Viktor Gerashchenko (chairman of the central bank) offers his resignation in a letter to Yeltsin and the president issues a decree formally endorsing it.

19 October 1994. Tatiana Paramonova is appointed temporary head of the central bank. (The State Duma rejected her permanent appointment on 23 November, but she stayed on.)

27 October 1994. A motion of 'no confidence' in the government fails to attain the requisite minimum 226 votes. The votes were 194 for the motion, fifty-four against and fifty-five abstentions.

Protest rallies take place across the country in response to an appeal by the Federation of Independent Trade Unions. Among the issues were the non-payment of wages, worsening economic conditions and widening income differentials. According to the union, more than 8 million people participated (*CDSP*, 1994, vol. XLVI, no. 43, p. 10).

4 November 1994. Alexander Shokhin, economics minister and deputy prime minister, tenders his resignation after the appointment of Vladimir Panskov as finance minister.

5 November 1994. Anatoli Chubais is appointed joint deputy prime minister in charge of economic policy.

8 November 1994. Yevgeni Yasin is appointed finance minister.

2 December 1994. Yeltsin's personal guard, which is commanded by Alexander Korzhakov, raids the headquarters of the Most group. This business group is headed by Vladimir Gusinsky, a close associate of Yuri Luzhkov (the mayor of Moscow).

12 January 1995. Chubais assumes overall responsibility for privatization.

18 February 1995. Boris Fyodorov organizes the first meeting of a new political movement called Forward Russia (Forza Rossiya).

Alexander Yakovlev forms the (pro-Yeltsin) Russian Party of Social Democracy.

2 April 1995. Alexander Rutskoi's political movement Derzhava (Power) nominates him as its presidential candidate.

7 April 1995. The Federal Counter-intelligence Service (limited to domestic operations) becomes the Federal Security Service, with expanded powers: (1) at home, for example, it is able to search homes and businesses without a warrant as well as to run its own prisons and (2) it is once again able, in conjunction with the Foreign Intelligence Service, to operate abroad.

12 May 1995. Chernomyrdin launches Our Home is Russia, a party with the stress on 'stability'.

23 May 1995. Yeltsin vetoes two State Duma decisions: (1) to maintain equal division of the 450 seats into party list and constituency candidates (Yeltsin wants a 150/300 split) and (2) to require candidates to step down from government office fifty days before the general election.

15 June 1995. The Council of the Federation votes in favour of the first State Duma decision. (Yeltsin was expected to agree with this in return for the State Duma abandoning its second decision.)

29 June 1995. A US shuttle links up with the Mir space station.

11 July 1995. Yeltsin is taken into hospital with heart trouble. (Yeltsin was expected to leave on 17 July, but his stay was extended until 24 July; he then spent some time in a sanatorium.)

26 October 1995. Yeltsin is once again hospitalized with heart trouble. (Initially the heart attack was claimed to be less serious than before, but it soon became apparent that this was not the case.)

3 November 1995. Prime minister Chernomyrdin, after a visit to Yeltsin, says that he will be temporarily 'co-ordinating' defence, interior, security and foreign affairs. 'The president has to be partially relieved of these duties to give him a better chance to recover ... But of course we seek the president's advice an all key questions.'

5 November 1995. Chernomyrdin backtracks: 'There was no handover of power by the president ... This is an absolutely erroneous interpretation because we did not talk of transferring authority. One can speak only about increasing my working schedule due to the president's illness and nothing else.'

8 November 1995. Yeltsin dismisses Tatiana Paramonova as acting head of the central bank. (Parliament has twice refused to approve her appointment. Her deputy, Alexander Khandruyev, was appointed temporary replacement, but on 14 November Yeltsin nominated Sergei Dubinin. He was approved by the State Duma on 22 November.)

27 November 1995. Yeltsin is discharged from hospital but moves to a sanatorium.

5 December 1995. The State Duma overrides a Council of the Federation veto. The draft law, defining how a new Council of the Federation is to be formed after the present one's term expires on 13 December 1995, now goes directly to the president. The draft law says that each of the eighty-nine regions will send two deputies to the chamber, one from the local council (or parliament) and one from the local executive body (*IHT*, 6 December 1995, p. 5).

According to a source in *CDSP* (1995, vol. XLVII, no. 49, p. 11), the upper chamber was to be formed from the heads of the legislative and executive bodies of power in the members of the federation. 'It is assumed that eventually the heads of the regions, who are still appointed by the president, will be elected instead. The law directs that these elections be held no later than December 1996.' Another source noted that Yeltsin signed the law on 6 December 1995. The term of office of the old upper chamber was to expire after 12 December 1995. 'The heads of the executive and legislative branches in the regions will automatically become new senators' (pp. 11–12).

15 December 1995. Yeltsin (still in the sanatorium) says that 'The most dangerous thing is that representatives of some parties want to return the country to the past'. Voters should support those who offer 'stability and accord in our common home – Russia'.

17 December 1995. Yeltsin is adamant that 'No circumstances could force me to abandon the course of reforms I have chosen'.

THE GENERAL ELECTION OF 17 DECEMBER 1995

By the deadline, which was midnight 22 October 1995, forty-three parties had registered. But checks were made as to the legality of the signatures collected. The supreme court overturned the central electoral commission's decision to disqualify Yabloko, Derzhava-Rutskoi and Democratic Russia, on relatively minor technical grounds, from running in the election of the proportional representation seats. There were various figures mentioned for the number of registered voters, e.g. 105,409,443 and 107,496,558.

There was once again a 5 per cent threshold for the 225 seats elected by proportional representation from national party lists. The other 225 seat were to be, as before, elected by single-member constituencies in a first-past-the-post system. The turnout needed to be at least 25 per cent but the actual figure was an impressive 64.4 per cent.

The parties, leading personalities and platforms

The reader is recommended to review the corresponding section devoted to the 12 December 1993 election as a supplement to the following:

The Communist Party of the Russian Federation. Gennadi Zyuganov. Economic policies include higher public spending (e.g. for social reasons and industrial subsidies), greater tariff protection for domestic industry, the regulation of basic food prices and slower privatization. An important role for the state sector, especially in strategic sectors (where there should be some renationalization). 'Illegal' privatization should be reversed. Direct foreign investment should be encouraged. The party has strong support from pensioners and also strongly targets the traditional working class. Advocates a voluntary revival of the former Soviet Union. In his 5 November 1995 speech commemorating the seventy-eighth anniversary of the Bolshevik Revolution, Zyuganov claimed that there are '20 million out of work, 15 million hungry, 6 million refugees, 2 million children not attending school and 1 million on the streets without parents. The only time Russia had such a situation was in the early 1920s'.

Gennadi Zyuganov outlined his party's policies in an article written after the election (*IHT*, 2 February 1996, p. 6): 'We have thus called for evolutionary reform consistent with Russian historical traditions and world trends ... Boris Yeltsin's regime has thoughtlessly tried to bring the "blessings" of neoliberalism to Russia, whose economy and character are quite different from those in the West. The results have been disastrous ... We would restore the might of the Russian state and its status in the world ... We would seek to restore our state's unique role as the pivot and fulcrum of a Eurasian continental bloc – and its consequent role as a necessary balance between East and West. We consider the disruption of military and strategic parity caused by the collapse of the Soviet Union dangerously destabilizing. And we see the restoration of the union of the former Soviet peoples – based on voluntary association – as a historical necessity dictated by Russia's needs and those of world security... we take an extremely negative view of plans to expand Nato into Eastern Europe, up to Russia's borders ... Any policy that counts on Russia remaining in its humiliating position, following in the American wake, is doomed to defeat ... We are ready to guarantee American investment and create better conditions for them than now exist.' Zyuganov is quoted in *IHT* (6 February 1996, p. 6) as saying that 'The state should control basic industries, energy, railroads, defence production, education, medical care'.

Our Home is Russia. Viktor Chernomyrdin. Advocates stability, continuity and competence.

Liberal Democratic Party of Russia. Leader, Vladimir Zhirinovsky. Extreme nationalist.

Yabloko. Grigori Yavlinsky and Vladimir Lukin. (Note that Yuri Boldyev has left Yabloko.) Close ties with the 'near abroad'. Yavlinsky: 'The main question in these elections is why did 5 per cent of the people get so much that it is impossible even to imagine it, while 95 per cent got nothing at all. The second question is whether this is the fault of the market economy or is this because of how reforms were carried out' (cited in the *FT*, 11 November 1995, p. 7; 11 December 1995, p. 2). 'If in the end you have only corruption and crime and collective farms and a small group of people – maybe 3 to 5 per cent, mainly the previous party leaders – who have gained from the reforms, then the other 95 per cent have no visible results' (cited in the *IHT*, 15 December 1995, p. 5).

Agrarian Party of Russia. Mikhail Lapshin. A left-wing party advocating strong support for agriculture and resistance to land reform (including land privatization).

Power to the People. Founded on 21 August 1995. Leader, Nikolai Ryzhkov. Other personalities include Sergei Baburin, Stanislav Terekhov, Yelena Shuvalova and Anatoli Karpov. 'The rebirth of a united Russia based on the restoration of the economy and traditional spiritual values and the reuniting of the nations and peoples that were part of the USSR.' Also advocates the building of a society that 'combines the social guarantees of the Soviet people with a mixed economy's effective market mechanisms that are acceptable to Russia'.

Democratic Choice of Russia – United Democrats. Radical economic reform. Liberal social and foreign policies. On 26 August 1995 a unifying agreement was signed by Democratic Choice of Russia (Yegor Gaidar and Sergei

Kovalyov) and the United Democrats (Alexander Yakovlev and Yuri Chernochenko).

Congress of Russian Communities. Yuri Skokov, Alexander Lebed, Sergei Glazyev and Ludmila Vartazarova. Moderate nationalist. Protection of the interests of ethnic Russians in the 'near abroad'. Advocates a 'socially-orientated market economy' and greater protection of domestic industry. Lebed has stressed policies against crime and corruption, has talked of reversing 'unfair' and 'illegal' privatization and advocates a smaller but all-professional army.

Women of Russia. Alevtina Fedulova. A centre-left party which advocates a strong welfare state.

Ivan Rybkin Bloc. Apart from Ivan Rybkin, leading personalities of the centre-left bloc include Stanislav Shatalin. Greater emphasis on social policy.

Forward Russia. Boris Fyodorov. Advocates radical economic reform but also preventing abuses of privatization. Appeals to nationalist reformers. Law and order.

Pamfilova/Gurov/Lysenko (Republican Party) Bloc. The slogan of Ella Pamfilova, Alexander Gurov and Vladimir Lysenko is 'Social justice, civilized federalism and fight crime'.

The result of the election

The results are shown in Table 12.2. Only four parties surmounted the 5 per cent threshold for party list seats, the Communist Party of the Russian Federation, the Liberal Democratic Party of Russia, Our Home is Russia and Yabloko. The 'reformist' vote was once again split.

As expected, the big winner was the Communist Party of the Russian Federation, profiting from the pain of political and economic transition experienced by large sections of the population. The party list vote was pretty much as predicted in opinion polls but it did better than expected in the constituency seats. The Communist Party fared much worse in the big cities of western Russia, e.g. in the party list seats it came second to Yabloko in St Petersburg and third in Moscow (where Our Home is Russia came first). (It is worth mentioning that there are 30 million pensioners in Russia: Flora Lewis, *IHT,* 22 December 1995, p. 8.)

Zhirinovsky's Liberal Democratic Party of Russia did much better than expected but worse than in the last election.

Prime minister Chernomyrdin made some expensive pre-election promises, e.g. the back payment of wages and pensions and compensation for those tricked by investment scams. But these did not have the required effect and he explained the disappointing (but not unexpected) share of the vote in terms of the newness of the party compared with that of the Communist Party. Nevertheless, Our Home is Russia ended up as the second largest party in the State Duma.

Table 12.2 Russia: the general election of 17 December 1995: the State Duma

Party or bloc	*Party list*		*Constituency seats*	*Total seats*
	% vote	*Seats*		
Communist Party of the Russian Federation	22.30	99	58	157
Our Home is Russia	10.13	45	10	55
Liberal Democratic Party of Russia	11.18	50	1	51
Yabloko	6.89	31	14	45
Agrarian Party of Russia	3.78		20	20
Power to the People	1.61		9	9
Democratic Choice of Russia–United Democrats	3.90		9	9
Congress of Russian Communities	4.29		5	5
Women of Russia	4.60		3	3
Ivan Rybkin	1.12		3	3
Forward Russia	1.96		3	3
Pamfilova/Gurov/Lysenko bloc	1.61		2	2
Eleven parties or blocs won one constituency seat each (in addition to LDPR)			11	11
Independents			77	77
Total		225	225	450

Source: White *et al.* (1997: 783); White (1998: 266); author's own calculations.

Yabloko did worse than expected, Yavlinsky explaining this in terms of his party being too liberal to attract many 'protest' votes. (When the votes started to be counted it looked as if Democratic Choice of Russia–United Democrats might scrape over the 5 per cent threshold for the party list seats. But this was not to be.)

Women of Russia did much worse than expected.

General Alexander Lebed faded badly after a promising start and his Congress of Russian Communities did much worse than expected. He accused the government of ballot rigging. But Lebed won a constituency seat in Tula.

Comments on the election

'It will be no surprise if the Russian government is handed a stinging defeat in the parliamentary elections … The people are burdened by an unending economic and social crisis. They resent the staggering government corruption that has compromised economic reform and led to several years of inflation and privations. Russia has always lacked a political tradition, even the rhetoric, of civic-mindedness. Few politicians even profess a standard of public service or public morality. Although virtually all post-communist states have experienced corruption scandals (largely because civil society is weak and still unorganized), Russia's corruption is singularly deep. One reason is that the Communist Party Central Committee, the breeding ground of much of today's leadership, was profoundly corrupt ... In the Soviet Union's waning years senior apparatchiks converted political power into financial stakes in the emerging market economy' (Jeffrey Sachs, *IHT*, 6 December 1995, p. 10).

On 19 December prime minister Chernomyrdin said that 'The government intends to continue its economic course. What is essential for us is stability and above all economic stability.' 'Changes, shifts, sackings – nothing of the sort will happen. Personnel changes have routinely taken place and will take place in the future, but they have nothing to do with this [the election].'

On 20 December 1995 Yeltsin pledged that Russia would continue with 'the same policies as before and not leave the path of reform'. He was quoted as saying, on 29 December 1995, that: 'The voters served notice to politicians. When reforming the economy, they should not forget about people' (*FT*, 30 December 1997, p. 1). Yeltsin's New Year message: 'It is in Russia's national interests to develop democracy, to strengthen law and order and to continue economic reforms ... The main task for 1996 is that those in Russia who today are poor should begin to live better. Life is difficult, but a turn for the better is already visible.'

Jerry Hough (*IHT*, 13 February 1996, p. 6) summarizes the results of a large-scale study conducted in Russia in December 1995:

1. Only 10 per cent of participants thought Russia was going in the right direction and many blamed the West. 'Russians are unhappy with the present course of policy. And when they look at the results of their reform in comparison with that of China, it is understandable that they might think that the West's intention must have been to undermine them. Western advice to keep on a fast and firm course toward free market economy, advice that comes paired with essential handouts from the International Monetary Fund, has caused enormous pain.' Only 3 per cent of participants said their financial situation improved a lot in 1995 and 13 per cent said that it had improved a little. More than 60 per cent reckoned they were worse off, with, for instance, nearly half of those employed saying that their salaries were rarely or never paid on time. 'Yet the Russians still favour gradual economic reform. Only on the issue of privatizing big enterprises has there been a swing, with a majority now opposing it.' Overall, Hough concludes that 'it is not surprising that those pushing market-based economic reforms have lost virtually all support'.

2. 'The Russians are astonishingly hopeful about democracy and are quite engaged.'

Hough believes that Gennadi Zyuganov 'has varied his message to different audiences'. 'Zyuganov must convince moderates that he is moving to the centre without losing his present supporters – no mean task. Because he is ambiguous there is no way of knowing what policy he would follow if elected. There has been so much privatization that Communist officials would have a difficult time returning to old-time socialism, but the natural resources industries would likely be renationalized. An industrial policy of state investment is nearly certain, as is import substitution policy with high tariffs.

There will also be great pressure to bring states of the former Soviet Union back into the economic fold.'

Political events after the December 1995 general election

26 December 1995. Yeltsin leaves the sanatorium.

29 December 1995. Yeltsin returns to the Kremlin.

5 January 1996. Andrei Kozyrev resigns as foreign minister. He is to take up his (Murmansk) constituency seat in the State Duma. (The constitution rules out cabinet members being deputies at the same time. Kozyrev was appointed foreign minister of the Russian Federation in October 1990, i.e. before the break-up of the Soviet Union.)

9 January 1996. Yevgeni Primakov, the head of the Foreign Intelligence Service, is appointed foreign minister.

16 January 1996. Anatoli Chubais resigns, saying that he believes Yeltin's evaluation of his work to be 'rather negative'. 'If the president considers my work unsatisfactory I should resign.' (While he was holding a press conference the president's press office announced that Chubais was being dismissed for 'not being exacting enough in his demands on the federal agencies under his jurisdiction and failing to carry out a number of instructions from the RF President': *CDSP*, 1996, vol. XLVIII, no. 3, p. 11.)

17 January 1996. Gennadi Seleznyov (Communist Party) is elected speaker of the State Duma.

24 January 1996. Sergei Kovalyov resigns as chairman of the president's human rights commission. (Sergei Kovalyov was appointed to the above post in October 1993.)

24 January 1996. Yegor Stroyev is elected chairman of the Council of the Federation.

25 January 1996. The Council of Europe's votes 164 to thirty-five (with fifteen abstentions) to accept Russia as its thirty-ninth member. (Russia was formally admitted on 28 February 1996 and on the same day signed the European Convention on Human Rights. The Council of Europe was set up in 1949 to safeguard democracy and human rights in Europe. Russia applied for membership in 1992, the Council of Europe broke off negotiations in February 1995 over Chechenia and negotiations were resumed in October 1995. Critics again raised issues such as Chechenia in the debate. Since 1995 the number of executions carried out has been increasing. On 16 May 1996 Yeltsin said that capital punishment would be gradually phased out.)

Vladimir Kadannikov replaces Chubais as first deputy prime minister in charge of the economy.

15 February 1996. Yeltsin announces that he is to be a candidate in the June 1996 presidential election: 'I am for reform but not at any price. I am for a corrective course but not for going backwards.'

23 February 1996. In his state of the nation address Yeltsin says that: 'The government, seeking to reach financial stabilization, has forgotten the needs of the people … and failed to protect them … We have long been urging the people to tighten their belts, and the people have been doing that, but their patience has run out.'

15 March 1996. The State Duma votes 250 to ninety-eight to annul the Belovezh (Belovezhskaya Forest) agreement of December 1991 signed by the presidents of Russia, Ukraine and Belarus dissolving the USSR, the vote being moved by the Communist Party of the Russian Federation. The Duma declares null and void the Russian Supreme Soviet's 12 December 1991 resolution 'On denouncing the treaty on the formation of the USSR' (*CDSP*, 1996, vol. XLVIII, no. 11, pp. 1–8; no. 12, pp. 6–9).

27 May 1996. The long-delayed economic programme of the National-Patriotic Front, which supports Zyuganov, is published.

Entitled 'From destruction to creation, Russia's path into the twenty-first century', the programme envisaged a three-stage process:

1. The first stage, to be completed by the end of 1997, envisages stimulating production by lowering of energy, raw materials and transport prices, increasing protection from foreign competition, increasing the working capital of enterprises and raising agricultural prices. The aim is to stop the decline in output and ensure a growth rate of about 7 per cent.

2. The second stage, to be implemented between 1998 and 2003, involves increases investment in manufacturing.

3. The third stage, from 1994 to 2010, envisages the creation of 'post industrial technologies' and Russia's integration into world markets by gradually reducing protectionist measures.

The programme aimed to stimulate industrial production, to achieve greater social justice, and to defend domestic manufacturers by raising tariffs, creating state-directed investment banks, halting capital flight and encouraging foreign investment in technological fields. Subsidies to agriculture would be increased. The concept of a 'multi-layered economy' is defended and a sweeping renationalization of 'legally' privatized enterprises was not envisaged. There would be a 'mixed economy', but the state would have a controlling interest in 'strategic' enterprises and have the 'leading role' in the economy. 'Privatization was conducted with violation of the laws. The rights of the new owners have not been legally established. Under the guise of privatization an unprecedented misappropriation has taken place.' Zyuganov said that Russia would regain control of its economic destiny, growth would be 5 per cent a year for the next two years and around 9 per cent a year by the turn of the century, and social justice would be provided to all. (John Thornhill, *FT*, 28 May 1996, p. 2; David Hoffman, *IHT*, 29 May 1996, p. 7; *CDSP*, 1996, vol. XLVIII, no. 21, p. 7.) While endorsing a mixed economy, Zyuganov pledges 'to restore in full the right of nationwide state ownership of the land and its natural resources' (Bruce Clark, *The World Today*, May 1996, vol. 52, no. 5, p. 121).

2 June 1996. In the second round of the election for mayor of St Petersburg, Vladimir Yakovlev narrowly beats Anatoli Sobchak. (Yakovlev, who was formerly Sobchak's deputy, won 47.5 per cent of the vote compared with 45.8 per cent for the latter. Sobchak won 28.8 per cent of the vote in the first round held on 19 May, while Yakovlev received 21.8 per cent.)

16 June 1996. The first round of the presidential election takes place, with a 69.8 per cent turnout of the 108,495,023 million registered voters (*CDSP*, 1996, vol. XLVIII, no. 25, p. 15). (Although there were many mutual accusations and predictions of cheating by opponents during the run-up to the election, international observers were generally satisfied. The chairman of OSCE's parliamentary assembly and head of the group of international parliamentary observers said that 'No major irregularities were recorded anywhere; on the whole the first round of the election was conducted fairly and honestly'. But observers did note the lack of equal opportunities for electioneering in the news media, with Yeltsin the clear favourite of the press: *CDSP*, 1996, vol. XLVIII, no. 24, pp. 4–5.) The results for the ten candidates are as follows: Boris Yeltsin, 35.28 per cent; Gennadi Zyuganov, 32.04 per cent; Alexander Lebed, 14.52 per cent; Grigori Yavlinsky, 7.34 per cent; Vladimir Zhirinovsky, 5.70 per cent; Svyatoslav Fyodorov, 0.92 per cent; Mikhail Gorbachev, 0.51 per cent; Martin Shakkum, 0.37 per cent; Yuri Vlasov, 0.20 per cent; Vladimir Bryntsalov, 0.16 per cent.

Yeltsin trailed badly early on in the campaign but ended in first position, although not gaining the 50 per cent needed to avoid a second round. (As of January 1996 only 6 per cent of voters planned to support Yeltsin, fewer than half the number intending to vote for Zyuganov: Treisman 1996: 64.) He ran a surprisingly energetic campaign, stressing that he was the only real alternative to the communist candidate. The media were overwhelmingly behind Yeltsin (leading to numerous complaints from other candidates, e.g. on 26 June Zyuganov complained to the central election commission about unfair media access), he made many expensive promises and he had the declared support of Anatoli Chubais (who played an active role in the campaign), Yegor Gaidar and Boris Fyodorov. The turnout was lower than Yeltsin had hoped for. Zyuganov could rely on a good turnout from the core communist voters (encouraged by good local party organization), but he largely failed to expand his appeal beyond the older disaffected sections of society. The major surprise was Alexander Lebed, who ran as an independent and pushed Vladimir Zhirinovsky into fifth place. ('In the fortnight preceding the first round, Alexander Lebed suddenly received positive exposure. When the results of that round became known, Yeltsin's spin doctors admitted assisting Lebed': Margot Light, *The World Today*, 1996, vol. 52, nos 8–9, p. 201.)

'The 1996 vote was ... Russia's last "revolutionary" election in which voters were asked to choose between two fundamentally different systems ... The majority of Russians in this vote preferred the current system, or the prospects offered by the current system, to the Soviet *ancien regime* … Yeltsin realized that he could win reelection only by first establishing himself as the only leader capable of uniting all of Russia's reformist forces, and then convincing Russian voters that he was the lesser of two evils' (McFaul 1996b: 319–20).

Yuri Luzhkov easily won the election for mayor of Moscow, with 89.65 per cent of the votes cast in a 67.8 per cent turnout.

18 June 1996. Defence minister Pavel Grachev (appointed 19 May 1992) is dismissed. Former general Alexander Lebed becomes secretary of the presidential 'security council' and national security adviser. (Lebed claimed that he had thwarted an attempt by five Russian generals to persuade Grachev to put the army on red alert in order to pressurize Yeltsin to retain Grachev as defence minister.) Mikhail Kolesnikov (chief of staff) is made acting defence minister.

Lebed justified his decision as follows: 'I faced two ideas: an old one which has long outlived itself and has caused much bloodshed and suffering, and a new one which has been carried out extremely poorly so far but which has a future. I have chosen the new idea.' Lebed's campaign slogan was 'truth and order'. He has always campaigned on a law and order platform and is passionately against crime and corruption.

20 June 1996. Yeltsin dismisses Alexander Korzhakov (head of the president's security organization), General Mikhail Barsukov (head of the Federal Security Service) and Oleg Soskovets (a first deputy prime minister). Yeltsin said that 'They began to take too much on themselves and to give too little'. But there were rumours that the three were planning to persuade the president to postpone the second round of the presidential election.

1 July 1996. A frail looking Yeltsin makes a brief prerecorded address on television. (Speculation about his health has resurfaced. He did not attend the G7 meeting held on 27–9 June, has not been seen in public since 26 June and cancelled public engagements on and after 28 June. On 20 September 1996 the heart surgeon Renat Akchurin reckoned that Yeltsin had had a heart attack, his third, in late June or early July and suggested that it had been hushed up for political reasons: 'Can you imagine what would happen if he told everyone he has had a heart attack and he is unable to work?')

3 July 1996. Yeltsin (53.82 per cent) wins the runoff against Zyuganov (40.31 per cent). (Those voting against both candidates accounted for 4.83 per cent of the vote.) The turnout is 68.89 per cent. (There was an option on the ballot paper for those voting against both candidates. International observers were generally happy with the way the election was conducted, but Zyuganov again expressed concern at bias in the media. Zhirinovsky supported Yeltsin and Yavlinsky, less directly, suggested that his supporters vote against Zyuganov. It was generally felt that many voted against Zyuganov rather than positively for Yeltsin. Yeltsin performed well among the younger sections of society and those living in large cities such as Moscow and St Petersburg.)

The bias in the national press stemmed partly from fear of the possibility of the reintroduction of controls if a communist president gained power. But others have pointed out that the situation locally was very different. Yegor Gaidar reckons that 'the Communists have 130 provincial newspapers, when Russia's Democratic Choice, for example, has none' (*CDSP,* 1996, vol. XLVIII, no. 29, p. 17).

'The clear and overwhelming message of the election is that Russians, whatever their political colouration, want a more deliberate, humane transition from communism to capitalism and a more orderly society. The country has lurched toward a free market under President Yeltsin, bringing incredible wealth to a small fraction of people, some benefits to a slowly developing middle class and hardship to millions of citizens, particularly the elderly. The government's privatization programme has been determined by corruption and favouritism. Large sectors of the Russian economy, including banking and transportation, have been manipulated by the Russian mafia. Violent crime has exploded across the country. Until Mr Yeltsin saw the threat to his campaign and started wildly passing out financial assistance, many Russian workers had not been paid for months. Given the inequities and disorder, it is a political miracle that Russians did not throw Mr Yeltsin out of office and elect a communist or fascist leader. His re-election is a tribute to their stoic patience and their enduring hope. Mr Yeltsin must now return the favour by delivering an honest, disciplined and compassionate government. Russia's democracy is imperfect, but considering the tyranny that prevailed until five years ago it stands as a remarkable achievement … For the first time in history a free Russia has freely chosen its leader' (leader comment by *The New York Times* in *IHT,* 5 July 1996, p. 6).

In mid-April 1996 Yeltsin doubled the minimum pension (effective as of 1 May 1996) and he signed a decree ordering compensation for those whose savings had been devalued by the 1992 hyperinflation (Treisman 1996: 67). Yeltsin 'declared war' on the problem of wage arrears. By early April 1996 those in the budget sector (a 'small fraction' of the total wage arrears) had been eliminated, although they began to recur in the following months (pp. 68–9). 'While the sort of social policy and largess Yeltsin could promise on the campaign trail would hardly change the values of voters or their understanding of concrete interests, they could win over those already inclined to support Yeltsin – either as a reformer, or out of deferrence to the incumbent – but who had been aggravated into supporting Zyuganov or not voting by unpaid wages, miserly pensions, and a sense that the president did not care. By paying people their back wages or increasing social aid, Yeltsin's team hoped to make it possible for generally sympathetic voters to vote out of hope – at least temporary hope – rather than annoyance … While the president's strategy of polarizing the electorate and raising the fear of a return to communist repression helped him beat out the "Third Force" centrist candidates for leadership of the non-communist camp, that alone probably would not have been enough to defeat Zyuganov. His campaigning with "populist" promises, generous social policy initiatives, and regional aid … played a crucial role in securing majority support' (pp. 75–6).

'Russia's political landscape has changed substantially since the July presidential election. First, the path to executive power has become much better defined. All the serious hopefuls are assuming that the next Kremlin ruler will come to power through the ballot box and not by some other method … Second, politics in Russia is no longer polarized between communists and anti-communists. From 1990 to 1996 the struggle between two fundamentally different systems shaped every national election. Polling from the July election showed unequivocally that voters were not choosing between two candidates but between two systems. Thus Mr Yeltsin could maintain negative approval ratings throughout the campaign and still win in a landslide. Most Russians did not want to go back to communism … Third, since Russia does not have interest-based ideological parties, personalities (rather than liberals, conservatives or social democrats) are ascendant … One factor that has not changed since the July elections is the divide between the winners and losers in Russia's transition to the market. The 30 million voters who supported Mr Zyuganov in July may no longer believe in communist restoration, but they are still suffering from actions of the current government, and thus oppose it. They are unlikely to back anyone identified with the status quo – Mr Chernomyrdin, Mr Luzhkov or … Anatoli Chubais. Mr Lebed's battles with his government colleagues make him the heir apparent to this protest vote … With the battle between communism and capitalism over, the greatest threat to market development in Russia is not a communist comeback but instability, democratic collapse and authoritarian rule' (Michael McFaul, *IHT*, 2 October 1996, p. 6).

Alexander Solzhenitsyn advised voters not to support either candidate. In November 1996 he stated: 'Former members of the communist elite, along with Russia's new rich, who amassed instant fortunes through banditry, have formed an exclusive … oligarchy of 150 to 200 people that run the country … The government enjoys the same impunity as the former communist power and cannot be called a democracy' (*The Times*, 28 November 1996, p. 16).

'Afraid it had no political allies, the desperate Yeltsin administration decided to create some. The Kremlin's vehicle was the shares-for-loans privatization scheme, which, over a few months in the autumn of 1995, transferred controlling stakes in some of Russia's most valuable companies to government insiders at a fraction of their potential worth … Yeltsin cruised to victory, aided by the vigorous organizational and material support of the small group of bankers he had made into billionaires' (Chrystia Freeland, *FT*, Survey, 9 April 1997, p. i).

10 July 1996. Yeltsin: 'The policy of reforms will be continued, but the economic course requires serious corrections. Factories must have orders, people must have work and we must ensure a rise in every Russian family's living standards. I see this as my main task.'

15 July 1996. Nikolai Yegorov is replaced as chief of staff by Anatoli Chubais.

17 July 1996. General Igor Rodionov (supported by Lebed) is appointed defence minister.

6 August 1996. Yeltsin returns to work.

7–8 August 1996. The founding congress of the National Patriotic Union (NPU) takes place. The NPU consists of many left-wing and nationalist parties, including the Communist Party of the Russian Federation and the Agrarian Party of Russia. Gennadi Zyuganov is appointed leader. The head of the NPU's organizing committee, Nikolai Ryzhkov, says: 'The aim of the movement is to achieve a transformation to save the country from national catastrophe and to create a force working for the rebirth of Russia as a great, independent and socially-orientated power.'

9 August 1996. A gaunt Boris Yeltsin is sworn in as president. (He plans a two-month holiday, allegedly due to 'colossal exhaustion'.) The low-key and shortened ceremony is held indoors, overshadowed by setbacks in heavy fighting in Chechenia.

Yeltsin renominates Chernomyrdin as prime minister (confirmed by the Duma the following day by 314 votes to eighty-five, with three abstentions).

15 August 1996. Three first deputy prime ministers are appointed: Aleksei Bolshakov (industry, construction, transport and communications, and use of mineral resources; deputizes for Chernomyrdin); Vladimir Potanin, head of Oneximbank (the economy; he replaces Vladimir Kadannikov); Alexander Livshits (finance).

22 August 1996. Yeltsin makes his first public appearance since 9 August.

Tatiana Dmitriyeva (health) becomes the only woman in the cabinet.

5 September 1996. In a television interview Yeltsin announces that he is to have an operation later in the month.

10 September 1996. Ministers in defence, security and intelligence are told that 'all questions that require a decision by the head of state' will be 'co-ordinated' by prime minister Chernomyrdin during Yeltin's 'leave' of absence. Yeltsin will retain control of the 'red button' relating to nuclear weapons.

19 September 1996. Yeltsin signs a decree promising to transfer all his presidential powers to prime minister Chernomyrdin during the former's operation. But Yeltsin needs to sign another decree authorizing this handover of power and yet another to take power back.

11 October 1996. Alexander Korzhakov gives a news conference: 'Some people who are now in the president's entourage really wanted to run him into the ground in order to get the situation which we have now. And, naturally, they wanted to manipulate him behind his back after that.' Korzhakov says he has 'compromising material' which he will reveal if he or is family are threatened. (Korzhakov has become the target of a criminal investigation after being accused of extortion. 'Some observers see the conflicting charges as part of the rivalry between Mr Chubais and Mr

Alexander Lebed, the popular security adviser who has befriended General Korzhakov': Chrystia Freeland, *FT*, 12 October 1996, p. 2.)

13 October 1996. Lebed and Korzhakov appear together at a public meeting in Tula. Lebed supports Korzhakov's candidacy for the former's old parliamentary seat at Tula (which he had to give up when promoted by Yeltsin).

17 October 1996. Yeltsin dismisses Lebed: "Some time ago he [Lebed] offered to resign, but I told him that he must learn to work together with all state organizations and leaders ... We parted and I did not accept his resignation, thinking that he would draw conclusions. He has not drawn conclusions. I must say that during this time he has made a series of mistakes which are simply unacceptable for Russia and damaging. Then some sort of election race is being created. The elections are not until 2000, but already now such a situation is being created that everybody seems to be striving for elections ... There must be a united team ... It is Lebed who is splitting them up, taking a series of actions that are not co-ordinated with the president. This is totally unacceptable. Korzhakov is out of office and he [Lebed] took him to Tula to present him there as his successor ... I have to relieve General Lebed of his position as secretary of the security council. A decree to this effect will be signed today to relieve Lebed ... of the position of secretary of the security council ... and assistant to the President ... on national security.'

Lebed's reply: 'I have no intention of carrying out a presidential campaign while there is a living president'; 'The decision was perfectly natural. The only question was when. I was the black sheep in this flock'; 'It would be a great pity if, as a result of the actions of individuals very close to where we are now, military action in Chechenia were to begin again. I have not the slightest regret at the loss of my first two posts. I am not made to be a bureaucrat – I cannot bow and scrape, I cannot be a servant. But I do regret the loss of the third duty [presidential representative to Chechenia]. I am very sorry about that'; 'I just got in the way of Chubais's attempts to establish a regency. He wants to be president'; 'My comrades in arms, my allies and people who I probably do not know in person – do not do anything abrupt. We act only using constitutional means.' (Lebed also claimed that the businessman Boris Berezovsky personally threatened him after the truce in Chechenia was signed because it harmed Berezovsky's business: *FT*, 18 October 1996, p. 1.)

18 October 1996. The State Duma approves Lebed's dismissal.

19 October 1996. Yeltsin appoints Ivan Rybkin (the former speaker of the State Duma) as secretary of the 'security council' and presidential envoy to Chechenia (but not national security adviser).

21 October 1996. Yeltsin announces the establishment of a consultative council to co-ordinate decision-making. Chernomyrdin and Chubais are to meet regularly with the speakers of the two houses of parliament (Gennadi Seleznyov of the State Duma and Yegor Stroyev of the Council of the Federation).

27 October 1996. A presidential decree strips Korzhakov of his military rank of lieutenant-general.

28 October 1996. A decree relieves Korzhakov of all his military duties because of 'a series of slanderous statements concerning the Russian president and members of his family' and the releasing of confidential information. (Korzhakov has said for example, that Yeltsin is being manipulated by his daughter Tatiana Dyachenko and his chief of staff Chubais: *IHT*, 29 October 1996, p. 5.)

All Yeltsin's meetings are cancelled for the rest of the week (today being a Tuesday) because of the need to conduct medical tests.

30 October 1996. The controversial businessman Boris Berezovsky is appointed deputy secretary of the 'security council'. This decision is criticized by Zyuganov and Yavlinsky and Gennadi Selezyov says that he will boycott the new consultative council until Yeltsin returns to work on the grounds that he cannot work with Chubais.

'The same tight-knit group of seven businessmen now meets weekly and works closely with Mr Chubais ... the group has placed two of its members – Mr Vladimir Potanin and Mr Boris Berezovsky – in important government positions ... Mr Berezovsky [is] head of a sprawling business empire comprising car dealerships, TV stations and a bank ... the business alliance funded Mr Yeltsin's reelection drive to the tune of about $3 million ... it appointed a ten-strong campaign team headed by Mr Chubais and also containing Ms Tatiana Dyachenko, Mr Yeltsin's daughter ... Apart from Mr Berezovsky the group of seven comprises: Mr Potanin, former head of Oneximbank and now first deputy prime minister for the economy; Mr Vladimir Gussinsky, head of the powerful Most banking and media group; Mr Mikhail Khodorkovsky, president of the Menatep financial and oil empire; Mr Peter Aven and Mr Mikhail Friedman of Alfa Bank; and Mr Alexander Smolensky of Stolichny Bank. Their six enterprises, according to Mr Berezovsky, control about 50 per cent of the economy ... Mr Berezovsky's appointment this week has sparked vigorous protests uniting the communist opposition and Russia's small band of liberal democrats. Critics say the businessmen represent an unelected oligarchy whose rise to power jeopardizes the country's chances of becoming a democratic state with an open market economy based on the rule of law ... Sergei Kovalyov, a leading human rights campaigner, said "It is very dangerous" ... Mr Kovalyov ... recalls a conversation a couple of years ago in which Mr Chubais complained bitterly about leading businessmen. "They steal and steal and steal ... But let them steal and take their property. They will then become owners and decent administrators of this property"' (Chrystia Freeland, John Thornhill and Andrew Gowers, *FT*, 1 November 1996, p. 17).

5 November 1996. President Yeltsin undergoes a seven-hour, quintuple heart bypass operation. He signs decree handing over presidential powers to Chernomyrdin. (Yeltsin signed another decree the following day taking them back.)

4 December 1996. Yeltsin moves out of the sanatorium and into a nearby government residence.

9 December 1996. Yeltsin moves to his country residence.

20 December 1996. Yeltsin is interviewed on television for the first time since his operation. He says that he will resume work at the Kremlin on 23 December 1996.

23 December 1996. Yeltsin returns to work at the Kremlin.

25 December 1996. Yeltsin addresses the nation on television.

27 December 1996. Alexander Lebed announces the formation of a new political party, the Russian Popular Republican Party. He says that this is a 'third force' avoiding the extremes of left and right: 'The real control of social and economic development should belong to the government responsible to parliament's lower house and formed according to the results of the parliamentary elections.'

8 January 1997. Yeltsin is admitted to hospital with the first signs of pneumonia.

20 January 1997. Yeltsin is discharged from hospital and moves into his country house outside Moscow in order to recuperate.

22 January 1997. Yeltsin unexpectedly returns to work at the Kremlin (but only for one day).

28 January 1997. Yeltsin goes to work at the Kremlin.

9 February 1997. Alexander Korzhakov wins the Duma by-election in Tula (held by Alexander Lebed before his resignation).

11 February 1997. It is announced that there will be no speedy return to the Kremlin by Yeltsin.

14 February 1997. Yeltsin addresses the nation on radio.

21 February 1997. US Secretary of State Madeleine Albright meets Yeltsin on the second day of her two-day visit to Russia.

3 March 1997. Yeltsin meets an EU delegation in Moscow.

6 March 1997. Yeltsin gives a vigorous state-of-the-nation speech. He lists an array of problems (including crime and corruption, arrears in pay and pensions, and the decline in living standards) and severely criticizes the government. 'Lack of will and indifference, irresponsibility and incompetence in dealing with state problems – that is how people assess the current government. I have to admit that they are right … The executive branch has turned out to be incapable of working without the president shouting at it.'

7 March 1997. Yeltsin makes Anatoli Chubais a first deputy prime minister (i.e. the fourth).

17 March 1997. Boris Nemtsov, the reformist governor of Nizhny Novgorod, is appointed as first deputy prime minister (one of only two). Nemtsov is to be in charge of social welfare (including wage and pension arrears) and the regulation of natural monopolies.

Anatoli Chubais takes over as finance minister (as well as of the economy). Alexander Livshits moves from finance to the post of deputy chief of the presidential staff. (Chubais has cancelled the tax privileges enjoyed by Norilsk Metal and Yukos: *FT*, 19 March 1997, p. 2.)

There are six deputy prime ministers: Yakov Urinson, industry and deputy economics minister; Alfred Kokh, privatization and budgetary revenue; Anatoli Kulikov, interior ministry, customs, police and tax enforcement; Oleg Sysuyev, regions; Valery Serov, relations with other CIS countries; Vladimir Bulgak, science and technology.

Vladimir Potanin (who returns to head Oneximbank), Viktor Ilyushin and Alexei Bolshakov lose their positions.

18 March 1997. Yeltsin vetoes the bill (passed by both houses of parliament) forbidding the return of most works of art seized in Germany at the end of the Second World War. Yeltsin supports the joint Russian-German commission looking into the matter. (On 4 April 1997 the Duma overturned Yeltsin's veto by far more than the required two-thirds majority, by 308 votes to fifteen. On 13 May 1997 the Council of the Federation also overturned Yeltsin's veto by more than the required two-thirds majority. On 6 April 1998 the constitutional court ruled against Yeltsin, saying that he had 'evaded' his constitutional responsibilities by not signing the bill. Under the new law the return of every item of war booty would be subject to individual parliamentary approval. The bill would introduce highly complicated procedures for the return of trophy art, requiring a formal request by a foreign government and approval by the Russian parliament: *IHT*, 7 April 1998, p. 5. Yeltsin signed the bill on 14 April 1998.)

26 March 1997. Yevgeni Yasin remains in the cabinet but as minister without portfolio. Yasin is to deal with longer-term economic strategy. Alexei Kudrin becomes first deputy finance minister.

24 April 1997. Nemtsov is awarded the fuel and energy ministry as well.

20 May–2 June 1997. Yeltsin attends all the sessions the meeting of the G7 ('the Summit of the Eight' in President Clinton's terminology) except the one dealing with international financial affairs. Russia is accepted as a member of the Paris Club of creditor governments. The final communiqué starts with 'We, eight industrialized democracies of the world'.

23 June 1997. The State Duma passes a controversial bill on religion ('On Freedom of Conscience and Religious Associations') by 300 votes to eight. The bill has to be approved by the Council of the Federation and by the president. (The bill was approved by the Council of the Federation. Yeltsin vetoed it on 22 July 1997 but submitted an essentially unchanged version. The State Duma passed the revised draft on 19 September 1997 by 358 votes to six. It was passed unanimously by the Council of the Federation on 24 September 1997 and signed by Yeltsin on 26 September 1997.)

One of the main arguments put forward is to curb extremists cults. 'Traditional' religions ('religious organizations') are unaffected. The Russian Orthodox Church is described as playing a 'special role' and being an 'inalienable part of Russian historical, spiritual and cultural heritage'.

Christianity, Islam, Buddhism and Judaism are described as 'respected' religions that are 'an integral part of the historical heritage of the peoples of Russia'. All religions will have to apply for registration before the end of 1998.

A religious association can be classified as all-Russian only if it has had at least 100,000 members and branches in at least half the provinces for at least fifty years. 'Religious groups' not qualifying in this way must obtain documents from local authorities showing that they have existed under special supervision for fifteen years in order to be registered as 'religious organizations'. Those 'religious groups' that fail this test will be subject to a number of restrictions, e.g. they will be banned from owning property; services cannot be conducted in public places (including hospitals, crematoria and prisons); they cannot publish, import or distribute religious literature; they cannot promote educational activity (including running schools); they cannot invite foreign preachers. Those religious associations already registered have to reregister every year for fifteen years.

The constitution guarantees that religions 'shall be equal before the law' (*IHT*, 24 June 1997, p. 5). The restriction of the right 'to spread a belief' to 'religious organizations' is 'a direct contradiction of the Russian constitution, which guarantees equality to all associations of believers and excludes restrictions of civil rights on grounds of religion'. Religious associations have the right to teach their religion only to 'their own successors', 'whereas the constitution guarantees every individual the right to spread religious disciplines and receive information and ideas'. The new law entitles only citizens of the Russian Federation to unite on the basis of religion, although 'the constitution extends this right to foreigners and those with no citizenship' (*Obshchaya Gazeta*, reprinted in *The Guardian*, 9 July 1997, p. 15).

25 June 1997. A robot supply ship crashes into the Mir space station.

30 June 1997. Yeltsin appoints his daughter Tatiana Dyachenko as an official adviser on questions of his public image.

13 August 1997. Alfred Kokh resigns as privatization minister and is replaced by Maxim Boycko. (Kokh was seemingly given an $100,000 advance from a Swiss company with ties to Oneximbank: *IHT*, 18 November 1997, p. 10.) (See Chapter 5 on privatization.)

18 August 1997. Mikhail Manevich, the deputy governor of St Petersburg and chairman of the St Petersburg committee for the management of city property, is assassinated.

1 September 1997. Yeltsin: 'My term ends in 2000. I will not run again.' (The constitution rules out a third term for any president. But some argue that since Yeltsin's first term started when the Soviet Union existed it does not count. On 2 October 1997, in reply to a question about a third term, Yeltsin was less certain: 'My supporters and friends have forbidden me to talk about this matter. There are still three years to go and it is too early to talk about it.' On 9 October 1997 he seemed certain once again: 'I will not present my candidacy for a third term.')

3 September 1997. The reopening of the Cathedral of Christ the Saviour in Moscow. (It was built to celebrate the victory over Napoleon in 1812, being completed in 1833, and destroyed by Stalin in 1931.)

5–7 September 1997. Mayor Yuri Luzhkov organizes a three-day spectacular to celebrate the 850th anniversary of Moscow.

14 September 1997. The security service receives a tip-off of a plot to assassinate Chubais. There are rumours that an oil company is involved.

15 September 1997. Yeltsin meets with six business tycoons to persuade them to stop quarrelling among themselves and to criticize those attacking members of the government (especially Chubais and Nemtsov). (Boris Berezovsky did not attend the meeting. Those present were Vladimir Potanin, Vladimir Gusinsky, Mikhail Friedman, Alexander Smolensky, Vladimir Vinogradov and Mikhail Khodorkovsky.)

17 September 1997. Russia becomes a member (the nineteenth) of the Paris Club of creditor nations.

24 September 1997. Yeltsin speaks to the Council of the Federation: 'Economic freedom alone is not enough for a transition to steady economic growth. We need a new economic order. And that requires strong and intelligent government and a sturdy state ... Today everyone agrees that we must increase the role of the state ... We are resolutely moving from a policy of "non-interference" to a policy of preemptive regulation of economic processes and oversight of vitally important branches of the economy and the effectiveness of budget spending. This is not, of course, a return to the time of Gosplan and Gossnab ... The government is establishing clear rules of economic behaviour that are the same for everyone ... The state will not tolerate any attempts at pressure by representatives of business and banks ... At the same time we will harshly suppress attempts by government officials to establish their own rules ... of operating in the market ... We have begun to chop away at the economic roots of corruption ... We are strengthening the Federal Treasury. Work with so-called authorized banks is being cut back. By the beginning of 1998 all federal budget accounts will be in the Federal Treasury, not in banks ... We are switching to a competitive system for all state purchases ... The handling of federal budget money and money in off-budget funds will also be shifted to a competitive basis ... We must energetically stimulate demand for the output of Russian enterprises. Of course we must not support all of them indiscriminately, only those that produce high quality goods.'

10 October 1997. France, Germany and Russia agree to hold annual summit meetings.

15 October 1997. A vote of no confidence in the government in the State Duma is postponed until 22 October.

21 October 1997. The Communist Party announces that it will withdraw its vote of no confidence, claiming that Yeltsin has made sufficient concessions. These include reconsideration of the new tax code (to be submitted to a commission of ministers and MPs), regular talks and extra time devoted on television and radio to the State Duma.

It is announced that a new diamond agreement has been reached with De Beers of South Africa, effective 1 December 1997. It will expire at the end of 1998 but can be extended for another two years if mutually agreed (*FT*, 22 October 1997, p. 41). (See entry for 23 February 1996.) (On 23 February 1996 Russia and De Beers signed a three-year 'memorandum of general principles' on the sale of diamonds. The old five-year agreement had expired at the end of 1995. On 1 January 1997 De beers broke off the agreement after failure to reach agreement. On 21 August 1998 it was announced that agreement had been reached with De Beers to extend the agreement for another three years: *FT*, 22 August 1998, p. 18. On 3 November 1998 it was announced that a marketing agreement had been signed between De Beers and Almazy Rossii-Sakha [Alrosa], extending for three years an agreement for De Beers to market diamonds. The Russian government owns 32 per cent of Alrosa, which produces 98 per cent of Russian rough diamonds. Russian diamonds make up about a quarter of total sales by De Beers, which in turn accounts for more than 60 per cent of the world trade in rough diamonds. Alrosa agreed to sell at least half its output through De beers, but could sell 5 per cent of its diamonds on the international market independently: *FT*, 4 November 1998, p. 40.)

5 November 1997. Boris Berezovsky is 'relieved of his duties [as deputy secretary of the 'security council', with responsibility for negotiations with Chechenia] ... in connection with his move to other work'. (Nemtsov: 'I think that this is an important step in Russia's effort to move away as far as possible from oligarchic capitalism.' Berezovsky accused Chubais of favouring Vladimir Potanin: 'The path Anatoli Chubais has taken seems to me to be totally hypocritical': *FT*, 6 November 1997, p. 2.)

14 November 1997. Yeltsin dismisses Alexander Kazakov, his deputy chief of staff. (Kazakov is one of five co-authors of a contracted book on privatization, the others being Anatoli Chubais, Maxim Boycko, Pyotr Mostovoi and Alfred Kokh. They had been paid large advances by a publishing company 51 per cent owned by Oneximbank. Vladimir Potanin, who heads Oneximbank, was successful in the sale of shares in the telephone holding company Svyazinvest in July 1997. On 13 November parliament voted for an investigation by the prosecutor-general. The total sum was apparently $450,000, so each co-author received $90,000. Chubais said that under the contract the co-authors were to donate 95 per cent of the money to the Foundation for the Defence of Private Property in Russia. Yegor Gaidar agreed to handle the donations.)

15 November 1997. Yeltsin dismisses Maxim Boycko (privatization minister) and Pyotr Mostovoi (head of the federal bankruptcy agency). Yeltsin calls Chubais's conduct 'impermissible' but rejects his offer of resignation.

19 November 1997. The State Duma approves a non-binding resolution (by 267 votes to four) calling for the dismissal of Chubais. Prime minister

Chernomyrdin says that deputy prime ministers will be stripped of their ministries (finance in the case of Chubais).

20 November 1997. Chubais formally loses the finance portfolio and Nemtsov loses the energy portfolio. The new appointments are Mikhail Zadornov (finance minister), Sergei Kiryenko (fuel and energy minister) and Tatiana Mitina (Yeltsin's deputy chief of staff).

25 November 1997. Yeltsin says that he 'won't give up Chubais'. 'This is not an unlawful act. It has nothing to do with the criminal code. This is a moral-ethical problem.'

10 December 1997. Yeltsin enters a sanatorium with 'an acute respiratory viral infection'. (Although he did some work in the sanatorium, there was renewed speculation about the seriousness of Yeltsin's health.)

23 December 1997. Yeltsin works for three hours in the Kremlin but returns to the sanatorium as planned.

26 December 1997. Yeltsin does a full day's work and remarks: 'Today it is obvious to the majority of people that there are few noticeable economic successes. We will correct mistakes and draw the necessary conclusions ... We have not lost the habit of thinking in accordance with [communist] clichés and rules. Only party slogans have been replaced with economic ones. Instead of exhortations to build the Dnieper power dam or the Magnita plant we called for "privatization at any price".'

Yeltsin and the State Duma agree to set up a working group to seek a compromise on the land code.

16 January 1998. Prime minister Chernomyrdin takes control of the fuel and energy industry (formerly under Nemtsov), the finance ministry, budget and monetary policy, development of the banking system, and government policy on the news media (formerly under Chubais). Chubais will concentrate on tax policy, while Nemtsov will concentrate on housing, pension, transport and electricity reform.

19 January 1998. Yeltsin claims that not all wage arrears to state employees were paid by the end-of-1997 deadline.

30 January 1998. Yeltsin says that he will not run again for the presidency (scheduled for 9 July 2000). 'I will not violate the constitution. However, I have already made up my mind about my successor. Now I have only one problem – when to announce it. Even the candidate does not know. He may dream about it but he does not know.' (Yeltsin is sixty-seven on 1 February 1998.)

The official commission confirms that the remains of Tsar Nicholas II and some members of his family and entourage (nine people altogether) unearthed in 1991 in Yekaterinburg (formerly Sverdlovsk) are genuine. Although the final decision rests with Yeltsin, the commission recommends that the remains of the royal family should be buried in St Petersburg (rather than Moscow or Yekaterinburg) on 17 July 1998 (the eightieth anniversary of their murder by the Bolsheviks). (On 27 February 1998 the government announced that the commission's recommendations had been accepted. The government recommended that the remains be buried in the Peter and Paul Fortress/Cathedral in St Petersburg. But the president had not yet given his approval and the Russian Orthodox Church still had doubts about the authenticity of the remains. Yeltsin gave his approval on 2 March.)

5 February 1998. Yeltsin: 'I will stand my ground. I am telling you, both [Chubais and Nemtsov] will continue working until the year 2000.'

9–11 February 1998. Yeltsin visits Italy and the Vatican.

12 February 1998. Pavel Popovskikh, a retired military intelligence officer (the former director of intelligence for the paratroop units), is arrested in connection with the murder of the journalist Dmitri Kholodov on 17 October 1994. Kholodov was investigation corruption in the Western Group of Forces (that part of the army formerly in East Germany).

17 February 1998. Yeltsin delivers his annual address to the State Duma and the Council of the Federation: 'We are stuck in the middle of a bridge. The inflationary past is behind us but we have failed to reach the investment future ... I am speaking about the need for a realistic budget, about ending non-payments, about industrial policy, about economizing. I will no longer repeat this. If the government is not able to solve these strategic tasks, then we will have to have another government ... The Russian government will further protect property, secure economic freedom and a market economy, retain low inflation and a firm rate for the rouble. But today that is not enough. We need stable and proper economic growth, a supported flow of investment ... Although the budget is already under discussion, nevertheless it should be made realistic this year by adopting amendments.'

28 February 1998. Yeltsin dismisses the deputy prime minister in charge of relations with the former Soviet republics, the minister of education and the minister of transport.

2 March 1998. Yeltsin deprives eleven deputy prime ministers (including Chubais and Nemtsov) and a deputy head of the presidential administration of their bodyguards, allegedly as a cost-saving measure.

Yeltsin appoints Ivan Rybkin as deputy prime minister overseeing relations with the former Soviet republics.

The nuclear energy minister is dismissed.

3 March 1998. Yeltsin appoints Andrei Kokoshin as secretary of the 'security council', replacing Ivan Rybkin.

13 March 1998. Yeltsin has an 'acute respiratory infection'. (He next turned up for work on 20 March.)

23 March 1998. Yeltsin dismisses the prime minister Chernomyrdin and the entire cabinet. (An April 1997 law states that the removal of a prime minister automatically entails the dissolution of the government: *The Telegraph*, 24 March 1998, p. 14.)

Yeltsin makes a television broadcast: 'Chernomyrdin is stepping down. I have worked with Viktor Stepanovich for more than five years, he has done a great deal for the country, and I value his thoroughness and reliability. I have never doubted his loyalty, his devotion to work or his human decency. The 2000 [presidential] election is very important to us. One might say that it is Russia's future. I have instructed Chernomyrdin to concentrate on political preparations for the election. The resignation of the government does not mean a change of course. It means our desire to impart more energy and efficiency to economic reforms, to give them an additional impetus, a fresh momentum. It is a natural process of renewal. No government is irreplaceable. The cabinet of ministers has, on the whole, accomplished the tasks that were set for it, but, unfortunately, it has not solved a number of key problems. Yes, we have made a certain amount of progress in the economy, but we are still lagging behind in the social sphere. Many people do not feel any change for the better. I believe that recently the government has been lacking in dynamism and initiative, fresh approaches and fresh ideas. Without those a powerful upsurge in the economy is not possible. In short, the country needs a new team that is capable of achieving real, tangible results. I think the members of the cabinet need to focus better on the solution of concrete economic and social issues. They should be less involved in politics.'

Yeltsin at first appointed himself as acting prime minister. But Yeltsin then appointed thirty-five-year-old Sergei Kiriyenko as acting prime minister. In May 1997 Kiriyenko had been appointed deputy fuel and energy minister and in November 1997 full minister, having been transferred from his post as president of an oil refinery in Nizhny Novgorod at the request of Boris Nemtsov. Kiriyenko: 'There will be no new government programme. There will be continuity of policy.'

Yeltsin dismisses Viktor Chernomyrdin, Anatoli Chubais, Anatoli Kulikov (interior minister) by name. The remainder of the cabinet will carry out their duties until a new government is formed. Chernomyrdin is to 'concentrate on political preparations' for the presidential election to be held in the year 2000.

Comments: 'Reform of Russia's business environment ... has been neglected ... Yeltsin is certainly aware of the need for these reforms. But his attention may be distracted by two other priorities. One is to keep up economic growth ... His other priority, of course, is political manoeuvring, ahead of the presidential elections in 2000. Mr Yeltsin has long been playing off Russia's political factions against each other, trying to prevent any of them from gaining too much power. The dismissal of the government, whatever reasons Mr Yeltsin gave, was certainly motivated by politics rather than economics' (*FT*, editorial, 24 March 1998, p. 23).

'Yet again, Mr Yeltsin has made himself Tsar of all he surveys. Nothing else makes sense ... As has happened before, the president has reasserted his authority so as to spread maximum confusion elsewhere ... By plunging Russia into political chaos, he has also put himself back at the centre of the most important game in town – the search for Russia's next president ... The once omnipotent Kremlin chief had found himself growing marginalized as the country focused not on him, but on his potential successors. Even the (to put it mildly) uncharismatic prime minister, Viktor Chernomyrdin, began to assume an independent political role, emerging, in the eyes of some observers, as one of Mr Yeltsin's most likely successors' (Chrystia Freeland, *FT*, 24 March 1998, p. 23).

'The Duma is set up in a way that has given it an investment in irresponsibility. Irresponsible opposition is virtually the only power available to it ... The president has more power than is good for him or for the state, functioning as a latter-day Czar. Behind his visible conflict with the Duma is the half-visible struggle among that handful of men who dominate the privatized economy, each with his favoured politicians, and each with his own publishing or media group' (William Pfaff, *IHT*, 22 April 1998, p. 9).

Some observers, says Leyla Boulton, have interpreted Yeltsin's move as a way of avoiding a (now cancelled) review of the government's performance scheduled by parliament for 10 April 1998 (*FT*, 24 March 1998, p. 2).

'Yeltsin's dismissal of all ... ministers was seen partly as a genuine attempt to revitalize Russia's sluggish reform process, and partly as a ploy to reestablish himself as the unchallenged ruler' (Richard Beeston, *The Times*, 24 March 1998, p. 1).

Boris Berezovsky's 'advice may have contributed to the president's decision to sack his government' (*FT*, 25 March 1998, p. 1).

'Newspapers that back Mr Chernomyrdin targeted Boris Berezovsky ... as the plotter ... Many commentators said a central motivation could have been his [Yeltsin's] awareness of Mr Chernomyrdin's growing political ambitions' (*IHT*, 25 March 1998, p. 12).

'Mr Chernomyrdin ... as prime minister ... was powerful enough to deal with them as equals ... Only if Mr Chernomyrdin were obliged to seek power without the patronage of the state at his disposal would the oligarchs have him at their mercy ... Did Mr Berezovsky engineer Mr Chernomyrdin's dismissal in order to take control of him? It is a possible reading of events ... There is another view ... Berezovsky's ... scheming may have gone badly wrong. By this reckoning, too, Mr Berezovsky identified Mr Chernomyrdin as "his candidate". But the two moved too quickly and carelessly ... It argues that Mr Yeltsin ... struck back. For the moment this version ranks as more plausible' (*The Economist*, 28 March 1998, p. 27).

'The struggle is largely between a small group of big-business owners who have amassed enormous fortunes as former state enterprises have been sold off and government aides who have pledged to bring a sense of fair play to Russia's anything-goes brand of capitalism. At the centre is Boris Berezovsky ... who has done more than anyone to mobilize the opposition to Mr Yeltsin ... Berezovsky has unleashed a furious media campaign against [Kiriyenko] ... On Tuesday [21 April] Mr Berezovsky's newspaper Nezavisimaya Gazeta openly proclaimed that a ... fight over the Kiriyenko nomination could be avoided only if Mr Yeltsin met the tycoons' conditions. The price: the abandonment of market reformers who have clashed with Mr Berezovsky by trying to regulate better the sale of state property ...Berezovsky has been so active that Mr Yeltsin reportedly warned him to limit his intrigues or leave the country, according to press reports ... He was ousted in a power struggle last year [1997] but has maintained a close working relationship with Tatiana Dyachenko, Mr Yeltsin's daughter and political advisor ... [Berezovsky is] at odds with Anatoli Chubias and Boris Nemtsov ... who has asserted that their goal was to break the grip that the "crony capitalists" had on the Russian economy. The dispute over the control of economic policy crested this year when the government began to arrange the auction of the state oil company Rosneft. For months Mr Berezovsky lobbied furiously to shape the conditions to his advantage – and lost. The official who drafted the terms was Mr Kiriyenko' (Michael Gordon, *IHT*, 23 April 1998, pp. 1, 10).

'The real struggle ... is between rival power-brokers and businessmen, and can be glimpsed indistinctly through the newspapers they control. Nezavisimaya Gazeta, owned by Boris Berezovsky, warns that Mr Kiriyenko can be confirmed only if the president accepts the conditions of "big Capital", getting rid of reformers who have tried to break up the big private monopolies. Komsomolskaya Pravda, owned by Vladimir Potanin, replies with the accusation that Mr Berezovsky has bribed some deputies, notably the supporters of the ultra-nationalist Vladimir Zhirinovsky, to vote against Mr Kiriyenko' (*FT*, editorial, 24 April 1998, p. 21).

'There are many in the West who think that Boris Yeltsin has gone mad ... But in fact President Yeltsin has acted in a completely rational and constitutional way. Clearly he was jealous of Mr Chernomyrdin, but the prime minister has usurped much of his power, contrary to the Russian constitution. Worse, he has ganged up with some unsavoury crony capitalists, notably the media tycoon Boris Berezovsky, who opposes competitive auctions of state companies perhaps because he prefers to buy them cheaply in inside deals. Mr Chernomyrdin and Mr Berezovsky together helped stall reforms last fall. With the appointment of Mr Kiriyenko, badly needed reforms can be restarted ... Mr Chernomyrdin successfully stalled on tax reform for years ... The government expanded by no less than 1.2 million bureaucrats during Mr Chernomyrdin's tenure. No wonder Russian and foreign businessmen complain that little can be done because of extraordinary red tape. In Soviet fashion Mr Chernomyrdin had one apparatchik for every reformer in the government. Mr Kiriyenko has demanded that half the bureaucracy be eliminated so that the other half can start working ... The most vocal criticism [of thirty-five year-old Kiriyenko, 'a young official largely unknown abroad'] has come from Mr Berezovsky, whose newspapers have tried to expound on all of his faults, without finding much. Mr Berezovsky's concerns appear to be that he is independent and opposes crony capitalism. Because such vested interests remain strong, progress is likely to come in small steps. But Mr Yeltsin took an important stride when he replaced his prime minister' (Anders Åslund, *IHT*, 29 April 1998, p. 10).

27 March 1998. Yeltsin nominates Sergei Kiriyenko as prime minister and threatens to dissolve parliament if he is not confirmed: 'I am not trying to scare anyone. I simply tell you as president, do not waste your time. Confirm him quickly. If you reject him once, twice, three times, then the fourth time means dissolution ... I have already warned Kiriyenko: he does not have any time to warm up. Social issues, which have been neglected, demand immediate solutions. We cannot allow wage arrears to accumulate.'

28 March 1998. Chernomyrdin announces that he is to be a candidate in the 2000 presidential election.

30 March 1998. Yeltsin: 'I am not taking part in the [2000 presidential] elections.' Justice minister Sergei Stepashin is named as acting interior minister.

4 April 1998. Anatoli Chubais is voted on to the fifteen-member board of directors of UES (United Energy Services), the electricity group (*FT*, 6 April 1998, p. 3).

UES owns the national transmission grid and controls about 80 per cent of generating capacity. The shareholding structure of UES is as follows: the state, 52 per cent; foreign investors, 30 per cent; management and employees, 7 per cent; other domestic shareholders, 11 per cent (*The Economist*, 11 April 1998, p. 66).

7 April 1998. Yeltsin meets parliamentary, regional and trade union representatives. He rules out a coalition government (the cabinet needing 'business-minded professionals') but offers to make 1998 a 'year without confrontation' (i.e. Yeltsin will not veto bills passed by parliament) if Kiriyenko is confirmed as prime minister.

8 April 1998. Vladimir Zhirinovsky: 'The essence of the conflict around the Jewish people is that when their number grows too much in some country, war breaks out there. That happened in Germany' (*The Independent*, 9 April 1998, p. 15).

9 April 1998. The national day of action, organized by the Federation of Independent Trade Unions and supported by the Communist Party, takes place against such things as the late payment of wages and pensions. Under the banner of 'Wages, Jobs and Legality', trade unions are demanding a rise in the minimum wage and legislation to defend workers' rights. The government is called upon to strengthen an article in the civil code, which should oblige enterprises to pay wages before taxes (*FT*, 9 April 1998, p. 2). But the day of action is poorly supported. Instead of the hoped for 20 million, estimates ranged from 2 million to 5 million (Moscow television; *The Guardian*, 10 April 1998) to only 'hundreds of thousands' (*IHT*, 10 April 1998, p. 1; *The Independent*, 10 April 1998, p. 13).

10 April 1998. Kiriyenko is rejected as prime minister by the State Duma in the first round of voting but by a smaller margin than generally expected, 143 'yes' votes (at least 226 are required) to 186 'no' votes. Yeltsin resubmits his nomination. Kiriyenko stresses the need to do something about pay arrears and for greater social protection. He says that almost one-third of the population are living at or below the poverty line (*IHT*, 11 April 1998, p. 4). Kiriyenko: 'Today more than 32 million people, about a quarter of the Russian population, have incomes below the official minimum subsistence level. That is the main question we must all answer' (*FT*, 11 April 1998, p. 2). (The vote was by secret ballot.)

13 April 1998. Yeltsin says he has told an aide to consider deputies' other concerns, apparently over housing and perquisites they receive in Moscow. But he makes it clear that such benefits will come only after Kiriyenko is confirmed (*IHT*, 14 April 1998, p. 5).

Yeltsin says that he had told the administrative department, which provides cars, housing and holiday cottages for the bureaucracy and the legislature, to 'solve the deputies' problems', but only 'if they show a constructive attitude' (*The Telegraph*, 14 April 1998, p. 13).

14 April 1998. Speaker of the State Duma Gennadi Seleznyov, after failing to convince Yeltsin of the need for a fresh candidate, recommends support for Kiriyenko: 'I think the majority of deputies will make the right choice – the Duma must be preserved. I sensed that I had done all I can. I could not change the president's mind.' 'The Duma's fate is a hundred times more important to me than the future of Kiriyenko. We must support Kiriyenko's candidacy.'

17 April 1998. Kiriyenko loses in the second round of voting by 271 votes to 115, i.e. by a larger margin than in the first round. Yeltsin resubmits his nomination. (There was an open vote on this occasion.)

22 April 1998. The Council of the Federation votes heavily in favour (with only ten against) of a resolution recommending that the State Duma approve Kiriyenko as prime minister.

Gennadi Zyuganov, after laying a wreath at Lenin's tomb on Red Square (to celebrate the one-hundred-and-twenty-eighth anniversary of Lenin's birth) again refuses to endorse Kiriyenko.

24 April 1998. In its third vote (which was secret) the State Duma approves Kiriyenko as prime minister. Only 276 deputies voted, with 251 'yes' votes and twenty-five 'no' votes. Grigori Yavlinsky, who has consistently declined to support Kiriyenko, says that the latter's appointment means 'a weak, authoritarian president, a helpless Duma and a new round of bribing Zhirinovsky' (*The Guardian*, 25 April 1998, p. 17).

28–30 April 1998. There are no first deputy prime ministers in the new, streamlined, generally young, reformist-looking government. Many members were reappointed.

The three deputy prime ministers were Boris Nemtsov (oil and gas as well as energy and transportation monopolies), Viktor Khristenko (who was formerly deputy finance minister dealing with relations between the regional and federal budgets) and Oleg Sisuyev (social affairs; formerly he was mayor of Samara and labour minister). Other important members were Mikhail Zadornov (finance minister), Yakov Urinson (economy minister), Yevgeni

Primakov (foreign minister), Sergei Stepashin (interior minister), Igor Sergeyev (defence minister), Sergei Generalov (fuel and energy minister) and Viktor Semyenov (agriculture).

(On 29 April 1998 the CIS leaders appointed Boris Berezovsky as executive secretary of the organization. On 30 April Anatoli Chubais was appointed chief executive of the electricity giant Unified Energy Systems, which is 53 per cent state owned. On 17 June 1998 Yeltsin appointed Chubais a deputy prime minister, although with no seat in the cabinet, with special responsibility for co-ordinating relations with international financial organizations.

The appointment was the result of the financial crisis. During May and June there also took place industrial action and protests by, for example, miners, teachers and doctors. Miners in particular were active, e.g. blocking railway lines. The Trans-Siberian blockade was ended on 24 May and that of the northern lines on 26 May after the government promised to pay wage arrears and to find and retrain workers for new jobs. But protests continued. On 22 May a presidential decree specified cuts in administration to help pay for wage arrears: *CDSP*, 1998, vol. 50, no. 21, pp. 10–11.)

5 May 1998. A presidential spokesman says that the Kiriyenko government will have more authority than the one dismissed in March (*RET*, 1998, no. 2, p. 66).

15–17 May 1998. Yeltsin attends the G8 meeting in the United Kingdom.

17 May 1998. Alexander Lebed is elected governor of Krasnoyarsk.

21 May 1998. Armed supporters of the chairman of the Union of Moslems of Russia temporarily take over government buildings in Makhachkala, the capital of Dagestan (*CDSP*, 1998, vol. 50, no. 21, pp. 1–3).

22 May 1998. The State Duma elects Oleg Mironov as human rights commissioner to replace Sergei Kovalyov, even though Kovalyov was one of the eleven candidates (*The Independent*, 23 May 1998, p. 15).

29 May 1998. Yeltsin dismisses the head of the tax service, replacing him with former finance minister Boris Fyodorov.

17 June 1998. Yeltsin appoints Anatoli Chubais as a deputy prime minister, although with no seat in the cabinet, with special responsibility for co-ordinating relations with international financial institutions. Chubais was recommended by the 'financial oligarchy', who decided to bury their differences during the financial crisis.

19 June 1998. Yeltsin replies to a question about whether he intends to run for a third term as president: 'No, this is not planned under the constitution. The constitution provides for only two terms.'

21 June 1998. Russia and India initial and thus revive a ten-year-old pact in which Russia will build two nuclear reactors in India.

3 July 1998. General Lev Rokhlin is shot dead. His wife confesses.

7 July 1998. A German commercial satellite is launched from a Russian nuclear submarine.

14 July 1998. Yeltsin: 'I would like Russia in the year 2000 to begin work peacefully with a new president.'

17 July 1998. The remains of Tsar Nicholas II, Tsarina Alexandra, three daughters and four attendants are buried in the Peter and Paul Cathedral in St Petersburg. (The remains of his son and one other daughter have not been found.) President Yeltsin (who only decided to attend the day before): 'The massacre in Yekaterinburg was one of the most shameful pages in our history.' (In 1977, as the local Communist Party chief, Yeltsin carried out orders to destroy the Ipatiev house in Sverdlovsk – now Yekaterinburg – where the murders by the Bolsheviks took place on 17 July 1918. Patriarch Alexei II of the Russian Orthodox Church did not attend the funeral on 17 July 1998, allegedly on the grounds that he was not convinced of the authenticity of the remains. Some important members of the Romanov family did not attend the ceremony either.)

22 July 1998. Prime minister Kiriyenko offers the trade and industry ministry to Yuri Maslyukov (Communist Party MP and head of Gosplan between 1988 and 1991). (He was appointed the following day.)

25 July 1998. Yeltsin dismisses Nikolai Kovalyov as head of the Federal Security Service. The replacement is Vladimir Putin.

17 August 1998. Boris Fyodorov adds to his duties by becoming deputy prime minister responsible for macroeconomic policy and the management of the state debt.

23 August 1998. Yeltsin (who is still on holiday after about five weeks) dismisses prime minister Kiriyenko and the entire government. Viktor Chernomyrdin is named as acting prime minister. (Yeltsin failed to gain State Duma approval of Chernomyrdin as prime minister.)

28 August 1998. Yeltsin dismisses Anatoli Chubais as deputy prime minister with special responsibility for co-ordinating relations with international financial institutions.

29 August 1998. Boris Fyodorov is appointed acting deputy prime minister with responsibility for financial affairs and negotiations with international financial organizations.

7 September 1998. Central bank governor Sergei Dubinin submits his resignation, which is welcomed by Yeltsin.

8 September 1998. Yevgeni Primakov: 'I am grateful to all those who have suggested my candidacy. However, I must unequivocally state: I cannot consent to this ... [I shall do] all that is possible in the interests of my country.'

10 September 1998. Yeltsin nominates acting foreign minister Yevgeni Primakov as prime minister.

11 September 1998. The State Duma approves Yevgeni Primakov as prime minister by 315 votes to sixty-three, with fifteen abstentions.

Yuri Maslyukov becomes first deputy prime minister responsible for economic policy. (Maslyukov was head of Gosplan 1988–91: *FT*, 14 September 1998, p. 2.)

Viktor Gerashchenko becomes chairman of the central bank for the second time.

15 September 1998. Alexander Shokhin (head of Our Home is Russia in parliament) is named as deputy prime minister in charge of finances (including negotiations with international institutions such as the IMF). He says that he will stay in the government only if he is able to modify policies that, in his view, will lead to inflation. He believes that a mass printing of roubles will lead to hyperinflation (*IHT*, 17 September 1998, p. 13).

'Summoned back from a decade of obscurity, a group of Gorbachev-era economists stood outside the headquarters building of the Russian government on Tuesday [15 September], waiting to give advice on how to rescue a floundering economy ... Among them were three top advisers to Mr Gorbachev – Leonid Abalkin [director of the Institute of Economics], Nikolai Petrakov and Oleg Bogomolov [director of the Institute for International Economic and Political Studies] ... Russia's new prime minister, a top economic aide and the new head of the central bank all served under Mr Gorbachev' (Celestine Bohlen, *IHT*, 16 September 1998, p. 6).

'A group of academic economists leaded by Leonid Abalkin, prominent in the late Soviet era, yesterday [15 September] claimed the government intended to adopt all the main points of their programme set out in an open letter to the Russian media ... [which] include the "controlled" emission of roubles. This should allow the government to pay off mounting wage and pension arrears and inject liquidity into Russia's cash-strapped industries' (Arkady Ostrovsky and John Thornhill, *FT*, 16 September 1998, p. 1).

On 14 September members of the economics department of the Russian Academy of Science (Dmitri Lvov, Leonid Abalkin, Oleg Bogomolov, Nikolai Petrakov and Stepan Sitaryan) published an open letter to the president, the federal assembly and the government. Among other things, they advocated the following: regular cost-of-living increases in wages and salaries, pensions and other social support payments; the mandatory sale of 100 per cent of foreign currency earnings to the central bank; 'special exporters' of strategic goods; the 'possibility of non-payment of state obligations' should be eliminated by means of a 'controlled currency emission' (*CDSP*, 1998, vol. 50, no. 37, p. 7).

25 September 1998. Alexander Shokhin resigns over the reappointment of Mikhail Zadornov as finance minister. It has been suggested that disagreement with the policies of Yuri Maslyukov was also a factor lying behind Shokhin's decision to resign (*CDSP*, 1998, vol. 50, no. 39, p. 6).

28 September 1998. Boris Fyodorov is dismissed (*IHT*, 29 September 1998, p. 2).

11 October 1998. Yeltsin begins a visit to Uzbekistan. He stumbled at one point and nearly fell over. He flew to Kazakhstan the following day but was instructed by his doctors to make an early return to Russia on the grounds of bronchitis. (He was advised to take the rest of the week off work.)

On 11 October a declaration on comprehensive co-operation between Russia, Uzbekistan and Tajikistan was signed. 'The document provides for the parties to provide assistance, including military assistance, in the event of aggression against any of the states. The presumed adversary is well known – the Taleban of Afghanistan ... The co-operation will be directed against not just foreign but also domestic enemies ... The declaration authorizes each country's special forces to operate on the other countries' territory. In other words, Uzbek state security agencies will be able to maintain surveillance of and, with the assistance of their Russian counterparts, arrest – in Moscow, for example – Uzbek nationals nationals whose actions are punishable under the Uzbek criminal code but are not considered a crime in Russia' (*CDSP*, 1998, vol. 50, no. 41, p. 4).

19 October 1998. Yeltsin cancels meetings in the Kremlin and remains in his residence outside Moscow.

26 October 1998. Yeltsin's one-day (formerly two-day) visit to Austria to meet EU leaders, scheduled for the following day, is called off. The official explanation talks of an 'asthenic condition' (general weakness). Prime minister Primakov is to go instead.

27 October 1998. Yeltsin enters a sanatorium.

28 October 1998. 'The president's withdrawal from day-to-day politics came as the government unveiled a few of the main elements of its long-awaited plans to tackle the economic crisis (*FT*, 29 October 1998, p. 1).

30 October 1998. Yeltsin begins a holiday on the Black Sea.

4 November 1998. Ivan Ortov, a correspondent for a right-wing nationalist magazine, drives a car up to the gates of the Kremlin. The car explodes.

A motion censuring General Albert Makashov (a member of the Communist Party's central committee) for antisemitic comments is defeated in the State Duma by 121 votes to 107, with three abstentions. Jews make up less than 0.5 per cent of the population. There are thought to be fewer than 500,000 Jews in the country (James meek, *The Guardian*, 5 November 1998, p. 16).

5 November 1998. 'The constitutional court ruled Thursday [5 November] that Boris Yeltsin could not seek a third term as president ... The court said in a widely expected decision that it was clear that Mr Yeltsin, sixty-seven, was serving his second and final term and did not examine the issue of whether he had a legal right to run for election again' (*IHT*, 6 November 1998, p. 5).

19 November 1998. Yuri Luzhkov holds the founding meeting of his new party, the Fatherland Party, whose creation he announced on television on 15 November.

20 November 1998. 'The killing in St Petersburg of Galina Starovoitova, a leading defender of Russia's democratic reforms [on 20 November] ... shocked her old allies, who claimed she was the latest victim of the country's lethally corrupt political climate ... Her press aide ... was seriously wounded ... Starovoitova ... was a spirited and visible leader of Russia's young democratic movement, who shared many a platform with Mr Yeltsin and the late human-rights campaigner Andrei Sakharov in the late 1980s and early

1990s. She was a co-founder of Democratic Russia … Most recently she had declared herself a candidate for governor of the region [Leningrad] outside St Petersburg' (Celestine Bohlen, *IHT*, 23 November 1998, p. 8). (There was a massive turnout for her funeral on 24 November.)

'Since 1993 seven members of the Duma have been killed, although in most cases as a result of financial disputes rather than politics … She had plenty of enemies. The Communists, obviously. She was planning to present to the Duma evidence of corruption by Communist members. She was loathed by the nationalists … She said recently that she would run for a governorship against Vladimir Zhirinovsky, a nationalist leader she accused of trying to build "a criminal dictatorship". She condemned antisemitic remarks made by a former general who now sits in the Duma. The army feared her. "Our military is not accountable to the civil society and does not even answer to the president", she once said … A problem for her enemies was that she could not be bought' (*The Economist*, 28 November 1998, p. 144).

23 November 1998. Yeltsin is hospitalized with pneumonia. He holds a meeting at the hospital with President Jiang Zemin of China (on a visit to Russia 22–4 November).

27 November 1998. A group of liberal politicians announce a centre-right coalition to fight the next election. They include Sergei Kiriyenko, Yegor Gaidar, Anatoli Chubais and Boris Nemtsov.

The presidential spokesman, Dmitri Yakushkin, reveals that Yeltsin suffered 'several heart attacks' during the 1996 presidential election campaign. Previously only one 'mild' heart attack had been admitted.

2 December 1998. The State Duma approves a draft resolution recommending that the Moscow city government restore the Felix Dzerzhinsky monument on Lubyanka Square. The monument was pulled off its base in the middle of the night of 22–23 August 1991 (*CDSP*, 1998, vol. 50, no. 48, p. 4).

7 December 1998. Yeltsin returns to the Kremlin from hospital for just three hours. He dismisses the head of the presidential administration (chief of staff) Valentin Yumashev and three of his deputies for their 'failure to take serious steps to combat political extremism and corruption'. Yumashev is replaced by the secretary of the 'security council', Nikolai Bordyuzha, who will now hold both positions. Yeltsin will take personal control of the justice ministry and the federal tax police, i.e. their heads will report directly to the president rather than the prime minister.

'The justice ministry and the federal tax police service were the last remaining force-wielding agencies … [to join] the ranks of the defence ministry, the internal affairs ministry, the federal agency for government communications and information, the intelligence and counterintelligence agencies and all the other ministries and services defending the security of the homeland' (*CDSP*, 1999, vol. 50, no. 49, p. 3).

9 December 1998. Yeltsin moves from hospital to a secluded country residence.

15 December 1998. The Duma's impeachment commission discusses the final charge against Boris Yeltsin, namely 'genocide against the Russian people'. Viktor Ilyukhin, security committee chairman, says that this 'large-scale genocide' would have had less serious consequences if 'members of the indigenous nationality instead of the Jewish nation alone, talented though that nation is, had predominated' in the president's inner circle (*CDSP*, 1999, vol. 50, no. 50, p. 9).

'A leading Russian Communist [Viktor Ilyukhin, head of the Duma's defence committee] told a parliamentary hearing that Jews were responsible for what he called the "genocide" of the Russian people' (*The Times*, 16 December 1998, p. 12).

6 and 20 December 1998. In both the first and second rounds of the election for the St Petersburg city (municipal) assembly Yabloko and other democratic parties did well.

Preliminary results after the second round showed that a group headed by Yuri Boldyrev led the poll, securing fifteen of the fifty city council seats. Yabloka was second with seven seats. Boldyrev was a co-founder of Yabloko but split with Grigori Yavlinsky over largely personal differences. Two deputies were elected from Galina Starovoitova's Soglasiye (Accord) party. (She was assassinated on 20 November 1998.) The Communist Party lost three of the five seats it had formerly held on the council. A communist ally won one seat (*FT*, 22 December 1998, p. 2).

17 January 1999. Yeltsin is hospitalized with a bleeding stomach ulcer.

19 January 1999. Yeltsin cancels a planned visit to France due to start on 28 January.

25 January 1999. Primakov sends a letter to the speaker of the State Duma in which he proposes that temporary restraint should be exercised in order to maintain 'political stability in the Russian Federation during the preelection period'. The proposals are as follows: (1) impeachment proceedings against Yeltsin be dropped and immunity from prosecution after leaving office be offered; (2) after retirement the president will have bodyguards for himself and his family, 80 per cent of presidential pay, life and medical insurance health care, domestic help, access to the government's exclusive phone system, a seat for life in the Council of the Federation and free travel on all forms of transport except taxis; (3) the president will promise not to dissolve parliament or dismiss the government during the run-up to the next general election in December 1999; (4) the State Duma will not pass any measures of no confidence in the government (*IHT*, 27 January 1999, p. 5, and 28 January 1999, p. 5; *The Guardian*, 27 January 1999, p. 15; *CDSP*, 1999, vol. 51, no. 4, p. 1).

The president's press service says that Yeltsin 'opposes any limitation on the constitutional rights' of the branches of government (*CDSP*, 1999, vol. 51, no. 4, p. 3).

27 January 1999. The President's spokesman says that Yeltsin 'would not mind' the halting of impeachment proceedings and the offer of immunity from prosecution, but not if he had to relinquish some of his broad authority (*IHT*, 28 January 1999, p. 5).

30 January 1999. Yeltsin moves from the hospital to a sanatorium.

1 February 1999. Yeltsin is sixty-eight.

2 February 1999. The constitutional court imposes a moratorium on capital punishment sentences until a new code is drawn up that will make such sentences the preserve of jury courts alone. Only nine of the eighty-nine regions currently operate trial by jury (*IHT*, 3 February 1999, p. 5).

Yeltsin briefly turns up at the Kremlin and makes some staff changes.

Yuri Skuratov resigns as chief prosecutor, 'for reasons of health'.

3 February 1999. 'Russia's acting chief prosecutor yesterday [3 February] criticised the country's courts for being too lenient, and said an explosion in corruption among officials ranked among the world's worst in that respect. "Corruption among Russian bureaucrats has reached unprecedented levels", said Yuri Chaika. Only Venezuela, Nigeria, Pakistan and Cameroon do worse than us" ... On Tuesday [2 February] a high-profile raid by the general presecutor's office ... took place at Sibneft, an oil group linked to the "oligarch" Boris Berezovsky' (*FT*, 4 February 1999, p. 2).

'Russia's chief prosecutor suddenly resigns, officially for health reasons ... In private conversations Kremlin aides acknowledged that there was more to Mr Skuratov's abrupt exit than a bad heart, the ailment with which he was admitted Monday [1 February] to the Kremlin hospital. They said Mr Yeltsin's displeasure had been a long time building, first over Mr Skuratov's failure to bring to the most publicized Russian crimes to trial and, more recently, over his failure to move against outspoken neo-fascist and antisemitic politicians ... The prosecutor's foot-dragging in bring a case against Albert Makashov – a communist member of parliament who in October called for Jews to be driven out of Russia – was linked to the resurgence last weekend of a small splinter neo-fascist group in Moscow ... The interior ministry announced Wednesday [3 February] that it had arrested a former justice minister, Valentin Kovalyov, on charges of embezzlement ... The police confirmed Wednesday night that they had found evidence of illegal wiretapping during a citywide raid of offices and apartments linked to Boris Berezovsky ... now the most public target of what seems to be prime minister Yevgeni Primakov's opening shot in a crackdown on economic crime and corruption. Mr Primakov sent out a warning last week when he said that an amnesty of 94,000 prisoners would free cells needed to house an incoming wave of corrupt officials and businessmen ... Armed Russian federation agents ... swooped this week through the offices of Sibneft, a Berezovsky-controlled oil company, and Atoll, a Berezovsky-controlled security company. Atoll has been accused of serving as Mr Berezovsky's private intelligence agency, secretly spying on top Russian officials and even members of President Boris Yeltsin's family. The raids [are] seen as the final blows to Mr Berezovsky's dwindling prestige and influence' (Celestine Bohlen, *IHT*, 5 February 1999, p. 5).

4 February 1999. 'Masked, camouflaged special troops raided an office affiliated with Aeroflot, the national airline in which Mr Berezovsky has had major interests. The raids Thursday [4 February] marked the second time this week that investigators stormed into a business linked to Mr Berezovsky. On Tuesday [2 February] they seized documents and videotapes from Sibneft, a leading oil company that also has ties to Mr Berezovsky. They said they found evidence there that he ran an intelligence operation to tap the phones of Mr Yeltsin's family' (*IHT*, 6 February 1999, p. 11).

Russia's highest court refuses to drop treason charges against Alexander Nikitin for exposing nuclear pollution by the northern fleet (*IHT*, 5 February 1999, p. 5).

Astronauts aboard Mir fail to a unfurl a fabric mirror in space to reflect the sun's rays to earth at night. A more modest space mirror test was carried out in 1993 but it was not visible from earth (*IHT*, 5 February 1999, p. 5). (The experiment was abandoned.)

5 February 1999. 'President Boris Yeltsin has accepted an agreement under which he would be stripped of the right to dismiss the prime minister without first winning parliament's consent ... Under the pact ratified earlier Friday [5 February] by Russia's "security council", Mr Yeltsin would keep the government in place until legislative elections in December while deputies would drop impeachment proceedings against the president. Mr Yeltsin has said that he will neither resign because of ill health nor agree to amendments stripping him of power before his term expires in eighteen months' (*IHT*, 6 February 1999, p. 2).

8 February 1999. Yeltsin, against medical device, flies to Jordan for the funeral of King Hussein. But he has to cut short his visit because of ill health.

13 February 1999. The Council on Foreign and Defence Policy is a 150-member, independent think-tank (*FT*, 15 February 1999, p. 2). '"I oppose the idea that the president should step down before his constitutional term expires", Mr Primakov told reporters at a meeting of the influential Council on Foreign and Defence policy, a private, elite group of politicians, analysts, scholars and businessmen. Mr Yeltsin should remain in office "for the sake of stability in Russia, for the normal running of the elections, so that all the conditions can be created for the elections", Mr Primakov said. His comments were significant because some council members prepared a discussion paper, debated behind closed doors, suggesting that Mr Yeltsin's leadership had become so weak that he is dragging down the Russian state. The paper was drafted by a working group co-ordinated by Sergei Karaganov, deputy director of the Institute of Europe and chairman of the council. Among other things, the discussion paper ... calls for him [Yeltsin] to step down for health reasons, followed by early elections. It suggests that Mr Primakov lead a coalition including ... Yuri Luzhkov ... However, Mr Karaganov said later that the council had not adopted this approach in its closed debate' (*IHT*, 15 February 1999, p. 5).

18 February 1999. Yeltsin meets Chancellor Schröder of Germany in Moscow.

26 February 1999. The founding congress of the Thatcherites of Russia takes place. '[The party] draws its inspiration from the political principles of the former British prime minister. The party, backed by a secretive group of businessmen alarmed at the state of modern Russia, is wedded to the concept of parliamentary democracy, privatization, monetarism, a flat tax rate of 20 per cent and the creation of a Russian version of the [British] House of Lords' (John Thornhill, *FT,* 27 February 1999, p. 2).

27 February 1999. Yeltsin returns to hospital with a recurrence of the ulcer problem.

4 March 1999. Yeltsin asks the other members of the CIS to agree to dismiss Boris Berezovsky as executive chairman of the CIS 'for exceeding his powers and failing to carry out orders'.

17 March 1999. The Council of the Federation refuses to accept the resignation of Yuri Skuratov.

Yuri Skuratov (in his speech to the Council of the Federation): 'I could sense almost physically that, for some people, the activity of law-enforcement agencies had become like a thorn in their side, that we had touched on a sore spot, so to speak. Especially when we started looking into instances in which enterprises had been privatized or converted into joint stock companies illegally, or into unlawful activity in the banking system, and into management of the economy and abuses by very high-ranking officials. I am very sorry to say that certain forces have skilfully managed to wedge themselves between the president and the prosecutor general ... First of all the influential people who made their mark in dubious operations in the market for GKOs [short-term government bonds] ... A big contribution to the process of getting me out of office was made by the oligarchs ... The cases they are most interested in are the ones involving the Aeroflot airline company, the AvtoVAZ [Volga Automotive Plant] joint stock company, the Atoll private security company and others' (*CDSP,* 1999, vol. 51, no. 11, p. 1).

'In his speech to the Federation Council Mr Skuratov had earlier denied that he was ill and said he would continue in his work if he was backed by parliament. He explained his resignation had been prompted by "certain forces" who had driven a wedge between him and the president. Mr Skuratov said his investigations had uncovered dubious practices in the government debt market ... Mr Skuratov implied that Boris Berezovsky ... had been one of those behind a campaign to discredit him ... Last month [February] he [Skuratov] disclosed that the central bank had channelled billions of dollars of its hard currency reserves through an obscure, Jersey-based fund management group called Fimaco' (*FT,* 18 March 1999, p. 3).

18 March 1999. 'After meeting Thursday [18 March] with both Mr Skuratov and prime minister Yevgeni Primakov, Mr Yeltsin directed the Russian security council to form a commission to investigate Mr Skuratov's alleged "misdeeds, which bring disgrace to the honour of a prosecutor, and his violations of the prosecutor's oath"' (*IHT*, 19 March 1999, p. 1).

Yeltsin leaves hospital.

19 March 1999. Yeltsin dismisses his chief of staff (and secretary of the 'security council') Nikolai Bordyuzha. The new chief of staff is Alexander Voloshin.

23 March 1999. Prosecutor-general Yuri Skuratov sends a team into the Kremlin to seize documents as part of a corruption probe. The documents seized concern the Kremlin's dealings with a Swiss construction firm, which renovated large parts of the Kremlin and other government buildings. There have been rumours of bribery in relation to the award of contracts (*The Guardian*, 24 March 1999, p. 17; *The Independent*, 24 March 1999, p. 13).

'Russia's chief prosecutor's office has confirmed that it is investigating corruption inside the Kremlin itself, aiming at members of President Yeltsin's inner circle. Acting on orders from Yuri Skuratov ... investigator's have seized documents from the offices of the presidential administration's powerful property-management office, headed by Pavel Borodin ... Until now Russia's periodic anti-corruption campaigns have steered clear of the Kremlin ... Mr Borodin's property-management office is a vast empire of office buildings, apartment blocks, clinics, country houses and vacation spas used by government employees. The investigation of the office followed a raid on 22 January by Swiss investigators of Mabetex, a construction company ... that does extensive business throughout the former Soviet Union ... Accusations that have surfaced during Mr Skuratov's investigation suggest that Mabetex paid Kremlin officials to secure the lucrative contracts' (Celestine Bohlen, *IHT*, 25 March 1999, p. 7).

30 March 1999. Yeltsin delivers his annual state of the nation speech: 'Nato strikes against Yugoslavia continue. In circumvention of the UN Security Council and in violation of its charter ... But the crisis in the Balkans calls for well-considered, responsible actions on our part, not emotional assessments. More and more political leaders understand that in such situations brute force does not achieve anything. Russia has made its choice. It will not allow itself to be drawn into a military conflict ... Our weight in the world arena depends on how we solve our problems at home. This means that we need order in government, accord in society, stability in the economy and the social sphere ... In July [1998] the government drafted its anti-crisis programme ... The State Duma rejected that programme ... The Duma sent a bad signal to investors, a signal telling them that Russia's authorities were unwilling to take responsibility for decisions that were difficult but that had to be made ... We are bogged down halfway between a planned, command economy and a workable market one. We have created a freakish model, a hybrid of the two systems ... A major achievement of ... is that we have not slipped into a much deeper crisis ... Now a fundamentally new phase must begin in the work of the government ... The time has come to establish new priorities, the most crucial of all is Russia's economic competitiveness ... Our people ... should have confidence in the power of law and the stability of economic rules' (*CDSP*, 1999, vol. 51, no. 13, p. 14; *IHT*, 31 March 1999, p. 6).

2 April 1999. Yeltsin suspends Yuri Skuratov from his position as chief prosecutor. The decision led to a debate about the legality of the move.

'Under the 1993 constitution the prosecutor is appointed and relieved from his post by the Federation Council on the nomination of the president. However, a separate law says that if the prosecutor is under investigation he can be suspended, which is the action that Mr Yeltsin took Friday [2 April]. The investigation of Mr Skuratov centres on who paid for the prostitutes [shown on a videotape with Skuratov], according to the news agency Interfax, which ... said a businessman paid for the prostitutes in exchange for Mr Skuratov's promise to delay three criminal cases against the businessman' (*IHT*, 3 April 1999, p. 2).

Yeltsin unilaterally dismisses Boris Berezovsky as executive secretary of the CIS. A plane carrying him from Paris was refused permission to enter Russian airspace and landed instead in Ukraine. At the CIS conference Yeltsin succeeded in winning confirmation of Yuri Yarov as the new executive secretary. Yarov became Yeltsin's first deputy chief of staff in the summer of 1996 but was dismissed in December 1998 (*CDSP*, 1999, vol. 51, no. 14, pp. 19–20).

6 April 1999. 'Russia's chief prosecutor issued an arrest warrant Tuesday [6 April] for Boris Berezovsky ... Officials in the prosecutor's office said Mr Berezovsky [who is in France] ... had been charged with money laundering and "illegal entrepreneurship" as part of a scheme that diverted Aeroflot's foreign currency proceeds to a Geneva-based company that they were said to control ... While Mr Yeltsin recently ordered Mr Skuratov be removed from his post a second time, corruption inquiries under Mr Skuratov's deputy seem to have continued apace' (*IHT*, 7 April 1999, p. 5).

'Mr Berezovsky ... lost his immunity from prosecution last week [2 April] when he was fired as secretary of the CIS and stripped of his diplomatic immunity. But Mr Berezovsky claimed he had been prevented from defending himself at a meeting of CIS leaders in Moscow when his aircraft was denied access to Russian airspace' (*FT*, 7 April 1999, p. 3).

'Russia's prosecutor general Yuri Skuratov issued arrest warrants for ... Boris Berezovsky, head of the conglomerate Logova, and Alexander Smolensky, head of the defunct bank SBS-Agro ... Both [were] charged with embezzlement' (*Business Central Europe*, May 1999, p. 12).

9 April 1999. Yeltsin: 'I believe that at the present time, at this stage, Primakov is useful. For how long we'll see, but today Primakov is useful. The fact that it is necessary to strengthen the government is another. That issue does need to be addressed' (*CDSP*, 1999, vol. 51, no. 15, p. 1).

'Interior minister Sergei Stepashin said Friday [9 April] that he would not arrest Boris Berezovsky even though there is a warrant out for the billionaire businessman … "Berezovsky will arrive in Russia, present his explanations and this, I hope, will be the end of the incident", Mr Stepashin said' (*IHT*, 10 April 1999, p. 2).

10 April 1999. Yeltsin: 'The main tasks set before the Russian Federation government in the area of government policy for the years 1998–99 have not been accomplished … The federal budget adopted for 1999 is contradictory … Particular attention should be paid to predicting the dynamics of the rouble exchange rate, the balance of payments and the inflation rate' (*CDSP*, 1999, vol. 51, no. 15, p. 17).

14 April 1999. The warrant for Berezovsky's arrest is withdrawn. (The arrest warrant for Alexander Smolensky was withdrawn on 20 April.)

18 April 1999. Berezovsky returns to Russia. (He went into hospital the following day.)

20 April 1999. The founding conference takes place of the regional bloc called *Voice of Russia*. Its co-ordinator is Samara province's governor Konstantin Titov. (On 22 April there took place a meeting of the co-ordinating committee of the bloc called *All Russia*. It is led by Tatarstan's Mintimir Shaimiyev and St Petersburg's Vladimir Yakovlev: *CDSP*, 1999, vol. 51, no. 16, p. 9.)

21 April 1999. For the second time the Council of the Federation votes (by seventy-nine to sixty-one) not to accept the resignation of Yuri Skuratov.

23 April 1999. Nato celebrates its fiftieth anniversary. (Nato was actually founded on 4 April 1949). Of the forty-three governments invited to attend the Nato summit only Russia declined the invitation, in protest at the Nato bombing of Yugoslavia.

26 April 1999. Boris Berezovsky is formally charged with money-laundering and barred from leaving Moscow while prosecutors investigate his case. He is accused of expatriating hard currency profits from the state airline Aeroflot to a shell company in Switzerland he had set up. It is alleged that he ran the state airline for several years by naming his cronies to the board of directors (*IHT*, 27 April 1999, p. 5). Berezovsky is charged with illegal business activities, money laundering and continuing business activities when he held a state post (*FT*, 27 April 1999, p. 3).

27 April 1999. Yeltsin dismisses Vadim Gustov, a deputy prime minister in charge of relations with the provinces and former Soviet republics. Interior minister Sergei Stepashin becomes first deputy prime minister and takes over Gustov's portfolio (*IHT*, 28 April 1999, p. 7).

5 May 1999. 'Georgia, Ukraine, Azerbaijan and Moldova signed a pact in Washington last week adding Uzbekistan to a year-old alliance, creating Guuam. The alliance is meant to strengthen members' political and economic ties to the West … Guuam's main task is to develop the area's rich oil and gas deposits to the exclusion of Russia, a goal partly achieved last month [April] with the opening of a pipeline carrying Caspian Sea oil to export through Azerbaijan and Georgia … Guuam's members have agreed to low-level military co-operation but insist the group is not a military alliance directed against a third party – namely, Russia. Moscow has grown increasingly worried since Georgia, Uzbekistan and Azerbaijan pulled out of the CIS collective security pact this spring [1999]. Ukraine and Moldova never were members' (*FT*, 6 May 1999, p. 2).

12 May 1999. President Yeltsin dismisses prime minister Yevgeni Primakov the day before the State Duma was to begin impeachment hearings against Yeltsin.

Yeltsin (in a televison address): 'Today [Wednesday 12 May] I made a difficult decision – I dismissed the government. Yevgeni Maximovich [Primakov] took over at a very difficult moment – a period of severe crisis in the country. His appointment was supported by all political forces. The crisis in the economy and the social sphere was then successfully slowed down. But assessments of the government's performance gradually changed. Its activity began to be associated solely with political stability. But today the situation is again far from stable – both in the economy and in politics. Yes, the credibility of the Primakov government is still high, but this is mainly because of the prime minister's personal qualities. Even in the most difficult situations he always shows striking restraint, calmness and composure. However, social tension in the regions is growing. Criticism of the government is increasing in all quarters ... The government has fully accomplished the tactical task that was set before it. But we still are not making any headway in the economy ... There is no foundation for serious and stable economic growth. The economic crisis will not resolve itself on its own. Therefore, the government must act. Last September [1998], when the political atmosphere was so heated and the economic situation was so difficult, Yevgeni Maximovich could not make any drastic moves. He fully demonstrated his great skill as a diplomat, showing caution and prudence. I respect him for not having given in to pressure from radicals, on either the left or the right. But today the situation is different. The prime minister's caution and his willingness to take only those measures that receive maximum approval and support are now beginning to do harm, since with elections coming up there will not be many people willing to support unpopular, tough economic decisions. Stabilization of poverty and economic decline is not what we need. We need a serious breakthrough ... It is high time for a switch to energetic action. We cannot put off necessary decisions until the election campaign is over ... I am convinced that right now delays and procrastination are striking the most severe blow to the economy and the social sphere. That is why I was forced to make the difficult but necessary decision to dismiss the government. Once again I want to convey to Yevgeni Primakov my most heartfelt thanks for everything he has done, and above all, of course, for the courage he showed in agreeing to become head of the government at a difficult time.'

A statement released by the president's press service: 'Today I made a difficult decision – I relieved Yevgeni Maximovich Primakov of his duties as chairman of the government. It is true that the government has fully accomplished the tactical task that was set before it. But the economic situation is still not improving. There have been delays and procrastination and I am convinced that this is what is currently striking the most severe blow to economic and political stability … Today, nine months later, the [government's] economic strategy is still an open question. We do not have the right to put off for another half a year – until the end of the election campaign – taking decisions that are necessary for the revival of the economy.'

Interior minister (and a first deputy prime minister since last week) Sergei Stepashin is named acting prime minister and is nominated by Yeltsin as a candidate to replace Primakov. Railway minister Nikolai Aksyenenko is named as an acting first deputy prime minister.

Sergei Stepashin: 'The government has really done a lot to stabilize the economic and political situation. We have only one goal today: to advance with clear and tough market reforms' (*FT*, 13 May 1999, p. 3).

'The RTS share index fell 37.9 to 199.2, nearly 20 per cent' (*FT*, 13 May 1999, p. 3).

The State Duma votes for a non-binding resolution, by 243 votes to twenty, calling on Yeltsin to resign.

A Kremlin spokesman: 'Yeltsin warned that Russia would withdraw from co-operation in negotiations if its proposals and mediation efforts for the Kosovo conflict were ignored' (*IHT*, 13 May 1999, p. 1).

13 May 1999. The State Duma begins impeachments hearings against Yeltsin.

The five articles of impeachment constituting the State Duma charges accuse Yeltsin of illegally conspiring to destroy the Soviet Union in 1991, overthrowing the constitutional order and violently dispersing the elected parliament in 1993, unleashing an illegal war in Chechenia, undermining national defence by ruining Russia's armed forces, and committing 'genocide' against the Russian people by pushing market reforms that led to falling birth rates, shortened life expectancy and widespread poverty.

14 May 1999. The day was set aside for invited 'experts' to comment on the impeachment proceedings. But only five turned up and big names were missing (such as Mikhail Gorbachev, Alexander Rutskoi, Ruslan Khasbulatov, Sergei Shakrai, Pavel Grachev and Viktor Yerin) (*CDSP*, 1999, vol. 51, no. 19, p. 10).

15 May 1999. All five charges fail to reach the minimum required 300 votes. Even the charge relating to Chechenia (generally considered the most likely to succeed) received only 283 votes. The genocide charge gained the lowest support, with only 238 votes.

'Only 348 of Russia's 450 MPs collected their ballot papers to vote on the five accusations' (*FT*, 17 May 1999, p. 2)

('Yuri Maslyukov … has already announced his resignation': *IHT*, 18 May 1999, p. 5.)

17 May 1999. A Moscow court dismisses charges of abusing power against Yuri Skuratov. The military prosecutor's office is to appeal to the supreme court's military chamber (*The Telegraph*, 18 May 1999, p. 18).

19 May 1999. Sergei Stepashin is approved as prime minister on the first vote by 301 to fifty-five, with fourteen abstentions.

21 May 1999. Igor Ivanov (foreign minister) and Igor Sergeyev (defence) retain their positions. But deputy interior minister Vladimir Rushailo becomes interior minister.

25 May 1999. Mikhail Zadornov becomes a first deputy prime minister and will take charge of financial policy. A deputy finance minister, Mikhail Kasyanov, becomes finance minister instead of Zadornov. Alexander Pochinok replaces Georgi Boos as head of the tax service.

28 May 1999. Mikhail Zadornov resigns.

'Mikhail Zadornov had been elevated by Mr Stepashin from finance minister to first deputy, a post in which he was to oversee macroeconomic issues and Russia's dealing with international financial institutions ... Mr Zadornov said he had quit because Mr Yeltsin had refused to combine his new job with his old duties as finance minister. Mr Stepashin seemed to confirm that arrangement earlier this week, only to see Mr Yeltsin appoint a new finance minister, Mikhail Kasyanov ... An underlying explanation widely accepted by political experts here ... is that Mr Zadornov was shoved out of the government by supporters of Boris Berezovsky ... [who] is said to be very close to Mr Yeltsin's daughter and senior adviser, Tatiana Dyachenko ... Mr Berezovsky seems to have staged a comeback ... In that view the losers Friday were the supporters of ... Anatoli Chubais ... Nikolai Aksyenenko is nominally first deputy prime minister for industrial policy, but he has repeatedly insisted that his job includes the government's entire fiscal portfolio, including the duties Mr Zadornov has now given up' (Michael Wines, *IHT*, 29 May 1999, p. 1).

'Aksyenenko ... [has] said that he would be in charge of everything in the government, including macroeconomics' (*CDSP*, 1999, vol. 51, no. 21, p. 7). 'Aksyenenko ... is bidding for control of everything that has even the slightest connection with material resources and cash flows' (*CDSP*, 1999, vol. 51, no. 22, p. 7). 'Stepashin officially confirmed [on 3 June] that Nikolai Alsyenenko will be first deputy prime minister number one and will stand in for the prime minister when he is out of the country' (p. 6).

'Mikhail Zadornov ... promoted to become first deputy prime minister in charge of the economy, said it was impossible to work in the current conditions ... "I am absolutely certain that we need a unified economic bloc in the government"' (John Thornhill, *FT*, 29 May 1999, p. 2). 'The most important political intrigue of them all [is] the struggle for pole position to succeed President Boris Yeltsin ... It has now become clearer than ever that the actual reason for Mr Primakov's dismissal were political. Yeltsin decided the left-leaning Primakov could not be trusted to succeed him ... The Yeltsin's "family", including his daughter, Tatiana Dyachenko, and two influential businessmen, Boris Berezovsky and Roman Abramovich [head of the oil company Sibneft], appear set on promoting the interests of Nikolai Aksyenenko ... A rival clan. led by Anatoli Chubais ... has opted for Sergei Stepashin' (p. 2).

29 May 1999. The opening congress of *Just Cause* takes place. Its leader is Boris Nemtsov. The merged parties include Democratic Choice of Russia (led by Yegor Gaidar), Forward Russia (led by Boris Fyodorov) and Common Case (led by Irina Khakamada). Other important members include Anatoli Chubais. Sergei Kiriyenko says that his New Force will be a partner but not a full member (*FT,* 31 May 1999, p. 2).

31 May 1999. 'The post of first deputy prime minister goes to Viktor Khristenko, forty-one, who had served in the reformist cabinet of Sergei Kiriyenko ... The job of finance minister has gone to Mikhail Kasyanov, the former deputy finance minister ... Mikhail Zadornov ... is to be the country's liaison with the international financial institutions ... The cabinet has a series of overlapping and potentially competing authorities. Nikolai Aksyenenko is the economics boss, while Mr Khristenko is a fellow first deputy prime minister but clearly subordinate. He has no clear brief ... To deepen the confusion Andrei Shapovalyants, another reformist figure, will continue to serve as minister for the economy' (*FT,* 1 June 1999, p. 2).

'Viktor Khristenko has become the second first deputy prime minister, in charge of macroeconomics and finance' (*CDSP,* 1999, vol. 51, no. 22, p. 2).

Ilya Klebanov becomes a deputy prime minister (making three in all).

Formal cabinet responsibilities are as follows: Nikolai Aksyenenko, control over the production sector of the economy, including natural monopolies; Viktor Khristenko, financial policy; Ilya Klebanov, the military-industrial complex; Mikhail Kasyanov, minister of finance; Andrei Shapovalyants, minister of economics (*CDSP,* 1999, vol. 51, no. 22, p. 4).

Nikolai Aksyenenko: issues relating to development of the production sector and industrial, structural and investment policy; anti-monopoly policy and the support of entrepreneurship; transportation; railways; fuel and power; construction and housing and municipal services; telecommunications. Viktor Khristenko: economics; finance (operational matters); state property; anti-monopoly policy; taxes and assessments; tax police; trade; currency and export controls; financial reorganization and bankruptcy; federal debt centre (*CDSP,* 1999, vol. 51, no. 23, pp. 9–10).

3 June 1999. Yeltsin signs a decree to commute the death sentences of all 716 convicts on death row, renewing pressure on parliament to abolish the death sentence altogether. In 1996 Russia ranked third in the world in number of executions (as many as 140). The president promised in 1996 to scrap the death penalty when Russia joined the Council of Europe. No one has been executed since then, although courts handed down death sentences until February 1999 (*IHT,* 4 June 1999, p. 7). Russia's last execution, administered by a bullet in the back of the neck, was carried out on 2 September 1996. The number of people executed since Yeltsin came to power in 1991 is 163 (*The Times*, 4 June 1999, p. 15).

'In August 1996 – after executing fifty-three people in eight months – Russia slapped a moratorium on capital punishment in line with commitments made on joining the Council of Europe earlier that year. In February [1999] the constitutional court banned death sentences unless passed in a jury trial. Last month [June] Boris Yeltsin commuted sentences on all 716 remaining prisoners on death row – but the next president could easily resort to execution' (*The Independent*, 3 July 1999, p. 17).

30 June 1999. Viktor Chernomyrdin is appointed chairman of Gazprom.

6 July 1999. The constitutional court rules that a prime minister has no right to dissolve parliament while standing in temporarily for the president. The court rules that a prime minister serving temporarily as president is also barred from proposing amendments to the constitution. The court says that the president can regain his powers in full he has handed them over only temporarily (*IHT*, 7 July 1999, p. 8).

Yeltsin signs a decree creating a new federal agency. The Russian Federation Ministry for the Press, Television and Radio Broadcasting and Mass Communications is to be headed by Mikhail Lesin. Concern is expressed about its broad powers (*CDSP*, 1999, vol. 51, no. 27, pp. 1–4).

20 July 1999. 'Russia's constitutional court ruled on Tuesday [20 July] that Moscow had the right to keep art treasures removed from Germany and the Nazi allies during World War II. But it left the door open to requests from Moscow's wartime allies for the repatriation of booty brought to Russia during and after the 1939–45 war. The court's ruling was the latest move in a long-running battle between President Boris Yeltsin and parliament over a controversial law halting the repatriation of war booty to Germany. Mr Yeltsin opposes the law and had asked the constitutional court to reject it. The court said parts of the law breached the constitution but decided not to throw it out completely. The constitutional court ruled that Russia's World War II enemies could not appeal for the return of art trophies because they were "aggressor countries". Those who could, Moscow's wartime allies, were given eighteen months to appeal for the return of their treasures, it said. Mr Yeltsin ... initially vetoed the law, but parliament overturned his veto. He then tried to veto it again, but the court said he did not have the right to veto laws twice. He then sought another ruling by the constitutional court, saying parliamentary procedures were violated when the law was passed by the State Duma' (*IHT*, 21 July 1999, p. 6).

'The eighty-page judgement made public yesterday upheld key elements of a law, passed by the Russian parliament, which sought to block any restitution of trophy art. The judgement overturned part of the law by ruling that victims of Nazism and the Holocaust could apply for restitution of objects over the coming eighteen months, but that "the aggressor states have no claim on the return of their cultural objects". It singled out Germany ... The head of the constitutional court said negotiations over the return of objects could continue. But he said the judgement supported most elements of the Russian parliament's law, which would require every German request for restitution to be debated case-by-case by politicians' (*FT*, 21 July 1999, p. 2).

(President Vladimir Putin approved the law on 25 May 2000.)

23 July 1999. Anatoli Chubais, Sergei Kiriyenko and Konstantin Titov (governor of Samara province) agree to form an electoral bloc (*CDSP*, 1999, vol. 51, no. 30, p. 5).

3 August 1999. The All Russia movement of regional leaders announces that it has decided to form a common platform with Yuri Luzhkov's Fatherland party to contest the December 1999 parliamentary election (*FT*, 4 August 1999, p. 2; *IHT*, 4 August 1999, p. 3). The co-chairmen of the co-ordinating council are Yuri Luzhkov and Vladimir Yalovlev (governor of St Petersburg) (*CDSP*, 1999, vol. 51, no. 31, p. 2).

'Sergei Zvyerev [deputy head of the presidential administration] yesterday quit the Kremlin and accused the presidential administration of plotting to frustrate free elections and muzzle the media. Mr Zvyerev ... claimed the administration was using the tax police to put pressure on the opposition media' (*FT*, 4 August 1999, p. 2).

4 August 1999. 'The mayor of Moscow forged an alliance Wednesday [4 August] with centrist regional leaders ... Mayor Yuri Luzhkov said his Fatherland party had offered Yevgeni Primakov the top position on its list of candidates for December's elections to the State Duma .... Mr Primakov has no party affiliation ... At a ceremony in a Moscow business complex Mr Luzhkov signed papers forming a coalition between his Fatherland party and the All Russia group of regional leaders ... Mr Yeltsin's chief of staff, Alexander Voloshin ... said that Mr Luzhkov was not the best choice for Russia. He said that Mr Luzhkov favoured an aggressive foreign policy toward Ukraine and had threatened to redistribute property that had been privatized over the past decade' (*IHT*, 5 August 1999, p. 7).

'Mintimir Shaimiyev [president of Tatarstan] leads the regional governors allied to Mr Luzhkov' (*The Economist*, 14 August 1999, p. 14).

'A left-of-centre party is now coalescing around the Our Fatherland is All Russia bloc founded by Yuri Luzhkov, Moscow's mayor, and several regional governors' (*FT*, 13 August 1999, p. 2).

'The Kremlin has failed to gain control of the formation of a central preelection bloc ... Boris Yeltsin's personal meeting with Mintimir Shaimiev, the unofficial leader of All Russia and presidential chief of staff Alexander Voloshin ... talks with governors did not help the Kremlin change the situation in its favour ... The politicians forming the bloc refused to fulfil the Kremlin's wish and offer prime minister Stepashin the number one slot on the new bloc's list [of Duma candidates]' (*Kommersant*, 5 August 1999, p. 1: cited in *CDSP*, 1999, vol. 51, no. 31, p. 3).

5 August 1999. 'Yesterday [5 August] ... Raf Shakiriv, the dismissed editor-in-chief of the Kommersant newspaper, stated that the publishing house was under the complete control of Boris Berezovsky ... In July (according to the official story) 85 per cent of the publishing house's stock was transferred to an American investment company called American Capital, and 15 per cent went to Boris Berezovsky ... Shakiriv ... interpreted what happened as confirmation of the rumours that American Capital was a "dummy firm" and that Kommersant was under the complete control of Boris Berezovsky' (*CDSP*, 1999, vol. 51, no. 32, p. 13). (On 3 July 1999 it was reported that 76 per cent of the Kommersant Publishing House had been sold to the American Capital Group. There was speculation that the real owner was Boris Berezovsky: *CDSP*, 1999, vo. 51, no. 27, pp. 4–6.)

6 August 1999. Boris Berezovsky (in a meeting with Kommersant journalists): 'Today [6 August] the process [of buying shares from American Capital] . The controlling block of has been transferred' (*CDSP*, 1999, vol. 51, no. 32, p. 13).

'Boris Berezovsky ... swept into the offices of the Kommersant newspaper on Friday [6 August] and explained to the assembled journalists that he had just bought their parent company ... Raf Shakirov, Kommersant's editor, had just been fired the previous day [5 August] ... Over the past few months he [Berezovsky] has been amassing an array of media assets. He is already believed to have won considerable influence over ORT, the main television channel, in which the state retains a 51 per cent stake. In addition, he has acquired a controlling interest in the TV-6 television company as well as the Noviye Isvestia and Nezavisimaya newspapers ... Mr Berezovsky appears to be targeting Media-Most, which was founded by Vladimir Gusinsky, a rival oligarch, and currently backs the political ambitions of Mr Luzhkov. Media-Most, which many regard as the most professional news organization in Russia, owns the NTV television station, the Sevodnya newspaper, the Echo Moskvy radio station and the Itogi news magazine. But in recent weeks its headquarters have been raided by the tax police and its credit lines have been cut off' (John Thornhill, *FT*, 9 August 1999, p. 3).

Prime minister Sergei Stepashin: 'I will not support any of the political groupings in the elections. My job does not allow that. Some of my predecessors initially said they would not take sides with any parties, let alone with the financial and industrial conglomerates. I am sure they were sincere, but gradually people felt they were beginning to conform to one or other of the groups behind the scenes' (*The Guardian*, 10 August 1999, p. 13).

9 August 1999. Yeltsin dismisses prime minister Sergei Stepashin (and thus the entire government). The president nominates Vladimir Putin as prime minister.

Putin was born on 7 October 1952 and became a middle-ranking KGB agent in the Soviet era. He worked in the GDR and learned to speak German. In the new Russia he became first deputy mayor of St Petersburg under Anatoli Sobchak, a leading reformer whose reputation was later sullied by corruption allegations. Among Putin's important duties was the attraction of foreign investment. On 25 July 1998 Putin was appointed head of the Federal Security Service and on 29 March 1999 he also became secretary of the 'security council'.

In 1990 Putin became an adviser to the chairman of the Leningrad city soviet. In 1991–2 he was chairman of the St Petersburg municipal administration's committee on foreign relations. In 1992–4 he was deputy mayor of St Petersburg and chairman of the foreign relations committee. In 1994 he became first vice-chairman of the St Petersburg city government and continued to serve as chairman of the foreign relations committee. In 1994–6 he was first deputy mayor of St Petersburg and chairman of the foreign relations committee. In 1996–7 he was deputy head of the Yeltsin's administrative office. In 1997–8 he was deputy chief of staff to Yeltsin. From May through July 1998 he was first deputy chief of staff (*CDSP*, 2000, vol. 52, no. 5, p. 5).

Yeltsin (television address): 'Today I signed a decree on the elections to the State Duma. They will be held on 19 December. Precisely in accordance with the time frame established by the constitution and by law ... The presidential election will be held exactly a year from now. And I have now decided to name a person who, in my opinion, is capable of consolidating our society and, with support from the broadest array of political forces, of ensuring the continuation of reforms in Russia. A person who will be able to rally around himself those who will face the task of renewing our great Russia in the twenty-first century. He is Vladimir Putin, secretary of the "security council" and director of the Russian federal security service. Today I decided to dismiss the government of Sergei Stepashin ... I have asked the State Duma to confirm Vladimir Putin as chairman of the Russian government. I am sure that he will accomplish much good for our country working in this post and that the citizens of Russia will be able to assess Putin's personal and professional qualities. I have confidence in him. But I also want all those who in July 2000 will go to the polling stations and make their choice to have confidence in him too. I think Putin will have enough time to show his worth ... A year from now, for the first time in our country's history, Russia's first president will transfer power to a fresh, newly elected president.'

The failure to prevent the Fatherland-All Russia bloc turning into an opposition centre of power was a commonly listed reason for Stepashin's dismissal.

'The official exchange rate reached 25.29 to the US dollar ... The [stock] market's initial reaction was negative, falling 11 per cent in the first hour of trading. However, it recovered later and was down only marginally at closing time' (*RET*, Monthly Update, 10 August 1999, pp. 13, 15).

'The rouble fell from 24.55 to the US dollar to 25.29, while the Moscow stock market closed down 5 per cent on the day' (*FT*, 10 August 1999, p. 1).

13 August 1999. Sergei Stepashin: 'I refused to service interests of a certain group, which decided I was not reliable enough' (*IHT*, 14 August 1999, p. 6);

'They threw me out because I am not for sale' (*The Times*, 14 August 1999, p. 15).

16 August 1999. The State Duma approves Vladimir Putin as prime minister in the first round of voting: 233 for and eighty-four against, with seventeen abstentions.

Vladimir Putin: 'The primary thing that should be concerning all of us equally right now is the stability and reliability of the governing authorities … Therefore, I have received the fundamental consent of the president of the Russian Federation to leave the majority of ministers in their positions. One of the government's main tasks is to ensure calm and order in the country and to hold honest and fair elections, both for Duma seats and for the presidency … The cabinet's economic policy will be, in many respects, a continuation of what was begun by the previous government … I intend to continue the reforms begun by my predecessors, but I want to stress that reforms per se are not, of course, an end in themselves. Reforms are only a mechanism for improving people's lives, the lives of ordinary citizens first and foremost … By October we will do everything within our power to pay off all pension arrears. And we will start gradually increasing pension amounts in stages. We will also make sure that employees in budget-funded sectors will receive their pay on schedule' (*CDSP*, 1999, vol. 51, no. 33, pp. 5–6).

17 August 1999. Yevgeni Primakov: 'Today the decision was made to elect me chairman of the co-ordinating council of the Fatherland-All Russia bloc. A few days earlier I received an official invitation to head the bloc's federal list in the State Duma elections. Today I would like to announce that I have accepted that invitation … The government needs to be a cabinet based on the State Duma majority … The next president … should turn some of his powers over to the government and the federal assembly. We need to institute a vice-president … It is essential … to guarantee complete safety and security and an appropriate standard of living for presidents after they leave office upon the expiration of their terms' (*CDSP*, 1999, vol. 51, no. 33, pp. 1–3). (Yuri Luzhkov is second on the list of candidates.)

'Mr Primakov … called for legal changes which would "guarantee former presidents complete safety and a dignified life" – a clear reference to the worries about prosecution that are spurring Mr Yeltsin's cronies and family to seek every possible way of hanging on to power … This week [17 August] the outgoing justice minister, Pavel Krashennikov … [said that] Mr Yeltsin had dismissed him for failing to find an excuse to ban the Communist Party and for enabling Mr Luzhkov's party, Fatherland, to register in time to take part in the elections' (*The Economist*, Saturday 21 August 1999, p. 27). (Yeltsin has been critical of Krashennikov's investigations into violations of the constitution by the Communist Party: *CDSP*, 1999, vol. 51, no. 33, p. 8.)

'The new alliance includes a group of regional bosses, among them the St Petersburg mayor, Vladimir Yakovlev, and the Tatarstan president, Mintimir Shaimiyev. It was joined Tuesday [17 August] by the head of the Agrarian

Party, Mikhail Lapshin, who had previously been an ally of the Communists ... Sergei Stepashin ... said Tuesday he would run for parliament from his native St Petersburg' (*IHT,* 18 August 1999, p. 4).

20 August 1999. Vladimir Putin: '[Nikolai Asyenenko] had been considered the number one first deputy [but now] there won't be any "first among firsts" ... There will no longer be any "firsts among the firsts" in the cabinet. That is no way to do business' (*CDSP,* 1999, vol. 51, no. 34, pp. 5–6). The two first deputy prime ministers are Nikolai Asyenenko and Viktor Khristenko (p. 7).

21 August 1999. 'Saturday [21 August] was expected to be the day when Sergei Stepashin ... announced he would be leading the projected [centrist electoral] alliance. Instead, Mr Stepashin surprised much of the country by declaring he had failed to pull together the disparate group of democrats. "Bringing people together who cannot be united is impossible ... Their personal ambitions are too big" ... Mr Stepashin will run for a seat in the parliament as a representative from St Petersburg ... Aides to Viktor Chernomyrdin [Our Home is Russia] disclosed Saturday that the coalition had begun to fall apart when Mr Chernomyrdin refused to include the Democratic Choice Party of Yegor Gaidar ... Another deal breaker was Mr Chernomyrdin's refusal to allow another former prime minister, Sergei Kiriyenko [New Force movement]... to be listed among the top three leaders of the alliance in the parliamentary slate' (*IHT,* 23 August 1999, p. 5).

'[There was a] failure to build a broad-based coalition over the weekend ... [a] collapse of talks to recruit ... Sergei Stepashin to a centre-right grouping along with two former prime ministers, Viktor Chernomurdin and Sergei Kiriyenko ... Sergei Stepashin ... said on Saturday [21 August] that he had resolved to stand in a personal capacity in his home city of St Petersburg ... Mr Kiriyenko said he planned to join forces with Anatoli Chubais ... Mr Chernomyrdin ruled out any such alliance for his Our Home is Russia' (*FT,* 23 August 1999, p. 2).

'Vladimir Yakovlev, the governor of St Petersburg, was elected head of the All Russia party on Saturday [21 August], although he does not plan to stand for a seat in December [1999]' (*FT,* 23 August 1999, p. 2).

22 August 1999. The Stalinist Bloc for the Soviet Union is formed. It will be led by Viktor Anpilov. Yevgeni Dzhugashvili, grandson of Joseph Stalin, will be number three in its parliamentary list (*FT,* 23 August 1999, p. 2).

The Stalinist Bloc for the USSR unites four factions of hardline communists and others on the far left. It advocates the abolition of the presidency, the return of power to the people and the return of 'stolen' property (*The Times*, 31 August 1999, p. 37).

(A new, extreme-left bloc called Communists and Working people of Russia for the Soviet Union was formed recently. It includes the Russian Communist Workers' Party, the Communists and Working Russia for the Soviet Union movement and the Soviet Homeland movement: *Nezavisimaya Gazeta*, 26 August 1999, p. 3; *CDSP,* 1999, vol. 51, no. 34, p. 16.)

24 August 1999. Sergei Stepashin and Yabloko form a new bloc. Stepashin is to be on Yabloko's list for the elections to the State Duma as the candidate in a single-seat district in St Petersburg (whose former deputy was the late Galina Starovoitova) (*CDSP,* 1999, vol. 51, no. 34, p. 7).

'Sergei Stepashin, who last week flirted with an alliance with Grigori Yavlinsky's ... Yabloko ... announced that he was striking out on his own and would stand as a deputy in St Petersburg. But within a day he had changed his mind: he has now formed an alliance with Yabloko and will run as the second name on the party list' (*The Times*, 26 August 1999, p. 18).

The Union of Rightist Forces is formed, led by Sergei Kiriyenko (New Force), Boris Nemtsov (Young Russia) and Irina Khakmada (Common Cause). Voice of Russia (headed by Samara province governor Konstantin Titov) agrees to form a bloc with it. The Voice of Russia leader is not planning to enter the State Duma himself (*CDSP,* 1999, vol. 51, no. 34, p. 8). (Other important figures include Yegor Gaidar, Anatoli Chubais, who is campaign manager, and Pavel Krashennikov.)

Sergei Kiriyenko says that Boris Nemtsov's Young Russia party is joining an alliance Kiriyenko has established with the Russia's Choice party of Anatoli Chubais (*IHT,* 25 August 1999, p. 6).

27 August 1999. The Agrarian Party joins the Fatherland-All-Russia bloc (*CDSP,* 1999. vol. 51, no. 34, p. 9).

'On the eve of its congress on Saturday [28 August] it [the Fatherland-All-Russia bloc] won a major boost when delegates from the Agrarian Party [led by Mikhail Lapshin] decided by a large majority to join forces with it' (*The Guardian*, 30 August 1999, p. 11).

28 August 1999. The Fatherland-All Russia bloc presents its election platform at a rally. These include the following: a major reduction in the powers of the president and a transfer of authority to a government reflecting a majority in the State Duma (the president should cease to be Russia's chief executive and an independent committee of doctors should decide when the president is unfit to serve); the recreation of the post of vice-president; a national minimum wage; the indexation of pensions (*The Guardian*, 30 August 1999, p. 11).

Yevgeni Primakov: 'The development of democracy and freedom of speech were and remain our values ... We do not want to go back to the command system which went bankrupt, nor do we want to nationalize everything, but we do want to use the levers of state to regulate the economy in the interests of growth, honest business and the welfare of taxpayers ... Supporters of a strong state do not strive to nationalize everything but to ensure effective management of state property ... [Retiring presidents should have] full security and a worthy life' (*FT,* 30 August 1999, p. 2; *The Times*, 30 August 1999, p. 12; *The Guardian*, 30 August 1999, p. 11).

2 September 1999. Mikhail Zadornov resigns as the president's special representative for relations with international financial organizations (his place being taken by finance minister Mikhail Kasyanov). Zadornov has joined Yabloko and intends to run for a seat in the State Duma (*CDSP*, 1999, vol. 51, no. 35, p. 16). (On 16 October 1999 first deputy prime minister Viktor Khristenko took over the role of special representative: *RET*, 1999, vol. 8, no. 4, p. 99.)

20 September 1999. Raisa Gorbachev dies of leukaemia.

24 September 1999. The formation is announced of the Unity governors' bloc, headed by emergency situations minister Sergei Shoigu. 'The new association is clearly the Kremlin's final attempt to get a "party of power" of its own into the running' (*CDSP*, 1999, vol. 51, no. 39, p. 13). On 24 October the pro-Yeltsin Unity bloc was also given the name Medved (Bear). Membership includes Alexander Rutskoi (*The Times*, 26 October 1999, p. 21).

9–11 October 1999. Yeltsin is treated in hospital for flu and a high temperature.

11 October 1999. The central election commission bans the party list for Vladimir Zhirinovsky's Liberal Democratic Party because the second and third candidates on the list failed to declare all their personal assets. (Election rules say that if any of the top three quit the race or are excluded the entire list is invalidated: *IHT*, 12 October 1999, p. 4.) Zhirinovsky and his sister registered under the name Zhirinovsky Block on 24 October (*The Times*, 26 October 1999, p. 21). The Zhirinovsky Block was formed on 13 October 1999 (*RET*, 1999, vol. 8, no. 4, p. 98).

20 October 1999. The United Social Democratic Party is launched, although too late to participate in the December 1999 election. Mikhail Gorbachev has agreed to head the party (*The Guardian*, 21 October 1999, p. 16).

23 November 1999. 'The Russian constitutional court eased a restriction in a controversial 1997 religion law on Tuesday [23 November 1999], but at the same time upheld the overall right of the government to limit the activity of religious faiths … The case involved Jehovah's Witnesses. In the town of Yaroslavl, north-east of Moscow, the local prosecutor had attempted to close down a branch of the Jehovah's Witnesses on the grounds that the local congregation did not have documents showing that it existed more than fifteen years ago, as the law requires. But the local congregation claimed that it did not need the documents because the Jehovah's Witnesses had already been certified in Moscow as meeting the requirement. The group says it has operated for more than fifty years in Russia but in Soviet times was hidden to avoid the authorities. The constitutional court backed the Jehovah's Witnesses, saying that the local congregation was correct … By some estimates there are more than 10,000 small religious groups that could feel the impact of these restrictions, which so far have not yet been fully enforced. In the decision Tuesday the court upheld the government's right to impose restrictions on religion. the court said these would have to be in the interest of public health, safety, order and morals, and protection of the rights of other persons … The court also approved of the state's right to set barriers before groups can be officially registered to prevent "the legalization of sects that violate human rights and commit unlawful and criminal deeds'" (*IHT*, 24 November 1999, p. 7).

The Jehovah's Witnesses (130,000 in Russia, of which 10,000 are in Moscow) are appearing before a Moscow civil court accused of inciting religious discord and threatened with a ban on their activities. A 1997 law on religion restricted non-traditional denominations. They are accused of violating the 1997 law by preaching religious discrimination, breaking up families and withholding medical treatment – all in the name of 'one true religion'. If they lose their legal status in Moscow other parts of Russia may follow and other religious groups could be affected (Celestine Bohlen, *IHT*, 12 February 1999, p. 5).

25 November 1999. Yeltsin is taken ill with 'a viral infection and acute bronchitis'. The signing of the reunification treaty with Belarus, scheduled for the following day, is postponed.

29 November 1999. Yeltsin is admitted to hospital with suspected pneumonia.

3 December 1999. Yevgeni Primakov accuses the Kremlin of offering bribes, promotions and free apartments to members of the Fatherland-All Russia bloc to pull out of the parliamentary election (*The Times*, 4 December 1999, p. 17).

6 December 1999. Yeltsin leaves hospital and pays a brief visit to the Kremlin.

8 December 1999. Yeltsin signs an agreement relating to unification with President Lukashenko of Belarus. During the signing ceremony Yeltsin was unsteady on his feet and seemed somewhat confused at times. Despite this Yeltsin flew off to China for a two-day visit.

17 December 1999. Yevgeni Primakov (openly backed by Yuri Luzkhkov), Grigori Yavlinksy and Vladimir Zhirinovsky announce they will run for the presidency.

19 December 1999. The general election takes place.

Half of the 450 seats in the State Duma were allotted on the basis of party lists. Parties that won at least 5 per cent of the vote shared these seats on a proportional basis. The other members were directly elected from 225 constituencies (although there was no constituency election in Chechenia because of the war there).

There were some 107–108 million voters. The actual turnout was 61.85 per cent, thus comfortably exceeding the minimum 25 per cent required.

Six (out of twenty-six) parties won enough seats in the party list section to enter the State Duma. The percentage of the vote and the number of seats won (225 in total) were as follows:

1. Russian Federation Communist Party, 24.29 per cent and sixty-seven.
2. Unity, 23.32 per cent and sixty-four.
3. Fatherland-All Russia, 13.33 per cent and thirty-seven.
4. Union of Rightist Forces, 8.52 per cent and twenty-four.
5. Zhirinovsky's Bloc, 5.98 per cent and seventeen.
6. Yabloko, 5.93 per cent and sixteen.

A total of 441 deputies were elected to the Duma, 225 from federal party lists and 216 in single-seat districts (*CDSP*, 1999, vol. 51, no. 52, pp. 5–6: results as of 29 December 1999).

The distribution of the 216 deputies in single-member districts was as follows: Russian Federation Communist Party, forty-seven; Unity, nine; Fatherland-All Russia, twenty-nine; Union of Rightist Forces, five; Zhirinovsky's Bloc, zero; Yabloko, four; other parties, seventeen; independents, 105. A second round of voting was scheduled for the eight single-member district seats where the majority of the electorate voted against all the candidates on the ballot paper. Elections were not held in Chechenia, the ninth vacant seat (Sakwa 2000: 101).

Although the Communist Party remained the largest single party in the State Duma, there was a dramatic, 'last-minute' increase in support for Unity and the Union of Rightist Forces. 'The surprise winners of the election were two parties [Unity and the Union of Rightist Forces] ... that emerged out of the political wilderness in the last few months, boosted by their backing of a popular war in Chechenia and supported by a ferocious propaganda campaign waged by the Kremlin and its allies' (Celestine Bohlen, *IHT*, 21 December 1999, p. 1). 'The big victor from the poll was undoubtedly Vladimir Putin, the prime minister, whose ruthless prosecution of the war in Chechenia has won him a dramatic rise in popularity. The bloc he invented, known as Unity, has emerged with almost as many votes as the Communist Party, despite having no policy platform, and no regional organization. It is simply the Kremlin's party' (*FT*, editorial, 21 December 1999, p. 18). Igor Shabdurasulov (Yeltsin's deputy chief of staff) commented after the election: 'In Russia a revolution has taken place, a peaceful one but a revolution all the same. This is a colossal breakthrough.'

Both Unity and the Union of Rightist Forces were overtly supported by prime minister Vladimir Putin, himself experiencing a rapid rise from obscurity to widespread popularity as a result of what was generally perceived to be a justified and successful prosecution of the war in Chechenia. He was widely perceived to be exercising strong leadership and restoring national pride.

The prospering of Unity and the Union of Rightist Forces mirrored the decline in the fortunes of Fatherland-All Russia. 'Mr Putin and his Kremlin allies showed great skill in destroying political opponents ... [Fatherland-All Russia] was widely expected just four months ago to lead at the polls. Under withering attack it won only third place ... The Kremlin used its control of the two leading television stations to smear Mr Luzhkov and his allies relentlessly with charges of corruption and murder, based on half-truths and outright fabrications. The government's tax authorities harassed media outlets which refused to hew the line. To be sure, Mr Luzhkov responded in kind, but it was an unfair battle. His media and financial resources pale compared with the Kremlin's' (Thomas Graham, *IHT*, 22 December 1999, p. 6). 'In the campaign both Mr Luzhkov and Mr Primakov were pummelled by a steady stream of negative, sometimes vicious, broadcasts on national television channels controlled by the Kremlin and its allies' (*IHT*, 21 December 1999, p. 1). 'The media was strongly opposed to the Fatherland-All Russia alliance' (*FT*, 21 December 1999, p. 18). 'The first and second television channels unashamedly favoured the Kremlin' (*The Independent*, 21 December 1999, p. 10).

The war in Chechenia hardly registered as a debating point during the election, although Yabloko suffered from Grigori Yavlinsky's call on 9 November 1999 for peace talks and a halt to the massive offensive, albeit subject to strict conditions. Economic issues were sidelined by war in Chechenia. 'The great issues facing Russia – in particular how to extricate the country from its prolonged socio-economic depression – were not even debated' (Thomas Graham, *IHT*, 22 December 1999, p. 6). But the war was not the only factor accounting for the muting of economic issues. The economy had returned to positive growth much more quickly than generally predicted after the crisis of August 1998, helped by the huge depreciation of the rouble (which improved the competitiveness of Russian products) and the marked increase in world oil prices. In addition, there had been a narrowing of views on economic policy. 'A study of the economic programmes of the main parties, conducted by the Carnegie Moscow Centre, found that there had been a notable convergence of thinking about the main economic challenges facing Russia and how to address them' (*FT*, 17 December 1999, p. 20).

The following parties finally ran (*CDSP*, 1999, vol. 51, no. 44, pp. 6–7):

Russian Federation Communist Party. Gennadi Zyuganov, Gennadi Seleznyov, Vasili Starodubtsev.

Unity (Yedinstvo) (Bear; Medved). Sergei Shoigu (minister for emergency situations), Alexander Karelin (Olympic gold-medal wrestler), Alexander Gurov (a former high police official).

'It was created only three months ago and has not even published a party programme' (*FT*, 17 December 1999, p. 20). 'It is difficult to believe that the strongly pro-government, military line taken by most of the Russian media towards ... Chechenia has not helped sway public opinion, in the process boosting the ratings for Unity, the party endorsed by Valdimir Putin, the prime minister' (*FT*, 18 December 1999, p. 7). 'Unity is three months old and has no political programme or regional infrastructure' (*The Guardian*, 18 December 1999, p. 15). Prime minister Putin endorsed Unity in late November 1999 (*IHT*, 22 December 1999, p. 6). 'The Unity bloc [is] an amalgam of statist, nationalist, liberal and even communist politicians. Unity's leadership even includes Alexander Rutskoi, who led an armed rebellion against Boris Yeltsin in October 1993, and Kirsan Ilyumzhinov, president of the republic of Kalmykia, who once threatened to secede from Russia' (Thomas Graham, *IHT*, 22 December 1999, p. 6)

Union of Rightist Forces. Sergei Kiriyenko, Boris Nemtsov, Irina Khakamada.

'Mr Putin ... said last week that he could agree with parts of the economic platform of the rightist party. Leaders of the Right Forces, who publicly have supported the prime minister's tough conduct of the Chechenia war despite the misgivings of some of their backers, have returned the compliment by endorsing Mr Putin for president' (*IHT*, Tuesday 21 December 1999, p. 1).

Fatherland-All Russia. Yevgeni Primakov, Yuri Luzhkov, Vladimir Yakovlev.

Yabloko. Grigori Yavlinsky, Sergei Stepshin, Vladimir Lukin.

Zhirinovsky's Bloc. Vladimir Zhirinovsky, Oleg Finko, Yegor Solomatin.

'Vladimir Zhirinovsky ... has supported the Kremlin on crucial votes' (*IHT*, 21 December 1999, p. 6). 'Mr Zhirinovsky ... has proved to be Mr Yeltsin's unfailing parliamentary ally' (*FT*, 21 December 1999, p. 6).

The others registered on 3 November were as follows:

Russia is Our Home. Viktor Chernomyrdin, Vladimir Ryzhlov, Dmitri Ayatskov.

Russian Party for the Defence of Women. Tatiana Roshchina, Zhanna Makhova, Irina Kremenets.

Congress of Russian Communities and Yuri Boldyrev's Movement. Yuri Boldyrev, Dmitri Rogozin, Viktor Glukhikh.

Conservative Movement of Russia. Lev Ubozhko, Vladimir Burenin, Anfrei Tishkov.

Spiritual Heritage. Aleksei Podberyozkin, Pyotr Proskurin, Valeri Vorotnikov.

Party of Peace and Unity. Sazki Umalatova, Viktor Stepanov, Nikolai Antoshkin.

Russian Union of All the People. Sergei Baburin, Nikolai Leonov, Nikolai Pavlov.

For Citizens's Dignity. Ella Pamfilova, Alexander Dondukov, Anatoli Shkirko.

Pensioners' Party. Yakov Ryabov,. Anatoli Kontashov, Rimma Markova.

Russian Socialist Party. Vladimir Bryntsalov, Igor Bryntsalov, Yuri Bryntsalov.

Movement in Support of the Army. Viktor Ilyukin, Albert Makashov, Yuri Saveliev.

Women of Russia. Alevtina Fedulova, Galina Karelova, Nina Veselova.

Movement of Patriotic Forces/Russian Cause. Oleg Ivanov, Yuri Petrov, Mikhail Sidorov.

General Andrei Nikolayev and Academician Svatoslav Fyodorov's Bloc. Andrei Nikolayev, Svatoslav Fyodorov, Tatiana Malyutina.

Peace, Labour, May. Alexander Burkov, Valeri Trushnikov, Alexander Tatarkin.

Socialist Party of Russia. Ivan Rubkin, Leonid Maiorov, Andrei Belishko.

Stalin Bloc for the USSR. Viktor Anpilov, Stanislav Terekhov, Yevgeni Dzhugashvili.

All-Russia Political Party of the People. Anzori Aksentyev, Tatiana Bure, Vladimir Shainsky.

Social Democrats. Their list has no federal section.

Communists and Working People of Russia for the Soviet Union. Viktor Tyulkin, Anatoli Kryuchkov, Vladislav Aseyev.

'International observers assessed the electoral campaign positively, while noting that state-run television had proved "very biased". "The electoral system in the Russian Federation has reached a new level in its journey to sophistication", said ... the head of the observer mission for OSCE' (*FT*, 21 December 1999, p. 1). 'Hundreds of observers co-ordinated by the European Parliament, the Council of Europe and OSCE ... reconvened in Moscow with a broadly positive view gained from witnesses across the country ... In a preliminary report they concluded the election was "competitive and pluralistic" and that a high turnout suggested "confidence in the democratic process" ... A smaller team of longer term observers [were concerned, for example, by] improper interference by regional authorities during the campaign ... But their biggest criticism was reserved for the Russian media. A study by the EU-funded European Institute for the Media concluded coverage of the elections had been biased, gave unequal time to the different parties and had deteriorated in character from the parliamentary campaign in 1995' (p. 6).

Yuri Luzhkov was reelected mayor of Moscow.

Boris Berezovsky won a seat in Karachayevo-Cherkessia in the north Caucasus.

'Both he and his business partner, Roman Abramovich, won seats in the Duma from remote regions and thus immunity from prosecution ... Perhaps Mr Berezovsky's most serious impact on the election was the creation of ... a party named Unity, which won the second-highest share of the seats in the Duma with a campaign in which it put forth no serious platform or policy positions ... He averred [on 22 December]... that he had something to do with it [the creation of Unity] ... He led a consortium that bought up 49 per cent of ORT, the state-owned television channel ... The channel is the only one that spans Russia's vast territory and Mr Berezovsky turned it into a propaganda weapon against his chief political enemies: Mr Primakov and ... Yuri Luzhkov ... As Mr Berezovsky was basking in success, the Luzhkov-Primakov party began splitting up. Mintimir Shaimiyev, the president of Tatarstan, and several other regional leaders said they would set up their own faction in parliament and would co-operate with the Putin government' (David Hoffman, *IHT*, 24 December 1999, p. 7).

'One in five of tomorrow's [19 December] candidates has a criminal past ... Duma deputies are immune from prosecution. The immunity clause ... has made the Duma a magnet for those with much to hide' (*The Times*, 18 December 1999, p. 12).

28 December 1999. Putin releases a policy statement: 'Russia will not soon become, if it will ever become, a second edition, say, of the USA or England, where liberal values have deep historical traditions. A strong state is not an anomaly for Russians, and not something that must be fought against, but on the contrary the source and guarantee of order, the initiator and main engine of any change ... [Russia] wants a restoration of a guiding and regulatory role of the state … Our state and its institutions have always played an exceptionally important role in the life of the country and its people … [There is need for] a comprehensive system of state regulation of the economy … [Russians] are not ready to abandon traditional dependence on the state and become self-reliant individuals … Russia has reached its limit of political and socio-economic upheaval, cataclysms and radical reforms … [There will be no resort to] experiments … radicalism … revolutionary extremism … [There is need for a long-term strategy of] market and democratic reforms implemented only by evolutionary, gradual and prudent methods … Everything depends on us, and us alone, on our ability to see the size of the threat, to pool forces and set our minds to hard and lengthy work … [Russia's decline has been caused by] our mistakes and miscalculations.'

31 December 1999. Boris Yeltsin unexpectedly announces his resignation as president at around mid-day. Prime minister Vladimir Putin becomes acting president (as of midday) until a presidential election is held. (The presidential has to be held within three months. Although 26 March 2000 was mentioned in the media, it is up to the Council of the Federation to fixed the exact day of the election. But that date was formally confirmed on 5 January.)

'Today I am addressing you for the last time as Russian president. I have made a decision. I have contemplated this long and hard. Today, on the last day of the outgoing century, I am retiring. Many times I have heard it said: Yeltsin will try to hold on to power by any means, he will not hand it over to anyone. That is all lies. That is not the case. I have always said that I would not take a single step away from the constitution, that the Duma elections should take place within the constitutional timescale. This has happened. Likewise, I would like the presidential elections to take place on schedule in June 2000. That was very important for Russia – we were creating a vital precedent of a civilized, voluntary handover of power, power from one president of Russia to another, newly elected one. And yet, I have taken a different decision. I am standing down. I am standing down earlier than scheduled. I have realized that I must do this. Russia must enter the new millennium with new faces, new intelligent, strong and energetic people. As for those of us who have been in power for many years, we must go. Seeing with what hope and belief people voted during the Duma elections for a new generation of politicians, I have understood that I had done the main job of my life. Russia will never return to the past. Russia will now always be moving forward. I must not stand in its way, in the way of the natural progress of history. Why hold on to power for another six months when the country has a strong person, fit to be president, with whom practically all Russians link their hopes for the future today? Why should I stand in his way? Why wait for another six months? … I want to ask you for forgiveness, because many of our hopes have not come true, because what we thought would be easy turned out to be painfully difficult. I ask you to forgive me for not fulfilling some hopes of those people who believed that we would be able to jump from the grey, stagnating, totalitarian past into a bright, rich and civilized future in one go. I myself believed this. But it could not be done in one fell swoop. In some respects I was too naive. Some of the problems were too complex. We struggled on through mistakes and failures. At this complex time many people experienced upheavals in their lives. But I want you to know that I never said this would be easy. Today it is important to me to tell you the following. I also experienced the pain that each of you experienced. I experienced it in my heart, with sleepless nights, agonizing over what needed to be done to ensure that people lived more easily and better, if only a little. I did not have any objective more important than that. I am leaving. I have done everything I could. I am not leaving because of my health, but because of all the problems taken together. A new generation is taking my place, the generation of those who can do more and do it better. In accordance with the constitution, as I go into retirement, I have signed a decree entrusting the duties of the president of Russia to prime minister Vladimir Vladimirovich Putin. For the next three months, again in accordance with the constitution, he will be head of state. Presidential elections will be held in three months' time. I have always had confidence in the amazing wisdom of Russian citizens. Therefore, I have no doubt what choice you will make at the end of March 2000.'

Acting President Putin signs a decree entitled 'On guarantees to the President of the Russian Federation after he leaves office and to the members of his family': 'After leaving office the President of the Russian Federation enjoys immunity. After leaving office the President of the Russian Federation may not be prosecuted on criminal charges, subjected to administrative penalties, detained, arrested or subjected to search, interrogation or personal inspection. The immunity enjoyed by the President of the Russian Federation after he leaves office extends to his places of residence and of work, the vehicles and means of communications he uses, all documents and baggage belonging to him and his correspondence.'

3 January 2000. Putin relieves Tatiana Dyachenko (Yeltsin's younger daughter) of her position as presidential adviser.

Putin renames Alexander Voloshin as presidential chief of staff. Dmitri Yakushkin, who is expected to take a job as Yeltsin's personal spokesman, is relieved of his position as presidential press secretary, and given another job as assistant to Voloshin (*IHT,* 4 January 2000, p. 7).

4 January 2000. Putin (in a television interview): 'This [Yeltsin's resignation] is linked first of all to the fact that he wanted the presidential campaign to proceed as he wanted. Let us be honest. He [Yeltsin] is providing me with a forum for the presidential campaign and doing so deliberately.'

Alexei Gromov is named as Putin's press secretary.

5 January 2000. 'The leaders of Mr Primakov's All-Russia movement, including the presidents of Tatarstan [Mintimir Shaimiyev], Bashkortostan [Murtaza Rakhimov] and Ingushetia [Ruslan Aushev], and the governor of

St Petersburg [Vladimir Yakovlev], said they had unanimously decided to support Mr Putin' (*FT*, 6 January 2000, p. 1).

6 January 2000. 'Vladimir Putin ... signed a decree that switched the focus of security to terrorism and the fight against organized crime' (*The Times*, 7 January 2000, p. 20).

9 January 2000. The position of governor of the Moscow region is won by Boris Gromov (who led the withdrawal of Soviet troops from Afghanistan), who was backed by Grigori Yavlinsky. His opponent, Gennadi Seleznyov (speaker of the outgoing State Duma), was backed by Putin.

10 January 2000. Putin makes cabinet changes.

Finance minister Mikhail Kasyanov becomes the only first deputy prime minister. He will act as the cabinet's 'technical co-ordinator' in the run-up to the presidential election on 26 March 2000. The new cabinet will have seven deputy prime ministers.

Pavel Borodin is demoted from head of the Kremlin's management office (which is in charge of a vast property empire) to become state secretary of the Russia-Belarus union. He is under investigation by Russian prosecutors in connection with allegations of bribes paid by a Swiss construction company for work done on the renovation of the Kremlin palace.

First deputy prime minister Nikolai Aksyenenko returns to his former post of railway minister. The other first deputy prime minister, Viktor Khristenko, is also demoted.

13 January 2000. Putin formally declares his candidacy for president.

'Yevgenni Primakov ... decided Thursday [13 January] to run for speaker of ... the State Duma. Mr Primakov did not comment publicly, but his plan was disclosed in a closed meeting of faction leaders' (*IHT*, 14 January 2000, p. 1).

18 January 2000. The opening day of the new State Duma.

Gennadi Seleznyov is reelected speaker.

Vladimir Putin addresses the Duma.

'Acting President Valdimir Putin urged lawmakers to stop fighting with the presidency and start tackling the country's problems' (*IHT*, 19 January 2000, p. 5)

'In his maiden speech to the new parliament Mr Putin ... called on it to approve legal codes on land, labour and civil and criminal court procedures that have languished unratified for years ... The ten-minute address ... set out fiscal reform and "the rights and freedoms of citizens" as top priorities ... He rejected suggestions that he plans to use the constitution to help him establish an elective dictatorship. "Those who speak about a possible dictatorship are themselves dreaming of it", he said after the speech ... Mr Putin insisted that dictatorship "is impossible in Russia"' (*The Times*, 19 January 2000, p. 17).

19 January 2000. 'Opposition lawmakers, fearing that they have been shut out by a deal between supporters of acting President Putin and the Communists, boycotted the new State Duma for a second day Wednesday [19 January] ...

Roughly 100 lawmakers walked out of the new Duma's opening session Tuesday [18 January] after the Communists and the pro-Putin Unity group formed an alliance to make Mr Seleznyov, a Communist, the speaker. They were also outraged by the two biggest factions taking control of most of the Duma's committees' (*IHT*, 20 January 2000, p. 5).

'Nearly a third of Russia's politicians boycotted parliament for a second day yesterday [19 January] in protest at the way in which the speaker and committee chairs had been divided between the Communists and the pro-Kremlin Unity party ... The centrist Fatherland-All Russia movement, the Union of Right Forces and Russia's Regions all strongly criticised the way the deal was done. The first three said they had formed a co-ordinating committee ... The four parties quit the Duma during its first session on Tuesday [18 January] after Unity agreed to support the reelection of Gennadi Seleznyov, the Communist speaker of the previous parliament, in exchange for receiving the majority of chairs in the specialist committees' (*FT*, 20 January 2000, p. 7).

'More than 100 deputies from smaller parties walked out of the voting in disgust' (*The Times*, 20 January 2000, p. 21).

'The Communists, with a fifth of the 450 seats, got a third of the chairmanships. Mr Putin's Unity, with 18 per cent of seats, got 26 per cent of the committee posts. Mr Primakov's Fatherland controls 10 per cent of seats and was offered one chairmanship, which it spurned' (*IHT*, 21 January 2000, p. 7).

'With just over a fifth of the deputies, the Communists also [in addition to the speaker] have the chairmanship of at least nine out of twenty-six committees ... Unity, which has slightly fewer members, won a deputy speakership and seven committees. A newly formed pro-Kremlin group of independents, called People's Deputies, ended up with five. Vladimir Zhirinovsky's Liberal Democrats, who usually vote the Kremlin line, have a deputy speakership and one committee' (*The Economist*, 22 January 2000, p. 45).

25 January 2000. 'A liberal pro-market party boycotting the session agreed to return in exchange for a promise to consider its legislative agenda. The Union of Right Forces agreed to go back to work, its leader said, after a meeting with acting President Vladimir Putin and the leader of .... Unity ... Boris Gryzlov. Sergei Kiriyenko, leader of the Union of Right Forces, said his faction had decided to return in exchange for a promise of prompt action on tax reform, passage of a land code, a labour law and legislation on the perks of legislators and limiting their right to immunity from criminal prosecution' (*IHT*, 26 January 2000, p. 6).

28 January 2000. 'Leaders of three Russian political parties have agreed to end their boycott of the Russian parliament on 9 February ... Mr Putin interceded in the dispute by meeting separately with two former prime ministers, Yevgeni Primakov and Sergei Kiriyenko. The two, along with Grigori Yavlinsky ... led a walkout last week ... Although the parties headed by Mr Primakov, Mr Kiriyenko and Mr Yavlinsky together hold about 140 of the 450 seats they had been given only two of the twenty-seven committees in parliament' (*IHT*, 29 January 2000, p. 2).

31 January 2000. The start of a three-day visit by US secretary of state Madeleine Albright.

4 February 2000. Yevgeni Primakov announces that he will not run in the forthcoming presidential election: 'During the elections, and as I began work in parliament, I sensed how far our society is from being a civil society and from being a true democracy.'

'On the opening day of the new parliament last month [January] a pro-Putin party known as Unity allied itself with the opposition Communists and took control of the parliament's top leadership positions. One goal of the manoeuvre, analysts say, was to block Mr Primakov from being elected speaker' (*IHT*, 5 February 2000, p. 5).

16 February 2000. Nato secretary-general George Robertson visits Russia. 'A joint statement issued after George Robertson … met Vladimir Putin … said the two sides aimed to intensify their contacts and become a cornerstone of European security' (*FT*, 17 February 2000, p. 12).

17 February 2000. Vladimir Zhirinovsky is barred from running in the presidential election on the grounds of a false property declaration (specifically failing to include a Moscow apartment owned by his son in his financial declaration). (The law requires candidates to declare their assets and those of their immediate family. But on 6 March the supreme court ordered Zhirinovsky to be registered as a candidate.)

20 February 2000. Anatoli Sobchak dies, seemingly of a heart attack.

25 February 2000. Putin publishes an open letter: 'The stronger the state, the freer the individual … [What is needed is] dictatorship of the law … It [the state] must set equal rules and comply with them … The essence of [economic] regulation is not to stifle the market and extend bureaucratic control into new branches – but quite the contrary … Our priority is to protect the market against illegal intervention, both bureaucratic and criminal.' (*FT*, 26 February 2000, p. 5, and 28 February 2000, p. 22; *IHT*, 3 March 2000. p. 5; *Business Central Europe*, April 2000, p. 44.)

'Little noticed by the West, Mr Putin, a former lieutenant colonel in the KGB, is rapidly remilitarizing society … Since Mr Putin took office on 31 December [1999] he has issued eleven presidential decrees. Six concerned the military … Mr Putin has also focussed on the military in his capacity as prime minister. His government's first legislative action reestablished military training in secondary schools, both public and private. Russian teenagers will once again become intimate with the Kalashnikov. The education ministry's plans to expand the school curriculum to twelve years will also have a military impact. Boys will graduate from high school at the conscription age of eighteen, and will not have time to try to gain acceptance to colleges that could grant draft exemptions … From now on military detachments will be encouraged to "adopt" boys of fourteen and older who are orphaned or have single mothers' (Masha Gessen, *IHT*, 1 March 2000, p. 11).

9 March 2000. A private aircraft crashes while taking off in Moscow. The nine dead include the investigative reporter Artyom Borovik, setting off speculation as to the cause of the crash.

11 March 2000. British prime minister Tony Blair visits Russia, the first visit by a Western leader since Vladimir Putin became acting president.

18 March 2000. 'The acting president admitted that he has not become a public politician. "You are supposed to look millions of people in the eye and make promises you know you cannot keep. I have not learned to do that." Vladimir Putin said that was why he had opted not to use campaign ads or take part in televised debates … Vladimir Putin plans to divided the oligarchs into "clean and unclean". The authorities will negotiate with the first (the "big businessmen"), but Putin promises to wage war on the rest (who are power hungry): "oligarchs of that kind will not exist as a class"' (*CDSP*, 2000, vol. 52, no. 12, p. 1).

'"Russia was founded as a super-centralized state from the very start. This is inherent in its genetic code, traditions and people's mentality", Mr Putin said before the presidential elections' (*FT*, Survey, 10 May 2000, p. v).

'Mr Putin said during the election campaign that if oligarchs "mean fusion, or those people who fuse, or help fusion of power and capital, there will be no oligarchs of this kind as a class" … The chief of the presidential administration Alexander Voloshin … is part of a Kremlin circle that helped bring Mr Putin to power. Under Mr Yeltsin the group also included former chief of staff Valentin Yumashev, Mr Yeltsin's daughter, Tatiana Dyachenko, and … Boris Berezovsky … Before and after the March presidential election the Kremlin group attempted to exert pressure on Vladimir Gusinsky, who created NTV commercial television and owns newspapers, radio stations and magazines … Mr Gusinsky's media outlets were viewed as sympathetic to … Moscow's mayor, Yuri Luzkkov, and former prime minister Yevgeni Primakov' (David Hoffman, *IHT*, 8 May 2000, p. 7).

22 March 2000. Putin: 'Experience has shown that at the time that treaty [with Tatarstan] was the right solution, and maybe even the only viable one … [But] the constitution stipulates that all Federation members are equal … [and] Tatarstan … understands that … [We have to] bring everything in conformity with the constitution' (*CDSP*, 2000, vol. 52, no. 12, p. 3).

26 March 2000. The presidential election is held. The total electorate was 109,209, 740 million. The turnout was 68.74 per cent.

There were eleven candidates, but the only thing in doubt was whether prime minister and acting president Vladimir Putin would win in the first round. In fact, he did. Although Putin did not formally campaign, he received a great deal of publicity in the media. The preliminary results were as follows:

Vladimir Putin, 52.94 per cent.

Gennadi Zyuganov (leader of the Russian Federation Communist Party), 29.21 per cent.

Grigori Yavlinsky (leader of Yabloko), 5.80 per cent.

Aman Tuleyev (leftist governor of Kemerovo province), 2.95 per cent.

Vladimir Zhirinovsky (leader of the Liberal Democratic Party of Russia), 2.70 per cent.

Option to vote against all candidates, 1.90 per cent.

Konstantin Titov (reformist governor of Samara province), 1.5 per cent. (Titov submitted his resignation as governor of Samara province on 4 April and it was accepted three days later. Titov won only 20.5 per cent of the vote for the presidency in Samara province, coming in third behind Putin and Zyuganov: *CDSP*, 2000, vol. 52, no. 14, p. 12.)

Ella Pamfilova (leader of the political movement For Citizens' Dignity and former social affairs minister), 1.02 per cent.

Stanislav Govorukhin (State Duma deputy and former film maker), 0.45 per cent.

Yuri Skuratov (suspended prosecutor general), 0.43 per cent.

Alexei Podberyozkin (leader of Spiritual Heritage; a cultural leftist), 0.14 per cent.

Umar Dzhabrailov (ethnic Chechen businessman), 0.08 per cent.

'In preliminary findings released yesterday [27 March] an observation team from OSCE concluded that it had seen no evidence of significant fraud that would have affected the outcome. In a more critical report the European Institute of the Media attacked the disproportionately large and favourable coverage given to Mr Putin on television and in newspapers' (*FT*, 28 March 2000, p. 10).

'On Monday [27 March] Western observers declared Russia's presidential election "free and fair" and dismissed accusations by Mr Zyuganov that there had been "large-scale falsification" to boost Mr Putin's vote total. While the balloting itself passed with "nothing serious" in the way of vote fraud, a joint mission of OSCE and the Council of Europe showed that Russia is not yet a full democracy with a free and fair press. "Important segments of the media, both state-controlled and private, failed to provide impartial and fair information", said ... [the] president of the Council of Europe's parliamentary assembly' (*IHT*, 28 March 2000, p. 7).

Gennadi Zyuganov: 'We will be able to prove that the election results were blatantly falsified in many regions' (*CDSP*, 2000, vol. 52, no. 13, p. 4).

'In an ugly burst of negative campaigning Russian state-owned television has asserted that the nation's leading liberal candidate is supported by Jews, foreigners and homosexuals ... The prime-time allegations against Grigori Yavlinsky ... were broadcast on Thursday night [23 March] by the ORT television network ... The Russian government formally owns 51 per cent of the ORT channel, whose reports are seen throughout Russia. Boris Berezovsky ... is a major owner ... Before the December parliamentary elections ... [ORT] conducted slashing attacks against Yevgeni Primakov ... and Yuri Luzhkov' (*IHT*, 25 March 2000, p. 7).

29 March 2000. The State Duma votes down a Communist Party resolution proposing a referral to the constitutional court of the immunity from prosecution granted to Yeltsin by Putin. The resolution failed to pass, with 144 opposed, 136 in favour and twenty-seven abstaining.

31 March 2000. Putin: 'The West misunderstands our thesis about a strong Russian state. It interprets it as an increase in the use of force, the law enforcement agencies and the security services. We have something completely different in mind, an effective state. It is a state which does not just stick to the rules of the game but is able to guarantee the same rule for everyone ... What we are talking about is a strong state where rules are secured by laws and their observation is guaranteed ... Strengthening the state and continuing market reforms are the principles on which the work of the government will be based ... Pro-market professionals [will be brought into government].'

12 April 2000. Putin appoints Andrei Illarionov as an adviser.

'The outspoken liberal economist ... is the thirty-eight-year-old director of the Institute of Economic Analysis, who has been fiercely critical of the government's economic policies. In 1998 Mr Illarionov provoked a storm of controversy by calling for a controlled devaluation of the rouble months before the government was forced to abandon its rigid exchange rate regime ... In the early 1990 Mr Illarionov worked as an adviser to Viktor Chernomyrdin ... but grew increasingly frustrated at the lack of real economic reforms' (*IHT,* 13 April 2000, p. 10).

16–17 April 2000. Putin visits the UK, his first visit to the West since his election as president.

19 April 2000. The Council of the Federation votes 133 to ten in favour of President-elect Vladimir Putin's recommendation to dismiss Yuri Skuratov as chief prosecutor. 'In January [2000] Mr Skuratov accused Mr Putin of shielding corrupt aides who had served under Mr Yeltsin' (*IHT,* 20 April 2000, p. 5).

7 May 2000. Vladimir Putin is sworn in as president. Putin: 'For the first time in all of Russian history supreme power is being handed over in the most democratic and simplest possible way – through the will of the people, legitimately and peacefully ... The peaceful transfer of power is a crucial element of the political stability that you and I have dreamed of, that we have striven for and tried to achieve.'

Putin names Mikhail Kasyanov as acting prime minister.

9 May 2000. The Victory Day celebration, commemorating the defeat of Nazi Germany in the 'Great Patriotic War', is presided over by President Putin. An estimated 27 million Soviet citizens lost their lives in the Second World War (*IHT,* 10 May 2000, p. 9).

10 May 2000. Putin nominates Kasyanov as prime minister.

11 May 2000. 'Armed and hooded Russian tax police yesterday [11 May] aided the Moscow headquarters of Media-Most, owner of the country's main independent television channel … The action against a company which has often taken a critical line towards the Kremlin administration provoked a strong outcry among liberal commentators in Russia … Officials from the federal tax police, the general prosecutors office and the FSB, the successor body to the KGB, all took part in the morning raid … Media-Most, controlled by the powerful business oligarch Vladimir Gusinsky, owns the TV station NTV, the radio station Echo, the daily newspaper Sevodnia and the news magazine Itogi … In late 1994 there was a similar raid on the company, which some saw as being revenge for its support of Yuri Luzhkov' (*FT*, 12 May 2000, p. 8).

12 May 2000. 'Mr Putin, in a written statement issued by the Kremlin in the aftermath of the raid against the Media-Most conglomerate, said: "A free press should exist as an important guarantee of society's democratic development … Freedom of speech and of mass media are among the basic values" … The general prosecutor's office, apparently using agents drawn from other departments, confiscated two computers and some video- and audiocassettes from the media empire controlled by the magnate Vladimir Gusinsky … A spokesman for the Federal Security Service … claimed late Thursday [11 May] that the raid was aimed at uncovering wiretapping by the Media-Most security department' (*IHT*, 13 May 2000, p. 2).

14 May 2000. Vladimir Yakovlev is reelected as governor of St Petersburg with over 70 per cent of the vote.

'At the start of the campaign the Russian president made clear his strong personal dislike for Mr Yakovlev, who became governor of St Petersburg in 1996 when he defeated the incumbent Anatoli Sobchak. Mr Putin initially supported the rival candidacy of Valentina Matvienko, the social securities minister, but she dropped out of the race' (*FT*, 15 May 2000, p. 13). (Valentina Matvienko said that Putin had asked her to withdraw her candidacy on 4 April 2000: *CDSP*, 2000, vol. 51, no. 5, p. 11.)

17 May 2000. The State Duma approves Mikhail Kasyanov as prime minister in the first round of voting. The voting was 325 to fifty-five, with fifteen abstentions.

A presidential decree abolishes the state committee for environmental protection and the federal forestry service. Both are incorporated into the ministry of natural resources. (Critics claim that ministry of natural resources is more concerned with economic development than the environment.)

18 May 2000. Alexei Kudrin is appointed finance minister and deputy prime minister. German Gref (director of the Centre for Strategic Planning, a policy research institute working on an economic reform programme) becomes minister of economic development and trade.

27 May 2000. Unity (Bear) holds its first congress. Emergencies minister Sergei Shoigu is voted leader of the party (*The Telegraph*, 30 May 2000, p. 16).

3–5 June 2000. President Clinton visits Russia. He holds his first summit with President Putin. The following was agreed on 4 June:

1. To establish a permanent joint early-warning centre in Moscow to prevent miscalculation about missile launches.

2. To cut by thirty-four tonnes each the stockpiles of weapons-grade plutonium.

The USA and Russia are each to convert to civilian use or bury thirty-four tonnes of plutonium. This will cost $5.7 billion over twenty years, with $4 billion of that being borne by the USA, which has already spent more that $3 billion since 1994 helping Russia dismantle warheads (*FT*, 5 June 2000, p. 24).

According to US officials, the thirty-four tonnes to be destroyed by each country represent about one quarter of Russia's military plutonium stockpile and about one third of that of the USA (*IHT*, 4 September 2000, p. 4).

The plutonium is sufficient for 7,000 nuclear warheads and constitutes about half the US stockpile and a third of Russia's (*The Times*, 5 June 2000, p. 19).

There was no agreement on the US proposal to amend the 1972 Anti-Ballistic Treaty by the USA setting up a limited National Missile Defence system on US soil to combat any attack from 'rogue' state such as North Korea, Iraq and Iran. Putin: 'We are against having a cure that is worse than the disease.' But a joint statement was issued by the two presidents: 'The international community is facing a dangerous and growing threat of proliferation of weapons of mass destruction and the means of delivery, including missiles and missile technologies, and stress their desire to reverse that process, including through existing and possible new international legal mechanisms. They agree that problems related to the menace must be considered and solved on the basis of mutual co-operation and account of each other's interests' (*IHT*, 5 June 2000, pp. 1, 4; *The Guardian*, 5 June 2000, p. 1).

On 5 June President Clinton addressed a joint session of the State Duma and the Council of the Federation, the first US president to do so.

Putin (5 June, on a visit to Italy): 'Russia proposes setting up, together with Europe and Nato, a common missile [defence] system.' (On 6 June Putin said that the Pope could visit Russia as soon as the Russian Orthodox Church and the Roman Catholic Church resolve their differences.)

13 June 2000. Vladimir Gusinsky (president of Media-Most) is arrested for alleged fraud (embezzlement of state funds). The formal charge was 'large-scale embezzlement'. The loss to the state comes to about $10 million and is related to the privatization at a low price of a St Petersburg television company (Channel 11).

In 1986 Vladimir Gusinsky (in partnership) opened a co-operative called Metall. In 1989 the Most joint venture was founded. In 1992 the Most Group was established. Most Bank became the Moscow city council's authorized bank. In 1993 Gusinsky became interested in the news media and the newspaper *Sevodnia* and the NTV television company were founded. Next came the magazines *Itogi* and *Sem Dnei*, and the radio station Ekho Moskvy also joined

Media-Most. The Most Bank office was raided in December 1994. In 1996 Gusinsky became president of the Russian Jewish Congress and played a very active role in the reelection of Boris Yeltsin as president. In 1999 Gusinsky stepped down as director general of Most Group and president of Most Bank and became president of Media-Most (*CDSP*, 2000, vol. 52, no. 24, p. 4).

There was widespread condemnation of the arrest across the political spectrum, claiming, for example, that the arrest was politically motivated and a threat to freedom of the press. 'Many interpreted the attack on Mr Gusinsky as Kremlin punishment for his defiance rather than the beginning of an effort to curb the tycoon's influence' (David Hoffman, *IHT*, 8 July 2000, p. 13).

The following day seventeen leading businessmen signed an open letter condemning the arrest: 'Until yesterday we used to think that we lived in a democratic country. Today we started to doubt it seriously .... Vladimir Gusinsky is regarded with mixed feelings in business circles. We acknowledge that law enforcement agencies may have questions about his activities ... Today that name [Vladimir Gusinky] is synonymous with a critical stance toward the regime and it symbolizes the independent news media in opposition ... Yesterday confirmed how fragile democracy is in Russia. A precedent was established for what appears to be the authorities taking reprisals against a political opponent. This precedent could be applied to opponents at the regional level or in government departments, and all of us can be listed as opponents – practically the whole business community ... We hope the authorities will find the courage to acknowledge that the danger to society posed by Vladimir Gusinky is not so great as to require him to be isolated from society by prison walls while he is under investigation. We are certain that Vladimir Gusinsky is prepared to co-operate with the investigators.' The seventeen included Vladimir Potanin (Interros), Anatoli Chubais (UES), Mikhail Friedman (Alfa Group), Pyotr Aven (Alfa Bank), Mikhail Khodorkovsky (Yukos), Rem Vyakhirev (Gazprom) and Vladimir Yevtushenkov (Systema). Among those who did not sign were Boris Berezovsky, Roman Abramovich and Vagit Alekperov.

'Seventeen signed ... The companies they represented include Sibneft, the oil group linked to Boris Berezovsky and Roman Abramovich [acknowledged leading shareholder and executive of the Sibneft oil group. He has recently played the leading role in the purchase and merger of different companies to create Russian Aluminium which controls 75 per cent of the country's output. Abramovich is also a deputy in the Duma]; Gazprom, the gas company which has helped fund Media-Most; Sistema, the holding company with connections to Yuri Luzhkov, the mayor of Moscow; and UES, the electricity utility. Both Alfa Group and Interros, which controls Norilsk Nickel, were also present' (*FT*, 1 July 2000, p. 8).

'Gazprom has come under close scrutiny recently, notably for the loans to and shares in Media-Most' (*FT*, 1 July 2000, p. 8). 'Recently Gazprom guaranteed a $211 million loan to Media-Most by a Western bank, and when the television company defaulted it stepped in and repaid the loan, reportedly receiving a large shareholding in Media-Most as collateral' (*FT*, 12 July 2000, p. 10). 'Gazprom presently has a 14.3 per cent stake in Media-Most but ... the media company's spokesman said that, if a settlement was reached on a share transfer, Gazprom's stake in Media-Most could be increased to over 25 per cent' (*FT*, 28 July 2000, p. 8). 'Gazprom ... has guaranteed loans to Media-Most totally about $380 million' (*IHT*, 12 July 2000, p. 4).

(Gusinsky was released from prison on 16 June.)

21 June 2000. 'A lawsuit launched in Moscow yesterday [21 June] centres on a vast Arctic mining complex ... The prosecutor's office formally announced it was suing the owners of Norilsk Nickel ... on the grounds that they robbed the state of hundreds of millions of dollars when taking control of the company three years ago ... An arbitration court has sent the lawsuit back to the prosecutor's office to be rewritten' (*The Times*, 22 June 2000, p. 16).

28 June 2000. 'Masked and armed police yesterday [28 June] raided a Siberian company controlled by two of Russia's influential business oligarchs ... TNK, an oil subsidiary of the Alfa group owned by Pyotr Aven and Mikhail Friedman ... The action was related to an investigation concerning the sale in 1997 to a subsidiary of Alfa of shares in TNK previously owned by the state ... Legal action was launched in Moscow last week against the Russian commodities group Norilsk Nickel ... A Moscow court [decided] to question the legality of the ... privatization of Norilsk Nickel, controlled by Vladimir Potanin' (*FT*, Thursday 29 June 2000, p. 10). 'The conduct of my company Interros is now being questioned by the Moscow prosecutor' (Vladimir Potanin, *FT*, 29 June 2000, p. 27).

'The Russian government yesterday [28 June] approved a pro-market economic reform programme running until the end of next year ... The sixty-point programme called for the modernization of the banking system, protection of minority shareholder rights, restructuring natural monopolies, controls on government spending and reforms to the tax system ... A second more detailed plan designed to cover policy reforms over the next decade would be adopted in the autumn following further discussions with academics, politicians and government officials' (*FT*, 29 June 2000, p. 10). 'A twenty-page document contains the outline of a government action programme for the next eighteen months, distilled from a far weightier tome with even more ambitious long-term goals, that was endorsed by the cabinet last week. There are calls for a shake-up of the tax and customs regime [including the introduction of a flat-rate income tax of 12 per cent, with a further 1 per cent unified social tax]; the breakup of the country's gas and electricity monopolies and the introduction of competition; the end of housing subsidies; and even a balanced budget from 2001 ... [The 400-page report] called for the creation of a "subsidiary state", in which an increasing proportion of medical and schooling facilities and pensions would be provided by private sector companies' (*FT*, Tuesday 4 July 2000, p. 9).

The governments adopts two economic programmes: 'Basic long-term tasks for social and economic policy' and 'Priority tasks of the government for 2000–2001'. They were written by the Centre for Strategic Studies opened in December 1999 under its head German Gref. The former programme will be subject to 'scholarly review' (*CDSP*, 2000, vol. 52, no. 26, pp. 4–7).

'A key element in Gref's strategy was the concept of a "new social contract". In Gref's view the state should finally withdraw from involvement in business altogether and stop directly and indirectly subsidizing inefficient enterprises. Such subsidizing slows the growth of unemployment and forces enterprises to shoulder the costs of municipal services for the public. In exchange the state should provide businesses and citizens with a stable set of ground rules, a coherent tax system, targeted social assistance, the decriminalization of the economy, and general law and order. For their part citizens should pay their taxes in full and not break the law' (*Kommersant*, 27 June 2000, p. 8; *CDSP*, 2000, vol. 52, no. 26, p. 7).

'The Russian government has made public its long-awaited plan … The programme was debated for months in government and in a research group led by the minister for trade and economy, German Gref, which drew up the plan … With the new economic blueprint … the Kremlin aims to slash the subsidies that have kept utility rates absurdly low. It will also wipe out the unpaid wages, tax breaks and other obligations that have sapped the government's already limited spending power. And it will devise an entirely new energy policy … Those are the major goals for this year. The rest of the plan proposes radical changes in everything from the nation's moribund banking system to its pension funds … The government's programme calls for raising energy prices, which still lag far behind the cost of production and for greater fiscal openness in the operations of … Gazprom. A private savings scheme for pensions could be instituted as early as next year, while action on bank reform … was put off until the fall … The proposed tax changes would reduce the burden on companies by 20 per cent this year' (*IHT*, 30 June 2000, p. 4).

'Russia has adopted the most liberal market-oriented economic programme attempted since the collapse of the Soviet Union in 1991 … For the next two years the plan calls for reducing the public sector share in the economy, with tight fiscal discipline; reforming state agencies to make it easier for businesses to start and function; modernizing the moribund banking system; and bringing more competition to the big natural gas, electricity and railway monopolies … Additional elements of the short-term plan include making budget spending more transparent and undertaking long-delayed structural reforms, such as overhauling the tax law and creating a new land code … The cabinet … adopted a ten-year economic strategy and a short-term plan for this year [2000] and next [2001]. The plans were the outgrowth of a research organization set up by Mr Putin before the March [2000] elections and headed by German Gref, now minister for economics and trade … Unlike many [economic plans] in the past, it was not written to satisfy criteria of the IMF. The fund has suspended lending to Russia and, with ample oil revenues, Moscow does not seem anxious to revive it' (David Hoffman, *IHT*, 8 July 2000, p. 13).

'The new programme ... consists of a list of priority measures to be implemented in the first eighteen months. The plan, which has been approved by the government, is based on free-market principles and calls for equal opportunities for all economic actors, guaranteed property rights and the elimination of bureaucratic constraints hindering business activity. Special features of the new programme include ... Import liberalization ... Import duties will be cut to a minimum ... Budgetary and tax reform. Tax revenues are to be centralized ... including 100 per cent of VAT ... Dividing tax revenues between the federal government and the provinces on a 50–50 basis will no longer be acceptable. Currently twelve rich provinces provide 66 per cent of all tax revenues collected in the Russian Federation's eighty-nine regions ... Social reform ... Direct and indirect state subsidies, including those on utility rates paid by companies, will be eliminated ... Deregulation. The procedure for registering companies will be simplified. A single agency will be responsible for registration and the list of activities subject to licensing will be cut significantly ... The breakup of electricity, natural gas and railway monopolies. The transport and distribution divisions of Gazprom ... will become financially independent. Electricity producers will be encouraged to join a wholesale electricity market. Non-paying customers will be cut off. Foreign companies will be able to compete in the railways, and passenger rail fares will be increased ... The government also plans to create markets for land and buildings' (*Transition*, 2000, vol. 11, nos 3–4, pp. 25–6).

'The programme consists of several parts, including priority measures for 2000–2001 and a section outlining longer-term economic reforms. According to trade and economic development minister German Gref, the priority measures aim at breaking up Gazprom, promoting independent electricity producers, solving the non-payments problems by mandatory electricity disconnections, increasing competition in rail transport, eliminating the threat of renationalization and enhancing property rights, improving bankruptcy procedures, eliminating tax privileges, reducing government interference in business, and introducing international accounting standards. The programme also calls for a gradual reduction in import tariffs, which would promote Russia's progress towards membership of the WTO' (*RET*, 2000, vol. 9, no. 2, p. 100).

2 July 2000. Konstantin Titov one again becomes governor of Samara province by winning a by-election.

8 July 2000. Putin (his first state of the nation speech): 'It must be admitted that the state itself has to a very large degree assisted in the dictatorship of the shadow economy and of "gray area" arrangements, for rampant corruption and for the huge outflow of capital abroad. It is responsible because it failed to make the rules clear and it imposed unwarranted restrictions ... The vacuum of power has led to private corporations and clans usurping state power ... The president of Russia must have the right to establish order and be able to interfere should regional leaders break federal laws ... For several years now the country's population has been decreasing by an average of 750,000 annually ... If this trend continues Russia's survival as a nation, as a people, will be in jeopardy ... Russia's economic weaknesses continues to be another serious problem. The widening gap between the advanced countries and Russia is pushing us into the ranks of third-world countries. The figures showing current economic growth should not put our minds at ease ... The current growth has very little to do with the revamping of the economic mechanism. It is largely the result of favourable foreign economic conditions ... Without truly free news media Russian democracy will simply not survive and we will not succeed in building a civil society ... [But] journalistic freedom has turned into a tempting little morsel for politicians and major financial groups and become a convenient tool in interclan warfare ... sometimes even to turn them into sources of mass disinformation and an instrument for fighting the state ... Only a strong ... an effective and democratic state can protect civil, political and economic freedoms ... The key role the government should play in the economy is, without a doubt, the protection of economic freedom. Our stategic policy is as follows: less administrative bureaucracy and more entrepreneurial freedom – freedom to produce, trade and invest ... The government's task is to co-ordinate the operations of state institutions that ensure the functioning of the market. We won't achieve stable development without genuinely independent courts and an effective system of law-enforcement agencies ... It won't be possible in the immediate future for the state to cease its involvement in the development of some sectors of our economy ... such as the defence-industry complex. The state will continue to keep strategically important branches of the economy under its constant attention ... Protection of ownership rights must be ensured ... A second area is ensuring equal conditions for competition ... A third area is freeing entrepreneurs from administrative oppression ... A fourth area is reducing the tax burden ... The customs system must be radically simplified and the duties on goods must be made uniform ... The fifth area is the development of the financial infrastructure ... The sixth area is a realistic social-welfare policy ... We are insisting on one kind of dictatorship – dictatorship of the law' (*CDSP*, 2000, vol. 52, no. 28, p. 6).

11 July 2000. 'Russian prosecutors searched the offices of Media-Most ... for the second time in two months ... The prosecutors also sought documents from Gazprom' (*IHT*, 12 July 2000, p. 4).

'Yesterday [11 July] Russian authorities ... accused the chairman of Lukoil, the country's largest oil company, of tax evasion. Tax administration officials said they ... were pursuing a criminal case against Vagit Alekperov, chairman, and the company's chief accountant ... The tax administration said funds were hidden from the authorities by Lukoil's management by receiving illegal refunds of value-added tax from fake exports of oil products which were never exported. Lukoil denied the charges, saying it had received an "honest tax payer of the year award" form the tax ministry last year [1999] ... Prosecutors yesterday also targeted Vladimir Potanin, chairman of Interros, the financial holding company that controls ... Norilsk Metal. They said Mr Potanin must pay $140 million to make up the amount they said he underpaid for a 38 per cent stake in the enterprise ... The case against Media-Most involves charges ranging from invasion of privacy by security guards to financial skullduggery. Authorities are especially interested in the links between the television company and Gazprom' (*FT*, 12 July 2000, p. 10).

'Officers of the Federal Security Service were again at the Media-Most holding company on Tuesday [11 July] and – for the first time – at the studios of ... [Gusinsky's television channel] NTV, seeking documents to build an embezzlement case against him. The police are also after Vagit Alekperov, the head of Lukoil ... for tax fraud, although in May [2000] he had been awarded a state prize as a model taxpayer. Vladimir Potanin has been ordered to pay the government $140 million or face charges of rigging a privatization auction for Norilsk Nickel' (*The Independent*, 13 July 2000, p. 17).

'Experts estimate that ... Vladimir Kadannikov [Avtovaz] "owes" the state something of the order of $840 million' (*CDSP*, 2000, vol. 52, no. 28, p. 3).

'Government agencies ... have demanded in a letter that the tycoon who owns 38 per cent of Norilsk Nickel ... pay the $140 million difference between the true value and the price paid when the company was privatized ... A similar complaint was filed in June [2000] against Tyumen Oil' (*IHT*, 17 June 2000, p. 4).

'The prosecutor general's office recommended to Potanin that he voluntarily pays "compensation for damages in the amount of $140 million", promising that if he complies, no further action will be taken against him' (*CDSP*, 2000, vol. 52, no. 28, p. 1).

12 July 2000. President Putin (in an address on television): 'We should not confuse democracy and anarchy. There are, of course, people who feel comfortable in conditions of disorder. You know we have a saying about catching fish in muddy [troubled] waters. Here there are fishermen who have already caught a lot and would like to preserve this state of affairs for the long term ... I do not think this is acceptable for the Russian people or for our partners abroad.'

'Russian authorities yesterday [12 July] launched their third big criminal tax investigation in a month, fresh evidence that President Vladimir Putin is mounting a serious attack against the country's most powerful businessmen, or oligarchs. The probe into an alleged $600 million tax fraud at Avtovaz, Russia's largest car maker, follows investigations into the tax affairs of Media-Most and of Vagit Alekperov, chairman of Lukoil, the country's biggest oil company ... The probe at Avtovaz is significant because the company has in the past been linked with Boris Berezovsky ... In a newspaper interview published on 8 July, the day after the case against Avtovaz was secretly launched, Berezovsky criticized the Kremlin for being "authoritarian" and announced plans to create a political party that would include business leaders and Russia's governors, who are also the targets of recent Kremlin attempts to roll back privatization. Yesterday Mr Berezovsky said he had ended his links with Avtovaz and denied claims by industry analysts that he retained control ... Mr Berezovsky's ties with Avtovaz started in the mid-1990s when he began marketing its cars ... The tax police said Avtovaz evaded roughly $600 million in taxes by producing cars with the same vehicle identification number. Avtovaz officials denied this and said the charge would imply they were making 40 per cent more cars than their books say' (*FT*, 13 July 2000, p. 10).

'Boris Berezovsky ... was once involved in a car-marketing company with shares in Avtovaz [which produces Ladas], but he says he no longer has any interest in the auto industry' (*The Independent*, 13 July 2000, p. 17).

'Officials allege that Avtovaz, which makes passenger cars in a factory made by Fiat, concealed the sale of more than 200,000 vehicles by duplicating identification numbers. The operation involved a value of about $600 million, officials said ... Avtovaz has been under investigation for tax evasion off and on for at least two years ... Avtovaz manufactures about 700,000 cars a year ... Boris Berezovsky ... made a fortune with the company in the early 1990s, but company officials said he no longer had any connections' (*IHT*, 14 July 2000, p. 4).

'Experts estimate that Vladimir Kadannikov [Avtovaz] "owes" the state something of the order of $840 million' (*CDSP*, 2000, vol. 52, no. 28, p. 3).

'Avtovaz's [Volga Automotive Plant's] main dealer is the Logovaz firm, which is closely associated with Boris Berezovsky' (*CDSP*, 2000, vol. 52, no. 28, p. 2).

'Vagit Alekperov, head of Lukoil, has links with several television stations and a joint stake, with Vladimir Potanin, in the daily newspaper *Izvestia*' (*The Guardian*, 14 July 2000, p. 20).

'Lukoil has extensive interests in newspapers and local television ... Vladimir Potanin is an investor in the national daily *Izvestia* ... Boris Berezovsky took control last year [1999] of Russia's most respected and powerful business newpaper, *Kommersant*' (*IHT*, 17 July 2000, p. 4).

'Mr Berezovsky controls several newspapers and has a 49 per cent stake in the state ORT television channel' (*FT*, 18 July 2000, p. 10). 'Apart from the *Kommersant* newspaper Mr Berezovsky also controls *Nezavisimaya Gazeta* and *Noviya Izvestia*' (*FT*, 24 August 2000, p. 5). 'Boris Berezovsky ... [owns] the daily *Nezavisimaya Gazeta* ... another network, as well as a 49 per cent stake in ORT, Russia's premier network and the only one to broadcast nationwide. The state own a controlling interest' (*IHT*, 19 July 2000, p. 4). 'The state owns 51 per cent of it [ORT: Public Russian Television], but Mr Berezovsky's allies outnumber the government's representatives on the board' (*IHT*, 5 September 2000, p. 4).

'Mr Gusinsky controls the daily newspaper *Sevodnia* and the news magazine *Itogi* as well as NTV' (*FT*, 24 August 2000, p. 5).

Komsomolskaya Pravda is controlled by Valdimir Potanin's Interros group (*FT*, 24 August 2000, p. 5).

'To some experts the challenges are distinguished by two traits: many involve owners of powerful media companies, and none touch those tycoons who are said to be closest to the Kremlin and the people who made Mr Putin president: the friends and relatives of Mr Yeltsin' (Michael Wines, *IHT*, 17 July 2000, p. 4).

The Zvezda (Star) service module is launched. It is Russia's main contribution to the International Space Station. The module has been at the Baikanur Cosmodrome in Kazakhstan for more than a year awaiting the launch. 'The $320 million space module was entirely financed by Russia, and it was repeatedly delayed because of money problems and two successive crashes of Proton boosters' (*IHT*, 12 July 2000, p. 4). '[The module is] a crucial piece of the International Space Station, speeding the construction of the $60 billion project after more than two years of delay ... [The module] has the living quarters and flight controls to enable crews to live and work on the station for months. While Russia will still build and deliver parts of the sixteen-nation project, delays can no longer set back work the way the Zvezda delay did ... Zvezda is scheduled to dock on 26 July by computer with two other space station components, Zarya and Unity, launched in 1998' (*IHT*, 13 July 2000, p. 8).

14 July 2000. The Audit Chamber, a parliamentary watchdog, announces it will investigate whether UES (Unified Energy System), the electricity monopoly headed by Anatoli Chubais, illegally sold more than 15 per cent of its shares to foreigners in 1992. The Audit Chamber is headed by Sergei Stepashin. (*The Times*, 15 July 2000, p. 16; *The Guardian*, 15 July 2000, p. 16; *FT*, 15 July 2000, p. 12; *IHT*, 17 July 2000, p. 4.)

16 July 2000. 'Russia's most prominent tycoon, Boris Berezovsky, has called upon the Kremlin to declare an amnesty that would embrace the super-rich. He said the wealthy were being persecuted for violating a set of laws which no one could possible follow, and added that the government ... should grant a general amnesty ... for all citizens ... In an interview with the *Financial Times* ... Mr Berezovsky ... said that ... only those who "have been asleep for the past ten years" are not at risk of going to jail. "If you want to bring charges against Mr Putin, when he was vice-mayor of St Petersburg, I am confident that this is possible"' (*FT*, 17 July 2000, p. 1).

17 July 2000. Boris Berezovsky announces his intention to give up his seat in the State Duma: 'I do not want to participate in Russia's collapse and the establishment of an authoritarian regime ... The Duma has turned into a legal department of the Kremlin that obediently rubber-stamps its decisions ...

Everybody accepted it [the proposal for regional reform] with hurrah, obediently… This campaign [against the oligarchs] is well orchestrated and is aimed at destroying major independent businesses in Russia … I intend to play on equal terms with other oligarchs in this campaign launched by the state against Russian business.'

'Mr Berezovsky said he was questioned by an investigator on Friday [14 July] in connection with the probe into Aeroflot, the national airline' (*FT*, 18 July 2000, p. 10).

He formally resigned his seat on 19 July.

19 July 2000. 'The prosecutor general's office seized the property of Vladimir Gusinsky yesterday [19 July]. The only property involved so far is Gusinsky's private home outside Moscow … all the property the house contains and the … lot on which it stands … But the prosecutor general's office has already said everything the man owns will be seized: from his real estate in foreign countries to his personal shares in media enterprises … The seizure will be in effect until the final verdict is handed down, at which point it will be learned whether the property is to be ultimately confiscated … Investigators plan to inventory all the property Gusinsky owns, including his possessions abroad. But the prosecutor general's office is particularly interested in Gusinsky's shares in over twenty media companies, including NTV [television], Ekho Moskvy [radio], [the newspaper] *Sevodnia* and [the weekly news magazine] *Itogi*' (*CDSP*, 2000, vol. 52, no. 29, p. 9).

23 July 2000. 'Alpha Group [is] a banking and industrial conglomerate … Mikhail Friedman, head of the group, said police last month [June] seized control of Alpha Group's 13 per cent stake in the Slavneft oil company in connection with a three-year old criminal investigation' (*FT*, 24 July 2000, p. 8).

27 July 2000. It is announced that the case against Vladimir Gusinsky is to be dropped, owing, prosecutors say, to 'lack of the fact of a crime'.

28 July 2000. Putin meets twenty-one leading businessmen. Boris Nemtsov conceived the idea. Among those not invited to attend were Boris Berezovsky, Roman Abramovich and Vladimir Gusinsky. Anatoli Chubais was in Finland on business.

Putin: 'I only want to draw your attention straight away to the fact that you have yourselves formed this very state through the political or quasi-political structures under your control. So perhaps what one should do least of all is blame the mirror … We have to discuss what is to be done so that relations [between business and government] can be democratic, absolutely civilized and transparent.'

A statement was released by the participants after the meeting: '[It] was the common opinion that privatization, with all its difficulties and drawbacks, was a natural and necessary step on the path toward building an efficient and competitive economy. It was stated in this connection that the authorities will not be conducting political campaigns to redistribute property and revise the results of privatization' (*IHT*, 29 July 2000, p. 5).

'The oligarchs issued a statement indicating that "companies and banks which uphold the state's interests while conducting their affairs will enjoy guaranteed support and wide-ranging help from the president"' (*IHT*, 5 August 2000, p. 6).

'The tycoons and Mr Putin agreed that all businessmen should be equally distanced from the Kremlin. The recent legal attacks have conspicuously bypassed the business interests of Roman Abramovich, who is considered to be the Kremlin's favourite. However, according to Boris Nemtsov ... the politician who initiated the meeting ... Mr Putin indicated that he really does mean to distance all oligarchs from the Kremlin when he asked why Sibneft, an oil company associated with Mr Abromovich and Boris Berezovsky, made such low profits and paid so little tax ... The Kremlin said in a statement Mr Putin and the business leaders had agreed to hold regular meetings' (*FT*, 29 July 2000, p. 7).

'*Kommersant* was told by a participant in the meeting that the president said everything they had expected him to. That it is necessary to strengthen the right of private ownership. That law enforcement agencies do not and will not have orders to harass businessmen, and that they are supposed to fight crime, not business. And, finally, that there has not been, nor will be, any revision of the outcomes of privatization ... [Putin] "Are you prepared, right now, to renounce the idea of installing your own people in government agencies?" ... Virtually the only guest he criticized personally was Sibneft president Yevgeni Shvidler. "Why is Sibneft paying so little in taxes?"' (*Kommersant*, 29 July 2000, p. 1; *CDSP*, 2000, vol. 52, no. 31, p. 8).

3 August 2000. 'The prosecutor general of Russia on Thursday [3 August] unexpectedly halted a criminal investigation into illegal business practices by senior executives at Russia's largest automaker, Avtovaz ... Avtovaz ... is run by a former first deputy prime minister, Vladimir Kadannikov, while its cars are distributed through the Logovaz network set up by Boris Berezovsky ... Tax officials on 7 July began an investigation ... Tax officials alleged that Avtovaz had hidden the sales of about 200,000 cars by assigning them all the same identification number. But the prosecutor's office told Interfax that an inquiry had shown that the tax police did not have sufficient evidence to begin a criminal inquiry' (*IHT*, 4 August 2000, p. 5).

10 August 2000. Tax police raid the headquarters of the oil company Sibneft and take away some documents. 'The action seemed to be a direct blow against Roman Abramovich, who has a controlling interest in Sibneft and has been named frequently by the Russian press as both a close confidant of the family circle of former president Boris Yeltsin and of those around Mr Putin. At a Kremlin meeting last month [July] other oligarchs raised the topic of favouritism in the tax authority's dealings, pointing out that while most had been raided, the business interests of Mr Abramvich had been untouched ... Lukoil claimed that the investigation against it had been triggered by rivals bidding for a controlling stake in the oil company Onaco. These rivals included Sibneft, which on Wednesday [9 August] formally announced a joint bid with other oil groups … There were already hints that Sibneft was coming to the close attention of Mr Putin when the ministry of finance accused the company of paying lower taxes than all of its competitors at the end of last month. A few days later Mr Putin singled out the company during a meeting with twenty-one oligarchs, stressing he wanted to distance himself from preferential treatment' (*FT*, 11 August 2000, p. 6).

11 August 2000. 'President Vladimir Putin has decided to unilaterally reduce Russia's nuclear arsenal and shift scarce financial resources to rebuild conventional forces, according to reports in the Russian news media … Mr Putin decided to let the number of Russia's nuclear warheads shrink to 1,500 … The status of the elite strategic rocket forces as a separate branch will be "reconsidered" and parts will fall under air force command within two years … He authorized an $80 million increase in this year's $4.5 billion defence budget' (*IHT*, 14 August 2000, p. 6).

12 August 2000. A Russian nuclear-powered submarine (the *Kursk*, launched as recently as 1994) sinks in the Barents Sea during a naval exercise. Only on 21 August (after Norwegian and British deep-sea divers had quickly opened the escape hatch, which the Russian rescue services, which had no such divers at hand, failed to do) was it announced that all 118 members of the crew had died. The two nuclear reactors automatically shut themselves down, but they will need to be dealt with as quickly as possible to prevent radioactive leaks.

'While it is true that all four Russian fleets are supposed to have their own teams of deep-sea divers, it turns out that they do not have personnel and their training programmes have been discontinued – for want of government funding, it is claimed' (*Nezavisimaya Gazeta*, 18 August 2000, pp. 1–2; *CDSP*, 2000, vol. 52, no. 33, p. 6).

The naval exercise was meant to be a forerunner of a high-profile show of force elsewhere. 'The Northern Fleets current exercises, during which the *Kursk* accident occurred … were supposed to be a dress rehearsal for a voyage by a group of navy attack aircraft carriers to the Atlantic Ocean and Mediterranean Sea planned for this fall' (*Vremya Novostei*, 18 August 2000, p. 1: *CDSP*, 2000, vol. 52, no. 33, p. 6). ('The commander of the Russian navy said Tuesday [10 October] that he has postponed indefinitely a major fleet exercise that would have sent an aircraft carrier task force to the Mediterranean Sea for the first time in years … The *Kursk* had been designated to take part in the Mediterranean display of Russian naval power. Since the disaster all submarines of its class have been ordered to stay in port until the safety of their weapons and operating systems could be assured': *IHT*, 11 October 2000, p. 7.)

Delayed, incomplete and misleading information and conflicting and confusing explanations about the timing and cause of the incident led to considerable criticism within Russia. For example, news of the sinking was announced only on 14 August and initially it was said that it took place on

13 August. Suggested causes included a collision, on-board explosions (seemingly two) and the former followed by the latter . At first Russia did not seek assistance from other countries, but on 16 August Britain and Norway were asked to help in the rescue operation. The USA's offer of technical assistance was taken up on 18 August. The delays in asking for Western assistance added to the criticism within Russia, especially as the Russian rescue attempts failed. ('President Vladimir Putin ... said last night [25 August] that the first offer of foreign help came on the 15 August, three days after the sinking': *The Independent*, 26 August 2000, p. 13. 'By yesterday evening [15 August] all the world's leading naval powers – the United States, Great Britain and France – had offered to help Moscow in its efforts to rescue the crew': *CDSP*, 2000, vol. 52, no. 33, p. 2; 'President Putin ... said [on 22 August] that foreign rescue personnel officially offered their assistance on 15 August. It was immediately accepted': *CDSP*, 2000, vol. 52, no. 34, p. 11.)

The reputation of President Putin was tarnished (although his overall domestic poll ratings did not suffer very much). 'Five days after the sinking of the nuclear submarine *Kursk*, Vladimir Putin deemed it possible to offer some comment [on 16 August] on the events taking place in the Barents Sea ... [He met] with a group of Russian journalists in Sochi, where he is currently vacationing' (*Vremya Novostei*, 17 August 2000, p. 1; *CDSP*, 2000, vol. 52, no. 33, p. 4). Putin stayed on holiday in the Black Sea resort of Sochi until 18 August.

Putin faced a fraught meeting with some of the relatives and others on 22 August. Putin attacked, without actually naming them, those oligarchs who he said were using their control of the media, for ulterior motives, to criticize the official handling of the crisis. The 23 August was designated as a day of national mourning.

Putin (23 August 2000): 'Even though I have occupied my office in the Kremlin for only just over 100 days, I have a great feeling of responsibility and guilt for this tragedy ... If someone is guilty they must without any doubt be punished. But we must receive an objective picture of the tragedy and the rescue operation ... We have to get an objective picture of the reason for this tragedy. Only after that can we make some decisions ... [We must wait until] a full understanding has been gained about what happened and why ... Our country has survived worse than this.'

Putin refused to accept the resignations of defence minister Igor Sergeyev, admiral-of-the-fleet Vladimir Kuroyedov and commander of the northern fleet Vyacheslav Popov.

Putin later announced the following:

1. Compensation for the families of the dead submariners.

2. Pay increases for the armed forces, police, prison guards, customs officials, the tax police and nuclear workers.

3. The creation of new naval rescue centres, one each for the Northern, the Baltic, the Black Sea and the Pacific Fleets.

'Submarines were the capital ships of the Soviet navy, but even during the best of times a syndrome of poor training, maintenance, construction and design made Soviet submarines hazardous. Fires, explosions and reactor accidents were common. Nine submarines have sunk since 1957, killing almost 300 sailors. In 1985 a reactor exploded during a refuelling, killing ten and releasing several million curies of radiation ... The Russian navy inherited all these problems and found some new ones ... In 1990 the Soviet navy had some 190 nuclear-powered submarines. Today the Russian fleet may have about fifty ... The retirement of Russia's nuclear submarines has compounded a large naval radioactive waste problem left over from Soviet days' (Joshua Handler, *IHT*, 28 August 2000, p. 1).

In 1989 the Komsomolets nuclear submarine went down in the Norwegian Sea, killing forty-two sailors (*The Times*, 29 August 2000, p. 13; *IHT*, 7 September 2000, p. 9).

14 August 2000. The Russian Orthodox Church makes saints of Tsar Nicholas II, his wife Alexandra and his five children (Alexei, Olga, Tatiana, Maria and Anastasia). They are canonized as 'passion bearers' (the lowest level of sainthood) for 'the meekness, patience and humility with which the Imperial Family endured their sufferings in captivity, and in their martyrs' death in Yekaterinburg'. (They were killed by the Bolsheviks on 17 July 1918.)

'Tsar Nicholas ... was canonized in 1981 by the Orthodox Church in exile, a decision condemned at the time by the church authorities in Moscow' (*FT*, 15 August 2000, p. 6).

(The ceremony was held on 20 August 2000 in the Cathedral of Christ the Saviour in Moscow.)

27–8 August 2000. The Ostankino television tower in Moscow is badly damaged by fire. Four people died. (The tower was built in 1967 to celebrate the fiftieth anniversary of the Bolshevik Revolution. It was then the tallest structure in the world and is still the second tallest.)

President Putin: 'This latest disaster shows what sort of condition our vital facilities and the country as a whole are in.'

3–5 September 2000. Putin visits Japan. No progress is made on the Kuril Islands issue.

'Back in 1956 the Soviets undertook to return two islands in return for a peace treaty, a commitment that Mr Putin has now reaffirmed. Japan wants sovereignty over all four islands, although it would allow Russian administration for the time being. And Japan will not accept a peace treaty that does not also deal with the islands' (*IHT*, 6 September 2000, p. 10). 'Russia is ready to discuss a Soviet-era offer to return two of the disputed Kuril Islands to Japan once the two sides sign a peace treaty formally ending World War II. Moscow is seeking talks with Tokyo about their interpretation of a 1956 agreement that restored diplomatic relations but fell short of a full-blown peace treaty' (*IHT*, 12 September 2000, p. 4).

4 September 2000. Boris Berezovsky (in an open letter to President Putin): 'Last week a high-ranking official on your staff issued me an ultimatum: to place under state management the block of shares in ORT [Russian Public Television] that I control, or to follow in the footsteps of Gusinsky – to all appearances Butyrka prison was meant … If I accept the ultimatum Russian will cease to have television news and in its place will have television propaganda controlled by your advisers … Building on the idea of creating a civil society I have decided to place the block of ORT shares that I control under the management of journalists and other members of the creative intelligentsia. I feel certain that a similar step by the state, an initiative that you could take, would enable our country's number one television channel to completely respond to its name – "Russian Public Television"' (*CDSP*, 2000, p. 52, no. 36, pp. 1–3). (On 7 September Berezovsky revealed that the official was the president's chief of staff, Alexander Voloshin: p. 5.)

'Mr Berezovsky … controls 49 per cent of the network … ORT is the most watched television channel … The state owns 51 per cent of it' (*IHT*, 5 September 2000, p. 4).

'Boris Berezovsky named "creative intellectuals" Thursday [7 September] to whom he would give control over his … 49 per cent share in ORT … He proposed turning them over in trust for four years to a committee of what he called creative intellectuals. Most of those on Mr Berezovsky's list worked at ORT or at newspapers he controls, although the list also included an employee of the US-funded Radio Liberty and a novelist' (*IHT*, 8 September 2000, p. 8). (Details are to be found in *CDSP*, 2000, vol. 52, no. 36, p. 4.)

6 September 2000. At the United Nations Millennium Summit President Putin proposes a UN conference in Moscow in 2001 on the prevention of military activities in space and calls for a ban on the production of weapons grade plutonium and uranium.

9 September 2000. There are accounts in the Western press of the *Moscow Times*'s claim that Putin would not have won outright in the first round of the presidential election held on 26 March 2000 without large-scale electoral fraud. For example, nearly 1.3 million new voters appeared between elections for the State Duma on 19 December 2000 and the presidential election. In Chechenia the electoral commission claimed that nearly 500,000 voters displaced by the war in Chechenia failed to vote in December but did vote for Putin in March 2000. (*The Independent*, 11 September 2000, p. 10; *The Times*, 11 September 2000, p. 13.)

12 September 2000. 'President Valdimir Putin yesterday [12 September] signed into force a national doctrine setting out the guiding principles on information security … the work of the increasingly influential "security council" … Observers said that although the wording of the doctrine was extremely vague, and it was unclear how it would be implemented, the doctrine could allow the Kremlin to control distribution of information and be used as a legal cover for political attacks on the Russian press. The doctrine follows an earlier decree that authorized the security services to tap telephone lines and personal computers without special court sanctions. The draft budget for next year also contains funds for a "top secret state media programme"' (*FT*, 13 September 2000, p. 10).

'Russia has published a new doctrine on "information security", approved by President Vladimir Putin, that analysts have described as another sign of the Kremlin's determination to reassert dominance over the news media ... Moreover, according to the Russian media, the federal security service ... has taken measures to allow them to monitor all email and internet activity' (*IHT*, 15 September 2000, p. 2).

'Individual provisions of it [the information security doctrine] can easily be used to substantiate claims that it either defends freedom of speech or seriously restricts it. For example, the Kremlin's desire to take over Boris Berezovsky's share in ORT [Russian Public Television] can be interpreted as unlawful "encroachment by government agencies on citizens' rights and freedoms in the realm of information" or, conversely, as completely legitimate opposition to "the spreading of disinformation about the Russian Federation's policies and the actions of government agencies". And the hushing up of the *Kursk* accident looks, at one and the same time, like both a threat to information security ("irrational, excessive restriction of access to information that the public needs to know") and a measure taken to ensure it ("the use of counter-propaganda to prevent adverse consequences from the spreading of disinformation about Russia's domestic policies"' (*Kommersant*, 13 September 2000, p. 1; *CDSP*, 2000, vol. 52, no. 37, pp. 6–7).

13 September 2000. The supreme court upholds Alexander Nikitin's acquittal despite attempts by the federal security service and the prosecutor general's office to have the case reopened.

18 September 2000. Putin dedicates a Jewish community centre and condemns antisemitism (*IHT*, 19 September 2000, p. 8).

19 September 2000. 'The Russian prosecutors office said Tuesday [19 September] it had begun investigating a claim that the country's biggest independent media group was trying to back out of a takeover agreement with the Gazprom natural gas monopoly. The investigation ... comes at Gazprom's request ... Gazprom is demanding that ... Vladimir Gusinsky ... honour a July agreement to yield control of his company [Media-Most] to settle debts to Gazprom. Mr Gusinsky says the agreement was forced on him at "gunpoint, so to say" and under pressure from the Kremlin. He has vowed not to sell out ... One of the provisions of the 20 July agreement, disclosed for the first time in documents made public Monday [18 September], suggest that the Kremlin was prepared to make a deal with Mr Gusinsky under which he would not be subject to prosecution as long as he remained silent and did not criticize the government ... In late July charges were dropped and Mr Gusinsky was permitted to leave the country. He has not returned to Russia [from Spain] ... Gazprom, which is 38 per cent owned by the state ... has made a $211 million loan secured by 20 per cent of Media-Most shares, and another loan, for $262 million, due next summer, is backed by another 20 per cent of the company… Media-Most … includes radio, print and a pay television system, as well as NTV. Mr Gusinsky's news magazine, *Itogi*, is a partner of *Newsweek* … On 20 July Mr Gusinsky signed a deal to settle all debts with Gazprom for $773 million, which comprised forgiveness of the outstanding $473 million in loans, plus an additional $300 in cash from Gazprom. But just two days earlier Mr Gusinsky made a sworn statement saying that he was being forced to make a deal by the press minister, Mikhail Lesin, a point man for the Kremlin' (*IHT*, 20 September 2000, p. 13).

'A secret appendix to the 20 July agreement to sell out to Gazprom … signed by Mikhail Lesin, the media minister … stipulated that the criminal investigation of Mr Gusinsky was being dropped and a travel ban lifted. It added that Mr Gusinsky and "leaders of the organization" – meaning the chief editors … were being granted "security guarantees, the protection of their rights and liberties, including the guaranteed right to move freely, to choose their place of residence, and to travel freely beyond the borders of the Russian Federation and to return to the Russian Federation without hindrance" … The document was signed by Mr Lesin and Alfred Kokh, the head of Gazprom's modest media holdings' (*The Guardian*, 20 September 2000, p. 17).

'Russia's press minister yesterday [20 September] admitted that he had endorsed a document this summer offering to drop criminal charges against Vladimir Gusinsky if he sold his Media-Most empire to … Gazprom … Mikhail Lesin said he had approved a contract between Mr Gusinsky and Alfred Kokh, the head of Gazprom's media arm, and acknowledged that he had made a "serious mistake" in so doing … Mr Lesin tried to assume personal responsibility by saying that he had taken the initiative on his own and had only informed [prime minister Mikhail] Kasyanov afterwards. Mr Lesin claimed that the freedom-for-asset pledge in the contract was an initiative of Mr Gusinsky… A senior executive of Media-Most said last night … that it was Mr Lesin who had proposed the contract' (*FT*, 21 September 2000, p. 11).

'The president, like prime minister Kasyanov, considers Mr Lesin's actions "unacceptable"' (*CDSP*, 2000, vol. 52, no. 39, p. 5). (For Gusinsky's statement of 18 July and other details, see *CDSP*, 2000, vol. 52, no. 38, pp. 1–6.)

28 September 2000. 'Russian prosecutors began a criminal embezzlement investigation Thursday [28 September] against the heads of companies belonging to Media-Most… The prosecutors were acting on accusations that Media-Most had hidden assets abroad to avoid having them seized by Gazprom' (*IHT*, 29 September 2000, p. 4). 'The deputy prosecutor said yesterday [28 September] that the fraud charges were made because Media-Most shares used as security for the [Gazprom] loan had been moved to offshore funds … Mikhail Kasyanov, the prime minister, said yesterday that Mr Lesin [the press minister] has "acted improperly in signing a document on relations between the two for-profit companies"' (*The Independent*, 29 September 2000, p. 14). 'The prosecutor general's office has instituted criminal proceedings in response to an appeal by Gazprom-Media. The company complained that this April nearly all of Media-Most's assets were transferred out of the holding company, leaving it no longer in possession of controlling stakes in its constituent companies. Meanwhile, Gazprom still holds 40 per cent of Media-Most as collateral for two loans to the company, one of $211 million, the other of $275 million. Gazprom executives contend that the withdrawal of assets has devalued its collateral and damaged its interests' (*CDSP*, 2000, vol. 52, no. 39, p. 5).

'Media-Most ... yesterday [18 October] said it had reached an outline agreement with Gazprom ... in a deal that would preserve its independence from the state. The vaguely worded statement ... also hinted that the heavily indebted Media-Most was in talks with a significant international investor' (*FT*, 19 October 2000, p. 11).

'Vladimir Gusinsky ... and Gazprom have agreed that Mr Gusinsky can pay off his debt to the monopoly in a way that will allow his media group to remain independent, according to officials on both sides. The deal means that Mr Gusinsky will be allowed to use company stock to settle his $211.6 million debt, plus interest of $36.9 million, as the two parties had originally envisioned' (*IHT*, 20 October 2000, p. 8).

3 October 2000. President Putin, while on a visit to India, signs an agreement entitled a Declaration of Strategic Partnership.

6 October 2000. Andrei Babitsky is convicted of using false documents. A small fine is imposed but even that will not be paid because it is covered by the May 2000 amnesty.

20 October 2000. The effort to recover bodies from the *Kursk* begins. 'The recovery effort is being run by the Norwegian arm of the US oil services company Halliburton, but the divers cutting their way into the hull are Russian ... [Divers] pierced the inner hull of the nuclear vessel for the first time yesterday [22 October]' (*The Guardian*, 23 October 2000, p. 14).

The first bodies were recovered on 25 October. A letter found on one of the bodies indicates that at least twenty-three of the crew survived the explosions for some time. The search ended on 7 November after twelve bodies were recovered. On 8 November it was announced that a second note had been found on another of the twelve bodies recovered.

'A senior Russian government official ... Ilya Klebanov, said [on 8 November] that video footage had reinforced the theory of a collision with another vessel, which Russian officials have repeatedly advanced as the reason for the disaster. They claim that the *Kursk* was struck by a foreign submarine or a World War II mine. Western and some Russian experts have expressed scepticism about this explanation, however, and said that the *Kursk* was sunk by an internal explosion that originated in the torpedo room. Mr Klebanov said that "we have managed to discover a very serious dent on the sub" in the forward two sections ...

Mr Klebanov said that the "inward depression" on the *Kursk* "could have been caused by a blow and nothing else. And also very serious streaks which suggest that something was moving alongside the sub, something was sliding along it after the blow, grazing off the rubber of the light [outer] hull" ... Mr Klebanov spoke after a special commission appointed by President Vladimir Putin to investigate the disaster met in Moscow. Mr Klebanov said it was possible that a conclusive answer to what sank the nuclear attack vessel would be forthcoming only after it is raised next summer, as planned. He said the commission had not yet reached a conclusion, but ruled out a crew mistake or testing of a "new torpedo". Some specialists have speculated about a new engine being tested on an older tropedo' (*IHT*, 9 November 2000, p. 8). (Western reports suggest that there were two internal explosions, a malfunctioning torpedo causing a second massive explosion of torpedos.)

'The Russian navy admitted for the first time yesterday [16 November] that one of the two explosions on the submarine was caused by a torpedo exploding on board. Admiral Vyacheslav Popov, commander of the Northern Fleet, said, however, that the cause of the first, smaller explosion was not yet clear' (*The Times*, 17 November 2000, p. 13).

21 October 2000. Alexander Rutskoi is barred by a local court from running for reelection as governor of Kursk province. 'He was accused of taking advantage of his official position during the election campaign and of providing false information about his real estate and vehicles' (*CDSP*, 2000, vol. 52, no. 43, p. 4).

25 October 2000. A Russian defence ministry plane crashes in Georgia with the loss of all eighty-six on board (including eight children).

31 October 2000. Two Russians and one American take off at the Baikonur station in Kazkahstan to become the first residents of the international space station. They docked on 2 November.

1 November 2000. 'Russia's general prosecutor yesterday [1 November] ... summoned ... Vladimir Gusinsky and Boris Berezovsky ... who are currently outside Russia ... to appear in Moscow on 13 November, with the threat of prison and international arrest warrants if they failed to show up ... for questioning about alleged criminal business dealings ... The general prosecutor's office said it now had sufficient proof [in the case of Boris Berezovsky] to bring charges of large-scale theft ... in relation to alleged embezzlement from the state airline Aeroflot ... Separately it accused Mr Gusinsky of "deceit and abuse of trust" and embezzlement in securing more than $300 million in loans from Gazprom' (*FT*, 2 November 2000, p. 12).

13 November 2000. 'Russian prosecutors yesterday [13 November] issued an arrest warrant for Vladimir Gusinsky ... as news emerged of a debt agreement which would see Mr Gusinsky lose control of key parts of his empire. Under a deal signed on Saturday [11 November] Gazprom ... will emerge as the largest single shareholder in NTV, Russia's leading private channel, with 46 per cent of the company's shares. An additional 19 per cent in NTV will be sold to outside investors … Russia's prosecutor yesterday ordered Mr Gusinsky's arrest on new charges of embezzlement … The prosecutor's press office said that Mr Gusinsky had deliberately failed to turn up for questioning yesterday … Media-Most owes a total of $473 million to Gazprom which has acted as a guarantor for two loans given to the media group by Credit Suisse First Boston … A person close to the negotiations said Gazprom would get a blocking stake of 25 per cent plus one share in all the businesses which comprise Media-Most and a 16 per cent stake in the NTV television channel in compensation for the $211 million loan and the $37.5 million on interest payments owed by Media-Most. Gazprom already holds a 30 per cent stake in NTV and the deal would take its holding to 46 per cent. Media-Most would also hand over 19 per cent of NTV and 25 per cent in some of its other businesses to Gazprom as security against CSFB's second loan of $262 million which comes for repayment next year. However, under the deal, Gazprom must sell the 19 per cent stake in NTV to a foreign shareholder. It is understood that Deutsche Bank would be appointed to find an outside investor in NTV' (*FT*, 14 November 2000, p. 9).

'Russian prosecutors issued an arrest warrant Monday [13 November] for Vladimir Gusinsky … accusing him of fraud, even as his company reached an agreement to settle its debts with … Gazprom … The prosecutors accuse Mr Gusinsky of misrepresenting assets in Media-Most when he accepted loans guaranteed by Gazprom … The agreement with Gazprom … is scheduled for approval in a local court here Tuesday [14 November] … A top executive at Gazprom, Alfred Kokh, said … that the gas company would take 46 per cent of Media-Most. Mr Gusinsky will retain 35 per cent of the company, while the remaining 19 per cent will be sold to a foreign investor' (*IHT*, 14 November 2000, p. 17).

'It is thought that he [Gusinsky] stand accused of misrepresenting Media-Most assets when he accepted bank loans … guaranteed by Gazprom. Prosecutors said that the group was bankrupt at the time. Medi-Most officials deny the claim' (*The Guardian*, 14 November 2000, p. 16).

'Boris Berezovsky … will also be summoned to appear in court tomorrow to face charges of embezzlement' (*The Times*, 14 November 2000, p. 20).

14 November 2000. '[Gazprom] on Tuesday [14 November] suddenly backed out of … [the] agreement … A lawyer for … Media-Most said Gazprom caved into pressure from the prosecutor's office … But a Gazprom official said the company pulled out on its own accord because the agreement was flawed' (*IHT*, 15 November 2000, p. 15).

15 November 2000. 'Boris Berezovsky yesterday [15 November] refused to attend a Moscow court to face charges of embezzlement' (*The Times*, 16 November 2000, p. 19). (Berezovsky, like Gusinsky, was still out of the country.)

17 November 2000. 'Media-Most … yesterday [17 November] said it had signed an agreement to swap its debt for equity with Gazprom. The deal …

would give him [Gusinsky], Gazprom and an outside investor yet to be found blocking stakes ... A Media-Most executive said the deal ... paved the way for a restructuring of the group's debts while preserving its independence from the dominance of any of the shareholders' (*FT*, 18 November 2000, p. 10).

'Vladimir Gusinsky agreed Friday [17 November] to give up a a large stake in the country's only independent television station on condition that it be sold, in part, to a foreign investor to ensure its independence from the government. Mr Gusinsky ... let his stake in the NTV television station fall to 49 per cent to pay off those debts. He also pledged more shares to cover debts due next year, and ultimately will be left with a 25 per cent stake in the station. The agreement reached Friday will make Gazprom the biggest shareholder in the station though it blocks the gas company – hence the government – from gaining a controlling stake ... Mr Putin may attempt to influence NTV policies through Gazprom, analysts said ... A similar deal collapsed earlier this week because of what many saw as political manoeuvring on behalf of the Kremlin and the federal prosecutor's office. The agreement Friday is different, the companies said, because it does not need court approval, which raises it out of the reach of the federal prosecutors. In addition to the NTV stake, Mr Gusinsky is to give Gazprom a 25 per cent stake in each one of his other media companies, which include a publishing house, a newspaper and a radio station. Another 25 per cent stake in each of these companies would be pledged as collateral' (*IHT*, 18 November 2000, p. 19).

CHAPTER THIRTEEN

MILITARY AND FOREIGN AFFAIRS, DISARMAMENT AGREEMENTS, PARTNERSHIP FOR PEACE, THE KOSOVO CRISIS AND NATO EXPANSION

THE ARMED FORCES

Lambeth (1995: 90) argues that the Russian military have largely remained above politics and helped to stabilize the nation amid reforms.

Alexander Lebed (26 September 1996): 'Russia does not have a historical tradition of military coups.'

The size of the armed forces and proposals for reduction

'Government spending on the military has shrunk from 30 per cent of GNP to about 3 per cent, or $16 billion for 1998' (Jim Hoagland, *IHT*, 8 January 1998, p. 8).

29 December 1993. Defence minister Pavel Grachev thinks that the target size of the armed forces should be 2.1 million instead of 1.5 million: 'We plan to have 2.1 million by the end of 1994 [no more than 150,000 men would go during 1994]. We'll keep the army at about that size, not at 1.5 million.' (The Soviet armed forces reached a peak of nearly 5 million in 1988.)

25 October 1994. Defence minister Grachev announces plans to reduce the army from 2.3 million (at the start of 1994) to 1.9 million by January 1995 and 1.7 million by the end of 1995.

14 November 1994. Yeltsin declares that the army should be reduced in size to 1,917,400 by 1 January 1995, 1.7 million by 1 January 1996 and, ultimately, 1.5 million.

February 1996. A German foreign office report stated that the Russian military had proposed a force of 1.92 million in 1995. But at the start of 1995 there were under 1.4 million members of the armed forces and by July 1995 the figure had fallen to 1.34 million (*IHT*, 17 February 1996, p. 1).

A survey in the *FT* (11 April 1996, p. v) cites an estimate by Mark Galeotti: defence ministry forces number 1.5 million to 1.7 million; other military units, including 200,000 border guards and 270,000 internal peacekeepers, may total almost 700,000.

(The head of the advisory defence council, Yuri Baturin, says that no one actually knows how big the army is. He estimates that there are 2.5 million servicemen, but this figure includes 'ghost troops' that do not appear in the official military budget: Tony Barber, *The Independent*, 13 November 1996, p. 11. Igor Rodionov says that approximately 1.5 million men are serving in the defence ministry's armed forces. He thinks that the armed forces can be reduced to 1.2 million by the end of 1997: *CDSP*, 1996, vol. XLVIII, no. 40, p. 6. Some 1.7 million supposedly serve, but most experts think the real number is far less. Yuri Baturin, secretary of the president's defence council, says that 'Nobody knows the exact strength of the armed forces': *IHT*, 1 March 1997, p. 2. According to the general staff, the army was reduced from 2.8 million men in 1992 to 1.7 million in 1996: *FT*, Survey, 15 April 1998, p. v.)

16 July 1997. Yeltsin signs a decree to reduce the size of the army from 1.7 million to 1.2 million by the end of 1998.

3 December 1997. In Brussels defence minister Igor Sergeyev confirms that the armed forces will be reduced by 300,000 in 1998, down to 1.2 million by the start of 1999 (*The Telegraph*, 4 December 1997, p. 24).

20 January 1998. Yeltsin says that the military cut the number of servicemen by 200,000 in 1997 (*The Times*, 21 January 1998, p. 13).

June 1998. Russian defence spending fell by over 90 per cent between 1988 and 1997 (*The Economist*, 20 June 1998, p. 148). Defence spending is declining, with procurement only 30 per cent of its 1991 level (*Newsbrief*, July 1998, vol. 18, no. 7, p. 55). (In November 1993 Yeltsin announced the creation of Rosvooruzhenie, Russian Armaments in English, thus placing responsibility for international arms sales in the hands of a single agency: p. 55.) Defence spending fell from 19 per cent of the federal budget in 1992 to 3 per cent in 1997. 'The army is overmanned, but cannot afford to retire officers, since it is obliged to provide retirees with apartments. The secrecy surrounding defence expenditure and procurement has hidden large-scale embezzlement by high level officers' (*RET*, Monthly Update, 2 July 1998, p. 3).

July 1999. 'Russia's military spending is projected this year [1999] at about $4 billion – compared with about $260 billion for the US armed forces' (*IHT*, 12 July 1999, p. 2).

January 2000. 'Russia still has a standing force of 1.5 million troops, slightly larger than the one maintained by the United States, but the budget this year [2000] will be only $4 billion, compared with the Pentagon's $284 billion' (*IHT*, 17 January 2000, p. 7),

'In the Soviet era … we were spending hundreds of billions a year on defence, not the current figure of $4 billion' (stated by Anatoli Adamishin, former deputy foreign minister, in May 2000: *CDSP*, 2000, vol. 52, no. 21, p. 12).

27 January 2000. 'Acting President Vladimir Putin approved plans Thursday [27 January] to sharply increase the purchase of new weapons and equipment to modernize the Russian military. Mr Putin … also said that the defence budget would be reallocated so that more money goes to develop high-technical conventional weapons … "The army has been underfinanced for several years, which has entailed negative consequences for the nation's defence potential", Mr Putin said … Mr Putin insisted that the new policy was not linked to Russia's stalled military campaign in Chechenia … While the new policy announced by Mr Putin does not call for an increase in the military budget of 146.35 billion roubles ($5.06 billion) for 2000, it authorizes a shift in spending priorities. Deputy prime minister Ilya Klebanov said the plan called for an increase in spending on weapons and development by up to 80 per cent in some categories. He said that spending on military supplies overall would increase by 50 per cent' (*IHT*, 28 January 2000, p. 5).

'In January [2000] the government announced a 50 per cent rise in defence procurement, to 62 billion roubles ($2.2 billion) … Even with the latest boost, Russia's procurement budget is only about 4 per cent of America's' (*The Economist*, 25 March 2000, p. 95).

'Since being appointed prime minister last August [1999], Mr Putin has … promised to increase the defence budget by 57 per cent' (*The Guardian*, 28 January 2000, p. 13).

May 2000. There are still more than 1.2 million in the armed forces and perhaps 3 million people are under arms altogether once other units (such as border guards) are included. 'On Nato estimates Russian defence spending has fallen from more than 10 per cent of GDP a decade ago to less than 5 per cent. The official defence budget, which excludes much spending on military technology, was as low as 2.3 per cent of GDP last year [1999] … Actual spending was higher, due to the costs of the Chechen war' (*FT*, Survey, 10 May 2000, p. viii). 'Russia spends about $5 billion a year on defence, compared with $300 billion for the USA' (*FT*, 23 August 2000, p. 18).

8 September 2000. Defence minister Igor Sergeyev confirms reports that the armed forces are to be reduced by around 350,000 (from the current total of about 1,200,000) to about 850,000 between and 2001 and 2003.

'[In] the heyday of the Soviet Union Moscow supported 4.3 million troops in uniform … Russia inherited a 2 million military establishment after the Soviet Union broke up in 1991 and President Boris Yeltsin struggled unsuccessfully to cut it to 1.5 million during his first term in office. After Mr Yeltsin's reelection in 1996 he appointed Marshal Sergeyev as defence minister and over the next four years was able to reduce the level from 1.7 million to 1.2 million … Marshal Sergeyev did not give a detailed breakdown of the cuts envisaged, but military officials have been quoted as saying that ground forces are to be cut by about 180,000, the navy by more than 50,000, the air force by about 40,000, interior ministry troops by 20,000, the federal security service and the government communications service by 25,000 and other security services by 15,000 or more' (*IHT*, 11 September 2000, p. 7).

The largest reductions are to come from the ground troops divisions, which are to lose some 180,000. The navy is to lose around 50,000 and the air force about 40,000. The remainder of the cuts will affect border guards and interior ministry troops (*The Guardian*, 9 September 2000, p. 20).

The Soviet armed forces numbered 5,130,000 in 1989 and 3,489,000 in 1991. Russian armed forces numbered 2,085,000 in 1994 and 1,200,000 in 2000 (*The Telegraph*, 9 September 2000, p. 17).

'Marshal Sergeyev ... cited cuts not only among land-based troops, the navy and air force, but also civilian personnel, border guards, ministry of interior troops and railway forces. Some argue that these categories – many of whom do not depend directly on the ministry of defence – bring the total number of people working in the armed forces to nearly 3 million ... Marshal Sergeyev said the number of divisions in the long-range nuclear strategic rocket force ... would be cut from twenty-two to twelve, and lose its separate command structure by 2006' (*FT*, 12 September 2000, p. 8).

Putin (speaking to the 'security council' on 27 September 2000): 'The leaders of all departments with military units have objections [to the reduction plan] ... There will be no wholesale massive reductions of the Russian armed forces ... Measured, calm and smooth work is needed to optimize the country's entire military machine ... It will take time to formulate decisions and work out their format ... [Defence cannot be addressed] by sheer enthusiasm [in budget cutting] ... [although] far too much [is being spent on the military] ... Our army must be mobile, effective, flexible and combat-capable.'

'Defence represents about 25 per cent of the Russian budget' (*IHT*, 28 September 2000, p. 5).

9 November 2000. 'Russia will cut its vast military by 600,000 people over the next five years to create more mobile and better equipped defence forces, the country's "security council" decided yesterday [9 November] ... The drastic cuts include 365,000 people from the 1.2 defence ministry forces, as well as 130,000 civilian staff and 105,000 military personnel that do not come under direct control of the defence ministry such as interior troops, border guards and railway troops' (*FT*, 10 November 2000, p. 12).

'The Kremlin said Thursday [9 November] that it planned to shrink its armed forces by 600,000 members, led by deep cuts in the main defence ministry forces ... The reductions total roughly a fifth of the 3 million or so Russians officially under arms ... The cuts include a long-expected reduction of the defence ministry forces by 365,000, to about 850,000, as well as layoffs of 235,000 civilian and military workers in eleven other armed branches not under the defence ministry's control ... The reductions were proposed long ago ... All told military and law-enforcement expenses eat up about 35 per cent of Russia's federal budget ... Sergei Ivanov ... who runs the "security council" ... said ... about 70 per cent of the military budget is being spent merely to maintain troops and bureaucrats ... leaving little to maintain equipment ... At least twelve agencies have official military organizations, from railway troops to spies to communication workers. And this does not count paramilitary organizations, such as the special Russian police units known as OMON, which fights in wars and wields authority but is maintained more or less off the books. The true number of Russian forces, still a state secret, probably totals from 4 million to 5 million' (*IHT*, 10 November 2000, p. 4).

'[The 600,000 means] reducing the total of 3.1 million military and civilian personnel by about a fifth' (*The Times*, 15 November 2000, p. 21).

'Russia has already announced that it is cutting its forces overseen by the defence ministry by 365,000. In addition the "security council" decided yesterday 105,000 military personnel from the eleven armed organizations, such as the interior ministry, would go, as would 130,000 civilian staff' (*The Independent*, 10 November 2000, p. 18).

'The Russian armed forces are bloated, top-heavy and weak. Nobody knows their real size because commanders systematically inflate the size of their units in order to pocket the pay, rations and equipment. There are far too many senior officers and bureaucrats and far too few front-line troops ... Of the 1,2 million troops that come under the defence ministry about 365,000 will go. Of the 1 million or so under other ministries around 105,000 will be cut. And of the 1 million-odd civil servants in defence and security some 130,000 will be shed. In all some 240,000 officers, including 380 generals, will be fired ... Ten civilian ministries (dealing with disasters, construction, railways, home affairs and so on) have their own military wings' (*The Economist*, 18 November 2000, pp. 68, 71).

The problems and future of conscription

More than 75 per cent of eligible Russian youths now routinely evade conscription (Lambeth 1995: 90). Less than 20 per cent of draft-age youths are joining up (Bruce Clark, *FT*, Survey, 10 April 1995, p. xiii). Around 84 per cent of eligible conscripts evaded military service in 1994 compared with 48 per cent in 1989 (including legal exemptions) (John Thornhill, *FT*, 2 May 1995, p. 3). The defence ministry estimates that only 20 per cent of the age group eligible for call-up is entering the army (*FT*, 17 May 1996, p. 2). A February 1996 German foreign office report stated that only 24 per cent of conscripts were being called up, between 50,000 and 70,000 conscripts refused to serve in 1993 and 1994, and 3,000 soldiers deserted in the first half of 1995 (*IHT*, 17 February 1996, p. 1).

30 April 1995. Yeltsin signs a decree extending military service from eighteen months to two years. (The shorter period was introduced in 1993.) In addition, only those students doing postgraduate scientific work or graduates immediately starting work in state organizations will be allowed to defer military service.

16 May 1996. Yeltsin issues two decrees:

1. From spring 2000 'the armed forces would be made up of voluntary, contracting citizens ... with conscription abandoned'.
2. With immediate effect, only volunteers will be sent to 'conflict areas'.

7 February 1997. General Igor Rodionov expresses the view that the transfer of the 1.7 million-strong armed forces from a conscription-based to a professional force over the next three years is wishful thinking (*FT,* 8 February 1997, p. 2.)

29 December 1998. 'Russia's 1.2 million member army is fed with 150,000 new draftees every six months. No one seems to have exact figures for the number of draft evaders, although only about half the conscripts actually end up in the service, said ... a defence ministry spokesman. About 15 per cent do not bother to respond to draft notices and an additional 20 per cent try to get out on health grounds ... The defence ministry says 42,000 deserters are on the lam at any time' (Daniel Williams, *IHT,* 30 December 1998, p. 5).

30 January 2000. 'There are no reliable figures on Russian draft dodgers, although the defence ministry last spring [1999] claimed their number in 1998 had been halved, to 20,000 from 40,000 nationally' (*IHT,* 31 January 2000, p. 8).

12 April 2000. 'The number of young men ... who have dodged military service has soared since ground warfare broke out in Chechenia last year [1999] ... according to a senior general. "The number of evaders increased by almost 50 per cent last fall", said Colonel General Vladislav Putilin, the chief of mobilization of the Russian general staff. "For the first time in four years the armed forces will experience a shortage of manpower" ... The problem is so severe that the Russian military has relaxed its standards for service in Chechenia. In September [1999] the government decreed that soldiers had to serve at least a year before they could be sent to Chechenia. Now that requirement is only six months ... Educational deferments are a way to avoid army service. So are health problems. And when all else fails young men simply refuse to show up when summoned. General Putilin said 49,000 men evaded reporting last autumn [1999], just under one-fifth of the number eventually conscripted ... The use of deferments, loopholes and outright bribery has led to a wide sense of unfairness. The poor, less well-connected and least educated shoulder an increasing share of the burden ... In an effort to encourage soldiers to volunteer for combat, the military counts every day fighting in Chechenia as the equivalent of two days of regular service' (Michael Gordon, *IHT,* 13 April 2000, p. 4).

November 2000. 'The draft ... produces people of the wrong kind and not even many of them. Only 13 per cent of those in the eligible age group (eighteen to twenty-seven) are actually conscripted ... and of those caught in the net 38 per cent have been unable to get either jobs or further education, nearly one-third are drunks or drug addicts, and 13 per cent have criminal records' (*The Economist,* 18 November 2000, p. 68).

The poor state of the Russian armed forces

24 September 1995. Prime minister Chernomyrdin bans any future power cuts to 'installations of the armed forces and the defence industry'. (On 21 September

1995 soldiers forced a restoration of electricity supply to a submarine base near Murmansk used for decommissioning nuclear vessels when the supply was cut off for non-payment of fuel bills. It was alleged that a nuclear accident was narrowly averted. Other incidents include the one in September 1994 when power was denied to a strategic nuclear missile command centre in the Moscow region.)

18 June 1996. Defence minister Pavel Grachev is dismissed.

17 July 1996. General Igor Rodionov (supported by Lebed) is appointed defence minister.

25 September 1996. Lebed comments on the situation in the armed forces: 'An armed uprising may take place this autumn … Not only soldiers, but even officers are in hospital with malnutrition. There is a huge number of suicides in the army. People are forced to beg and steal.'

Christopher Bellamy (*The Independent*, 26 September 1996, p. 13) comments as follows: 'One-and-a-half million men who have not been paid for three months are still serving, 500,000 of them officers. But Mr Lebed … was probably exaggerating the form such a "mutiny" might take, though not the problems which might cause it … the forces are unlikely to turn on the government, or soldiers on their officers. If the mutiny of which Mr Lebed gave warning happens, most will just pack up and drift away to the part-time businesses on which they now rely to feed their families … The army and navy have been worst hit, although the Strategic Missile troops, airforce and even the troops of the interior ministry and the FSK, the former KGB, have not been immune. There were even cases of missile command posts closing because the Russian MoD had not paid the electricity bill. Most alarmingly, there has been a 20 per cent increase in suicides among military personnel and a 28 per cent rise among officers. The failure to pay conscripts has resulted in delays to their discharge … Officers are the most likely to mutiny. The armed forces comprise 800,000 eighteen-to-twenty-year-old conscripts, 250,000 longer-service contract soldiers and 500,000 officers with degree-level qualifications, most of whom joined expecting a great career in the armed forces of a superpower … The military press has repeatedly said Russia is returning to an army "of workers and peasants", meaning that bright or well-off youngsters can wrangle exemption … At the end of last year the forces had not been paid for months, and Mr Yeltsin ensured they did receive their salaries in time for the election. Since then they have not been paid. The ravages of inflation mean majors and colonels now earn less than bus drivers, so many now moonlight. Often the work is loading and unloading trucks, or stacking supermarket shelves.'

26 September 1996. Alexander Lebed: 'The army is in fact on the brink of mutiny.'

1 October 1996. Defence minister Igor Rodionov describes the poor state of the armed forces: many servicemen have not even received their July wages; more than 110.000 soldiers lack adequate housing; entire units are losing their combat capability; there is the danger that service personnel will not turn up at their post and seek income elsewhere or sell their weapons. 'We must find a way out of this extremely difficult and critical situation which the army is in today because of the lack of funding. If things go on like this the situation will become intolerable. The defence ministry cannot guarantee that no undesirable and uncontrollable processes will develop in the armed forces, that is, the army will stop performing its direct duties. Russia may lose its armed forces as an integral and viable state structure with all the consequences that this may have.' (Yeltsin responded by ordering the prime minister to convene a special cabinet meeting on army financing and by announcing the first meeting, on 4 October, of the newly formed defence council. Lebed did not attend: see entry for 3 October 1996 in the section on Chechenia in Chapter 11.)

25 October 1996. Defence minister Igor Rodionov: 'The country's leadership and society should know that chronic underfunding has taken the armed forces to the brink of undesirable and even uncontrollable developments. If the 1997 defence budget is not changed, Russia may lose the armed forces as an integral and capable state structure and will have to face the consequences.'

12 November 1996. Defence minister Igor Rodionov: 'If extreme measures are not taken to reform the army in the near future, the consequences for the state could be catastrophic ... The armed forces have reached a point beyond which any further reduction in their combat readiness may lead to unpredictable, tragic consequences.'

11 December 1996. Yeltsin decrees that Igor Rodionov is retired from the army (he recently turned sixty) and thus becomes a civilian defence minister.

7 February 1997. Defence minister Igor Rodionov: 'No one today can guarantee the reliability of our control systems. Russia might soon reach the threshold beyond which its missiles and nuclear systems cannot be controlled ... I am becoming a spectator of the destructive process in the army and can do nothing about it.'

22 May 1997. Yeltsin dismisses defence minister Igor Rodionov for failing to carry out reforms in the armed forces. General Igor Sergeyev, commander of the Strategic Nuclear Forces, becomes acting defence minister. (Chief of the general staff General Viktor Samsonov was to have been replaced by General Viktor Chechevatov, but the latter declined. Instead General Anatoli Kvashnin took over the post.)

20 September 1997. The Movement to Support the Army is established, led by Lev Rokhlin. (On 26 September 1997 the State Duma voted to retain him as head of its defence committee despite the fact that on 9 September he had been ousted from Our Home is Russia for opposing plans for reforming the military. Rokhlin was shot dead on 3 July 1998, his wife confessing to the crime.)

The threat of the theft of nuclear and other material

21 August 1994. Theo Waigel, the German finance minister, says that 'Our financial aid to Russia will depend on Moscow's willingness to co-operate with us in the fight against the international smuggling of nuclear materials. I hope other industrialized countries will align themselves with us.'

Since May 1994 Germany had been the scene of four such incidents, the most serious on 10 August (although there was later to be an inquiry into allegations that the German security services themselves had set it up; three smugglers were given prison sentences on 17 July 1995, but the German judge expressed concern at the role of a paid agent of German intelligence in luring the smugglers). The sources and significance of these nuclear materials were the subject of considerable debate, but on 22 August German and Russian negotiators came to a preliminary agreement to co-operate. On 24 February 1995 the Russian interior ministry reported that 80 per cent of storage sites lacked basic equipment at their gates for detecting radioactive materials.

20 October 1994. The funeral takes place of the *Moskovsky Komsomolets* journalist Dmitri Kholodov. He was killed (on 17 October) by a bomb in a briefcase he thought contained information on corruption (such as the illegal sale of equipment) in the Western Group of Forces (that part of the army formerly in East Germany). He was due to appear at a parliamentary hearing.

9 September 1997. Alexei Yablokov (a former adviser to Yeltsin): 'The statement by Alexander Lebed concerning suitcases with nuclear bombs is definitely not groundless.' (This was a few days after Lebed had made the claim that some of these bombs were unaccounted for: *IHT,* 23 September 1997, p. 10.)

7 February 2000. 'In a major agreement aimed at safeguarding nuclear fuel to make weapons, Russian has promised to stop making plutonium out of fuel from its civilian power reactors as part of a $100 million joint research and aid package from the United States ... The United States has not reprocessed nuclear fuel since 1978. Part of the accord – $25 million for long-term joint research – is contingent on an end to new sales and transfers of nuclear technology to Iran. Washington says those transactions are helping Tehran acquire nuclear weapons ... But the bulk of the money will be given in exchange for Russia's decision to stop reprocessing nuclear fuel from its twenty-nine civilian power reactors. This will include, if Congress approves, $45 million to better secure spent fuel already stored at Mayak, a formerly closed nuclear complex in the southern Urals, and to build a large dry storage site elsewhere in Russia. Yevgeni Adamov, Russia's atomic energy minister insisted ... that despite the agreement Russia would not stop competing to sell new light-water power rectors to Iran. But he also said Russia had lived up to commitments made to Washington last year [1999] not to provide sensitive material or technology to Iran ... Russia, officials say, already possesses about 150 metric tons of plutonium and 1,200 tonnes of highly enriched uranium, both of which can be used in nuclear weapons ... Normally Russia would send this material [spent fuel from civilian reactors] to Mayak for reprocessing – that is the separation of plutonium, which can be used for weapons, from the rest of the fuel. But under the new agreement the plutonium will not be separated out. Instead, the unreprocessed material will be stored at a new site somewhere in Russia that the United States will finance' (*IHT*, 8 February 2000, p. 3).

DEFENCE DOCTRINE

'The end of the Cold War has produced an alarming nuclear irony. Russia is now more dependent on its nuclear weapons than ever, and at the same time those weapons are more vulnerable ... Domestic politics, economic problems and general neglect of the military have left Russia with a hollow conventional force. As that force has deteriorated, Russian military planners have placed increased emphasis on nuclear weapons, which are less expensive to maintain. But steeply declining defence budgets have left even some of those weapons dangerously exposed. Most Russian ballistic-missile submarines are kept in port because it costs less to keep them idle than to put them to sea. That makes it easier for another country to knock out Russia's submarine fleet' (editorial, *The New York Times* in *IHT*, 13 January 1998, p. 8).

2 November 1993. Russia formally announces a new military doctrine: (1) a defensive posture is adopted, with no country considered to be an adversary; (2) the 'no first use' of nuclear weapons pledge is abandoned (first made in 1982 by Brezhnev for generally perceived propaganda purposes rather than as a credible policy); (3) no reference is made to the final desired size of the armed forces (previously set at 1.5 million); (4) regional conflicts are considered the main danger and so the priority will be rapid deployment forces; (5) the use of the armed forces is permitted when Russia's security is threatened from within by nationalist or separatist forces, when the constitutional order is in danger of being undermined by force, when, for example, nuclear or chemical installations are attacked, or against illegal armed groups; (6) in the interests of Russia and of other CIS members (and by mutual consent) there may be cases where Russian forces and equipment are based outside Russia; (7) the armed forces may undertake peacekeeping operations for the UN or as a result of bilateral or multilateral deals.

10 January 2000. A new national security doctrine is decreed by acting president Vladimir Putin.

In December 1997 Yeltsin's strategy declared that nuclear weapons would only be used 'in the case of a threat to the very existence of the Russian Federation as a sovereign state'. The new doctrine states: 'The Russian Federation considers it possible to use military force to guarantee its national security according to the following principles: the use of all forces and equipment at its disposal, including nuclear weapons, in case of the need to repel armed aggression if all other means of resolving the crisis have been exhausted or proved ineffective.'

There are now two 'mutually exclusive tendencies', that of a 'multi-polar world' and that of a 'uni-polar [world] ... Western countries led by the USA want to create a world in which they would dominate and make decisions based on military force, ignoring international law'. The USA is trying to create 'unilateral' solutions to global problems with military force and 'sidelining the basic founding standards of international law'.

'The level and scale of the military threat in the military sphere is increasing.' (*IHT*, 15 January 2000, pp. 1, 5; *The Times*, 15 January 2000, p. 15; *The Independent*, 15 January 2000, p. 15; *The Guardian*, 14 January 2000, p. 1.)

21 April 2000. The 'security council' approves a new military doctrine.

'President-elect Vladimir Putin ... met with his security advisers Friday [21 April] and formally approved a new national security strategy that warns of potential threat from Amercian military preeminence and the expansion of the Western military alliance closer to Russia's frontiers. The document enshrines a new doctrine that would authorize Russian forces to use nuclear weapons first in conflict where they faced "large-scale aggression" or suffered an attack from "weapons of mass destruction" ... The new military doctrine approved on Friday by the Russian security advisers in intended to replace a 1993 version' (*IHT*, 22 April 2000, pp. 1, 4).

'The national "security council" approved a new military doctrine, which recognizes the potential threats posed by both Nato and Islamic terrorism, and broadens the criteria that would permit Russia to employ nuclear weapons' (*FT*, 22 April 2000, p. 6).

14 July 2000. 'President Vladimir Putin said Friday [14 July] that ... "There is no reorganization [of the missile forces] ... These decisions cannot be taken in a closed way, on the one hand. On the other, they cannot be put up for a nationwide vote" ... The defence minister, Marshal Igor Sergeyev [is] a staunch defender of keeping the missile troops as a separate branch of the military ... [On 12 July] the chief of the general staff, General Anatoli Kvashnin, proposed subordinating the missile troops – now an independent branch – to the regular army and slashing the number of personnel ... The proposal alarmed Marshal Sergeyev, a former head of the missile troops, which oversee Russia's land-based intercontinental ballistic missiles. (The navy and airforce separately handle weapons on submarines and airplanes.) ... The two military leaders have been sparring for some time. General Kvashnin is seen by many military observers as lobbying for Marshal Sergeyev's job' (*IHT*, 15 July 2000, pp. 1, 4).

'[Kvashnin's] plan calls for shrinking the Strategic Missile Forces from nineteen to four by 2003 and transforming the SMF into a centrally commanded service, then reducing it further to two divisions and merging it with the Air Force by 2016' (*CDSP*, 2000, vol. 52, no. 29, p. 1).

'The general staff ... saw a deadly threat in the defence minister's proposals to bring all nuclear weapons, including those controlled by the army, navy and air force, under the separate rocket forces. So General Kvashnin counter-attacked' (*The Economist*, 22 June 2000, p. 49).

'A section of Russia's top military commanders are actively canvassing the possibility of Russia joining Nato, according to sources in Russian business circles. This strategy ... lies behind the smouldering dispute between Igor Sergeyev ... and Anatoli Kvashnin ... General Kvashnin has told senior figures in the Moscow political and business establishment that he believes Russia can no longer sustain a posture of distance from Nato and that it should consider a closer relationship – even the possibility of becoming a member of the pact in the future ... A senior business figure ... said the proposal was at the root of the disagreement between the two commanders and that General Kvashnin's approach was more in tune with that of President Vladimir Putin' (John Lloyd, *FT*, 17 July 2000, p. 19).

31 July 2000. 'President Vladimir Putin fired six senior generals Monday [31 July] ... The six generals were all seen as allies of the defence minister, Marshal Igor Sergeyev' (*IHT*, 1 August 2000, p. 8).

INTERNATIONAL TREATIES AND AGREEMENTS AND NATO EXPANSION

The Nuclear Non-proliferation Treaty (NNPT) was signed in 1968 and came into effect in 1970. Gorbachev's contribution to arms reductions has already been dealt with in Chapter 10.

On 29 December 1992 the US secretary of state, Lawrence Eagleburger, and the Russian foreign minister, Andrei Kozyrev, announced that an agreement on the second Strategic Arms Reduction Treaty (Start 2) had been reached and that a treaty would be presented to their presidents for signing (which Bush and Yeltsin duly did on 3 January 1993). Whereas Start 1 (signed in July 1991) aimed finally to reduce strategic (long-range) nuclear warheads by approximately a third, Start 2 aimed to reduce them by two-thirds. By the year 2003 the USA was to have some 3,500 warheads left (about the level of the early 1960s) and Russia was to have around 3,000 (roughly the level of the mid-1970s; the deadline could be reached three years earlier if sufficient US help was given for dismantling). Long-range, land-based missiles with multiple warheads were to be eliminated. Belarus, Kazakhstan and Ukraine had earlier agreed to become non-nuclear states, but implementation was another matter. Start 1 needed to be fully ratified before Start 2 could come into effect. Ukraine, for example, had not even ratified Start 1, although President Kravchuk expressed confidence that parliament would do so. (In 1990 the USA had 12,646 strategic nuclear warheads and the Soviet Union had 11,012. Start 1 would reduce the totals to 8,556 and 6,163 respectively, while Start 2 would reduce them further to 3,500 and 3,000 respectively: *The Times* 4 January 1993, p. 1.)

10–11 January 1994. The Partnership for Peace policy is formally agreed at the Nato summit.

30 May 1994. It is announced that Russia and the USA are no longer targeting each other with long-range nuclear missiles.

22 June 1994. Russia becomes the twenty-first signatory of the Partnership for Peace with Nato. Russia and Nato also agree to (but do not actually sign) a separate document ('summary of conclusions'), involving 'enhanced dialogue' on broader political and security matters (such as nuclear disarmament and non-proliferation). The document establishes the following: (1) 'the development of a far-reaching co-operative Nato-Russia relationship, both inside and outside Partnership for Peace'; (2) recognition of Russia as 'a major European, international and nuclear power'; (3) information-sharing, political consultations and security co-operation. (Other countries have simply signed the Partnership for Peace and only later begun to refine their links with Nato.)

2 September 1994. Russian and US troops begin (nine-day) joint exercises in Russia for UN peacekeeping purposes.

President Jiang Jemin of China begins a four-day visit (the first by a head of state since Mao Tse-Tung in 1957). Presidents Yeltsin and Jiang Jemin agree on the following: Russia and China to cease targeting each other with strategic nuclear weapons; not to use force against each other; to reduce the number of troops stationed along the border; the disputed western part of the border is finally settled; to enhance trade and economic co-operation in general.

1 December 1994. Kozyrev objects to the Partnership for Peace proposals and refuses to finalize plans for military co-operation.

4 December 1994. Yeltsin speaks against Nato's encroachment on Eastern Europe.

5–6 December 1994. At the OSCE conference in Budapest Yeltsin again criticized Nato: 'Europe is in danger of plunging into a cold peace.'

16 February 1995. In his state-of-the-nation speech Yeltsin talked of: 'Upholding Russia's position within the framework of OSCE and increasing the role of this organization in the interests of all its members ... Russia does not claim a right to "veto" the entry of new members into Nato, but it will not agree to the hasty expansion of that alliance either ... The creation of a stable security mechanism for the twenty-first century is at the centre of political interaction with the European states. That mechanism could rely on existing organizations and institutions, above all OSCE's potential and possibilities' (*CDSP*, 1995, vol. XLVII, no. 8, p. 14).

20 March 1995. Kozyrev on Nato: 'Why rush things if we run the risk of creating new lines of division? ... [Nato] should be replaced by a new model based on comprehensive security ... The gap between Nato's very active moves to study potential enlargement and its passive attitude in developing this new model of comprehensive security is a very wide one and it could be dangerous.'

11 May 1995. The Nuclear Non-proliferation Treaty is extended indefinitely.

31 May 1995. Russia agrees (1) to join the Partnership for Peace and (2) to a second document involving a 'special relationship' with Nato (arrangements for an 'enhanced dialogue' over matters such as nuclear proliferation and peacekeeping). But Andrei Kozyrev still objects to Nato's ideas on expansion in Eastern Europe.

8 September 1995. Yeltsin: 'Those who insist on the expansion of Nato are making a major political mistake. The flames of war could ignite across the whole of Europe.' If Nato were to expand Russia would 'immediately establish constructive ties with all ex-Soviet republics and form a bloc'.

1 December 1995. China's last border questions with Russia are resolved, with Russia ceding about 1,100 ha in the Far East (*IHT,* 30 December 1995, p. 5).

26 April 1996. Russia, China, Kazakhstan, Kyrgyzstan and Tajikistan sign a border treaty. A 100 km-wide zone on each side of the border is to be demarcated. The countries will inform each other about troop movements within the zone and about the personnel and weapons stationed there. Military forces will not attack or direct exercises against one another (with observers present to monitor exercises).

20 August 1996. India formally vetoes the Comprehensive [nuclear] Test Ban Treaty. (India conducted a nuclear test in 1974. India conducted three underground nuclear tests on 11 May 1998 and two more two days later. On 28 May 1998 Pakistan tested five nuclear devices and another one two days later.)

10 October 1996. The Comprehensive Test Ban Treaty is approved by the 185-member UN General Assembly by 158 votes to three (India, Bhutan and Libya were against), with five abstentions (Cuba, Lebanon, Syria, Tanzania and Mauritius). The treaty cannot come into force (become international law) unless all forty-four countries with nuclear arms or nuclear power stations have signed and ratified it. But individual signatories can hold to the treaty and it has moral force.

24 September 1996. At the fifty-first session of the United Nations General Assembly the Comprehensive Test Ban Treaty is signed by the USA, Russia, China, France, the UK, Japan and other countries.

The first atomic bomb was exploded on 16 July 1945 in the New Mexico desert in the USA. Between 1945 and 1996 2,046 nuclear tests were carried out. The distribution by country was as follows: USA, 1,032; Soviet Union, 715; France, 210; United Kingdom, forty-five; China, forty-four. The 1963 partial test ban treaty, signed by the USA, the Soviet Union and the United Kingdom, forbade atmospheric testing but permitted underground tests. China exploded its first nuclear weapon in October 1964 (*IHT,* 12 May 1998, pp. 1, 4).

27 December 1996. Russia and China announce that there will be an (unspecified) reduction in military forces along their common border. (A formal agreement was to be signed in April 1997, when the two countries would be joined by Kazakhstan, Kyrgyzstan and Tajikistan.) (On 13 January

1997 Yeltsin wrote to the president of Belarus about possible union. This may have been meant as a warning to Nato about expansion eastwards.)

6 March 1997. Yeltsin: The eastward expansion of Nato could cause 'direct damage to our security', its purpose being 'the desire to oust Russia from Europe, to achieve its strategic isolation'.

20–1 March 1997. Presidents Yeltsin and Clinton agree to begin talks on Start 3 (but only after the Russian State Duma ratifies Start 2), which will aim to reduce strategic nuclear warheads to 2,000–2,500 by the end of 2007. The USA also agrees to extend the Start 2 deadline for Russia to destroy its multiple-warhead missiles from 2003 to 2007.

President Clinton says that Russia will attend the next meeting of the G7 from the beginning, forming 'the Summit of the Eight'. (Yeltsin attended all the sessions held on 20–22 June 1997 except the one dealing with international financial affairs.)

24 April 1997. Russia, China, Kazakhstan, Kyrgyzstan and Tajikistan sign an agreement fixing ceilings for troops and weapons within a 100 kilometre frontier band. (It seems as though there will be no actual reduction in troop numbers since present numbers are already low enough.)

25 April 1997. The US Senate approves the Chemical Weapons Convention by seventy-four votes to twenty-six (i.e. by more than the required two-thirds majority). But the State Duma postpones its vote owing to 'very difficult economic conditions'. (The convention was originally signed by 130 countries, including Russia and the USA, on 13 January 1993. The convention, now signed by additional countries, will take effect 29 April 1997.) (The convention was ratified by the State Duma on 31 October 1997 and by the Council of the Federation on 5 November 1997.)

14 May 1997. Nato secretary-general Javier Solana and Russian foreign minister Yevgeni Primakov announce that agreement has been reached on a Founding Act on Mutual Relations, Co-operation and Security between Nato and the Russian Federation as a way of gaining Russia's acceptance of Nato's proposed eastward enlargement.

1. 'Nato and Russia do not consider each other as adversaries.'

2. The term 'Founding Act' implies (as did the 1975 Helsinki Final Act) that the document will be politically as opposed to legally binding. Thus it will be signed by political leaders on 27 May 1997 and will not need to be ratified by individual parliaments.

3. 'The member states of Nato reiterate that they have no intention, no plan and no reason to deploy nuclear weapons on the territory of new member states … and do not foresee any future need to do so.' 'In the current foreseeable security environment' Nato will not station 'substantial combat forces' on the territory of new member states. There will be no storage sites for nuclear weapons there. Military infrastructure in new member states will 'suit the strategic environment', i.e. adequate to ensure inter-operability between member forces and rapid deployment. Nato and Russia agree 'to

prevent any potentially threatening build-up of conventional forces' in Central and Eastern Europe. Talks on modifying the 1990 Conventional Forces in Europe Treaty will continue.

4. A Nato-Russia Permanent Joint Council will be created on which Nato and Russia will discuss 'any issues of common interest related to security and stability in the Euro-Atlantic area', e.g. peacekeeping, arms control, nuclear safety, nuclear and conventional military doctrine, terrorism and drugs trafficking. The council will 'provide a mechanism for consultations, co-ordination and, where appropriate, for joint decisions and action ... to identify and pursue as many opportunities for joint action as possible'. There will be a three-person chair, namely the Nato secretary-general, the Russian ambassador to Nato and a Nato envoy who will rotate among existing members. Liaison officers will be exchanged and allowed to operate in some command headquarters. 'Provisions of this document do not provide Nato or Russia in any way with a right of veto over the actions of the other, nor do they infringe upon or restrict the rights of Nato or Russia to independent decision-making and action.' The Founding Act says that there can be no 'new dividing lines or spheres of influence limiting the sovereignty of any states'. All states have an 'inherent right to choose the means to ensure their own security'.

27 May 1997. The Founding Act is signed in Paris Yeltsin and the sixteen Nato leaders.

8 July 1997. Nato's secretary general Javier Solana Madariaga: 'Today heads of state and government have agreed to invite the Czech Republic, Hungary and Poland to begin accession talks with Nato. Our goal is to sign the protocol of accession at the time of the ministerial meetings in December 1997 and to see the ratification process completed in time for membership to become effective by the fiftieth anniversary of the Washington Treaty in April 1999. We affirm that Nato remains open to new members under Article 10 of the North Atlantic Treaty... The alliance expects to extend further invitations in coming years ... No European democratic country whose admission would fulfil the objectives of the treaty will be excluded from consideration ... We will review the process at our next meeting in 1999. With regard to the aspiring members, we recognize with great interest and take account of the positive developments toward democracy and the rule of law in a number of south-eastern European countries, especially Romania and Slovenia ... At the same time we recognize the progress achieved by the states in the Baltic region who are also aspiring members.'

Yeltsin refused an invitation to attend the Nato meeting and Russia was represented by a deputy prime minister. Russian foreign minister Primakov states (in Moscow) that: 'Nato enlargement is a big mistake, possibly the biggest mistake since the end of the Second World War.'

A majority of the sixteen Nato countries (led by France) supported the inclusion of Romania and Slovenia in the first wave of invitations. But the

USA was adamant that only three countries would be invited to become members of Nato in the first wave.

9 July 1997. The first meeting of the Euro-Atlantic Partnership Council takes place. (Defence and security matters are discussed by the sixteen Nato countries and twenty-eight other countries.)

16 July 1997. The European Commission recommends that Estonia, Cyprus, the Czech Republic, Hungary, Poland and Slovenia open negotiations in early 1998 for entry to the EU.

23 July 1997. General agreement is reached on amending the CFE (Conventional Forces in Europe) Treaty. Although details are not given it seems that the total amount of equipment will be reduced and each country will be given its own individual ceiling.

26 September 1997. The first meeting of the Permanent Joint Council takes place.

An agreement is signed by the USA, Russia, Belarus, Kazakhstan and Belarus to extend the deadline for implementing the 1993 Start 2 Treaty from the beginning 2003 to the end of 2007. Launch and delivery systems must be disabled by 2003 and dismantled by the end of 2007. (Start 2 was ratified by the US Senate in 1996 but has still not been ratified by the State Duma.)

Agreement is reached between the USA, Russia, Ukraine, Kazakhstan and Belarus to amend the 1972 anti-ballistic missile treaty, allowing the building of defences against shorter-range missiles.

1–2 November 1997. The prime minister of Japan visits Russia for informal talks with Yeltsin. Much is made of economic co-operation and 'maximum efforts' will be made to conclude a Second World War peace treaty by the year 2000. (Yeltsin paid a return visit on 18–19 April 1998.)

Yeltsin made a long-delayed visit to Japan on 11–13 October 1993. He promised to withdraw the remaining 5,000 troops from the disputed Kuril Islands. (The Kuril Islands were settled by Russians, following exploration in the seventeenth and eighteenth centuries. In 1855 Japan seized a group of the southern islands and in 1875 took possession of the entire chain. In 1945 the islands were ceded to Russia as part of the Yalta agreement. '[On 12 November 1998] Mr Yeltsin presented proposals, kept secret [to the visiting prime minister of Japan] to end the dispute over four Pacific Ocean islands, which are called the Southern Kurils in Russia and the Northern Territories in Japan ... The dispute over the four islands, seized by Soviet forces at the end of the Second World War, has prevented Russia and Japan from signing a formal peace treaty to end hostilities. Mr Yeltsin proposed the creation of a committee to consider the border between the two countries and jointly manage the economies of the islands': *FT*, 13 November 1998, p. 3.)

10 November 1997. Russia and China sign a declaration on the demarcation of their 2,800-mile (4,300-kilometre) border. ('The short western border, only 50 miles long, is still under negotiation': *IHT*, 11 November 1997, p. 4.) (There was also an agreement in principle to build a gas pipeline from Siberia to China's Pacific coast.) (In October 1995 Russia and China demarcated the last 54 km of disputed border, their total border being 4,380 km long: *The Economist*, 21 October 1995, p. 6. The last border questions with China have been resolved, with Russia ceding about 1,100 ha in the Far East: *IHT*, 30 December 1995, p. 5.) ('In September [1998] the two sides [Russia and China] announced that the demarcation of the final, western sector of their common border had been completed. This covered a mountainous stretch between the Altai republic and the Xinjiang-Uighur autonomous region. In 1997 the 4,000 kilometre section from the Sea of Japan to Mongolia was completed. Only two islands in the Amur River and one in the Argun remain in limbo' (*FEER: Asia 1999 Yearbook*, 1999, p. 190.)

27 November 1997. Nato accepts that it will cost existing members of the alliance some $1.3 billion over ten years to admit the Czech Republic, Hungary and Poland (*IHT*, 28 November 1997, p. 7); the range is $1.3–1.5 billion (*IHT*, 2 December 1997, p. 14). (Note that this estimate is well below the initial one. Opponents of Nato expansion have complained that the cost of Nato expansion has been massaged down massively in order to justify expansion.)

'The [US] Senate has no idea whether Nato expansion will cost $1.5 billion, as the Pentagon predicts, or $125 billion, the price once cited by the Congressional Budget Office. Nor does it know how much of that burden Washington will have to bear' (*The New York Times*, editorial in *IHT*, 25 April 1998, p. 6).

30 November 1997. Chancellor Kohl of Germany pays a one-day visit to Russia. He and Yeltsin agree to hold (in Russia) the first in a series of Russia-Germany-France summits in the first half of 1998.

2 December 1997. At the start of a three-day visit to Sweden Yeltsin makes another unexpected statement on nuclear arms: 'I announce here, for the first time, that we are going to reduce unilaterally the quantity of nuclear warheads by a further one-third ... It is time for us to take this matter to its natural conclusion and destroy nuclear weapons altogether.' (A presidential spokesman later played down the significant of the announcement.)

3 December 1997. Yeltsin in a speech to the Swedish parliament: 'From 1 January 1999 Russia will unilaterally reduce – and I am saying this for the first time – by more than 40 per cent its land and naval units, especially in north-western Russia.' Foreign minister Primakov says that the figure of 40 per cent refers only to north-western Russia.

3–4 December 1997. The treaty banning the use, production stockpiling and transfer of anti-personnel mines is signed by 121 countries. Among those not signing are Russia, the USA, China, India, Pakistan, Iraq, Iran, Syria, Israel and Afghanistan. But Russia extends a ban on the export of anti-personnel mines that do not automatically self-destruct and that are impossible to detect.

17 December 1997. Yeltsin signs a national security 'concept' which states that: 'Russia reserves to itself the right to use all the means and powers it has in its possession, including nuclear weapons, if as a result of unleashing an armed aggression there will appear a threat to the very existence of the state.' Russia's influence in the world has 'considerably decreased'. 'The crisis-like state of the economy is the major reason for the appearance of a threat to the national security of the Russian Federation.' Russia faces 'centrifugal aspirations' that could cause the country to disintegrate. Some regions already ignore the constitution (David Hoffman, *IHT*, 26 December 1997, pp. 1, 5).

26 March 1998. A summit meeting is held in Moscow between President Yeltsin, Chancellor Kohl of Germany and President Chirac of France.

21 June 1998. Russia and India initial and thus revive a ten-year-old pact in which Russia will build two nuclear reactors in India.

16 July 1998. The USA announces that it will impose trade sanctions on nine Russian companies and institutions that are considered to have been helping Iran with its missile development programme (*IHT*, 17 July 1998, p. 7).

24 July 1998. Alexander Lebed (governor of Krasnoyarsk) writes an open letter to the prime minister: 'Officers of the Uzhursk [nuclear] missile base have not received their wages for five months and their wives have been assailing the unit's headquarters. The officers are hungry, the officers are very angry. I am seriously thinking about taking the base under the region's jurisdiction. We, the people of Krasnoyarsk, are not yet a rich people. But in exchange for the status of a nuclear territory, we will, if you like, feed the unit, becoming, along with India and Pakistan, a headache for the world community. One comes to the sad conclusion that the government considers lands to the east of the Urals as something alien. It is rather weird since 60 per cent of the country's territory and 80 per cent of its resources lie there.'

1–2 September 1998. President Clinton visits Russia. He and President Yeltsin sign two arms agreements (*IHT*, 2 September 1998, p. 8):

1. Each nation will inform the other of missile and space vehicle launching around the world. This extends to long-range missiles a protocol previously adopted for shorter-range missiles.
2. A reduction in plutonium stockpiles (plutonium recovered from dismantled weapons).

22 September 1998. Russia and the United States sign an accord allowing US companies to help modernize secret 'nuclear cities'. These were among the most secret facilities in the former Soviet Union where scientists worked on the design and production of nuclear weapons. US companies will invest in work in the cities to ensure that the 600,000 employees are not driven elsewhere through lack of work (*IHT*, 23 September 1998, p. 6). 'A House-Senate conference panel last week approved $20 million for the programme, Initiatives for Proliferation Prevention, … Also called the "nuclear cities" programme, it will provide seed money "to move scientists into commercial roles" ... The roughly 1.5 million employees involved in Russian nuclear weapons development and production work in facilities in ten specially constructed cities, closed to foreigners, and twenty-five other sites spread across the country ... The initial "nuclear cities" programme contracts were signed in 1994 with $35 million funding ... More than 3,000 weapons scientists, engineers and technicians have been involved in 375 projects funded by the project' (*IHT*, 21 September 1998, p. 5).

Russia says that it will open ten secret cities at the core of its nuclear weapons complex to foreign investment in a US-backed effort aimed at redeploying highly skilled workers in the civil economy. The Russia-USA accord includes $30 million of US funding in 1999 to bring jobs to the cities' 600,000 inhabitants (*FT*, 23 September 1998, p. 2).

6 October 1998. Yuri Maslyukov (first deputy prime minister): 'The state does not have the means to maintain the present level of several thousand warheads. The maximum we can hope for is a level of several hundred nuclear charges in 2007–2010. In seven or eight years time Russia will not have a single missile, submarine or bomber built in Soviet times.' He says that the State Duma should jointly agree a programme that from 2000 would add at least thirty-five Topol-M (single-warhead, land-based) missiles annually, bring into service several new Yuri Dolgoruky-class nuclear submarines, and modernize command and attack warning systems.

29 October 1998. 'For the first time in history a Russian court has thrown out treason charges brought by the federal security service (FSB), the successor organization to the KGB ... A St Petersburg judge yesterday [29 October] rejected the case against Alexander Nikitin, a former navy captain and environmental campaigner, saying the prosecution had not presented sufficiently clear evidence to support its accusations. But the judge added that the FSB should continue its investigations into allegations that Mr Nikitin had betrayed state secrets by passing on information about Russian nuclear submarines to a Norwegian environmental agency ... Mr Nikitin was arrested in February 1996 by the FSB on suspicion of spying ... His response was that all of the "secrets" he revealed in a report for Bellona, the Norwegian environment group which commissioned Mr Nikitin's research, had already been published ... Another Russian environmentalist, Grigori Pasko, faces similar charges for passing documents and videos to the Japanese media describing the Russian navy's dumping of nuclear waste' (*FT*, 30 October 1998, p. 3).

(On 28 December 1999 Alexander Nikitin was acquitted by a St Petersburg court of charges of espionage – brought by the Federal Security Service – for disclosing nuclear safety hazards aboard Russian atomic submarines for the Norwegian environmental group Bellona. He was accused under military orders that were secret and were adopted only after his arrest. The judge said the use of the secret orders was a 'direct violation of the constitution. We are discussing the period August to September 1995. Later it became possible to apply new legislative acts, but not at that time': *IHT*, 30 December 1999, pp. 1, 4. Nikitin was arrested in February 1999: *FT*, 30 December 1999, p. 4. In April 2000 the supreme court upheld the St Petersburg court's decision.)

('A crusading Russian journalist was freed from a Vladivostok jail Tuesday [20 July] after a military court ruled he had abused his power but was entitled to an amnesty. Captain Grigori Pasko spent twenty months in prison after reporting on environmental abuses by the Russian navy ... Kept in solitary confinement, Captain Pasko had been charged with treason for disclosing state secrets and faced a possible prison term of twelve years. After international human rights and press freedom organizations protested to the Kremlin, however, the military judges convicted Captain Pasko of a lesser crime, sentenced him to three years in prison and ordered an amnesty ... A career naval officer and military journalist, Captain Pasko chronicled environmental abuses by the Russian navy for ... the newspaper of the Russian Pacific Fleet. He also worked as a freelancer for NHK, the largest television network in Japan, and provided the network with a video tape about the dumping of nuclear waste at sea. Captain Pasko was arrested at Vladivostok airport in 1997 following a trip to Japan': *IHT*, 21 July 1999, p. 6. 'The Vladivostok military court rejected the charge of high treason levelled against Mr Pasko by the security services, but sentenced him to three years in prison on a lesser charge of abusing his service commission as a naval officer ... Mr Pasko was arrested in November 1997 and charged with passing secret information about Russia's far-east nuclear fleet to the Japanese media. He said he had only gathered publicly available information about the ecological dangers posed by the nuclear fleet': *FT*, 21 July 1999, p. 2.)

20 November 1998. The first piece of an international space station is successfully launched in Kazakhstan. The joint project involves the USA, Russia, Europe, Canada and Japan. 'The United States, by far the biggest partner in the station, paid the Russian government $240 million to build the Zarya [sunrise] module' (*IHT*, 21 November 1998, p. 4).

Russia subsequently fell behind on its delivery schedule. The USA blamed factors such as Russia using its very limited resources on maintaining the Mir space station in operation. On 22 January 1999 Russian announced that the Mir space station was to be kept in orbit for another three years. (The base block was launched 20 February 1986 and its service life lasted much longer than the forecast five years.)

Since then Mir's fortunes have ebbed and flowed:

1. On 27 August 1999 the last three astronauts left the Mir space station.

2. On 4 April 2000 two cosmonauts blasted off on a mission to the Mir space station.

'Vladimir Putin ... recently reversed plans to scrap the fourteen-year-old orbiting space laboratory ... "The reasons for maintaining Mir are convincing and we will work to put them into action", Mr Putin said last month [March] ... Mir's twentieth-century viability was further boosted by the decision in

January [2000] of a group of American millionaires to invest up to $200 million in the project to exploit Mir's commercial potential ... The American business men, who revitalized the space station's prospects in January by offering to invest $20 million and trying to raise up to $200 million for future missions, announced yesterday [4 April] that they were looking for business partners around the world to make Mir fit for space tourism, advertising in space and for the development of hi-tech products ... Mir-Corp [is] the firm set up by the American businessmen to rent the space station form the Russians' (*The Guardian*, 5 April 2000, p. 18).

'The world's first privately-funded manned space mission docked on schedule with Russia's Mir space station [on 6 April] ... Yesterday's successful docking also triggered the signature by the director's of Mir-Corp, the Bermuda-registered vehicle, on an agreement to pump what one said amounted to a further $50 million of private sector support into the venture ... [An] Indian entrepreneur is one of the two existing backers. The other is Gold & Appel, a British Virgin Islands-based investment fund ... which has already put up $20 million. Together they own 40 per cent of Mir-Corp, with the remaining 60 per cent owned by Energiya, a privatized Russian company in which the state still retains a 38 per cent share. And they claim that this year or next they could cover annual operating costs, which they estimate at less than $200 million' (*FT*, 7 April 2000, p. 10).

On 16 November 2000 it was announced that Mir would be destroyed at the end of February 2001 in a controlled descent.

17 December 1998. Russia condemns the air strikes on Iraq by the USA and the UK which started the previous day.

18 December 1998. 'Russia recalled its ambassadors to Washington and London on Friday [18 December] to protest the US and British air strikes on Iraq ... Russia's withdrawal of its ambassadors ... was one of Moscow's angriest ripostes since the end of the Cold War. Interfax news agency said it was the first time Moscow had recalled an ambassador to the United States since World War II and the first time it had withdrawn its envoy to Britain since 1971 ... Russia's Communist-led parliament registered its dissent by shelving plans to ratify Start 2 ... A vote on the treaty, which was widely expected to be approved, was scheduled for next Friday' (*IHT*, 19 December 1998, p. 4).

22 December 1998. The State Duma delays consideration of the Start 2 treaty until at least its spring 1999 session partly as a consequence of the bombing of Iraq. 'Russia's nuclear arsenal is falling way below Start 2 levels because of obsolescence and lack of money ...Without the treaty Russia's nuclear arsenal is expected to fall below 1,000 warheads seven years from now as missiles, submarines and bombers are retired, while the USA would be entitled to remain at previous levels of about 6,000 warheads' (David Hoffman, *IHT*, 23 December 1998, p. 7).

27 December 1998. 'Russia placed on combat duty Sunday [27 December] the first regiment of its new single-warhead intercontinental ballistic missile, the

Topol-M … The first group of ten solid-fuel Topol-M missiles [was] located at a base in the Saratov region south-east of Moscow … The weapon is designed to replace the multiple-warhead land-based missiles … banned by the Start 2 strategic arms treaty, which has still not been ratified by the Russian parliament …. Nuclear forces have become the backbone of its deterrent as conventional armies and weapons are seriously deteriorating … The Topol-M has been one of the very few modernization projects carried out … [and] the first developed within Russia; Soviet models relied heavily on Ukraine' (David Hoffman, *IHT*, 28 December 1998, p. 5).

12 January 1999. Lieutenant-General Anatoli Sokolov (commander of missile attack prevention division, the early warning system) writes in a letter to Colonel-General Vladimir Yakovlev (commander of the strategic rocket forces): 'Given your biased attitude to our branch of the military and personal animosity to me, I consider further service in the armed forces to be pointless' (*The Telegraph*, 13 January 1999, p. 13). 'Three of his deputies also resigned in protest at being brought under the control of the strategic missile troops' (*The Times*, 13 January 1999, p. 10).

The USA imposes economic penalties on three institutions, accusing them of assisting Iran with nuclear and missile technology (*IHT*, 13 January 1999, p. 1). ('Deputy prime minister Yuri Maslyukov … undercut Russia's previous denials that its scientists had passed on long-range missile technology to Tehran. He said in a television interview that "some of the cases" that the United States has presented "turned out to be true". To punish the technology transfer the Clinton administration has placed sanctions on a dozen Russian scientific institutions and threatened to forbid US companies from launching satellites on Russian boosters': *IHT*, 23 January 1999, p. 2.)

24 March 1999. Nato starts bombing the Federal Republic of Yugoslavia as a result of the failure to resolve the Kosovo crisis diplomatically. Russia suspends co-operation with Nato and participation in the Partnership for Peace programme.

23 April 1999. Nato celebrates its fiftieth anniversary.[1] But Russia declines the invitation to attend. (For the role of Russia in ending the Kosovo crisis, see the following section.)

29 April 1999. 'Russia announced yesterday [29 April] it would put more emphasis on developing tactical nuclear weapons in framing its national security needs up to 2010. The move signals Moscow may be preparing to lower the threshold for using nuclear weapons to to battlefield situations' (*FT*, 30 April 1999, p. 2)

'Boris Yeltsin … yesterday ordered the development of new tactical nuclear weapons … Yesterday's meeting of the advisory security council was a public effort by Mr Yeltsin to show his anger at the Nato [bombing] campaign in Kosovo … The proposed development of smaller tactical missiles is significant because it signals a radical shift in Russian defence strategy toward a nuclear first-strike capability' (*The Guardian*, 30 April 1999, p. 14).

5 May 1999. 'Georgia, Ukraine, Azerbaijan and Moldova signed a pact in Washington last week adding Uzbekistan to a year-old alliance, creating Guuam. The alliance is meant to strengthen members' political and economic ties to the West ... Guuam's main task is to develop the area's rich oil and gas deposits to the exclusion of Russia, a goal partly achieved last month [April] with the opening of a pipeline carrying Caspian Sea oil to export through Azerbaijan and Georgia ... Guuam's members have agreed to low-level military co-operation but insist the group is not a military alliance directed against a third party – namely, Russia. Moscow has grown increasingly worried since Georgia, Uzbekistan and Azerbaijan pulled out of the CIS collective security pact this spring [1999]. Ukraine and Moldova never were members' (*FT*, 6 May 1999, p. 2).

26 July 1999. The US secretary of state and the Russian foreign minister agree to create a 'hot line' (direct telephone link) between their two offices.

17–19 August 1999. The USA and Russia held three days of talks in Moscow on the prospects for additional nuclear weapons cuts. The issue of a Start 3 treaty was raised that could cut arsenals to 2,000 to 2,500 warheads. The existing Start 2 treaty, signed in 1993 but not yet ratified by the State Duma, calls for both countries to scale back to 3,000 to 3,500 warheads each. Russia agreed to listen to US proposals to amend the 1972 Anti-Ballistic Missile Treaty (ABM) in order to build missile defences currently banned under the treaty. The USA fears that missile programmes are being developed by countries like Iran and North Korea (*IHT*, 18 August 1999, p. 4; *IHT*, 21 August 1999, p. 4).

Russia proposed reducing the number of nuclear warheads allowed to each side under Start 3 to 1,500 at most (*IHT*, 20 August 1999, p. 5).

No substantial progress was reported on the talks. The next round of talks is due to begin in September 1999 (*FT*, 21 August 1999, p. 2; *IHT*, 21 August 1999, p. 5).

25–6 August 1999. The presidents of Russia, China, Kazakhstan Kyrgyzstan and Tajikistan meet in Bishkek (the capital of Kyrgyzstan). The five countries are called the 'Shanghai Five', named after the Chinese city where a treaty on easing border tension was signed in 1996. A declaration is signed: 'The importance of fighting international terrorism, the illegal drugs trade, arms trafficking, illegal migration and other forms of transborder crime, separatism and religious extremism [is stressed]... The signatories also consider that creating a multi-polar world is the common path for development and will ensure long-term stability' (*IHT*, 26 August 1999, p. i).

'Under pressure from Jiang Zemin, the following clause was inserted in the fnal Bishek document: "Human rights should not be used as a pretext for interfering in a state's internal affairs"' (*CDSP*, 1999, vol. 51, no. 34, p. 15).

2–6 October 1999. 'China and Russia held their first joint naval exercises. A guided-missile escort vessel from the Russian Pacific fleet took part in the 2–6 October manoeuvres, held 50 kilometres off Shanghai ... On 2 October China began ... unprecedented joint naval exercises with Russia' (*FEER*, 14 October 1999, pp. 16, 27).

13 October 1999. The US Senate rejects the Comprehensive Test Ban Treaty by fifty-one votes to forty-eight. (A minimum two-thirds majority, i.e. sixty-seven votes, is needed to ratify the treaty.) President Clinton vowed to continue abiding by the obligations of the treaty.

17 October 1999. 'The United States is now offering to help Russian complete a large missile-tracking radar [near Irkutsk] if Moscow agrees to renegotiate ... the 1972 Anti-Ballistic Missile Treaty ... American officials have also suggested that Washington might upgrade a Russian-controlled radar in Azerbaijan ... Deputy secretary of state Strobe Talbot has held a series of high-level meetings with the Russians ... In January [1999] ... President Bill Clinton sent President Boris Yeltsin a letter asking Russia to renegotiate the treaty to permit a limited system of defence ... because nations like North Korea and Iran were developing the means to manufacture ocean-spanning ballistic missiles' (*IHT*, 18 October 1999, pp. 1, 10).

18–19 November 1999. The purpose of the fifty-four nation OSCE (Organization for Security and Co-operation in Europe) summit meeting in Istanbul was to map out the principles and role of OSCE in the twenty-first century and to sign a new conventional arms accord. There was heavy criticism of what was described as Russia's indiscriminate bombing campaign in Chechenia and the resultant large numbers of refugees.

A revised Conventional Forces in Europe (CFE) Treaty was signed on 19 November 1999. Aimed at eliminating the risk of surprise attack, it sets limits for tanks, armoured vehicles, artillery pieces, combat aircraft and attack helicopters. But, unlike the 1990 document, it sets national ceilings, with sub-limits in flanking regions, rather than bloc-to-bloc limits between Nato and the former Warsaw Pact. Thirty countries 'from the Atlantic to the Urals' were involved in the signing, but the treaty is now open to others to join (*IHT*, 20 November 1999, p. 2; *FT*, 20 November 1999, p. 5). 'The updated conventional arms treaty ... halves the numbers of warplanes, tanks and other heavy non-nuclear weapons in much of Europe ... Unlike its predecessor of 1990 ... which led to the destruction of over 50,000 pieces of heavy weaponry, the new arrangements set limits on a state-by-state, rather than bloc-by-bloc basis. It also provides for more verification' (*The Independent*, 20 November 1999, p. 16). '[The revised treaty] gives Russia more leeway on its southern flank' (*FT*, 20 November 1999, p. 5).

The USA and other counties (including France, Germany and the UK) said that they would seek ratification only when Russia met the military commitments, currently exceeded by its forces fighting in Chechenia.

A Charter for European Security was signed by all fifty-four OSCE members, mapping out the principles and role of OSCE. 'The idea [of a] ... pan-European security charter ... was conceived several years ago by Russia as a means of reinforcing OSCE to counter or overshadow Nato enlargement ...

[The charter] formalizes existing norms about security and observance of human rights, and reinforces OSCE capacity to send civilian help to crises' (*FT*, 20 November 1999, p. 5). 'The organization's new security charter was originally sought by Russia to keep an expanding Nato at bay and safeguard the rights of its ethnic minorities in the now independent Baltic States' (*The Guardian*, 20 November 1999, p. 22). '[The charter] ... insists that although decisions among all fifty-four members of OSCE will still be taken by consensus, flexibility should remain at the heart of the "co-operative and inclusive approach to common and indivisible security"' (*The Times*, 20 November 1999, p. 15).

The charter includes the following: 'Participating states are accountable to their citizens and responsible to each other for their implementation of their OSCE commitments. We regard these commitments as our common achievement and, therefore, to be matters of immediate and legitimate concern to all participating states' (*IHT*, 20 November 1999, p. 2).

Russia agreed to reduce its troops in Georgia. 'The CFE Treaty [revised in Istanbul] ... requires that a state cannot deploy forces in another state without the host country's consent ... Russia agreed ... to dismantle two of its four bases in Georgia by mid-2001' (*FT*, 20 November 1999, p. 5). Russia agreed to remove its troops in Moldova completely by the end of 2002. 'Russia agreed ... to pull all its estimated 2,600-strong contingent out of Moldova by 2002' (*FT*, 20 November 1999, p. 5).

9 December 1999. President Yeltsin of Russia visits China and signs two border agreements with China. Provision is made for demarcation in the western region and along the eastern river frontiers. Economic co-operation across the border also featured (*The Guardian*, 10 December 1999, p. 15; *IHT*, 10 December 1999, p. 5).

31 March 2000. President-elect Vladimir Putin: 'Russia is conducting and will continue to conduct talks on reducing strategic offensive weapons further. We are tackling the task of freeing the world from excessive weapons stockpiles. Our aim is to make our nuclear weapons complex safer and more effective. We will preserve and strengthen the Russian nuclear weapons complex, even though there is no question of building it up.'

'President-elect Vladimir Putin ... called on the State Duma to quickly ratify the stalled 1993 Start 2 treaty' (*The Guardian*, 1 April 2000, p. 15).

Russia currently has about 6,000 warheads (*IHT*, 1 April 2000, p. 2).

'Russia admitted that destruction of its chemical weapons stockpiles had not begun yet and pleaded for increased Western financial aid to help it meet its commitments under the Chemical Weapons Convention' (*The Times*, 1 April 2000, p. 13).

14 April 2000. The State Duma ratifies the Start 2 treaty by 288 votes to 131, with four abstentions. Under the treaty the number of nuclear warheads will be reduced from 6,000 to between 3,000 and 3,500 on each side by the end of 2007. Multiple-warhead land-based missiles are banned under the treaty (because of the temptation to use these missiles, themselves vulnerable to a first strike, to carry out a devastating first strike). The Council of the Federation has to approve the treaty. The approval is conditional, e.g. on the US Senate approving several protocols to the treaty, on the USA not withdrawing from or violating the 26 May 1972 Anti-Ballistic Missile (ABM) Treaty, and on Nato not deploying nuclear weapons in the new Nato countries (Hungary, the Czech Republic and Poland).

President Putin (address to the State Duma prior to the vote): 'Ratification does not lead to our unilateral disarmament. After a decision on Start 2 is made, our nuclear forces will still be able at any moment and any point on the planet to destroy any enemy several times over, even if we have to fight several nuclear powers. It will preserve a powerful nuclear shield, but also allows us to channel funds to the support of conventional forces, allowing us to make our army more combat ready. Considering the present situation in the world, local conflicts will pose the main threats to Russia. We do not need an arms race. We faced one before and if we allow it again it will be worse than last time. Ratification of Start 2 will link this treaty to the 1972 ABM Treaty. I want to stress that in this case we will have the chance and we will withdraw not only from the Start 2 treaty but from the whole system of treaties on the limitation and control of strategic and conventional weapons. When Start 2 takes effect in a package with ABM, the United States will face a choice between being obviously to blame for destroying the fundamentals of strategic stability and giving up the deployment of a national anti-missile system.'

(The Council of the Federation ratified the treaty on 19 April 2000 by 112 votes to fifteen, with seven abstentions.)

Russia has rejected the US proposal to set up a national missile defence (NMD) system, a missile shield to defend the whole of US territory against a small number of strategic (intercontinental) nuclear missiles from what are now called 'states of concern' (formerly 'rogue states') such as North Korea, Iran and Iraq. China also rejects the US proposal and is particularly concerned that its own, relatively limited number of nuclear missiles will become less effective. Russia has suggested collaboration with Europe and the USA to jointly develop a programme using theatre anti-missile systems allowed under the 1972 ABM treaty to shoot down missiles just after launching (in the so-called 'boost phase'). The USA says that this system would be too slow in setting up and would involve US anti-missile systems outside US territory.

On 18 July 2000 President Putin of Russia and President Jiang Zemin signed a joint statement during the former's 17–19 July visit to China: 'The [US] plan to develop a national missile defence (NMD) system seeks unilateral military and security advantages that will pose the most grave, adverse consequences not only to the national security of Russia and China and other countries but to the security and international strategic stability of the US itself … [It] will trigger a new arms race … [Incorporating Taiwan] in any foreign missile defence system is unacceptable.'

President Vladimir Putin of Russia visited North Korea on 19–20 July 2000. 'The first [visit] by a Kremlin leader – Soviet or Russian' (*IHT*, 17 July 2000, p. 1). Putin used the occasion to add weight to the anti-NMD case. Putin (19 July): '[Kim Jong Il] voiced an idea under which North Korea is even prepared to use exclusively the rocket equipment of other countries for peaceful space research if they offered it ... North Korea is even prepared to use exclusively the technology of other countries if it is offered rocket boosters for peaceful space research ... One should expect other countries, if they assert that the DPRK poses a threat for them, would support this project. One can minimize the threat by supplying the DPRK with its rocket boosters.' (It was not exactly clear what was involved. The USA indicated that it would be prepared to launch satellites for peaceful purposes on North Korea's behalf but would not transfer rockets or technology to North Korea for the purpose.) 'Mr Putin last week said any North Korean missile threat could be reduced by "extending real security guarantees"' (*FT*, Thursday 20 July 2000, p. 10).

On 8 July 2000 the third test of the NMD system failed. There had been a previous failure and even the one allegedly successful test brought forth doubts about its meaning (allegations of rigging, for example).

President Clinton (1 September 2000): 'I simply cannot conclude, with the information I have today, that we have enough confidence in the technology and operational effectiveness of the entire NMD system to move forward to deployment ... Therefore I have decided not to authorize deployment of a National Missile Defence at this time... We can never afford to overlook the fact that the actions and reactions of others in this increasingly interdependent world bear upon our security ... We will continue to work with our allies and to strengthen the understanding ... [to] explore creative ways we can co-operate to enhance their security... [There is a] need to avoid stimulating an already dangerous regional nuclear capability from China to South Asia ... [We will] continue a robust programme of testing [the NMD].'

21 April 2000. The State Duma ratifies the Comprehensive Test Ban Treaty by 298 votes to seventy-four.

'A Russian patrol opened fire on a Japanese fishing vessel in waters around the disputed Kuril Islands between the two countries. Russian officials claimed the boat was in Russian territory, was unidentified and refused requests to halt' (*FT*, 22 April 2000, p. 6).

'The Russian coast guard on Friday [21 April] chased a Japanese fishing boat and opened fire on the vessel before seizing it near Hokkaido ... and took it back into Russian waters ... The incident threatens to revive tensions between the two counties, which have disputed maritime borders and possession of several small islands in the area since the end of World War II ... According to Russian officials, the fishing boat disobeyed a Russian patrol vessel's orders to stop for inspection in international waters between the two countries. "The intruder was shelled when it attempted to escape from Russian economic zone into neutral waters", the Itar-Tass news agency said.

The Russian authorities said that the Japanese ship was operating with its name and identification numbers concealed and that it had tried to escape after being summoned. The Japanese authorities gave an entirely different version of the incident, saying the fishing boat was operating in Japanese waters near what Japan calls its Northern Territories' (*IHT*, 22 April 2000, p. 4).

24 April–19 May 2000. An implementation review begins of the 1968 Nuclear Non-proliferation Treaty. (The treaty went into effect in 1970 and was extended indefinitely in 1995: *IHT*, 22 May 2000, p. 6.)

'A total of 187 countries have ratified the nonproliferation treaty, which took effect in 1970; India, Pakistan, Israel and Cuba have not … Three of these (India, Pakistan and Israel) are capable of producing nuclear weapons … The treaty allowed only the five declared nuclear powers (the United States, Russia, China, France and Britain) to keep their weapons, while pursuing disarmament' (*IHT*, 25 April 2000, pp. 4, 6). Article VI requires action to achieve complete disarmament (*IHT*, 26 April 2000, p. 8).

On 1 May 2000 the five main nuclear powers (the USA, Russia, France, Britain and China) issued a statement promising (without setting a timetable) 'our unequivocal commitment to the ultimate goals of a complete elimination of nuclear weapons and a treaty on general and complete disarmament under strict and effective international controls' (*IHT*, 2 May 2000, p. 4).

'Late on Saturday [20 May] … 187 countries signed the Nuclear Nonproliferation Treaty … which included a commitment from Britain, China, France, Russian and the United States … to "an unequivocal undertaking by the nuclear-weapon states to accomplish the total elimination of their nuclear arsenals, leading to nuclear disarmament" … [although the agreement does not set] a timetable for action' (*The Times*, 22 May 2000, p. 13).

31 May 2000. 'The Yeltsin decree of 1992 stated that Russia could only export nuclear equipment and materials to countries which do not possess nuclear weapons and whose entire nuclear activities are under the guarantees of the IAEA [International Atomic Energy Agency, based in Vienna]. The Putin decree revises this. The Russian government "in exceptional circumstances" can decide to export nuclear weapons to a country which has no nuclear weapons but which has not placed all its nuclear activity under IAEA safeguards. The client government has to give assurances that the equipment will not be diverted for nuclear weapons purposes' (*The Guardian*, 1 June 2000, p. 2).

3–5 June 2000. See entry in Chapter 12.

10 July 2000. A new foreign policy doctrine is published, the first revision since 23 April 1993. It was signed by President Putin on 28 June 2000.

Foreign minister Igor Ivanov: 'There is an increasing tendency towards the creation of a uni-polar world under the economic and military domination of the United States … Russia will promote the formation of a multi-polar system of international relations … [Russian foreign policy can be described as] pragmatic … Today our foreign policy resources are limited. We will concentrate them first and foremost on areas of vital importance to use … At the centre of our entire foreign policy activities [is] the pursuance of national interests … One of the key ideas of the concept is that foreign policy should actively assist in solving internal problems at the current largely crucial stage in Russia's development … [As regards economic interests] first of all the fuel and energy area … [The provision of] favourable conditions for Russia's economic growth … What we are aiming to do is to make it [foreign policy] more rational, more sustainable politically and economically.' (*CDSP*, 2000, vol. 52, no. 28, p. 5.)

President Valdimir Putin (8 July 2000): 'A foreign policy doctrine was recently approved. It acknowledges that domestic policy goals take precedence over foreign policy objectives … Pragmatism, economic effectiveness and the priority of national tasks form the foundation of this policy' (*CDSP*, 2000 vol. 52, no. 28, p. 5).

13 November 2000. Putin: 'As is well known we proposed to the United States, including the highest level, to aim toward a radical cut in nuclear warheads of our countries to 1,500, which is prefectly feasible by 2008. But this is not the limit. We are ready in the future to look at further reductions … Russia is prepared to pursue the dialogue begun more than a year ago concerning the ABM issues we disagree about. The obligation to examine all aspects of the ABM treaty is written into the agreement itself.'

Russia and the Kosovo crisis

9 March 1998. The 'contact group' of countries (the USA, Russia, France, Germany, the United Kingdom and Italy) meet in London (and agree to meet in Washington on 25 March). Although Russia is represented by its deputy foreign minister, foreign minister Yevgeni Primakov is contacted by telephone.

The six countries agree to ask the United Nations Security Council to impose a comprehensive arms embargo on the Federal Republic of Yugoslavia and also agree to stop supplying equipment that could be used for internal suppression and terrorism.

The five Western countries agree to deny visas to those responsible for repression in Kosovo and to halt government-financed export credits for trade and investment (including funding for privatization, the proceeds of which are considered to be used to finance the Milosevic regime). (Russia will reconsider these points if the repression continues.) Yugoslav assets abroad will be frozen by the five countries after 25 March 1998 if the repression continues.

The 'contact group' condemns the 'unacceptable use of force' by Serbia and the 'deplorable' actions of the Serbian police. It also condemns the 'terrorist actions' of the Kosovo Liberation Army (KLO) and agrees that Kosovo should be granted autonomy but not independence.

The six countries issue a statement, which says that within ten days Milosevic should take 'rapid and effective steps to stop the violence and engage in a commitment to find a political solution to the issue of Kosovo through dialogue'. Special police units should be withdrawn from Kosovo. Access to Kosovo should be allowed to OSCE, the International Committee of the Red Cross, 'contact group' diplomats and the UN High Commissioner for Refugees. Milosevic should commit himself publicly 'to begin a process of dialogue'. The international war crimes tribunal in the Hague should consider extending its enquiries to Kosovo. (*IHT,* 10 March 1998, pp. 1, 6; *The Independent,* 10 March 1998, p. 9; *The Guardian,* 10 March 1998, p. 2; *FT,* 10 March 1998, p. 1.)

25 March 1998. The 'contact group' agree to extend the deadline for compliance of their demands (including the full withdrawal of special police units and unconditional dialogue with ethnic Albanians). 'We expect President Milosevic to implement the process of unconditional dialogue and take political responsibility for ensuring that Belgrade engages in serious negotiations on Kosovo's status. If Belgrade fails to meet the London benchmarks and if the dialogue does not get under way within the next four weeks we shall take steps to apply further measures.' US Secretary of State Madeleine Albright: 'Mr Milosevic ... must embrace dialogue publicly, enter it without preconditions, accept outside participation and take political responsibility for making it work.' The 'contact group' countries will try to reach agreement on the terms of an arms embargo by 31 March. (*IHT,* 26 March 1998, pp. 1, 4; *FT,* 26 March 1998, p. 3; *The Telegraph,* 26 March 1998, p. 19.)

31 March 1998. The UN Security Council imposes an arms embargo on the Federal Republic of Yugoslavia. A resolution condemns the 'excessive force' used by Serbia and urges 'the authorities in Belgrade and the leadership of the Kosovar Albanian community to enter into a meaningful dialogue on political status issues'. The outcome of a dialogue should include 'an enhanced status for Kosovo which would include a substantially greater degree of autonomy and meaningful self-administration'.

29 April 1998. The 'contact group' agrees to freeze Yugoslav assets held abroad. But Russia dissents from a threat to block new foreign investments if Serbia does not sign up to a framework of talks on Kosovo by 9 May. (The ban on investment was implemented on 9 May.)

18 May 1998. The 'contact group' declares that the ban on foreign investments 'will not be put into effect'.

12 June 1998. The foreign ministers of the 'contact group' (including Russia) condemn the 'massive and disproportionate use of force'. They make four demands of Milosevic: 'immediate action' to end the repressive action by Serb military forces against the civilian ethnic Albanian population in Kosovo and the withdrawal of 'security units used for civilian repression' (i.e. special police and the army); unimpeded access for international monitors and observers; measures to help refugees return home; 'rapid progress' in talks with the Albanian leadership. If the demands are not met there will be 'moves to further measures to halt the violence and protect the civilian population, including those that may require the authorization of a United Nations Security Council resolution'. 'Kosovo Albanian extremists' are warned to refrain from violent acts.

Action will be postponed until Milosevic meets Yeltsin in Moscow on 15–16 June.

16 June 1998. Milosevic agrees to the following after talks with Yeltsin in Moscow:

1. There is a need to restart talks with Rugova but 'I see no reason to negotiate with terrorists'. Talks will include the subject of autonomy.

2. 'No repressive action will be taken against the civilian population.' Refugees will be allowed home and state aid will be allocated for rebuilding 'destroyed homes'.

3. Diplomats and international organizations such as the International Committee of the Red Cross and the United Nations High Commissioner for Refugees (but not journalists) will be allowed access to Kosovo. There will be free access to humanitarian aid.

4. 'Any withdrawal of units of the Yugoslav army ... is out of the question.' 'Serb security forces will reduce their presence outside their normal bases according to the degree to which terrorist activity diminishes.' 'There has been no ethnic cleansing. The security forces declared that there had been no civilian casualties at all in the last operation. Terrorist groups have used several villages, expelling civilians beforehand to turn houses into fortresses ... It is clear that all actions by the Serbian police were only against terrorist groups, not against civilians.' (*IHT*, 17 June 1998, pp. 1, 6; *FT*, 17 June 1998, p. 22; *The Guardian*, 17 June 1998, pp. 14, 19; *The Times*, 17 June 1998, p. 13; *The Telegraph*, 17 June 1998, p. 17.)

2 July 1998. The US announces the formation of a monitoring unit, comprising US, Russian, Austrian and Polish diplomats (*The Independent*, 3 July 1998, p. 14).

3 July 1998. Richard Holbrooke begins a fresh series of talks in the region. (He was later joined by the Russian deputy foreign minister Nikolai Afanasyevsky.)

6 July 1998. The diplomats (accredited in Yugoslavia and agreed in the 16 June 1998 talks in Moscow) begin their patrols in Kosovo.

8 July 1998. The 'contact group' meets. The group is to put the basic elements of a political settlement to the parties (although details are not given) and will work for a UN Security Council resolution calling for a ceasefire 'to permit a meaningful dialogue between the parties'. There is recognition that the Serbs have been more 'restrained' of late. A statement includes the following: 'Although the primary responsibility for the situation in Kosovo rests with Belgrade, the Contact Group acknowledges that armed

Kosovo Albanian groups also have a responsibility to avoid violence and all armed activities. The Contact Group reiterated that violence is inadmissible and will not solve the problem of Kosovo. Indeed, it will only make it more difficult to achieve a political solution. The Contact Group also concluded that all concerned on the Kosovo Albanian side should commit themselves to dialogue and a peaceful settlement and reject violence and acts of terrorism. The Contact Group insisted that those outside the Federal Republic of Yugoslavia who are supplying financial support, arms or training for armed Kosovo Albanian groups should cease doing so immediately. It is clear that the Kosovo Albanian team for all these talks must be fully representative of their community in order to speak authoritatively.'

8 August 1998. The 'contact group' presents plans for a constitutional settlement that will give the People of Kosovo control of their own internal affairs, control over their own security and real autonomy (*The Guardian*, 10 August 1998, p. 11).

The 'contact group' puts forward the following proposals: Kosovo should be given broad autonomy as a 'special part' of Serbia or a 'constituent unit' of the Federal Republic of Yugoslavia; 'Kosovo would be obligated not to secede unilaterally and Belgrade would be obligated not to alter Kosovo's status unilaterally; Kosovo should have 'constitutionally protected significant legislative, executive and judicial powers, including control of local police'; Kosovo should have its own taxation, flag and emblems and 'international relations in particular areas'. The 'contact group' expresses 'its willingness to provide political, economic, technical and other support for the implementation of such an agreement' (*FT*, 13 August 1998, p. 2).

17 August 1998. A five-day Nato exercise begins in Albania, involving troops from eleven Nato countries, Russia, Albania and Lithuania (*IHT*, 18 August 1998, p. 5).

23 September 1998. The UN Security Council approves (with China abstaining) a France-UK resolution demanding an immediate ceasefire, an end to 'all action by security forces affecting civilians', the immediate withdrawal of 'security units used for civilian repression' and 'rapid progress on a clear timetable' for peace talks. 'Further action and additional measures' will be taken in the event of non-compliance. The situation in Kosovo 'constitutes a threat to peace and security in the region'. The resolution refers to 'enforcement provisions' of Chapter 7 of the UN Charter. (Under the UN Charter a Chapter 7 resolution is militarily enforceable: *IHT*, 24 September 1998, p. 7. 'Chapter 7 of the UN Charter [is] that part of the treaty which envisages the use of force in order to stop a situation which may threaten international security': *Newsbrief*, 1998, vol. 18, no. 10, p. 74.) The resolution demands that the promises Milosevic made to President Yeltsin of Russia in June 1998 be kept. (The promises included allowing EU observers into Kosovo, guaranteed access to aid agencies and the safe return of refugees.) There should be taken 'immediate steps to avert an impending catastrophe'.

The resolution also demands that the Kosovo Albanian leadership condemn all terrorist action.

5 October 1998. Igor Sergeyev (Russia's defence minister) says that if Nato uses force against Serbia 'there would be a retreat to the Cold War' and the prospects for ratification of Start 2 would be diminished.

8 October 1998. The 'contact group' meets in London. In effect the elements of the 23 September UN Security Council resolution are reiterated. But Russia once again stresses that it will veto any Security Council recommending the use of force against Serbia.

22 January 1999. The 'contact group' officials meet in London and 'set the goal of early negotiations on a political settlement with direct international involvement'. They condemn the 'mass murder' in Racak.

'A set of principles [was] endorsed Friday [22 January] in London by the contact group ... Officials say the principles include effective self-government for the Kosovar Albanians – their own political, legal, judicial and police powers – in parallel structures to the existing Serbian ones. The point is to provide a form of political autonomy within the Yugoslav federation, but without independence, with the final status of Kosovo to be decided at least three years later through some form of referendum' (*IHT,* 25 January 1999, p. 6).

26 January 1999. The US secretary of state and the Russian foreign minister issue a joint statement urging Milosevic to allow the war crimes tribunal to investigate the massacre at Racak (*IHT,* 27 January 1999, p. 5).

29 January 1999. The 'contact group' issues a statement in London, 'summoning representatives of the Yugoslav and Serbian governments and of the Kosovo Albanians' to a conference starting no later than 6 February in Rambouillet (the chateau) near Paris. A maximum of three weeks is given for the achievement of a negotiated settlement. The representatives are expected to make adequate progress on a deal involving 'substantial autonomy' (though not independence) for Kosovo within seven days and to conclude the deal by no more than seven days after that. The conference will be co-chaired by the British and French foreign secretaries (Robin Cook and Hubert Vedrine). They will be helped by three international observers, the US envoy Christopher Hill, the EU envoy Wolfgang Petritsch and a Russian official (as yet unnamed).

'Russia ... opposes the use of force to back up the contact group's demands, which is why the threat of Nato action was not stated explicitly ... In deference to Russia, Mr Cook and Mr Vedrine declined to specify what would happen if the 19 February deadline for accepting a settlement was not met ... Mrs Albright was less restrained ... "We have committed ourselves to doing what is necessary to secure compliance from both sides. And we will maintain the credible use of force, which has proven again and again to be the only language President Milosevic understands"' (*IHT,* 30 January 1999, pp. 1, 4).

4 February 1999. The Serbian parliament votes 227 to three with three abstentions to send delegates to the talks. But the following is also passed: 'We do not accept foreign troops in our territory under any pretext of implementing an agreement that is reached.'

6 February 1999. The talks start on the scheduled date of 6 February, albeit three hours late owing to the late arrival of the ethnic Albanian delegation. Both the Yugoslav and Albanian delegations agree on a statement 'condemning in the strongest terms' a bomb attack on an Albanian-owned food store in Pristina on Saturday evening in which three ethnic Albanians were killed (including a woman and a child). 'This cowardly act, like others before, is aimed at obstructing the efforts begun today at the Rambouillet negotiations', said the statement. (There have been a series of attacks recently on both Serbian and Albanian cafés in Pristina.)

18 February 1999. President Yeltsin: 'I gave my opinion, both in writing and on the phone to Clinton, that it [bombing] won't work. This is all. This is our whole reply. We will not allow Kosovo to be touched.' The US administration says that there has been no recent communications between the two presidents (*IHT*, 19 February 1999, p. 5).

20 February 1999. The talks, scheduled to end at noon Saturday 20 February, are extended until 23 February (2 p.m. GMT). The sticking points are the Serbian objections to a Nato peacekeeping force and ethnic Albanian demands for a referendum on Kosovo's future status after three years. (There were reports on 20 February of fighting in Kosovo.)

'The Kosovo talks plunged into crisis as secretary of state Madeleine Albright said Sunday [21 February] that both Serbians and ethnic Albanians were refusing key points in the peace plan … "We had never said that there would be bombing of the Serbs if there was a no answer also from the Albanians" … The ethnic Albanian delegation balked Saturday [20 February] … Mrs Albright also berated him [Milosevic] for refusing to discuss the plan for Nato forces … The international political blueprint for Kosovo … was accepted by Serbia's president, Milan Milutinovic … The Kosovo delegation insisted that the plan should include a referendum on Kosovo's future status, which would virtually guarantee a vote for independence … Western governments … have insisted that the peace plan not prejudge the province's final status … After a three-year period of autonomy Kosovo would get international support in negotiating its future status with Belgrade … The Kosovar delegation … seemed ready to accept the deal earlier in the week … Air strikes against Serbia are "not going to help" provide stability in Kosovo if the ethnic Albanians refuse to accept the autonomy offer at Rambouillet, Robin Cook, Britain's foreign secretary, said' (*IHT*, 22 February 1999, pp. 1, 4).

23 February 1999. The peace talks are suspended until 15 March 1999, when a 'peace implementation conference' will be convened in France.

International mediators said that there was a 'consensus' on a political agreement on autonomy for Kosovo, but neither side signed any agreement.

The ethnic Albanian delegation said that it needed to hold 'technical consultations' with its 'political and military' base in Kosovo. The document does not refer to a referendum after three years. Instead, there is reference to 'taking into account the political will of the local population' and the 1975 Helsinki Final Act. The Serbs said that they were ready to 'discuss the scope and character of an international presence'.

'Under the terms of an agreement cobbled together less than two hours before the talks ended Tuesday [23 February] the ethnic Albanians said they supported the agreement "in principle" but need until 15 March to discuss the terms inside Kosovo and gauge popular reaction ... The chief opponent of the accord is Adem Demaci, a KLA political spokesman who initially opposed the negotiations and urged the commanders who took part to reject the draft accord ... After hearing Mr Demaci's arguments various military commanders telephoned ... to raise objections. These calls had a particular impact on Hashim Thaci ... Mr Thaci attempted to pressure other delegates to oppose the deal and raised objections up to the last few minutes of the talks ... His efforts came as a surprise to Western diplomats ... US officials assigned part of the blame for the failure to achieve a final settlement to Adem Demaci ... who refused to attend the talks .... Mr Demaci met Friday morning [19 February] in Slovenia with Mr Thaci and encouraged him to take a hardline tack ... It was Hashim Thaci ... who surprised Western diplomats by refusing to give his unconditional approval to the accord ...The result has been to defer by at least three weeks a Western plan to gain the ethnic Albanians' approval and use it as a lever to pressure the Belgrade government and its Serbian counterpart into also saying yes – a strategy that would be backed up by the threat of Nato air strikes' (R. Jeffrey Smith, *IHT*, 25 February 1999, pp. 1, 6).

15 March 1999. The peace talks reconvene in France (this time in Paris).

The ethnic Albanian delegation says that it is willing to sign the agreement.

Politically, the proposals involve a three-year period of autonomy. Kosovo will remain part of Serbia, which will control its economy, money, defences and foreign relations (William Pfaff, *IHT*, 11 February 1999, p. 8). Self-government will centre on elected bodies:

1. A 100-seat assembly controlling taxes and budgets representing all communities.
2. Parliament will elect a president, who will name a prime minister.
3. Thirty local councils responsible for such issues as law enforcement, schools, medical care and land use. This system will accommodate the Serbs, estimated at 5 per cent of the population of Kosovo (*IHT*, 12 February 1999, p. 10).

Kosovo will have its own judiciary.

The whole arrangement will be reviewed in three years. The draft peace plan says that 'an international meeting' will be held after three years 'to determine a mechanism for a final solution to Kosovo on the basis of the will of the people' and other factors (*FT*, 16 March 1999, p. 3). An international meeting will take account of the 'will of the people' and the 'opinions of relevant authorities' (*IHT*, 16 March 1999, p. 8).

The political plan is to be enforced by a Nato-led force (Kosovo Peace Implementation Force or Kfor) comprising around 28,000 troops. Yugoslav armed forces will have to leave the province except for 1,500 border guards, who will have to stay in their frontier positions under rules enforced by Nato troops. They will be confined to a 5 kilometre zone bordering Albania and Macedonia. Yugoslav paramilitary police will be limited to 2,575. They will stay for one year only, operating under the direct control of the international verification commission. By the end of the year a 3,000-member new local police force will have been trained. These men, now in the KLA, will be required to surrender their heavy weapons to storage depots under Nato supervision and will be banned from carrying light weapons or wearing insignia (*IHT*, 11 February 1999, p. 8, and 12 February 1999, p. 10). The Rambouillet timetable will remove all special police after a year and all army after six months, except for 1,500 border troops (*FT*, 1 April 1999, p. 2).

'Under an annex of the Rambouillet accords that were to govern the behaviour of the purely Nato forces, they were to be given full access to go anywhere they wanted in the Federal Republic of Yugoslavia and will be immune from any legal process (*IHT*, 5 June 1999, p. 4). The annex says: 'Nato personnel shall enjoy, together with their vehicles, vessels, aircraft and equipment, free and unrestricted passage and unimpeded access throughout the FRY, including associated airspace and territorial waters' (*IHT*, 11 June 1999, p. 7).

16 March 1999. The Serbian delegation's request for extensive changes to the political draft is denied by the international mediators.

18 March 1999. Representatives of the ethnic Albanian delegation sign the agreement. Russia's mediator, Boris Mayorsky, refuses to sign as a witness.

19 March 1999. The talks in Paris are called off.

The 1,380 OSCE verifiers prepare to leave the following day (*FT*, 20 March 1999, p. 2).

23 March 1999. Russian prime minister Yevgeni Primakov, on his way to a visit to the USA, turns around in mid-flight over the Atlantic after telephone discussion with US Vice-President Al Gore. A US official says: 'The Vice-President could not assure Primakov that bombing would not take place while he was here.'

It is announced that Azerbaijan has detained a Russian cargo plane (which stopped to refuel) carrying MiG fighters that may have been bound for Yugoslavia. (The following day Kazakhstan claimed ownership of the MiGs, saying they were bound for the Czech Republic.)

24 March 1999. Nato begins missile and air attacks on Yugoslavia.

'The decision by Nato to attack a sovereign nation for the first time in its fifty-year history represents a momentous transformation for a defensive alliance conceived to protect Western Europe from an invasion by the Soviet Union' (*IHT*, 24 March 1999, p. 1).

German planes take part in combat for the first time since the end of the Second World War.

Russian suspends co-operation with Nato and participation in the Partnership for Peace programme.

Nato did not seek a UN Security Council resolution to approve the bombing campaign because both Russia and China would have opposed it. Instead, Nato argued that its actions were in the spirit of previous resolutions.

26 March 1999. The UN Security Council rejects by twelve votes to three a Russian resolution calling for an immediate cessation of bombing and a return to negotiations. The three votes belonged to Russia, China and India.

Russia expels two Nato representatives.

The Russian contingent in Sfor in Bosnia opts out of US command in favour of its own command headquarters (*EEN*, 1999, vol. 12, no. 16, p. 9).

28 March 1999. Gunmen fire on the US embassy in Moscow after failing to launch a grenade.

29 March 1999. It is announced that prime minister Yevgeni Primakov is to lead a delegation to Belgrade starting the following day.

30 March 1999. In talks in Belgrade Primakov and Milosevic produce a six-point plan, including a ceasefire and an offer to withdraw some Serbian forces from Kosovo if Nato halts its air offensive and permission for 'all peaceful refugees' to return 'if they are Yugoslav citizens'. A statement from Milosevic followed: 'To open up a space for a political solution the aggression on our country has to cease immediately ... the Yugoslav leadership will accept the Russian proposal that after the cessation of bombing ... [the leadership will] begin decreasing the presence of part of its forces that are in Kosovo.' He also calls for Nato troops in Macedonia to be removed and for 'the complete cessation of Nato's support for the separatists'.

Primakov then flew to Germany, but Chancellor Schröder said: 'The proposals brought by prime minister Primakov are no basis for a political settlement ... The first and most significant signal must be the complete withdrawal of military and paramilitary forces from Kosovo so that the killing in this part of Europe can be stopped.'

Yeltsin delivers his annual state of the nation speech: 'Nato strikes against Yugoslavia continue. In circumvention of the UN Security Council and in violation of its charter ... But the crisis in the Balkans calls for well-considered, responsible actions on our part, not emotional assessments. More and more political leaders understand that in such situations brute force does not achieve anything. Russia has made its choice. It will not allow itself to be drawn into a military conflict' (*CDSP*, 1999, vol. 51, no. 13, p. 15).

31 March 1999. Russia says it is sending a reconnaissance ship to the Adriatic to gather information and is considering sending up to six more from its Black Sea fleet. ('Moscow confirmed yesterday [1 April] that intelligence information gleaned by a reconnaissance ship … would be passed to Belgrade to help counter the air campaign': *The Times*, 2 April 1999, p. 1.)

1 April 1999. Nato rejects a proposal from Boris Yeltsin calling for a meeting of foreign ministers of the Group of Eight countries.

7 April 1999. Nato says that five questions have to be answered affirmitively by Milosevic for bombing to stop:

1. Is he ready for a verifiable cessation of all military activity?
2. Is he ready to withdraw troops, police and paramilitary units from Kosovo?
3. Is he ready to accept the deployment of an international security force?
4. Will he permit the unconditional return of all refugees and unimpeded access for humanitarian aid?
5. Will he accept a political agreement based on the Rambouillet peace agreement?

9 April 1999. President Boris Yeltsin: 'I told Nato, the Americans, the Germans, do not push us towards military action. Otherwise there will be a European war for sure and possibly world war. We are against this … Russia will not get involved if the Americans do not push us. They want to use ground troops, take over Yugoslavia, make it their protectorate. We cannot allow this. Russia and the access to the Mediterranean Sea are nearby, so we can by no means give Yugoslavia away.'

US spokesman: 'We have been officially assured that Russia will not be drawn into the conflict' (*FT*, 10 April 1999, p. 1).

'The Russian leadership sent out dangerously contradictory messages on Yugoslavia yesterday after President Boris Yeltsin was reported to have ordered the country's missiles to be targeted on Nato countries involved in air strikes, before other senior officers denied any action had been taken. Gennadi Seleznyov, Communist speaker of the [State] Duma, the lower house of parliament, said in the morning that Mr Yeltsin had told him … that he had ordered nuclear weapons to be retargeted on the West … [But] by late afternoon Igor Ivanov, foreign minister, was emphasizing that he was unaware of "any orders concerning missiles"' (*FT*, 10 April 1999, p. 2). Igor Ivanov: 'As far as we know in the foreign ministry, no orders concerning missiles have been issued' (*IHT*, 10 April 1999, p. 1).

12 April 1999. 'In a joint statement from nineteen Nato foreign ministers the alliance declared Monday [12 April] that Nato "will hold President Milosevic and the Belgrade leadership responsible for the well-being of all civilians in Kosovo"' (*IHT*, 13 April 1999, p. 1). 'The Nato ministers restated their desire to "work constructively with Russia in reaching a political solution" to the crisis … Officials said an offer to Russia could include having Russian troops on an international peacekeeping force, which, according to defence minister Alain Richard of France, need not necessarily come under Nato authority … The foreign minister insisted that air strikes would continue until Mr Milosevic acceded to five conditions:

1. Ensure a verifiable stop to all military action and the immediate ending of violence and repression.
2. Agree to the stationing in Kosovo of an international military presence.
3. Ensure the withdrawal from Kosovo of the military, police and paramilitary forces.
4. Agree to the unconditional and safe return of all refugees and displaced persons, and unhindered access to them by humanitarian aid organizations.
5. Provide credible assurance of his willingness to work on the basis of the Rambouillet accords in the establishment for Kosovo in conformity with international law and the charter of the United Nations.

'Nato foreign ministers ... urged Russia first to help broker and then to police a peace settlement that could give Kosovo "internationally protected status"' (*The Independent*, 13 April 1999, p. 2).

The Yugoslav parliament votes in favour of a political union with Russia and Belarus. '[But] representatives of the Yugoslav republic of Montenegro boycotted the vote' (*FT*, 13 April 1999, p. 1). 'It was Gennadi Seleznyov, the Communist speaker of the Duma ... who raised the idea of a union last Friday [9 April] after meeting Mr Milosevic. Mr Seleznyov also suggested that the idea had been received positively by President Boris Yeltsin. Striking a note of caution, however ... Mr Yeltsin's chief foreign policy adviser said yesterday [12 April] that ... the inclusion of other countries [other than Russia and Belarus] could be taken "only after in-depth analysis of the entire legal situation and considering the national interests of Russia"' (p. 2).

13 April 1999. US secretary of state Madeleine Albright (after meeting Russian foreign minister Igor Ivanov): 'Our sense is that it [an international military presence] has to have a Nato core, with other countries providing other aspects, or working in co-operation with it.'

14 April 1999. Yeltsin appoints Viktor Chernomyrdin as his special envoy on the Kosovo crisis.

19 April 1999. Yeltsin comments on television: 'Bill Clinton hopes to win. He hopes Milosevic will capitulate, give up the whole of Yugoslavia, make it an America's protectorate. We will not allow this. This is a strategic place, the Balkans.'

Presidents Clinton and Yeltsin then have a long telephone conversation. Yeltsin reiterates that Russia is willing to mediate and that Russia will not intervene militarily. Russia will not send any more naval ships to join the reconnaissance ship already in the Adriatic. He says that ethnic Albanian refugees must be allowed to return home.

20 April 1999. 'President Yeltsin [in Russian newspaper reports on 20 April] again stressed Moscow's readiness to play the role of intermediary ... He urged journalists not to exaggerate the prospects of a union linking Russia, Belarus and Yugoslavia, a proposal that has been enthusiastically endorsed by the opposition-dominated Russian parliament. "We will consider it ... We cannot discard it now because we would abandon Milosovic. And we want to embrace him a bit more closely. And hold him a bit tight"' (*IHT*, 21 April 1999, p. 8).

The Russian Patriarch Alexei II visits Belgrade.

22 April 1999. 'Russia and Yugoslavia were reported last night [22 April] to have proposed an international presence in Kosovo under the auspices of the United Nations ... The new development ... came after talks in Belgrade between Viktor Chernomyrdin [the Russian special envoy] ... and Slobodan Milosevic ... Mr Chernomyrdin was reported to have said that Mr Milosevic, who had previously opposed the presence of foreign troops in Kosovo, was ready to allow "international forces" in Kosovo. But one condition was that Russia would have to take part' (*FT*, 23 April 1999, p. 1). '"Yugoslavia has agreed to the presence in Kosovo of forces from other countries", he [Chernomyrdin] said on returning to Moscow. "Military forces. There is a war going on there." But the Yugoslav foreign ministry said yesterday [23 April] Mr Milosevic had agreed to "a UN, unarmed presence, an observer presence in Kosovo"' (*FT*, 24 April 1999, p. 2). 'Such a force would include Russian troops and fly a UN flag, Mr Chernomyrdin said ... But in Belgrade the foreign ministry spokesman [said on 23 April that this refers to] "a UN unarmed presence in Kosovo"' (*IHT*, 24 April 1999, p. 4).

23 April 1999. Nato celebrates its fiftieth anniversary. (Nato was actually founded on 4 April 1949). Of the forty-three governments invited to attend the Nato summit only Russia declined the invitation, in protest at the Nato bombing of Yugoslavia.

25 April 1999. The end of the three-day Nato summit. There was agreement to intensify the bombing campaign. Madeleine Albright (US secretary of state): 'There was really genuine support for an intensified air campaign.'

'[Nato] Leaders met their counterparts in the seven states neighbouring Yugoslavia. The Nato spokesman said the alliance had given security assurances to the frontline states ... He said two of the seven countries, Romania and Slovenia, had granted access to their air space, while a parliamentary vote was expected tomorrow [27 April] in Bulgaria on the same issue ... Nato's military command is now drafting details of a naval blockade ordered Friday [23 April] by allied leaders. But many Nato ministers said the scope of the measure, including whether it would affect Russia and other non-Nato shipping, was still under discussion' (*FT*, 26 April 1999, p. 1). 'Nato yesterday [25 April] pledged to protect the frontline states around Kosovo against any Yugoslav aggression and launched a wider strategy to rebuild the Balkans ... Looking beyond the war Nato said it planned to upgrade its security relations with Balkan countries, principally through its partnership for peace programmes, while EU members of Nato said the EU would similarly help Balkan countries with aid and trade preferences ... US President Bill Clinton suggested south-east Europe needed regional co-operation as well as outside aid. The US and Europe "should do more to draw these countries closer to each other and relate them to all the institutions of

Europe, the US and Canada" ... The Washington summit stressed the need for all international organizations – chiefly Nato, the EU and OSCE – to play their part in reconstructing democracy and prosperity in the Balkans' (p. 2).

27 April 1999. 'This week Moscow has bounced back into the limelight as Western leaders seek Russia's help in concluding a political settlement to the conflict' (*FT,* 28 April 1999, p. 2).

2 May 1999. 'A further peace initiative was launched in Vienna by members of the US Congress and the Duma, Russia's parliament. Their talks were attended by Dragomir Karic, a Yugoslav businessman and friend of Mr Milosevic, acting as an adviser to the Russian delegation ... The joint Congress-Duma statement seeks an end to Nato bombing of Yugoslavia, withdrawal of Serbian troops from Kosovo and cessation of military activities of the KLA. Under the proposals the make-up of the international force would be discussed by the five permanent members of the United Nations Security Council, Macedonia, Albania, Yugoslavia and the "recognized leadership of Kosovo"' (*FT,* 3 May 1999, p. 1).

3 May 1999. Russian special envoy Viktor Chernomyrdin meets President Clinton in Washington.

6 May 1999. Foreign ministers of the G8 countries adopt the following general principles on the political solution to the Kosovo crisis:

1. Immediate, verifiable end of violence and repression in Kosovo.
2. Withdrawal from Kosovo of military, police and paramilitary forces.
3. Deployment in Kosovo of effective international civil and security presences, endorsed and adopted by the United Nations, capable of guaranteeing the achievement of the common objective.
4. Establishment of an interim administration for Kosovo to be decided by the Security Council of the United Nations to ensure conditions for a peaceful and normal life for all inhabitants in Kosovo.
5. The safe and free return of all displaced persons and unimpeded access to Kosovo by humanitarian aid organizations.
6. A political process towards the establishment of an interim political framework agreement providing a substantial self-government for Kosovo, taking full account of the Rambouillet accords and the principles of sovereignty and territorial integrity of the Federal Republic of Yugoslavia and the other countries of the region. Also the demilitarization of the UCK (Kosovo Liberation Army).
7. Comprehensive approach to the economic developments and stabilization of the crisis region.

In order to implement these principles the G8 foreign ministers instructed their political directors to prepare elements of a UN Security Council resolution.

The G8 presidency will inform the Chinese government of the results of today's meeting.

'Russia's foreign minister, Igor Ivanov, said his country would insist on the interpretation that Yugoslavia's sovereignty meant Nato troops could not take part in the international security presence without Yugoslavia's consent. "Without the agreement of the state nothing is possible", he said' (*IHT*, 7 May 1999, p. 5).

'In Belgrade President Milosevic was quoted as saying in an interview that he could accept a UN peace mission armed with "self-defence weapons" but it must not include any of the nineteen Nato countries. "We cannot accept an occupation force, not under a Nato flag or a UN flag", Mr Milosevic said. He said Yugoslavia would be willing to invite non-Nato countries, such as Russia, Ukraine, Belarus or even Ireland, but could not accept the presence of troops from any of the allied nations that participated in the bombing campaign' (*IHT*, 7 May 1999, p. 5).

7 May 1999. The Chinese embassy in Belgrade is bombed.

Nato described the bombing as a 'terrible accident'. It was the result of 'faulty information' as regards targeting, mistaking the building for the federal directorate of supply and procurement (a military office). (It was later revealed that an outdated map had been used.) Three Chinese journalists were killed. Angry demonstrations followed in China, including three days of mob attacks on US and UK embassies. On 10 May China suspended co-operation with the USA on stopping proliferation of weapons of mass destruction, discussions about human rights and high level military contacts. On 15 June a US delegation arrived in Beijing to explain the bombing. But the following day China announced that it had found the explanation 'unconvincing'.)

11 May 1999. Viktor Chernomyrdin visits Beijing. '"The bombings must stop" before a peace proposal can be considered, Mr Chernomyrdin said … "This is Russia's and China's basic attitude"' (*IHT*, 12 May 1999, p. 1).

12 May 1999. President Yeltsin dismisses prime minister Yevgeni Primakov.

A Kremlin spokesman: 'Yeltsin warned that Russia would withdraw from co-operation in negotiations if its proposals and mediation efforts for the Kosovo conflict were ignored' (*IHT*, 13 May 1999, p. 1).

27 May 1999. The UN's International Criminal Tribunal for the Former Yugoslavia indicts Slobodan Milosevic (and four others), the first time that this has happened to a sitting head of state. The charge: 'The accused planned, instigated, ordered, committed or otherwise aided and abetted in a campaign of terror and violence directed at Kosovo Albanian citizens.'

28 May 1999. 'Russia has agreed to tell Slobodan Milosevic that Nato forces must be at the core of an international force in postwar Kosovo … Western diplomats said. Until now Moscow has never challenged Mr Milosevic's position of accepting a lightly armed peacekeeping force, including Russian forces and troops from neutral nations, but excluding units from Nato countries that have fought against Serbia' (*IHT*, 29 May 1999, p. 1).

2 June 1999. The International Court of Justice in The Hague rejects Yugoslavia's request for an interim injunction ('provisional measures') against Nato's bombing campaign. The vote was twelve to three (the three being the judges from Yugoslavia, Russia and China).

Viktor Chernomyrdin and Finnish president and EU envoy Martti Ahtisaari fly to Belgrade after extensive talks in Bonn at an EU summit (which included US deputy secretary of state Strobe Talbott) which resulted in an international peace plan to be presented to Slobodan Milosevic. Martti Ahtisaari: 'It is neither negotiations nor an ultimatum. It is making an offer for peace and spelling out in no uncertain terms what the conditions are.' They arrive later than planned and had only a brief meeting with Slobodan Milosevic.

3 June 1999. The Yugoslav government and Serbian parliament accept the international peace plan brought by Martti Ahtisaari and Viktor Chernomyrdin. (Note that the footnote mentioned in point 10 was not voted upon: *IHT*, 8 June 1999, p. 8.)

The text of the document is as follows:

1. Immediate and verifiable end of violence and repression in Kosovo.

2. Verifiable withdrawal from Kosovo of all military, police and paramilitary forces according to a rapid time schedule.

3. Deployment in Kosovo, under the aegis of the United Nations, of effective international civilian and security presences.

4. The international security presence with substantial Nato participation must be deployed under unified command and control and authorized to establish a safe environment for all people in Kosovo and to facilitate the safe return to their homes of all displaced persons and refugees.

5. Establishment of an interim administration for Kosovo as part of the international civilian presence under which the people of Kosovo can enjoy substantial autonomy within the FRY [Federal Republic of Yugoslavia] to be decided by the Security Council of the United Nations. Interim administration to provide transitional administration while establishing and overseeing the development of provisional democratic self-governing institutions to ensure conditions for a peaceful and normal life of all inhabitants in Kosovo.

6. After withdrawal an agreed number of Yugoslav and Serbian personnel will be permitted to return to perform the following functions: liaison with international civil mission and international presence; marking/clearing minefields; maintaining a presence at Serb patrimonial sites; maintaining a presence at key border crossings.

7. Safe and free return of all refugees and displaced persons under the supervision of the UNHCR and unimpeded access to Kosovo by humanitarian aid organizations

8. A political process towards the establishment of an interim political framework agreement providing for a substantial self-government for Kosovo, taking full account of the Rambouillet accords and the principles of sovereignty and territorial integrity of the FRY and the other countries of

the region, and the demilitarization of the UCK [KLA]. Negotiations between the parties for a settlement should not delay or disrupt the establishment of democratic self-governing institutions.

9. Comprehensive approach to the economic development and stabilization of the crisis region. This will include the implementation of a Stability Pact for South-Eastern Europe with broad international participation in order to further promotion of democracy, economic prosperity, stability and regional co-operation.

10. Suspension of military activity will require acceptance of the principles set forth above in addition to agreement to other, previously identified, required elements, which are specified in the footnote. A military-technical agreement will then be rapidly concluded.

Withdrawal: Procedures for withdrawals, including the phased, detailed schedule and delineation of a buffer area in Serbia beyond which forces will be withdrawn.

Returning personnel: Equipment associated [with] the returning personnel; Terms of reference for their functional responsibilities; Timetable for their return; Delineation of their geographical areas of operation; Rules governing their relationship to international security presence and international civil mission.

Other required elements:

Rapid and precise timetable for withdrawals meaning, e.g. seven days to complete withdrawal; air defence weapons withdrawn outside a 25 km mutual safety zone within forty-eight hours.

Return of personnel for the four functions specified above will be under the supervision of the international security presence and will be limited to a small agreed number (hundreds not thousands).

Suspension of military activity will occur after the beginning of verifiable withdrawals.

The discussion and achieving of a military-technical agreement shall not extend the previously determined time for completion of withdrawals.

A second footnote refers to the composition of the international force. It is understood that Nato considers an international security force with 'substantial Nato participation' to mean unified command and control and having Nato at the core. This in turn means a unified Nato chain of command under the political direction of the North Atlantic Council in consultation with non-Nato force contributors. All Nato countries, partners and other countries will be eligible to contribute to the international security force. Nato units will be under Nato command. It is understood that Russia's position is that the Russian contingent will not be under Nato command and its relationship to the international presence will be governed by relevant additional agreements.

7 June 1999. Foreign ministers of the G8 countries (i.e. the G7 countries plus Russia) announce that agreement has been reached on seventeen of the twenty points in a resolution to be placed before the UN Security Council. Talks will resume tomorrow.

8 June 1999. Foreign ministers of the G8 countries agree on a draft resolution to be presented to the UN Security Council. The following sequence of events is envisaged: (1) signature of the military-technical agreement; (2) verifiable start of the Serb military withdrawal; (3) a pause in Nato bombing; (4) adoption of the resolution by the UN Security Council; (5) deployment of peacekeeping forces; (6) formal end of the Nato air campaign upon completion of the Serb withdrawal. Events 2, 3 and 4 are meant to be almost simultaneous. This will allow fulfilment of the demand by Russia and China for a halt in bombing before the passing of the resolution.

Key portions of the draft resolution are as follows:

> The Security Council:
> Demands in particular that the Federal Republic of Yugoslavia put an immediate and verifiable end to violence and repression in Kosovo and begin/complete verifiable phased withdrawals from Kosovo of all military, police and paramilitary forces according to a rapid timetable, with which the deployment of the international security presence in Kosovo will be synchronized. (Note that an aim here is to avoid a vacuum which the KLA might try to fill. Another aim is to prevent withdrawing Yugoslav troops taking revenge on ethnic Albanians.)
>
> Confirms that after the withdrawal an agreed number of Yugoslav and Serb military and police personnel will be permitted to return to Kosovo to perform the functions in accordance with Annex 2.
>
> Decides on the deployment in Kosovo, under UN auspices, of civil and security presences, with appropriate equipment and personnel as required.
>
> Requests the secretary-general to appoint in consultation with the Security Council a special representative to control the implementation of the civil presence, and further requests the secretary-general to instruct his special representative to co-ordinate closely with the international security presence to ensure that both presences operate towards the same goals and in a mutually supportive manner. (The tasks of the 'special representative' include 'promoting the establishment, pending a final settlement, of substantial autonomy and self-government in Kosovo': quoted in *IHT*, 14 June 1999, p. 8.)
>
> Authorizes member states and relevant international organizations to establish the international security presence in Kosovo as set out in point 4 of Annex 2. ('All necessary means' implies that military action may be used if necessary, as laid out under Chapter 7 of the UN charter. Chapter 7 authorizes the Security Council to intervene against a sovereign state in the interests of international peace.)
>
> Decides that the responsibilities of the international security presence to be deployed in Kosovo will include: demilitarizing the Kosovo

Liberation Army (KLA); establishing a secure environment in which refugees and displaced persons can return home in safety; supervising de-mining until the international civil presence can take responsibility for this task; border-monitoring duties.

Authorizes the secretary-general to establish an international civil presence in Kosovo in order to provide an interim administration under which the people of Kosovo can enjoy substantial autonomy.

Demands full co-operation by all concerned, including the international security presence, with the International Criminal Tribunal for the Former Yugoslavia.

Demands that the KLA and other armed Kosovo Albanian groups end immediately all offensive actions and comply with the requirements for demilitarization as laid down by the head of the international security presence.

Decides that the civil and security presences, established for an initial period of twelve months, are to continue thereafter unless the Security Council decides otherwise.

Annex 1:
Petersberg Principles, 6 May 1999 (excerpts):

The G8 foreign ministers adopted the following general principles on the political solution to the Kosovo crisis:

Deployment in Kosovo of effective international civil and security presences, endorsed and adopted by the United Nations, capable of guaranteeing the achievement of the common objectives.

The safe and free return of all refugees and displaced persons and unimpeded access to Kosovo by humanitarian aid organizations.

A political process towards the establishment of an interim political framework agreement providing for a substantial self-government for Kosovo.

Annex 2 (3 June 1999 agreement):
Agreement should be reached on the following principles to move toward a resolution of the Kosovo crisis:

Verifiable withdrawal from Kosovo of all military, police and paramilitary forces according to a rapid time schedule.

Deployment in Kosovo, under UN auspices, of effective international civilian and security presences.

The international security presence with substantial Nato participation must be deployed under unified command and control.

Establishment of an interim administration for Kosovo as part of the international civilian presence under which the people of Kosovo can enjoy substantial autonomy.

After withdrawal an agreed number of Yugoslav and Serbian personnel will be permitted to return to perform the following functions: liaison with international civil mission and international presence; marking/clearing minefields; maintaining a presence at Serb patrimonial sites; maintaining a presence at key border crossings.

Safe and free return of all refugees and displaced persons.

A political process towards the establishment of an interim political framework agreement providing for a substantial self-government for Kosovo, taking full account of the Rambouillet accords and the principles of sovereignty and territorial integrity of the Federal Republic of Yugoslavia and the other countries of the region, and the demilitarization of the KLA.

Suspension of military activity will require acceptance of the principles set forth above in addition to agreement to other, previously identified, required elements.

Rapid and precise timetable for withdrawals; air defence weapons withdrawn outside a 25 km mutual safety zone within forty-eight hours.

Return of personnel for the four functions specified above will be under the supervision of the international security presence and will be limited to a small agreed number (hundreds not thousands).

Suspension of military activity will occur after the beginning of verifiable withdrawals.

The discussion and achieving of a military-technical agreement shall not extend the previously determined time for completion of withdrawals.

The exact relationship with Russian forces will be the subject of negotiations between Nato and Russia.

9 June 1999. The military-technical agreement is signed on behalf of Nato by Lieutenant-General Michael Jackson (the British general in charge of the allied rapid reaction force and of Kfor). Two Yugoslav generals sign on behalf of the FRY. (Dragoljub Ojdanovic, chief of the general staff of the armed forces of the FRY, did not attend the talks because he has been indicted as a war criminal by the international court.)

10 June 1999. A formal suspension of Nato bombing is announced after a start to the Yugoslav withdrawal was verified. (But Nato air strikes actually stopped when the military technical agreement was signed.) This was followed by the UN Security Council approving the resolution (with only minor amendments) by fourteen to zero, with China abstaining.

'[The bombing campaign ended with] the lack of a single allied casualty in combat' (*IHT,* 11 June 1999, p. 1).

11 June 1999. 'Nato military commanders were caught by surprise Friday [11 June] when Russia sent the first foreign peacekeeping troops into Yugoslavia ... A Russian convoy consisting of about fifty vehicles and up to 200 soldiers crossed the Yugoslav border from Bosnia early in the day... The battalion was drawn from some 1,300 Russian soldiers who are based in the northern Bosnian town of Ugljevik ... The US deputy secretary of state Trobe Talbott ... reversed course in mid-air and flew back to Moscow Friday after hearing about the Russian troop movement ... Foreign minister Igor Ivanov ... said the Russian soldiers were preparing to assume positions along the northern rim of Kosovo but did not plan to enter Kosovo without co-ordinating their moves with allied commanders ... Russia insists on having its own sector, preferably in the north where Serbian religious shrines and many of the province's Serb inhabitants are located. But Nato commanders fear that a Russian sector would quickly lead to the de facto partition of Kosovo ... Nato military authorities have divided the Kosovo map into five sectors that would be controlled by allied forces from Britain, France, Italy, Germany and the United States ... As of Friday 19,300 Nato soldiers had assembled inside Macedonia while another 7,300 were on the ground in Albania' (*IHT*, 12 June 1999, pp. 1, 4). 'The sudden move by this Russian unit, which left the Nato-led peacekeeping force in Bosnia and headed for Kosovo, seemed to fit the political defiance in Moscow led by a hard-line military commander, General Leonid Ivashov ... General Ivashov handled the military side of negotiations with Belgrade involving Viktor Chernomyrdin ... who had overall responsibility for them and has been criticized in Moscow for failing to win more for Russia ... General Ivashov had confronted US envoy, deputy secretary of state Strobe Talbott, on Russia's role in postwar Kosovo in talks this week in Moscow, which ended in deadlock after the Russian general was quoted as saying that Russian wanted to run a sector in the north of Kosovo, an area with a heavy population of ethnic Serbs ... Mr Talbott ... insisted publicly after two days of difficult talks in Moscow that Nato could not accept Russia's demands for a separate zone in northern Russia because it would amount to disguised partition' (p. 4).

'It was confirmed yesterday [14 June] that Moscow had tried to fly additional troops from Russia into Kosovo on Friday evening [11 June] ... Hungary's prime minister said he had rejected a request from Moscow to allow six aircraft, containing 600 paratroops, to use Hungarian air space. Bulgaria said yesterday [14 June] it had also refused aceess to Russian military aircraft' (*FT*, 15 June 1999, p. 4).

'So far Bulgaria, Romania and Hungary ... have resisted Russian requests to use their airspace, saying that they are waiting clarification about the disposition of the peacekeeping force' (*IHT*, 16 June 1999, p. 1).

12–13 June 1999. The Russian troops arrived at Pristina airport in the early hours of Saturday 12 June, while Nato forces did not start moving into Kosovo until dawn. The Russian troops were welcomed by ethnic Serbs and Nato forces by ethnic Albanians. The Russian forces blocked off the airport, which led to a standoff with Nato forces.

'Only after a tense face-off and a three-hour negotiation between officers from the opposing sides was agreement reached to divide control of the Pristina airport' (*IHT*, 14 June 1999, p. 10).

It was unclear who had issued the orders for the rapid advance of Russian troops.

'[Russian] foreign minister Igor Ivanov initially said that the deployment was a mistake and that the troops would be withdrawn, suggesting that the defence ministry had acted on its own. But as dawn broke and the troops stayed put military officials issued their own statement saying that the operation had been cleared at the highest level' (*IHT*, 14 June 1999, p. 10). 'The Russians ... have vowed not to send additional troops without prior agreement' (p. 10).

'On Sunday [13 June] Mr Ivanov ... told CNN that the Russian contingent had been ordered to leave Pristina ... In fact Mr Yeltsin later said he approved of the manoeuvre. Mr Ivanov told reporters that the movement of the troops was "something of a surprise for me" but brushed aside the matter as insignificant and "technical". "In the final count the foreign minister is not obligated to follow by the minute all these issues of troops being sent and so forth"' (*IHT*, 14 June 1999, p. 10).

'In the early hours of Saturday morning [12 June] Mr Ivanov issued a statement claiming the troop deployment was a "mistake" ... President Boris Yeltsin personally authorized the decision to move 200 Bosnian-based peacekeeping troops into Kosovo before Nato forces arrived, Russia's foreign ministry said yesterday [13 June]. [Although] Igor Ivanov ... admitted his ministry had not been informed about the move' (*FT*, 14 June 1999, p. 2). 'Nato officials did note that Russia had broken an agreement [relating to Sfor in Bosnia] by sending its troops from Bosnia' (*FT*, 16 June 1999, p. 2).

Sevodnya (14 June 1999, p. 1): 'According to our information, [Lieutenant General Viktor] Zavarin's column got its orders from chief of the general staff Anatoli Kvashnin, who in turn had received his orders from the Kremlin' (*CDSP*, 1999, vol. 51, no. 24, p. 1).

Nezavisimaya Gazeta (16 June 1999, p. 1): 'Plans for the operation ... were drawn up by a group of officers attached to the first administration of the chief operations administration of the Russian armed forces' general staff ... After the plan was approved by chief of the general staff Anatoli Kvashnin and defence minister Igor Sergeyev, the document was submitted to Boris Yeltsin on 10 June ... [The president] immediately gave the military the go-ahead' (*CDSP*, 1999, vol. 51, no. 24, p. 4).

'British paratroopers could have been at the Pristina airport long before the Russians had the [US] White House not imposed a twenty-four-hour delay so that European forces would not enter Kosovo before the US marines and steal the televised glory' (William Pfaff, *IHT*, 17 June 1999, p. 8).

15 June 1999. 'Russia sent a convoy of eleven vehicles and twenty-nine men from its peacekeeping duties in Bosnia on a journey across Yugoslavia yesterday [15 June] to take food and water [fuel and money] to its troops holding Pristina airport' (*FT*, 16 June 1999, p. 2).

'The Russians showed no signs Tuesday [15 June] of leaving the Pristina airport. Indeed, a convoy of eleven vehicles is en route from Bosbia through

Serbia to resupply the approximately 200 Russians in Pristina with fuel and food. But Nato officials said they were encouraged that this time the Russians requested permission from the Nato commanders in Bosnia to leave their posts and take the supplies. Last week when the Russians left Bosnia for Kosovo, they did so without informing the commanders in Bosnia' (*IHT*, 17 June 1999, p. 4).

18 June 1999. 'Late Friday [18 June] the US secretary of defence, William Cohen, reached an agreement with Russian officials, including the defence minister, Marshal Igor Sergeyev, to add 3,600 Russian troops to the peacekeeping force, which will ultimately total more than 50,000. Russia will deploy troops in the American, German and French sectors and control the grounds of Pristina airport, while leaving air control to Nato forces' (*IHT*, 21 June 1999, p. 5). 'The agreement provides that the Russian troops will operate within the US, German and French sectors of Kosovo, plus Pristina's airport in the British sector ... British forces will direct air traffic ... With no separate Russian sector there will be no obvious geographic basis for partition. Russian troops will serve under Russian commanders, who in turn will report to the top Nato officers of their sectors' (p. 8). Russian troops will not have to apprehend people accused of committing war crimes (*IHT*, 1 July 1999, p. 5).

'Moscow would control its own soldiers, but would co-ordinate all activities with the respective national commanders of the sectors, who in turn would answer to Nato's chief commander in Kosovo, British General Mike Jackson ... Britain has committed about 13,000 troops, France 9,000, Germany 8,000 and the USA 7,500' (*IHT*, 19 June 1999, p. 1).

20 June 1999. 'Javier Solana said Sunday [20 June] that all Serbian troops and police had left Kosovo province in compliance with the agreement signed 9 June and that he was, therefore, officially terminating Nato's bombing campaign against Yugoslavia ... Yugoslav forces completed their pullout eleven hours before the midnight deadline' (*IHT*, 21 June 1999, p. 5).

'Lieutenant General Sir Mike Jackson, the Kfor commander, had reported Kosovo clear of all uniformed Yugoslav forces – except for a few stragglers – by 1 pm local time yesterday [20 June] ... eleven hours ahead of the deadline of midnight local time' (*FT*, 21 June 1999, p. 1).

18–20 June 1999. The G8 countries meet in Cologne, although President Yeltsin of Russia made an appearance only on the final day.

'Although Western leaders took great pains to welcome Russia as an equal partner, Russia failed to persuade other leaders to change their minds on how to deal with President Slobodan Milosevic of Yugoslavia. Mr Clinton and other leaders adamantly refused to channel reconstruction funds to Serbia as long as Mr Milosevic remained in office' (*IHT*, 21 June 1999, p. 1). 'In a symbolic achievement Russia managed to delete a strongly phrased warning from the final communiqué that made clear that Serbia could not expect reconstruction aid as long as Mr Milosevic remained in office. But he [prime minister Sergei Stepashin of Russia] did not change the positions of the

United States, Britain and France. The Cologne declaration, however, opens the way for immediate humanitarian aid to the entire Balkan region, conditioning "reconstruction" aid to democratic reforms in Serbia. The eight leaders endorsed the creation of a "stability pact" for the Balkans, an initiative of the EU' (p. 6). 'The European Commission, meanwhile, announced it would set up a special agency in Pristina that would handle about Ecu 500 million ($520 million) a year of humanitarian aid for the next three years, on an unconditional basis ... Further aid will have to wait a donors conference, to be held during July... Only later in the year will the broader reconstruction issue be addressed, with a second donors conference being convened ... A senior EU financial official said Western financial support would be concentrated on Kosovo in a first stage, to be followed by other countries affected by the war and finally by the Balkan region as a whole ... How much the United States will spend on Kosovo reconstruction remains unclear, although Europe has indicated that it will bear most of the burden' (p. 6).

'The leaders affirmed their strong support for the EU-led stability pact for the reconstruction of south-east Europe ... There were no specifics on how much money would be involved, although it was accepted that Europe should pay the lion's share ... Samual Berger, national security adviser to President Clinton, said there was a line between humanitarian aid and reconstruction aid. But "where that line is, is not self-evident. Is getting electric lights back on for the winter humanitarian aid or reconstruction?"' (*FT*, 21 June 1999, p. 3).

Leaders from the G8 countries, the EU and Balkan countries plan to meet in Sarajevo in the summer to discuss the future of the region and an EU stability pact for south-east Europe (*FT*, 22 June 1999, p. 24).

21 June 1999. Nato and the KLA announce a detailed demilitarization agreement drawn up by Nato officers and KLA commanders. The agreement is signed by Lieutenant-General Sir Michael Jackson and Hashim Thaci.

4 July 1999. 'A Nato delegation flew to Moscow on Sunday [4 July] in hopes of resolving the latest disagreement over the role of Russian peacekeepers in Kosovo. Moscow had planned to send more peacekeeping troops to Yugoslavia on Sunday, but the United States convinced Romania, Bulgaria and Hungary to deny Russia an air corridor. The United States and Nato insist that the details of the Russian mission be worked out first' (*IHT*, Monday 5 July 1999, p. 1). 'Two weeks after an agreement reached in Helsinki Russian military negotiators last week sought to alter it by having their troops in Kosovo take orders only from Russian officers, rather than be under the formal command of Nato. Russia also wants to station forces in the Italian as well as French, American and German sectors ... Allied officials has expected to settle the details of Russia's peacekeeping role at high-level military talks ... last week ... The Russian zone in the German sector borders on the Italian sector in western Kosovo and allied officials say that the Russians want to operate in that sector as well' (p. 4). 'Officials worked out an agreement last month [June] in Helsinki on peacekeeping operations in Kosovo. But the accord was somewhat vague and the two sides have interpreted it differently. The United States, for example, acknowledges that Russian peacekeepers will not formally report to Nato commanders. But Washington says Russian forces should be prepared to follow instructions from Nato commanders in the field. Moscow, though, has underscored that its troops will be under a separate Russian command, and it has never been clear how closely the Russian military is prepared to co-operate with Nato. Moscow has ordered an American military attaché to leave the country… The American officer left Russia Thursday evening [1 July] … One Clinton administration official speculated that the expulsion might have been a response to a recent decision by the United States to expel a Russian official from the United States on accusations of spying… Recently the Russian held a Cold-War-style military exercise in which two old Tupolev-95 Bear bombers approached Iceland' (p. 5). 'The TU-95 Bear bombers were intercepted by four US F-15 fighters and a P–3 patrol plan near Iceland on Friday [25 June] and escorted in a clockwise flight around the island … Norway, which like Iceland is a Nato member, also scrambled jets to meet two other TU-140 Blackjack bombers that flew down the Norwegian coastline, but Russian reports said the interceptors failed to reach the bombers before they turned back. US officials said the flights formed part of extensive exercises by the Russian armed forces last week. Though Russian bombers often probed Western defences during the Cold War, officials said no such activity had been reported in a decade … The bomber flights occurred five days into what Russia said was a previously scheduled exercise, West '99, that involved up to 50,000 troops from five military districts and three naval fleets. The exercise involved more than thirty ships, four submarines … as well as the Russian air force and navy aircraft. US defence officials noted that it was the largest Russian military exercise since Russia restructured its air forces at the end of the Cold War' (*IHT*, Friday 2 July, pp. 1, 4).

5 July 1999. 'Negotiators for Nato and the Kremlin agreed on terms Monday [5 July] for deploying peacekeepers in Kosovo … The accord appeared to settle at least some aspects of a weeks-long dispute over precisely who would issue orders to the Russian troops and where they would serve … But neither side would disclose details of the negotiations … The nature of the compromise that allowed Monday's agreement was not clear … Russian officials said … that a Russian liaison at Nato headquarters in Belgium would continue to work on other points of the deployment… A workable formula for the operation seemed to have been devised last month. The accord stated that Russian troops would not serve under a direct Nato command, but instead would accept – and by and large execute – Nato orders issued through a liaison. But after the signing Moscow began arguing that its troops should be allowed to follow Russian orders, not Nato's, according to Western officials. The Russians sought to alter the boundaries of the regions in which they were stationed so that troops in French- and German-controlled sectors of Kosovo could effectively act as one force' (*IHT*, 6 July 1999, pp. 1, 4).

'The deal was understood to include a concession to Russia that it could deploy two battalions – equivalent to about 1,000 soldiers – rather than one in the German-run zone of Kosovo. There had been suggestions earlier that Russia aimed to deploy one of the two battalions originally due to serve within the US zone in the Italian zone instead' (*FT*, 6 July 1999, p. 2).

23 July 1999. Russia ends its boycott on contacts with Nato, attending a meeting in Brussels. Ambassadors from Russia and Nato's nineteen member nations hold two hours of discussion about how to improve co-operation within Kfor. The Permanent Joint Council was established two years ago. In a brief statement after the meeting Nato and Russia pledged to 'do their utmost to ensure equal treatment for all inhabitants of Kosovo, regardless of their ethnic, political or religious affiliations' (*IHT*, 24 July 1999, pp. 1, 4).

1 September 1999. Russia's representative at Nato headquarters returns to Brussels but only to consult about Russia's participation in peacekeeping duties.

16 February 2000. Nato secretary-general George Robertson visits Russia. 'A joint statement issued after George Robertson … met Vladimir Putin … said the two sides aimed to intensify their contacts and become a cornerstone of European security' (*FT*, 17 February 2000, p. 12).

NOTE

1 On 12 March 1999 the Czech Republic, Hungary and Poland became members of Nato.

CONCLUSION

GDP growth in 2001 will be lower than in 2000 (when it was 8.3 per cent) but the rate will still be relatively good for the Russian economy. In the first quarter of 2001 the year-on-year GDP growth rate was 4.9 per cent (*RET*, Monthly Update, 17 September 2001, p. 2). Barter has declined significantly but is still a problem. One factor in the decline is the need for cash payments by a government hit by the August 1998 financial crisis as regards borrowing from foreigners (*Business Central Europe*, April 2001, p. 59). 'Business surveys show that the use of barter and other non-monetary means of payment continue to decline in favour of money-based transactions, and the share of cash in enterprise payments is well above 70 per cent. However, the share has stayed at roughly the same level for some time already. That points to serious structural problems due to lack of restructuring of enterprises, which is hampering further decline in the share of non-monetary forms of payment' (*RET*, Monthly Update, 17 September 2001, p. 1). (Arrears have declined significantly as well.)

Russia is currently not borrowing new funds from the IMF and repayments to that organization have increased. In early 2001 Russia tried to pressure the Paris Club of creditor nations into formally rescheduling debt. But this tactic did not succeed, especially given Russia's healthy growth of output and foreign exchange reserves in 1999 and 2000. The budget was amended in February 2001 to provide sufficient funds. There has been further liberalization of the foreign exchange regime.

Corruption is still a major problem, but there are some encouraging signs. The tax system has been improved (see below) and in July 2001 the State Duma approved on second reading a bill to combat money-laundering. (Capital flight is still significant.)

Foreign direct investment was a relatively good $4.4 billion in 2000 (*RET*, 2000, vol. 9, no. 4, p. 41). But it is still a comparatively small figure, especially in *per capita* terms. 'The total … [of] inward foreign investment … since 1991 amounts to only $22 billion 11 half the figure for Poland' (*The Economist*, Survey, 21 July 2001, p. 17). In 2000 foreign direct investment per person was as follows: Russia, $2.7; USA, $316.5; China, $39.0; Poland, $9.6 (p. 5).

As regards privatization, there has been greater transparency in sales. The climate has improved for private activity in general. An important factor is tax legislation. Scheduled to begin in 2002, the State Duma (in June 2001) approved a uniform profit tax regime and a reduction in the rate of profit tax from 35 per cent to 24 per cent. The elimination of tax exemptions is an important anti-corruption step and an important step in the direction of a less arbitrary tax system. In July 2001 approval was given for an increase in excise taxes and for the introduction of a new law on the taxation of mineral resources. (There was also the introduction at the start of 2001 of a flat rate 13 per cent income tax.)

There have been reports of improvements in corporate governance (e.g. *FT*, 18 September 2001, p. 21). President Vladimir Putin has seemingly allowed the financial oligarchs to retain their often dubiously gained wealth in return for paying taxes and ceasing to try to interfere in government. This has encouraged a more long-term business outlook and thus greater attention to factors such as reinvestment and an improved attitude to small shareholders (including dividend payments).

The fiscal situation is generally healthy. 'The State Duma passes [on 14 December 2000] the 2001 budget in the fourth and final reading. For the first time in post-Soviet history the budget is scheduled to be balanced. It is based on an estimated annual inflation rate of 12 per cent and a GDP growth rate of 4 per cent. The average exchange rate in 2001 is forecast at 30 roubles to the dollar' (*RET*, 2000, vol. 9, no. 4, p. 68). '[In 2000] for the first time in post-Soviet history the federal budget ran a surplus, due to high revenues related to increased exports and rapid economic growth. Budget revenue exceeded targets by almost 40 per cent' (p. 5). In 2000 the federal budget surplus was 2.5 per cent of GDP (the primary budget surplus being 5 per cent of GDP) (p. 53). Previously there were federal budget deficits: 1996, 117.9 per cent of GDP; 1997, 116.7 per cent of GDP; 1998, 114.9 per cent of GDP' 1999, 111.7 per cent of GDP (*RET*, Monthly Update, 20 March 2001, p. 2). 'The lower house approved [on 6 October 2000] the country's first ever balanced budget ... The Duma approved the budget in the first reading' (*FT*, 7 October 2000, p. 8). For 2002 the draft federal budget aims for a surplus (after debt service) of 1.26 per cent of GDP (*RET*, 2001, vol. 10, no. 1, p. 60).

President Vladimir Putin remains very popular within Russia, not least because he embodies greater stability. But there are concerns, including continuing problems in Chechenia. On 25 January 2001 the Council of Europe adopted a motion expressing 'grave concern' about human rights abuses in Chechenia. But the assembly still voted to restore Russia's voting rights.)

There are concerns over President Putin's sensitivity to criticism and his moves to exercise greater control over the media. Vladimir Gusinsky and Boris Berezovsky are out in the cold politically and out of the country physically. In April 2001 Spain refused to extradite Gusinsky to Russia. (On 12 December he had been arrested on an international warrant issued by

Russia via Interpol and on the grounds that he had misrepresented his assets when obtaining a loan from Gazprom.) Critical elements of the media have been assailed by tax and health audits. In April 2001 Gazprom (a company in which the state has reasserted its control over management) gained control over Gusinsky's television station NTV (the only independent nation-wide television station). As far as the ORT television company (previously 51 per cent owned by the state and 49 per cent owned by Berezovsky) is concerned, Gazprom took control in a deal arranged in February 2001. In April 2001 the prestigious daily newspaper *Sevodnia* was closed down. In May 2001 Gazprom attempted to control *Ekho Moskvy* (an independent radio station) and in July succeeded. Critics see Gazprom as a means of indirectly securing state control over those parts of the independent media critical of the president and the government.

'President Putin signs [on 4 September 2000] a decree on the establishment of the new "state council". The council will include governors and leaders of the regions and will be headed by the president. The council will include governors and leaders of the regions and will be headed by the president. The presidium of the council will consist of the governors of the seven new federal areas and will be renewed every six months' (*RET*, 2000, vol. 9, no. 3, p. 77). 'The presidium of the "state council" opens [on 29 September] ... [and] will be formed in accordance with the rotation principle ... Putin stresses that the best option in current circumstances is for the "state council" to act as a consultative body' (*RET*, 2000, vol. 9, no. 3, p. 81). In June 2001 a commission was set up to look at the delimitation of power between the federal, regional and local levels.

Local elections have generally been supportive of President Putin. In November 2000 Bashkortostan introduced a new constitution, one in line with federal laws. Putin used the severe energy crisis in the far east to help secure the resignation of Yevgeni Nazdratenko, governor of the Maritime region, in February 2001 (although the latter was given the post of chairman of the state fisheries commission).

In May 2001 the Russian Academy of Sciences issued instructions requiring its scientists to report any contacts with foreigners.

Party consolidation has been taking place. On 12 April 2001 Unity and Fatherland-All Russia announced that they were to merge in November of that year. Other parties announced they would like to join the new party. In May 2001 the Union of Rightist Forces was announced, to be led by Boris Nemtsov. The parties concerned included Nemtsov's Young Russia, Yegor Gaidar's Russia's Democratic Choice and Sergei Kiriyenko's New Force.

In June 2001 a bill was approved aimed at reducing the number of political parties. Among other criticisms was the claim that it would be difficult to form regional parties.

In his 3 April 2001 state of the nation speech President Putin emphasized the need for economic and legal reforms. To date it seems as though he had been concentrating more on accumulating power than implementing such reforms. Critics detect an air of indecisiveness on occasion. The Land Code relating to the sale of agricultural land has still not been approved by the State Duma, for example. (Legislation relating to the sale of other land was approved by the State Duma in September 2001.) But notable economic reforms include, as discussed above, those concerning taxation. President Putin has set Russia firmly on the path of economic reform in the context of a much more stable political environment and a more law-based society.

On 16 July 2001 the Good Neighbourly Treaty of Friendship and Co-operation was signed with China. Very little of the border remains in dispute (e.g. some islands in the Amur River).

Even before 11 September 2001 President Putin seemed to get on well personally with President George W. Bush (inaugurated in January 2001). But the terrorist attacks on the World Trade Centre in New York and on the Pentagon in Washington on 11 September 2001 proved to be something of a watershed in relations between Russia and the USA. President Putin immediately condemned the attacks and was actually the first international leader to telephone President Bush. This is not to underestimate problems such as national missile defence and Nato expansion (ever more likely to include the Baltic States of Estonia, Latvia and Lithuania). But even these sorts of problems seem much more manageable and President Putin is popular enough to combat resistance emanating from domestic sources such as the military. One major issue is Chechenia, where President Putin is hypersensitive to criticism at home and abroad (critics drawing a distinction between the legitimate aims of the elected Chechen president, Aslan Maskhadov, and terrorists such as Khattab). Russia stresses the links between Osama bin Laden, the Moslem fundamentalist who is the USA's number one target, with rebels in Chechenia. Limited renewed contacts between Russian officials and representatives of Aslan Maskhadov have so far come to nothing. Those concerned with human rights fear that the West may soften is criticism of Russia's campaign in Chechenia too much in the interest of the global war against international terrorism, while President Putin will feel disappointed if he does not receive what he perceives as adequate support from the West in what he regards as his war against terrorism.

BIBLIOGRAPHY

CDSP Current Digest of the Soviet Press (since 5 February 1992 *Post-Soviet*)
EEN Eastern Europe Newsletter
FEER Far Eastern Economic Review
FT Financial Times
IHT International Herald Tribune
RET Russian Economic Trends

Note the following changes of title: *Soviet Economy* to *Post-Soviet Studies*; *Soviet Studies* to *Europe-Asia Studies.*

BOOKS AND JOURNALS

Adirim, I. (1989) 'A note on the current level, pattern and trends of unemployment in the USSR', *Soviet Studies*, vol. XLI, no. 3.

Afanasyev, Y. (1994) 'Russian reform is dead', *Foreign Affairs*, vol. 73, no. 2.

Aganbegyan, A. (1988a) 'The economics of *perestroika*', *International Affairs* (London), vol. 64, no. 2.

—— (1988b) *The Challenge: Economics of Perestroika*, London: Hutchinson.

—— (1989) *Moving the Mountain: Inside the Perestroika Revolution*, London: Bantam Press.

Aghion, P. and Blanchard, O. (1994) *On the Speed of Transition in Central Europe*, Nuffield College Oxford: Discussion Paper no. 87.

Allison, G. and Blackwill, R. (1991) 'America's stake in the Soviet future', *Foreign Affairs*, vol. 70, no. 3.

Amelina, M. (1999) 'The (not so) mysterious resilience of Russia's agricultural collectives', *Transition*, vol. 10, no. 6.

Arnot, B. (1988) *Controlling Soviet Labour*, London: Macmillan.

Ash, T. (1993) 'Agriculture in the former centrally-planned economies in transition', *Economics of Transition*, vol. 1, no. 4.

Ash, T. and Hare, P. (1994) 'Privatization in the Russian Federation: changing enterprise behaviour in the transition period', *Cambridge Journal of Economics*, vol. 18, no. 6.

Åslund, A. (1985) *Private Enterprise in Eastern Europe*, London: Macmillan.

—— (1989) *Gorbachev's Struggle for Economic Reform: The Soviet Reform Process, 1985–88*, 1st edn, London: Pinter.

—— (1991a) *Gorbachev's Struggle for Economic Reform: The Soviet Reform Process, 1985–88*, 2nd edn, London: Pinter.

—— (1991b) 'Gorbachev, *perestroyka*, and economic crisis', *Problems of Communism*, January–April.

—— (ed.) (1992a) *The Post-Soviet Economy; Soviet and Western Perspectives*, London: Pinter.

—— (1992b) 'A critique of Soviet reform plans' in Åslund (1992a).

—— (1994a) 'Lessons of the first four years of systemic change in Eastern Europe', *Journal of Comparative Economics*, vol. 19, no. 1.

—— (1994b) 'Russia's success story', *Foreign Affairs*, vol. 73, no. 5.

—— (1996) 'Introduction: the Balkan transformation in perspective' in Jeffries (1996).

—— (1999a) 'Russia's current economic dilemma', *Post-Soviet Affairs*, vol. 15, no. 1.

—— (1999b) 'Russia's collapse', *Foreign Affairs*, vol. 78, no. 5.

Åslund, A. and Layard, R. (eds) (1993) *Changing the Economic System in Russia*, London: Pinter.

Åslund, A., Boone, P. and Johnson, S. (1996) 'How to stabilize: lessons from post-communist countries', *Brookings Papers on Economic Activity*, no. 1.

Balcerowicz, L. (1993) 'Transition to market economy: Central and East European countries in comparative perspective', *British Review of Economic Issues*, vol. 15, no. 37.

—— (1994) 'Common fallacies in the debate on the transition to a market economy', *Economic Policy*, no. 19 (Supplement).

Balino, T. (1998) 'Monetary policy in Russia', *Finance and Development*, December.

Bartholdy, K. and Szegvari, I. (1993) 'Statistical review', *Economics of Transition*, vol. 1, no. 1.

Bergson, A. (ed.) (1953) *Soviet Economic Growth*, New York: Row Peterson.

—— (1961) *The Real National Income of Soviet Russia since 1928*, Cambridge, Mass.: Harvard University Press.

Berkowitz, D., Berliner, J., Gregory, P., Linz, S. and Millar, R. (1993) 'An evaluation of the CIA's analysis of Soviet economic performance', *Comparative Economic Studies*, vol. XXXV, no. 2.

Berliner, J. (1976) *The Innovation Decision in Soviet Industry*, Cambridge, Mass.: MIT Press.

Bideleux, R. (1987) *Communism and Development*, London: Methuen.

Bideleux, R. and Jeffries, I. (1998) *A History of Eastern Europe: Crisis and Change*, London: Routledge.

Birman, I. (1978) 'From the achieved level', *Soviet Studies*, vol. XXXI, no. 2.

Blanchard, O., Dornbusch, R., Krugman, P., Layard, R. and Summers, L. (1991) *Reform in Eastern Europe*, Cambridge, Mass.: MIT Press.

Bleaney, M. (1988) *Do Socialist Economies Work? The Soviet and East European Experience*, Oxford: Basil Blackwell.

Boone, P. and Fedorov, B. (1997) 'The ups and down of Russian economic reforms' in Woo *et al.* (1997)

Boycko, M. (1991) 'Price decontrol: the microeconomic case for the "big bang" approach', *Oxford Review of Economic Policy*, vol. 7, no. 4.

Boycko, M., Shleifer, A. and Vishny, R. (1994) 'Voucher privatization', *Journal of Financial Economics*, vol. 35, no. 2.

—— (1996) 'A theory of privatization', *Economic Journal*, vol. 106, no. 435.

Brada, J. and Wädekin, K-E. (1988) *Socialist Agriculture in Transition: Organizational Response to Failing Performance*, Boulder: Westview Press.

Brooks, K. (1990a) 'Soviet agriculture's halting reform', *Problems of Communism*, March–April.

—— (1990b) 'Soviet agricultural policy and pricing under Gorbachev' in Gray (1990).

—— (1990c) 'Perestroika in the countryside: agricultural reform in the Gorbachev era', *Comparative Economic Studies*, vol. XXXII, no. 2.
—— (1992) 'Stabilization, sectoral adjustment and enterprise reform in the agricultural sector of Russia', *American Journal of Agricultural Economics*, vol. 74, no. 5.
Brooks, K., Guash, L., Braverman, A. and Csaki, C. (1991) 'Agriculture and the transition to the market', *Journal of Economic Perspectives*, vol. 5, no. 4.
Brown, A., Ickes, B. and Ryterman, R. (1994) *The Myth of Monopoly: a New View of Industrial Structure in Russia*, World Bank: Policy Research Working Paper no. 1331.
Brown, D.J. and Earle, J. (1999) 'Evaluating enterprise privatization in Russia', *RET*, 1999, vol. 8, no. 3.
Brzezinski, Z. (1994) 'The premature partnership', *Foreign Affairs*, vol. 73, no. 2.
Buck, T., Filatotchev, I. and Wright, M. (1994) 'Employee buy-outs and the transformation of Russian industry', *Comparative Economic Studies*, vol. XXXVI, no. 2.
Burawoy, M. (1996) 'The state and economic involution: Russia through a China lens', *World Development*, vol. 24, no. 6.
Business Central Europe (1995) *The Annual*, London: The Economist Group.
—— (1997) *The Annual: 1997–98*, London: The Economist Group.
—— (1998) *The Annual: 1998–99*, London: The Economist Group.
Butterfield, J. (1990) 'Devolution in decision-making and organizational change in Soviet agriculture', *Comparative Economic Studies*, vol. XXXII, no. 2.
Chapman, J. (1988) 'Gorbachev's wage reform', *Soviet Economy*, vol. 4, no. 4.
—— (1989) 'Income distribution and social justice in the Soviet Union', *Comparative Economic Studies*, vol. XXXI, no. 1.
Chen, L., Wittgenstein, F. and McKeon, E. (1996) 'The upsurge of mortality in Russia: causes and implications', *Population and Development Review*, vol. 22, no. 3.
Chubais, A. and Vishnevskaya, M. (1993) 'Main issues of privatization in Russia' in Åslund and Layard (1993).
Clague, C. and Rausser, G. (eds) (1992) *The Emergence of Market Economies in Eastern Europe*, Oxford: Blackwell.
Cochrane, N. (1988) 'The private sector in East European agriculture', *Problems of Communism*, March–April.
—— (1990) 'Reforming socialist agriculture: Bulgarian and Hungarian experience and implications for the USSR' in Wädekin (1990b).
Desai, P. (2000) 'Why did the rouble collapse in August 1998?', *American Economic Review*, Papers and Proceedings, May.
Desai, R. and Goldberg, I. (2000) 'Shareholders, governance and the Russian enterprise dilemma', *Finance and Development*, vol. 37, no. 2.
Dyker, D. (1981) *The Process of Investment in the Soviet Union*, Cambridge: Cambridge University Press.
—— (1985) *The Future of the Soviet Planning System*, London: Croom Helm.
—— (ed.) (1987) *The Soviet Union under Gorbachev: Prospects for Reform*, Chapters 3, 'Industrial planning', and 4, 'Agriculture', London: Croom Helm.
EBRD (1994) *Transition Report*, London: European Bank for Reconstruction and Development.
—— (1995a) *Transition Report Update* (April), London: European Bank for Reconstruction and Development.
—— (1995b) *Transition Report*, London: European Bank for Reconstruction and Development.
—— (1996a) *Transition Report Update* (April), London: European Bank for Reconstruction and Development.

—— (1996b) *Transition Report*, London: European Bank for Reconstruction and Development.
—— (1997a) *Transition Report Update* (April), London: European Bank for Reconstruction and Development.
—— (1997b) *Transition Report*, London: European Bank for Reconstruction and Development.
—— (1998a) *Transition Report Update* (April), London: European Bank for Reconstruction and Development.
—— (1998b) *Transition Report*, London: European Bank for Reconstruction and Development.
—— (1999a) *Transition Report Update* (April), London: European Bank for Reconstruction and Development.
—— (1999b) *Transition Report*, London: European Bank for Reconstruction and Development.
—— (2000a) *Transition Report Update* (May), London: European Bank for Reconstruction and Development.
—— (2000b) *Transition Report*, London: European Bank for Reconstruction and Development.
Economic Commission for Europe (1989) *Economic Reform in the European Centrally Planned Economies*, Economic Studies no. 1, New York: UN.
Economist Surveys:
—— (1988) 'The Soviet Economy', 9 April.
—— (1989) 'Russia's anti-drink campaign', 23 December
—— (1990) '*Perestroika*', 28 April.
—— (1990) 'The Soviet Union', 20 October.
—— (1992) 'Russia', 5 December.
—— (1995) 'Russia's emerging market', 8 April.
—— (1997) 'Russia', 12 July.
Ellman, M. (1979) *Socialist Planning*, London: Cambridge University Press.
—— (1989) *The USSR in the 1990s*, London: EIU.
—— (1993) 'General aspects of transition' in Ellman *et al.* (1993).
—— (1994) 'The increase of death and disease under "katastroika"', *Cambridge Journal of Economics*, vol. 18, no. 4.
—— (1997) 'The political economy of transition', *Oxford Review of Economic Policy*, vol. 13, no. 2.
Ellman, M., Gaidar, E. and Kolodko, G. (editor Admiraal, P.) (1993) *Economic Transition in Eastern Europe*, Oxford: Blackwell.
Ericson, R. (1998) 'Six years after the collapse of the USSR: the Russian economy', *Post-Soviet Affairs*, vol. 14, np. 1.
Fan, Q. and Schaffer, M. (1994) 'Government financial transfers and enterprise adjustments in Russia, with comparisons to Central and Eastern Europe', *Economics of Transition*, vol. 2, no. 2.
Filatotchev, I., Buck, T. and Wright, M. (1992) 'Privatization and buy-outs in the USSR', *Soviet Studies*, vol. 44, no. 2.
Filatotchev, I., Wright, M. and Bleaney, M. (1999a) 'Privatization, insider control and managerial entrenchment in Russia', *Economics of Transition*, vol. 7 no. 2.
—— (1999b) 'Insider-controlled firms in Russia', *Economics of Planning*, vol. 32, no. 2.
Filtzer, D. (1989) 'The Soviet wage reform of 1956–62', *Soviet Studies*, vol. XLI, no. 1.
—— (1991) 'The contradictions of the marketless market: self-financing in the Soviet industrial enterprise 1986–90', *Soviet Studies*, vol. 43, no. 6.
Financial Times (various surveys):

Russia: 13 May 1992; 27 May 1993; 27 June 1994; 10 April 1995; 11 April 1996; 9 April 1997; 17 September 1997 (Moscow); 15 April 1998; 30 April 1999; 10 May 2000.
Soviet Union: 12 March 1990.

Fischer, S. (1992a) 'Stabilization and economic reform in Russia', *Brookings Papers on Economic Activity*, no. 1.

—— (1992b) 'Privatization in East European transformation' in Clague and Rausser (1992).

Fischer, S. and Frenkel, J. (1992) 'Macroeconomic issues of Soviet reform', *American Economic Review*, Papers and Proceedings, May.

Fischer, S. and Gelb, A. (1991) 'The process of socialist economic transformation' *Journal of Economic Perspectives*, vol. 5, no. 4.

Fischer, S., Sahay, R. and Vegh, C. (1996) 'Stabilization and growth in transition economies: the early experience', *Journal of Economic Perspectives*, vol. 10, no. 2.

Flemming, J. and Matthews, R. (1994) 'Economic reform in Russia', *National Institute Economic Review*, no. 149.

Freeland, C. (2000) 'To Russia with Love', *The New Statesman*, 19 June 2000, p. 13).

Gaddy, C. and Ickes, B. (1998a) 'Why are Russian enterprises not restructuring', *Transition*, vol. 9, no. 4.

—— (1998b) 'Russia's virtual economy', *Foreign Affairs*, vol. 77, no. 5.

Gagnon, V. (1987) 'Gorbachev and the collective contract brigade', *Soviet Studies*, vol. XXXIX, no. 1.

Gaidar, Y. (1997) 'The IMF and Russia', *American Economic Review*, Papers and Proceedings, vol. 87, no. 2.

Gerschenkron, A. (1962) *Economic Backwardness in Historical Perspective*, Cambridge, Mass.: Harvard University Press.

Gorbachev, M. (1987) *Perestroika: New Thinking for our Country and the World*, London: Collins; New York: Harper & Row.

Granick, D. (1975) *Enterprise Guidance in Eastern Europe*, Princeton, NJ: Princeton University Press.

Gray, E. (ed.) (1990) *Soviet Agriculture: Comparative Perspectives*, Ames, Ia: Iowa State University Press.

Gregory, P. (1989a) 'Soviet bureaucratic behaviour: *khozyaistvenniki* and *apparatchiki*', *Soviet Studies*, vol. XLI, no. 4.

—— (1989b) 'The Soviet bureaucracy and *perestroika*', *Comparative Economic Studies*, vol. XXXI, no. 1.

Gregory, P. and Collier, I. (1988) 'Unemployment in the Soviet Union: evidence from the Soviet interview project', *American Economic Review*, September.

Gregory, P. and Stuart, R. (1990) *Soviet Economic Structure and Performance*, 4th edn, New York: Harper & Row (2nd edn 1981 and 3rd edn 1986).

—— (1994) *Soviet and Post-Soviet Economic Structure and Performance*, 5th edn, New York: Harper Collins.

Hanauer, L. (1996) 'Tatarstan's bid for autonomy: Tatarstan as a model for the devolution of power in the Russian Federation', *Journal of Communist Studies and Transition Politics*, vol. 12, no. 1.

Handelman, S. (1994) 'The Russian mafiya', *Foreign Affairs*, vol. 73, no. 2.

Hanson, P. (1989a) 'The Soviet economy at the end of year IV', *Detente*, no. 14.

—— (1989b) 'Capitalism or socialism?', *Detente*, no. 16.

—— (1990a) 'Gorbachev's policies after four years' in T. Hasegawa and A. Pravda (eds) *Perestroika: Soviet Domestic and Foreign Policies*, London: Sage (Royal Institute of International Affairs).

—— (1990b) 'Property rights in the new phase of reforms', *Soviet Economy*, vol. 6, no. 2.
—— (1999) 'The Russian economic crisis and the future of Russian economic reform', *Europe-Asia Studies*, vol. 51, no. 7.
Hansson, A. (1993) 'The trouble with the rouble: monetary reform in the former Soviet Union' in Åslund and Layard (1993).
Hare, P. (1987) 'Resource allocation without prices: the Soviet economy', *The Economic Review*, vol. 5, no. 2.
Havrylyshyn, O. Miller, M. and Perraudin, W. (1994) 'Deficits, inflation and the political economy of Ukraine', *Economic Policy*, no. 19.
Healey, N., Leksin, V. and Svetsov, A. (1999) 'The municipalization of enterprise-owned "social assets" in Russia', *Post-Soviet Affairs*, vol. 15, no. 3.
Herd, G. (1998) 'Regional meltdown?', *The World Today*, vol. 54, no. 10.
Hewett, E. (1988) *Reforming the Soviet Economy: Equality versus Efficiency*, Washington, DC: Brookings Institution.
—— (1989) '*Perestroika* and the Congress of People's Deputies', *Soviet Economy*, vol. 5, no. 1.
—— (1990) 'The new Soviet plan', *Foreign Affairs*, vol. 69, no. 5
Holzman, F. (1976) *International Trade under Communism*, New York: Basic Books.
—— (1986a) 'The significance of Soviet subsidies to Eastern Europe', *Comparative Economic Studies*, vol. 28, no. 1.
—— (1986b) 'Further thoughts on the significance of Soviet subsidies to Eastern Europe', *Comparative Economic Studies*, vol. 28, no. 3.
—— (1987) *The Economics of Soviet Bloc Trade and Finance*, Boulder and London: Westview Press.
—— (1991) 'Moving towards rouble convertibility', *Comparative Economic Studies*, vol. XXXIII, no. 3.
Hough, J. (1994) 'The Russian general election of 1993: public attitudes toward economic reform and democratization', *Post-Soviet Affairs*, vol. 10, no. 1.
Ickes, B. and Ryterman, R. (1993) 'Road block to economic reform: inter-enterprise debt and the transition to markets', *Post-Soviet Affairs*, vol. 9, no. 3.
Ickes, B., Murrell, P. and Ryterman, R. (1997) 'End of the tunnel?: the effects of financial stabilization in Russia', *Post-Soviet Affairs*, vol. 13, no. 2.
IMF, World Bank, OECD and EBRD (1990) *The Economy of the USSR*, Washington, DC: The World Bank.
International Herald Tribune (various surveys):
Russia: 8 December 1993; 2 December 1994'; 19 September 1997.
Soviet Union: 7–8 November 1985; 7 November 1988.
Jeffries, I. (ed.) (1981) *The Industrial Enterprise in Eastern Europe*, New York: Praeger.
—— (1990) *A Guide to the Socialist Economies*, London: Routledge.
—— (ed.) (1992) *Industrial Reform in Socialist Countries: from Restructuring to Revolution*, Aldershot: Edward Elgar.
—— (1993) *Socialist Economies and the Transition to the Market: a Guide*, London: Routledge.
—— (1996) *A Guide to the Economies in Transition*, London: Routledge.
—— (ed.) (1996) *Problems of Economic and Political Transformation in the Balkans*, London: Pinter.
Johnson, J. (1997) 'Russia's emerging financial-industrial groups', *Post-Soviet Affairs*, vol. 13, no. 4.
Jones, A. and Moskoff, W. (1989) 'New co-operatives in the USSR', *Problems of Communism*, November–December.

Joskow, P., Schmalensee, R. and Tsukanova, N. (1994) 'Competition policy in Russia during and after privatization', *Brookings Papers on Economic Activity (Microeconomics)*, Washington, DC: Brookings Institution.
Kaplan, N. (1953) 'Capital formation and allocation' in Bergson (1953).
Kempton, D. (1996) 'The republic of Sakha (Yakutia): the evolution of centre-periphery relations in the Russian Federation', *Europe-Asia Studies*, vol. 48, no. 4.
Kipp. J. (1994) 'The Zhirinovsky threat', *Foreign Affairs*, vol. 73, no. 3.
Kitching, G. (1998) 'The development of agrarian capitalism in Russia 1991–97: some observations from fieldwork', *The Journal of Peasant Studies*, vol. 25, no. 3.
Kornai, J. (1992a) *The Socialist System: the Political Economy of Communism*, Oxford: Oxford University Press.
—— (1992b) 'The postsocialist transition and the state: reflections in the light of Hungarian fiscal problems', *American Economic Review*, Papers and Proceedings, May.
Kostakov, V. (1988) 'Labour problems in the light of *perestroyka*', *Soviet Economy*, vol. 4 (January–March).
Kroll, H. (1988) 'The role of contracts in the Soviet economy', *Soviet Studies*, vol. XL, no. 3.
Krueger, G. (1995) 'Transition strategies of former state-owned enterprises in Russia', *Comparative Economic Studies*, vol. 37, no. 4.
Kushnirsky, F. (1989) 'The new role of normatives in Soviet economic planning', *Soviet Studies*, vol. XLI, no. 4.
—— (1991) 'Conversion, civilian production, and goods quality in the Soviet Union', *Comparative Economic Studies*, vol. XXXIII, no. 1.
Lambeth, B. (1995) 'Russia's wounded military', *Foreign Affairs*, vol. 74, p. 2.
Lapidus, G. (1998) 'Six years after the collapse of the USSR: Russian policy-making', *Post-Soviet Affairs*, vol. 14, no. 1.
Le Houerou, P. and Rutkowski, M. (1996) 'Federal transfers in Russia: their impact on regional revenues and incomes', *Comparative Economic Studies*, vol. XXXVIII, nos 2 and 3.
Lenin, V. (1964) *Collective Works*, Vol. 21, Moscow: Progress Publishers.
Levine, H. (1997) 'Five years after the collapse of the USSR', *Post-Soviet Affairs*, vol. 13, no. 1.
Light, M. (1998) 'Russia's permanent crisis', *Global Emerging Markets (Deutsche Bank Research)*, vol. 1, no. 2.
Linz, S. (1988) 'Managerial autonomy in Soviet firms', *Soviet Studies*, vol. XL, no. 2.
Linz, S. and Moskoff, W. (eds) (1988) *Reorganisation and Reform in the Soviet Union*, Armonk, NY, and London: M.E. Sharpe.
Lipton, D. and Sachs, J. (1992) 'Prospects for Russia's economic reforms', *Brookings Papers on Economic Activity*, no. 2.
Malleret, T., Orlova, N. and Romanov, V. (1999) 'What loaded and triggered the Russian crisis?', *Post-Soviet Affairs*, vol. 15, no. 2.
Marrese, M. (1990) '*Perestroika* and socialist privatization; a comment', *Comparative Economic Studies*, vol. XXII, no. 3.
McFarlane, B. (1988) *Yugoslavia: Politics, Economics and Society*, London: Pinter.
McFaul, M. (1995) 'Eurasia letter: Russian politics after Chechnya', *Foreign Policy*, no. 99.
—— (1996a) 'The allocation of property rights in Russia: the first round', *Communist and Post-Communist Studies*, vol. 29, no. 3.
—— (1996b) 'Russia's 1996 presidential elections', *Post-Soviet Affairs*, vol. 12, no. 4.

McKinnon, R. (1992a) 'Taxation, money, and credit in a liberalizing socialist economy', *Economics of Planning*, vol. 25, no. 1.
—— (1992b) 'Taxation, money and credit in a liberalizing socialist economy' in Clague and Rausser (1992).
—— (1994) 'Financial growth and macroeconomic stability in China, 1978–92: implications for Russia and other transitional economies', *Journal of Comparative Economics*, vol. 18, no. 3.
McKinsey Global Institute (1999) *Unlocking Economic Growth in Russia*, Moscow: McKinsey Global Institute.
Michalopoulos, C. and Tarr, D. (1993) 'Energizing trade of the states of the former Soviet Union', *Finance and Development*, March.
Murrell, P. (1990) *The Nature of Socialist Economies: Lessons from Eastern European Foreign Trade*, Princeton, NJ: Princeton University Press.
—— (1992a) 'Evolutionary and radical approaches to economic reform', *Economics of Planning*, vol. 25, no. 1.
—— (1992b) 'Evolution in economics and in the economic reform of the centrally planned economies' in Clague and Rausser (1992).
—— (1993) 'What is shock therapy? What did it do in Poland and Russia?', *Post-Soviet Affairs*, vol. 9, no. 2.
Nellis, J. (1999) 'Time to rethink privatization in transition economies?', *Finance and Development*, vol. 36, no. 2.
Nikonov, A. (1992) 'Agricultural transition in Russia and the other former states of the USSR', *American Journal of Agricultural Economics*, vol. 74, no. 5.
Nolan, P. (1992) *Transforming Stalinist Systems: China's Reforms in the Light of Russian and East European Experience*, University of Cambridge: Discussion Paper on Economic Transition DPET 9203.
—— (1996) 'China's rise, Russia's fall', *Journal of Peasant Studies*, vol. 24, nos 1 and 2.
Nove, A. (1961) *The Soviet Economy*, London: Allen & Unwin.
—— (1977) 'The Soviet Economic System, 1st edn, London: Allen & Unwin.
—— (1981) 'The Soviet industrial enterprise' in Jeffries (1981).
—— (1986) *The Soviet Economic System*, 3rd edn, London: Allen & Unwin.
—— (1987) 'Soviet agriculture: light at the end of the tunnel?', *Detente*, nos 9–10.
—— (1994) 'A gap in transition models? A comment on Gomulka', *Europe-Asia Studies*, vol. 46, no. 5.
Ofer, G. (1987) 'Soviet economic growth, 1928–85', *Journal of Economic Literature*, vol. XXV (December).
Orlowski, L. (1993) 'Indirect transfers in trade among former Soviet Union republics: sources, patterns and policy responses in the post-Soviet period', *Europe-Asia Studies*, vol. 45, no. 6.
Oxenstierna, S. (1992) 'Trends in employment and unemployment' in Åslund (1992a).
Pallot, J. (1993) 'Update on the Russian Federation land reform', *Post-Soviet Geography*, vol. XXXIV, no. 3.
Panova, G. (1988) 'Recent developments in Soviet banking', *National Westminster Bank Quarterly Review*, August.
Plokker, K. (1990) 'The development of individual and co-operative labour activity in the Soviet Union', *Soviet Studies*, vol. 42, no. 3.
Pryor, F. (1992) *The Red and the Green: the Rise and the Fall of Collectivized Agriculture in Marxist Regimes*, Princeton, NJ: Princeton University Press.
Sachs, J. (1994) *Poland's Jump to the Market Economy*, Cambridge, Mass.: MIT Press.
—— (1995) 'Consolidating capitalism', *Foreign Policy*, no. 98.

—— (1996a) 'The transition at mid-decade', *American Economic Review*, Papers and Proceedings (May).

—— (1996b) 'Economic transition and the exchange rate regime', *American Economic Review*, Papers and Proceedings (May).

—— (1997) 'An overview of stabilization issues facing economies in transition' in Woo *et al.* (1997).

Sachs, J. and Woo, W. (1994) 'Structural factors in the economic reforms of China, Eastern Europe and the former Soviet Union', *Economic Policy*, no. 18.

Sakwa, R. (1995) 'The Russian elections of 1993', *Europe-Asia Studies*, vol. 47, no. 2.

—— (2000) 'Russia's "permanent" (uninterrupted) elections of 1999–2000', *Communist Studies and Transition Politics*, vol. 16, no. 3.

Sakwa, R. and Webber, M. (1999) 'The Commonwealth of Independent States, 1991–98: stagnation and survival', *Europe–Asia Studies*, vol. 51, no. 3.

Schroeder, G. (1982) 'Soviet economic reform decrees: more steps on the treadmill', US Congress, Joint Economic Committee, Washington, DC: Government Printing Office.

—— (1986) *The System versus Progress: Soviet Economic Problems*, London: Centre for Research into Communist Economies.

—— (1988a) 'Organisations and hierarchies: the perennial search for solutions' in Linz and Moskoff (1988).

—— (1988b) 'Property rights issues in economic reforms in socialist countries', *Studies in Comparative Communism*, vol. XXI, no. 2.

—— (1992) 'The Soviet industrial enterprise in the 1980s' in Jeffries (1992).

Sharma, A. (1996) 'Inside Russia's true economy', *Foreign Policy*, no. 103.

Shaw, D. (1992) 'Further progress with land reform', *Post-Soviet Geography*, vol. XXXIII, no. 8.

Shlapentokh, V. (1993) 'Privatization debates in Russia, 1989–92', *Comparative Economic Studies*, vol. XXXV, no. 2.

Shleifer, A. (1997) 'Government in transition', *European Economic Review*, vol. 41, nos 3–5.

Shleifer, A. and Vishny, R. (1991) 'Reversing the Soviet economic collapse', *Brookings Papers on Economic Activity*, no. 2.

Siszov, A. (1993) 'Land reform developments in Russia', *Economics of Transition*, vol. 1, no. 4.

Slider, D. (1987) 'The brigade system in Soviet industry: an effort to restructure the labour force', *Soviet Studies*, vol. XXXIX, no. 3.

—— (1991) 'Embattled entrepreneurs: Soviet co-operatives in an unreformed society', *Soviet Studies*, vol. 43, no. 5.

Smith, A. H. (1983) *The Planned Economies of Eastern Europe*, London: Croom Helm.

—— (1993) *Russia and the World Economy: Problems of Integration*, London: Routledge.

Solnick, S. (1998) 'Gubernatorial elections in Russia, 1996–97', *Post-Soviet Affairs*, vol. 14, no. 1.

Somogyi, L. (ed.) (1993) *The Political Economy of the Transition Process in Eastern Europe*, Aldershot: Edward Elgar.

Stalin, J. (1955a) *Works*, Vol. 12, Moscow: Foreign Languages Publishing House.

—— (1955b) *Works*, Vol. 13, Moscow: Foreign Languages Publishing House.

—— (1955c) *Works*, Vol. 14, Moscow: Foreign Languages Publishing House.

Stepan, A. (2000) 'Russian federalism in comparative perspective', *Post-Soviet Affairs*, vol. 16, no. 2.

Sutela, P. (1994) 'Insider privatization in Russia: speculations on systemic change', *Europe-Asia Studies*, vol. 46, no. 3.

Sutherland, D. and Hanson, P. (1996) 'Structural change in the economies of Russia's regions', *Europe-Asia Studies*, vol. 48, no. 3.
Tarr, D. (1994) 'The terms-of-trade effects of moving to world prices on the countries of the former Soviet Union', *Journal of Comparative Economics*, vol. 18, no. 1.
Tesche, J. (1994) 'Fiscal decentralization in the Russian Federation', *Comparative Economic Studies*, vol. XXXVI, no. 3.
Tompson, W. (1999) 'The price of everything and the value of nothing? Unravelling the workings of Russia's "virtual economy"', *Economy and Society*, vol. 28, no. 2.
—— (2000a) 'Putin's power play', *The World Today*, vol. 56, no. 7.
—— (2000b) 'Financial backwardness in contemporary perspective: prospects for the development of financial intermediation in Russia', *Europe-Asia Studies*, vol. 52, no. 4.
Trehub, A. (1987) 'Social and economic rights in the Soviet Union', *Survey*, vol. 29, no. 4.
Treisman, D. (1996) 'Why Yeltsin won', *Foreign Affairs*, vol. 75, no. 5.
—— (1998) 'Russia's taxing problem', *Foreign Policy*, no. 112.
Treml, V. (1989) 'The most recent input-output table: a milestone in Soviet statistics', *Soviet Economy*, vol. 5, no. 4.
United Nations (1993) *World Economic Survey 1993*, New York: United Nations.
United Nations Economic Commission for Europe (1992) *Economic Survey of Europe in 1991–92*, New York: United Nations.
—— (1993) *Economic Survey of Europe in 1992–93*, New York: United Nations.
—— (1994) *Economic Survey of Europe in 1993–94*, New York: United Nations.
—— (1995) *Economic Survey of Europe in 1994–95*, New York: United Nations.
—— (1996) *Economic Survey of Europe in 1995–96*, New York: United Nations.
—— (1997) *Economic Survey of Europe in 1996–97*, New York: United Nations.
—— (1998a) *Economic Survey of Europe 1998*, No. 1, New York: United Nations.
—— (1998b) *Economic Survey of Europe 1998*, No. 2, New York: United Nations.
—— (1998c) *Economic Survey of Europe 1998*, No. 3, New York: United Nations.
US Congress, Joint Economic Committee (1977) *East European Economies Post-Helsinki*, Washington, DC: US Government Printing Office.
—— (1979) *Soviet Economy in a Time of Change*, Washington, DC: US Government Printing Office.
—— (1982) *Soviet Economy in the 1980s: Problems and Prospects*, Washington, DC: US Government Printing Office.
—— (1986) *East European Economies: Slow Growth in the 1980s*, vol. 3: Country Studies on Eastern Europe and Yugoslavia, Washington, DC: US Government Printing Office.
Van Atta, D. (1994) 'Agrarian reform in post-Soviet Russia', *Post-Soviet Affairs*, vol. 10, no. 2.
Van Brabant, J. (1980) *Socialist Economic Integration*, Cambridge: Cambridge University Press.
—— (1988) 'Planned economies in the GATT framework: the Soviet case', *Soviet Economy*, vol. 4 (January-March).
—— (1989) *Economic Integration in Eastern Europe*, London: Harvester Wheatsheaf.
Wädekin, K-E. (1982) *Agrarian Policies in Communist Europe*, Totowa, NJ: Rowman & Allanheld (1982).
—— (1988) 'Soviet agriculture: a brighter prospect' in P. Wiles (ed.), *The Soviet Economy on the Brink of Reform*, London: Unwin Hyman.
—— (ed.) (1990a) *Communist Agriculture: Farming in the Far East and Cuba*, London: Routledge.
—— (1990b) *Communist Agriculture: Farming in the Soviet Union and Eastern Europe*, London: Routledge.

—— (1990c) 'Private agriculture in socialist countries: implications for the USSR' in Gray (1990).

Wallace, W. and Clarke, R. (1986) *Comecon, Trade and the West*, London: Pinter.

Wanniski, J. (1992) 'The future of Russian capitalism', *Foreign Affairs*, vol. 71, no. 2.

Watson, J. (1996) 'Foreign investment in Russia: the case of the oil industry', *Europe-Asia Studies*, vol. 48, no. 3.

Wegren, S. (1992a) 'Private farming and agrarian reform in Russia', *Problems of Communism*, May-June.

—— (1992b) 'Agricultural reform in the nonchernozem zone; the case of Kostroma oblast', *Post-Soviet Geography*, vol. XXIII, no. 10.

—— (1994) 'Rural reform and political culture', *Europe-Asia Studies*, vol. 46, no. 2.

—— (1996) 'The politics of private farming in Russia', *Journal of Peasant Studies*, vol. 23, no. 4.

—— (1997) 'Land reform and the land market in Russia: operation, constraints and prospects', *Europe-Asia Studies*, vol. 49, no. 6.

—— (1998) 'Russian agrarian reform and rural capitalism reconsidered', *Journal of Peasant Studies*, vol. 26, no. 1.

White, S. (1998) 'Electoral statistics, 1993–96', *Communist Studies and Transition Politics*, vol. 14, nos 1 and 2.

White, S., Wyman, M. and Oates, S. (1997) 'Parties and voters in the 1995 Russian Duma election', *Europe-Asia Studies*, vol. 49, no. 5.

Woo, W. (1994) 'The art of reforming centrally planned economies: comparing China, Poland and Russia', *Journal of Comparative Economics*, vol. 18, no. 3.

Woo, W., Parker, S. and Sachs, J. (eds) (1997) *Economies in Transition: Comparing Asia and Eastern Europe*, London: MIT Press.

World Bank (1996) *World Development Report: From Plan to Market*, New York: Oxford University Press.

Yavlinsky, G. (1998) 'Russia's phony capitalism', *Foreign Affairs*, vol. 77, no. 3.

INDEX